WATERFOWL
Ducks, Geese & Swans of the World

BY FRANK S. TODD

A SEA WORLD PRESS PUBLICATION

HARCOURT BRACE JOVANOVICH, New York and London

Sea World Press engaged Constellation Phoenix, Inc.,
San Diego, California to assist in the preparation of this
book and to provide the services of:

John Bonnett Wexo, Editorial Director
Eldon P. Slick, Graphics Director
Joan M. Hubert, Art Director
Barbara K. McDowell, Associate Editor
Barbara D. Friesen, Production Coordinator

Typography by Robert D. Dehm, Thompson Type
San Diego, California
Printed in the United States of America
by Graphic Arts Center, Portland, Oregon

Todd, Frank Sturtevant, 1942-
    Waterfowl: Ducks, Geese, and Swans of the World

Library of Congress Catalog Card Number: 79-63521

ISBN 0-15-004036-9

First edition

A   B   C   D   E

Table of Contents

Foreword

WATERFOWL: Ducks, Geese, and Swans of the World, by Frank S. Todd, is the first major work by a recognized authority on the waterfowl of the world that includes quality color photographs of virtually every species and subspecies of wildfowl. As such, it fills a major gap in the iconography of the family Anatidae (waterfowl) and the closely allied Anhimidae (screamers).

The four volumes of my work, "The Waterfowl of the World," illustrated by Sir Peter Scott, were published between 1954 and 1964. As we had hoped, a number of new studies—and even books—of a local, special, and general nature have appeared since, adding considerably to our knowledge of these highly interesting birds. Colored drawings are, in my opinion, essential to the complex descriptions in detailed ornithological works, as only these can depict the specific characteristics of the different species and subspecies with sufficient accuracy and detail. But in a totally different and often superior way, high-quality color photographs are just as important, since they can show, often amazingly well, the shapes, postures, and colors of these marvelous birds.

The text which accompanies Frank Todd's photographic plates is of high quality. It is accurate and to the point, and it contains much new information about the behavior of a number of species. This was only to be expected from the author, whose achievements as curator of birds, first at the Los Angeles Zoo and now at Sea World, have demonstrated that he has knowledge, skill, and good taste. Readers will not only enjoy this book, they will benefit from it.

Jean Delacour
Cleres, France

Preface

I can't say for certain when my curiosity about birds was initially aroused, but it could easily have been the day many years ago when my attention was drawn to an inviting hole in a large termite nest atop a very tall tree in the Republic of Panama. I climbed the tree and foolishly thrust my hand into the hole. The indignant orange-chinned parakeet nesting inside was not particularly impressed with my boyish curiosity, and firmly (and painfully) sank its beak into my finger. Thus began my life-long fascination with birds.

As a young man growing up in the jungles of Central America, I had numerous opportunities to enjoy and learn from the tropical biological paradise that surrounded me. My parents were very tolerant of my rather unorthodox activities, although I must confess that they did look with some disfavor on the collection of poisonous snakes that I kept under my bed. (It seems that most biologists begin their careers with reptiles—perhaps because these creatures are the easiest to catch.) Over the years, my folks gradually came to realize that I was apparently never going to grow up, and finally, they recognized that such peculiar behavior was the way of an aspiring biologist. I do believe that they were greatly relieved, however, when my enthusiasm for snakes waned and my interest in birds intensified.

Although I have spent my professional life studying all birds, and have been fortunate enough to observe thousands of species, the waterfowl as a group remain my favorites, for reasons that will become apparent as this book is read. Few people will ever be privileged to view all 147 living species or all 245 surviving subspecies of ducks, geese, and swans; and this is truly unfortunate, because the wildfowl are among the most spectacular of all birds.

Traditionally, wildfowl have been popular literary subjects, and many hundreds of books have been devoted to them. The past few years have been particularly fruitful, with the appearance of such beautiful and informative works as Johnsgard's *Ducks, Geese and Swans of the World*, Frith's *Waterfowl of Australia*, Ogilvie's *Ducks of Britain and Europe*, Bellrose's updating of the Kortright classic, *Ducks, Geese and Swans of North America*, and the long awaited publication of the second and third waterfowl volumes of the *Handbook of North American Birds* series, edited by Ralph Palmer. However, these books are mainly regional in scope, or may be too technical for most readers.

The primary purpose of this book is to increase public appreciation of waterfowl by providing a single volume that photographically depicts virtually *all* species and subspecies of waterfowl in color—a book that will be of value not only to the professional, but to every interested person as well. To this end, lengthy descriptions of courtship displays, which are sometimes involved and complicated, have been avoided where possible. Range maps, measurements, vocalizations, and detailed written descriptions of the different plumages (except where controversy exists) have likewise been omitted. This kind of technical information is readily available in other more scholarly works for those who have the need for it. The major emphasis here is placed on natural history.

To illustrate more clearly the sometimes subtle differences between various forms, particularly those which are closely related, pictures of drakes in breeding plumage were selected in most cases. Numerous species were photographed in the wild, but as a matter of practicality, many photographs were taken under controlled conditions. The large and comprehensive wildfowl collection at Sea World in San Diego was the main source, but it was my privilege to work with a number of other outstanding collections as well. Without the assistance and enthusiasm of the aviculturists associated with these collections, this book could not have been produced. I am grateful to all these dedicated individuals, but I must especially acknowledge the *tremendous* help and hospitality of Mike Lubbock, Assistant Director (Aviculture) of the Wildfowl Trust, Slimbridge, England; and his staff as well.

It is impossible to list by name all of the persons who assisted in some way, but Winston Guest, John DeJose, Bill Makins, Mickey Ollson, Jane Dawson, Mike and Mary Dam, Chris Marler, K. C. Lint, Allison Jane Stewart, Gus Griswold, Eddie Asper, Dr. Jesus Estudillo, George Allen, Jr., Chuck Pilling, Joanna Lubbock, Dan Southwick, Don Bruning, Kerry Muller, Steve Wylie, and Guy Greenwell are among the many aviculturists who not only put up with me, but went out of their way to see to it that I obtained the required material.

Federal and state biologists also unhesitatingly assisted, and I should like to particularly acknowledge the help of Don Tiller, John Hall, Bob Gill, Margaret Peterson, Glen Smart, Ah Fat Lee, John Sarvis, Chris and Carla Dau, and Fish and Wildlife Service Special Agent Robert Prather. Dr. Gordon R. Williams, the director of the New Zealand Wildlife Service and his staff, particularly Colin Roderick and Rodney Russ, gave freely of their time and expertise. The Argentine ornithologist Maurice Rumboll was most helpful, as was the staff of the Patuxent Wildlife Research Center. Ricardo Mata and Francois Berger greatly assisted me with my Guatemalan fieldwork. I am also grateful for the assistance of the master and crew of the National Science Foundation Research Vessel *Hero*.

The great majority of the pictures were selected from my own photographic files, but the pictorial contributions of Paul Johnsgard, Dr. Salim Ali, Lady Philippa Scott, Karl Kenyon, Joe Jehl, Ken Fink, Tony Mercieca, Father A. E. Ames, Chris Spiker, Phil Stanton, Andre Chauveau, the California Department of Fish and Game, the New Zealand Wildlife Service, the U.S. Fish and Wildlife Service, and others have greatly enhanced the book, and I am most appreciative.

With a family of birds as large and diverse as the waterfowl, it is inevitable that some representatives are either so rare or so little known that usable photographs of the living birds are impossible to obtain. Some species and subspecies have become extinct (or nearly so) in historical times. In an attempt to make this book as complete as possible, it was necessary to refer to museum material, and in this regard, I wish to thank Dr. Ralph Schrieber of the Los Angeles County Museum of Natural History for his assistance, as well as the ornithological staff of the National Museum of Natural History, Smithsonian Institution.

Drs. Jean Delacour, Paul Johnsgard, Lanny Cornell, and Joe Jehl Jr., as well as Glen Smart, James King, Chris Dau, and Mike Lubbock commented on preliminary drafts of the manuscript and provided numerous helpful suggestions. My good friend, Dave Siddon, offered invaluable and constructive editorial advice. Dr. Nate Gale and Richard Chrisman were instrumental in getting the project started, and Dr. George Llano (formerly Acting Chief Scientist, Office of Polar Programs, National Science Foundation) was helpful in countless ways.

The staff and management of Sea World—in particular, Frank Powell, Dave DeMotte, and Leon Drew—have been most understanding, and have also offered a great deal of encouragement when it was needed. My tireless secretaries, Cary Duffin and Judi Myers, who typed and retyped drafts time and again, deserve very special recognition, as does my outstanding avicultural staff. The gentle prodding and enthusiastic encouragement of my long-time friend Dr. Jean Delacour, the patriarch of 20th Century ornithologists, provided the primary inspiration for this book. My editor, John Wexo, and designer Paul Slick were particularly helpful during the final stages. (Naturally, since all of the aforementioned individuals have unselfishly given of their time and expertise, they are largely responsible for any virtues that this work may possess. But any shortcomings are solely my responsibility.)

Finally, it is with great pleasure that I dedicate this book to my patient and incredibly understanding wife, Sherlyn, and to my often fatherless children, Suzy and Jody, who have repeatedly had to put up with my travels to the far ends of the earth. No biologist has been more fortunate.

Frank S. Todd
San Diego, California

Dedicated With Love to
SHERLYN, SUZY, AND JODY

1
Introduction
to the
True Waterfowl

Ducks, geese, and swans are among the most beautiful and striking birds that ever graced this planet. Known to Americans as waterfowl and to the British as wildfowl, these magnificent birds are all very closely related and are all members of the avian family Anatidae—a group which most ornithologists simply refer to as the anatids. Of all the birds, waterfowl are perhaps the most spectacular and fascinating to observe, and indeed, there are relatively few individuals who will not readily admit to having at least a passing interest in these colorful and fascinating winged creatures.

In essence, the waterfowl collectively combine many of the qualities that man finds most aesthetically pleasing about birds. Often, they have brightly colored plumages which may be boldly patterned, and they occur in a great variety of diverse shapes, sizes, and forms. Their relatively large sizes and highly social natures quickly draws our attention to them, and their dynamic lifestyles are such that sooner or later, most people are exposed to them. Furthermore, their center of distribution lies in the Northern Hemisphere, not in the tropics like many families of exotic birds, and some 55 to 60 forms inhabit or are frequently encountered in North America alone.

Casual observers may assume that all water birds are waterfowl, but the 147 living species of ducks, geese, and swans stand alone.

1.2

1.1 (Opposite Page) *Barnacle goose in flight. Most geese have an effortless flight style, and their capabilities in the air are legendary.*

1.2 *American wigeon drake. As a group, waterfowl are powerful fliers, and even high mountain ranges and large oceans have had little effect on their distribution. Reportedly, one species (the bar-headed goose) is even capable of flying over Mt. Everest at an altitude of 29,000 feet.*

Even though they may resemble other groups of aquatic birds in many respects, these similarities are merely superficial and have resulted because of similar lifestyles. Coots, grebes, and loons also live on water, and are not unlike waterfowl in profile, but they are not even distantly related. Stilts, sandpipers, and avocets are shorebirds rather than wildfowl. Likewise, egrets, herons, flamingos, and storks are more correctly thought of as waders; while cormorants, gulls, penguins, pelicans, and puffins are loosely called "sea birds."

The closest living relatives of wildfowl are, in fact, the bizarre screamers of South America. This relationship is quite puzzling to non-biologists, because screamers don't even remotely resemble a duck or a goose, but the kinship is nevertheless so close that screamers occupy a family position in the same taxonomic order, the Anseriformes. Some contemporary specialists believe that flamingos may also be an ancient offshoot of the waterfowl line, and based on anatomical and behavioral similarities, some ornithologists even suggest that flamingos should be included in the same order as waterfowl. The vocalizations of flamingos are distinctly goose-like, and even their feather parasites suggest an affinity with geese—and interestingly, newly-hatched downy flamingo chicks are superficially very

1.4

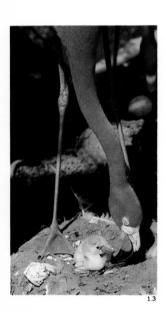

1.3

1.5

1.3 *Caribbean flamingo with two-day-old chick. Flamingos are rather closely related to waterfowl, and some authorities believe that they should be included in the same taxonomic order. In many ways, recently hatched flamingo chicks closely resemble young goslings.*

1.4 *Black-necked screamer. Even though screamers superficially resemble gamebirds, they are the closest surviving relatives of the waterfowl.*

1.5 *California brown pelican with eggs and young. These birds, as well as those illustrated in plates 1.6 and 1.7, are water birds — but they are not even remotely related to waterfowl.*

1.6 *Portrait of a horned puffin.*

1.7 *Emperor penguin with quarter-grown chick.*

1.6

1.7

similar to young goslings. In addition to these fairly close relationships with screamers and flamingos, there are also numerous anatomical similarities between the waterfowl and some gamebirds, and the anatids were probably derived originally from a gallinaceous ancestor that may have been remotely related to the present-day cracids.

The origin of waterfowl dates back perhaps as much as 80 million years, and although this makes them relative newcomers when compared to many life forms, they have a far more ancient lineage than does man. Life has been present on Earth for more than two billion years, but man as we know him has only existed for two million years or less. As a group, birds are believed to have evolved from reptiles and, in fact, paleontologists sometimes refer to them as "glorified reptiles." It appears that they began to branch off from the reptilian line approximately 150 million years ago, shortly before the emergence of the first mammals (which also evolved from reptiles, but independently). The famous *Archaeopteryx* is the earliest recognized avian fossil, dating from the Jurassic Period, approximately 140 million years ago—but undoubtedly, there were earlier birds or bird-like creatures whose remains are yet to be discovered.

Fossil remains of waterfowl and other birds are scarce, because birds are of necessity relatively frail creatures. For one thing, their bones must be hollow if they are to be able to fly, and such hollow and lightweight structures do not stand the test of time very well. Consequently, most fossil waterfowl species have been described mainly from pieces of only a few disarticulated bones. The earliest recognizable wildfowl fossil on which most experts agree comes from the upper Eocene Period, dating back perhaps 40 to 50 million years. Altogether, avian paleontologists have thus far identified about a hundred extinct forms of waterfowl.

The never-ending process of evolution has been particularly productive with birds. Thousands (and perhaps millions) of species evolved and ultimately disappeared before man arrived on the scene, and today there are approximately 8650 living species of birds, which are divided by biologists into 27 orders and 115 families. The anatids, which comprise but one of these orders and families, exhibit considerable diversity in external appearance, size, plumage, pattern, behavior, and ecology, but they are nonetheless among the most homogenous of all avian groups. Despite great differences in size, for example—from the tiny pygmy goose weighing but ten ounces to the massive trumpeter swan which may reach almost 40 pounds, and have a wing span of eight to ten feet—all species are still readily identified as waterfowl.

Ducks, geese, and swans were among the first birds to be domesticated by man. The greylag goose was apparently domesticated as much as 4500 years ago, and may in fact be the first of all domestic birds. Originally, waterfowl were undoubtedly maintained as a food source, but later they were kept strictly for ornamental and aesthetic purposes as well. Written allusions to them date back at least 2500 years, and they were depicted in paintings even earlier. Cro-Magnon man fashioned primitive rock carvings of swans in northern Russia, and cave paintings of waterfowl have also been unearthed in neolithic sites that were inhabited no less than 20,000 years ago in Spain, France, and Italy.

Waterfowl are just as intriguing to modern man, and more has probably been written about them than about any other single avian group. Even so, our knowledge about them can still be considered very far from complete; indeed, in the case of some species the

1.8

1.9

1.8 *Western greylag goose. Greylag geese are believed to have been one of the first birds to be domesticated — perhaps as long ago as the third millenium B.C.*

1.9 *Male green pygmy goose with an Australian jacana or lily-trotter. These little ducks are among the smallest of the waterfowl.*

1.10 *Pair of trumpeter swans, with the bird on the right in a typical sleeping posture. These magnificent birds are considered to be the largest of all wildfowl, and may weigh more than 60 times as much as the pygmy goose illustrated in plate 1.9.*

1.10

1.11

1.12

1.13

1.11 *Underwater view of the feet of a Canada goose. As a foot of this type is pushed backward, the webs expand and the foot acts as a paddle. During the return stroke, the webs are held together and offer less resistance, reducing drag to a minimum.*

1.12 *The well-webbed feet of this whooper swan typify the normal wildfowl foot. One might assume that such large feet would be cumbersome when walking, and this is true to some degree — but many forms of waterfowl are surprisingly agile when ashore, particularly geese.*

1.13 *The foot webbing is significantly reduced on a very few species of waterfowl, because the birds involved have shifted to a much more terrestrial lifestyle. The feet of the Nene goose shown here, for example, are adapted for walking on the steep volcanic slopes of Hawaii.*

almost complete lack of accurate life history data is scandalous. (For example, most of our knowledge about the reproductive biology of the American black scoter and the surf scoter dates back to the turn of the century.)

In general, ducks, geese, and swans have probably been admired more and exploited to a greater degree than most other bird groups. From an economic standpoint, certainly, they are among the most valuable of all birds, and many people the world over are very dependent on wildfowl and their eggs as a food source. In the western world, the rearing of these birds for food is not of major importance, but in less affluent regions (particularly Asia) domestic ducks are frequently as common as chickens are in America. Waterfowl hunting is a major sport in North America and Europe, an "industry" which contributes billions of dollars to the economy each year. The preoccupation of waterfowl hunters with wetland habitat protection has resulted in many benefits to the quarry species (and to numerous other life forms as well). At the same time, however, the escalating conflict between hunters and protectionists has spawned a great deal of conflict in recent years.

Anatids are cosmopolitan in distribution, inhabiting all continents except Antarctica; and even there, they may sometimes be rare stragglers. (A South Georgia pintail, for example, was observed in January of 1975 on a small island adjacent to the Antarctic Peninsula, near the United States Antarctic Research Station Palmer.) Topographic barriers such as mountain ranges or oceans are not major factors in determining their distribution, since most species can fly over them. As a group, in fact, wildfowl exploit a tremendous variety of ecological niches, and while some individual species are very widely distributed, others occupy extremely small areas. The ranges of the common mallard and northern pintail, for example, encompass most of the Northern Hemisphere and parts of the Southern Hemisphere, whereas the white-eyed duck of Madagascar and Bernier's teal are restricted to a few lakes on a single island. While waterfowl may have originated in tropical or southern regions, they have most successfully colonized the extensive grasslands and tundras of the north temperate and arctic zones.

Waterfowl are fairly long-lived in captivity, where they are afforded greater protection and have easier lives, and twenty- to thirty-year-old captive geese and swans are not particularly uncommon. Mortality in the wild, however, is very high, and the potential life spans suggested by some captive specimens are rarely attained under natural conditions. For most of the smaller duck species, two or three (possibly up to six) breeding seasons is the average life span that can be expected; and between 60 and 75 percent of the annual hatch is lost during the first year, with 90 to 95 percent gone within three years. Yet, banding records indicate that some wild geese have survived at least 18 years, and ducks as long as 16 years.

Most waterfowl have comparatively short legs and strongly webbed front toes, and are excellent swimmers. Exceptions are the Nene, magpie, and Cape Barren geese, which have adapted to terrestrial lifestyles and consequently exhibit reduced foot webbing. To aid in swimming, the legs of many waterfowl are placed far back on the body. While this undoubtedly increases the efficiency of aquatic propulsion, it also forces the birds to move with a waddling gait when they are ashore, since they must shift their center of gravity to a position above the supporting leg to maintain balance. Because of their wide bodies and relatively short legs, this displacement of the center of

1.14

1.15

1.16

1.17

1.18

1.19

gravity can only be accomplished by a rotation and shifting to the side, which in turn brings about the characteristic waddle.

The normal swimming speed of waterfowl is between two and three miles per hour, although they can swim much faster if pursued. As each webbed foot is thrust backward, the webs spread apart, thus presenting the maximum surface to the water, while during the forward stroke the webs are closed and offer less resistance. Buoyancy in the water is due mainly to internal air sacs (not to air trapped in the feathers as some writers suggest). These air sacs, which are connected to the lungs, extend into the body cavity and even into some of the long bones as well. As with many diving birds, the air sacs of waterfowl can be inflated or deflated to alter buoyancy.

Many species typically roost ashore, where they will commonly doze while standing on one leg, with the head turned back and the bill usually inserted into the scapular feathers on the same side as the lifted foot. Other species, including some of the sea ducks, seldom come

ashore, preferring instead to sleep on the water for security. As a rule, wildfowl have relatively long necks and flattened, broad bills which are perhaps their most characteristic feature. Indeed, their bills alone are so distinctive that it is very difficult to confuse them with any other bird type. Typically, they are blunt and often somewhat spatulate in shape, are covered with a thin soft membrane, and have a hard nail at the tip of the upper mandible. Mergansers (or "sawbills") are different from other waterfowl in that they have long, hard, slender bills, with tooth-like serrations along the edges that aid them in holding slippery fish securely. In general, variations of bill shape reflect different feeding techniques.

All ducks, geese, and swans are thickly feathered and are noted for their compact waterproof plumage, as well as the dense coat of insulating down beneath. The number of feathers varies greatly, however, and while a whistling swan may have over 25,000 feathers (most of them covering the neck), a green-winged teal may have as few as

1.14 *Sleeping western greylag goose in the rain. When resting ashore, wildfowl will frequently stand on one leg. Often, the head is turned back and the bill is inserted into the scapular feathers on the same side as the raised leg.*

1.15 *Dozing trumpeter swan. On occasion, some waterfowl will sleep ashore standing on both legs.*

1.16 *Drake northern cinnamon teal, a species that has a typical duck bill.*

1.17 *Female goosander, one of the mergansers or fish ducks. Unlike other waterfowl, mergansers have evolved a bill that is long and cylindrical, with a number of saw-like serrations along the edges. Such a bill is obviously advantageous for fish-eating birds that must be able to hold onto struggling, slippery fish. Merganser bills are probably the least typical of all the different types of wildfowl bills.*

1.18 *Trumpeter swan. Most swans have huge, powerful bills that are very effective when pulling up masses of aquatic vegetation from underwater.*

1.19 *Thick-billed bean goose. Many geese are noted for their extreme grazing tendencies and their bills are ideally suited for cropping and cutting grass, as well as other vegetation.*

1.20

1.21

1.22

1.20 *Two drake mallards on the wing. The wings of waterfowl are small in relation to the weight of their bodies, and indeed, the ratio of wing area to body weight is among the lowest of flying birds. But the power of the wing stroke compensates for this apparent disadvantage.*

1.21 *Barnacle goose coming in for a landing. The aerial acrobatics of these birds, particularly when they are landing rapidly, are so unbelievable that they must be observed firsthand to be fully appreciated.*

1.22 *Wandering albatross. Like waterfowl, albatrosses are well known for their unparalleled flying ability, but whereas the albatross is noted for gliding and soaring, waterfowl flap their wings continuously — as rapidly as 300 or more strokes per minute in some cases.*

11,500. Ten or eleven primary feathers and twelve to twenty-four tail feathers are typical. Not surprisingly, most wildfowl are powerful fliers, although there are a few species which are totally flightless, such as two of the three forms of South American steamer ducks. Generally, waterfowl fly with their necks extended and their legs trailing. They propel themselves through the air with continuous wing beats, and unlike species such as condors or albatrosses, they are not noted for any soaring ability.

The voices of waterfowl vary considerably in intensity, tone, and quality. Most people are familiar with the well-known quack of the female mallard, and it is considered by many to be the typical duck call. Waterfowl that honk, hiss, and trumpet are also not totally unfamiliar. But very few people are aware that some species may huff, grunt, bark, squeak, cluck, and coo as well. Vocalizations are used for courtship, communication, defense, warning, recognition, flocking signals, and for other social purposes.

In many cases, the sexes have different voices, with that of the female usually being lower; and contrary to popular belief, no species is totally mute—not even the so-called "mute" swan. Swans exhibit the greatest vocal variety, ranging from the insignificant voice of the mute swan to the clear, melodic, far-carrying cry of the trumpeter swan. Not surprisingly, many anatids derive their descriptive vernacular names from their voices; whistling ducks obviously whistle, Cape Barren geese (known also as pig geese) grunt, and trumpeter swans trumpet. The coscoroba swan possesses a distinct ringing "cos-cor-oo" call, and the Eskimo name "hohohalik" for the oldsquaw duck suggests its yodel-like call.

The waterfowl family exhibits a great deal of variation in the size and shape of the syrinx or vocal organ. Males of many species are characterized by the development of a symmetrical bony enlargement (or bulla) at the base of the trachea, and the size and shape of this bony sound chamber (or lack of it altogether) is instrumental in determining the sound and quality of the vocalization produced. In the words of the noted waterfowl behaviorist Paul Johnsgard, the bulla ". . . operates in much the same manner as a mechanical whistle, producing a whistling note as air is rapidly passed by it through the trachea. Female ducks and males of species that lack such bullas, instead apparently rely on the vibration of the soft tympanic membranes located between the base of the trachea and the bronchi. These thin membranes are readily vibrated by the passage of air across them, and pitch is apparently regulated by varying the tension on the membranes through the use of two opposing pairs of muscles." Systematists consider the shape of the bulla to be very significant taxonomically.

A number of species produce mechanical sounds as well. Male ruddy ducks, for example, have specialized tracheal air sacs in the neck, which can be inflated and beaten upon with the bill during courtship to create a distinct drumming sound. Some whistling ducks emit a characteristic whistling sound in flight that is created by the vibration of peculiarly shaped outer primary feathers. The rushing wing beats of mute swans may be audible for over a hundred yards, and probably assist the birds in maintaining auditory contact with each other in flight when visibility is limited. In contrast, the other northern swans produce no significant mechanical sounds while in flight, relying instead on vocal contact.

Waterfowl feed on a great variety of food items, and as a result, a great many feeding adaptations and techniques have evolved. Bill shapes, for example, have been modified to suit specific feeding

1.23 *Northern black-bellied whistling duck vocalizing. Waterfowl have a large variety of different types of calls. Not surprisingly, the vernacular name of this bird is derived from the whistling notes it produces.*

1.24 *Drake wood duck calling. In most instances, male and female wildfowl have different voices. With wood ducks, drakes are noted for their low goldfinch-like calls, while females call out with an owl-like call in flight and may utter a sharp-noted whistle during courtship.*

1.25 *Jankowski's swan vocalizing. Northern swans are famous for their incredible vocal capabilities, and their calls carry considerable distances across the tundra. It may be that such loud calls are important in maintaining and defending the enormous territories that these birds typically establish.*

1.26 *Nene goose calling at dusk. Usually, the call of this species is a low moaning sound, but they are also capable of producing a more typical goose-like yelping call.*

1.24

1.25

1.23

1.26

1.27

1.30

1.28

1.27 *Lesser Bahama pintail upending. This technique makes it possible for many waterfowl to feed in deeper water.*

1.28 *Ruddy shelduck.*

1.29 *Pair of mute swans.*

1.30 *Taverner's Canada goose.*

1.29

requirements, and not surprisingly, the most extreme modifications have evolved on those species which tend to be the most specialized. Basically, there are three main methods of feeding: diving, grazing, and surface feeding. Surface feeding is the most common, and is utilized by not only the least specialized of waterfowl but by some of the most specialized as well. Dabbling ducks (sometimes known as river or puddle ducks) are primarily surface feeders, typically ingesting material from the surface of a pond, lake, or river; but they will often tip up, or upend, to obtain their food from the bottom as well. Diving ducks submerge for their food, and rarely leave the security of the water because the rearward position of their legs makes it difficult to move on land. Many diving ducks forage on living organisms in the water, and although most rarely go down any further than 10 to 20 feet, several species (such as the oldsquaw and king eider) are reported to dive deeper than 180 feet. (These deep divers, however, do not come close to matching the unbelievable 800-foot dives of the emperor penguin.) Practically all waterfowl can (and do) dive when forced to do so, even those which are not adapted to such a lifestyle. Sea ducks feed chiefly in salt water, and many have evolved specialized nasal salt glands that facilitate the discharge of excess salt. With

1.31 *A number of species of ducks, such as this northern ruddy duck, are effective divers. All diving species depend on their relatively large feet for underwater propulsion, and some utilize their wings as well. To ascend, diving ducks merely stop pumping their feet and bob to the surface like corks.* PHOTO BY TONY MERCIECA

1.32 *Some waterfowl, including the pink-eared duck shown, have bills that are adapted to their very specialized feeding requirements. Pink-eared ducks use their broadened spatulate bills to filter-feed from the surface of the water. The soft flaps which extend below the lower mandible make it possible to more effectively strain floating planktonic organisms and blue-green algae.*

1.33 *Northern shoveler female. Surface-feeding ducks are noted for lamellae that line the mandibles, an adaptation which enables them to strain minute food organisms out of the water.*

1.34 *Russian bean goose grazing. Most geese are very effective grazers, and the size and shape of the bill is usually a fairly accurate indication of the type of vegetation that a species feeds on — short grass, long grass, roots, etc.*

1.35 *Drake surf scoter. Waterfowl that frequent the sea or salt water habitats often have specialized supra-orbital glands. These glands make it possible for the birds to ingest salt water because they secrete excess salt. With scoters and some other species, the salt glands can be quite large and may alter the shape of the head profile.*

some species, the presence of these glands may affect the shape of their profiles.

The type of food selected by the various wildfowl depends somewhat on their method of feeding. Relatively nonselective feeders such as mallards consume almost anything edible that they encounter. Shovelers and pink-eared ducks are more specialized, and filter minute aquatic organisms from the surface of the water. True geese are noted for their extreme grazing habits and spend a great deal of time ashore. All waterfowl except mergansers have a highly sensitive functional tongue that is lined with many small spiny projections. The action of the tongue, working against rows of horny lamellae that line the mandibles, serves as an efficient food-sifting mechanism. (This is particularly true of dabbling ducks, which have twice as many lamellae as diving ducks.) The peculiar sound emitted during feeding is sometimes referred to as "chattering." Except for the flamingos, no other birds feed in this specialized manner.

Grass, seeds, cultivated grain, and aquatic vegetation (such as duck weed and algae) are favored by some species, while others prefer fish, molluscs, crustaceans, insects, and other miscellaneous small, succulent creatures. Aquatic invertebrates are particularly important for

1.36 *Red-breasted goose. With most waterfowl species, brightly-colored and boldly-patterned plumage is generally restricted to the males. With geese, however, both sexes are usually similar in color.*

1.37 *Pacific harlequin ducks — three drakes in full color and a female. Despite their gorgeous coloration and gaudy pattern, these ducks can be surprisingly difficult to observe, particularly when at sea.*

1.38 *Western greylag goose with goslings. Geese are typically rather somber in color, and for the most part, they are not distinctly patterned.*

1.39 *Drake wood duck. Considered by many to be the most exquisite of wildfowl, wood ducks once faced extinction — partly because their colorful feathers were much in demand for human fashions.*

many ducklings or goslings, although as adults they may feed primarily on herbaceous material. A few species are even carnivorous, and may feed on carcasses at times. In sum—ducks, geese, and swans exploit almost every available food source.

Waterfowl weights are subject to a significant amount of fluctuation. During incubation, for example, it is not unusual for some female geese (and other waterfowl as well) to lose up to 40 percent of their peak weight (which is attained just prior to their northward spring migration). Weights also tend to drop during the molt, particularly with males. As a rule, seasonal weight differences are not nearly as severe with nonmigratory species.

The beauty and variety of their coloration is one of the most attractive features of the world's waterfowl, giving endless pleasure to the beholder. The colors of their plumages span the full spectrum, from the exquisitely caparisoned wood duck to the rather nondescript greylag goose. Generally, males are more ornate and brighter than females, yet in some species, such as the Siberian red-breasted goose, both sexes are boldly colored and patterned. Among the most strikingly patterned and colorful wildfowl are the wood duck, harlequin duck, and Baikal teal, which are so brilliantly garbed that they appear almost artificial.

In addition to the abundant supply of color that nature has provided most waterfowl in their livery, their beauty is often further enhanced by a metallic and iridescent wing speculum—a lustrous area that is sometimes called a "wing window." The velvety appearance of the eiders and some of the scoters also produces a unique visual effect. Some waterfowl have developed other attractive adornments as well. These may take the form of modifications of the shape of a single feather, or of whole regions of plumage—as with the distinctive forward-curling tail feather of the mallard drake or the strongly undulated innermost wing feathers of the black swan. Muscovy ducks are noted for curled hoods, crested ducks and mergansers for crests, plumed tree ducks for elongated flank feathers, falcated ducks for trailing sickle-like wing feathers, mandarin ducks for sail-like inner secondaries, and pintail and oldsquaw ducks for long, thin tail feathers.

Fleshy modifications are not unusual either. For instance, black-necked swans and drake king eiders have highly developed colored knobs on the top of their upper mandibles, and European shelduck drakes and rosy-billed pochards are noted for bright facial shields. The bills of some species are brilliantly colored, and the color may vary greatly depending on the season—as when the beautiful powder blue bill of the courting ruddy duck drake fades to a dull greyish brown during the nonbreeding season.

The question arises why many of the drakes, particularly in the north, are so brightly dressed to begin with. It may initially appear, for instance, that bright colors would run counter to the need for camouflage in the wild. But, in fact, distinctive colors and contrasting patterns may enable an animal to visually blend into its surroundings by de-emphasizing its shape. For example, as gaudy as the male harlequin duck is at close range, it is surprisingly difficult to see from a distance. At other times, bright colors may serve to protect females and young, as when a brightly colored male attracts a potential predator and draws it away from an incubating hen. Obviously, gay colors and conspicuous patterns also play a significant role in courtship, and many males use their fancy plumage to attract a mate. It has also been suggested that ornamental plumage could be a device to prevent hybridization, but this theory is weakened by the existence of numer-

1.40 *Speculum of a bronze-winged duck. Many ducks, particularly dabbling ducks, have a beautiful lustrous area like this on the wing. With a number of dull and nondescript species, this metallic and iridescent "wing window" is the only hint of color on the bird. The speculum is generally restricted to the secondaries and adorns the wings of both sexes. It probably has several purposes, but there is no doubt that it functions as a flashing flight signal which aids in maintaining flock cohesion. Depending on the species, speculum colors vary significantly, from deep blues and purples to green and bronze.*

1.41

1.42

1.43

1.44

1.45

1.41 *Drake spectacled eider. Many waterfowl are noted for peculiarly-shaped feathers or fleshy modifications, and the distinctive "spectacles" of these eiders are among the most distinctive and beautiful of these.*

1.42 *Drake oldsquaw duck in breeding plumage. The vernacular names of waterfowl are frequently based on their physical appearance. Oldsquaw, for example, are often referred to as long-tailed ducks (for obvious reasons).*

1.43 *Male muscovy duck. Quite a few species of waterfowl have ornamental facial structures and crests.*

1.44 *Northern pintail drake in full color. This species obviously derived its descriptive vernacular name from its long, thin tail feathers.*

1.45 *Three adult male hooded mergansers with a female to the right. The hoods, which are carried by both sexes, are erectile — but they can also be flattened along the back of the neck.*

1.46 Drake mandarin duck. These birds are perhaps best known for their distinctive crests, their orange-chestnut "side whiskers," and the peculiar orange "sails" that extend up along their flanks.

1.47 During the breeding season, there is a dramatic increase in both the color intensity and the size of the fleshy bulbous knob atop the upper mandible of the drake rosybill pochard.

1.48 Adult male ruddy duck. When these ducks are out of breeding color, their bills lose the distinctive powder-blue color for which they are perhaps best known, and their ruddy plumage is replaced by a duller and more somber coloration.

1.49 Adult ruddy duck drake in full breeding color.

1.50 The fleshy knob of the mute swan cob increases in size significantly and its color becomes more intense when the bird is in breeding condition.

1.46

1.47

1.48

1.49

1.50

1.51

1.52

1.53

1.54

1.51 *Drake Baikal teal in full breeding plumage. Compare this colorful drake with the males in eclipse plumage that are shown in plate 1.55.*

1.52 *Female mallard with ducklings. With many duck species, females are more somber in color and lack the patterns of their brightly-colored mates (see plate 1.54).*

1.53 *The dark color and concealing pattern of this incubating Steller's eider female combine to provide an extremely effective camouflage. Often, incubating hens increase the effectiveness of this camouflage still further by flattening themselves out on the ground. In such a position, they are practically invisible, even when nesting on the exposed tundra.*

1.54 *Drake northern mallard in the spring. The bright colors and contrasting patterns of many northern ducks are of obvious importance in pair bond formation.*

ous nondescript species of waterfowl and some forms that exhibit no external sexual dimorphism at all. If prevention of hybridization is involved, one must wonder why *all* waterfowl are not brightly colored—or for that matter, why not all birds.

Female ducks are usually cryptically dressed with inconspicuous colors, predominantly browns and greys. This coloration is an advantage to a bird sitting on a ground nest because it provides a degree of camouflage. In summer, drakes of many northern species acquire an "eclipse plumage," and their brilliant colors and patterns are replaced by a dull plumage similar to that of the female. During the molt, many drakes can be difficult for the casual observer (and many experienced observers as well) to identify because their plumage is significantly altered. Obviously, a grounded camouflaged bird stands a much greater chance of survival than a conspicuously colored flightless bird.

The molt is necessary because feathers wear out and must be replaced, and normally the body feathers of ducks are shed twice a

year, while the wing feathers are molted but once. All of the flight feathers on the wing are lost simultaneously, and the birds are flightless for one to two months. Interestingly, the large flight feathers are usually not dropped until the male is well into eclipse plumage, and therefore the bird is not completely devoid of its flying abilities until it has assumed a complete protective coloration. Sometimes, with geese and swans that rear the young together, both sexes do not molt simultaneously, so that one of the pair is always in a position to provide greater care and protection for the young.

The Australian magpie goose is unique among the waterfowl in that it has a graduated wing molt, and thus bypasses the typical anatid flightless period. Most wildfowl tend to seek large bodies of water when flightless during the molt, and spend a great deal of time (or the whole time) in the water in an effort to escape predation. As the wing feathers are replaced, the growth of "blood feathers" makes the wings very heavy, and this is a very dangerous time to handle wildfowl, since

1.56

1.55 *Baikal teal males in eclipse plumage. After the breeding season, northern ducks in particular shed their bright nuptial feathers and assume a dull nondescript coloration similar to that of their mates. During the molt, the flight feathers are lost and the birds become flightless for several weeks. It is believed that the eclipse plumage gives the drakes a degree of camouflage while they are grounded.*

1.56 *Nene goose with blood feathers. As new flight feathers grow in, they are richly supplied with blood and are consequently very heavy and delicate. It can be dangerous to handle waterfowl during this time, because a bird will bleed profusely if a blood feather is broken. Once the feathers are fully grown, nourishment is no longer required and they are essentially dead. At this point, they can even be cut without fear of harm to the bird.*

1.55

the breaking of a blood feather can result in a substantial amount of bleeding.

Thousands of waterfowl are banded by biologists annually during the period of flightlessness. In the past, this was done in a rather haphazard manner, but now all official banding in North America is a coordinated, computerized operation, and approximately 300,000 ducks, geese, and swans are banded each year in North America alone. The data that are gathered in this massive operation shed a great deal of light on the biology and lifestyles of many species, providing new information on life spans, population dynamics, effects of hunting pressure, migratory routes, and other matters that in turn are important when it comes to determining the length of hunting seasons, bag limits, protection policies regarding some species, and what land to acquire and preserve to protect both breeding and wintering habitat. Modern aircraft, banding, biotelemetry, and computers have provided many new and more efficient ways to obtain, analyze, store, and retrieve voluminous amounts of valuable field data, adding significantly to our knowledge of waterfowl.

Since they spend a great part of their lives in water, waterfowl must be waterproofed to the extent that water will bead up and roll off their backs like droplets of mercury. For this, they are equipped with a large and highly developed tufted oil gland at the base of the tail, which is known as the uropygial gland. Frequent preening and oiling are vital to maintain the feathers in prime condition and to keep them waterproofed, and to help preserve the surface of the bill and legs as well. After bathing, waterfowl may preen for hours, a process that can be fascinating to observe. The feathers are "combed out" using the serrated edges of the bill, and often, feathers that appear to be damaged can be repaired when properly preened. If the birds fail to keep themselves in good condition, especially if the feathers are not maintained and oiled, they run the risk of chilling and sinking—and perhaps even drowning. Further, an un-oiled duck, which must stay out of water to avoid chilling or drowning, is more likely to become a meal for an alert predator.

Northern waterfowl in particular can be extremely gregarious, and many species tend to assemble in tremendous flocks, especially during migration and on the wintering grounds. This has a number of advantages, not the least of which is the greater survival potential it confers on each bird by combining the senses and actions of a large group. On the other hand, it also increases their vulnerability to oil spills and other forms of pollution, as well as contagious diseases.

The biannual migratory treks of many of the northern species are well documented. Not all waterfowl migrate, but those that inhabit the higher latitudes usually do, and each fall millions of ducks, geese, and swans move down from their ancestral breeding grounds in the Arctic to spend the winter in more favorable southern climates. The melodic, far-carrying call of the Canada goose winging its way south on a crisp autumn morning is unforgettable, and is a sure sign that winter is not far behind. The phenomenon of migration also occurs in the Southern Hemisphere but is not such a grand spectacle. The seasons are reversed south of the equator, and the southern (or austral) summer occurs at the same time as the northern winter.

1.58

1.57 (Opposite Page) *U.S. Fish and Wildlife Service biologists banding ducks. Banding has proved to be an effective wildlife management tool and has been instrumental in providing biologists with much valuable information about the often-elusive lifestyles of many species. Most major banding operations are conducted early in the molt when the birds are flightless (and when they are often gregarious). The procedure is harmless to the bird. Note that one biologist is holding a string of bands which are numbered sequentially. An effective banding team is usually composed of at least three individuals: one to hold the birds, one to band, and one to record the data (which includes the band number, species, sex, weight, measurements, etc.).* PHOTO BY U.S.F.&W.S.

1.58 *Western greylag goose bathing. When waterfowl are properly waterproofed, water should bead up or easily sheet off them. Frequent bathing is required to maintain a bird in prime condition. Bathing waterfowl may furiously flail or beat the surface of the water with their wings and may even roll over on their backs.*

1.59

1.60

1.63

1.61

1.62

1.64

Bathing waterfowl

1.59 *Western greylag goose.*
1.60 *Fulvous whistling duck.*
1.61 *Russian bean goose with goslings.*
1.62 *Javan whistling duck.*
1.63 *Drake wood duck.*
1.64 *Orinoco goose.*
1.65 *White-faced whistling duck.*
1.66 *Drake ruddy duck.*
1.67 *Male spur-winged goose.*
1.68 *Northern black-bellied whistling duck.*
1.69 *Greater snow goose.*

1.65

1.66

1.67

1.68

1.69

19

1.71 *Western greylag goose preening. Waterfowl have a highly-developed tufted oil gland (or uropygial gland) which is located at the base of the tail. Oil from this gland is used to waterproof the feathers, and this goose is oiling its bill for that purpose. Feather maintenance is of primary importance to species that are powerful fliers and which spend a great deal of time in the water. During preening, waterfowl may assume a number of peculiar postures.*

1.71

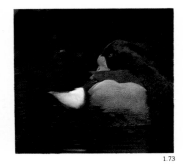

1.72

1.73

Preening waterfowl

1.70 *Male North American ruddy duck. It may initially appear that "duck bills" are ill-suited for detailed tasks such as preening, but they are actually very efficient tools for the purpose.*

1.72 *Coscoroba swan. Preening is the single most important part of feather care.*

1.73 *Drake rosy-billed pochard. Preening almost invariably follows bathing, and involves the arrangement, cleansing, and general maintenance of the feather structure by the bill.*

1.70

Preening waterfowl

1.74 *Female northern shoveler.*

1.75 *Drake European shelduck. Nibbling (or mandibulating) is the most thorough and accurate preening method. During such activity, the bird deals with an individual feather, seizing it in the tips of the bill and passing it between them, working from base to tip.*

1.76 *Mute swan. Preening is particularly important during the molt, when old feathers are worked loose and discarded. At times, great masses of feathers surround a swan that has been preening for several hours.*

1.77 *Puna teal. When the feathers are oiled during preening, the uropygial gland is stimulated with the bill to initiate the "flow" of oil. The tail is characteristically fanned and twisted to one side.*

1.78 (Opposite Page) *Egyptian goose preening in the water. During preening, the feathers are "combed out" and even feathers which may initially appear to be damaged beyond repair can often be brought back into condition. Frequent preening is also required to preserve the surface of the bills and legs. At times, such activity may go on for hours.*

1.79 *Preening male gadwall.*

1.80 *Cuban whistling duck preening neck feathers.*

1.81 *Preening black-necked swans often roll over on their sides. Most preening activity of these swans takes place in the water because the species is almost totally aquatic.*

1.82 *Like most animals, wildfowl frequently stretch (as this drake redhead duck is doing). This behavior is a comfort movement, and should not be confused with feather maintenance or courtship activity.*

1.79

1.80

1.81

1.82

Migration may be triggered by variations in climatic conditions at high latitudes, and the effect that these changes have on food availability. Presumably, adverse weather by itself is of no great consequence, but freezing waters will encourage southward movement (although some eiders winter at the very edge of the arctic ice pack, and a few mallards winter in arctic Alaska where warm springs keep water open, even when the ambient air temperature plummets to 50°F below zero). Both sexes generally migrate to the same area but there are some exceptions, such as the European goldeneye. While most waterfowl stop to rest and feed during migration, certain elements of the populations of several species may undertake nonstop flights of 2000 or even 3000 miles. At an average speed of 50 miles per hour, a 2000-mile flight would keep them in the air continuously for about 40 hours.

Mass migrational movements may appear to be random, but they are far from that. Well-established aerial highways or corridors known as flyways are utilized year after year, and in North America four major migration routes are recognized: the Atlantic, Mississippi, Central, and Pacific flyways. These administrative flyways overlap considerably, so their boundaries cannot be precisely defined, and they may also vary somewhat from year to year depending on climatic (and perhaps other) conditions. Millions of waterfowl come from Canada and Alaska to winter in southern states, and large numbers move on to Central and South America as well. As an example, a tiny blue-winged teal banded in Canada was recovered six months later in Peru, some 7000 miles away. (While this is remarkable for a duck, it can't begin to compare with the exploits of the arctic tern, which migrates between the Arctic and the Antarctic and makes an annual trip of about 25,000 miles.)

Flyways exist in Europe and Asia as well, but they are more difficult to delineate than those of the New World because relations between many countries in the Eastern Hemisphere are simply not as harmonious as they are in the west, and consequently, coordinated scientific work is fraught with political difficulties. (There are signs of improvement in this situation, however.)

International protection for waterfowl is critical because their flyways and ranges are much older than mankind and cross over many man-made political boundaries. Any abuse of the waterfowl resource in one country can directly affect the utilization and enjoyment of that resource by citizens of other countries. In North America, the passage of the Migratory Bird Treaty Act in 1916 was the first major step in providing some means of international protection for waterfowl; and today, Canada, Mexico, and the United States work jointly in solving the problems that affect wildfowl and other migratory birds. To illustrate the importance of such cooperation, it is enough to note that as many as 80 percent of all North American waterfowl are produced in Canada, and many of these birds winter in Mexico. Recently-signed treaties with Japan and the Soviet Union will increase international protection. Interestingly, no country in Europe has hunting laws as strict as those in North America, and while access to guns is much easier in the United States, access to waterfowl is much more difficult.

If a sizable population of gamebirds is well managed, a surplus portion of that population can be "harvested" each year without adversely affecting the survival potential of that species. In North America, this surplus is taken into account when hunting regulations are established, and since bird populations tend to fluctuate, bag limits

1.84

1.85

1.86

1.86 *Alaskan pond habitat. Many species of waterfowl (and other forms of wildlife) greatly depend on the Arctic for breeding areas. Since many of these species are migratory, it is imperative that both their northern breeding grounds and southern wintering areas be preserved. Without appropriate habitat, wildlife cannot survive, no matter how much "protection" individual species are officially afforded.*

1.87 *Sharp-winged teal copulating. Breeding normally takes place in deeper water, but sometimes in their zeal the birds find themselves grounded.*

1.87

are established annually and may vary from year to year. The length of the hunting season is also subject to variation, and if a specific species has had a poor reproductive year, it is conceivable that the limit will be reduced and the season shortened for that particular species. If a population crash is severe enough, total protection may be warranted until numbers recover enough to absorb a certain amount of hunting pressure. Always, hunting is legal only in the fall, long after the breeding season has terminated. Removal of a portion of the population in the fall also reduces feeding pressure on the remaining birds, and assures that they will have a more ample food supply to see them through the winter.

The uncanny ability of birds to navigate accurately for long distances has been the subject of intense investigation and controversy for hundreds of years, and while our knowledge of this phenomenon increases annually, our understanding of it is still rather rudimentary. Undoubtedly, the positions of the sun, moon, and stars serve as navigation aids, but there must be many other factors involved as well (such as possible subtle differences in the magnetic field of the Earth). During migration, waterfowl tend to fly higher than they do in local flights—on the average, they cruise between 1000 and 3000 feet, but on occasion they climb as high as 20,000 or more feet.

In the spring, northern migrants return to the arctic to breed and rear their young, and this northward movement may be triggered by certain physiological stimuli (including a tremendous increase in the size of the gonads). The timing of the reproductive cycles of these birds is such that the young are hatched and reared during the time of maximum solar radiation. Probably, the amount of daylight (or photoperiod) is extremely important to this process, because it may play some role in stimulating breeding activity. In the higher latitudes, these optimal conditions exist only during the brief warm spring and summer months. Interestingly, at these latitudes (both north and south), there are fewer species compared to temperate or tropical regions, while the *number* of individuals in each species is far greater as a rule.

Seasonal variation in the abundance of specific food items has a direct effect on waterfowl feeding habits, and for nearly all species this means an increase in animal food during the spring and summer, when more invertebrates are available. Mosquitos, which make life on the tundra unbearable for human intruders, are important dietary items for young arctic waterfowl, although their diets as adults will be totally different.

Ducks, geese, and swans are well-known for their highly ritualized courtship behaviors, which may range from the very subtle and intricate to the extremely showy and elaborate. Actual mating usually takes place in the water, and is often referred to as "treading." With many species, the female may be almost completely submerged during the process, and on occasion she may even be drowned. Copulation is somewhat difficult for birds in general, and in the case of waterfowl, the act is complicated further by the instability of the water's surface. Most other avian groups merely require cloacal contact for fertilization to result, but penetration is necessary for waterfowl—and as a result, males have evolved a distinct erectile penis. Due to the presence of this organ, it is possible to accurately sex wildfowl by inspecting the vent, even at one day of age.

Most anatids are monogamous, and polygamous behavior is confined to only a few species. The pair bond varies considerably, how-

1.88

1.89

1.90

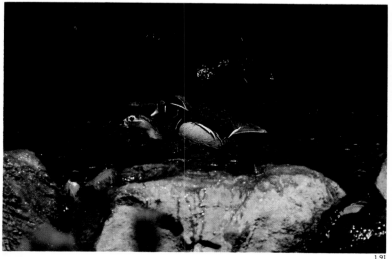

1.91

1.92

1.93

Breeding waterfowl

1.88 *Hooded merganser. During mating, it is not uncommon for females to be completely submerged. From time to time, they may even be drowned.*

1.89 *Bufflehead.*

1.90 *American goldeneye. Once copulation is complete, the drake usually swims around the female several times while still grasping her neck feathers.*

1.91 *Wood duck.*

1.92 *Northern mallard.*

1.93 *European goldeneye.*

Courtship behavior

1.94 *Falkland Island flightless steamer ducks. The female is calling in the stretch posture.*

1.95 *Ruddy duck drake "bubbling." During courtship, many waterfowl often engage in complicated movements and postures, and they tend to be more vocal than usual. The ritualistic bubbling display of the ruddy is elaborate and complex, and it may be used as both a courtship display and as a threat to other males. When bubbling, the bird erects its "horns," inflates its neck, cocks its tail, and beats its bill against the inflated neck, producing a hollow tapping sound. Air is forced out from under the feathers and causes bubbles to appear.*

1.96 *American goldeneye. This drake is in the midst of the head-throw, part of a very elaborate display. A rattling sound is usually simultaneously produced.*

1.97 *Lesser Bahama pintail performing the down-up-head-up-tail-up display.*

1.98 *American goldeneye female. Just prior to actual copulation, the females of most wildfowl species flatten out on top of the water in this fashion. This behavior suggests that she is receptive.*

1.99 *Mergansers possess a large courting repertoire. This red-breasted merganser is performing the salute and curtsy. In this display, a swimming bird suddenly jerks its head diagonally in such a manner that the head, bill, and neck form a straight line (the salute). Then the head is immediately jerked downward until the base of the neck is underwater and the twisted head is above it. The tail is pointed downward, and a distinct cat-like call is produced.*

1.94

1.95

1.96

1.97

1.98

1.99

1.100

1.101

ever, from lifelong (with the swans and geese) to almost nonexistent (with muscovy ducks). Pair forming and courtship activities have received a significant amount of attention from animal behaviorists in recent years, but these highly stereotyped rituals are sometimes so subtle and complicated that many of the sequences can be very difficult to interpret. Students of wildfowl behavior have nevertheless coined special terms which rather graphically describe specific displays, such as: triumph ceremony, display shake, bill-down display, incitement, grunt-whistle, head throw, kinked-neck posture, bowsprit, rear-end display, salute, curtsy, pushing, head-pumping, bubbling, burping, and gesture of repulsion. Many of these diverse movements may be joined together into a kind of dance by a male seeking to attract a female. In some species, females may initiate courtship by inciting the males, and typically, they will flatten out on the surface of the water prior to copulation, almost as if they are soliciting the attention of the drake.

With many ducks of the Northern Hemisphere, there are usually more males than females. Just why this is so has yet to be fully understood, but the phenomenon may have something to do with assuring mates for re-nesting females that have lost clutches; or perhaps an excess of males in the population stimulates breeding activity and strengthens pair bonds.

Once the pair bond is established, nest building generally commences, although pair formation with many nontropical migratory species may occur long before nesting and often far from breeding areas. In the far north, the typical waterfowl nest is located on rolling tundra in a marshy area, near fresh water. Sometimes, more than a dozen species may nest in relatively close proximity to one another, particularly on small islands that are surrounded by the melting pack ice, where the various species are afforded security from terrestrial predators. More often, waterfowl nests are scattered, because most species are not particularly gregarious during nesting. Some wildfowl (such as snow geese, black brant, red-breasted geese, and some eiders) are colonial nesters, but they are exceptions. A number of species nest in association with large gulls or terns, and this apparently offers them some protection from other predators when they are on the eggs. However, in the case of larger gulls, this protection is lost once the young hatch, when the ducklings may be readily preyed upon by their former benefactors.

Many anatids nest in the open, while others lay their eggs in the cavities of trees or in underground burrows. Swans and some of the stiff-tails are noted for elaborate nests, but more typically, nest construction is rather rudimentary, because waterfowl lack the instinct to carry nesting material. Generally, most species merely reach forward from the nest site, grasp a beakful of material, pass it over their backs, and drop it—and as a consequence, usually only material that is within reach is used. The most atypical nester of all is the parasitic South American black-headed duck, which builds no nest at all and deposits its eggs instead in the nest of a host species.

Waterfowl eggs are generally white or off-white, pale green, or brownish in color, and they are never spotted or patterned. The female alone incubates (except for magpie geese, some black swans, whistling ducks, and white-backed ducks), and incubation periods vary from 20 to 44 days, with high-latitude species tending to have shorter incubation periods than their tropical or temperate counterparts. Interestingly, the size of the bird does not always appear to be related to the length of incubation, and some northern geese have

1.102

1.100 *Incubating spectacled eider. Waterfowl nest in a variety of ways, but those that breed on the treeless tundra must nest on the ground. As a rule, waterfowl do not build elaborate nests, and only material that is within reach is used in nest construction. Spectacled eider nests are generally quite exposed early in the season, but they usually become more concealed as temperatures rise and new vegetation grows.*

1.101 *At times, hooded merganser drakes may court collectively. This species is noted for its many displays, which may include extreme neck-stretching, head-throws with expanded crests, and extreme expansion of the neck. Some displays may be accompanied by a rolling frog-like call.*

1.102 *Typical waterfowl nesting habitat in Alaska.*

1.103 *Nesting barnacle geese. In typical goose fashion, only the female incubates but the gander remains nearby on guard.*

1.104 *Cackling goose female. When threatened, incubating geese will often lie low on the nest and may hiss in a menacing manner.*

1.105 *Incubating black brant. When nesting, this species frequently seeks small peninsulas that extend into tundra ponds. Peninsula nest sites, while not as secure or predator-free as an island, do afford a degree of security from terrestrial predators (such as arctic foxes) because they can only approach from one side.*

incubation periods that are as short as that of the much smaller teal. Obviously, incubation in this case is adapted to the very brief breeding season in the north, since the young must be fledged and capable of departing before the icy fingers of winter tighten their grip.

Most waterfowl generally line the nest and cover their eggs with the down that underlies their breast feathers. Significantly, this nest down is plucked from a region of the breast that will later be held against the eggs during nesting, and thus the eggs are brought into a relatively closer contact with the warm skin. At the same time, this is not the typical "brood patch" of many other bird groups, in which the egg actually does come in contact with naked skin, since it is not in the best interest of an aquatic bird to have an area of bare skin below the waterline. When males assist with incubation (as some swans and whistling ducks do), little down is used, because the eggs will be covered most of the time. Lining of the nest sometimes commences as the clutch is being set, but most species wait until the final egg is laid and incubation begins.

As a rule, eggs are laid during the early morning hours, and while smaller species usually lay one egg a day, an egg every other day is more typical with larger species such as geese and swans. It is interesting that species which nest in the open, and whose eggs require a protective cover, have mostly dark brown down; while cavity or hole nesters, which have little need to conceal their eggs, have white down. For example, the American merganser (a cavity nester) has white down, whereas a closely related ground nester, the red-breasted merganser, has dark brown down.

During incubation, nests are protected in a variety of ways. A number of species depend on their drab disruptive plumage to keep them concealed, and when the female is off the nest, the eggs may be covered with down to provide warmth and camouflage. In the case of some cavity-nesting species, incubating females may hiss like a snake, a ploy that frequently discourages all but the most persistent intruders. Others may attempt to draw off a potential predator by feigning an injury such as a broken wing, and the broken wing technique has been reported for at least 58 wildfowl species. Swans and some geese will often stand and fight intruders. If frightened off the nest, many ducks (particularly eiders) will defecate on the eggs, and the foul odor may either serve to discourage predation or function as a camouflage mechanism, or both. However, whatever tactics are used, the evidence shows that they are not always successful, because egg predation is surprisingly high. To compensate for such losses, many wildfowl lay large clutches.

In most cases, once incubation commences the hens are reluctant to depart the nest. Some northern species reportedly eat nothing during the entire incubation period and may not desert the nest unless ejected by an intruder. More commonly, however, females will cautiously sneak away from the nest for brief periods during the early morning or late afternoon to feed, drink, and bathe. As hatching approaches, the diligent hens flee the nest only as a last resort. Recent evidence suggests that some communication between the incubating adult and the unhatched egg may take place just prior to pipping—and this in turn suggests that some form of audio imprinting may occur before the young are even hatched.

As pipping commences, a small star-shaped crack appears on the egg, and it is frequently possible to actually hear the bird calling from within the shell. Faint tapping sounds are also audible, as the chick

Waterfowl nests and eggs

1.106 *Mexican duck.*

1.107 *Flying steamer duck. Note the copious amount of down used to line the nest.* PHOTO BY JOE JEHL

1.108 *Red-breasted merganser.* PHOTO BY EDDIE ASPER

1.109 *Pacific greater scaup.*

1.110 *Northern pintail.*

1.111

1.112

1.113

1.114

Waterfowl nests and eggs
1.111 *American green-*
winged teal.
1.112 *Barnacle goose.*
1.113 *Black brant.*
1.114 *Oldsquaw duck.*
1.115 *Whistling swan.*
1.116 *Bar-headed goose.*

1.115

1.116

bangs against the shell with the tip of its bill. An egg tooth at the tip of the bill is provided for this purpose, which is shed shortly after hatching. Once pipped, the top of the egg is chipped away as the hatchling rotates within the shell, and this results in the detachment of a whole section of the larger end, which falls away in the form of a cap. Breaking out of an egg demands a tremendous amount of energy, and the exhausted newly hatched young normally sleep for some time subsequent to emerging. At first, they are wet and slimy, but as soon as they dry off, they fluff up.

There is usually an interval of 16 to 18 hours (or more) between pipping and emergence, and as much as 24 hours may be required. Since incubation of the total clutch generally commences at the same time, most of the eggs hatch within a day or two of each other, and this synchronized timing increases survival potential by allowing the female (or both parents in the case of some species) to turn their attention to caring for all the young as soon as possible. The young are extremely appealing, and the thick down which covers them may be strikingly colored and patterned. They hatch with their eyes open, and become active as soon as they dry off and fluff up. Down-covered young are better adapted for maintaining a constant body temperature than naked ones, and even though waterfowl young depend on their parents for protection, they are not nearly as helpless as the blind and naked chicks of other avian groups, such as songbirds, woodpeckers, pelicans, or hummingbirds.

Usually, the downy young begin to forage within a day or so after hatching, although they possess sufficient reserve fats to sustain them for several days without external nourishment if necessary. The young of some species even swim and dive within hours after abandoning the nest. As a rule, tropical species grow more slowly than birds from higher latitudes. Some of the smaller species can fly (or are fledged) at approximately 40 days of age, but larger birds usually require two to three months. There are notable exceptions, however, and the young of some high arctic geese, such as Ross's goose, fledge in the incredibly short period of four weeks or less.

Once in the water, ducklings feed themselves by randomly pecking at any object that attracts their attention, and apparently learn what is edible by trial and error. Interestingly, the eyes of most ducklings are protected against the random pecking of their nest mates by the patterning of their down. They typically have either a dark stripe extending through the eye, a completely dark head, or a dark cap which extends down below the eyes, and this tends to obscure the position of the shiny eyes, which might otherwise attract the attention of another hungry or curious duckling. (Goslings, on the other hand, are not patterned at all, and tend to be rather uniform in color.)

The role of the hen during the rearing period is essentially that of a guardian and watchdog. She remains ever alert for danger, and diligently attempts to keep the brood from scattering too widely. Often, a mother will maintain the cohesion of the brood by using a gentle call, to which the ducklings respond with a distinct cheeping of their own. With geese, swans, whistling ducks, and a few others, both parents participate in the rearing of the young. During the first week or so of life, young waterfowl are very vulnerable to chilling, and this, along with starvation, is one of the major mortality factors; therefore, at night when temperatures may drop, the young are often brooded under the wings of the female. Generally, a dense soft down (usually duller, drabber, or paler) begins to appear in the second week, as the natal down is shed. When feathers begin to emerge, they appear first

1.117

1.119

1.121

1.122

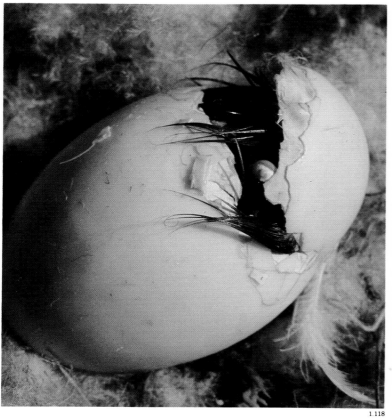

1.118

1.120

1.117 Nene goose at the initial hatching stage, just after pipping. The egg tooth (visible on the tip of the bill) facilitates the hatchling's emergence from the shell and is shed shortly afterward.

1.118 Wood duck breaking its way out of the egg. Typically, waterfowl young rotate in the egg and chip away the shell until the large end of the egg is detached in the form of a cap.

1.119 Recently-hatched northern pintail. Upon hatching, waterfowl are wet and slimy, but they rapidly dry off and fluff up.

1.120 Northern versicolor teal duckling. Once they leave the nest, most waterfowl are relatively independent. They feed themselves, and other than protection and brooding, they require little care.

1.121 Arctic loon nest and eggs. While waterfowl eggs are generally light colored and unpatterned, the eggs of other species may be more cryptically colored and are usually dark and spotted (or otherwise patterned).

1.122 California brown pelican as it emerges from the egg. Unlike waterfowl, many birds produce young that are blind, naked, and totally helpless upon hatching. Young of this type require a great deal of parental attention.

Waterfowl young

1.123 *Dozing cape teal female with day-old ducklings.*

1.124 *Argentine red shoveler female with brood.*

1.125 *Ruddy-headed goose.*

on the body. Down on the head, neck, and back is the last to go, and the young are usually well feathered on the body by the time the flight feathers come in.

The flying abilities of waterfowl are practically unsurpassed in the avian world. Their skill, speed, and maneuverability have long captured the imagination of earth-bound man, and their spectacular aerial antics have been praised in song and verse down through the ages. Again and again, many of the world's most creative writers and poets have tried to describe the flight of a wild goose and failed—perhaps because something so beautiful and awe-inspiring is simply beyond the powers of verbal or written description. To me, geese are the most exciting of the wildfowl to observe on the wing, not only because they generally move in huge masses and are extremely vocal, but also because they often employ unorthodox aerial maneuvers just prior to landing. In an effort to decrease air speed, they may sideslip, tumble, or even backflap. With ducks, the sky may start humming simultaneously with thousands of flying forms, sweeping around and suddenly dropping down with set wings to land with an enormous splash.

Although I have been privileged to repeatedly view the spectacle of migrating waterfowl, when many thousands of birds are on the move simultaneously, the sight never fails to stir me. One experiences a

1.126

1.127

1.128

1.129

1.130

1.131

1.126 Pair of bar-headed geese with gosling. With all geese, both parents participate in the rearing of the young.

1.127 European wigeon female with brood.

1.128 Family of ringed teal (male on the right).

1.129 Snow geese with half-grown goslings.

1.130 Female gadwall with ducklings.

1.131 Pair of western greylag geese with goslings.

1.132

1.133

1.134

1.135

1.137

1.136

Waterfowl young

1.132 *Pink-footed goose.*

1.133 *Northern mallard female with brood.*

1.134 *Family of fulvous whistling ducks.*
As is typical with whistling ducks,
both parents are involved in brood care.

1.135 *Lesser white-fronted goose gosling.*

1.136 *European pochard female and young.*

1.137 *Chiloe wigeon with large ducklings.*

1.138

1.139

1.140

1.141

Waterfowl young

1.138 *White-winged wood duck.*

1.139 *Lesser Bahama pintail.*

1.140 *Andean goose.*

1.141 *Florida duck.*

1.142 *Hooded merganser.*

1.143 *Family of northern black-bellied whistling ducks.*

1.142

1.143

1.144

1.145

1.146

Waterfowl young

1.144 *North American ruddy duck.*

1.145 *Emperor goose.*

1.146 *Muscovy duck.*

1.147 *Cackling goose.*

1.148 *Spotted whistling duck.*

1.149 *Female goldeneye with a single large duckling.*
PHOTO BY KEN FINK

1.147

1.148

1.149

1.150

1.151

1.152

1.153

Waterfowl young

1.150 *Orinoco goose.*
1.151 *Greater Brazilian teal.*
1.152 *Fulvous whistling duck.*
1.153 *Barnacle geese.*
1.154 *Patagonian crested duck.*
PHOTO BY JOE JEHL
1.155 *Hawaiian duck.*
1.156 *Magpie goose.*

1.154

1.155

1.156

39

1.157

1.157 *Half-grown cape shelduck ducklings. Generally, by the second week of life the more distinctive natal down has been replaced by a duller, drabber, or paler down, which is dense and soft.*

1.58 *Barnacle goose female brooding goslings under her right wing. This provides them with a secure and warm sanctuary.*

1.159 *Female goosander leading brood.* PHOTO BY KEN FINK

1.158

1.159

1.160 *Drake wood duck taking off from the surface of the water. Many duck species are able to spring up from the water and become airborne almost instantly. Other species, such as heavy swans, can only attain flight with considerable difficulty.* PHOTO BY TONY MERCIECA

1.161 *Flock of emperor geese in flight.*

1.162 *Part of a large concentration of wintering northern pintail.*

longing to join them on the adventurous and often hazardous journey that lies ahead. To be sure, wildfowl are noted for their grace and beauty on the water, but it is not until they cast aside the bonds of earth and effortlessly drift upward that their true spirit emerges.

The manner in which they take off is arresting in itself. Mallards and other dabblers jump up from the water or ground and become airborne immediately—and if startled, they may explode upward like a guided missile, often protesting with a loud quack. For other species, becoming airborne is much more laborious. Swans, for example, are forced to run along the surface of the water (usually into the wind) before they gain enough speed to take off, and diving ducks skitter rapidly over the water before attaining flight speed.

Although they are known as powerful fliers, waterfowl have wings that are *relatively* small and their bodies are heavy; in fact, the ratio of wing surface area to body weight is among the lowest of flying birds. But the *power* of the wing stroke compensates for this apparent disadvantage. The wing beat of swans in flight is approximately 160 strokes per minute, but in some ducks it may exceed 300, and these powerful wing strokes even make flight possible in heavy headwinds when other birds are grounded. Flight speeds are difficult to ascertain with any degree of accuracy, and after missing an apparently easy shot, chagrined hunters will unhesitatingly suggest that some ducks fly at speeds exceeding 200 miles per hour. These claims, however, fall into the same category as the tales of the "fish that got away"—interesting, but not substantiated. The canvasback, one of the swiftest of all wildfowl, has been reliably clocked at over 70 miles per hour, but most waterfowl cruise at 25 to 35 miles per hour under normal conditions.

Man's effect on waterfowl has been largely negative and the total North American wildfowl population has generally decreased during the past century. Hunting abuses were excessive during the Nineteenth Century and the early part of the Twentieth Century, and legal bag limits once exceeded 25 ducks per day. The limit today, however, may be but two or three per day in some flyways, and widespread and indiscriminate habitat destruction and loss has replaced hunting and direct persecution as the most detrimental human-caused factor affecting waterfowl.

1.163

1.163 *Flock of Steller's eiders (mostly immatures) running across the surface of the water to gain sufficient speed for flight. With large flocks, there is a great deal of splashing and noise before the birds become airborne.*

1.164 *Pacific harlequin ducks skittering over the surface of the water prior to flight. Most sea ducks are capable of taking off only after a preliminary run across the top of the water. But even when running on the water, they can move with surprising rapidity.*

1.165 *Pair of northern versicolor teal taking to the wing. As with most dabbling ducks, these teal can explode upward from the surface of the water without a moment's hesitation. If startled, their rapid departure is often accompanied by a loud protesting quack.*

1.166 (Opposite Page) *Drake canvasback. The nesting habitat requirements of these ducks are rather specific. If appropriate habitat is lost or altered, either through man's activities or natural causes, the reproductive potential of a specialized species can be severely compromised.*

1.167 (Opposite Page) *Pristine tundra pond in Alaska. Ponds such as these are important to the survival of a number of species.*

1.164

1.165

Remarkably, most American anatid populations are presently fairly stable and some of the more adaptable species are presently more numerous than they were one hundred years ago as a result of refined wildlife management techniques. Stringent protection, habitat preservation and restoration, and a greater understanding of their biological requirements have contributed to the substantial increase of some species, with the ubiquitous mallard being perhaps the best example of this. The mallard has benefited because it is among the most adaptable of all waterfowl, with habitat requirements and lifestyles that are not particularly specialized. But the more specialized canvasback, which is greatly dependent on the presence of prairie potholes in the north central United States and Canada, has not fared as well.

1.166

Prairie potholes are the backbone of duck production in North America—to such an extent that some biologists refer to them as "duck factories." The pothole country was created by advancing and retreating glaciers of the recent ice ages, and encompasses some 300,000 square miles; and while this unique habitat constitutes only ten percent of waterfowl breeding grounds, *over 50 percent* of North American ducks that hatch annually are produced in this region. Unfortunately, these vitally important lands are being rapidly usurped for agricultural and other purposes.

Ducks nesting in agricultural areas are often disrupted by farm machinery, since many crops are harvested during the spring breeding season; and even though most farmers are sympathetic to the needs of waterfowl, nests may be inadvertently destroyed by mowing operations. Incubating hens that refuse to flush can be lost, and a mowed-over nest is invariably a failure, even if the eggs are not molested. Generally, the female deserts the site immediately and the eggs are taken by predators—and even if the nest is not abandoned, the lack of cover inevitably dooms the nesting attempt.

In pastures, particularly those which are overgrazed, the birds must contend with the probability that restless cattle will trample the nests. In itself, the destruction of nests by trampling is rather insignificant, but the total negative effect of agricultural activities can be very great. On the credit side, however, agriculture helps to maintain countless thousands of ducks and geese by providing rice, corn, and wheat during the growing season and following the harvest. Harvesting machines tend to lose rather substantial amounts of grain, and this excess has been a great boon to waterfowl in recent decades.

1.167

1.168 *In the Arctic, prime waterfowl breeding habitat may consist of vast wetlands dotted with numerous small islands. These little islands provide ideal nesting sites because they afford the birds a degree of security from marauding terrestrial predators.*

1.169 *Typical waterfowl breeding habitat in northern Alaska.*

1.170 *During the late spring and the summer months, a great deal of the arctic terrain appears to be under water. Habitat of this type is typical of the Yukon-Kuskokwim Delta, an area noted for its incredibly dense population of nesting waterfowl.*

1.168

1.169

1.170

While many of man's activities can be extremely detrimental to the lifestyles of a number of species, they are not the only negative factors that all wildlife must face every day. Adverse weather, diseases, parasites, predators, and the scarcity of appropriate food constantly affect their survival—and even though many people persist in believing that animals in the wild, far from human habitation, lead idyllic lives in a wilderness utopia, this "Bambi syndrome" is a myth. To be sure, the gauntlet of hunters that waterfowl must run each fall takes its toll, but nature exacts an even higher toll, albeit in a more subtle fashion. For example, a species such as the canvasback, which has relatively narrow habitat requirements, can experience severe (and even total) reproductive failure as a result of natural conditions, such as severe and widespread droughts. While totally accurate figures are not available, it is believed that some 100 million waterfowl move south to wintering grounds each year in North America—and of these, only 40 million make it back. Approximately 20 million are taken by hunters, but the other 40 million are lost as a result of natural causes.

All animals, except those at the top of the food chain, are potential prey of predators; and if man can be considered a predator, even the largest animals that ever existed, the great whales, are preyed upon. The predators of North American wildfowl alone are legion, and include marauding feral dogs and cats in areas of human habitation, coyotes, wolves, foxes, black bears, skunks, otters, racoons, weasels, mink, ground squirrels, cranes, gulls, birds of prey, magpies, crows, snakes, alligators—and even fish, such as bass, pike, and catfish. Eggs are favored by many predators, while others (such as turtles, bullfrogs, and fish) concentrate on ducklings in the water. Adults are not immune to predation either, and an unwary duck is usually a dead duck. In the Arctic, during years when the rodent population has crashed, fox predation can have a disastrous impact. Eggs are usually taken, but if incubating females can be caught unaware, they are consumed as well. There are even accounts of killer whales preying on black brant, of southern sea lions taking steamer ducks, and of caribou making off with the eggs of lesser snow geese and black brant.

Interestingly, the alligators of Louisiana have recently learned to capitalize on the presence of waterfowl hunters who use decoys. Since afforded protection, alligators have made a remarkable comeback and some 300,000 inhabit the coastal waters of Louisiana alone. Some opportunistic gators lie in wait among the decoys, and as the ducks are decoyed in and shot the reptiles immediately claim them. They are apparently associating the gunshots and subsequent splashes with food. Canine retrievers are not immune either, and at least one hunting dog has been taken by an alligator.

The gregarious habits of waterfowl during the winter make them extremely susceptible to a number of deadly diseases. Two of the most dreaded in North America are botulism and fowl cholera. Botulism is sometimes called "western duck sickness," because mortalities were first described from the west, but it is not a disease in the true sense of the word. Rather, it is a form of food poisoning that is caused by the extraordinarily toxic metabolic by-products of the anaerobic bacterium *Clostridium botulinum*. Neurotoxins released by the bacteria are absorbed into the blood and lymph circulatory systems from the digestive tract, where they block the transmission of nerve impulses to the muscles and bring about a loss of coordination. Progressive paralysis follows, and death may result from drowning when the bird is in the water, since it may become unable to keep its head above the surface. Ashore, death may be due to respiratory failure, exposure, or

Waterfowl predators

1.171 *Sandhill crane. These birds do not hesitate to consume young waterfowl, and since cranes frequently breed in the same areas as wildfowl, they can have an impact.*

1.172 *Incubating long-tailed jaeger. Jaegers are major avian predators in the Arctic.*

1.173 *Arctic fox pup. These foxes probably constitute the greatest threat to arctic-nesting waterfowl. They most often prey on eggs and young but will take adults as well if they can catch them unaware.*

1.171

1.172

1.173

1.174

Waterfowl predators

1.174 *Golden eagles strike waterfowl in the air at times. These huge raptors are probably not a significant wildfowl predator, but they may have a local impact.*

1.175 *Great blue heron (with a brown pelican flying overhead). In some areas, these herons prey heavily on wildfowl, particularly the young. At times, they remain motionless at the edge of a waterway, waiting for a family of ducks to move into range and then snatching a duckling with lightning speed.*

1.175

1.176

1.177

1.178

1.179

Waterfowl predators

1.176 *Cottonmouth or water moccasin. These and many other snakes will feed upon waterfowl if the opportunity arises.*

1.177 *Timber wolf.*

1.178 *Coyote pup. Coyotes are opportunists and are quick to take nesting waterfowl or their young.*

1.179 *Bobcat.*

1.180

1.181

Waterfowl predators

1.180 *Protesting arctic ground squirrel at the entrance of its burrow. While they are not predators in the true sense of the word, ground squirrels (and some other rodents as well) will take eggs if the opportunity arises. Their overall impact is probably relatively minor, however.*

1.181 *American fisher. Like most agile carnivores, these mustelids will prey on waterfowl from time to time, although such fare undoubtedly constitutes a very small portion of their diet. The fisher is better known for its ability to successfully prey on porcupines.*

1.182 *North American badger. These powerful burrowing carnivores consume almost anything they encounter, waterfowl included. Like some of the other opportunistic predators, they appear to be quite fond of eggs.*

1.182

1.184

Waterfowl predators

1.183 *American black bear cub. Bears readily consume a wide variety of food items, but they are particularly fond of eggs.*

1.184 *Downy great horned owl. In North America at least, these owls are major waterfowl predators. Hunting in the dark and flying noiselessly, they seldom fail to take their prey. Even waterfowl in captivity are not secure from attack, and in some areas propagators consider owls to be the most cunning and effective of predators. For some unknown reason, horned owls will inevitably take the rarest and most expensive bird in a collection.*

1.183

1.185 *American alligator. This alligator has successfully taken a common egret — but it could just as easily have been a duck or goose. Alligators lurking on the surface of the water closely resemble floating logs, and unsuspecting birds may actually swim to them. Once a bird is grabbed by these powerful crocodilians, the end is quick.*

1.186 *(Opposite Page) Mallards killed by botulism. More than 40 million waterfowl die every year in North America alone from this and other natural causes.*
PHOTO BY CALIFORNIA DEPARTMENT OF FISH AND GAME

1.185

starvation. This affliction is occasionally referred to as "limberneck," because affected birds are unable to control their neck muscles. Treatment consists of flushing out the digestive tract with fresh water, and antitoxin injections slightly increase the number of survivors.

Thousands of ducks succumb to botulism annually, but some years are decidedly worse than others. In 1932, for example, over 250,000 ducks perished at the north end of the Great Salt Lake in Utah alone; in 1910, millions died throughout the United States. During the late 1960s, some 250,000 mortalities occurred in the Central Valley of California. To be sure, a great deal has been learned about botulism since the turn of the century, but it continues to be a major cause of mortality. Among the many factors that determine its occurrence and severity are summer temperatures, falling water levels that result in extended exposures of shoreline, and an anaerobic intermix of soil, dead insect bodies, or other organic matter. Some waterfowl refuges have been able to partially control the disease by periodically raising and lowering water levels.

Fowl cholera (*Pasteurella multocida*) has affected the poultry industry for more than 200 years, but the first known outbreak among wild ducks occurred in California and Texas in 1944. Losses fluctuate annually, but during the winter of 1955-56, over 60,000 ducks died from fowl cholera in Texas alone. In February of 1970, over 88,000 birds died in the Chesapeake Bay area, including at least 62,100 oldsquaw, 19,000 white-winged scoters, 500 black scoters, 2500 bufflehead, and 900 whistling swans. As recently as the spring of 1975, some 20,000 anatids perished in Nebraska of the disease, and annually some 5000 to 70,000 are stricken in the state of California. As large as these numbers may be, they do not really reflect the total death toll, since large numbers of wildfowl perish daily in isolated

groups that are not noticed, and mortality counts are usually only made when mass die-offs occur in particular localities.

Duck virus enteritis (D.V.E.) was not a significant problem in North America until the late 1960s, but even though it is generally considered a disease of domestic or semi-domestic waterfowl, "duck plague" can sometimes strike wild populations. D.V.E. has not been a major wild waterfowl mortality factor in North America thus far, but some 40,000 wild ducks succumbed in South Dakota in 1973 alone, and the potential for greater outbreaks exists. Unfortunately, the survivors of an outbreak can become carriers, and the deadly virus can undergo extended periods of latency. If a carrier becomes stressed, the virus can be shed. Some species appear to be much more susceptible than others.

To many people, these seemingly huge losses from natural causes may appear to be wasteful, unnecessary, and perhaps even cruel— but that is not the case at all, because all wild populations must be strictly governed by checks and balances if they are to remain healthy and viable. If, for example, all the young that hatched in a given year were to survive, the entire population of a species could be placed in jeopardy because the available food sources would soon prove inadequate to feed all. Some *must* die so that the majority may survive.

Certainly, the emergence of man as a dominant force affecting waterfowl population dynamics is most *un*natural, and almost everywhere it has resulted in biological chaos. But fortunately, since nature can be resilient and can absorb abuse up to a point, the picture is not totally hopeless. If given half a chance, most waterfowl populations stand a fair chance of survival—although admittedly, their survival may be in spite of man, rather than because of him.

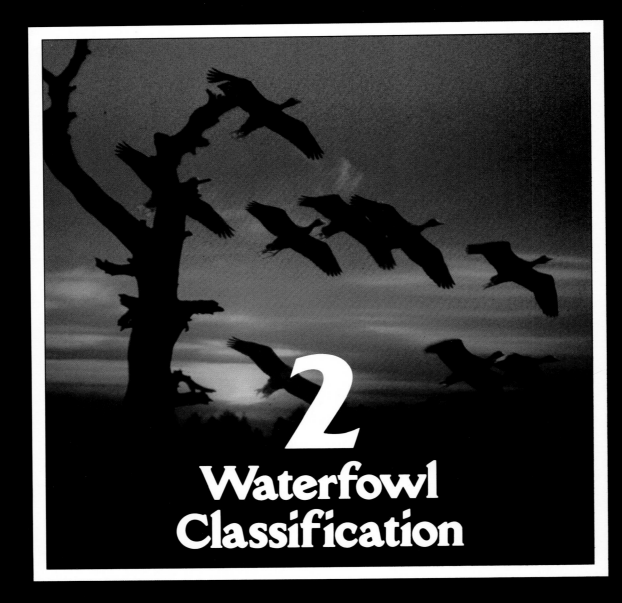

2
Waterfowl Classification

The wildfowl constitute a well-defined and easily identifiable group of birds, but the proper scientific classification of the group is nevertheless most perplexing, and has been a great challenge for avian taxonomists for hundreds of years. Many questions are unanswered to this day, and it appears likely that a number of species will remain taxonomically troublesome for years to come. Most contemporary specialists recognize 151 species of waterfowl (four of which are recently extinct)—or 247 forms, if all subspecies (or races) are considered. But not all authorities agree on the relationships between many species, or even on the number of tribes and the relationships between them.

Unfortunately, we cannot expect a resolution of these questions in the near future, since a great deal more must be discovered about the waterfowl before our classifications will truly represent accurate reflections of their evolutionary history or genetic relationships. There are, for example, some aberrant groups and species which are presently placed within specific groups on the slimmest of scientific grounds, as much for convenience sake as for any other reason. Then too, wildfowl are such an ancient and diversified assortment of birds that there

2.2

2.1 (Opposite Page) Northern black-bellied whistling ducks in flight at sunset.

2.2 Pair of flying steamer ducks in Patagonia. Common or vernacular names can be confusing, and while flying steamer ducks are sometimes referred to as "canvasbacks" by the inhabitants of the Falkland Islands, the true canvasback is a highly sought gamebird of North America.

are many forms of intermediate ancestry, and this greatly complicates the taxonomists' task. Size, form, and bill shape are usually the most obvious external physical criteria used to segregate the ducks and geese, but there are many other more subtle factors which are just as important in determining true relationships. Many of the obscure differences between the various waterfowl will be dealt with in greater detail in the chapters ahead, as specific tribes are discussed.

Most ornithologists accept the classification system proposed by the eminent ornithologists Jean Delacour and Ernst Mayr in their classic paper, "The Family Anatidae" (1945), although some taxonomists have since modified its organization. Essentially, Delacour and Mayr attempted to lump together those wildfowl which appeared to be most closely related, basing the groupings on behavioral and anatomical similarities. (In recent years, the use of behavioral comparisons has become an even more important systematic tool, and the detailed comparative study of the distinctive and elaborate displays of many of the waterfowl has contributed a great deal to our knowledge of waterfowl relationships.)

Closely related wildfowl groups are placed in collective units called tribes—a unique term that is not used with any other avian family. (It was formerly customary to fragment the family into numerous subfamilies instead.) Some systematists will undoubtedly challenge my use of the ten traditional tribes of Delacour and Mayr, but the thinking regarding the use of this particular taxonomic arrangement is not totally inconsistent with the philosophy of other contemporary waterfowl specialists. The structure of this book is based on the following taxonomic schema:

CLASS: AVES (Birds)
ORDER: ANSERIFORMES
FAMILY: Anatidae

SUBFAMILY: Anseranatinae		
	Tribe: Anseranatini	Magpie Goose
SUBFAMILY: Anserinae		
	Tribe: Dendrocygnini	Whistling Ducks
	Tribe: Anserini	Swans and True Geese
SUBFAMILY: Anatinae		
	Tribe: Tadornini	Shelducks and Sheldgeese
	Tribe: Anatini	Dabbling Ducks
	Tribe: Somateriini	Eiders
	Tribe: Aythyini	Pochards
	Tribe: Cairinini	Perching Ducks
	Tribe: Mergini	Sea Ducks
	Tribe: Oxyurini	Stiff-Tailed Ducks

Because our knowledge of waterfowl is constantly growing and taxonomy is essentially a fluid science, numerous changes in the original Delacour-Mayr system have been proposed. The noted waterfowl behavioralist Dr. Paul Johnsgard has, in fact, already totally reorganized the family based on intensive behavioral, biochemical, and anatomical studies (including tracheal comparisons). While some of his proposals may initially appear to be radical and perhaps even unfounded, that is not necessarily the case once the hard evidence is examined. In fact, there can be no doubt that many (if not all) of the Johngard recommendations will be accepted in the near future. Following Johnsgard's thinking, the tribal organization of the family would appear as follows:

FAMILY: Anatidae

SUBFAMILY: Anseranatinae		
	Tribe: Anseranatini	Magpie Goose
SUBFAMILY: Anserinae		
	Tribe: Dendrocygnini	Whistling Ducks
	Tribe: Anserini	Swans and True Geese
	Tribe: Cereopsini	Cape Barren Goose
	Tribe: Stictonettini	Freckled Duck
SUBFAMILY: Anatinae		
	Tribe: Tadornini	Shelducks and Sheldgeese
	Tribe: Tachyerini	Steamer Ducks
	Tribe: Cairinini	Perching Ducks
	Tribe: Merganettini	Torrent Ducks
	Tribe: Anatini	Dabbling Ducks
	Tribe: Aythyini	Pochards
	Tribe: Mergini	Sea Ducks
	Tribe: Oxyurini	Stiff-Tailed Ducks

You will note the number of tribes has been increased from 10 to 13 (with 43 genera and 148 species). Major changes include the creation of four new tribes (Cape Barren Goose, freckled duck, steamer ducks and torrent ducks), a merging of the eiders with the sea ducks, with the consequent elimination of the tribe Somateriini. In addition, the perching ducks have been shifted from a position behind the pochards to one in front of the dabbling ducks. Some species have also been moved from one tribe to another, with the white-backed ducks shifting from the stiff-tails to the whistling ducks, and the crested ducks from the shelduck tribe to the dabbling duck tribe.

For the layman, terminology can be a problem. Even the commonly used terms "ducks" and "geese" can be vague and misleading. Most people, for example, think of geese as being larger than ducks, but "pygmy geese" are among the smallest of all the waterfowl. To make things more confusing still, these little birds are not geese at all, but specialized perching ducks. On the other hand, spur-winged geese, which are also perching ducks, happen to be among the *largest* of waterfowl.

The inconsistencies in English terminology and popular nomenclature are responsible for constant confusion. While they may be of limited value locally, such names are not standardized, and a single species may be referred to by many different common names in different regions . . . or different species may be called by the same common name. For example, the bird that is called a canvasback in North America is totally different from the duck that is referred to as a canvasback in the Falkland Islands, and the latter is really the flying steamer duck. Therefore, to the biologist, the scientific or Latin name is invaluable because it has world-wide recognition. The Latin name for the common mallard, for instance, is *Anas platyrhynchos*. And while there are at least 34 vernacular or local names for the mallard, ranging from "frosty-back" and "twister" to "ringneck" and "ice duck," *Anas platyrhynchos* always applies to the same duck, regardless of who is referring to it. Thus, the accepted scientific classification of the Greenland race of the mallard would be:

PHYLUM:	Chordata
CLASS:	Aves
ORDER:	Anseriformes
FAMILY:	Anatidae
SUBFAMILY:	Anatinae
TRIBE:	Anatini
GENUS:	*Anas*
SPECIES:	*platyrhynchos*
SUBSPECIES:	*conboschas*

Anas platyrhynchos conboschas = Greenland mallard

As much as possible, the use of scientific names has been minimized in the text of this book to make it more readable, but the serious student of waterfowl will find all of the necessary systematic material in detail in the reference section at the back of the book.

2.3 *Barrow's goldeneye drake in nuptial plumage, consuming ice at a wintery icefall.*

2.3

3
Magpie Goose
Anseranatini

The tropics of northern Australia and southern New Guinea are enriched by the presence of the strange magpie goose. Although this species is clearly anserine in much of its behavior and anatomy, it deviates from the rest of the waterfowl in so many ways that a number of specialists believe it should be placed in a separate family all by itself. As it is, a separate subfamily (Anseranatinae) has been created for it, and even its scientific name—*Anseranas semipalmata*—reflects some of its physical peculiarities. (Literally translated, it means, "half-webbed goose-duck.") Sometimes called the semipalmated goose because of its unusual semi-webbed feet, the magpie goose is more commonly known in Australia as the pied goose because of its distinctive black and white plumage.

3.2

3.1 (Opposite Page) *The magpie goose is essentially a terrestrial species, but it is nevertheless very much at ease in an aquatic environment.*

3.2 *Magpie geese are not among the more accomplished of waterfowl swimmers. They have a very distinctive profile in the water, with their posteriors typically held rather high. They rarely swim, and are more often found away from water than in it.*

It is interesting to note that Australia is not particularly rich in wildfowl species, but of the 19 that can be considered native, a surprising number are quite unique. At least four—magpie goose, Cape Barren goose, freckled duck, and pink-eared duck—are so peculiar that they remain, even to this day, perplexing in a taxonomical sense.

Magpie geese are unquestionably the most generalized of living waterfowl, retaining many primitive characteristics. As a consequence, this species probably represents the closest surviving link between the wildfowl and other bird groups. Some ornithologists are of the opinion that magpie geese may be more closely related to African spur-winged geese, which they superficially resemble, than is currently accepted.

Recent studies of feather proteins and behavior, on the other hand, suggest that these odd birds also share some affinities with the semi-terrestrial screamers of South America, particularly the crested screamer (*Chauna torquata*). Screamers are rather closely related to true waterfowl, and have been afforded a position in the same taxonomic order, despite a number of distinct gamebird characteristics that they clearly possess as well. It may be that both the magpie goose and the screamers represent major stages in the evolution of typical waterfowl from a gallinaceous-type ancestor.

The faces of magpie geese are featherless back to the eyes, a feature they share with most swans. Their tails are quite long and the plumage is boldly patterned in black and white, with the white feathers sometimes heavily stained by reddish clay or stagnant water, particularly during the dry season. There is no seasonal variation in plumage.

3.3 Somewhat like a typical northern goose in its proportions, the magpie goose is not closely related and is not really a goose. This distinctive species is characterized by its partially webbed feet and its bold black and white plumage.

3.3

Immature birds resemble adults, except that the white is more or less mottled with brown or grey.

Almost exclusively herbivorous, these birds have a specialized strongly-hooked reddish yellow bill, which is used to dig out food from hard baked clay during the dry season. Curiously, the bill surface is very uneven, almost "pebbled" in appearance. They sometimes filter feed in the mud or may utilize their feet to bend down grasses so that the seeds are more accessible. The magpie goose is most active during the early morning and late afternoon, and prefers to feed in open areas well away from cover, presumably as protection from predators. Dingos, the wild dogs of Australia, have been observed rushing from cover and attacking foraging geese, sometimes successfully.

The bright yellow-orange legs are relatively long, and the feet are notable for a particularly long hind toe located on the same plane as the three front toes—a most unusual feature for waterfowl. Also, the amount of webbing between the toes is significantly reduced. Both of these structural peculiarities of the foot indicate a lifestyle in which walking and perching predominate over swimming, and indeed, magpie geese are accomplished walkers and rather infrequent swimmers.

They may, however, readily seek the security of the water when leading young. (When they do swim, they often float high, and unlike most other waterfowl, they have never been observed diving.)

It is not particularly uncommon for magpie geese to perch in tall trees (even on surprisingly thin twigs), and this has led some specialists to believe that their partially-webbed feet evolved as a perching adaptation. But they spend less time perching than walking, and so it seems more likely that the modified foot structure has evolved as an adaptation to their terrestrial existence. They walk with a peculiar slow and deliberate gait, and during the dry season may spend considerable time traversing arid areas; often, they must climb over dense swampy vegetation, and fully-webbed feet could be rather unwieldy for such activity. The feet are also used in the construction of rather elaborate nests.

Determining the gender of magpie geese is an interesting exercise. The sexes are quite similar externally, and both are characterized by a high head crown, or cranial knob. This knob usually reaches greater development in the somewhat larger males, but its size alone cannot always be used to reliably ascertain sex, since it is also an indication of age in both sexes. As a rule, the higher the knob, the older the individual, and I have seen females with crowns almost as large as those of adult males.

Strange as it may seem, one of the most accurate methods for determining the sex has to do with the development of the windpipe, or trachea. The greatly elongated windpipe of adult males (which can be up to 150 cm long) can usually be felt looped under the skin, extending down the left side (rarely the right) of the breast. In females or juveniles, the trachea does not penetrate the area between the breast muscle and the skin, although very old females may have one very small loop close to the neck. The only other avian group with external trachial loops that can be felt under the skin are the cracids, a family of specialized arboreal gamebirds of the American tropics. (Older male Australian freckled ducks may also have a tracheal coil outside the sternum, although its relative length is less than that of the magpie goose.)

The length of the trachea is undoubtedly responsible for the different vocal qualities of the two sexes. Both have loud and resonant honks, but the calls of the male are louder and lower (although in some of the literature they are said to be higher in pitch). The longer trachea of the gander probably functions as an effective resonator of low-frequency sounds. Younger goslings of both sexes have high-pitched whistles or may utter chittering sounds, but by the eighth month even immature birds can be accurately sexed by voice. Adult vocalization may take the form of a series of spaced, deliberate monotonic calls, or may consist of rapid repetitive honks. Ganders have also been known to hiss when defending the nest. Frequently, both sexes will vocalize in unison, and calling in flight is not unusual.

Magpie geese are noted for a strong and unpleasant musky odor, and it is said that the distinctive smell can betray their presence from a considerable distance. *Anseranas* is almost instantly recognizable on the wing. The flight of these birds is relatively slow and labored, with heavy and distinct wing beats, and their broad rounded wings give them the appearance in flight of a stork or a large bird of prey.

Most aberrant of their many atypical anatid traits, magpie geese molt gradually, instead of simultaneously shedding all of their flight feathers. Thus, they are able to bypass the period of flightless vulnerability that plagues *all* other wildfowl species. This deviation from the norm is probably necessary to reduce their susceptibility to predation, since the geese are birds of semi-open habitats and molting commences at the end of the breeding season when the swamps are rapidly drying out. If left flightless for even a short period, they could easily find themselves helplessly stranded in a dry swamp.

Habitat preferences of magpie geese vary, and they move seasonally in response to changing water conditions. In general, they are more often found away from water than in it. During the breeding season, however, they tend to favor billabongs or swampy areas, along the flood plains of tropical rivers, usually within 50 miles of the coast. The denser, more vegetated parts of spike-rush swamps are most preferred. In exceptionally dry years, extensive wandering can occur and they may drift as far south as southern Australia, even rarely to Tasmania.

Unlike most of their near relatives, magpie geese are polygamous. Males take two (sometimes even three) mates, and the bond between

3.4 *Adult ganders, such as this one, typically have more fully developed cranial knobs than their mates. Both sexes have peculiar bills that have a rather "pebbled" look to them. Like most swans, their faces are featherless back to the eyes.*

3.5 *The helmeted curassow, one of the cracids. This family of tropical gamebirds is similar in a number of ways to the magpie goose.*

3.6 *When landing, magpie geese appear to be ungainly and cumbersome.*

3.7

the mated trios is very strong, perhaps even life long. It has been suggested that more than two parents may be advantageous because the young grow surprisingly rapidly, and also because of the relative impermanence of the breeding habitat. Apparently, successful breeding does not occur until at least the third year. Copulation most often takes place on the nest platform (rarely in the water), and the male does not grasp the nape feathers of the female during mating—both atypical traits for wildfowl. The only other waterfowl that habitually copulate ashore or at the water's edge are the Nene and Cape Barren geese—and these birds, like the magpie goose, are semi-terrestrial with reduced foot webbing.

Depending on climatic conditions, breeding behavior usually commences in October or November, and arrival of the austral spring rains will generally stimulate courtship activity. However, actual nest construction and egg laying may be delayed until March or April, at the end of the wet season. Breeding habitat requirements are very specific and this delay may be associated with the need for optimum water depth, which in turn affects the density and height of the vegetation.

Ganders defend nesting territories of approximately half an acre in size, and magpie geese tend to nest in loose colonies, which vary in size from a few acres to several square miles. In one study, nest density in a typical colony consisted of 135 nests per 100 acres. Nests usually consist of huge mounds of semifloating vegetation, which is trampled

down and then piled up in a manner similar to that of most swans. The more elaborate nests are even woven and have a deep depression on the top. Males assume most of the responsibility for nest construction, although both sexes participate and all of the females lay in the same nest. For reasons not clearly understood, several preliminary nests (dummy nests) may be built before the nest that will actually be used is constructed. It may be that such activity strengthens the pair bond.

Typically, four to nine oval creamy-white eggs are produced, and these are subject to a great deal of predation. As many as 70 percent may be lost to such opportunists as eagles, crows, snakes and monitor lizards. Unlike swans and true geese, magpie geese do not use their wings for nest defense, but depend instead on their powerful bills, which can be very effective weapons. All members of the nesting group are involved in incubation, which takes from 24 to 28 days. The male is apparently responsible for most of the nocturnal incubation, and all group members assist in rearing the young. The nest is lined with little or no down, but because both sexes incubate, the eggs are usually never left uncovered or unattended from the time incubation begins.

It is of great interest that parent magpie geese feed the newly-hatched goslings from their beaks—behavior that has been observed in only one other waterfowl species, the equally strange Australian musk duck. (All other waterfowl young must forage for themselves from the very beginning.) Tidbits of food, which may be brought up from underwater, are dropped in front of the goslings in the manner of some gamebirds. Parental feeding is most conspicuous during the first week after hatching, but has been observed up to six weeks of age. Parents also obtain food for the young either by upending or by bending seedheads down with their feet to bring the seeds within reach of the goslings.

In many respects, the appearance and behavior of *Anseranas* goslings vaguely recalls that of a coot or gallinule chick. Their bright yellow-orange bills are proportionally large and their peculiar cinnamon-red heads are totally unique among downy waterfowl young. It seems obvious that these peculiar physical features are associated in some way with their specialized parental feeding requirements, and may possibly serve as a target for the adults. It is also conceivable that the goslings' loud and sibilant calls, which are uttered with open bills, may trigger a parental feeding response that prevents the adults from swallowing the food.

Brood nests may be "constructed" for the young up to several weeks of age. A sitting bird of either sex literally pulls such a nest together, heaping vegetation up around it and often totally covering the goslings—a practice that once again does not conform with typical waterfowl behavior. Goslings grow rapidly and fledge in 10 to 12 weeks, but may remain with the adults until the next breeding season. They can be aggressive to one another, and when food is in short supply, the less dominant young may perish. If the swamps dry up prematurely and the young have not yet fledged when the adults depart, it is unlikely that they will survive—in low water years, mortality of this type can be incredibly high.

Magpie geese are routinely observed in groups of 200 to 300, or even as many as 5000 individuals, but massive flocks of up to 80,000 birds have been recorded. Despite these huge flocks, there is no evidence of any social structure larger than the male-dominated family unit. Threatening and fighting between individuals is apparently frequent.

Even though their range has decreased significantly since the early 1900s, and they have been essentially extinct in southern Australia since the early decades of this century, magpie geese are still regarded as relatively common throughout some portions of their range, particularly in the subcoastal plains of northern Australia. Not too long ago, rather large flocks were attracted to flooded rice fields, and farmers considered them a double nuisance, since the geese not only grazed on the rice, but trampled it down as well. The problem was partially solved in many areas (although not in all) by regulating the amount of water in the fields in such a way that the croplands no longer met the specific feeding requirements of the geese. Formerly, they were poisoned in large numbers.

Magpie geese are, by nature, relatively tame and easy to approach, and this has made them particularly vulnerable to hunters in the past. New Guinea natives formerly hunted them with spears. Australian aborigines still supplement their diet with goose eggs and hunt the geese by skillfully hitting flying birds with throwing sticks, but their activities have had no significant impact on the population. Some legal sport hunting does take place in the Northern Territory, but the geese are totally protected elsewhere.

Far more detrimental than hunting are the harmful side effects of civilization. Control of the rivers and waterways may benefit man, but the resultant loss of habitat has had a decidedly negative effect on

3.8

wildlife in general and waterfowl in particular. Nevertheless, recent evidence does suggest that even though magpie geese may be declining in numbers, and are less common than they once were in some of their strongholds, the overall population remains healthy, particularly in tropical areas. Their continued survival, of course, is contingent on the preservation of remaining coastal wetlands.

Relatively few magpie geese are maintained in zoological collections outside Australia. Partly, this is because regulations regarding the exportation of any Australian wildlife are very strict. Beyond this, the captive breeding of magpie geese outside Australia has been only sporadically successful (although results during the past few years have been more encouraging). For the serious student, the scarcity of magpie geese in waterfowl collections is rather unfortunate because, in many respects, the magpie goose is one of the most interesting of the waterfowl. These birds may possess distinct personalities and are very impressive—even though they can be aggressive at times and have been known to attack humans. In some collections they are kept full-winged because they tend not to wander far and do present a spectacular sight as they fly about the grounds.

Outside Australia, young have definitely been produced at the Wildfowl Trust in England, the San Diego Zoo in the United States, and the magnificent Delacour collection in Normandy, France. They may also have been produced on one occasion in at least one private

collection some years ago, but the evidence for this is incomplete.

Curiously, most of the captive breedings have involved birds that would normally be considered quite ancient by most avian standards. One of the Wildfowl Trust birds, for example, was at least 20 years old when she began producing eggs, and the French geese were in the collection for some 15 years prior to breeding. However, banding recovery data from the wild suggest that magpie geese are rather long-lived: at least 11 individuals have been recovered after ten years, and two after almost 19 years.

In a number of cases, the successful captive breeders were full-winged (including some in Australian collections), but this does not necessarily imply that pinioning compromises breeding potential since pinioned birds have bred as well. At times, breeding behavior corresponded to that observed in the wild, and nesting trios were formed at the Wildfowl Trust. In at least one instance, two females laid in a single nest and continued to lay as the eggs were collected, ultimately producing 18 eggs.

Only recently have magpie geese begun to produce young once again in North America. In 1945, six eggs were laid at the San Diego Zoo and of these, five hatched and four were ultimately reared by the parents. The following year, three eggs were laid, and after they were transferred to a broody bantam two hatched and one was reared. Thirty-two years were then to pass before the species was bred again.

During the summer of 1978, a pair of proven breeders, at least 11 years old, was imported from Australia by the San Diego Zoo. This pair was placed with two old females, one of which was acquired in 1951 and the other in 1966. The new male bred with the older female and a clutch of five eggs resulted. Only one was fertile, and unfortunately it failed to hatch. The same female then laid an additional clutch of five eggs. Again, only one was fertile, but this time a female gosling was hatched in an incubator. Although this gosling was initially weak and had crooked toes, the toes were straightened by taping them for several days, and she was ultimately reared without incident.

In October of the same year, a third clutch was produced by the same adult female. However, she did not incubate attentively and the other females continually interfered, so the four eggs were removed from the nest. To increase the chances of success, two eggs were placed in the zoo incubator and the other two were deposited in the Sea World incubator. Both of the zoo eggs were fertile but one embryo died midway through incubation and the other succumbed while pipping.

Only one of the Sea World eggs was fertile. Because of the general weakness of the gosling hatched previously by the zoo and the problems experienced with the most recent eggs, this remaining egg was subjected to a relative humidity somewhat higher than is normal for most waterfowl. For several days prior to actual pipping, the rather loud "cheeps" of the chick were clearly audible from within the egg. Pipping was a day behind the zoo egg and this, coupled with the information that one of their goslings had died during pipping, prompted the Sea World aviculturists to open the egg and remove the youngster. At best, this procedure is very risky and should only be considered as a last resort, but in this case the decision proved to be correct, because the egg shell was very hard and it is possible that the gosling would not have been strong enough to emerge on its own. Happily, it was a male and was reared without difficulty. (It should be noted that during the process of rearing, goslings of this species are very prone to imprint, and great care must be exercised to prevent it.)

Incredibly, in mid-November of 1978, yet another clutch of three eggs was laid by the same aged female. These proved to be infertile, but all the same, it is almost beyond belief that this geriatric bird of no less than 28 years of age was able to not only lay some fertile eggs, but also to produce four full clutches in such a relatively brief period.

There can be no question that the recent production of young in at least two collections (San Diego Zoo and Cleres, France) will do much to increase future breeding potential. It is not known at what age magpie geese cease producing fertile eggs, but certainly the addition of young birds is essential if the species is to continue outside of Australia in the absence of additional exportations. ◢▬▬▬

3.10

3.11

3.12

3.13

3.14

3.9 (Opposite Page) *Usually, magpie geese are encountered in flocks of several thousand individuals — but in areas of prime habitat, congregations may be significantly larger (i.e., tens of thousands). Even though magpie geese are obviously gregarious, there can be much threatening and fighting between individuals.* PHOTO BY A. EAMES

3.10 *Magpie goose gosling (male) at one day of age. The peculiar head and bill coloring is clearly evident.*

3.11 *Male at 30 days of age. At this stage, the young are very uncoordinated and clumsy. (By the 14th day, the color of the legs and bill has faded to grey.)*

3.12 *Male at 41 days of age. Beginning to feather out, and to assume the appearance of a magpie goose.*

3.13 *Male at 57 days of age, essentially in immature plumage. Note that the bill is still dark and that its surface is smooth, but that the leg color is lightening.*

3.14 *Female magpie goose at 100 days of age. At this age, the bill is changing color and the legs have assumed the adult coloration.*

4
Whistling or Tree Ducks
Dendrocygnini

Of the two widely used vernacular names for ducks of this tribe, whistling ducks is the one that is perhaps the most appropriate and descriptive, since all species vocalize with unique, very unduck-like multisyllabic whistles. Their strange calls range from distinctive high-pitched shrill sounds to clear or squeaky whistles, and they are often extremely vocal. A number of species call continuously, even on the wing, and some occasionally even twitter like song birds. The name tree duck, on the other hand, is really descriptive in only a limited sense, since some whistling ducks are more arboreal than others, and ducks from other tribes (such as the perching ducks) are more likely to regularly perch and nest in trees.

Whistling ducks differ so strikingly from most other waterfowl that some consideration has been given to the formation of a separate subfamily. In general, they have longer legs and necks than "typical" ducks and are behaviorally much more like swans or geese. Males and females are externally similar in appearance, but vocalizations of the sexes may differ slightly, with females characteristically having somewhat lower calls, and curiously, females often weigh more than their

4.2

4.1 (Opposite Page) *Northern black-bellied whistling duck. Better known for their whistling calls than for their perching ability, some whistling ducks do nevertheless perch readily.*

4.2 *This dozing but alert Eyton's whistling duck illustrates the two unique features of this species: yellow-orange eyes and long lanceolate flank feathers. Many of the whistling ducks are nocturnal and commonly sleep during the day.*

mates. In some species, such as the plumed whistling duck, the flank feathers have become elongated and are highly ornamental.

Geographical distribution of the dendrocygnids covers most of the tropics and subtropics of both the Old and New Worlds, but they are essentially restricted to the warm lowland areas of their range. One tribal representative, the fulvous whistling duck, is among the most cosmopolitan of *all* birds, occupying four continents and numerous islands with no significant variation in size or color—and this absence of valid subspecific differences over such a globe-spanning range is quite extraordinary from an evolutionary point of view. In addition, this remarkable duck is the *only* waterfowl species that naturally breeds in all hemispheres.

Also unusual is the range of the white-faced whistling duck, with a discontinuous distribution in both South Africa and South America and, once again, no discernable subspecific differentiation anywhere. The fulvous and black-bellied whistling ducks are the only members of the tribe that occur in the United States, the former usually associated with rice fields and marshes, and the latter with lakes and savannahs.

Whistling ducks are well known for the incredibly large clutches of eggs they sometimes produce. Normal-sized clutches generally consist

of 10 to 15 eggs, but some nests have been discovered containing more than 100 eggs, obviously the work of a number of females. As many as 17 females have been observed laying in a single nest in one day. Nests of this type are usually referred to as "dump nests" and they are not often incubated. When they are, however, a surprisingly large number of eggs may hatch, with broods of more than 30 young not being particularly uncommon. But many ducklings from such "super clutches" are usually lost within the first few days, probably as a result of the inability of the adults to effectively brood so many.

Usually, nests are built on the ground, but low bushes or trees are also utilized. Abandoned nests of other species are sometimes occupied or a tree hollow may be selected, but whistling ducks as a group are not generally considered cavity nesters. A substantial nest is normally constructed and, unlike most waterfowl nests, it is not heavily lined with down.

As with northern geese, the pair bond is very strong (it may last for life), and both sexes share equally in care of the young. Incubation periods vary from 27 to 32 days, and in some cases, the male may even incubate, possibly spending more time on the nest than its mate. Newly-hatched downy young are noted for contrasting color patterns, particularly those of the red-billed whistling duck.

Fulvous and black-bellied whistling ducks are often almost military-like in their mannerisms and it is not unusual to see a perfectly straight line of them swimming across the water. If startled, dendrocygnids frequently stand rigidly still, with their long necks up-stretched, and in this position they may easily be mistaken for standing stalks of surrounding vegetation. For the greater part of the year, whistling ducks are rather gregarious. Tropical species are essentially sedentary, while the more temperate forms are at least partially migratory.

The flight posture of whistling ducks is very characteristic—the short rounded wings beat slowly, the long neck is extended, the shoulders are "hunched" with the long legs trailing behind, and the overall flight silhouette is somewhat reminiscent of a flying crane or ibis. They have the curious habit of hovering, with their necks craned below their feet, prior to landing. Due to their relatively slow flight, and because they can be overly confident at times, most forms are not considered superior gamebirds by seasoned waterfowlers; they even seem to have a tendency to circle when one of their number has been shot. (Oddly, they may at other times be very shy and retiring, and difficult to approach.)

The rumps of many whistling ducks are pale colored and thus very conspicuous in flight. This contrasting coloration, which is typical of most true geese as well, may function as a visual signal to maintain flock cohesiveness in flight. Several species are noted for distinctive mechanical whistling noises that are produced when they fly, and these sounds are apparently caused by vibrations of the indented inner vanes of the outermost primary feathers.

In general, most whistling ducks swim rather low in the water. They usually feed on the water's surface, but are very efficient (albeit somewhat awkward) divers as well. Many species are nocturnal feeders, and although they are collectively thought of as omnivorous, most apparently prefer to forage on vegetation. Several types are prone to graze ashore, and are considered detrimental to crops in some regions. At times, when flocks of whistling ducks are grubbing and poking in the mud, they rather resemble huge foraging shorebirds.

Most captive waterfowl collections are enhanced by the presence of at least one pair of whistling ducks, and some species breed readily. As

4.3 (Opposite Page) *Southern black-bellied whistling duck. All whistling ducks have a flight style that is unlike that of most waterfowl. Most diagnostic is the distinct "hump backed" posture.*

4.4 *Fulvous whistling duck. Most dendrocygnids tend to float rather low in the water, and while they are not regarded as superior divers, they unhesitatingly engage in such activity.*

4.5 *Many waterfowl species have young that are very distinctive and attractive, but few can match the vivid color and pattern of the black-bellied whistling duck.*

4.6 *The prominent white upper wing surfaces of these northern black-bellied whistling ducks in Guatemala — and their continuous whistles — quickly call attention to them.*

a group they are considered to be quite ornamental and tame, and all species have been propagated in captivity at one time or another. With the possible exception of the spotted and Cuban whistling ducks, they are generally not overly aggressive to other ducks, although some can be spiteful from time to time (especially during the breeding season). Some aviculturists maintain whistling ducks in a full-winged state, and the birds tend not to wander very far. At the same time, it should be noted that the primaries and secondaries are almost of equal length and pinioned birds can frequently fly surprisingly well.

The tribe has traditionally consisted of the single genus *Dendrocygna*, but Johnsgard has recently suggested the inclusion of another genus by shifting the peculiar white-backed ducks (*Thalassornis*) from the stiff-tail tribe to the whistling ducks. This move cannot be justified on the basis of appearance, since the white-backed ducks superficially have nothing in common with whistling ducks. But anatomical and behavioral similarities, combined with definite relationships that have been clearly established by analysis of feather proteins, do strongly indicate that the white-backed ducks may be more appropriately classified with the whistling ducks.

The little **spotted whistling duck** (*Dendrocygna guttata*) is not well known, either in the wild or in captivity, despite its apparent local abundance in appropriate habitat and its alleged status as the most numerous and widespread of New Guinea ducks. These handsome ducks have dusky red bills, legs, and feet, as well as small inconspicuous crests that can be partially raised during periods of excitement. Their unusually large eyes suggest a nocturnal existence.

Spotted whistling ducks are among the most arboreal members of the tribe, and may nest in tree hollows. They can be gregarious, and flocks numbering in the hundreds have been documented; they may also roost collectively. When they fly, a distinct and noisy whirring sound is produced as air passes through the notched primary feathers. Reportedly, these birds are not as vocal as some other species, but I have observed that just the opposite is true, at least in the case of some captive pairs. In many ways, these birds look rather like miniature Cuban whistling ducks, but they are apparently more closely related to Eyton's whistling ducks.

Over the years, relatively few spotted whistling ducks have been maintained in wildfowl collections, perhaps because they tend to be somewhat aggressive—especially to other whistling ducks—and because they are extremely difficult to obtain. The species was first bred in captivity in 1959 at the Wildfowl Trust, and in recent years they have become slightly more available, although they are still far from common.

Superficially, the **Cuban or black-billed whistling duck** (*Dendrocygna arborea*) of the West Indies appears to be a larger version of the spotted whistling duck, but it is probably more closely related to the red-billed whistling duck. Brackish water mangrove and fresh water swamps are the favored habitat of this species. They frequently feed on the fruit of the royal palm and palms are sometimes selected for nesting as well. (A duck feeding in a palm tree, it goes without saying, is a strange sight to see.) Cuban whistling ducks are the largest, but among the least vocal of the eight whistling duck species.

Although they may still be locally abundant, these ducks are declining in numbers and are regarded as endangered. But despite the fact that they are "officially protected," hunting still occurs regularly on some Caribbean Islands, eggs are taken, and man has subjected them to a great deal of indirect persecution by altering or destroying their habitat. In addition, the predatory activities of the introduced mongoose have had a detrimental effect on some islands.

Temperaments of Cuban whistling ducks can vary greatly, and some of these birds can be best described as vicious, especially during the breeding season. Particularly pugnacious birds have been known to kill large swans in waterfowl collections by riding their backs and ultimately drowning them, a sight that must be seen to be believed. Some other individuals, on the other hand, can be reasonably docile and seldom intimidating to other species. While not particularly uncommon in collections, Cuban whistling ducks cannot be considered prolific breeders, even though a number of aviculturists have been very successful with them.

The **plumed whistling duck** (*Dendrocygna eytoni*) is a tropical grassland species that inhabits eastern Australia, with rare stragglers reported in Tasmania, New Guinea and even New Zealand. Appropriately enough, Australians often call these birds grass whistle ducks, and this local name distinguishes them from the other Australian *Dendrocygna*, which is known as the water whistle duck. (Both of these vernacular names are obviously derived from the different habitat preferences of the two species.)

In America, grass whistle ducks are more commonly known as Eyton's whistling ducks. Among the most handsome and attractive members of the tribe, these ducks possess elongated lanceolate flank feathers and distinctive yellow or orange eyes (which contrast with the dark brown eyes of the other whistling duck species). The flank feathers of the drakes may be slightly more pronounced and may possibly extend upward to a greater degree than those of the females, but this is not really a reliable indicator of sex, particularly with older birds. Legs and feet of both sexes are pink, and the bill is pink mottled with black. Immature birds resemble adults, but can be recognized by their paler color, less distinct side barring, and broader blackish margins on the flank feathers.

Eyton's whistling ducks are clearly adapted to a cursorial lifestyle; they seldom perch, and are somewhat awkward when they do. Rather slow and inefficient swimmers, they avoid deep water habitats and do not dive nearly as readily as some of their relatives, except when

4.8

4.9

4.8 *Preening Eyton's whistling duck. A highly nomadic species, these ducks are most frequently associated with tropical grassland regions. They are among the very few Australian waterfowl that have taken advantage of man's domination of the continent, and indeed, their population has increased in some areas.*

4.9 *Cuban whistling ducks are not nearly as numerous as they formerly were, and the population decline has been such that they are considered endangered. Although these birds are fully protected throughout most of their range, some are shot nevertheless (particularly in Cuba). Over-hunting, habitat destruction, and the introduction of the carnivorous mongoose are all factors working against this fine duck.*

4.10

4.10 *Part of a loafing flock of approximately 6000 Eyton's whistling ducks in northern Australia. The gregarious nature of the species is obvious. During the day, they characteristically gather at communal roosting sites such as this and most of their foraging activity takes place at night. A few red-backed radjah shelducks can be seen in the foreground.*
PHOTO BY A. EAMES

wounded. Strongly nomadic, they display a tendency to congregate in large flocks at communal roosting sites (particularly during the dry season). Mainly night feeders, these birds appear to be among the most wary of the whistling ducks. They tend to twitter continually and their wings whistle in flight.

As with many Australian avian species, breeding success is dependent on the arrival of the life-giving austral spring rains. During exceptionally wet seasons, the entire adult population may breed and productivity can be high, but if it is a dry year, the length of the season will be greatly reduced—and breeding may not take place at all if conditions are severe enough.

Eyton's whistling ducks are not presently threatened and the overall population may even have benefited to some extent from human settlement. The growth of the Australian cattle industry has been particularly beneficial, because it has necessitated the creation of cattle watering holes that provide water year round, and because grazing cattle tend to keep the tall coarse grass down to a level where it can be

utilized by the ducks.

Even though they are well established in waterfowl collections, Eyton's whistling ducks are not overly abundant and are at best sporadic breeders—at least in North America. There is an unusually high incidence of infertility, and many of the young produced are not very viable. Possibly, many of the captive birds are inbred and an infusion of new imported blood may be required to revitalize this population.

The three similar subspecies of the **wandering whistling duck** (*Dendrocygna arcuata*) are resident throughout a wide area, from the Philippines south to Australia, and while their movements are mainly local, they may sometimes wander considerable distances—hence the origin of their vernacular name. In appearance and behavior, this species resembles the more familiar fulvous whistling duck, but differs in that the crown is nearly black, neck striping is absent, and the bill is blackish rather than bluish grey. In addition, the first primary feather is distinctly notched, and a characteristic whirr is produced when the

4.11 *Eyton's whistling duck. Note that the ornamental flank feathers are not nearly as prominent as those of the duck depicted in 4.2. There can be much variation in this regard.*

4.12 *East Indian wandering whistling duck. These birds have a cleaner, crisper look than the more familiar, slightly larger fulvous whistling duck, and they are easily differentiated by their black crowns, blackish bills, and a lack of neck striping.*

4.13 *Of the three races of wandering whistling ducks, only the East Indian birds are well established in captivity. Like all waterfowl, they commonly rest standing on one leg.*

4.14 *The dainty lesser wandering whistling duck is an insular bird with a rather limited distribution. Introduced predators such as the mongoose have been responsible for a significant population reduction, and this duck may already be gone from Fiji.*

wing is in motion. As a group, wandering whistling ducks are particularly active and alert birds which feed extensively in the water.

The Australian race (*D. a. australis*) is the largest of the three forms, whereas the lesser wandering whistling duck (*D. a. pygmaea*) is very small, scarcely larger than the diminutive Javan whistling duck. Predation by the introduced mongoose may be responsible for the apparent extirpation of the lesser wandering whistling duck in Fiji (although it was seen there as recently as 1959), and possibly in New Caledonia as well. The Australian birds (water whistle ducks) are highly regarded gamebirds, which are widely distributed throughout the northern tropics, and usually encountered in constantly moving dense flocks. The lifestyle of these tropical ducks is greatly influenced by the occurrence of the cyclic rains, and they tend to move inland to breed during the rainy season.

In captivity, it is unwise to maintain them with fulvous whistling ducks because the two forms will readily interbreed. In my experience, if given the chance, wandering whistling ducks will actively join with their near relatives in preference to one of their own kind. The Australian and Fiji races have seldom been available to aviculturists, but the intermediate-sized East Indian birds (*D. a. arcuata*) have become fairly well established in collections in recent years.

Possibly the most numerous and widespread of the dendrocygnids is the **fulvous whistling duck** (*Dendrocygna bicolor*). Throughout their huge cosmopolitan range they occupy a wide variety of habitats, from lowlands on up to 5000-foot altitudes. Flattened crowns and short tails give both sexes a rather dumpy appearance, and although females are slightly smaller and duller than males, these differences are barely discernable. They dive readily (especially the ducklings), but are not noted for grace or style when doing so. Their habitat of squealing as they take to the wing has earned them the descriptive vernacular name of "Mexican squealer." Once airborne, they tend to fly in irregular formations.

Some farmers regard fulvous whistling ducks as agricultural pests and destroy every nest they encounter. In some regions, these ducks

may nest colonially, but this is probably more the exception than the rule. Nests typically consist of mats of aquatic vegetation trampled down to form a platform above the water, with the tops usually concealed from above by overhanging grass.

A rather nomadic species, the fulvous whistling duck has been recorded in at least 20 states, as well as some Canadian provinces. Normally, however, the northern extreme of their range barely extends into Texas and Louisiana. This northern population declined rapidly during the 1960's (from thousands to several hundred), apparently because toxic pesticides, such as aldrin, were being indiscriminately applied to rice crops. Since the use of such non-selective chlorinated hydrocarbon pesticides has been significantly reduced, the ducks are responding favorably and this population has apparently begun to recover.

Almost every waterfowl collection contains at least one pair of these enchanting ducks, and they breed very readily—practically year round in southern climates. In comparing them to other whistling ducks, Delacour comments that they are "quiet and rather dull." But I consider them somewhat noisy myself, and some individuals can be fairly aggressive.

The **white-faced whistling duck** (*Dendrocygna viduata*) is one of the most distinctive and attractive representatives of the tribe. As the popular name implies, the faces of adults are a conspicuous white, although those of immature birds are grey. They demonstrate very little inclination to perch in trees, and during the day are much more apt to be found loafing in large numbers on sand bars near the water's edge. They are particularly fond of flood plains and large lagoons, and usually do not frequent forested areas.

Relatively quiet during the day, white-faced whistling ducks are likely to be loquacious at night while feeding. When swimming, they float higher in the water than most dendrocygnids, with their heads held high. Pairs (and sometimes trios) engage in a great deal of mutual preening, and although allopreening is not particularly uncommon among whistling ducks in general, these birds seem to be especially attentive to each other. They have a wide range, can be fairly abundant locally, and in Africa are said to be one of the most common ducks. Their good looks and docile nature make them very desirable for waterfowl collections, and they are well established; unfortunately, they do not breed as readily as some of their near relatives.

The **black-bellied or red-billed whistling duck** (*Dendrocygna autumnalis*) is the only whistling duck with a bright red bill. Blessed as well with truly elegant plumage and a graceful shape, these ducks are almost heron-like in their posture. On the wing, they are often very vocal, emitting a peculiar whistling "pe-che-che-ne" sound—a call that is the origin of one native name for them. Their vocalizations are considered to be the most musical of the tribe, and they are also known for their constant twittering. In Mexico, natives may call them "patos maizal" or cornfield ducks, a name that refers to the substantial crop damage they are reported to cause. Ninety percent of their food is vegetation.

Essentially a species of the neotropical lowlands, red-billed whistling ducks do range as far north as southern Texas, and in recent years appear to have been expanding their range even further northward. This range expansion may be in response to the increased number of stock ponds provided by cattlemen, as well as to the enlargement of Lake Corpus Christi—since both developments have created additional suitable nesting habitat.

4.16

4.15 (Opposite Page) *White-faced whistling ducks are a highly social species, and are among the most beautiful of the dendrocygnids. Less apt to perch than some of the other species, they are inclined to pass much of the day roosting on mudflats or sandbars. Due to their wide distribution in Africa and South America, and their rather broad ecological tolerances, these lovely birds are not really endangered in any part of their range.*

4.16 *Like most waterfowl, white-faced whistling ducks must bathe frequently if their plumage is to be maintained in top condition. During such activity, the wings may flail the surface of the water to such a degree that an observer who is unfamiliar with wildfowl behavior might think that the bathing bird is injured. Many of the favored food items of these birds are obtained by diving, including a wide variety of small crustaceans, molluscs, aquatic insects, and other small invertebrates. Food of vegetable origin is also consumed.*

4.19

4.18   4.20

4.17 (Opposite Page) *The fulvous whistling duck is noted for an enormous cosmopolitan distribution, which encompasses four continents, and it is the only one of the waterfowl species that naturally breeds in all hemispheres. As with the other whistling ducks, the sexes are similar in appearance, although females may be slightly smaller and duller. This species is not as gregarious as some of the others and is not often encountered in large flocks.*

4.18 *Black-bellied whistling duck. The long legs and neck and large feet which are characteristic of all whistling ducks are clearly illustrated here. This species walks with a very erect posture that is possibly a reflection of its rather terrestrial way of life. Generally avoiding deep water areas, they are more likely to seek mudflats and sandbars. They are often associated with tropical coastal areas, and while not generally considered a salt water species, they are frequently encountered in salt water mangrove swamps. Birds of the northern race can be distinguished from their close southern relatives by their slightly larger size and the lack of grey on the breast.*

4.19 *Northern black-bellied whistling duck. Not surprisingly, this species is sometimes known as the red-billed tree duck. When viewed at close range, their white eye rings can be quite prominent. Unlike the other whistling ducks, an extensive portion of their upper wing surface is white, a condition that is particularly obvious in flight.*

4.20 *Mutual preening is not uncommon with whistling ducks in general, and this activity is highly developed with white-faced whistling ducks. The affectionate behavior may be associated with pair bond formation and might serve to strengthen the bond once it is formed. This species typically nests on the ground, and pairs with broods may not be obvious because they have a tendency to hide their ducklings in aquatic vegetation.*

4.21 *Javan whistling ducks, smallest of the dendrocygnids, are delicate-looking little ducks. Very common throughout the jungles and swamps of Asia, they are surprisingly rare in wildfowl collections. They feed fairly extensively on snails and other small invertebrates, but also gather in rice paddies, where their tendency to graze on young rice shoots is looked upon with some disfavor by rice farmers. They frequent backwaters, swamps, and lakes where there is an abundant growth of vegetation, and they are often encountered in flocks of 50 or more. In especially favored habitat in India, they may gather in huge flocks, surpassing in number all other ducks.*

4.21

Because they are extremely curious and habitually start to chatter loudly whenever disturbed, these handsome birds are often kept as house pets and watch birds in Central and South America. The brightly-colored and unusually-marked ducklings, which have occasionally been observed riding on the backs of swimming adults, are among the most attractive of all waterfowl young.

Two distinct regional races of this species (a southern and a northern) are recognized, with ranges that converge in Panama. Some biologists have suggested that there may be as many as four separate races, but two of the proposed subspecies have never gained widespread acceptance. Both of the currently acknowledged races are somewhat similar, but the southern birds (*D. a. discolor*) tend to be slightly smaller and are greyer on the breast. In American wildfowl collections, the southern subspecies is poorly represented but northern birds (*D. a. autumnalis*) are quite abundant, while in European collections the situation is reversed. Both forms are easy to maintain and propagation presents no real challenge.

The **Javan or lesser whistling duck** (*Dendrocygna javanica*), also known as the Indian whistling duck, is extremely numerous in India and Ceylon. Flocks numbering in the hundreds of thousands were reported at the turn of the century, and in the past, these birds were sold by the thousands in the markets of Calcutta, Singapore and Saigon. This being the case, it is curious to note that they are currently quite scarce in captive waterfowl collections and can be considered very rare in North America.

Delicate and dainty, the smallest of the dendrocygnids, Javan whistling ducks are characterized by a narrow yellow eye ring that is quite conspicuous when viewed at close range. Often, these birds are observed in the company of fulvous whistling ducks or Asian pygmy geese. Their flight has been described as particularly noisy and feeble—or even "rail-like." Essentially diurnal, they may nevertheless feed extensively at night. Their flesh is said to be unpalatable, probably because they consume more animal food (such as fresh water snails) than most of the whistling ducks, and this has afforded them some protection from meat hunters.

They tend to avoid open water and large rivers as well as brackish estuaries or coastal lagoons—and although they may be seen rarely on the ocean just beyond the surf line, they are generally encountered in jungle swamps. The presence or absence of appropriate roosting trees near the water may be a major determining factor in their distribution.

Javan whistling ducks are apparently not overly particular about nesting sites and will deposit their eggs in almost any location—among reeds or canes, on the ground, in low bushes, in forks and hollows of trees, and even in the abandoned nests of crows, herons or kites. Peak breeding activity coincides with the summer rainy season.

The reluctance of these ducks to breed in captivity is a source of concern to those aviculturists who are fortunate enough to have them. Just why they should be more difficult to propagate than other whistling ducks is a mystery.

4.22

4.23

4.22 *Southern black-bellied whistling duck. These birds can be very curious and will often select a high perch to give them a better vantage point. This species usually nests in tree cavities instead of on the ground. Pairs are very protective of their young, and when swimming, one parent leads while the other brings up the rear—a behavior that is distinctly goose-like. On occasion, the young may climb onto the back of a parent.*

4.23 *Pair of Javan whistling ducks.*

5
Swans
Anserini

Largest and most majestic of the waterfowl, swans are among the most familiar and long-lived of all birds. They are indigenous to every continent except Antarctica and Africa, and although most of them inhabit the Northern Hemisphere, three distinct species occur south of the equator as well.

Swans have had a long association with man. Indeed, archaeologists have discovered drawings of swan-like creatures dating back at least as far as the Stone Age. It seems that these magnificent birds have always been viewed as sacred creatures possessing magical qualities, perhaps because of their snow white plumage and regal bearing.

Down through the ages, they have played a prominent role in mythology, inspiring hundreds of legends, including the memorable ancient Greek myth of Leda and the swan. According to this legend,

5.2

5.1 (Opposite Page) *Pair of black-necked swans at dusk.*

5.2 *Whistling swans nest on the arctic tundra, but migrate some 2000 miles south to pass the winter. While extremely territorial on the breeding grounds, they become gregarious during the winter and may flock up in the thousands. These are considered to be among the more numerous of northern swans, with a population that may approximate 100,000 swans, and apparently their numbers have increased slightly over the past quarter century.*

on the eve of her wedding to King Tyndareus of Sparta, Leda was visited by the great god Zeus, who assumed the form of a swan. Zeus seduced her, and she subsequently bore two sets of twins, each pair enclosed in an egg. One set of twins was said to be the progeny of Zeus, while the other twins were the mortal children of Tyndareus. Uncounted works of art have been inspired by this classic legend, including a magnificent painting by Michelangelo that is one of the world's greatest art treasures.

The ancient Greeks were apparently also responsible for the origin of the so-called "swan song." They believed that a swan "sang" a song of death when its life was about to end. Many people still hold this belief, including some ornithologists—and it is conceivable that a prolonged exhalation of air from the trachea of a dying swan could produce a series of "musical" notes.

Some time prior to the 12th Century, the mute swan was domesticated in Great Britain. For hundreds of years, these birds were considered to be the exclusive property of the Crown and could only be raised by persons possessing a permit from the Royal Swan Master. The Crown later granted "royalties" enabling certain corporate bodies to own swans and to mark their bills with registered symbols or "swan marks." Usually the swan marks consisted of a pattern of notches cut into the upper mandible of the bill, and any unmarked mute swans on the River Thames were considered the property of the Crown. Young swans were captured annually for marking in a colorful traditional ceremony known as "swan-upping."

Much of this ancient tradition is still carried on today in Great Britain, and the royal status of the mute swan is much the same as it was during medieval times. The only two organizations that continue to mark mute swans are the Worshipful companies of Dyers and Vintners. (The Vintners' Company received their swan mark from the Crown in 1472 and the Dyers' Company shortly thereafter in 1473.) On the Monday of the third week of July, the swan-upping rites commence, and even though the royal swans are no longer marked, the Queen's Swan Keeper is still a principle participant in the ceremony. Adolescent swans are caught with a bent pole that is somewhat reminiscent of a shepherd's staff, are marked according to the mark of their parents and pinioned at the same time. The entire process is quite painless, but swan-upping has nevertheless come under attack recently from protectionist groups who allege that it is cruel. As a result, this ancient ceremony may soon become a thing of the past.

Although man has identified with swans through the ages, his feelings of admiration have not deterred him from exploiting them. Throughout historic times, swans have been harvested for food and sport, and even their eggs have been marketed. Fortunately, they have fared better in recent times, and instances of direct persecution, such as hunting and egg harvesting, are less common than they once were. But they are still regarded as legal gamebirds in some areas, and despite the toughness and relatively poor quality of their flesh, a number are killed each year.

Tragically, indiscriminate destruction of habitat still continues at an alarming rate—and the consequences of such irresponsible "development" could be irreversible. In addition, widespread pollution, oil spills, and collisions with aircraft or power lines are becoming ever more prominent as significant causes of mortality. Hundreds of mute swans are killed each year in England alone by flying into power lines and pylons.

Most authorities recognize eight types of swans. Trumpeter, whistling, whooper, and Bewick's swans are generally thought of as the "northern swans." The mute swan, although admittedly a resident of the northern hemisphere, is both behaviorally and anatomically so distinct from the rest of the northern swan complex that it is usually regarded separately. The remaining three swans, the black swan, the black-necked swan, and the coscoroba swan, all occur south of the equator. All species, from both Northern and Southern hemispheres, are related closely enough to be placed in the single genus *Cygnus*, with the sole exception of the aberrant South American coscoroba, which has been assigned to the separate genus *Coscoroba*.

Some ornithologists have challenged the placement of swans and true geese together in the tribe Anserini, and have advocated the creation of a separate swan tribe, the Cygnini. But this proposal has not gained widespread acceptance, and the numerous behavioral and anatomical similarities between geese and swans cannot be ignored.

Male swans are called cobs, females are known as pens, and the downy young are referred to as cygnets. Both sexes are similar, but cobs tend to be larger and more aggressive. Swans have a far greater number of cervical, or neck, vertebrae than any other warm-blooded animal; while all mammals, including even the long-necked giraffes, have but seven, swans possess either 24 or 25. In light of this, the incredible flexibility of their necks should not be at all surprising.

All mature swans, with the obvious exceptions of black-necked and black swans, are essentially snow white, although immature birds are brownish grey. It is a curious fact that Europeans were so conditioned

to the image of the white swan that they simply would not believe in the existence of the Australian black swan when it was first reported in the late 17th Century. Its discoverer was widely ridiculed and told that such a creature was a natural impossibility.

Most swans are highly migratory, and this is particularly true of the Northern Hemisphere species. During migration, swans tend to fly high and fast, often in "V" formation or irregular lines. Flight speeds of 35 to 50 miles per hour are typical, but swans with a stiff tail wind can exceed 70 miles per hour. Young birds remain with their parents for their first year and during that time have an opportunity to learn the well established migration routes.

Prone to move at night, swans may fly as high as 10,000 feet, probably to avoid the turbulence that is sometimes associated with lower altitudes. It has been said that they fly so high that ice crystals

5.3

may form on their wings, and there is one account of "hundreds" being forced down in Pennsylvania in the spring of 1879 when their wings became "laden with ice." They generally fly with their legs trailing behind them, but when it is bitter cold some birds will tuck their feet forward into their belly feathers. On occasion, swans and aircraft have met in flight, with disastrous results—in 1962, for instance, an airliner collided with a flock of whistling swans and crashed, with a loss of 17 human lives.

Essentially vegetarian, swans feed extensively on a wide variety of aquatic plants. The characteristic long neck is a specialized adaptation that makes it possible for the birds to forage in relatively deep water, often by upending. Swans are, by the way, known to be wasteful feeders, and other less specialized opportunistic aquatic birds often capitalize on the remains of food dredged up by foraging swans.

Many northern swans habitually come ashore to feed on tundra vegetation and muskeg berries, and whistling swan families are often observed some distance from water. As with many other species of ducks and geese, wintering swans may readily forage in cultivated fields, and although the overall impact is minimal, this behavior does little to increase their popularity with local farmers.

The literature is filled with colorful accounts concerning the fidelity of swans. Many people mistakenly believe that a swan will never accept another mate if its original partner is lost. Undeniably, the pair bond between swans is very strong, but a surviving bird will not pine away and ultimately die, as has been suggested. Sooner or later, a new mate will usually be taken.

5.3 Mute swans are awkward and cumbersome on the ground, but on the wing they are very graceful and strong fliers. Unlike the other swans of the north, these birds are relatively nonvocal, and as a result, they depend on the loud whistling or swishing sounds produced by their powerful wings to maintain aerial flock contact, particularly when flying at night or during inclement weather.

5.4

5.5

5.6

5.4 *As with most swans, whistling swans line their nests with little or no down. The eggs are white or yellowish when fresh, but as incubation progresses they become scratched and stained. Swan eggs are among the largest laid by any bird.*

5.5 *Mute swan foraging underwater. The extremely long and flexible necks of swans enable them to exploit deeper food sources than those generally available to other waterfowl. Primarily vegetarian, mute swans feed extensively on a wide variety of aquatic plants, but they can also be considered opportunistic feeders and wintering birds are even prone to graze in cultivated fields.*

5.6 *Deep water feeding is accomplished by upending, as illustrated by this pair of whistling swans. In the case of the huge trumpeter swans, vegetation as deep as three and a half feet beneath the surface can be reached. Foraging swans tend to be wasteful, and are often surrounded by floating vegetation dredged up from the bottom. As a result, less specialized birds tend to mingle with the feeding swans to capitalize on these leftovers. In Chesapeake Bay, wintering whistling swans sometimes feed on clams, and interestingly, opportunistic gulls may steal their food.*

Swans are well known for the huge nests they construct. Both sexes participate in nest building, and frequently the male selects the site and actually initiates construction. Whistling swans generally build the bases of their nests on solid ground, often some distance from the water, whereas trumpeter swans usually construct floating nests. When both species inhabit the same area, as in Alaska, these differences provide an excellent way to accurately identify the nests of each species during aerial surveys. With the sole exception of the coscoroba swan, swans do not use any great amount of down to line their nests.

Of all the waterfowl, swans are the most inclined to establish a large territory and defend it, and a cob defending its nest or young can be a very formidable adversary. Fights between rival males can be vicious and on rare occasions may result in the death of the losing combatant. Territorial defense may even involve fierce aerial battles. (In Great Britain, on the other hand, some mute swans exist in a semi-domesticated state and are not nearly as territorial; they may even nest colonially.)

Humans are not immune to attack. Arms have been broken by the powerful flailing wings of a defensive mute swan, and there are a few records of swans actually killing young children who were tormenting them. Mute swan cobs threaten with their wings partially opened and raised, forming a graceful arch over their backs with their head and neck thrown back—a posture that is known as "busking" or "swanning." Neck and body feathers are also ruffled up, making the birds appear larger and presumably more formidable. During this obviously aggressive display, they swim with violent simultaneous thrusts of both feet, moving forward in a characteristically jerky fashion.

Swan eggs are among the largest of any flying bird. Clutch sizes may vary from one to fourteen eggs, but three to six eggs appear to be most typical. Those of the mute swan are similar in appearance to the eggs of the nearly extinct California condor, and this close resemblance has led in the past to a rather bizarre variety of fraud. During the early part of the 20th Century, interest in oology (the study of eggs) was at its height, and a lucrative egg trade flourished. Because California condors have always been rare in historical times, and because they have the lowest reproductive potential of any North American bird (they normally lay only one egg every other year), a condor egg was the ultimate acquisition for an egg collector. Prices of two and even three thousand dollars per egg were not uncommon—an astronomical sum at the turn of the century. It is small wonder, therefore, that some unscrupulous egg dealers attempted to palm off readily available swan eggs for the almost unobtainable condor eggs!

The incubation periods of swans vary between 29 and 36 days. Usually, incubation commences with the laying of the final egg, thus assuring the nearly simultaneous hatching of the entire clutch and increasing the survival potential of all the young. Most waterfowl hatch over a one- to three-day period, with the egg laid last usually hatching first because it has never cooled. Late hatchers and spoiled (addled) eggs are usually abandoned.

In some species, such as the black swan, both sexes incubate, and in *all* species both parents engage in the complexities of rearing the young. Newly-hatched cygnets do not require any food for several days, making it possible for the first bird hatched to survive in the nest until the later ones hatch. On occasion, black swan cobs may care for the first young to hatch while the female continues to incubate the remaining eggs. In rare cases, if an incubating female dies, the male may assume the task of hatching and rearing the young by himself. For

5.7 (Opposite Page) *Both sexes of black swans generally incubate, and as a result, the eggs are seldom left unattended. During periods of inclement weather, it is particularly important for the eggs to be covered. Unlike most swans, this species is not highly territorial and in some locales they may even nest colonially.*

5.8 *With swans, both parents are involved in rearing the young, and the defensive behavior of these whistling swans typifies the aggressiveness of most breeding swans. The recently hatched cygnets are being brooded under the left wing of the pen.*

5.9 *Mute swan eggs were occasionally sold in the past to unsuspecting egg collectors as the eggs of the rapidly disappearing California condor, shown here.*

5.10 *Whistling swans and their near relatives construct large nests, and the building and reinforcement of the nest may continue throughout incubation. In contrast to most waterfowl, both sexes construct the nest.*

5.11 *Bewick's swan.*

5.8

5.9

5.10

5.11

some weeks after the cygnets hatch, swans may return to the nest at night to brood the young.

Young swans are very appealing when they first emerge from the egg and fluff up—little more than puffs of down, weighing between four and eight ounces. As they begin to mature, they progress to the famous "ugly duckling" stage, and are transformed at last into the classic shape and beauty of the adult swan. Cygnets of species that breed in temperate climates are able to fly at about three months of age, with arctic nesting species tending to fledge much more rapidly. Reportedly, young Bewick's swans are capable of flight in the unbelievably brief period of 45 days, but this requires further documentation.

Despite their massive size, mature swans are noted for their gracefulness in the water. On land, their movements appear to be more clumsy and labored, but they are far from helpless. Capturing a molting flightless swan on the tundra, for food or for scientific purposes, is a challenge that has tested the mettle of many a northern Eskimo . . . and many a biologist.

One of the most enchanting aspects of swan behavior is the habit that the cygnets of some species have of climbing onto the backs of their parents. This peculiar and specialized behavior is most pronounced in the black-necked and mute swans, and affords the young a great deal of protection by providing them with a warm and safe sanctuary. It also enables the parents to regain the weight lost during the rigors of courtship, egg laying, incubation, and territory defense, by allowing them to feed while they simultaneously brood their young.

This interesting phenomenon is not restricted to swans. It has been reliably reported that at least nine other species of waterfowl carry their young, and from time to time, accounts appear of waterfowl that even carry their progeny in flight. In fact, parental carrying of young in flight has been reported for at least 16 species of wildfowl, with bill carrying and back riding most common. Observations such as these have traditionally been discounted, but a growing quantity of evidence suggests that in some cases the carrying of young in flight may be not only possible but probable.

The relatively recent discovery that male tropical sungrebes transport their chicks in "pouches" under their wings in flight has helped to alter thinking about what is or is not physically possible for birds. There are also reliable reports of woodcocks carrying their young for short distances on rare occasions, gripping them tightly between their legs and thighs.

Swans tend to be long-lived birds and some have survived 30 years and more in captivity; there are a number of unsubstantiated reports of life spans exceeding 100 years. In the wild, however, it is probable that 95 percent of northern swans are lost by their tenth year. This figure can be misleading, however, since the juvenile mortality rate of arctic nesting swans tends to be very high, particularly with those birds that are poorly developed at the time of their first southern migration. In general, immature swans tend to be very accident prone, and when this high juvenile mortality rate is included in the overall rate, it results in a median life expectancy of only ten years. But it is probable that swans which survive long enough to become established breeders have a much higher life expectancy. As a rule, swans do not breed until their fourth year, and with northern swans the fifth or sixth summer may arrive before *successful* breeding is achieved.

Swans can be extremely vocal, and the various species produce a wide variety of calls. With northern swans, the calls of both sexes are

5.13

5.14

5.15

5.12 (Opposite Page) *A defensive mute swan cob can be considered a formidable and dangerous adversary. When they threaten in the "busking" position, the wings are held high, the neck feathers are fluffed, and the head is laid well back.*

5.13 *A brood consisting of both normal and Polish mute cygnets. The leucistic Polish young do not assume the typical grey-brown plumage of the subadult, but pass directly into the snow white dress of the adults.*

5.14 *Black-necked swans are so well adapted to an aquatic lifestyle that they seldom come ashore except to nest. The young are brooded on the backs of their parents, and this appealing behavior makes it possible for adults to feed while simultaneously brooding their cygnets.*

5.15 *Bewick swan family. This species migrates some 2600 miles north to relatively inaccessible breeding habitat on the high Siberian tundra. Preferred nesting sites consist of small islets in shallow tundra ponds or the tops of small hummocks, where the swans have a good view of the flat terrain.*

5.12

5.16

5.16 *Polish mute swans differ from normal mute swans in that their feet are pale grey or pinkish rather than black or dark grey. The trumpeter swans which nest in the Rocky Mountain region are also known for leucistic cygnets that are white as immatures. The white coloration of these subadult birds may have afforded them some protection from meat hunters of an earlier era, who tended to shoot the more typical grey subadults because immature birds are more tender. Any bird that was white was thought to be an adult and therefore tough.*

similar, although the female's may have a higher pitch. The loud vocalizations of these swans may possibly aid in maintaining flock contact during migration, and calling certainly plays a prominent role during courtship. Even mute swans are not totally mute; when irritated, they produce a loud hoarse hiss or snort, and on occasion they have even been known to produce a relatively loud trumpet-like note.

Some swan species are also noted for extraordinarily long and convoluted windpipes. This development is carried to its furthest extreme by the trumpeter swan, with a windpipe that not only coils around within the sternum (breast bone) but that also has an extra hump. The length and shape of the windpipe has a direct relationship to the loudness and tone of the voice, and the trumpeter swan, with the longest and most convoluted windpipe, is not surprisingly the loudest of the swans. The voice of the mute swan, on the other hand, is insignificant because the windpipe is straight and does not coil into the sternum at all. Interestingly, the swans with the loudest voices also tend to be the most territorial, and their vocalizations are no doubt important in maintaining enormous territories.

Some early investigators suggested that northern swans have such bizarre looped tracheal arrangements because they are high-altitude fliers. They theorized that the longer windpipes might be necessary to warm freezing air before it reached the lungs and air sacs. Few contemporary biologists subscribe to this interesting but unlikely hypothesis, since it appears far more probable that the lengthened looping tracheas evolved merely to increase vocal capabilities.

Swans have traditionally been favorites in city parks, zoological gardens, country estates, and private waterfowl collections the world over. Aesthetically, few things can compare with the grace and beauty of a swan on a pond. All species are relatively easy to keep if a large expanse of water is available. However, during the breeding season temperaments may alter and some individuals can turn vicious, so great care must be exercised if they are maintained with other birds. Mute, black, and whooper swans are considered to be reliable and prolific breeders. Coscoroba, black-necked, and trumpeter swans are bred more sporadically, and whistling and Bewick's swans are seldom raised in captivity—although in recent years the Wildfowl Trust has

been quite successful with them, particularly with the latter species. One breeding female Bewick's swan at the Trust was known to be at least 30 years old when she ceased producing fertile eggs.

Interestingly, while there are numerous whistling swans in waterfowl collections, relatively few have been raised. Most of the captive population of whistling swans consists of birds that have been shot by hunters but not killed, and as with many forms of waterfowl, adults taken in the wild are not prone to breed readily. However, if eggs are collected, hatched, and reared by a skilled aviculturist, it is likely that the resulting hatched birds will produce. Recent breeding success with hand-raised whistling swans supports this premise and they are currently being bred with greater frequency. The northern swans will hybridize, and during 1977, a trumpeter and a whistler were crossed in an Alaskan collection. For lack of a better name, the resultant offspring have been dubbed "trumplers" or "trumplings."

The far-ranging Eurasian **mute swan** (*Cygnus olor*) is undoubtedly the most familiar of the swans; indeed, it may be the most widely recognized bird in the world. Among the heaviest of flying birds, it vies

with the trumpeter swan for the distinction of being the largest of all waterfowl. The heaviest recorded mute swan was a cob that weighed an unbelievable 50.7 pounds, but such extraordinary weights cannot be considered normal, since many mute swans exist in a semi-domesticated state and may be overfed. More typically, an average sized male weighs between 25 and 30 pounds, with cobs being significantly larger and heavier than their mates.

Unlike the other northern swans, which tend to hold their long necks erect, mute swans usually assume a posture in which the neck is gracefully curved, with the bill pointing downward. A bright red-orange bill and a black knob on the forehead are characteristic of the species, although the size of the knob is significantly reduced and the bill fades to a pale pink when the birds are not in breeding condition. Curiously, in spite of the mute swans' pure white plumage and northern distribution, their closest relatives appear to be the Australian black swans.

Mute swans frequently swim with one foot raised out of the water and resting upon the lower part of their backs (even cygnets demon-

5.17 *When relaxing, mute swans (and other species as well) may swim with one foot raised out of the water. Mute swans in the water are easily distinguishable from the other northern swans because they frequently carry their proportionally thicker necks in a graceful S-shaped curve, with their heads slightly lowered.*

strate this inclination), and many observers unfamiliar with swan behavior often assume incorrectly that a swan swimming in such a fashion is crippled. Like most swans, these birds are powerful fliers, but their great weight makes it somewhat difficult for them to take off. They must literally run across the surface of the water for some distance (usually into the wind) before achieving sufficient speed to become airborne. The loud pattering of their feet on the water is sometimes audible for great distances and spray ten feet high can be kicked up behind them.

The powerful motion of their wings in flight produces a strange whistling or swishing sound that can be heard for a mile or more in still air. It is possible that these mechanical flight sounds serve as a form of communication to maintain aerial contact at night or in bad weather, since these swans have only limited vocal capabilities. In some parts of their range, mute swans are highly migratory, whereas other populations are rather sedentary. The young are fledged between 120 and 150 days of age—a relatively long fledging period that is clearly a response to more southerly nesting localities which give them longer periods of favorable climate.

When ashore, these swans walk with an awkward waddle and the only swan that surpasses them in terrestrial clumsiness is the almost totally aquatic black-necked swan. Essentially vegetarian, mute swans may occasionally ingest (perhaps accidentally) small frogs, toads, tadpoles, molluscs, worms, and insects.

Strangely, there is an albino phase of this great white bird that has come to be known as the Polish mute swan. The legs and feet of albinistic adults are pinkish grey instead of black, and the down of the cygnets is white instead of the normal brownish grey; even as immatures, their plumage is atypically white, instead of the usual brownish grey. Polish mute swans occur with greatest frequency in eastern Europe and are thought to be the result of inbreeding.

Well-established feral populations of mute swans occur in both the northeastern United States and New Zealand. The North American population may exceed 4000 and is beginning to cause some concern, because the dominating mute swans tend to drive native whistling swans away from good winter feeding areas, especially in Chesapeake Bay. All the same, the mute swan is universally so highly regarded as an ornamental bird that it has been translocated to all continents— except, of course, the Antarctic. They tame readily and generally tend to flourish in association with civilization. In marked contrast to the other white swans, moderate disruption of habitat apparently has not yet seriously affected the overall population.

As the vernacular name implies, the **black swan** (*Cygnus atratus*) is indeed basically black, although the black may have a slight brownish tinge. This dark plumage is accentuated by a contrasting crimson red-orange bill, adorned with a conspicuous white band near the tip, and by piercing bright red eyes. During the breeding season, the eyes of some males are said to turn white. In flight, snow white distal secondary and primary feathers are revealed, flashing brilliantly against the black. Interestingly, the greater wing coverts are uniquely broadened in a peculiar undulating fashion that gives the appearance of a ruffled cloak. Subadults have mottled greyish brown plumage and paler bills.

Black swans have proportionally longer necks than other swans. The sexes are similar in appearance, but males are somewhat larger (weighing up to 20 pounds), and they have a tendency to hold their necks slightly more erect than females, particularly when swimming. In

5.18

5.19   5.20

5.18 *Portrait of a black swan. The high and thick crimson-red bill and red eyes contrast with the almost black plumage of this beautiful species.*

5.19 *Black swans are distinctive in the water. They frequently swim with the basal portion of their particularly long and snake-like necks resting on their upper backs.*

5.20 *In flight, the white primaries and distal secondaries of the black swan are very conspicuous. When the bird is at rest, they are not visible.*

5.21

5.22

5.21 Black swans are more gregarious and less territorial than most swans. In some areas, such as Lake Ellesmere in New Zealand (where they have been introduced), black swans may be encountered in large numbers year round. The swan population of this Lake may sometimes reach 100,000 birds, and this has necessitated some control measures, such as hunting seasons and egg harvesting. The population is so dense that the swans nest colonially. Colonial nesting also takes place in Tasmania, where one of the most significant cygnet predators is the Tasmanian devil.

5.22 Because of their great weight, mute swans require a long run over the surface of the water (usually into the wind) prior to becoming airborne.

addition, their eyes and bill color are slightly brighter, their heads are longer, and they have straighter upper mandibles. Compared to most northern swans, the vocal capabilities of black swans are rather limited. Males produce a higher and longer call that, with some practice, is relatively easy to distinguish from that of the female.

Native to Australia, these beautiful birds were successfully introduced into New Zealand 175 years ago, and until recently had prospered so well there that they were considered a nuisance in some localities. At times, control measures have proved necessary, such as hunting and egg harvesting, and even swan drives. The most sizeable and famous New Zealand concentration is at Lake Ellesmere on South Island, and at one time the swan population of this lake exceeded 100,000. In 1966 alone over 43,000 eggs were harvested from the area, but in 1968 the devastating storm "Wahine" drastically altered the swan breeding potential of the lake. The principal swan food source, lake weed, was uprooted in vast quantities and has failed to recover to prestorm levels. The lack of dense weed beds in the lake has not only created a food shortage, but has also deprived the cygnets of protected calm water areas in which to shelter during storms.

These are the least territorial of swans and in some areas, as at Lake Ellesmere and in parts of Tasmania, they may nest in colonies, with nests scarcely a yard apart. Breeding readily in captivity, particularly during the northern winter, many pairs produce young throughout the year. Black swans can be aggressive toward other species, but are not as dangerous in this regard as some of the larger swans.

The **black-necked swan** (*Cygnus melanocoryphus*) is the largest of South American waterfowl. Much admired as an ornamental bird, it is possibly the most beautiful of the swans. During the latter part of the 18th Century, thousands were trapped for their strikingly patterned skins, which were used to fashion women's garments in Europe; but fortunately, they are no longer subjected to such senseless exploitation.

Although not overly abundant in captivity, these magnificent creatures are relatively common in parts of their range, which covers much of the southern third of South America and includes even the Falkland Islands. Their wings are relatively short, which would seem to rule out the possibility of long nonstop flights, but an emaciated individual was seen on one of the South Shetland Islands, just north of the Antarctic Peninsula, during the austral summer of 1916-17—a distance of 500 to 600 miles from its usual habitat. In flight, their wings produce a distinct whistling sound.

Out of water, black-necked swans are the most awkward of swans because their legs are located far back on their bodies, an adaptation that increases their swimming efficiency. They are so clumsy ashore that they will occasionally push themselves forward on their breasts, not unlike a stranded loon or grebe. Cobs are noticeably larger than their mates, and during the breeding season the conspicuous red knob or carbuncle at the base of the upper mandible of the male may enlarge somewhat. The voice of the black-necked swan is a soft musical wheezy whistling note that is repeated often and may be sounded on the wing.

During the austral winter, these swans become more gregarious and I have seen thousands on a single lake in Argentina, but during the breeding season, they are significantly more territorial and may be considered aggressive. In captivity, they can also be pugnacious, and although I consider much of their threat behavior to be little more than bluff, they easily intimidate other birds. In some collections, these

5.24

5.25

5.26

5.23 (Opposite Page) *Black swan family. The greatest overall deterrent to nesting success in many areas is flooding. But predators can also be troublesome, and swamp harriers, Australian ravens, sea eagles, and swamp rats regularly steal eggs.*

5.24 *Despite the fact that they have relatively short wings, black-necked swans are among the fastest flying swans. In flight, their wings produce a loud rustling sound, and they frequently vocalize on the wing.*

5.25 *Family of black-necked swans. This species is noted for the red base of the leaden blue bill, which expands to form a large scarlet fleshy carbuncle that may be double-lobed. In addition, they have a variable white streak extending from the base of the bill, through their dark eyes, to the nape of the neck. Newly-hatched cygnets are among the whitest of all swan young.*

5.26 *During the nonbreeding season, black-necked swans tend to be more gregarious, and many migrate north to pass the winter. During such times, they can be encountered in large flocks on the lakes and lagoons to the south of Buenos Aires, Argentina. They often congregate with numerous other wintering aquatic birds, including red-gartered, white-winged, and red-fronted coots.*

swans have been known to harass flamingos (even to death), and when nesting, some particularly aggressive cobs may rush over the water to threaten human intruders. They are particularly intolerant of European shelducks, perhaps because of their similar appearance.

On the other hand, black-necked swans are charming to see when they have young, because the cygnets spend a good portion of their time on the backs of both parents, with the male carrying the burden most often. In some instances, I have seen such large young swans being carried that the back of the adult on which they were riding was

5.27

practically underwater. Adults of this species rarely come ashore, except when nesting, and this adaptation to waterborne brooding fits right in with their lifestyle. As adults, these lovely swans apparently have few natural enemies, but kelp gulls are considered to be serious egg predators, at least on the Falkland Islands.

Coscoroba swans (*Coscoroba coscoroba*), the smallest of swans, look rather like huge white ducks with long necks and conspicuous flattened duck-like red bills. Unquestionably, they are the least swan-like of the swans, and in some respects their appearance suggests that of a large misshapen Pekin duck. The entire face is feathered, a very unique feature for a swan, and their pink legs are quite long, so they are much more at ease out of the water than other swans. Also, they are different from their near relatives in that they use significant amounts of down to line their nests. Despite all of these peculiarities, however, their overall behavior is essentially swan-like.

Coscorobas demonstrate some similarities to whistling ducks; in particular, their downy young are clearly patterned like those of whistling ducks, whereas the cygnets of all other swans are of one color with no suggestion of a pattern. This resemblance does not necessarily imply that there is a particularly close relationship between the coscoroba swan and whistling ducks, as some specialists have suggested. It may simply be that the aberrant coscoroba represents an ancestral link between the more typical swans and the ducks and geese.

South American Indians originally derived the name coscoroba from the bird's peculiar call. The vocalizations of the female are significantly lower, and since the sexes are very similar in appearance, this difference can be an aid in determining gender. Adult males supposedly have yellow to reddish eyes, while those of the female are generally dark brown; but there is considerable color overlap and I have not found this to be a reliable sexing criterion.

Coscorobas tend to be quite wary and will usually take flight before other birds have become alarmed. I have seldom been able to approach closer to them than 200 yards. In contrast to other swans, they are able to rise directly from the surface of the water without running to gain flight speed. Their wings are short and broad, and the black distal portions of the outer six primary feathers contrast with the otherwise snow white plumage.

With a range that corresponds roughly to that of the black-necked swan, their greatest concentration appears to be in Chile, and they also appear to be gaining in numbers in the Falkland Islands (although nesting there has yet to be documented). These swans are less gregarious than their black-necked relatives, and can be rather common in some regions. There is no indication that the population is declining anywhere, even though their nests in some areas are vulnerable to cattle trampling. Fortunately, they are not highly sought gamebirds.

While coscoroba swans are fairly well represented in waterfowl collections, they cannot be considered abundant and are bred only infrequently—but once a pair commences breeding, they are usually dependable producers for years. Some individuals can be aggressive and may be troublesome to other birds.

The remainder of the swans make up the so-called northern swan complex. Remarkably similar to one another in appearance, these forms differ mainly in size and shape, and in the varying amounts of color (mainly yellow) on the bill. Their wings are somewhat larger than those of swans inhabiting the more temperate regions, an obvious adaptation for the long-distance migrations that are an integral part of their existence.

Each of the two northern continental masses, Eurasia and North America, possess two distinct but closely related populations of swans. Whooper and Bewick's are Old World forms, and trumpeter and whistling swans are their counterparts in America. Taxonomists disagree about the relationships of the various forms of northern swans. Delacour, for example, lumped the whooper and trumpeter swans into a single species with two races, but many contemporary specialists tend to view them as separate species.

The massive **trumpeter swan** (*Cygnus cygnus buccinator*) is the largest, and perhaps the most magnificent, of all the waterfowl. Tragically, it has been subjected to the most abuse. This incredible bird was commercially slaughtered for years, not only for food, but more reprehensibly for its feathers, which were formerly in great demand for such "necessities" as powder puffs and fashionable feathered boas. In addition, the quills of the flight feathers were eagerly sought for use as writing pens.

Between 1820 and 1880, over 108,000 swan skins were marketed by a single company, and most of these were taken from trumpeter swans. The trusting swans were easy prey for hunters, and their habit of circling over an intruder when flushed was particularly suicidal. By 1933, biologists estimated that their numbers had declined to a mere 66 individuals, exclusive of the then unknown Alaskan population. Strict federal protection and the establishment of sanctuaries came just

5.28

5.29

5.28 Pair of coscoroba swans. These birds are the least swan-like of the swans, and in many respects are more like whistling ducks. Extremely defensive during the breeding season, they engage in territorial disputes that on occasion may result in the death of the loser. Unlike the other swans, they build substantial nests and line them rather heavily with down. Preferred nesting sites consist of small islands of floating vegetation, and the nest may be partly ashore and partly in the water.

5.29 Coscoroba cygnets. No other swan produces young which are multi-colored or patterned. The young grow relatively slowly, and up to eight months may be required for them to attain adult size.

5.30 The peculiar coscoroba swan has a duck-like face and in Argentina it is sometimes known as the "white goose." Because of its relatively strong and long legs, this species is very much at ease ashore. Coscoroba swans feed mainly while wading in shallow water, foraging extensively on the leaves and stems of submerged and floating aquatic plants, as well as seeds and fruits. Those birds that live along the coast also consume aquatic insects, fish, and even small crustaceans.

5.30

5.31

5.31 *Certainly, the most majestic of all waterfowl (perhaps of all birds) is the trumpeter swan. Two separate populations exist: a large migratory one in Alaska and a smaller sedentary one in the Rocky Mountain region of Montana and Wyoming. The southern population was literally pulled back from the brink of extinction. Mercilessly slaughtered for food and plumage, they were reduced to less than 70 swans in 1933, even though they formerly were widespread throughout the Great Plains marshlands. Their huge flight feathers were eagerly sought for writing quills and Audubon himself wrote: "The quills are so hard and yet so elastic that the best steel pen of the present day might have blushed, if it could, to be compared with them." Fortunately, the tenacious swans responded favorably to the total protection that was finally offered to them, and the Rocky Mountain population now numbers some 1500 birds.*

5.32 *Trumpeters are the tallest and most statuesque of the swans, and they typically hold their long necks very erect. When angry, they may energetically flap their half-opened quivering wings and pump their heads up and down. They are unbelievably powerful birds, and can be considered dangerous to man or beast when nesting or with young. They viciously defend their enormous territories, and at times, mated pairs will pursue an invading swan that violates the air space above their territory.*

5.32

in time, and the southern population of trumpeter swans now numbers some 1500 birds.

This southern group was formerly widespread across the Great Plains marshlands, from central Canada east to Hudson Bay, and as far south as Iowa and Missouri. Contrary to persistent popular opinion, however, trumpeter swans were never adapted to mountain lake habitats. As recent study has shown, at least four months of frost-free weather are necessary for optimum breeding success, and premature cold weather, combined with the lack of appropriate nesting habitat, is probably responsible for the relatively low reproductive success of the non-migratory swans of Grand Teton National Park and surrounding areas. The largest segment of the Rocky Mountain population inhabits this region, where warm springs make ice-free water available year round, even in the coldest winters, and eliminate the need to migrate.

Trumpeter swans fared somewhat better in Alaska, and some 4500 trumpeters currently reside there during the summer (4170 were actually counted during the 1975 aerial survey). This population is migratory and winters along the Pacific coast from Alaska south to the Columbia River. The species is no longer considered endangered, but must still be classified as rare and threatened. Human activity in the form of oil drilling, mining, pipeline construction, and urban and recreational development is increasing in Alaskan swan country, and this activity will undoubtedly have a negative impact on the swans unless a well-planned land use policy is established soon.

While trumpeter swans are now afforded strict federal protection, some are nevertheless shot every year by careless "weekend hunters" who inevitably claim they mistook the trumpeters for whistling swans (which are a legal game species in some areas), or for large snow geese. The superficial similarities of trumpeter and whistling swans can make it easy to confuse the two in the field.

The most reliable way to tell them apart is by their voices, since the syrinx, or voice box, of the trumpeter is considerably longer, and this gives it a deeper and more resonant call. Another means of identification is bill coloration. Trumpeter swans never exhibit any yellow on the bill, whereas whistling swans usually have varying amounts of yellow near the base of the bill in front of the eye (although individuals exhibiting no yellow at all are not particularly uncommon).

Trumpeter swans are also considerably larger. Males average in excess of 26 pounds, and maximum weights may approach 38 pounds, whereas even a large whistling swan will rarely exceed 20 pounds. The necks of trumpeters are twice as long as the body, and a distinct red line (called the lipstick line) extends down the length of the bill between the upper and lower mandible. This red line may also be present on whistlers, but is not nearly so prominent. The distance between the tip of the bill and nostril on a trumpeter should be at least two inches, whereas the whistler's bill is relatively shorter and the nostrils are closer to the tip. More subtly, the whistling swan's head is somewhat more rounded. The heads and upper necks of both whistling and trumpeter swans, by the way, are frequently stained a rusty color from contact with ferrous minerals in the soils of marsh bottoms during their search for food.

There are few sights and sounds in nature that can be compared to those associated with courting trumpeter swans. The beautiful synchronized movements of the pair, combined with their melodic duetting, is truly unforgettable. (When heard at close range, however, their calls can be ear shattering!)

As with most swans, trumpeters defend huge territories and may occupy the same nest site year after year. In regions where muskrats occur, the swans may nest on top of one of their lodges. The base of the nest may be greater than 12 feet in diameter, and because the area around the base is cleared of aquatic vegetation during construction, there is often a distinctive moat surrounding the nest site.

Immature birds have mouse-grey plumage, with muted pink bills that have black borders and patchy black areas around the base and nostrils. Curiously, white downy cygnets are sometimes produced by birds of the Rocky Mountain population, instead of the more typical greyish cygnets. As adults, however, these birds are indistinguishable from their normal-colored nest mates.

Trumpeter swans still remain among the least common of the swans in captive waterfowl collections. However, they are presently being bred with greater frequency and can be considered reasonably well established. If a collection is fortunate enough to include a pair, a great deal of space is required because the swans can be savage to other birds during the breeding season.

Whistling swans (*Cygnus columbianus columbianus*) are quite obviously misnamed, for they do not whistle at all. Instead, they produce a variety of high-pitched hooting vocalizations. Main breeding concentrations are located in Alaska and the low Canadian arctic, and these birds are very important to some of the northern natives, who value them not only as a necessary source of food, but also for their down, which is used in clothing. The Eskimos of the Yukon-

5.33 *When viewed at close range, a trumpeter swan can be readily differentiated from the similar but smaller whistling swan. Their massive black bills are adorned with a distinct red line that extends down between the mandibles. In addition, there is a concave depression on each side of the bill. (They also have 24 tail feathers compared to 20 for the whistler.)*

5.34 *Pair of courting trumpeter swans. The loud staccato trumpeting calls must be heard firsthand to be fully appreciated, and to my mind there are few sounds in nature that better exemplify the wilderness spirit.*

5.35 *Immature trumpeter swan. At this age, the young are characterized by brownish grey plumage and fleshy pink bills. Interestingly, young swans dive with surprising ease. If the weather turns cold prematurely, subadults are subject to starvation, and a number may be injured on ice while attempting their first flights.*

5.37

Kuskokwim delta, for example, harvested approximately 5600 swans in 1964 alone.

Like their Eurasian counterpart, the Bewick's swan, whistlers may migrate more than 2000 miles. These long-distance movements have been documented more fully in recent years by an extensive colored neck-collaring program. Most of the northern Canadian nesting swans regularly winter in Maryland and North Carolina, while those of western Alaska tend to migrate to California and Utah. It has also been recently reported that a small flock of about 300 birds winter over on the warm water springs of Unimak Island, the easternmost of the Aleutian Islands.

Compared with the other northern swans, whistling swans are relatively common, and the population may exceed 100,000. On the wintering grounds, they tend to congregate in tremendous numbers, and during the early morning hours the air literally vibrates with the voices of hundreds of calling swans. This spectacle is one that an onlooker is not likely to soon forget.

5.38

5.39

5.40

5.41

5.42

Despite the objections of some people, a limited swan hunting season was authorized a number of years ago. When the season opened in Utah in October of 1962, some 320 whistling swans were taken. But as large as this figure may initially appear to be, it is probably not a great deal larger than the presumed illegal kill in that state in some previous years.

Strange as it may seem, whistling swans have, from time to time, been swept to their deaths over Niagara Falls. In some years, the current is so swift that the swans are trapped before they realize that they are in danger. On March 15, 1908, for example, no less than 100 swans were swept over the falls and lost.

The **whooper swan** (*Cygnus cygnus cygnus*), second largest of the northern swans, is also named for its incredible vocal capabilities. Its loud voice has a trumpet or bugle-like quality and is distinctly deeper and louder than the vocalization of the similar but smaller Bewick's swan. The dissimilar calls of the two species can, in fact, be considered a fairly reliable method of field identification for anyone with a good ear.

The entire base of the mature whooper's bill and the lores are distinctly colored a bright lemon yellow. Subadult birds are ashy brown, and the base of the bill, which is destined to become yellow, is pinkish. Whoopers tend to be relatively shy and are primarily associated with fresh water, but they will sometimes utilize marine habitats, such as land-locked seas or sheltered inlets. As with many other swans, they may re-use a nest in successive seasons, rebuilding it year after year.

The early Icelandic people revered the whooper swan, believing that it possessed supernatural powers. When the swans departed on their migration, it was thought that they were returning to their ancestral homeland in Valhalla, or to the moon. (Interestingly, up to a quarter of the Icelandic swan population does not migrate.)

The range of the species encompasses a huge area extending from Iceland eastward to the Pacific coast of Asia. In fact, several dozen whoopers normally cross the Bering Strait to pass the winter in the Aleutian Islands or the Pribilof Islands, and on a few occasions they have even nested in Alaska. A fairly large segment of the eastern

5.36 (Opposite Page) *Whistling swans are generally wary birds, but they can be inquisitive. From a distance, they can sometimes be separated from trumpeter swans because their movements are slightly faster and they tend to be somewhat more excitable.*

5.37 (Opposite Page) *Pair of whooper swans. Like their near relatives, this species is noted for its incomparable vocal capabilities. During the late winter, the calls of courting pairs have an infectious effect on the flock, and they all start calling — creating a delightful spectacle.*

5.38 *The yellow patch in front of the eye of the whistling swan is highly variable. It can be prominent, minute, or lacking altogether. This variability is clearly evident on the whistling swans illustrated here and in plates 5.36 and 5.41.*

5.39 *Wintering whistling swans taking off from the Great Salt Lake, Utah.*

5.40 *Adult whooper swans are readily identified by the prominent triangular-shaped bright yellow basal portion of their bills.*

5.41 *During the breeding season in the high arctic, territories as large as one and a half square miles may be established by a pair of whistling swans. While they are very protective of their young, a number fall prey to such predators as coyotes, arctic foxes, and even golden eagles. The young do not tend to be afraid of man, but if handled between two and four months of age they may play dead.*

5.42 *As is typical with all swans in flight, whistling swans fly with their long necks extended forward and their black legs and feet trailing behind.*

5.43

5.44

5.45

5.46

5.43 *Whistling swan on the wing.*

5.44 *The alert nature of these whooper swans in Scotland is readily apparent. Approximately 2000 of these swans normally fly from Iceland to Scotland to pass the winter, a 700-mile non-stop flight that takes 14 to 15 hours. (This is probably the longest non-stop flight of any of the swans.)*

5.45 *This hybrid cygnet resulted from a cross between a trumpeter swan and a whistling swan. For lack of a better name, such hybrids have been referred to as "trumplers" or "trumplings."*

5.46 *Jankowski's swan. Even though many authorities do not consider these birds separable from the Bewick's swan, they typically have longer, broader, and higher bills, as well as a slightly brighter and more extensive region of yellow on the bill.*

population regularly winters on the Japanese island of Honshu, where the swans are highly regarded and even pampered by the local inhabitants. The Russian population apparently suffered a significant decline during the 19th Century, but appears to be recovering. Although the total population is undoubtedly less than 100,000 birds, whooper swans are now afforded protection everywhere, and their future at this time is therefore reasonably secure.

Smallest and most terrestrial of the northern swans is the **Bewick's swan** (*Cygnus columbianus bewickii*), a bird that looks rather like a miniature whooper swan in many respects. Despite the obvious difference in the sizes of the two birds, however, Bewick's swans are sometimes confused with whoopers in the field. The larger whooper swans have proportionally longer necks and flatter heads; also, the area of yellow on their bills is much greater and extends below the nostrils at an acute angle, whereas the color on a Bewick's swan ends bluntly in front of the nostrils. The breeding range of the Bewick's swan somewhat overlaps that of the whooper, but it does not extend as far to the west and *bewickii* seldom nests south of the Arctic Circle. No hybrids between these two species have been documented.

Newly-hatched Bewick's swans are uniformly grey-brown overall, with flesh-colored bills and greyish legs. By spring, however, the darker plumage is intermingled with white, the basal portion of the bill has turned whitish, and the legs and feet tend to be blackish. At one and a half years of age, the immatures are practically indistinguishable from adults, save for a few grey feathers on the neck.

The yellow on the bills of Bewick's swans is subject to a significant amount of individual variation. Detailed observations made over the years at the Wildfowl Trust in Slimbridge, England have confirmed that the amount of yellow and the pattern formed on the bill is much like a human fingerprint, in that no two are exactly alike. As a result, individual swans can be readily identified by closely examining the striking variations in the yellow and black bill patterns. Thus far, no less than 2600 individual swans have been "bill-printed" and can be specifically identified by qualified observers.

The call of a Bewick's swan is reminiscent of the whistling swan, but is slightly softer and a bit more melodious. Pair bonds are exceptionally strong, and it is of interest to note that of the hundreds of wintering Bewick's swans that have been studied at the Wildfowl Trust, very few (if any) cases of "divorce" have been documented. If one of a mated pair was lost, up to three years were often required for re-pairing to occur, although in some cases, new pair bonds were established much sooner. A number of swan connoisseurs, comparing the shapes and postures of the various northern swans, suggest that Bewick's swan is the least attractive, but I do not necessarily agree.

These swans breed exclusively on the inaccessible and essentially uninhabited Siberian tundra, between the Pechora Delta and Lena Delta—and for this reason, a great deal remains to be learned about their breeding biology. Despite their aggressiveness, they may nest in loose "colonies" in regions of prime habitat. The 29- to 30-day incubation period is somewhat shorter than that of the other swans and this is surely a reflection of the relatively brief breeding season in the far north. Cygnets are preyed upon by arctic foxes, martins, stoats, and gyrfalcons.

Until recently, Bewick's swans were reasonably secure on their remote breeding grounds. Some were taken from time to time by Laplanders and their dogs, as the nomads passed through the region with their reindeer herds, and they were also exploited by the Russians

5.47

5.48

5.47 *Pair of Bewick's swans in southeastern England. Bewick's (pronounced "Buicks") are the smallest of the northern swans, and are among the most terrestrial. They are also somewhat maritime, and appear to favor brackish coastal waters as wintering areas in Germany, the Netherlands, Britain, and Ireland. As these areas are usurped by man for other purposes, this beautiful swan will become increasingly vulnerable, with the flocks squeezing into the diminishing remaining habitat. In addition, significant mortality can be attributed to shooting, oil pollution, and aerial collisions with trees, television antennas, and telephone wires.*

5.48 *Bewick's swan is a dainty species which is roughly a third of the size of the huge whooper swan. It is among the least common of the swans, with a population which may not exceed 10,000 individuals. It is possible, however, that they were never more numerous than this.*

5.49 *Trio of trumpeter swans in the snow.*

5.50 (Opposite Page) *Mute swan in flight.*

(who valued their tough skins and made them into caps and jackets). During the 19th century, Europeans harvested them for their beautiful down, which was used in the creation of fashionable feathered boas and other trimmings for ladies' clothing. In recent years, however, the breeding habitat of these swans has been increasingly subjected to the disturbance and disruption that is associated with the never-ending quest for oil. In addition, many of their favored traditional wet pasturelands are rapidly disappearing and wintering swans are being forced to concentrate in the appropriate areas that remain—a development that makes them even more vulnerable. Furthermore, even though they are totally protected by law throughout most of their range, over 40 percent of live adult swans that were x-rayed in Great Britain were found to be carrying at least one shotgun pellet.

Bewick's swans are not considered common, either in the wild or in captivity, and they are virtually absent from American waterfowl collections. The total extent of the population is not known, although the western segment is probably at least 10,000 birds (which may be as high as it ever has been). Some taxonomists have divided the eastern and western populations of Bewick's swans into two separate subspe-

cies. The Asian birds, which are known as Jankowski's swans (*Cygnus cygnus jankowskii*), are said to be somewhat larger, and their bills are theoretically longer, broader, higher, and more intensely yellow. But in regions where the two races overlap, birds of intermediate size are often produced, and this further complicates matters. Whether or not the Jankowski's swan will be recognized in the future as a bona fide race remains to be seen, but few specialists acknowledge it as separable at this time. There is reason to believe that the *jankowskii* segment of the population may be more extensive than that to the west. These swans breed between the Lena and Kolyman Deltas and winter in Korea, Japan, and western China; and they are afforded total protection in Russia and Japan.

Whistling, Bewick's, and Jankowski's swans have traditionally been considered races of a single species and are collectively known as the tundra swans. There is some evidence to suggest that perhaps the whistling and Bewick's swans deserve full species status; but whatever the outcome of this academic debate, it is still clear that the two forms are ecological counterparts.

6

True Geese and Brents
Anserini

I ntermediate in size between the swans and ducks, all 15 species of true geese and brents inhabit the Northern Hemisphere. Most are rather closely related, but can be neatly divided into two diverse groups. On the one hand, the true geese or "grey" geese are generally thought of as members of the genus *Anser;* while on the other hand, the Canada goose complex—as well as the Hawaiian, barnacle, red-breasted and sea geese—are placed in the genus *Branta*, and collectively are often referred to as the brents (brants) or "black" geese.

Some species, such as the wide-ranging Eurasian bean goose and the Canada goose, have been subdivided into numerous subspecies, with differences frequently so subtle that only an expert can accurately sort them out—and sometimes even experts are hard pressed to do so. Indeed, in some cases the differences are so very minor, and

6.2

6.1 (Opposite Page) *Snow geese in the sunset.*

6.2 *Bar-headed goose. Even though they are regarded as more terrestrial than most waterfowl, northern geese are very much at ease in the water and are accomplished swimmers. They are even surprisingly capable divers if need be. When they are flightless during the molt, or when they have young, geese tend to depend more on the security of the water.*

require so many exact measurements, that the validity of the races based on such criteria must be considered highly debatable.

Comparatively large heads are typical of geese, particularly those that are noted for extensive grazing. The shape of the bill is also diagnostic, in that it tends to be high and thick with a number of distinct serrations along the edges—obviously another adaptation to a grazing lifestyle. The serrations or "teeth" on the bill are used to great advantage in cutting grass, and the various bill shapes and sizes reflect different food preferences and feeding techniques. Greylag geese, for example, are characterized by large heavy bills which are well suited for digging out roots, whereas the bill of the red-breasted goose is relatively small and ideal for grazing on short grass.

As a rule, the coloration of northern geese is rather somber, although there are some startling exceptions. In the case of the Holarctic genus *Anser*, legs and feet are brightly colored, varying from yellow to orange and pink. The plumage is predominantly brown, grey, or white, and is quite uniform. Representatives of the *Branta* complex, on the other hand, typically have black legs and bills, while their plumage is more boldly patterned in black, dark brown or white—or even a rich red, as in the case of the red-breasted goose. Unlike ducks, which undergo a biannual molt, geese molt only once each year.

All but three species have white above and beneath the tail, which contrasts greatly with their dark backs and tails and probably functions as a visual flight signal when flocks are airborne. Snow and Ross's geese are exceptions, but since their plumage is essentially all white, they are probably always quite visible. Another exception, the emperor goose, does not usually engage in long migrations, and flock cohesiveness would therefore be of less importance.

Like swans and whistling ducks, geese exhibit little sexual dimorphism, and behavioral differences between the sexes are relatively slight. Likewise, the voices of both males and females are similar, although the gander's is usually higher-pitched and more metallic sounding. Although geese are accomplished swimmers, they do not habitually feed in the water, with the exception of the brant. When they resort to water that is too deep for effective surface feeding, they will sometimes pump their feet up and down to agitate the water and circulate otherwise inaccessible food particles to the surface—a technique also employed by a number of foraging swans and ducks. Most geese dive surprisingly well, and diving tactics are employed if danger threatens while in the flightless molt, or when they are merely engaged in "play" activities. At the same time, because many of the northern geese are accomplished grazers, they are much more adapted for walking than most of the other waterfowl, and consequently are very much at ease ashore. Notoriously wary, almost uncannily vigilant and alert, they can seldom be taken unaware.

Wild geese are well-known for their tendency to fly in a "V" or in long diagonal lines—formations that probably reduce drag and lessen the possibility of collisions between flying birds. During migration, family units remain intact. Extremely gregarious, northern geese frequently gather in great numbers during migration and when on the southern wintering grounds. During the southward migration, some species may mass together in the tens of thousands in staging areas, and in parts of their winter range the sky can be literally blackened with flying geese. The sound of 50,000 or more geese taking to the wing simultaneously is deafening and, combined with their loud and clamoring calls, creates a truly unforgettable wildlife spectacle. To witness a massive flock rising from a grain field or passing overhead during migration is to experience one of the grandest and most spell-binding thrills to be found in nature.

If northern geese are spectacular on the wing, they are no less spectacular in their landing behavior, often engaging in complex aerial maneuvers and acrobatics. They may plunge earthward in spiral nose dives or side-slip downward with half-folded wings, moving from side to side in a way that calls to mind huge falling autumn leaves (a maneuver that is sometimes known as wiffling). As strange as these movements may appear, they are in fact very purposeful, since they quickly empty air from the wings and facilitate a more rapid descent. And even though the birds may sometimes seem to be out of control when wiffling, in actuality these complex gyrations require exceptional skill and coordination. Incredible as it may seem, geese can even flip over on their backs, managing somehow to keep their heads upright.

When flocks or "gaggles" of geese descend like a storm cloud on grain fields, the visitation can spell disaster for a farmer, since large flocks can consume tons of grain in a single day. In an effort to protect farmers, many of the waterfowl refuges that have been established throughout North America on federal land have been planted in grain in an attempt to draw the birds away from croplands—but this has been only partially successful. As a result of their foraging activities in open, often cultivated areas, the true geese are sometimes collectively known as field geese. In some areas, such as Great Britain, wintering geese are more likely to feed at night, especially if there is hunting pressure.

All geese are extremely protective of their nests and young—as any inquisitive farm boy will attest. Domestic geese in particular are noted for hissing loudly when provoked, and will not hesitate to attack, even

6.3 Nesting geese can be very feisty, and incubating females may hiss in a threatening manner at an intruder. Ganders are particularly protective and often will attack an invader, viciously beating it with their powerful wings. The mandibular serrations can be clearly seen on this incubating pink-footed goose.

6.4 Migrating lesser snow geese in "V" formation.

6.5 On their wintering grounds, in southern California and elsewhere, huge masses of lesser snow geese flock up in the remaining wetlands. At times, concentrations can be so dense that the sun is obscured by the massive flocks passing overhead.

6.6 (Opposite Page) Atlantic Canada geese with set wings coming in for a landing, a sight that can mesmerize the nature lover.

to 80 days for a pair to construct a nest, lay eggs, incubate and rear the young, and the snow-free period in the breeding habitat averages only 75 days. Abundant food is available, however, and 24-hour sunlight from the midnight sun in midsummer makes almost continuous feeding possible, so the goslings grow very rapidly. Nevertheless, during exceptionally cold springs when the snow melt is delayed, the geese may not breed at all.

Like swans, both sexes *may* engage in nest building, with the female frequently doing most of it. Incubating geese usually lie so low on the nest that they can be very difficult to detect, and when nesting birds are off the nest, the eggs are covered with thick down to keep them warm and to camouflage the nest site. Incubation periods vary from 22 to 30 days and the downy goslings are capable of taking to the water shortly after hatching. Ganders assist in rearing the young, and goslings are generally led by one parent while the other protectively brings up the rear. The young birds are brooded under the wings of the female in a warm and dark sanctuary for several weeks, and at times the nest may be used as a brood site.

Geese have long been popular in captivity and adapt very well if managed properly. Some rare captive specimens, nearly fifty years old, have reportedly been known to breed regularly. Two species, the greylag and the swan goose, may have been completely domesticated prior to even chickens and ducks, perhaps as long ago as 1000 years prior to the time of Christ. Young geese are well-known for their tendency to imprint on human beings, and it is therefore not totally inconceivable that goslings could have simply followed early man back to his shelter or cave, and thereby initiated the concept of bird domestication. The greylag goose was possibly the first of domesticated birds, and was depicted on Egyptian frescoes more than 4500 years ago, along with red-breasted and white-fronted geese. The reproduction of the geese is so accurate that there is cause to believe that they must have existed in at least a semi-domesticated state.

Greylag and swan geese are the wild ancestors of all present-day domestic geese—the swan goose of Chinese and African knob-bill geese, and the greylag of all other domestic breeds. Domestic forms still resemble their wild ancestors, but tend to vary greatly in color, to be flightless and more awkward, and to be much heavier. An exceptionally large wild greylag goose may weigh 10 pounds, for example, whereas some domestic counterparts weigh as much as 30 pounds. Numerous domestic breeds have been developed over the years with such descriptive names as crested, Roman, Pilgrim, Embden, buff, Toulouse, Sebastapol, and bantam. These domestic geese are not only prized as a food source, but also because they may possess very endearing personalities. Their alert nature has prompted people to use them as "watchdogs" for perhaps thousands of years, and even today, with all the modern burglar alarms available, they are still used in this capacity. One particularly interesting instance of this is the flock of geese that guard a Scottish whiskey distillery.

The two subspecies of **greylag geese** (*Anser anser*) range over much of Europe and Asia, and some may even winter in North Africa. Both races are similar, and tend to be among the tamest of geese. The two distinct races undoubtedly evolved originally as a result of the separation between east and west that occurred at the time of the most recent ice age. But, as the British biologist, Ogilvie, cleverly notes, the birds have rather spoilt things since the ice retreated, by merging together again and interbreeding, thus producing all shades of plumage and bill color. The pinkish bill of the larger and paler eastern

if the intruder is human. When excited, many geese tend to extend their necks and lower them to the ground with the head slightly raised, vocalizing loudly. Some species have neck feathers that are arranged in vertical furrows, and when threatened they are capable of vibrating these, thus appearing more formidable. Goose bites can be painful, but their powerful flailing wings are far more dangerous. An enraged gander on the attack can easily knock a man to the ground.

Generally, geese nest in vegetation near water, and the female alone incubates while the gander remains nearby on guard. Some of the smaller species are capable of breeding at two years of age, but in most cases at least three years pass before maturity. The pair bond is lifelong, so there is little need for the elaborate courtship displays and bright plumage that typify the many duck species which must annually renew pair bonds.

For a number of high arctic breeding geese, nesting may actually commence prior to the onset of the annual spring thaw. Nest sites are selected on snow-free patches of ground, and egg laying commences almost immediately, because timing at such latitudes is critically important. In the case of brant geese, for example, it takes approximately 70

6.9

6.11

6.9 *Barnacle geese leading goslings. As is typical with most geese, one parent (usually the female) leads and the other parent follows. Goslings are capable of walking, running, or swimming as soon as they leave the nest. For the first several weeks after hatching, they are very vulnerable, and during that time predators and cold, wet weather may cause many losses.*

6.10 *Adult western greylag goose. As a result of long-standing persecution by man, this species has a discontinuous and scattered distribution in Europe. Formerly widespread, they now have a breeding range that is greatly reduced, although it still extends farther south in Europe than that of any other goose. Breeding habitat varies, but nests are typically located close to the water, and wooded islands are favored in many areas. Up to eight or nine weeks are required for fledging, which is significantly longer than any arctic nesting geese require. Almost all domestic geese are descended from the greylag, and its raucous call closely resembles the honk of many farmyard geese.*

6.11 *Western greylag goose dozing in the rain.*

6.10

6.12

6.12 *Western greylag geese in Scotland. While some greylags do nest in Scotland, the population swells considerably during the winter after the arrival of migrants from Iceland. For the past decade, this influx has varied between 61,000 and 76,500 geese, representing virtually the entire breeding population of Iceland.*

greylag goose (*A. a. rubrirostris*) distinguishes it from the orange-billed western birds (*A. a. anser*), but even though pure examples of the two races are easy enough to separate from one another, a color and size gradation exists between them that can complicate accurate identification.

The western greylag goose is a bird of open country, and has the distinction of being the only breeding goose indigenous to the British Isles. Some of the British birds are not truly migratory, and consequently lag behind other geese as they move north—and this, combined with their color, resulted in their strange but descriptive vernacular name. Their flight appears laborious but is, in actuality, both powerful and swift. These geese, which formerly had a much more extensive range throughout Europe, have been adversely affected by human interference, but the number of wintering birds has apparently been increasing in recent years nevertheless. In Scotland, they are not highly regarded by some farmers, because they may eat turnips and potatoes when bad weather prevents other more conventional foraging; and in Iceland, they allegedly cause considerable damage by trampling growing barley crops. The species is not particu-

larly common in North American wildfowl collections, probably because they closely resemble domestic forms, but they frequently appear in European collections and are bred often, especially the western race. Greylags readily hybridize with other geese, and fertile offspring are sometimes produced.

Swan geese (*Anser cygnoides*) are Asian in origin, and undoubtedly derive their vernacular name from an outward appearance that seems to combine both goose and swan characteristics. They do not, however, represent an ancestral line between these two groups, even though they are considered to be the most primitive of the geese. Birds of the interior, they have a breeding range that encompasses huge regions of thinly populated, often mountainous country in eastern Russia, Mongolia, and China, and they appear to prefer lake and river habitat in the steppe and forest steppe zones. Little is known of their population status, but there is some reason to believe that a significant decline has occurred in recent years. Certainly, these geese are subjected to hunting pressure throughout much of their range, and this, combined with human disturbance and loss of favored habitat, has clearly had an adverse effect. Formerly a common winter visitor to

6.14

6.15

6.13 *The swan goose is one of the largest and most distinctive of geese and is best known for its very long, straight bill. It is feared that this species has suffered a steady and significant decline throughout much of its wide range. Accurate population estimates are not available, but it is clear that the number of wintering swan geese in Japan and Korea has decreased substantially. Unfortunately, the swan goose is regarded as a quarry species throughout much of its range, although hunting has not been as detrimental as the loss of much of its favored habitat.*

6.14 - 6.15 *Eastern greylag geese. As a rule, these geese are easily differentiated from their western relatives by their pinkish bills, larger size, and overall lighter color.*

6.13

Japan, they are extremely rare there now, and they have apparently disappeared from Korea altogether. Unfortunately, the political situation in eastern Asia is such that comprehensive field studies by western biologists to clarify matters are out of the question at this time.

Swan geese are fairly common in waterfowl collections, but unhappily, most have been mixed with domestic birds over the years and there are pitifully few totally pure specimens in captivity, at least not in North America. Pure swan geese are very trim birds with long sloping foreheads and incredibly long and straight bills. Domestic varieties, on the other hand, are huge and cumbersome, with a large frontal knob and much longer necks. Some domestic varieties, which have large lappets or dewlaps, are more commonly referred to as "African geese." The sexes of pure birds are similar, but the female is smaller, with a more slender bill and neck.

The various forms of bean geese and the pink-footed goose vaguely resemble both greylag and swan geese. **Bean geese** (*Anser fabalis*) were so named because of their fondness for beans, which in former times was a major crop in the areas they inhabit. Five separate races have been described, although the limits of some of their ranges have

yet to be fully determined, and there appears to be a great deal of overlap, both physically and geographically.

Delacour recognizes two different types of populations: "the forest bean geese, breeding in the southern wooded part of the range, elongate in shape with long slender bills, the lower mandible almost straight and the nail at the tip rounded; and the tundra bean geese, nesting farther north in the tundra belt along the Arctic Ocean, stockier in shape, with the bill shorter and higher near the base, the lower mandible deep and distinctly curved outward, the nail long, oval and tapering."

The overall Eurasian range of the various races of these geese is huge, and as a rule, they tend to decrease in size from east to west. Western, Johansen's, and Middendorf's bean geese are thought to be forest forms; while the Russian and thick-billed bean geese are considered tundra birds. The bills of all forms are multicolored, with varying amounts of black and yellow, and they are among the least vocal of geese. The shorter and higher bills of the more northerly forms probably reflect an adaptation for feeding on short tundra vegetation. Not surprisingly, those that breed in forested regions are capable of rising

109

6.16

6.17

6.18

6.16 *Russian bean goose. These birds theoretically have rounder heads and shorter bills than their larger western relatives, and the orange-yellow coloration is essentially restricted to a narrow band over the top of the upper mandible.*

6.17 *Bean geese enjoy one of the most extensive ranges of any goose species, but only the western bean goose is well-known, and it is virtually the only one in captivity in the New World. Because of the extensive amount of yellow or orange on the elongated bill, this race is also known as the yellow-billed bean goose. As a group, bean geese are among the least vocal of geese, both on the ground and in the air.*

6.18 *Russian bean goose gosling. As is the case with a number of other species, the fine down of recently-hatched goslings is noted for a shiny, lustrous look that is lost after a few days. Even at an early age, the goslings can be very alert.*

6.19 (Opposite Page) *Middendorf's bean goose — a poorly-defined race that is supposedly comprised of birds with relatively long, slender, and straight bills. No population estimates are available.*

6.20 (Opposite Page) *Thick-billed bean goose. Characteristically, these geese have rather large and heavy bills that may have a considerable "gape" between the upper and lower mandibles.*

6.21 (Opposite Page) *Superficially similar to the bean geese, pink-footed geese have shorter necks, short black and pink bills, and pink legs. They are also swifter on the wing and usually fly in "V" formation.*

6.22 (Opposite Page) *Pink-footed geese can be partially colonial nesters, and nest sites are often selected on frost mounds. Ideal territories also include an additional mound nearby that the vigilant gander can use as a lookout perch.*

very steeply from confined places. Bean geese sometimes drift across the Bering Strait and have been recorded on the Pribilof and Aleutian Islands, as well as St. Lawrence Island in Alaska.

Generally, the differences between the various forms of bean geese are so subtle that few observers (if any) can accurately separate the various races in the field. The easiest to identify is the western or yellow-billed bean goose (*A. f. fabalis*), because of the extensive amount of yellow on its rather longish bill, and some individuals of this race may also have a patch of white feathers at the base of the bill. Johansen's bean geese (*A. f. johanseni*) supposedly have larger, less yellow bills than western bean geese, but it is possible that this latter race may ultimately prove to be inseparable. Thick-billed bean geese (*A. f. serrirostris*) have moderately long and massive bills which are quite high near the base. Individuals of the Russian race (*A. f. rossicus*) are similar to the thick-billed birds, but tend to be slightly smaller with shorter and less heavy bills. Middendorf's (or taiga) bean geese (*A. f. middendorfi*) are supposedly distinguished by long and slender straight bills.

In all probability, the so-called "Sushkin's goose" (*A. f. neglectus*) that sometimes appears in the literature merely represents a color phase of intergrade birds that resulted from crosses between thick-billed and Russian bean geese, or possibly even with pink-footed geese.

Bean geese are surprisingly rare in North American waterfowl collections, although the yellow-billed race is reasonably well represented. There are a number of thick-billed bean geese in collections in Europe, but very few are considered to be totally pure. Russian bean geese are somewhat more common, while Middendorf's bean geese are almost nonexistent anywhere in captivity. It seems unlikely that the Johansen form has ever been kept at any time.

The **pink-footed goose** (*Anser brachyrhynchus*) is obviously named for its colorful legs and feet (although these may also be almost purple). Formerly, it was considered a race of the bean goose complex, but it is now afforded full specific rank. Compared with bean geese, these birds are shorter and more compact, have shorter bills, and are generally more attractive. Three distinct breeding populations are known: a small group in Spitsbergen (Svalbard), and two others of larger size in Iceland and Greenland.

Sometimes, these birds select nesting sites in Iceland on relatively inaccessible ledges and cliffs above river gorges, presumably as protection against mammalian predators such as foxes; more typically, they breed on the open tundra. Nesting colonies are loose in most instances, but in some localities colonies can be quite dense, with as many as 1400 nests per square mile. Colonial nesting can be considered a predator deterrent, since many pairs of eyes searching for potential danger are obviously more effective than two pairs.

Some wintering pink-footed geese in northern England have developed a taste for carrots, much to the displeasure of the carrot farmers. Undoubtedly the most popular of the bean goose group in captivity, these attractive birds are bred fairly regularly in Europe and less frequently in America. As a rule, they mix well with other waterfowl and are not troublesome.

The North American representatives of the true geese are the well-known snow and white-fronted geese, and the less familiar Ross's and emperor geese. **Snow geese** (*Anser caerulescens*) are considered by some observers to be the most vociferous of all waterfowl, calling with a shrill honk that has a falsetto quality—a sound that has been

6.19

6.20

6.21

6.22

compared to the yelp of a fox terrier. They are also noted for a distinct black area along each side of the mandible (the so-called "grinning patch"). Spectacular fliers, they have been observed on at least one occasion migrating at an altitude of 20,000 feet.

There are two separate subspecies, commonly known as lesser and greater snow geese, with very little range overlap between the two races and only rare interbreeding. Although they are generally characterized as white geese with jet-black primaries, lesser snow geese (*A. c. caerulescens*) are well-known for an alternative color phase, in which they can be ashy blue-grey with white heads and are commonly referred to as blue geese. These color variants have long been troublesome to taxonomists, and even as recently as 1961, blue geese were still considered a separate species.

Blue geese breed in mixed colonies with their white counterparts, and interbreeding may take place, although they apparently have some preference for pairing with individuals of their own color. Nu-

6.26

merous color phases between the blue and the white forms have been recorded, but how and why the blue color phase evolved in the first place is not known. A blue color phase apparently occurs only very rarely (if at all) with the greater snow geese.

The majority of the blue goose population winters in the coastal regions of the Gulf of Mexico, chiefly in Louisiana. They are common in the Hudson Bay population, but rare in western Canada and Siberia—and since wintering snow geese in California migrate from these latter populations, it should come as no great surprise that the blue goose is seldom observed in the American west. All the same, blue geese have been expanding their breeding range westward in recent years.

Judging from the numbers of recovered neck-marked and leg-banded birds, it appears that the majority of lesser snow geese that nest in Siberia winter in North America—yet another graphic example of the need for international protection and cooperation. A population formerly wintered in Japan, but since the late 1860s they have been progressively depleted and are probably now gone.

Lesser snow geese may be the most abundant of all wild geese, with a population numbering in the millions, perhaps as many as 2,500,000. Their overall population has undergone a substantial increase since the late 1940s in some areas, particularly in the eastern Canadian arctic, and at present, most populations are relatively stable,

6.23 *Lesser snow geese are superb fliers, and are known for a powerful and fluid flight style. When landing, they may tumble and twist downward in spectacular fashion, with a tearing noise that is created as air spills from their outspread flight feathers. On the wing, their jet-black pinions are particularly conspicuous.*

6.24 *White phase immature lesser snow geese resemble adults, but they are mottled with grey, and their bills, legs, and feet are dusky instead of dull red. The polymorphic goslings exist in no less than five color phases, ranging from greenish yellow to dark brown to almost black.*

6.25 *The blue goose, long thought to be a separate species, is now merely considered a color variant of the lesser snow goose. Essentially an eastern bird, it is not frequently seen in the American west.*

6.26 *Wintering lesser snow geese in central California are occasionally encountered in tule rushes. In some years, more than 400,000 may winter in the Central Valley.*

6.23

6.24

6.25

6.27 *The presence of the inconspicuous incubating female blue goose is inadvertently betrayed by the alert gander on guard. Breeding blue geese are still much more common in eastern colonies. During the 1950s and early 1960s, they began to spread west, but this trend has slowed or even stopped during the past decade. The breeding range expansion corresponded with a general warming trend that was taking place at that time in the Canadian arctic. This region is cooling again, a condition that appears to favor the white phase birds.*

6.27

6.28 *Lesser snow geese are among the most numerous of all geese. Unlike most species, these geese are highly gregarious during the breeding season, and the sheer size of some of their larger colonies staggers the imagination. During the 1960s, for example, the Wrangle Island colony was thought to contain 200,000 pairs, although it is considerably less than that now. Some 163,000 pairs breed along the McConnell River, and another 100,000 pairs nest on Banks Island; there are also a number of other large colonies that contain between 20,000 and 95,000 pairs.*

6.29 *An intergrade lesser snow goose, showing characteristics of both blue and white phase birds. No less than seven different color phases have been described.*

6.29

while some continue to increase. (On the other hand, during the past ten years, the population on Wrangel Island in eastern Siberia, once one of the largest colonies, has apparently suffered.) It is unwise to be lulled into a false sense of security by the currently thriving overall status of these birds, since they remain extremely vulnerable. The continued need to exploit arctic oil and mineral riches is an increasingly dangerous threat, and the very real possibility of a contagious disease that could quickly decimate the huge wintering concentrations should not be overlooked. Also, several successive seasons of adverse weather could cause a substantially reduced level of breeding productivity.

Unlike most anatids, lesser snow geese tend to be very colonial during the breeding season, and nesting densities of up to 3000 nests per square mile have been recorded. The extent of such concentrations is almost beyond belief, and in some cases, colonies may contain more than 100,000 nests—making them perhaps the densest of all waterfowl colonies (with the possible exception of common eiders). Nesting may commence within days after arrival on their arctic breeding grounds, if snow-free areas are available. Their extreme northern breeding range has prompted some of the more poetic waterfowl enthusiasts to dub these birds "the geese that nest beyond the North Wind."

6.30

6.30 *Greater snow geese are somewhat larger than their lesser relatives and are not nearly as abundant. They have a much more restricted breeding range, and generally tend to nest farther north. The population has been steadily increasing during this century, to the point that these birds may presently be a hundredfold more numerous than they were in 1900.*

6.31 *Ross's geese are rather like miniature snow geese. While sometimes difficult to separate in the field, Ross's geese are easy to recognize at close range because of their tiny reddish bills with a warty bluish base, and their small heads. Their necks are also appreciably shorter and they are not much larger than a mallard overall. They also have higher-pitched calls — but this difference is generally only apparent when both species are calling together.*

Wintering flocks (which sometimes contain tens of thousands of geese) have in recent years tended to utilize coastal regions less than they used to, perhaps because most of the salt and brackish water marshes have been usurped by man for other purposes. As a consequence, the hungry geese have become increasingly dependent on inland crops and pastures, and this has generated some conflict between goose lovers and farmers.

In the field, it is very difficult to distinguish the two races of snow geese from each other. Greater snow geese (*A. c. atlanticus*) are obviously larger, weighing between 6 and 10.5 pounds, while their smaller relatives have an average weight of 4 to 6.25 pounds. The bills of the larger geese are also proportionally heavier and longer, and a snow goose with a bill exceeding 65.6 millimeters in length will probably prove to be a greater snow goose.

Greater snow geese are not nearly as widespread as the lesser race, and the entire breeding population is restricted to a relatively small portion of northwest Greenland and several arctic islands (Baffin, Devon, and possibly Grinnell) in extreme northeastern Canada. However, their numbers have increased dramatically since the turn of the century, when it was estimated that there were no more than 2000 to 3000 of them in existence. By 1950, the population had risen to approximately 48,000, and some people believe that it may currently exceed 200,000 geese (but this latter estimate may be somewhat optimistic). Most of the population winters along the Atlantic coast from Maryland south to North Carolina.

Interestingly, there are apparently very few pure greater snow geese in wildfowl collections; most appear to have lesser blood in them. Lesser snow geese, on the other hand, are very abundant and are among the most popular and prolific of all geese in captivity.

Ross's geese (*Anser rossii*) are essentially very small and petite snow geese weighing between 2.25 to 3.25 pounds. Adults (particularly older males) are noted for conspicuous warty protuberances near the base of the bill, whereas young birds lack this warty look, as do some females. The comparatively short, stubby red bills of these geese are bluish at the base, and they lack the distinct "grinning patch" that is so typical of their larger relatives. They also have shorter necks, a more rapid wing beat, and a much higher-pitched, less musical call. These vocalizations have prompted some goose hunters to nickname them "squealers"—but as a rule, they are less apt to call in flight than snow geese.

In a comparative sense, Ross's geese are relatively scarce, both in the wild and in waterfowl collections, but they are not nearly as rare as previously published figures suggest. The total population numbers between 50,000 and 70,000, and even these figures may be conser-

6.32

vative. Undoubtedly, Ross's geese have always been reasonably common but have simply been overlooked in the masses of wintering snow geese. Formerly, they spent the winter almost exclusively in the Central Valley of California, but their winter range has been somewhat expanded in recent years and a number have wandered as far east as New Mexico, and even down into Old Mexico.

It wasn't until June of 1938 that their nesting grounds along the Perry River Delta in the Northwest Territories of Canada were discovered. Often, Ross's geese breed in association with lesser snow geese and nesting territories may be as small as 150 square feet. Nest sites are fiercely defended, although the geese can be considered very docile during the remainder of the year.

As with the downy young of snow geese, goslings are polymorphic, and color graduations range from pure yellow to grey, with darker shades predominating by about two to one. When goslings are approached, they usually crouch down with the head and neck flat on the ground, and since they tend to blend into the surrounding terrain in this posture, it can be surprisingly difficult to locate them. Major predators include gulls, jaegers, and arctic foxes. At approximately three weeks of age, different broods may combine to form large aggregations of up to 200 young, and this early dissolution of the family unit deviates significantly from typical goose behavior. The fledging period is approximately 40 days.

Recent documentation has shown that adult Ross's geese, like lesser snow geese, also have a distinct blue phase. A few wintering adults have been collected in California that are perfectly valid Ross's geese with respect to their measurements, but which nevertheless look like miniature blue geese. Hybrids between Ross's geese and lesser snow geese have been recorded, and it is conceivable that the dark individuals are the result of a cross, but it is more likely that the little blue form of *rossii* represents a mutation.

At the same time, true hybrids are probably more common than reported, since white geese of intermediate size could be easily overlooked. To further complicate matters, Ross's and lesser snow geese nest together in some areas, and as a result of competition for nest sites, the different species may dump eggs in each other's nests. Naturally, the offspring from these mixed clutches will imprint on whichever parent rears them, thereby further increasing the tendency to interbreed.

Because of their delicate proportions and pleasant dispositions, Ross's geese are among the most desirable of captive geese. But despite the relative success that some propagators have had with them in recent years, they are still not overly abundant in collections. Like some of the other arctic geese (such as emperor, red-breasted, and brant geese), they do best when maintained in small flocks on fresh lawn grass.

The highly social **emperor or Alaskan goose** (*Anser canagicus*) is fairly common in Alaska, but is seldom observed elsewhere in North America. Two distinct populations exist: A Russian group breeding in Siberia adjacent to the Bering and Chukchi Seas (which may be in a state of decline), and an Alaskan group (which is apparently stable, currently numbering in excess of 100,000 geese). The relatively restricted range of these geese may be due in part to competition with more successful, less specialized goose species. Occasionally, emperor geese stray as far south as Oregon or northern California, and incredibly, stragglers have even been reported in Hawaii. (Some of these out-of-range vagrants may be the result of emperor geese dumping eggs into the nests of Pacific white-fronted geese, with the resulting young then migrating south with their foster parents.)

Emperor geese vaguely resemble blue geese, but have a cleaner, more delicate appearance, with recently-molted birds being significantly bluer and brighter than those in worn plumage. The black and white barring of the body feathers produces a striking scaled effect, and their deep yellow legs and feet and pale pink mandibles are most attractive. Immature birds are duller overall than their parents, and have brown, rather than black, barring on their backs. The heads and necks of these young birds are typically mottled with grey, their bills are black, and their legs and feet lack the bright yellow coloration of the adults.

Because these geese have littoral foraging tendencies, they are sometimes known as beach geese. A maritime species, they feed extensively on seaweed, shellfish and other marine organisms during the winter, and this is said to give their flesh a rank and unpleasant flavor. At low tide, they commonly feed among the rocks and kelp beds of their winter range, and they may gather in flocks after severe storms to capitalize on kelp and other marine vegetation that is washed ashore. I have often observed them foraging on mud flats, thrusting their heads deep into the mud, apparently in quest of small mussels or clams. Like swans and some other northern geese, their pure white heads are often stained a deep orange-yellow by iron deposits in the water, a condition known as "adventitious coloring." During the summer they also consume berries, sedges, and other more conventional goose fare.

Characteristically, emperor geese fly low over the water in uneven lateral lines, and their high-pitched calls are often given when airborne, making them easy to identify even in flight. They have comparatively short wings, and even though these beat rather rapidly, they are not particularly swift fliers. Their slow and low flight, combined with their unwariness, makes them vulnerable to sport hunting pressure in the few places where hunters can get at them, and Eskimos both hunt them extensively and prize them highly. Luckily, most of their habitat is rough, uninhabited country and few people, even in Alaska, ever see them in the wild. In fact, the emperor goose is one of the few geese whose entire range remains pristine, essentially free from the influence of man.

Traditionally, they nest near the coast, seldom more than ten miles inland. Almost all of the Alaskan population nests in the coastal areas of the Yukon-Kuskokwim Delta, and migrates southwest to the Aleutian Islands, where some 120,000 geese may pass the winter. More than 20,000 of these birds fly north after the breeding season to molt in the vicinity of St. Lawrence Island, midway between Siberia and Alaska—but why they do so is a mystery.

6.34

6.33

6.35

6.33 *Among the most desirable of geese in captivity, Ross's geese are highly regarded because of their delicate proportions and docile dispositions.*

6.34 *Emperor goose winging over the tundra. The white head and neck has been stained rusty orange-yellow as a result of iron deposits in the water.*

6.35 *Flock of emperor geese in flight along the Alaskan Peninsula.*

6.36 *Cackling goose nest and eggs. Most geese normally construct substantial nests, which are well-lined with thick down.*

6.37 *Emperor goose nest and eggs. This species typically uses less down than other geese. Why emperor geese should be different in this regard is unknown, but it is difficult to see how it could be advantageous. Indeed, at least one Russian biologist has suggested that the low insulation of the nest and the poor resistance of the goslings to cold may limit the northward range expansion of the species.*

6.38 *This emperor goose female has just left her nest, which is well-concealed in the tall grass directly to her right. The location of the nest on a small peninsula extending into a tundra pool is typical of the species.*

The average clutch size is four to six eggs, with an incubation period of 24 to 25 days. Less down is used in their nests than with most goose species, a trait that aids biologists in nest identification. At times, broods may merge, and in some areas, where emperor geese nest side by side with Pacific black brant, this tendency can make it very difficult to tell goslings apart, since the downy young of both species are very similar in appearance. Gulls and jaegers are the main egg and gosling predators, while bald eagles are said to sometimes capture adults in flight with seeming ease.

Because of their attractive appearance and docile nature, emperor geese have long been extremely popular with aviculturists, and even though they cannot yet be considered common in collections, they have been bred with greater frequency the past few years and are becoming more established. They can easily be mixed with other species without fear of serious conflict. As with many captive geese, they have a tendency to become fat, and if their weights are not controlled, they may not breed.

The four (or possibly five) races of **white-fronted geese** (*Anser albifrons*) are circumpolar in distribution, and they are essentially birds of the high arctic tundra, with ranges which may be the most extensive of any geese. Their vernacular name is derived from the distinctive white patch which surrounds the upper mandible, but their high-pitched pleasant voices have also earned them the popular name "laughing geese" in some European countries. Collectively, they are among the most vociferous of all geese.

In North America, the Pacific white-fronted goose (*A. a. frontalis*) is commonly known to goose hunters as the "speckle-belly," because of its relatively dark blotchy breast. Immature birds are basically a dusky brown overall with no white facial patches, and they lack distinctive breast markings. As adults, their orange legs and feet are quite attractive.

In Alaska, Pacific white-fronted geese are most likely to nest along the coast, but they also breed in low densities throughout much of the interior. They are almost exclusively western in distribution, and even wintering birds rarely venture east of the Mississippi River. Interestingly, the young of the previous season may accompany their parents back to the breeding grounds, and may even remain in the vicinity of the nesting territory, perhaps serving in some way as predator deterrents. As a rule, these geese rarely congregate in large flocks except during migration, and in flight they tend to form lines or chevrons. Highly regarded as gamebirds, Pacific white-fronts are considered by

6.39
6.40

many to be the most tasty of all geese. They are well represented in American waterfowl collections (less so in Europe), and are bred with a fair degree of regularity.

Largest and least known of the white-fronted geese are the rare and possibly endangered tule geese. Some authorities, to this day, do not acknowledge them as a distinct race, but recent evidence suggests that there may actually be *two* races—one that winters in central California, and another that winters along the Gulf Coast (coastal Texas, Louisiana, and northern Mexico). If the most recent taxonomic proposal gains acceptance, the Gulf Coast wintering population will be designated Gambel's or interior white-fronted geese (*A. a. gambelli*), whereas the darker California birds will be known as tule geese (*A. a. elgasi*). I personally cannot understand the controversy over the validity of these subspecies, for I am familiar with all the races of white-fronted geese, and to me both of these races are far more distinct from the Pacific white-fronted goose than is the European subspecies—yet, the European white-fronted goose has been considered a valid race for years.

It is believed that the total population of the tule (or Elgas) white-fronted goose is dangerously small, probably under 1500 individuals, but it is impossible to afford them adequate protection until more is known about their distribution. Biologists are desperately attempting to discover the breeding grounds of these elusive birds, and tiny transmitters have even been fitted onto individuals captured on the winter range in California, in the hope that radio signals could be picked up by receiver aircraft when the geese returned to the arctic. Thus far, little information has been obtained, but it is thought that this

population may breed in the forested taiga zone, just south of the Alaskan tundra. The most logical biotelemetric technique to attempt next would be transmitter signals that can be picked up by orbiting satellites, but prohibitive costs probably make this impractical.

Tule geese appear to be less wary and fly lower than birds of the more common Pacific race, which would make them more susceptible to hunting pressure. Indeed, some 100 to 150 are killed annually, possibly accounting for ten percent of the population. Their wintering habitat preferences differ from the more common *A. a. frontalis* and they seek small ponds with heavy reed growth. Captively raised for the first time in the private collection of Bob Elgas in Montana in 1976, they are represented in only a handful of collections. (Elgas, by the way, is the discoverer and main champion of the race.)

Gambel's white-fronted geese are apparently not much more common than tule geese—in the wild, this race may number no more than 2000 individuals. There is little definite data concerning the extent of their breeding range, but it is believed that they nest in the Old Crow Flat Marshes of the MacKenzie River Basin in western Canada and adjacent areas of Alaska. They were also first raised in captivity in the Elgas collection and are currently being reared at the Wildfowl Trust as well.

Greenland white-fronted geese (*A. a. flavirostris*) are distinctive because they are said to be much darker overall than the other races (although I have seen some tule geese which were significantly darker). The white facial patches of the Greenland race are not quite as large, and unlike the other races, their bills tend to be more yellowish orange than pink or flesh-colored. The black belly bars are very

6.41

6.39 *The Greenland white-fronted goose is distinctive because of its orange-yellow bill (rather than pink or flesh-colored), and its overall dark coloration.*

6.40 *Pacific white-fronted geese are well-known to North American hunters, who regard them as one of the most tasty geese. Their flesh-colored bills have a faint orange-yellow stripe at the top. Almost identical to geese of the European race, they are said to be separable on the basis of bill length, which averages 52mm (compared to 47mm for the European subspecies) — but there can be considerable overlap.*

6.41 *Breeding Pacific white-fronted geese utilize both coastal areas and slightly hilly upland tundra habitat. They are more likely to build nests along willow or shrub-lined ponds and streams than most of the other arctic-nesting geese.*

119

6.42

6.44

6.43

6.45

6.42 Greenland white-fronted goose stretching.

6.43 The lesser white-fronted goose is the most attractive of the white-fronted geese. These birds are easily identified by their small size, small round heads, tiny pink bills, large white facial patches (which often extend up to the crown) — and most of all, by their conspicuous yellow eye rings, which are visible from a considerable distance.

6.44 Tule geese are rare, and possibly endangered. They are essentially indistinguishable from Pacific white-fronts in flight, but they tend to fly lower and are less wary. Because of the resemblance, tule geese suffer heavy shooting losses. The only way to adequately protect them would be to close their entire wintering range to the hunting of all white-fronted geese.

6.45 The Gambel's white-fronted goose is a little-known race which is believed to be rare. The total population may number no more than 2000 birds.

extensive and add to the overall darkness of the bird. The total population of these geese is not large, probably only 12,000 to 15,000 individuals, with some indication of a slight decline in recent years.

It is curious that Greenland white-fronted geese undertake a hazardous migratory journey across the often hostile North Atlantic to winter in Europe, when appropriate wintering areas in North America are obviously much closer. It may be that the race spread to Greenland from northwestern Europe sometime after the most recent ice age, and the migrating geese are simply returning to their ancestral areas of origin to winter. This race, along with the following subspecies, is poorly represented in American collections, but is reasonably common and regularly bred in Europe.

European white-fronted geese (*A. a. albifrons*) are comparatively small with relatively short necks. In general, they are extremely similar to birds of the Pacific race, but show little or no trace of a yellow eye ring. According to Delacour, the differences between these two races may not readily be apparent when museum study skins are examined, but are somewhat more evident with living birds, because the varying proportions of the neck and bill are more obvious in life. To complicate matters, however, Pacific and European white-fronted geese interbreed where their ranges overlap in Siberia, and intermediate hybrids may be produced.

Smallest of the white-fronted geese is the Eurasian **lesser white-fronted goose** (*Anser erythropus*). Noted for a small rounded head and a very short bill, its most conspicuous feature is a very large and swollen yellow or orange-yellow eye ring. The white facial patch also extends further up the head, sometimes even to the crown. Yearlings lack the white forehead and black breast blotching of the adults, but their yellow eye rings are quite apparent. These dainty geese are distinct enough to be considered a separate species, and no wild hybrids with *A. albifrons* have been reported. Although their range overlaps slightly with that of the European white-fronted goose, they remain separate because of different habitat requirements.

Their high-pitched disyllabic or trisyllabic calls, which are sometimes uttered in rather long series, have prompted the Russians to refer to them as "peepers" or "squeakers." Preferred breeding habitat appears to consist of subarctic willow regions, particularly in hilly terrain with dwarf shrub bogs. As a breeding species, they are not limited to the tundra like their larger relatives, and may also utilize mountainous or even alpine habitat. Nests are well-lined with down, and may be situated on a ridge close to water or on an islet.

Lesser white-fronted geese are apparently still common in Siberia, but the East Asian population seems to be less extensive than it once was. The lack of definitive data from China, Korea, and eastern Russia makes it impossible to come up with an accurate population figure, but it may be on the order of 100,000 geese overall. These little geese are well represented in European collections, but surprisingly are still relatively uncommon in America, even though they are the most desirable of the white-fronted complex. They adapt well to captivity and breed rather freely.

Certainly the most striking of the grey geese is the **bar-headed goose** (*Anser indicus*), which derives its vernacular name from the two distinct horseshoe-shaped brownish black bars on its head. These geese possess a slightly larger wing area than most species, perhaps because they migrate at very high altitudes over the Himalayas, which separate their breeding ground in Tibet, Russia, and China from the winter range on the plains of northern India, Pakistan, and Bangla-

6.46

6.47

6.46 *European white-fronted geese enjoy a huge breeding range that extends across much of arctic Eurasia. The total extent of the overall population is unknown, but it is interesting to note that the number of birds wintering in western Europe alone increased from 66,000 during the winter of 1959/60 to 120,000 in 1975/76. At the same time, however, they have decreased in Britain in recent years. This localized decline may have resulted from a larger number of wintering birds remaining farther east, particularly in the goose refuges of Holland.*

6.47 *The dainty lesser white-fronted goose is much more active than its larger relatives, and can easily be picked out of a mixed flock because of its rapid movements. These geese are solitary nesters, and the four to six eggs are generally laid at the end of May. As with a number of arctic-nesting geese, the young fledge very rapidly, usually within 35 to 40 days.*

6.48 - 6.49 *Most attractive of the "grey" geese are the bar-headed geese. Unfortunately, the numbers of these beautiful geese have apparently declined significantly in recent years. Even when the breeding season has been particularly productive, there does not appear to be an appreciable population increase the following year, suggesting heavy migration and wintering losses. Predation, flooding, hunting, and loss of habitat are all factors that are working against them.*

desh. Reportedly, these incredible birds have even been observed flying over the summit of Mt. Everest itself, some 29,000 feet above sea level—a feat which would seem to be impossible.

Why, one wonders, would they select the highest region of the Himalayas to cross, when only a few miles away there are mountain passes at much lower altitudes? One explanation is that turbulent and unpredictable air currents associated with lower elevations are avoided at higher altitudes. It is also conceivable that the Himalayas have not always been the barrier that they presently are, and some writers have suggested that the migration route may have existed before the mountains rose to their present height. As the growth of the mountains continued in the middle of the traditional migration route, the bar-headed geese were forced to fly higher and higher, generation by generation. Just how they have solved the intricate physiological problems associated with such a fantastic venture has not been fully resolved, but it appears that they only spend very brief periods at these higher altitudes.

Mainly crepuscular or even nocturnal feeders, bar-headed geese are said to cause considerable damage to winter crops. Like most geese, they are essentially vegetarian, but when foraging in coastal regions may consume crustaceans and perhaps other invertebrates as well. Where hunted, these geese are very wary; when unmolested, they tend to be reasonably tame. The somewhat low nasal voice consists of a sonorous honk which has a rather musical quality.

A highly social species, they typically nest on small islands in marshy lakes or on rocky outcrops, but on occasion, some pairs nest in trees. They have also been known to take over the cliff nests of hawks, falcons, and ravens. The island nests are adversely affected by flooding, and a need to initiate more realistic water management programs is clear. Much of their breeding range is in high altitude regions, up to

and sometimes exceeding 15,000 feet, and they may nest singly or in colonies consisting of thousands of geese. Nest predation by ravens, crows, kites, sea eagles, and foxes can be severe. Due to the Red Chinese occupation of Tibet, the population of these geese is not thought to be as secure as it once was, and there are indications that they may be experiencing a severe decline, particularly in the northern portion of their range. (The Russian population currently numbers no more than 2000, although the Mongolian population seems to be holding its own.) The Tibetans were traditionally Buddhists, who had high regard for all life forms and thus protected the geese. The current presence of armed Indian and Chinese troops has put great pressure on the edible wildlife of the region—and the geese are regarded as important gamebirds. Eggs are also collected to supplement diets in Tibet. Fortunately, however, bar-headed geese are well established in captivity; they can be considered prolific breeders, and goslings are easily reared. There was, at one time, an introduced feral population in Sweden but it has apparently died out.

The remainder of the northern hemisphere geese have been incorporated into the genus *Branta*, including the specialized sea geese. Although closely related to the true geese (*Anser*), the five distinct species and numerous assorted races of the brant complex are distinguished by a more elegant pattern and decidedly less somber coloration—indeed, the Siberian red-breasted goose is considered by many to be the most beautiful of all waterfowl. Compared to the grey geese, these birds have necks which are proportionally longer and thinner and bills which are smaller and smoother, with much less prominent tooth-like serrations on the mandible. As a rule, they are more aggressive and demonstrative than their near relations.

Canada geese (*Branta canadensis*) are among the most easily recognized of all wild geese (at least in North America), and honkers are almost legendary as gamebirds. The numerous races occupy a wide variety of habitats, from the temperate woods, prairies, and semi-deserts of interior North America, to the ocean shores and tundra of the far north. There are few among us who will not cast our eyes skyward when a "V" or skein of honkers passes overhead, and the deep clear call of a Canada goose inevitably quickens the pulse of an outdoorsman.

In general, Canada geese are rather feisty birds. When annoyed, they characteristically twist their long necks into an "S" shape and hiss loudly. During the breeding season, they can become extremely aggressive and spiteful, and a defending gander may even pursue an invading rival into the air. In southeast Alaska it is said that some defensive individuals of the Vancouver race actually pursue and strike bald eagles in the air if the raptors fly over their nests.

As with most geese, they generally nest on the ground, but occasionally they may even occupy old heron or osprey nests in trees as high up as 100 feet. In some instances, the geese may even displace great blue herons from their nests; and in at least one unusual case, western Canada geese, great blue herons, and great horned owls were all observed nesting together in the same "colony." These geese probably utilize a greater variety of nesting sites than almost all the other species of wildfowl, and many of them readily accept even artificial man-made nesting structures.

For many years, Canada geese have been exposed to man-associated persecution, and with the exception of but two forms, all have coped with the pressure surprisingly well. Realistic wildlife management programs have contributed to a near doubling of the overall

6.50

6.51

6.52

6.50 In flight, bar-headed geese appear to be rather pale overall, but their relatively long wings have dark trailing edges.

6.51 The giant Canada goose, the largest of the 12 races of Canada geese, was at one time thought to be extinct. Currently, it is believed that the population exceeds 54,000 birds and is secure.

6.52 A flight of migrating Atlantic Canada geese.

population between 1955 and 1974 and most Canada goose populations are probably more numerous today than they were when America was colonized by European man. In part, this is because Canada geese have apparently benefited from the agricultural activities and products of man to a greater extent than any other North American anatid.

Taxonomists have literally had a field day with the Canada goose—no less than 12 subspecies are generally recognized at present, and up to 30 have been proposed. (Some contemporary workers, on the other hand, acknowledge only eight or even fewer races.) Unfortunately, the various forms do not fit into neat, well-defined categories, and there can be considerable overlap. Even for the most experienced goose biologists, the Canada goose complex has proven to be extremely confusing and perplexing, and has caused a great deal of controversy that continues to this day.

As a rule, descriptions of the different races have been based not only on geographical ranges, but also on size, shape of head, bill and neck, intensity of color, and voice, as well as proportions and posture. All races have large conspicuous white cheek patches. In general, however, the further north a race breeds, the smaller its body, and the further west, the darker its plumage. The geese range in size from almost as large as a small whistling swan to scarcely larger than a mallard. As for vocal differences, it can usually be said that the larger the race the longer is its call, the lower the pitch, and the more sonorous the quality. In captivity, most of the various races will readily hybridize and should be maintained separately. Many subspecies are well represented in collections and are bred on a regular basis, but some others are quite rare.

The giant Canada goose (*B. c. maxima*) is the largest and perhaps most distinctive of the honkers. Once thought to be extinct, they were "rediscovered" in Minnesota in 1962. Ganders average between 14 and 16 pounds, and some may weigh as much as 24 pounds. Their bodies are rather elongated, with proportionally long necks. Usually, they have conspicuous white spots above the eyes, rather light underparts, and a white ring may be present at the base of the neck. The cheek patches extend upward to the point where they almost meet behind the head, and some individuals have a black line at the throat that divides the white patches under the chin. Unlike most other races, the giant Canada goose is relatively nonmigratory.

Atlantic Canada geese (*B. c. canadensis*) are relatively large birds which almost never exhibit a white neck ring. The base of the neck and upper breast, as well as the extreme upper back, are creamy white, forming an ill-defined but complete broad collar; the rest of the underparts are only slightly darker. Although the literature indicates that geese of this race were introduced very successfully into Great Britain in the 1670s and more recently to New Zealand and Scandinavia, it is becoming increasingly evident that a number of other races, such as Great Basin and interior Canada geese, may have been involved as well. Some of these introduced geese have attained weights almost approaching those of the giant Canada goose. The feral population in Britain has steadily risen from 3500 in 1953 to 10,500 in 1968 to 19,500 in 1976. Some agricultural damage has been associated with the increase, and control measures are being considered. In Sweden, they have increased from several hundred in the 1930s to as many as 15,000 in 1975, and the New Zealand population is currently between 15,000 and 20,000 geese.

Moffitt's Canada goose (*B. c. moffitti*), sometimes also referred to as the Great Basin or western Canada goose, is often larger but proportionally trimmer in shape than geese of the Atlantic race; it also tends to be darker and less "scaley or scalloped" ventrally. Ganders weigh

between 8 and 13 pounds and their long thin necks are particularly distinctive. The race is not noted for the presence of a white neck ring. Interior Canada geese (*B. c. interior*), also known as Todd's or Hudson Bay Canada geese, are very similar to the Atlantic race, but tend to be generally darker overall and smaller. Shaped somewhat like interior Canada geese, lesser Canada geese (*B. c. parvipes*) are significantly smaller, and ganders seldom exceed seven pounds. A highly variable subspecies, they apparently represent an intermediate form between the larger Canadas of the southern forests and prairie regions, and the smaller, more northerly Canadian geese.

The dusky Canada goose (*B. c. occidentalis*) is among the darkest of the group, and is noted for a comparatively short and high bill. It is, in my opinion, the most striking of all the Canada geese. Another variety, the Vancouver or Queen Charlotte Canada goose (*B. c. fulva*), is not quite so dark and the slightly larger ganders of this race weigh between 10 and 13 pounds, as opposed to 8 to 9.5 pounds for dusky Canada geese. Proportionally, the bills of *fulva* are slightly smaller and their legs are somewhat longer.

Dusky Canada geese nest along the Copper River Delta in Alaska and winter in Oregon. During migration, they overfly the entire range of the nonmigratory Vancouver race (a situation taxonomists find rather perplexing). The total population may be suffering a decline, since they are subjected to a significant amount of hunting pressure, and their breeding range is beginning to receive some development pressure. Certainly, these lovely geese deserve a greater amount of protection than they have received in the past. Pure specimens are rather scarce in wildfowl collections.

Taverner's or Alaska Canada geese (*B. c. taverneri*) are smaller and generally darker than the lesser Canadas—a five-pound gander would be considered large—and the bill and neck are somewhat shorter. Varying greatly in color intensity, they often exhibit a narrow or incomplete white neck ring. Richardson's or Baffin Island Canada geese (*B. c. hutchinsii*) are slightly larger than Taverner's but generally tend to be lighter in color, particularly on the chest. Ganders average between four and six pounds, and their bills are somewhat larger. White neck rings are not uncommon, but may nevertheless occur.

Smallest and perhaps best-proportioned of the Canada geese are the cackling geese (*B. c. minima*), which seldom exceed four pounds. Their heads and bills are tiny compared to those of the other races, and while they are often said to be the darkest of the Canadas, I have seen some dusky Canada geese that were as dark or darker. White neck rings vary; they can be very prominent, or just slightly indicated, or absent altogether. I have also seen a few cackling geese that had a region of white between and above the eyes, but this condition does not appear to be widespread.

Their habit of chattering constantly and loudly is responsible for their rather descriptive vernacular name, and they can be easily distinguished from other Canada geese (even in flight) by the high pitch of their call. These attractive little geese nest primarily along the coastal regions of western Alaska, and winter from southern British Columbia south to California, where they are frequently found in association with lesser snow geese. Occasional stragglers turn up in Japan. In some cases, they may nest in loose colonies, with concentrations as dense as 100 or more nests per square mile.

The Aleutian Canada goose (*B. c. leucopareia*) is considered an endangered species, with a breeding range that is essentially limited at present to tiny Buldir Island (only 4250 acres), at the western tip of the

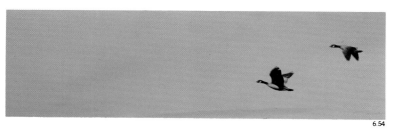
6.54

6.55

6.56

6.57

6.58

6.53 (Opposite Page) *Atlantic Canada goose flying over the wetlands of New Zealand, where the species has been introduced.*

6.54 *Pair of cackling geese in flight.*

6.55 *Interior Canada goose.*

6.56 *Lesser Canada goose.*

6.57 *Vancouver Canada goose.*

6.58 *Wintering Moffitt's Canada geese in association with lesser snow geese and pintails. Birds of this race are noted for fairly elongated bodies and long slender necks.*

6.59

6.60

6.61

6.59 Among the darkest of the various races of Canada geese, the dusky Canada goose may be in a state of decline.

6.60 Cackling geese are named for their distinctive call. They are the smallest and perhaps most attractive of the Canada geese.

6.61 Pair of Taverner's Canada geese at nest site.

6.62 Richardson's Canada goose.

6.63 Cackling goose and goslings.

6.63

6.62

Aleutian island chain. At one time thought to be extinct by some biologists, these geese were reduced to only 300 individuals by 1963, even though they formerly bred by the thousands throughout the outer two-thirds of the Aleutians, and may have even occupied the western Alaska coast. The Russian islands of Commander and Kuril once supported populations as well, but by 1914 they were gone. In former times, these geese wintered in Japan in large numbers, but in the latter part of the 19th Century they went into a rapid decline. (It may be that this Japanese population was derived from the Commander and Kuril colonies.) Aleutian Canada geese were said to be relatively common in Japanese wildfowl collections at one time, but unfortunately, they were all apparently consumed during the food shortages of the Second World War.

Aleutian Canada geese somewhat resemble cackling geese, but are usually not as dark and weigh between 4.5 and 5 pounds. A very extensive white neck ring is the most diagnostic feature of this race, although it may be insignificant on immatures. The black neck is relatively short and thick, and the back of the neck is sometimes sprinkled with white feathers. Bills tend to be short and high, with a long and pointed bill nail.

Recent data suggest that at least 80 to 90 percent of the population have a dark area under the chin, which exists because the white cheek patches do not merge at that point (a rather atypical feature for Canada geese)—but even with this identifying characteristic, measurements are still frequently required to determine with absolute certainty whether or not a given specimen is a member of the Aleutian

6.64

6.65

6.64 *The rare and endangered Aleutian Canada goose has fared better in recent years. In 1963, the population may have dipped as low as 300 individuals, but by 1977 it had apparently risen to 1600 birds. Total protection on the wintering grounds and the supplementing of the wild population with captive-reared birds have done much to brighten the once bleak picture. For the moment at least, the future of these birds appears assured.*

6.65 *Aleutian Canada goose gosling.*

race. Compared to many other northern geese, these birds are relatively nonvocal, and unlike typical Canada geese, they may nest on incredibly steep sea cliffs under tall vegetation.

The decline of this subspecies can be traced to a number of causes, among them a breeding range that was rather limited to begin with, indiscriminate hunting by northern natives, and—undoubtedly the most detrimental of all—the intentional introduction of the blue phase arctic fox (*Alopex lagopus*) and the red fox (*Vulpes vulpes*) to virtually all of the birds' island strongholds by fur farmers between the 1830s and 1930s.

World War II and reduced fur prices all but terminated commercial fur farming in the Aleutians, but unfortunately, the foxes remained. Although eradication of these elusive carnivores has been attempted on some of the islands, this effort has met with no great success to date. Military occupation of the islands during World War II must also be considered a negative factor, and Norway rats inadvertently introduced from ships have been particularly troublesome to ground-nesting birds, as have dogs and cats that were intentionally released. Other predators include bald eagles and glaucous-winged gulls (which prey upon eggs), but these natural predators have not posed as great a threat because the geese have always had to cope with them.

Luckily, the inaccessibility of Buldir Island and its lack of a good harbor prevented the introduction of foxes there, and a tiny remnant breeding population of Aleutian Canada geese survived. Using this population as a base, U.S. Fish and Wildlife Service biologists have been working diligently with Aleutian Canada geese for a number of years, and have successfully reared hundreds of them in captivity. Eighteen goslings were captured on Buldir Island in 1963 and the rearing program at the Patuxent Wildlife Research Center in Maryland commenced at that time. An additional 21 young were collected in 1971 and 20 more in 1975. Breeding flocks have also been established at the Northern Prairie Wildlife Research Center in North Dakota, and more recently on Amchitka Island in the Aleutians.

Captive breeding of this race has been a rather challenging task because Aleutian Canada geese, unlike their near relatives, are surprisingly difficult to propagate. Egg production is high but hatchability can be discouragingly low. (For example, during the 1976 season, 119 eggs were produced by 16 females at Patuxent, but only 35 hatched.) All the same, between 1966 and 1975 some 325 young were captively produced.

The 1977 season was not particularly gratifying at Patuxent. Twenty-seven pairs produced a total of 192 eggs, but only 27 hatched and only 24 of these were successfully reared. As a result of this apparent lack of success, management and husbandry techniques, as well as design of breeding pens and facilities, were altered significantly the following season. This resulted in a three-fold improvement over 1977. Some 243 eggs were laid, and all 71 goslings hatched were successfully reared. In addition, the captive flock on Amchitka, which in 1978 consisted of about 30 pairs, produced 95 out of 97 goslings, and an additional 15 to 20 young were reared at Northern Prairie Wildlife Research Center.

Thus, more than 180 Aleutian Canada geese were reared by the three federal facilities in 1978, a number which is rapidly approaching the stated goal of 200 young a year. To accomplish this, new blood from Buldir Island may be required from time to time, because only wild or first-generation birds are used as breeders.

Releases of captive-reared stock commenced in 1971 on Amchitka Island. This was followed by an additional attempt in 1976 and one on Agattu Island in 1974. It appears that some limited breeding success has been achieved, at least among the geese released on Agattu, possibly because bald eagles are less prevalent there. (Of the 41 geese released in 1974, five pairs formed, four females laid, and two pairs successfully reared five young.) Failure to successfully fledge young thus far on Amchitka has been attributed to the predatory activity of bald eagles.

All of the birds reared in captivity during 1978 will be acclaimed on Amchitka prior to a release sometime in the future. The release site will probably be on either Amchitka or Agattu, but could be on an island not yet designated, which hopefully will be cleared of foxes. In 1978, 139 captive-reared geese were released on Agattu, along with 22 wild adults that were captured in Northern California. These wild adults were necessary to serve as guides for the young to lead them to appropriate wintering grounds in California. Numbered neck collars, conspicuously colored, were fitted on a number of the young to facilitate easy field identification.

While many captive-reared birds have been liberated to date, it is doubtful that these attempts have had any *significant* effect on the total population thus far, although the original Buldir Island population appears to be increasing (75 active nests could be accounted for in 1975). The closing of selected areas in California to hunting probably has had more beneficial effect on the overall population than release programs at this stage. Federal biologists contend that much of the credit for the population increase must go to the California Depart-

6.66 *Aleutian Canada goose. These geese nest on steep slopes because the good visibility aids them in their defense against gulls and other predators. On Buldir Island, they apparently obtain most of their fresh water from plants and fog droplets.*

6.67 - 6.68 *The Nene, largest native bird of Hawaii, was at one time practically extinct. By 1948, no more than 50 existed, but today there are over 1000. The saga of restoration of the Nene through captive propagation is perhaps the most encouraging example of aviculture as a conservation tool.*

ment of Fish and Game, for their excellent cooperation in closing recommended areas to the hunting of all dark geese during the periods when the Aleutian Canada geese are likely to occur there. The California sportsmen who accepted these restrictions without complaint have also been cited as a contributing factor to the continuing success of this program. Most of the geese winter in California, and in the spring virtually the entire population gathers in the vicinity of Crescent City in northern California prior to the northward migration.

They have increased there from 790 in 1975 to almost 1600 during the fall of 1977, and it appears that the population is currently in fairly good shape.

The Bering Island Canada goose (*B. c. asiatica*) was last seen in 1914 and must be considered extinct. Individuals of this alleged race were very similar to the Aleutian subspecies, but were said to have an even more extensive white neck ring and to be slightly paler overall. The validity of this subspecies has been challenged repeatedly, since it was described from only two specimens, and only five museum specimens are currently known to exist. Certainly, since all known specimens were obtained within the northern range of the Aleutian race, the Bering Island birds appear to merely represent aberrant Aleutian Canada geese. Delacour himself no longer believes the race to be valid.

The **Nene or Hawaiian goose** (*Branta sandvicensis*) is closely related to the more familiar Canada goose, although some workers have suggested that it is distinct enough to warrant placement in the monotypic genus *Nesochen*. Inhabiting the tropical islands of the Hawaiian Archipelago, the species is nonmigratory (a unique distinction among northern geese). Deep furrows are formed by the neck feathers of these birds, producing a peculiar and impressive striped effect. They are not nearly as vocal as their mainland relatives, and their call consists of a low mournful moan.

Nene geese are residents of the highland lava-covered slopes of Mauna Kea, and of the Mauna Loa and Hualalai volcanoes on the big island of Hawaii. Recently, they have also been introduced to Halaeakala Crater on the Island of Maui. Undoubtedly, the dry and hostile environment, and the steep volcanic slopes, brought about stronger and larger legs and toes, as well as significantly reduced foot webs. The toes are also more mobile, giving the geese greater agility, which is undoubtedly a necessary adaptation for climbing about on the rough lava.

6.69

6.70

6.71

6.69 *Barnacle goose in the sunset.*

6.70 *Barnacle goose in molt. Note that the flight feathers have not fully regrown.*

6.71 *Pair of barnacle geese at dusk.*

6.72 (Opposite Page) *Barnacle goose in flight. From time to time, white individuals of this species are seen. These white birds are not true albinos, however, since they retain normally-colored eyes, bills, and legs.*

In such habitat, the only available water to be found is in small and often temporary pools (although the highlands are often covered with low damp clouds and the dew can be very heavy), and under these semi-arid conditions, it is not surprising that Nene are not particularly efficient swimmers. Like the Cape Barren goose (another terrestrial species), they normally copulate ashore or at the shoreline instead of in the water.

As recently as 25 years ago, the continued existence of the Nene was in doubt, but their plight has been mitigated considerably by carefully controlled captive breeding and release programs. Restoration of the species back into the highlands of Hawaii has been in progress for many years, and the project presently appears to be taking hold. (This effort has been discussed more fully in Chapter Fifteen.) Appropriately, the Nene has been designated the state bird of Hawaii.

Barnacle geese (*Branta leucopsis*) are closely related to and somewhat resemble Canada geese in many ways; but they are not as wary, and this has worked against them over the years. Despite a recent increase in the population from 30,000 in 1959 to at least 50,000 (and possibly 70,000 to 80,000) in the late 1970s, they remain one of the rarer geese, and population levels tend to be cyclic.

According to ancient legend, these birds hatched from floating barnacles, and this explains the origin of their peculiar vernacular name. Their northern nesting haunts remained unknown for hundreds of years, and so they seemed to "miraculously" appear on their wintering grounds each fall. In some way this caused people to consider them as "fish" rather than "fowl," and they were even permitted as food on Friday or during Lent, when meat was forbidden to those of the Catholic faith.

Extremely vocal, barnacle geese chatter noisily, and the sound of a flock can best be compared to a pack of yelping terriers. A defensive species, they may also hiss, with the tongue raised and showing threateningly, while they simultaneously move their necks in the manner of a serpent. They are nocturnally very active, and often feed after dark. Large flocks sometimes react to flying predators (such as peregrine falcons), or even a low-flying aircraft, as a flock of shorebirds would—twisting and turning in unison as they fly and creating a totally unforgettable spectacle.

During the nonbreeding season, barnacle geese can be considered essentially a maritime species, foraging mainly on tidal flats or in coastal marshes and adjoining grassy areas. At such times, they often gather in large flocks, rarely associating with other geese. Their high northern breeding grounds are located in east Greenland, Spitsbergen, and Novaya Zemlya in arctic Russia. There appears to be a distinct separation of these three breeding populations, even on the wintering grounds in Scotland, Ireland, and the Netherlands—but oddly, there is no indication of subspecific differentiation, despite the widespread geographical breeding separation. Stragglers are occasionally sighted off the Atlantic coast of North America.

Barnacle geese often breed in colonies and may nest in spectacular places—on precarious ledges high on the faces of steep cliffs, in holes and niches on a cliff face, or on outlying spurs of rock projecting over valleys and rocky gorges. They have also been known to nest in seabird colonies or in close proximity to gyrfalcon nests. Some of the nest sites may be 300 or more feet above the ground, and the same sites are often used year after year. (They may also nest on the ground in more typical goose fashion, and island sites are favored.)

Ledge nesting undoubtedly reduces predation, but it presents the geese with some interesting challenges. Landing on the smaller ledges can be difficult, for example, and goslings may also experience some trouble getting to the ground. It has been speculated that adults may carry them down in their bills or on their backs, but even though this is conceivable, it is not very probable. In all likelihood, the young merely tumble down the steep cliffs. The down of the goslings is very dense, and this would probably prevent serious injury during descent.

Compared to other goose species, the reproductive potential of barnacle geese appears to be rather low, suggesting a high incidence

6.73

6.73 *The nesting haunts of barnacle geese remained unknown until 1891, when nests were discovered in Greenland. Goslings may be preyed upon by large gulls, and experienced adults seldom leave their young unattended.*

of breeding failure. However, they adapt readily to captive conditions and are highly regarded by aviculturists. At the Wildfowl Trust, several hundred full-wing pairs nest on the grounds.

The stunning Siberian **red-breasted goose** (*Branta ruficollis*) is the smallest of the northern geese and is among the most boldly patterned of all birds. Depictions of these beautiful geese have been found in early Egyptian art—and, in fact, a tomb frescoe illustrating a red-breasted goose is thought to be one of the oldest known paintings in the world, dating from the early Fourth Dynasty (approximately 4500 years ago).

These dainty little birds have a delicate, almost hand-painted look about them. They possess a very high-pitched, rather distinctive and musical call, and during the breeding season they can be particularly vocal. Wintering red-breasted geese often associate with European and lesser white-fronted geese, and may roost on salt water at night. Immatures resemble adults, but are noted for greyer backs and less distinct white markings, pale or greyish chestnut cheeks, and white-tipped tail feathers. (Curiously, some subadults lack the prominent cheek patches.) As adults, they have lengthened nape feathers which form an indistinct mane.

These little geese are known to be rapid and agile fliers. Often, they fly in irregular groups and occasionally may form in diagonal lines—rarely, they may fly in "V" formation or single file. They appear to be more terrestrial and less aquatic than most of the northern geese. Feeding flocks can be noisy and quarrelsome, and when they graze they typically move their heads remarkably fast.

Unfortunately, it appears that red-breasted geese are in trouble. One of the rarest of geese, they probably number no more than 15,000 to 25,000 individuals, and recent population trends are far from encouraging. Without question, they have declined significantly during the past few decades—some specialists estimate as much as 50 percent. These geese formerly wintered almost exclusively along the coasts of the Caspian Sea (where more than 40,000 were accounted for in 1956), but due to changes in agricultural practices and drainage of marshlands, they have been rarely seen there in recent years. In December of 1968, some 25,000 red-breasted geese were wintering in Rumania, but such large numbers have not been seen since, and this has contributed to the belief that a catastrophic decline may have taken place. (No more than 6000 geese have been seen in the area in recent surveys.)

It may be, however, that the reduction of the population has not been as drastic as initially feared. In 1975, over 15,000 were observed migrating between the Caspian and Black seas. Also, the present extent of their wintering range is not fully known, and there are undoubtedly other, more inaccessible wintering areas to the east (probably in Turkey, Iraq, and perhaps Iran). Quite possibly, the geese have simply retreated to these areas.

Another major factor that could be having a negative influence on the population occurs on the breeding grounds. Red-breasted geese breed in a relatively restricted and almost totally inaccessible region of northern Siberia, mainly on the moss- and lichen-covered tundra of the western Taymyr Peninsula (as well as the adjacent Yamal and Gydan Peninsulas), along the deltas of the Ob and Khatanga Rivers. Apparently, the geese are greatly dependent on the presence of nesting peregrine falcons (or other birds of prey, such as rough-legged hawks or even large gulls), since they tend to form small colonies of from three to twenty nests around the raptors' nests.

Ground nesting is necessary in this area because islands and cliffs are rare, and this makes the goose nests vulnerable to predation. By constructing their nests only 10 to 30 feet away from the breeding peregrines, the little geese may gain some protection from arctic foxes, skuas, and other predators. Just why the falcons do not prey on the geese is not known, but perhaps it is because the geese are too large, and other more easily taken food may be readily available. The geese may also benefit the falcons to some degree by alerting them to impending danger.

As a result of the indiscriminate use of chlorinated hydrocarbon pesticides (such as DDT), the overall population of peregrine falcons has crashed. Because they are at the top of the food chain, these predators are particularly susceptible to this type of insidious poisoning. Can it be that the disappearance of the falcon has had a negative influence on the reproductive potential of the geese? In my opinion, this is a very real possibility, and clearly illustrates how sensitive an ecosystem can be. One species is adversely affected by nonselective poison originally applied for other purposes far from its breeding stronghold, and as a result subsequently disappears—and this in turn brings about the possible decline of yet another species.

Until more is known about the population dynamics and migratory movements of red-breasted geese, it seems prudent to consider them an endangered species and treat them accordingly. Incredible as it may seem, these geese are still regarded as a legal game species throughout much of their wintering range (even though a hunting ban was imposed in 1959), and considering their current population level,

6.75

6.74

6.74 The dainty red-breasted goose is perhaps the most beautiful of all waterfowl, noted for its distinctive color and pattern. It is among the most desirable of all geese in captivity — but unfortunately, it is rather rare, particularly in North America. While these gorgeous birds may bicker among themselves and frequently chase one another, they have relatively docile natures and can easily be mixed with other species without fear of harm. They are hardy and long-lived, but breed reluctantly in captivity. In a flock, they are delightful, particularly when they vocalize in unison.

6.75 Like most arctic nesters, red-breasted geese must complete their reproductive activities within a relatively brief period of time — just over 100 days. Favored nesting habitat on their relatively restricted breeding grounds consists of high and dry areas along steep river banks, low rocky crags, or gullies. Nest sites are generally open and quite often are visible from some distance away. Despite their small size, these feisty little geese are rather aggressive to one another, and when threatening they may vibrate their mane feathers. The six or seven eggs are incubated by the female alone, but the gander remains nearby throughout the 23- to 25-day incubation period. As the young begin to hatch in July, the adults generally commence their molt. By the end of August, the young are flying, and this suggests a short fledging period.

6.76 *Peregrine falcon. The breeding strategy of the red-breasted goose may be intricately linked with the presence of nesting peregrine falcons. The geese frequently nest in rather close association with the falcons, and are afforded protection from predators because the falcons will unhesitatingly drive any intruder from their territory. Unfortunately, the falcon has been adversely affected by chemical pesticides and has largely disappeared.*

6.77 *Pair of red-breasted geese.*

6.76

6.77

this is simply inexcusable. The discovery of oil in the breeding range of *ruficollis* will no doubt also add to its woes.

In sum, factors influencing the decline of these geese appear to be related to loss of appropriate wintering habitat, disappearance of the peregrine falcon, disturbance by man, and excessive hunting. The cumulative effect of all these pressures may very well result in the irrevocable loss of one of the world's most beautiful birds. A species simply cannot experience extreme pressure on both its breeding and wintering grounds and be expected to survive indefinitely.

In captivity, red-breasted geese are by far the rarest and most desirable of all geese—and also, unfortunately, among the most difficult to persuade to breed. Like most geese, they do best when an abundant supply of fresh grass is available, and small colonies are more apt to breed than single pairs. They appear to be rather susceptible to disturbance, and as with other arctic geese, their reluctance to breed in more temperate climates may be related to the different period of daytime light. In Europe they are fairly well established, but in America they are generally seen in only the more sophisticated collections.

The sea geese are, as the name implies, the most marine of the northern geese. In Europe, they are commonly called **brents** (*Branta bernicla*) and in America are known as **brant**—names that may be derived from their distinctive rolling call. Small and delicate geese, they are not much larger than a mallard drake, but despite this, their very rapid wing beats make them one of the fastest flying geese, with ground speeds that sometimes exceed 60 miles per hour. Typically, sea geese fly just above the waves in wide, irregular, and undulating lines, but they may also fly in tight flocks, often twisting and turning simultaneously. During migration, they prefer to fly around projecting spits of land rather than over them. They can be noisy when on the wing, and when flightless during the molt they dive readily. Swimming birds are noted for a stern-high posture, which reveals and accentuates their white undertails. Highly developed salt glands enable them to drink sea water and consume coastal vegetation with high salt content, such as eelgrass and algae, as well as small shellfish and other invertebrates.

Members of the Atlantic race are among the northernmost of breeding birds in the world, and nesting habitat for all brant geese is fairly far north—along arctic seashores, on islands, and on the marshy tundra. Generally arriving on the breeding grounds prior to the spring thaw, they locate their nests in a scrape or hollow and line them with copious amounts of very fine dark down. In the opinion of some people, brant down equals (or even exceeds) the quality of eider down, and is so cohesive that even strong tundra winds will not blow it away. The nest may also be supplemented with mosses and lichens, but usually not.

Because these geese breed along the lowland coastal tundra, never far from the tidal zone, storm tides may cause mass destruction of nests, and late winter storms sometimes promote nest desertion. During the breeding season, brant are more gregarious than most geese, particularly black brant (*B. b. orientalis*). In some areas of Alaska, black brant can be considered partially colonial nesters, and although nest densities vary, there may be as many as 144 per square mile (on the Yukon-Kuskokwim Delta, the average is five to nine nests per acre). Egging is still practiced by northern natives, and the *local* impact can be significant.

Shortly after goslings hatch, adults may take them to sea, where they are immediately able to swim and dive—but as a rule, they will

6.78 *Pacific or black brant. These are high arctic nesters, and as a rule, they have breeding ranges which extend farther north than any other goose. Almost exclusively marine during the winter, they may raft up in large flocks. These flocks can be noisy, and the high-pitched resonant din may increase in volume as other groups alight, as the tide changes, or when the birds become alarmed.*

remain in fresh or brackish water until the young fledge. Youngsters grow rapidly and are capable of flight in 35 to 40 days. Broods are sometimes merged. This western North American race may intergrade with Atlantic brant in northern Canada.

Black or Pacific brant were, at one time, common winter residents along the shores of southern California. But an advancing civilization has forced them to move farther south into Baja California, Mexico, where great numbers of them can be observed wintering in large sheltered Pacific lagoons, along with courting and calving California gray whales. (In recent years, a number have been observed wintering in the Sea of Cortez, particularly along the west coast of mainland Mexico.) In the spring, like their leviathan companions, Pacific brant commence the long trek back to the Arctic. Sea geese probably spend more time on the wing than any other American goose.

During both the spring and fall migration, more than 200,000 black brant assemble at Izembek Bay, along the north coast of the Alaska Peninsula, in one of the largest and most extensive eelgrass beds in the world. These concentrations may represent the total population of black brant, and the importance of Izembek Bay as a staging and wintering area for waterfowl is immense, so it is fortunate that the area is part of the National Wildlife Refuge System. The region is also

used extensively by emperor geese, Steller's eiders, and oldsquaw ducks—and just offshore, countless numbers of king and Pacific eiders, as well as white-winged scoters, pass the winter.

During the 1930s and 1940s, there was a catastrophic reduction in the population of Atlantic or light-bellied brant (*B. b. hrota*), when most of the eelgrass (*Zostera*) along the east coast of North America died off, probably as a result of disease. While they are now recovering, this eastern race is still far short of their former numbers. The disappearance of eelgrass also caused the population of the Russian brant (*B. b. bernicla*) to crash, with a loss of perhaps 75 percent of their number. Fortunately, the geese were able to modify their food requirements and presently appear to prefer sea lettuce; obviously, they were not as specialized in their dietary preferences as previously believed. As a result of this shift in diet, however, Atlantic brant in particular are not the highly-regarded gamebirds they once were, because some hunters claim that sea lettuce taints the flesh. During times when natural food is scarce, wintering birds may take to feeding on inland crops.

Russian or dark-bellied brant are the Eurasian representatives of the sea geese. During the winter, large numbers migrate to the coastal regions of England and northwest Europe, and while the *bernicla*

population has increased significantly in recent years, it is subject to much fluctuation (i.e., 34,000 in 1971, 120,000 in 1975, and 90,000 in 1977).

A fourth race, Lawrence's brant (*B. b. nigricans*), has been described, but is not generally regarded as valid because it is based on only three specimens. These birds may merely represent an intergrade between the Pacific and Atlantic race—and this taxonomic question may be academic anyway, since Lawrence's brant goose is possibly already gone. If this suspect race is cast aside, the black brant of western North America and eastern Siberia will become known solely as *B. b. nigricans*. However, Johnsgard has apparently split the black brant, and recognizes the brant which breed from the Lena River Delta to the Anadyr Basin of Siberia as the Pacific brant (*B. b. orientalis*)—thus adding somewhat to the confusion.

The three universally accepted races of brant are fairly easy to distinguish from one another, and are also geographically distinct. Pacific black brant, the darkest of the group, have an extensive white neck ring which almost totally encircles the neck. Russian brant have dark underparts and flanks, and this quickly differentiates them from the Atlantic (or light-bellied) race, which is characteristically much lighter along the sides and ventrally. (Curiously, Delacour indicates that albinistic specimens of the Atlantic race are not particularly uncommon, with some birds having brownish heads and necks, and mottled white and pale brown dorsal surfaces—but it seems more likely that this condition is due to worn plumage.)

Although they are not prolific breeders, brant geese do very well in captivity and are easily converted to foraging on terrestrial grasses. But unfortunately, they are not readily available and are, as a result, relatively poorly represented in most collections. If maintained in a small flock, they can be very charming and amusing, and they mix easily with other species. They are rarely bred, although in some collections they produce annually. Russian brant are seldom kept in American collections and are practically unknown to New World aviculturists.

6.79 *California gray whale. Black brant and gray whales can be encountered with one another on both the wintering grounds in Mexico and the offshore waters of the breeding range in the Arctic. However, the breeding seasons of the two species are reversed. The whales court and calve during the winter, but spend the summer foraging extensively in the rich arctic waters while the brant breed. The trek of the whales from the Arctic to Mexico and back constitutes the longest known regular migration for any mammal.*

6.80 *Atlantic or light-bellied brant goose. In flight, the bellies of these geese appear pale greyish, silvery, or even white — making them easy to distinguish from the black brant, which has dark underparts.*

6.81 *Like other geese, black brant are very aggressive when they have young. At such times, a defensive gander may hiss or growl and hold its head and neck in a sigmoid curve close to the ground or water. The head usually points upward slightly, the bill is opened wide, and the tongue is elevated.*

6.82 *(Opposite Page) Russian or dark-bellied brant goose. These geese breed in the Eurasian arctic and winter mainly along the coasts of England and northwestern Europe.*

7

Shelducks and Sheldgeese
Tadornini

As a group, members of the tribe Tadornini are clearly more closely related to one another behaviorally than they are anatomically. Taxonomically situated between the northern geese and typical dabbling ducks, this group has also traditionally included several very aberrant and puzzling species such as the Cape Barren goose, the crested ducks, and the peculiar steamer ducks—but the systematic positions of these aberrants must be regarded as very tentative and subject to modification as more definitive information about them becomes available. Indeed, in his latest taxonomic revision of the family, Johnsgard has removed the three of them from this tribe altogether, and two (Cape Barren geese and steamer ducks) have been elevated to new tribes.

Shelducks and sheldgeese are primarily southern hemispheric in distribution and inhabit tropical or temperate areas. Several of the shelducks, however, have successfully invaded northern regions and all continents have at least one resident species except North America and Antarctica. Very pugnacious as a rule, particularly during the

7.2

7.1 (Opposite Page) *Flock of lesser Magellan geese in Tierra del Fuego, Argentina.*

7.2 *Family of ruddy-headed geese. Sheldgeese are excellent parents, and energetically defend their young against almost any potential predator. Like some of the other South American sheldgeese, this species is noted for a large white wing patch which is usually not visible when the bird is relaxed. However, when threatened, they display this conspicuous wing patch prominently, leaving no doubt about their intentions.*

breeding season, most members of the tribe are often intolerant of other birds, including individuals of their own kind. In all cases, males are somewhat larger and frequently do not resemble their mates at all in either color or pattern. Many species have a hard spur-like knob at the bend of the wing and, as a rule, their tails are relatively long. Sheldgeese tend to be mainly vegetarian, whereas shelducks are more omnivorous; and neither group is nearly as gregarious or social as the true geese. Generally, most shelducks and sheldgeese spend considerable time ashore and are at ease on land, walking and running with grace. Interestingly, at least two species (the Orinoco goose and the radjah shelduck) perch in trees—and both the Egyptian goose and the ashy-headed goose also exhibit some arboreal tendencies.

None of the sheldgeese are highly migratory, but seasonal movements may be undertaken. Neither are they the most accomplished of waterfowl swimmers, although they do not necessarily shun the water. Vocalizations of the sexes are dissimilar, with males emitting high-pitched soft whistles and females producing hoarse cackles. The pair bond is very strong, probably lifelong, and even though only females incubate, ganders stand by to fiercely defend the nest and young. Most forms are not considered to be top-quality gamebirds, since they are rather unpalatable and fly relatively slowly. Six of the eight species of

sheldgeese occur in South America, and of these, five inhabit the colder southern regions; the other two species are African. With the sole exception of the coastal kelp goose, all South American sheldgeese are noted for extensive grazing activities.

As mentioned previously, all sheldgeese are very defensive and bad-tempered, but the **Andean goose** (*Chloëphaga melanoptera*) is one of the worst in this regard. During the breeding season, males of this species can only be described as savage—although some individuals may tame quickly, and it is not unusual to encounter them in a semi-domesticated state around native dwellings.

The sexes are similar in appearance, with both possessing an exquisite deep metallic violet-purple wing speculum, but males are significantly larger and bulkier. Both sexes are essentially white, with black tails, primaries, and tertials, and both have orange legs and feet. Compared to other sheldgeese, their necks are relatively short and their coral-red bills are rather hooked, giving them something of the appearance of a bird of prey. While they are not very social, Andean geese do sometimes gather in loose flocks.

During courtship, the elegant ganders strut around with their chests thrust out like cocky prizefighters, chattering and displaying before the females almost continually. These geese nest at high altitudes, up to the snow line, and usually remain above 10,000 feet for most of the year—but in the southern portion of their range in northern Chile, they may move down to the damp meadows and marshes at the base of the Andes during the austral winter. They are even less aquatic than some of the other sheldgeese, although newly-hatched goslings are usually led to the nearest water.

Andean geese can be locally common in many parts of their range, but some conservationists believe the overall population has shown a downward trend in recent years. Little definitive data are available concerning their status, but it seems probable that the relative inaccessibility of their mountainous habitat affords them some protection, and that the population is stable and reasonably secure for the time being. Most large waterfowl collections contain at least one pair, but Andean geese are not overly popular because, due to their dispositions, they usually have to be maintained separate from other waterfowl. They are bred regularly by some propagators, but not commonly.

Ashy-headed geese (*Chloëphaga poliocephala*) and **ruddy-headed geese** (*Chloëphaga rubidiceps*) are rather similar in appearance, but as their vernacular names imply, they have different head colors. With both species, the sexes are alike (although males are slightly larger), and both have prominent eye rings. Ashy-headed geese prefer the more wooded areas of the interior, although they may also be encountered along the coast. Ruddy-headed geese, on the other hand, are much more apt to occupy coastal regions, particularly open plains and grassland meadows. Both species appear to have a rather prolonged molt, and since this could leave a number of them with some of their flight feathers intact at any given time, it could reduce (or perhaps even eliminate) the flightless period—although at least some segments of the southwest Argentine *poliocephala* population do undergo a period of definite flightlessness.

Somewhat gregarious, ashy-headed geese are usually observed grazing in small parties. Often seen in the company of Magellan geese, they frequent low-lying areas, river valleys, lakes, and estuaries—but they also occupy certain ecological niches in the highlands. They perch fairly readily, and have the un-goose-like habit of nesting in the hollows of burned-out tree trunks or branches, sometimes even in tree

7.5

.7.4

7.3 (Opposite Page) *Pair of ashy-headed geese with fledged young at the extreme southern tip of South America. In some frontier districts, it is said that these geese are relatively easy to tame and natives may even keep them together with domestic ducks, geese, and turkeys.*

7.4 *Ashy-headed geese inhabit some of the most beautiful country on earth, including regions that are thickly covered with forests of southern beech. Not infrequently, they can be encountered during the nonbreeding season in sheltered coastal lagoons.*

7.5 *Male Andean goose. A violent and defensive species, these geese frequently call out with a whistling vocalization that is uttered with the head and neck diagonally outstretched. They are high-altitude breeders and nests are typically situated amidst sparse vegetation, usually on hilly slopes overlooking water, but at times on bare ground just below the snow line. Relatively tame in their mountain strongholds, Andean geese become more wary when they move down to lower altitudes during the winter, and grazing birds tend to stay in the center of fields, well away from hunters.*

7.6

7.6 *Ruddy-headed goose with young. While this species may nest in the same kinds of locations as the Magellan goose, their nests are easily distinguishable because of their cinnamon-colored down linings.*

7.7 *Smallest and one of the most attractive of the sheldgeese, the ruddy-headed goose is also unfortunately one of the most threatened. While these birds are still relatively abundant on the Falkland Islands, the continental contingent has undergone a severe decline and may number no more than 1000 birds. The introduction of the Patagonian gray fox has been particularly detrimental.*

7.7

crotches. Goslings of this species tend to run for wooded cover rather than the water when threatened, unlike the young of the larger Magellan geese.

Some of the literature indicates that ashy-headed geese may be relatively rare in Tierra del Fuego, but I have not found this to be necessarily true—at least not on the Argentine side of Isla Grande, where I have encountered reasonably large flocks, even during the late austral summer in April. Their center of distribution appears to be in Chile. Despite their rather feisty temperaments, these attractive birds have long been popular with aviculturists and are not infrequently bred.

Unlike their close relatives, ruddy-headed geese are not common in wildfowl collections, although a few more have become available during the past few years, and their captive status has become somewhat more secure than it once was. These little geese, the smallest of the sheldgeese, can be extremely combative and aggressive, and may readily challenge much larger birds (although I have kept some individuals that were most gentle). Females, as a rule, are much more vocal than their mates. Rich chestnut undertail coverts are particularly noticeable when these geese swim, as the tail is generally held well elevated. Nests are usually situated on the ground, but in the Falkland Islands ruddy-headed geese may also nest in abandoned Magellanic penguin burrows. They are somewhat migratory, and the continental population moves to the north to spend the winter.

The rapid and apparently drastic decline of this species in recent years is cause for great alarm. As recently as 1970, thousands were observed in Tierra del Fuego, and in the 1950s they were considered to be the most numerous of the sheldgeese in some portions of their range. Unfortunately, this is no longer the case, and sightings are becoming increasingly rare, except on the Falkland Islands, where the geese appear to be holding their own (at least for the present). Population estimates for the Falkland Islands suggest that up to 40,000 may occur there, but I view these figures as perhaps overly optimistic. While still not officially designated as such, the evidence suggests that the continental population of ruddy-headed geese is gravely endangered. Possibly it may number no more than 100 individuals, and may be on the verge of extirpation.

To illustrate the seriousness of the situation, it is only necessary to disclose that the prominent Argentine ornithologist, Maurice Rumboll, could account for only 30 ruddy-headed geese in a census taken between October and November of 1973 on the east side of Isla Grande, Tierra del Fuego. At the same time, he was able to record two to three thousand ashy-headed geese and up to 30,000 Magellan geese. In 1975, a census was conducted on the wintering grounds in the southeast portion of Buenos Aires Province, and ruddy-headed geese represented but one half of one percent of all geese observed. A similar survey in 1976 showed they had declined further to only 0.45 percent of the wintering population.

Local nonselective bounties, instituted primarily against the Magellan goose, have obviously had an adverse effect, but far more serious have been the detrimental results of the intentional introduction of the Patagonian grey fox in the late 1940s. The foxes were introduced to control rabbits, which had also been introduced and had subsequently become major pests. (On Isla Grande, the foxes are controlled to some extent by the Argentines on their side of the island—but unbelievably, they are *protected* by the Chileans on the west side of the island. Not surprisingly, the fox eradication program has had little success.) Unlike the ashy-headed goose, ruddy-headed geese nest in the open grasslands, and therefore undoubtedly suffer greater nest predation. There can be no question that these geese are suitable candidates for endangered species status and should be afforded total protection *now*.

The two races of **Magellan geese** (*Chloëphaga picta*), more commonly known as upland geese by the natives, have been the most ruthlessly persecuted of the sheldgeese. Essentially a species that prefers semi-arid open grassland, they are quite trusting by nature and have been slaughtered in large numbers with sticks and clubs, presumably to prevent them from eating grass that is intended for live-

stock. South American sheep ranchers claim that seven to ten geese can consume as much grass as a single sheep—and apparently, this is too much from the rancher's point of view. (The geese do appear to prefer the close cropped grass, and this would tend to concentrate them in sheep grazing areas.)

As recently as 1972, Magellan geese were declared a "national plague" in Tierra del Fuego and Patagonia. The local government offered a bounty of five cents for each egg, gosling, or pair of female legs, and during the 1972-73 breeding season alone, more than 150,000 eggs were destroyed. In a number of districts, a bounty on both birds and eggs is still in effect, and at times the geese are even harassed and driven by planes.

But despite such dedicated and cold-blooded persecution, the tenacious Magellan geese have demonstrated remarkable resiliency. They have managed to hold their own, particularly in the less inhabited areas—although even there they are not totally secure. In 1977, while walking along a remote beach in the Beagle Channel (Tierra del Fuego), I counted a minimum of 20 dead upland geese within a 150-yard stretch, some hanging on fence posts. All had presumably been shot.

7.8 *Lesser Magellan geese are polymorphic and ganders may be either completely white ventrally or, as in the case of this male, distinctly barred.*

7.9 *In recent years, ruddy-headed geese have become somewhat more common in captivity. The acquisition of fertile eggs from the Falkland Islands did much to revitalize the captive stock and these attractive geese are currently breeding on a more regular basis.*

7.10 *While South American sheep ranchers have treated lesser Magellan geese very shabbily, it may be that these tenacious geese are more numerous today than before the ranchers arrived on the scene, at least in Chile. Ironically, it was the ranchers' conversion of the forests into pastures that brought geese and ranchers into direct conflict. The carnage, which continues to this day, staggers the imagination, and as many as 50,000 eggs have been destroyed on a single ranch during one breeding season.*

7.11

7.12

7.13

7.14

7.11 *Greater Magellan goose male with gosling. On the Falkland Islands, as on the mainland, Magellan geese are looked upon with disfavor by sheep ranchers. The geese are hunted to some extent for human consumption and are said to be tastiest in the late summer and autumn, when they are feeding mainly on diddle-dee, tea, and wild strawberries.*

7.12 *In some areas, goslings may be preyed upon by skuas, gull-like birds that behave in many respects like birds of prey.*

7.13 *Female greater Magellan geese are larger and more attractive than females of the lesser race. Toward the end of December, while the young are still incapable of flight, the adults commence their molt and shed all their flight feathers, thus becoming flightless. At such times, they will readily take to the water if disturbed.*

7.14 *Female lesser Magellan goose. The head color may vary from deep brown to dirty grey.*

A striking parallel to this senseless destruction exists in North America, where the much-publicized "war on the wily coyote" continues to this day. As with the geese, the coyote's existence is primarily challenged by sheep-raising interests. Nonetheless, both forms persist, and in some cases even seem to prosper in spite of man's efforts. Paradoxically, the Magellan goose remains the most abundant of all the sheldgeese.

Greater Magellan or Falkland upland geese (*C. p. leucoptera*), the larger and rarer of the two races, are in the minds of many specialists restricted to the Falkland Islands, but small numbers also inhabit regions of Tierra del Fuego and southern Patagonia. They apparently do not nest in association with birds of the lesser race (*C. p. picta*), and this nesting separation suggests that they may be deserving of full species status. Males of the greater race are always white ventrally—whereas ganders of the lesser subspecies are polymorphic, and can be either completely white below, or distinctly barred black and white, or inbetween. It is said that barred males of the lesser race are more common in southern portions of the range and white males are more abundant in the north.

Females of both races are considered by some observers to be more attractive than their mates, and are polymorphic as well; those of the lesser race usually have pale sandy-brown heads, while the greater Magellan females have larger heads that are colored a warm medium brown. In addition, the underparts of lesser females appear to be darker and less reddish because the black ventral bars are almost twice as wide as the cinnamon bars; just the opposite of *leucoptera*. Females of both races superficially resemble ruddy-headed geese—with which they sometimes associate—but ruddy-headed geese are significantly smaller and trimmer, have a more prominent eye ring, and are noted for much finer barring on the body.

Ganders have particularly hard knobs located at the bend of the wing, which are put to use when they engage in battle—an activity that occurs almost continually, at least in captivity. The prominent white upper wing patch is one of the most conspicuous flight characteristics of both sexes. As with the other sheldgeese, males and females have dissimilar calls; the gander uttering a soft whistle, and its mate generating a deep harsh cackle.

Goslings hatched by the Magellan geese that nest along the coast are subject to much predation by skuas and kelp gulls. These preda-

144

tors may snatch an unwary gosling by the loose skin of the neck, carry it up to a height of 20 to 30 feet, and drop it repeatedly until it succumbs. The brain is then consumed and the rest discarded, as the opportunist departs in search of another meal. In at least one case, a peregrine falcon was observed to take a ten-day-old gosling from the water. Adults generally avoid water except when protecting their young or during the molt, when they will readily seek the security of the sea if threatened.

Magellan geese were introduced to South Georgia Island in the South Atlantic as a food source for whalers and sealers in 1910 and 1911, but by 1950 they had been extirpated. An additional introduction some years later also ended in failure. Both races are well established in waterfowl collections, but lesser Magellan geese are far more common in America. (In Europe, *leucoptera* is more common.) They breed readily, but many propagators are reluctant to keep them because of their belligerent nature.

Perhaps the strangest of the sheldgeese are the two races of **kelp geese** (*Chloëphaga hybrida*). Males are pure white, and aside from the totally white northern swans, they are the only waterfowl with all-white plumage. Females are distinctly striped with different hues of brown, and are so well camouflaged and wary that they can be extremely difficult to see against the dark rocks—although their presence is inevitably betrayed by the conspicuous, ever-present white ganders. The Falkland Island birds (*C. h. malvinarum*) are somewhat larger than their Patagonian counterparts (*C. h. hybrida*), with longer legs, wings, and bills. In addition, the white barring on the females is significantly broader. First-year males are dark and superficially resemble females, but by their second year they are totally white, except for dark-tipped primary feathers. Both sexes have bright lemon-yellow legs, and the short black bill of the male has a distinct pinkish or crimson spot on the top.

The kelp goose lifestyle is totally different from that of most waterfowl (except perhaps the emperor goose), since they have evolved toward a life on rocky ocean shores and have been extremely successful within a *very* narrow ecological niche. Contrary to their vernacular name, these geese do not utilize the leathery inshore kelp as a food source, but prefer instead to forage on sea lettuce. They also eat other forms of seaweed, aquatic vegetation, and possibly even molluscs; and some individuals of the Falkland race have evolved toward grassland grazing.

Kelp geese are reluctant fliers, and their flight is somewhat labored. But during courtship, pairs sometimes fly in unison, throwing back their heads and simultaneously thrusting out their chests while vocalizing. Males whistle repeatedly, while females honk or sometimes snort. Unless accompanying young, these geese usually spend little time actually in the water, preferring instead to forage at the water's edge. Some observers suggest that they may not be as waterproof as other waterfowl, but I have repeatedly observed them in the water, and have not seen any evidence which supports such an idea.

Nests are located within 30 feet of the high tide line (with rare exceptions), and only the female incubates. Although four to six goslings may hatch, mortality can be unusually high, and seldom do more than two of the young survive to fledge. Both parents rear the goslings, which appear to have a very slow growth rate. Since the young feed most intensively during low tide periods on exposed filamentous algae, it may be that this limitation of optimum feeding periods is responsible for their slow rate of growth.

7.15

7.16

7.17

7.15 Gander of the greater Magellan goose race. Individuals of this subspecies are larger than their lesser relatives, with longer legs and necks. Their underparts are never barred.

7.16 Falkland kelp goose male. Kelp geese are restricted to rocky coasts and shingle beaches, but may frequent freshwater ponds to bathe and drink. Their isolated habitat, combined with the fact that they are practically inedible, has afforded them a significant amount of protection from direct persecution by man.

7.17 Pair of Patagonian kelp geese engaged in courtship flight. Their courtship behavior has yet to be subjected to intense scientific study, but it does appear that mated pairs may fly in unison around their territory, throwing back their heads and calling as they do so.
PHOTO BY MAURICE RUMBOLL

7.18 *Pair of Patagonian kelp geese. Their short legs and large feet have undoubtedly evolved as an adaptation to their specialized way of life and probably enable them to walk and stand on wet and slippery rocks. The function of the non-concealing color of the gander is unknown, but it may serve an important function with regard to territory establishment and defense. A defensive gander on its territory is highly visible, and this may cause other males to avoid an encounter. The limited shoreline food resources may be at least partially responsible for the fairly low population density of the species.*

7.19 *Falkland or greater kelp goose gander.*

7.20 *Family of kelp geese on the Falkland Islands with roosting rock shags. It is easy to see how the extremely well-camouflaged female can be overlooked.*

7.18

7.19

7.20

Kelp geese are sedentary, and pairs rarely leave their home shore any time during the year, although I have noted some flocking tendencies (particularly with immatures) among feeding birds during the nonbreeding season. There is some scanty data in the literature suggesting that the continental population engages in a substantial northward migration during the winter. I have not yet visited their southern range in the middle of the winter, but I have been there during the onset of that season and have observed no activity at all that would indicate any strong migratory urge. While it may take place, it requires further documentation.

Unlike some of the other forms of South American sheldgeese, kelp geese have suffered relatively little persecution by man, probably because they inhabit often inaccessible coastal areas and, more importantly, because they do not compete with sheep for grass. Also, both the geese and their eggs are generally considered unpalatable, and for this reason have not been extensively hunted. (The sealers of a bygone era described the "sea goose" as edible only for a starving man.) Fuegian Indians did formerly trap them with snares fashioned from guanaco sinew or from shreds of whale baleen (which commonly washes up on the beach)—but ironically, the indians themselves disappeared after the arrival of the white man, while the specialized geese have survived.

Kelp geese have rarely been kept in captivity and are notoriously difficult to maintain, being apparently very susceptible to a number of diseases, especially aspergillosis. Developing an adequate diet for them has also been most challenging—although their dietary requirements may not be quite as strict as often implied, since I have frequently observed large numbers of Patagonian kelp geese foraging at sewage outlets. Mainland or lesser kelp geese appear to be slightly more hardy, and a pair survived for many years at the San Diego Zoo mixed in with many other species of waterfowl. Sadly, no kelp geese currently exist in any collection, although they were bred on at least one occasion in the past.

The remaining South American sheldgoose, the **Orinoco goose** (*Neochen jubatus*), inhabits the banks of dense jungle-lined rivers and streams in the more tropical lowlands, and is said to be one of the most common waterfowl of the Orinoco River. These birds may represent an ancestral link between the sheldgeese and the smaller shelducks. The sexes are similar in appearance, but the somewhat larger male can often be identified by the noticeably longer neck feathers, which may be erected when the bird becomes agitated. While they are not brightly colored or boldly patterned, their cherry-red or salmon-colored legs are very conspicuous. Immatures closely resemble their parents, but are somewhat paler overall. Orinoco geese are neither very aquatic nor are they particularly graceful fliers, and their wings reportedly produce a rattling sound during take-off. As adults, these birds are undoubtedly essentially vegetarian, but they do not appear to be reluctant to capitalize on the presence of small molluscs, worms, larvae, and aquatic insects when these are available.

These sedentary geese do not appear to be overly gregarious and for the greater part of the year are usually observed only in pairs or family groups (although a number may gather together during the molt). Pairs are very affectionate and engage in a great deal of mutual preening, particularly around the head. Ganders display by throwing their heads back, inflating and throwing out their chests, and calling with strong whistling notes. So energetically do they thrust out their chests, in fact, that they must frequently balance on their toes to keep

7.21 *The inshore waters of the Falkland Islands are frequently clogged with thick leathery kelp which, despite their vernacular name, kelp geese do not eat. Gosling mortality is quite high, as evidenced by the fact that only one young bird remains with this family.*

7.22 *Portrait of an adult gander Falkland Island kelp goose.*

7.23 - 7.24 *The Orinoco goose is perhaps the most arboreal of the sheldgeese. Normally nesting in hollow trees, these geese will readily nest on the ground amidst vegetation in captivity. These tropical lowland sheldgeese are more social than their near relatives, and frequently engage in mutual nibbling of the head feathers. Social preening is not limited to paired birds and may involve birds of the same or opposite sex; at times, three geese may engage in such activity. Generally shy and inconspicuous for much of the year, these birds become increasingly aggressive as the breeding season approaches. When threatened, both sexes erect their elongated neck feathers, making their necks appear very thick.*

from falling over backwards! Apparently, nests are normally located in tree hollows and lined with white down, which is typical of cavity nesters. The downy goslings, although patterned like sheldgeese, are noteworthy because they have large dark cheek patches.

Orinoco geese are popular with aviculturists, but are not overly common in collections because they are not generally available. Their sometimes aggressive behavior is a minor negative factor, but this is usually overlooked because they are more social than other sheldgeese and are in many respects a charming and entertaining species. As a rule, they are rather reluctant to breed, but when pairs do commence producing they can be prolific and dependable for years.

The **Abyssinian blue-winged goose** (*Cyanochen cyanopterus*) occupies a very restricted area in East Africa, usually at elevations above 8000 feet. These birds have the smallest range of all the sheldgeese and the total population is believed to be relatively small. They most frequently occur along highland Ethiopian rivers, but they may also inhabit tablelands where there are brooks and puddles, or meadows at the edge of swamps that are not too heavily overgrown with vegetation. Apparently not at all gregarious, they are usually encountered in pairs or family groups, and are not easily approachable. As with Andean geese, ganders strut about with their chests out, and some individuals can be both very bad-tempered and very vocal. (This similarity is interesting because Andean geese may be their closest relatives.) Unlike typical sheldgeese, both sexes of these birds have voices that are very similar, consisting of high-pitched, almost whistling, calls.

Blue-winged geese are essentially nocturnal feeders and, although mainly vegetarian, will not ignore such animal fare as worms, insects, snails, and even reptiles. Breeding biology has been little studied in the wild, only a few nests have been described, and the current status of the species is not really known. In particular, it is not known what effect (if any) the recent bloody war in the area may have had on the population. Blue-winged geese are fairly well established in captivity, but are not particularly popular because they can be extremely quarrelsome (ganders have been known to kill their exhibit mates). Some

7.25 *Male Egyptian goose. These sub-tropical African birds fly freely within and over forests. They spend much of the day on the flat shores of permanent lakes, and toward sunset they usually fly out to spend a few hours at communal grazing grounds. During the breeding season, they become highly territorial. The Egyptian goose was introduced to England during the 18th Century, and a feral population still exists there.*

7.25

breeders are very successful with them, but they are not widely bred.

The other African representative, the **Egyptian goose** (*Alopochen aegyptiacus*), was sacred to the ancient Egyptians. Occurring throughout most of the African tropics from sea level to 13,000 feet

(and very infrequently in southern Europe as well), they have adapted well to man's encroachment and are relatively common. In fact, they are accused of causing considerable crop damage and are considered agricultural pests in some areas. Essentially a species of inland freshwater areas, they are seldom observed in coastal habitats.

In many ways, Egyptian geese are more like huge shelducks than sheldgeese, particularly with respect to the patterning of the downy young. Ganders are not only larger and somewhat brighter in color than their mates, but generally have a darker and larger chestnut patch on the breast as well. The conspicuous dark patches surrounding the yellow eyes of both sexes are diagnostic of the species, although eye and chest patches are absent on juvenile birds. The mottled flesh-colored bills of the ganders swell up at the base when they are in breeding condition. The species is noted for two color phases, one much greyer dorsally than the other. Males are characteristically noisy and quarrelsome birds, with hoarse hollow voices that are reminiscent of husky asthmatic breathing or a steam engine—a sound that is, at any rate, very unlike the typical whistling call of most male sheldgeese.

A variety of nest sites are utilized, including trees up to 80 feet in height (sometimes even palm trees), and the geese may occupy the old deserted nests of large birds, such as fish eagles and goliath herons. In one case, a pair actually nested inside a huge hammerkop nest which was still in use by the storks, and they have also been known to nest on buildings and among colonies of cliff-nesting vultures.

After a prolonged and irregular breeding season, Egyptian geese often gather in large flocks to molt, and may associate with other species—including crocodiles and hippopotamuses—apparently without concern. From time to time, the geese may even perch on the back of a dozing hippo. (These two species don't readily mix in captivity, however, for every time I attempted it, the geese ended up in the mouths of the hippos.) On occasion, molting flocks number in the thousands. Essentially terrestrial, they swim well and are surprisingly capable divers. They feed both at night and during the day, and may forage at a considerable distance from water.

These geese are very common in captivity and are noted for being among the most vicious of all waterfowl, particularly when nesting. They have been introduced into England, where a small feral population still exists. A captive albinistic strain has been developed that is known as the white Egyptian goose, and while I personally do not find them very attractive, they are surprisingly popular with some aviculturists.

The peculiar **Cape Barren or Cereopsis goose** (*Cereopsis novae-hollandiae*) has no close surviving relative, and although it shares some similarities with the true geese, it has traditionally been considered more like a sheldgoose than anything else. But recent studies suggest that this odd bird is not particularly closely related to either true geese or sheldgeese, and while it does have traits in common with both groups, it probably represents a transitional species. As a result, Johnsgard has removed the Cereopsis goose from the Tadornini and placed it in the new monotypic tribe Cereopsini.

Cape Barren geese are so strange in appearance that the first Europeans to observe them believed they were immature black swans. Their short thick bills are covered by peculiar conspicuous waxy greenish yellow ceres, and the Latin name *Cereopsis* ("wax-like") refers to this. Their ash-grey color is unusual, and in flight black-tipped flight feathers are evident. They also have relatively long and surprisingly sharp claws, and bony knobs at the wrist which make

7.26

7.27

7.28

7.29

7.26 *Family of Cape Barren geese. At one time greatly endangered, these birds appear to be currently thriving. However, like their taxonomic status, their numerical status is controversial, and depending on the source, population figures range between 5000 and 20,000. Whatever the number, there can be no question that the population has increased considerably since the 1950s, when it was believed that no more than 900 existed.*

7.27 *Cape Barren goose goslings are most appealing. These geese breed on desolate, wind-swept islands in the Bass Strait. Nest sites are often located on rocky prominences that afford the geese a good lookout point. The nest itself is usually situated in tussock grass, bushes, or rocks.*

7.28 *Male Abyssinian blue-winged goose. These geese, which appear to have little fear of man, have the most restricted range of any of the sheldgeese. Ganders have a peculiar stance and commonly parade about with their heads almost resting on their backs, with feathers fluffed out around them. Unlike most members of this tribe, the upperwing coverts of these birds are pale blue instead of white.*

7.29 *Flock of Egyptian geese.*

7.30 *The Cape Barren goose is unique in its possession of a short bill and pale greenish yellow cere. These birds are essentially dove grey overall, but their heads are paler and they generally have a white crown. The sexes are basically the same in appearance but ganders can be slightly larger. Eye color is sometimes described as hazel brown in the literature, but eyes I have seen are more peach-colored. Established breeders are generally encountered in pairs, but non-breeding birds tend to be gregarious and may form flocks of up to 300 geese. Very defensive during the breeding season, these birds establish territories between one and 1½ acres in extent. Some local farmers consider them to be pests, but despite this, there seems to be very little poaching.*

7.30

their wings formidable weapons—both features that are painfully well-known to anyone who has handled one of these powerful birds.

As a breeding species, Cape Barren geese are restricted to small and windswept, often uninhabited, islands off the south Australian coast. The largest breeding concentration appears to be in the Furneaux Island group, which contains islands varying in size from 20 to 2500 acres. These islands are incapable of providing enough food for the geese on a year-round basis, so they flock up and move to coastal regions of the mainland during the nonbreeding season. Essentially grazing birds, they seldom enter the water, except when wounded, molting, or pursued with their young; and the greatly reduced webbing on their feet reflects an evolutionary trend toward a semi-terrestrial existence. Their salt glands are reasonably well developed, and they are therefore able to survive in regions with little or no fresh water.

The gander's voice is a loud trumpeting call, but the female's is an often-repeated low swine-like grunt that is responsible for the vernacular name "pig goose." Except for this difference in voices and the slightly superior size of the male, the sexes are identical. On the wing, they vocalize frequently.

Unlike most waterfowl, these geese generally copulate ashore. The ganders usually do most of the nest building, and while ground nesting is typical, they will upon occasion take to tree nesting. Upon hatching, the striking black and white goslings are most appealing. Their preen glands apparently do not become functional until they are approximately two weeks old, and the female may therefore rub the young with oil from her uropygial gland in an attempt to waterproof them. At approximately six weeks of age, young from different broods may merge to form nursery flocks, and up to 50 goslings have been recorded in such amalgamated groups.

In the wild, Cape Barren geese are apt to be wary and alert, and are not easily approached, but in captivity most tend to tame readily. During the breeding season (which occurs during the northern winter), they typically become extremely defensive, almost to the point of being violent, and propagators must exercise great care when maintaining them with other species of comparable size. They are not particularly uncommon in captivity and are bred on a fairly regular basis, but there are some signs that inbreeding may be a problem. In 1977, a number were imported from Australia into the United States by the Game Bird Center in Salt Lake City, Utah, in an attempt to strengthen blood lines. The imported wild birds were somewhat larger than the captive American birds, and it is believed that the new blood will greatly improve the reproductive potential.

Cape Barren geese are controversial with respect to status. Depending on one's source, the species is either considered endangered or abundant. It is believed that the initial decline of the species coincided with the emergence of the sealing industry in the Bass Strait. By the 1920s, sealing was no longer profitable, but by then some of the islands were inhabited by people who had developed a taste for these handsome geese and their eggs, and the population may have dipped as low as 900 individuals during the 1950s. Since that time, however, it has increased substantially.

Those who believe the birds are currently endangered suggest that no more than 5000 exist. But Tasmanian biologists (who are undoubtedly better acquainted with the situation) contend that the geese are far from endangered and are probably more numerous now than they have been at any time since the colonization of Australia by European man; the population, in fact, may even be increasing. Their conservative estimates set the total population at 16,000 to 20,000 birds. Agricultural activities on a number of the islands have proved to be beneficial to the geese, and they have responded favorably—perhaps too favorably on some islands, since they are now competing with those same agricultural activities. This has necessitated some population control, and approximately 750 geese were legally taken by hunters on Flinders Island in 1977, an action that caused a storm of protest. Cape Barren geese were introduced to the South Island of New Zealand during the late 1880s, and although this attempt met with little success, a few can still be encountered from time to time in the Otago region.

Shelducks are smaller than sheldgeese and generally more colorful, more adapted to an aquatic lifestyle, and significantly more omnivorous. Their bills are flatter, curved decidedly upward near the tip, and fitted with conspicuous lamellae. Drakes are usually slightly larger than the hens. Strong pair bonds are formed but are not as permanent as those of their larger relatives. Holes, cavities, or other sheltered locations are favorite nesting locales, and they lay a rather large number of eggs.

It is not uncommon among shelducks (and a number of sheldgeese as well) for females to initiate courtship, and they may incite a number of males in an apparent effort to get them to fight. Usually, when a female incites, the male immediately threatens and will often attack the indicated competitor. As a result, some propagators prefer to keep more than one drake, believing that the competition may increase breeding potential.

Depending on the species, shelduck males and females may or may not be similar in color and pattern, and in the case of the **New Zealand or paradise shelduck** (*Tadorna variegata*) the dissimilarities are striking. The almost totally black male is so unlike the more attractive white-headed female that they appear to be of different species. All shelducks apparently have two body molts each year, but with paradise shelducks, eclipse plumage is only really evident on the female. During the nonbreeding season, the rich chestnut color is replaced with a greyish plumage that is similar to that of the male, but the white head is retained at all times. Immatures resemble males somewhat, but young females may have some irregular white feathering on the head.

Paradise shelducks are the largest and most conspicuous of the indigenous New Zealand waterfowl, and are among the fiercest and

7.31

7.33

7.32

7.31 *Female Australian shelduck. Breeding pairs often return to the same nest site year after year. The 10 to 14 eggs are incubated by the female alone for 30 to 32 days. Young require some 50 to 70 days to fledge, at the end of which time the family group dissolves. During the molt, Australian shelducks tend to flock up at specific sites, which may be located as much as 400 miles from their nesting territories.*

7.32 *Pair of paradise shelducks. In flight, conspicuous white upperwing coverts form a prominent wing patch that is generally not visible when the birds are at rest. These shelducks frequently call on the wing. Although they have been subjected to pressure associated with habitat loss, there are some positive signs that they are adapting to the presence of pasture lands. Nests are generally well concealed on the ground or are located in tree hollows up to 20 feet above the ground.*

7.33 *Newly-hatched paradise shelduck. Like the young of other shelducks, the ducklings are boldly patterned and colored.*

151

most pugnacious of the shelducks. I once saw a pair savagely attack a family of grey ducks on a mud flat in New Zealand and quickly kill several ducklings for no apparent reason. These shelducks have been persecuted for years by both the Maoris and white men, and although they are highly adaptable and remain fairly widespread (and even common in some districts), the overall population has declined, probably due to over-hunting—this despite the fact that they are totally protected in many areas. The Maoris reportedly captured up to 5000 at a time when the birds were flightless during the molt. In general, however, they have been less affected by the presence of man than most forms of New Zealand wildfowl.

Exceedingly noisy birds, paradise shelducks tend to call in a duet whenever alarmed or excited, and at all times they chatter so much that even Delacour describes the noise as "positively tiresome." The low voice of the drake consists of raucous grunting sounds, whereas females repeatedly utter a loud, high-pitched, trumpeting call. The occurrence of these birds in wildfowl collections is somewhat sporadic, although in recent years some propagators have been particularly successful with them, and they have become more abundant in North America. However, considering the *total* captive population, the species is rather infrequently bred, and there appears to be a rather high incidence of infertility. It can be risky mixing them with other birds, particularly during the breeding season.

Largest of the shelducks is the **Australian shelduck** (*Tadorna tadornoides*) which is commonly known as the mountain duck in Australia and Tasmania. This local popular name is a misnomer, however, for contrary to a persistent belief that most of these birds move to the highlands during the breeding season, the species is actually much more abundant along the coast—even though a small segment of the population may shift to upland areas (up to 6000 feet) to breed. Shy and wary ducks, they are fond of salt and brackish water habitats, but may fly long distances seeking fresh water. For most of the year, they are not at all gregarious and typically are quite aggressive. Flocks consisting of a thousand or more birds have been documented, but it is probable that these larger aggregations consist primarily of molting birds.

The sexes are somewhat similar, but the male is larger. Also, females have a distinctive, highly variable white eye ring and a broad white patch at the base of the bill that the drakes lack. (These two white areas may be continuous in some cases, forming a large single area of white.) Drakes have an all-black head and a broad white ring at the base of the neck, as well as deep buff breasts that contrast with the more chestnut-colored breasts of the females, and a narrow white neck ring (which some females may also possess). When the male is in eclipse plumage, the buff color may turn to more of a yellowish brown, while the neck ring may become less clearly defined.

Australian shelducks are very vocal, especially on the wing. Characteristically, they tend to fly in long skeins, or even in "V" formation, and this is one way to readily identify them from a distance, since the only other Australian waterfowl that habitually fly in such a manner are the very different black swans. In flight, the large white wing patches of both sexes are particularly conspicuous. Outside of the breeding season, Australian shelducks are only rarely seen in trees, although they may perch on occasion.

As with most shelducks, the pair bond is very strong. Typically, the nest site is located in a tree hollow, often 60 to 70 feet above the ground (100 feet in at least one instance). But nest sites are variable,

7.34 *Pair of Australian shelducks; female on the right.*

7.35 *Pair of cape or South African shelducks with a half-grown duckling; the drake is on the right.*

and where trees are not available, rabbit burrows, caves, and limestone crevices are favored. The 5 to 14 white eggs are incubated by the female alone, and while she is so engaged, the male establishes a separate territory where the young will be reared. This brood territory may be up to three miles from the nest site and is rigorously defended. Upon hatching, the young are led overland and the family is reunited at the drake's territory. Territoriality breaks down somewhat as the young mature, and different broods may combine; at times, the ducklings are even abandoned by their parents prior to fledging.

In some areas, such as Victoria, these ducks are prone to cause agricultural damage, particularly to cereal and vegetable crops. They are not highly regarded as gamebirds, but may nevertheless be subjected to some local hunting pressure; at the present time, however, there is no need for concern over their status. Australian shelducks are not particularly uncommon in captivity, but they are not prolific breeders. Imported Australian stock has not reached America for many years, and it may be that an infusion of new blood is required to reinvigorate the captive gene pool.

The **South African or cape shelduck** (*Tadorna cana*) is essentially a sedentary and shy species, which is, despite its fairly restricted range, not particularly uncommon. Known as "berggans" to the South Africans, they are most often associated with marsh and river bank habitat. Some individuals live around farms in a semi-domesticated state, although in a number of regions they may be regarded as agricultural pests. The sexes are dissimilar, and an irregular white blotch on the face of the female easily distinguishes her from the significantly larger grey-headed drake.

Even though birds of this species are monogamous, females may outnumber males by as much as four to one—a very curious situation. When nesting, cape shelducks sometimes utilize abandoned aardvark or porcupine burrows that may be located more than a half-mile from water, and in some cases, the nest itself may be placed 20 feet back from the entrance of the usurped burrow. Pairs with up to thirteen young have been reported, but eight appears to be more typical.

Seasonally gregarious, particularly during the flightless molt, cape shelducks are at other times almost as pugnacious as paradise shelducks. But because they are handsome and ornamental, they have become popular avicultural birds all the same. Some of them possess very distinct personalities and can develop into real "characters." For example, a female at Sea World was continuously underfoot and followed staff members everywhere, even into the office. This pesky bird chattered continuously and loudly, and in the opinion of most who had to put up with her, excessively. In captivity, cape shelducks should not be kept with the closely-related ruddy shelducks, as they will readily hybridize. The species is well established and commonly bred.

The wide-ranging **ruddy shelduck** (*Tadorna ferruginea*) is greatly admired for its indescribably beautiful buff and cinnamon coloration and glossy iridescent green speculum, as well as for its black bill, legs, and feet. Females may be darker than their mates, with paler faces, and they lack the small black collar which is typical of the drakes. There can be a great deal of individual variation in these collars, as they may be narrow and indistinct or quite broad—and during the nonbreeding season, they may disappear altogether or become very obscure. Interestingly, ducklings that have the palest down when they hatch develop into the adults with the most richly colored plumage, becoming more attractive than their nest mates.

7.36

7.37

7.38

7.36 *Ruddy shelducks. The nests of this species may be located in a variety of places, but they are essentially cavity nesters. As with many hole-nesting ducks, incubating females will often hiss like a snake to discourage intruders, and a defending drake may fly at the intruder in a threatening manner.*

7.37 *Male cape shelduck. The low position in the water is typical of the species.*

7.38 *Female cape shelduck. These birds commonly congregate on islands or mudbanks, where they spend most of the day sleeping or preening. Nesting birds are fond of aardvark burrows and, in at least one case, a nest was located 27 feet inside the entrance of such a burrow.*

7.39

7.39 *Drake ruddy shelduck.*

7.40 *Black-backed or Moluccan radjah shelduck. These birds are very vocal, and in the thickly vegetated areas where they occur, they are generally heard before they are seen.*

7.40

Also known as brahminy ducks, these birds have adapted themselves to a wide variety of habitats, and are a most successful species. Their range is extensive, and breeding strongholds extend from the Black Sea through most of southern Russia to Mongolia and China, with a separate population in northeast Africa. Considered essentially a freshwater species, they seldom visit maritime coastal habitats. Unfortunately, there appears to be a drastic decline in numbers occurring at the limits of their range, and some fears have been expressed regarding their continued status as a breeding bird of Europe. In Nepal, they are said to fly about and land like pigeons on rocky pinnacles high up on forbidding mountainsides, and in some areas they may nest as high as 17,000 feet. Out-of-range stragglers have occasionally been observed in Greenland and Iceland.

Like their close relatives the cape shelducks, ruddy shelducks generally swim with the head erect, but with the front half of the body riding low in the water and the posterior held high. They are, however, very terrestrial and can often be found some distances from water. They may perch on rocks and even in trees. Essentially omnivorous nocturnal feeders, these birds have allegedly been observed feeding on the remains of human bodies thrown into the Ganges River in India, and they will also readily resort to feeding on garbage.

Jealous and quarrelsome birds, they can be dreadfully noisy, and their treatment of other waterfowl species often leaves a great deal to be desired. While they may flock up to some degree during the winter or when molting, they are essentially an aggressive and anti-social species.

The voices of the two sexes are similar, but the male's is not as loud and can best be described as a high-pitched nasal whooping call. Nest sites vary, but include holes in cliffs, in banks or trees, in crevices in the walls of abandoned buildings, or even in old raptor nests. Natives of Tibet and Mongolia consider ruddy shelducks to be sacred and regard them as excellent watchdogs since they raise a fuss whenever disturbed. In India, on the other hand, they are held in disdain by some hunters because their calls warn other animals when a stalk is in progress. Almost all waterfowl collections include at least one pair of these shelducks, and it is relatively easy to get them to breed; indeed, at times it is difficult to stop them.

The two races of **Radjah shelducks** (*Tadorna radjah*) from Australia, New Guinea, and some surrounding islands, are perhaps the most beautiful and specialized of the six living species of shelducks. Smallest of the tribe as well, these little ducks are noisy and fussy, but not nearly as foul-tempered as some of their near relatives. Both sexes are similar in appearance, and both can be quite vocal, even on the wing. The call of the female resembles a harsh rattle, and the male's can best be described as a hoarse whistle. They commonly nest in tree cavities, and perch readily. Their flight is relatively strong and maneuverable, and they prefer to fly through wooded areas rather than over them.

Favored habitats appear to be brackish water mudflats and the mangrove-fringed lower reaches of tropical rivers, but they may also frequent freshwater swamps and lagoons during the wet season. As a rule, however, their movements are quite restricted and they do not tend to wander far. Usually encountered in small groups (probably family parties), they may form small flocks during the dry season. Preferred food appears to be invertebrates (mostly small molluscs), but they do consume limited amounts of algae and other vegetation as well. As a rule, these birds feed ashore or in shallow water that usually does not exceed several inches in depth.

The Australian race (*T. r. rufitergum*) is presently confined to the coastal tropics of northern Australia, although their range was formerly more extensive. Thus far, they have suffered a great deal from direct persecution (such as shooting), and comparatively little from habitat destruction. Unfortunately, they make tempting targets, and many are shot in spite of the fact that they are not legal gamebirds and are not even particularly good eating. In the long run, however, loss of habitat in the coastal tropical wetlands will be far more detrimental.

Sometimes referred to as red-backed radjahs or burdekin ducks by the Aussies, pure Australian birds are extremely rare in American wildfowl collections (possibly no more than two aged males as of early 1979), and it may be that no more than one or two exist in Europe. Moluccan or black-backed radjah shelducks (*T. r. radjah*), on the other hand, are frequently maintained, and while they are usually difficult to breed initially, they can be considered prolific once they do commence. Despite their reputation as very aggressive and territorial birds in the wild, these are among the most desirable and popular of the shelducks, for they are by far the gentlest in captivity. Their secondary feathers are surprisingly long, and as a result, even pinioned birds are capable of sustained flight—an ability that has taken some propagators by surprise. Even as full-winged birds, however, they generally remain on the grounds.

Common or European shelducks (*Tadorna tadorna*) demonstrate a decided preference for salt water, and frequent sandy and muddy coasts and estuaries. Unlike other shelducks, they are quite gregarious. Ranging widely throughout Europe and Asia, they generally wander inland only during migration, and are usually encountered no more than a mile in either direction from the coast — although stragglers have been sighted from time to time off Iceland and even Massachusetts.

Their bright red bills and the bold colors and patterns of the adults have long made European shelducks avicultural favorites, and they

7.41 *Like most waterfowl, ruddy shelducks may engage in vigorous wing flapping after preening or bathing.*

7.42 *Australian or red-backed radjah shelduck. An arboreal species, these birds usually roost in green trees and appear to prefer the paperbark tree. Although they are not a legal game species, a number of red-backed radjahs are shot nonetheless, presumably because they are conspicuous and are slow to leave the ground.*

7.43 *Pair of European shelducks. These are rather gregarious birds, except during the spring and early summer.*

7.44 *Moluccan radjah shelduck duckling.*

7.45 When their young are threatened, European shelducks may attempt to draw the intruder away by flying about in a conspicuous manner and vocalizing loudly.

7.46 Pair of European shelducks with the female in the foreground preening. The large, fleshy, blood-red knob on the drake's upcurved bill is easy to see. After the young hatch, they are led to feeding areas, where they remain with their parents for about two and a half weeks and then may join groups of up to 100 young. Adults may remain with their broods until they fledge (45 to 50 days), but such behavior is apparently uncommon. Some broods are largely independent at 15 to 20 days of age and manage to survive without adult assistance.

are common in wildfowl collections everywhere. During the breeding season, the knob at the base of the bill on larger males becomes enlarged and fleshy, and brilliant carmine-red in color. Due to their pattern and coloration, these birds are extremely conspicuous, and possibly their preference for feeding primarily at dusk is an effort to escape the attention of predators. Unlike other shelducks, their calls are soft and high-pitched melodious whistles.

European shelducks feed extensively on small saltwater snails, and the size of their territories may be directly related to the density of the preferred molluscs. Like some other avian species, they may stamp their feet on the ground, and this has been interpreted by some as an attempt to bring worms or other invertebrates to the surface. However, it is more likely that this action loosens the soil structure so that the birds can dip their bills into the mud more easily in their quest for food.

The coastal people of Germany refer to these shelducks as "cave geese" because they are particularly fond of burrows as nesting sites. They do not excavate the holes, but rather use the abandoned tunnels of rabbits, foxes, or marmots. On occasion, haystacks or even farm buildings may be utilized, often some distance from water. Sometimes more than one female will lay in the same nest, perhaps as the result of a shortage of adequate nesting sites. The typical clutch size is 10 or 11

eggs, but up to 50 have been recorded from a single dump nest. Only one female incubates these multiple clutches, and not infrequently, most of the eggs successfully hatch. Reportedly, clutches may even be laid in the active nests of other wildfowl species, such as goosanders or red-breasted mergansers. If the nest or young are threatened, the adults may fly about in a conspicuous manner, attempting to draw the intruder away. After hatching takes place, the family moves to salt or brackish water.

Many adults may desert their half-grown young to engage in a molt migration, and when this happens the ducklings of many pairs often gather together in large groups, which are sometimes referred to as crèches. The crèches are generally left in the charge of a few adult-plumaged birds, and it is possible that these "guardians" may be nonbreeding subadults. On some occasions, such an assemblage of young may exceed 100 individuals. Most of the European population migrates to the North Sea to molt, and up to 100,000 ducks may gather in traditional areas, while another 30,000 choose to molt at Mediterranean or Black Sea sites.

A seventh species, the **crested Korean or Kuroda's shelduck** (*Tadorna cristata*), is known from only four specimens (one Russian, three Korean) and has probably been extinct since the 1920s—although it is possible that a small population may still cling to exis-

7.47

7.48

7.47 *Pair of Patagonian crested ducks. While the crest is obvious in this picture, it is held down along the back of the neck much of the time and is not easy to see. After the breeding season, these birds can often be encountered in small groups in coastal areas. They forage extensively among the rocks and kelp that are exposed by the falling tide, feeding mainly on items of animal origin. These opportunistic feeders take advantage of offal from slaughter houses, or even feed on the leftovers found in areas of human habitation.*

7.48 *This mount of a "Korean crested shelduck" is a composite of a number of different birds. Only three true specimens of this extinct crested shelduck are known to exist.*
PHOTO PROVIDED BY
GLEN SMART

tence in some remote portion of eastern Russia. The first described specimen, a male taken in 1877 near Vladivostok, Russia, was believed at that time to be a hybrid, perhaps between a falcated duck and a ruddy shelduck. The second, a female, was collected in 1917, and shortly thereafter another drake was taken. The last bird, also a male, was collected in 1924. The original Vladivostok specimen is currently housed in the Copenhagen Museum, whereas two of the others are in Tokyo, Japan. The remaining specimen has apparently disappeared over the years.

There was an unconfirmed sighting by two Russian students of a trio of Korean crested shelducks (one male and two females) amongst a flock of harlequin ducks southwest of Vladivostok in 1964, and still another unsubstantiated sighting occurred in 1943. In 1917, three were allegedly dropped from a flock of six in northwestern Korea, but unfortunately none of these were salvaged for science. Interestingly, the preserved specimens are in every respect identical to figures in ancient Japanese prints and Chinese tapestries (indicating that the species was indeed valid), and old Japanese records suggest that Korean shelducks were regularly imported to Japan from Korea during the early part of the 18th Century. Why they died out is not known.

Korean crested shelducks were very attractive birds. Drakes had a long drooping crest which was colored a glossy greenish black, and their crowns, foreheads, napes, and hind necks were similarly colored. But for a small black patch on the chin, the rest of the head and neck was grey. The breast and upper mantle were greenish black, the rump and tail were black with cinnamon rufous under the tail, and the remainder of the plumage was essentially grey. Males had red bills and feet, whereas those of the female were apparently fleshy pink (although some of the literature describes the legs as yellow). In both sexes, the iris was brown.

The plumage of the female differed markedly from the male's, and in many ways, females were more attractive than their mates. The crown, crest, and hind neck were black, and a distinct black line extended in front of and below the eye, producing an eyeglass-like effect. The remainder of the head and neck was white, and body plumage was a dull brown clearly lined with white. The coloration of the wing was similar to that of other shelducks. Immatures, ducklings, and eggs have apparently never been seen or described.

The two races of South American **crested ducks** (*Lophonetta specularioides*) are rather sedentary and aggressive birds. They are noted for slim bodies, relatively long tails, and bright metallic black speculums, which are washed with purplish or greenish bronze. (The speculums are remarkably similar to those of bronze-winged ducks.) In general, drakes tend to be larger and may be more brightly colored.

7.49 *Pair of Andean crested ducks. These high-altitude birds may be more common than believed, and in Chile they are said to be the most abundant duck of the "puna" zone. Vegetation at that altitude is scanty, so nests are generally located in grassy areas around the edges of lakes, or on individual tussocks in boggy areas near lagoons or salt marshes.*

7.50 *A small flock of Patagonian crested ducks with a pair of Chiloe wigeons in the Beagle Channel, Tierra del Fuego, Argentina.*

7.51 *Andean crested ducks are larger, lighter in color, and more aggressive than their Patagonian counterparts, and they can be easily differentiated by their yellow (rather than red) eyes. Note that the crest is being held down along the neck and is not obvious.*

7.52 *(Opposite Page) A family of Falkland Island flightless steamer ducks in the thick, leathery inshore kelp (Macrocystes). Kelp which is this dense is difficult to swim through and swimming birds often avoid it.*

Both sexes have ragged or irregular crests, and although the male's is larger, this is not always obvious, since the crests are often held down along the back of the neck.

Crested ducks are most peculiar birds, and it is possible that they are more closely related to bronze-winged ducks than to shelducks. Females do incite the males, which is a typical shelduck behavior, but the extreme overall aggressiveness of these birds is probably more a result of their feeding ecology than of any close relationship to the equally aggressive shelducks. Johnsgard suggests that crested ducks and bronze-winged ducks bridge the evolutionary gap between the typical mallard-like ducks and the pintail group, basing his opinion partly on the appearance of the downy young. As a result, he has shifted *Lophonetta* to the dabbling duck tribe and placed them in the large genus *Anas*. (They were formerly in this genus, but Delacour argued that the crested ducks were a transitional species, and based on their unusual shape and proportions, as well as their shelduck-like behavior, he maintained that they were deserving of a separate genus—*Lophonetta*.) A relationship with marbled teal is possible, but this has yet to be documented.

Patagonian crested ducks (*L. s. specularioides*) are characterized by their brilliant ruby-red eyes. They are frequently observed in salt water

along the southern coast of Argentina and Chile, and on the Falkland Islands. During the nonbreeding season, they gather together in small groups to forage among the rocks and kelp beds that are exposed by the tides. Essentially carnivorous, they will consume almost anything of animal origin they encounter. This even seems to include offal from local slaughter houses, although it may be that the ducks are really feeding on the invertebrates (such as crustaceans, isopods, larvae, and the like) that are associated with floating offal. Patagonian crested ducks are not generally thought to be overly gregarious, but I have seen fairly large flocks of them during the austral fall in Tierra del Fuego. (It is possible, of course, that these groups were composed primarily of subadults.)

Birds of the yellow-eyed Andean race (*L. s. alticola*) inhabit areas surrounding mountain lakes at altitudes between 10,000 and 15,000 feet, and appear to be most common in the Chilean Andes. They are somewhat larger and lighter in color than the lowland birds, and their speculums tend to be darker and more purplish without the greenish reflection. Both races tend to be highly territorial, bad tempered, and solitary during the breeding season, and will clear their nesting territory of other birds (although the reputation of *alticola* is worse in this regard than that of *specularioides*).

During courtship, the drakes frequently swim backwards, seemingly without effort. Males can be quite vocal and frequently utter buzzy

7.53 *Flightless steamer ducks are huge birds with massive heads and broad powerful bills. During the breeding season, they are very aggressive, to the point of being violent. They dive extremely well and feed extensively on molluscs, crustaceans, and even small fish. Eating mainly at high tide, they forage heavily in shellfish banks or in the extensive kelp beds that are common in southern waters.*

whistling sounds, whereas females sometimes sound vaguely like barking dogs, and in this respect are very much like bronze-winged ducks. Crested ducks will sometimes use an abandoned nest, such as that of a horned coot, instead of constructing one of their own. Both sexes participate in the rearing of the young. The Patagonian race is more common in wildfowl collections and breeds with great frequency. In captivity, their aggressive nature is such that they should not be maintained with other waterfowl if the exhibit is small.

The final group of tadornids, the massive primitive steamer ducks of southern South America and the Falkland Islands, are very peculiar in many respects, and have frustrated anatid taxonomists over the years. Currently, three distinct species are recognized, two of which are virtually flightless. All three are remarkably similar in appearance, and the flightlessness of two was the source of much early taxonomic confusion—because it led to the belief that young birds were capable of flight, but lost this ability as they matured. Not surprisingly, the flying species is considerably smaller and trimmer than the other two, with significantly longer wings.

Steamer ducks are probably the most specialized of all the diving ducks, and have an undeniable superficial resemblance to the eiders of the north. However, the two groups are not even distantly related, and the resemblance is strictly the result of convergent evolution. Traditionally, steamer ducks have been linked with shelducks and sheldgeese because of similarities of downy young, white wing specu-

lums, bony wing knobs, aggressive behavior, and permanent pair bonds. Feather protein analysis also indicates that they should be classified with the shelduck tribe. On the other hand, their skeletons suggest that steamer ducks may be, in fact, aberrant dabbling ducks. Johnsgard considers them bizarre enough and distinct enough to warrant a separate tribe of their own—the Tachyerini. But in the minds of some biologists, their taxonomic status is still far from being resolved.

Flying steamer ducks (*Tachyeres patachonicus*) inhabit the Falkland Islands and Tierra del Fuego, as well as mainland South America northward through Patagonia to Peninsula Valdez on the Argentine side and north to about 37° south latitude on the Chilean west coast. **Falkland Island steamer ducks** (*Tachyeres brachypterus*) are theoretically restricted to those islands, and for many years it has been accepted that **Magellanic steamer ducks** (*Tachyeres pteneres*) range along the coast of South America in an area roughly corresponding to that of the flying steamer duck. But Maurice Rumboll, the leading specialist on Argentine waterfowl, is of the opinion that nearly all of the flightless steamer ducks which occur from the Lamarie Channel (between the tip of South America and Staten Island) northward to the Valdez Peninsula are either Falkland Island steamer ducks or are representatives of an undescribed species (or, at the very least, a subspecies). If the Atlantic coast birds do ultimately prove to be Falkland Island steamers, one is forced to speculate on how the same flightless birds could have gotten there. Did they evolve on the mainland and somehow make their way to the Falkland Islands, or vice versa? (Rumboll also suggests that the birds which are currently accepted as Magellanic steamers are, in fact, restricted to the Beagle Channel and points west.)

Numerous early accounts claimed that flightless steamer ducks weighed up to 22 pounds, and Captain Cook himself reported weights between 29 and 30 pounds. These are obviously exaggerations, and 12 to 14 pounds for male Magellanic steamers is much more realistic—although a 14-pound duck is nevertheless huge. Females are somewhat smaller. When "steaming," these powerful ducks lower their heads and furiously thrash the water with their wings and feet, moving forward at a surprisingly rapid rate and creating a large wake as they do so. They swim so low in the water that sometimes their backs are awash, and speeds of 10 to 15 knots have been recorded. Undoubtedly, their huge feet help them to achieve such speeds; in the case of the Magellanic steamer, the spread webs may span six inches across. Early sailors suggested that the speed and tremendous foaming of these birds was reminiscent of a 19th Century side-wheeler steam boat traveling at full tilt, and this was the origin of their descriptive vernacular name. (Their incredibly huge heads have prompted the native residents to also call them loggerheads.)

Males have a variety of peculiar vocalizations, including cough-like sneezes, bullfrog-like grunts, rasping grunts, mechanical-sounding "ticking" grunts, and whistle-like sibilant grunts. Females also grunt, usually repeating a long series of low-pitched calls. Many of these calls must be heard to be believed; they simply defy written or verbal description.

While steamer ducks are excellent divers, they commonly up-end to forage as well. They may also use their wings for swimming under water. Shellfish and other marine organisms constitute their main diet, but they have been known to feed on offal as well. Their massive bills are well designed for crushing large, tough invertebrates, and birds I have collected often had their crops crammed full of two- to three-inch-long mussels. These are unbelievably powerful and tough birds, and no-one who has ever had to skin one for a museum will ever forget the experience. The job is so difficult that museum preparators consider one such task to be one too many—and from firsthand experience, I certainly agree.

Drakes assist the hens in rearing the young, but due to the greatly reduced wing size that is associated with flightlessness, females cannot very effectively brood larger ducklings, and the young may consequently bunch closely together for warmth. The downy ducklings somewhat resemble shelduck young, but have less spotting and less contrasting colors. They are capable of diving shortly after hatching.

Steamer ducks probably do not breed until at least their second year. They are long-lived, and apparently they mate for life, remaining together the entire time. Territorial fights can be vicious and bloody confrontations; often, both partners of a pair gang up on an intruder, and on occasion the loser is drowned. Nests are most often located near water, are generally well concealed, and much down is used to line them.

Flightlessness usually indicates a lack of terrestrial predators, and is a condition generally associated with island species, but Magellanic flightless steamer ducks successfully inhabit mainland South America, where land carnivores are not infrequent. Undoubtedly, their large size and incredibly savage dispositions contribute to their success.

7.54

7.55

7.56

7.54 *Flightless steamer ducks sometimes attack using the submerged sneak, in which only the head, bill, and top of the back are out of the water. They can move surprisingly fast when swimming in such a manner.*

7.55 *When "steaming," steamer ducks beat the water with their powerful feet while striking the surface with alternate wing strokes, churning up much water in the process. The birds to the left are shags.*

7.56 *Male Falkland Island steamer duck, with a brood of young to the left. Magellanic penguins and steamer ducks are commonly found in the same area.*

7.57

7.58

7.57 *Family of flying steamer ducks.*

7.58 *Pair of flying steamer ducks with Patagonian kelp geese.*

7.59 *Female flying steamer duck in flight, displaying the prominent white wing patches.*
PHOTO BY JOE JEHL

7.60 *Incubating female flying steamer duck in Argentina. The five to nine eggs are incubated by the female alone, but the vigilant drake remains in the vicinity. The eggs are much smaller and have thinner shells than those of their larger flightless relatives.*
PHOTO BY JOE JEHL

7.61 *(Opposite Page) Pair of Magellanic flightless steamer ducks with several male Patagonian kelp geese in Tierra del Fuego.*

7.59

7.60

Adults are sometimes victims of foxes, however, and eggs are apparently regularly taken by foxes and caracaras. Skuas and kelp gulls also prey upon downy young.

The Magellanic species is not only the largest and heaviest of the steamer ducks, it is the coarsest and palest in color as well. Females are considerably smaller than males, have browner heads, and are more wine-colored dorsally. Drakes of all three species are noted for conspicuous orange-yellow bills, while females have bills which are more yellowish or yellow-green (except for flying females, whose bills are yellow or reddish, shading to blue). The tails of all three species are distinctly curled, particularly on drakes.

Falkland Island flightless steamer ducks have much more red on the head and throat than their mainland counterparts, and are somewhat more attractive. Younger drakes of this species have grey and white heads, but older males may have pure white heads. Females typically have dark brown heads with distinct eye rings and eye streaks, and they are generally more reddish than their mates. Most of the feathers are edged with maroon, and the sides of the head and neck are brownish.

From a distance, Magellanic flightless steamer ducks can be difficult to accurately separate from male flying steamer ducks, although the smaller and trimmer flying birds have proportionally smaller bills and a white speculum that is much more extensive. The flying birds are not nearly as aggressive, and they are the only steamer duck that is considered edible—which may account for their relative scarcity in the Falkland Islands, where they are locally known as canvasbacks. Surprisingly, some observers have told me that these ducks can rise from the water with the ease of a mallard, but I have never seen any evidence of this ability.

Unlike the other two steamer ducks, which are strictly coastal in distribution, flying steamer ducks tend to frequent inland rivers and freshwater lakes when nesting, sometimes at relatively high elevations. During the nonbreeding season, however, I have often observed both Magellanic and flying steamer ducks side by side in the same coastal habitat. When nesting, flying steamer ducks appear to prefer small islets instead of shore locations.

Steamer duck nests are usually fairly well concealed within tussock grass or amidst dry kelp, and can be difficult to locate. From time to time, unoccupied Magellanic penguin burrows may be taken over by the Falkland Island birds. These large ducks (*brachypterus*) are often indifferent to human presence, and I have frequently observed them in the Port Stanley harbor, sometimes even loafing along the shore in town. While it has not been well-documented, these ducks may be regularly preyed upon by southern sea lions.

Steamer ducks are not rare in the wild, although some populations may be subjected to local persecution. Crab fishermen in the Beagle Channel, for example, have recently adopted the disgusting and repugnant practice of baiting their traps with steamer duck carcasses. In waterfowl collections, steamer ducks are rare—but even if they were readily available, it is unlikely that they would be very popular because of their intolerable and savage dispositions. Under no circumstances can these hostile ducks be mixed with any wildfowl (or most other birds), as they would kill them instantly, regardless of size. (In one case, an albatross was attacked and killed, and even swans have been killed.) Their captive scarcity is rather unfortunate nonetheless, because in spite of their obvious temperamental shortcomings, most captive steamer ducks that I am familiar with were extremely endearing. A few Falkland Island birds have been reared in Europe in recent years, but steamer ducks were first bred in captivity in 1966 at the Philadelphia Zoo. As of early 1979, I could only account for one steamer duck in North America (at Sea World in San Diego).

8
Dabbling
or
Surface-Feeding Ducks
Anatini

orty-five species (and 58 subspecies) make up this, the largest and most diverse of the ten traditional waterfowl tribes, and the huge and geographically widespread genus *Anas* alone consists of 38 species with some 52 subspecies—including ducks that are among the most numerous of all waterfowl. The diversity and relative abundance of dabblers makes it obvious that they are the most successful of all waterfowl; and in fact, the wild ducks familiar to most people fall within this group. For the most part, dabblers are relatively unspecialized and have been able to exploit a wide variety of environmental conditions. Cosmopolitan in distribution, they even inhabit numerous tiny remote oceanic islands, and some show transcontinental migration patterns. Many are mallard-like in form and behavior, but a number of aberrant debatable species are tentatively included in the group as well. Males are commonly referred to as drakes, while the female or hen is simply known as the duck.

Collectively, dabblers are smaller and have relatively shorter tails than the shelducks of the preceding chapter. More aquatic as well, they have shorter legs that are located farther back on their bodies, and they walk with more of a waddling gait as a result. In approximately half of the dabbler species, males and females are similar in appearance, with both sexes usually rather somber in coloration (and sometimes both brightly colored)—whereas the remaining species are

8.2

8.1 (Opposite Page) *South Georgia pintail on a small tarn on South Georgia Island.*

8.2 *Drake mallard and gadwall in flight. Most dabbling ducks are powerful and swift fliers, and those which nest in the far north generally undertake substantial migrations.*

as most people think of ducks, with males brightly, often brilliantly, colored and females cryptically colored and rather dull. The breeding or nuptial plumage of some species can also be highly ornamental. Males of most northern species molt into an obscure eclipse plumage shortly after the breeding season and resemble their mates for usually two to three months (although males of some species, such as the garganey teal, may retain the dull plumage for up to nine or ten months). Accurate species recognition during this period can be most perplexing, even for experienced waterfowl enthusiasts.

An iridescent, metallic, mirror-like speculum (or "wing window") is typical of most dabblers. This conspicuous wing patch is not restricted to males, and it may function as a flashing flight signal that helps to maintain the cohesion of a flock in flight. In most cases, dabbling duck wings are fairly long and pointed, allowing the birds to become airborne readily, without the preliminary run over the surface of the water that is necessary for some other waterfowl groups.

8.3 *Dozing American black ducks. Mainly surface feeders, black ducks do dive on occasion as deep as ten feet. A hardy species, these are primarily resident in the boreal forest zone; but during the winter, much of the population occupies marine habitat. They seldom travel in large flocks.*

8.4 *Drake Greenland mallard. Larger and lighter in color than common mallards, these ducks are nonmigratory and generally move to the coast during the winter — usually to areas where the current is swift enough to prevent ice from forming.*

Also known as river or puddle ducks, dabblers prefer freshwater habitats as a rule, but may frequent salt water as well, particularly during migration. Seldom, however, do they nest close to the sea-shore. Normally surface feeders, they also often reach under the water as far as they can stretch to obtain specific food items, and it is not uncommon to observe them feeding upended with only their bottoms exposed. As a group, they are not regarded as accomplished divers, but they may occasionally dive, and most ducklings do so readily.

Most members of this tribe typically breed during their first year and lay relatively large clutches of eggs. In fact, definite pair bond behavior has been recorded within six months of hatching with some species, such as the mallard. Unlike swans and geese, however, the pair bond is not particularly strong, and a different mate is usually courted annually. As a rule, the hen alone incubates and cares for the brood, but predictably, there are notable exceptions. Females usually have louder voices and typically quack harshly, while males generally emit whistling or wheezy vocalizations.

Perhaps the most typical duck of the tribe is the **common or northern mallard** (*Anas p. platyrhynchos*), which is probably the best known and most easily recognized of all wild ducks — and possibly the most popular of all gamebirds as well. Mallards rank among the most successful of all avian species, and throughout their wide distribution (which emcompasses most of the Northern Hemisphere) they occupy a tremendous variety of habitats. No wild duck is more tolerant of human presence or even disturbance, and they have been able to adjust well to a fast-changing, human-dominated world; with the result that they are almost everywhere the most abundant duck. Generally considered ground nesters, they will sometimes use a tree cavity and will also take quickly to man-made nest boxes, especially if these are over water.

As the progenitor of the domestic duck, mallards were well-known to ancient man. Just when they were initially domesticated remains a mystery, but the Egyptians certainly kept them several centuries be-fore Christ. The Chinese were probably maintaining them even ear-lier, and some historians believe that the mallard may have been the first domesticated bird, pre-dating even the chicken. *All* domestic duck breeds, with the sole exception of the barnyard muscovy, can be traced back to the mallard, and many of the domestic varieties still retain the characteristic metallic green head and curled tail of the wild mallard drake. (The best known of all the domestic varieties, of course, is the omnipresent white Pekin duck, which children recognize as the "Easter duck," and which looks nothing like a mallard.)

Mallards thrive in captivity and reproduce readily; in fact, too readily from an avicultural standpoint. Because many of the dabbling ducks are quite closely related to the mallard, interbreeding is not infrequent, even in the wild, and at least 45 mallard hybrid types have been documented. In captivity, mallards and their near relatives will breed with almost any duck species, and crosses can occur easily and quickly if a collection is not properly managed. Hybridization can be most unfortunate and should be discouraged, because one of the major responsibilities of a sincere propagator is the maintenance of pure bloodlines. Mallards, in their zeal, make this task most difficult and challenging.

Mallards that inhabit the coastal regions of southern Greenland tend to be larger and lighter in color, and are considered to be a distinct subspecies (*A. p. conboschas*). Birds of this race are associated with a marine habitat most of the year, and this may explain why they

8.5

possess much larger nasal glands, since this adaptation facilitates the discharge of excess salt. During the breeding season, the habitat preferences of these ducks shift, and they seek freshwater lakes and streams, as well as fiord islands. Unlike the typical mallard, these birds have a greatly reduced migratory urge, and their movements can be considered essentially local—a somewhat unique trait for a northern species. It is curious to note that the sexual maturity for both sexes may require up to two years. Why they should be so different in this regard from the nominate race is unclear.

Most fresh-water food sources are covered by ice during the winter, so Greenland mallards depend entirely upon the sea for sustenance at that time, and during particularly severe winters many may die of starvation. When occupying coastal habitat, they feed extensively on marine invertebrates. This race is not overly familiar to aviculturists, although they are bred fairly regularly at the Wildfowl Trust. (As a point of interest, the North American mallard is said to be slightly larger than its Eurasian counterpart, but is not considered subspecifically distinct.)

The Hawaiian duck, Laysan teal, Mexican duck, Florida duck, and American black duck are all regarded as ancient offshoots of the common mallard, and some authorities unglamorously describe the island forms as insular, degenerate, and inbred mallards. However, the **American black duck** (*Anas rubripes*) is considered distinct enough to warrant full species status. Actually, these ducks are not

black, but rather a dark brownish color, so their popular name is a misnomer, and it might be more appropriate to revert to the old name of dusky duck. Drakes in nuptial plumage are slightly darker than their mates, and have clear yellowish green bills (as opposed to the olive color of the female). They have a speculum that tends to be more purple than the classic deep blue of the common mallard, and leg colorations may range from reddish orange to greenish, depending on the season, age, and sex. (Formerly, the red-legged birds were thought to constitute a "northern" race.)

Some waterfowlers consider black ducks to be the most intelligent, wildest, and most wary of North American ducks, regarding them highly as gamebirds. They make greater use of wooded habitats than do most of the other North American ducks in the genus *Anas*. When the inland waters freeze up, they shift to coastal waters and marshes to pass the winter. Demonstrating a greater fondness for salt water than do mallards, they will tolerate fairly rough seas. Black ducks also feed on more animal food than their close relatives do, particularly during the winter months.

In the eastern United States, these ducks may be the most numerous of the dabblers, but in regions where their ranges overlap, mallards will readily hybridize with them—a disturbing trend that appears to be on the increase. The overall population may be declining, and it is becoming clear that the more adaptable mallard is pushing the black ducks out. Black ducks are well established in captivity, but are not particularly popular because of their nondescript appearance and mallard-like habits.

The **Mexican duck** (*Anas p. diazi*), was formerly known as the New Mexican duck and accorded full specific status, but is presently thought to be merely a mallard race. Unlike mallards, however, these ducks are essentially nonmigratory and much more wary. The sexes are similar, but can be separated by bill color—that of the male being olive-green, while the female's has a black ridge along the top which shades to a light olive-green, with a minute amount of orange at the base.

Currently, the center of distribution is in central Mexico, where these ducks can be found in wetlands that are scattered throughout the otherwise arid environment. Much of their marsh habitat in the central uplands of Mexico has been usurped for other purposes, although man has slightly compensated the ducks for this loss by creating artificial lakes and impoundments. During times when abundant surface water is available, the reproductive potential is high, but it plummets during a drought.

The Mexican duck is not common, and may never have been overly abundant (the population was estimated to be roughly 5000 in the early 1960s). Until recently, many biologists believed the species to be endangered, but the current total population probably numbers between 16,000 and 40,000 birds, with fewer than 1000 in the United States. (While this may initially appear to be a large number, consider that the population of northern mallards in North America alone may exceed some 12,000,000 individuals.)

It has recently been established that most of the "Mexican ducks" inhabiting the United States are in reality probably mallard hybrids; and some 90 percent of *diazi* collected north of Mexico for museums are undoubtedly hybrids as well. The decline of the genetically pure

8.6 *Female Florida duck. Birds of this nondescript mallard race tend to stand more erect than their larger relatives.*

8.7 *Pair of Mexican ducks. These birds are considered to be wary and difficult to approach, and they are said to fly faster and more strongly than common mallards.*

8.8 *Pair of Laysan teal. Presently confined to Laysan Island, these obscure little ducks may have also occupied Lisianski Island at one time. They are considered to be endangered and the population is subject to extreme fluctuation. Even during the best of times, it has probably not exceeded 700 ducks.*

Mexican duck is mainly attributed to loss of habitat, hybridization with mallards, and (in the past) over-hunting. A number of birds have been reared in captivity and released to supplement the wild population, including more than 300 reared and released by the New Mexico Fish and Game Department between 1963 and 1970. Because of their dull appearance and their susceptibility to hybridization, these ducks are maintained in relatively few collections.

The **Florida duck** (*Anas p. fulvigula*) is similar in color to a female mallard, but is decidedly lighter than a black duck. The bill of the male is a bright yellow with a characteristic black spot at the base, whereas the female's is sprinkled with small black spots. Considered one of the most carnivorous of North American puddle ducks, these birds readily consume molluscs, insects, and reportedly, even small fish. They are nonmigratory and range throughout central and southern Florida, where they are generally encountered in pairs or small family groups. Prime breeding habitat consists of coastal marshes and prairies. Perhaps as a result of the less severe climatic conditions, the breeding season can be rather extended.

Most contemporary taxonomists consider the Florida duck to be a race of the mallard, but others believe them to be distinct enough to warrant full specific rank, complete with a subspecies of their own. However, this latter race, the so-called mottled duck (*A. f. maculosa*), is not generally regarded as separable. (However, *maculosa* does tend to have a shorter neck and darker head.) While some of these dull forms are fairly well established in captivity, they are not particularly popular, because they are so similar to other mallard races and must be maintained separately to avoid hybridization.

Both the **Hawaiian duck or Koloa** (*Anas wyvilliana*) and the **Laysan teal** (*Anas laysanensis*) are considered endangered in the wild state, partly as a result of island distributions that were limited to begin with, but primarily due to modern man's invasion of their island domain. However, the skill and diligence of waterfowl propagators over the years has resulted in the establishment of a large captive gene pool of these two forms. (Their current status has been more fully discussed in Chapter Fifteen.) Since the first captive breeding of Laysan teal in 1959, they have become common in waterfowl collections everywhere; indeed, a single pair acquired by the Wildfowl Trust in 1958 was responsible for over 400 descendants. Laysan teal exhibit

a great deal of individual variation with respect to the white on the head, but as a rule, older birds tend to have whiter heads.

In the case of the Hawaiian duck, it is my opinion that pitifully few *totally* pure individuals exist in collections outside of Hawaii, and most captive birds appear to be more reddish in color than the wild birds. Apparently, the native population is currently restricted to a wetland refuge in the Hanalei Valley on the island of Kauai, and their occurrence on other Hawaiian islands is casual, even though they once occupied all of the islands except Lanai and Kahoolawe. Captive-reared birds have been liberated on Oahu and Hawaii.

The shaky status of the Hawaiian duck (3000 estimated in 1967) is attributed to both habitat destruction brought about by the draining of their principal breeding and feeding areas and to the introduction of the predatory mongoose. Until recently, the mongoose did not occupy Kauai, but it is apparently established there now and presents a real threat. In former times, the primary cause for the population decline was over-hunting (back in the early 1920s the bag limit was 25 ducks a day).

8.9

The three Asian **spotbill ducks** (*Anas poecilorhyncha*) are so named for the large prominent yellow spot at the tip of the bill. Mallard-like in shape, they have proportionally longer necks. Strictly freshwater birds of lower altitudes, their habits are essentially the same as the common mallard. They are not such accomplished fliers, but since only one race is migratory, strong long-distance flight capability does not appear to be essential. There is some scanty evidence which suggests that males *may* participate in brood care.

The Indian spotbill (*A. p. poecilorhyncha*) is the most numerous of the spotbills in captivity, and in the wild is a highly sought gamebird. It is characterized by a prominent swollen orange-red spot at the base of the bill and a greenish blue speculum, as well as by a white band on the trailing edge of the secondaries. Chinese spotbills (*A. p. zonorhyncha*), on the other hand, have a blue speculum, lack the red bill spot, and are somewhat less distinctive overall. Out-of-range stragglers have been sighted in the Aleutian Islands, Alaska. This race is currently less numerous in captivity than *poecilorhyncha*, but formerly was the most common form, at least in Europe. More have become available in recent years, however, and it seems that they are becoming established again.

Burmese spotbills (*A. p. haringtoni*) may merely represent an intergrade population between the Indian and Chinese subspecies, and they could conceivably constitute a specious race, although Delacour believes it is valid. They more closely resemble the Indian birds than those of Chinese origin, even though the red spot at the base of the bill is usually absent. While they are totally unknown to aviculturists of this era, Delacour imported some from Japan to France in 1926, and prior to World War II they were relatively plentiful.

The **grey (or black) duck** complex (*Anas superciliosa*) inhabits the islands of the South Pacific. Mallard-like in appearance, these insular ducks are not particularly colorful but have striking buff and black facial lines. Some contemporary specialists also include the spotbilled ducks in this complex, considering them as merely the continental representatives.

The New Zealand grey duck (*A. s. superciliosa*) is not endangered in the true sense of the word, but may be in danger of being lost as a pure form in some regions. Mallards from Great Britain were first introduced into New Zealand in 1867, and following the liberation of hand-reared stock from North America between 1920 and 1940, they flourished. Once established, the mallards rapidly began to hybridize with the closely related indigenous grey ducks, and predictably, mallards are possibly now the most numerous and widespread of New

8.10

8.9 *Pair of pure Hawaiian ducks at Pohakuloa. Also an endangered species, these birds have been adversely affected by introduced predators.*

8.10 *The New Zealand grey duck is considered to be the most attractive of the three races of grey ducks.*

8.11 *Indian spotbill.*

8.12 *Chinese spotbill.*

169

8.13 *Pair of Pelew Island or lesser grey ducks. Dainty and attractive little ducks, these birds are rather wary and are very mallard-like in behavior, habits, voice, and display. Where subjected to persecution, they tend to become nocturnal.*

8.14 *Australian black (grey) duck. Widespread throughout Australia (except for the dry inland areas), these ducks nest in a wide variety of situations, including even deserted ibis nests or the nests of other aquatic birds. The birds which nest inland rarely nest on the ground and typically select sites in tree cavities or other elevated locations.*

Zealand's waterfowl. In many cases, the results of hybridization are obvious, but frequently they are not.

Nevertheless, sooner or later the mallards can be expected to dominate many populations, thus effectively absorbing the native grey duck. Recent studies do suggest, however, that mallards and subsequent hybrids may merely be occupying disrupted ecological niches which would otherwise be devoid of ducks as a result of human activity. (This is certainly the case along the River Avon where it flows through downtown Christchurch.) Fortunately, the integrity of the more remote New Zealand grey duck populations appears to be secure, and there is also a wild and wary population that occurs on Campbell Island which is said to be fairly abundant. Yet another population of grey ducks (probably *superciliosa*) resides on the subantarctic island of Macquarie, just north of the Antarctic Convergence.

The closely related Australian black duck (*A. s. rogersi*) is rather similar in size and appearance to *superciliosa* and enjoys a widespread distribution throughout the continent (except for the inland deserts). Possibly, these are the most abundant ducks of that country—but, as in New Zealand, introduced mallards are threatening some segments of the native population through absorption. The birds which occur on Pelew Island and other South Pacific islands (*A. s. pelewensis*) are the smallest of the grey ducks, and due to the varying size of birds inhabiting different islands, it is possible that more intensive study will encourage biologists to propose additional subspecies. All three races of grey ducks are fairly well established in captivity, but great care is required to prevent hybridization. The New Zealand birds are perhaps the most desirable, because of their distinctly and neatly marked faces.

The so-called Marianas mallard, or Oustalets duck (*Anas [p.] oustaleti*), which sometimes appears in the literature, is not a valid species, or even a race, but merely represents a hybrid between the common mallard of the north and the black duck of the south (*A. platyrhynchos* x *A. superciliosa*). They inhabit the islands of Guam, Saipan, and Tinian (although by 1974 those on Guam were thought to be gone). Because some Washington bureaucrats and their advisors consider these birds to be an "endangered species," plans are being formulated to insure their survival—perhaps even through captive propagation. Personally, I question the wisdom of attempting to preserve an artificial "species," when the money and effort that such a venture will require could undoubtedly be much better spent on the preservation of bona fide endangered species that really need the help. Opinion is divided on this issue, and there may of course be some scientific value in protecting this "species." A contrary view to my own was expressed by waterfowl authority Janet Kear (of the Wildfowl Trust), who has said that "the scientific interest of this natural experiment in the evolution of a species is felt to be such that the population deserves protection whatever its taxonomic status."

The **Philippine mallard** (*Anas luzonica*) is considered to be one of the most beautiful of the mallards. With bright rusty cinnamon heads and necks, these ducks have a slender and elegant shape that is rather uncharacteristic of the mallard group. Their crowns and napes are darker, and a conspicuous dark stripe extends from the bill back through the eye. Apparently, their closest relatives are the spotbilled ducks. It is believed by some conservationists that they are no longer common and may be declining, but their status is not really known and *luzonica* has been described as both rare and "very abundant." They do appear to be widespread in their distribution, and this can be considered a positive factor.

8.15

8.16

8.17

Curiously, little field work has been conducted with the Philippine mallard, and no wild nests or eggs have been recorded. They are relatively abundant in wildfowl collections and breed readily, but they must be closely watched, as they are prone to hybridize with related ducks. This may be developing into a real problem, since I have seen fewer and fewer totally pure captive specimens in recent years. In my opinion, propagators are going to have to pay greater attention to the Philippine duck now, lest it be lost as a pure form in captivity.

The center of distribution for the little-known **Meller's duck** (*Anas melleri*) appears to be in eastern Madagascar (Malagasy Republic), where it ranges from sea level up to 6000 feet; although these birds also occur on the Indian Ocean island of Mauritius and were formerly found on La Réunion Island as well. It has been suggested that this duck was introduced by man to these latter islands some 200 years ago, but they could just as easily have immigrated there on their own, since cyclonic winds are not uncommon in that part of the world. Some authorities do not believe them to be deserving of full specific status.

Meller's ducks resemble female mallards and are about the same size (perhaps a bit larger). But they are more reddish brown in overall color; their dull, dark olive-green bills are relatively broad and high with a black nail and base; and their metallic green speculums are bordered with narrow bands of white. As adults, drakes are noted for conspicuous reddish orange or pinkish feet and legs, while those of the females and immatures are yellowish, tinged with brown. Otherwise, the sexes are essentially the same.

These obscure ducks are extremely wary and elusive, and they can be aggressive. Generally encountered in pairs or small groups, they frequent open ponds, bays, and sluggish streams in the more humid areas of Madagascar, while on Mauritius they apparently prefer wooded streams and isolated pools on the central volcanic plateau. They may also forage in cultivated rice fields.

Sadly, these interesting birds have been little studied, and nests and eggs in the wild remain unrecorded. In the rather recent past, they were considered to be relatively common, but their present status is far from encouraging. There are conflicting opinions regarding the future

8.15 *The Philippine duck, perhaps the most beautiful representative of the mallard complex, may be declining, but there is little definitive information regarding its status. Mainly local in distribution, these birds are not generally thought to be common. They breed freely in captivity but are very prone to hybridize with their close relatives.*

8.16 *Subadult Meller's duck. Undoubtedly rare and probably endangered, this duck has been little studied in the wild and is unfamiliar to most people.* PHOTO BY ANDRÉ CHAUVEAU

8.17 *Ducklings of Meller's duck. The ducklings in the background are New Zealand shovelers.*

of the species, but current evidence suggests that it may be greatly endangered, primarily due to hunting pressure and other forms of human interference. Accurate population figures are not available, and this scarcity of information clearly indicates that the population should be closely monitored, since its limited range and the deterioration of its habitat are certainly negative factors. On the other hand, many of the mallard-like ducks have exhibited a remarkable degree of adaptability and tenacity, and this will hopefully be a major point in favor of Meller's duck.

On Mauritius, the population numbered some 20 pairs in 1977, but they formerly were much more abundant and it is believed that several hundred pairs inhabited the island in the 1930s. The human population of the island is steadily increasing, and the ducks should be placed under official protection. But whether or not *melleri* is afforded such protection may be academic, since the human population of a protein-starved country is most concerned with its own survival, and any animal—endangered or not—is considered fair game.

Meller's ducks have traditionally been poorly represented in wildfowl collections, although a number were collected by Delacour prior to the Second World War, and some were subsequently reared by him. He once described them to me in typical Delacourian fashion as "dull, but interesting." Due to their quarrelsome nature, these ducks may be somewhat troublesome, but it appears at this point that their continued survival might lie in the skills of dedicated and capable aviculturists. Some breeding success has been achieved in Mauritius in recent years, and two pair have been sent out to the Wildfowl Trust and the zoo on the Isle of Jersey. These birds bred within a year or so, suggesting that Meller's duck could easily be re-established in captivity if a few more birds become available.

The two subspecies of African **yellow-billed ducks** (*Anas undulata*) are more slender and graceful than the other mallards and are named for their conspicuous brilliant yellow bills, which have a black patch on the ridge. With both races, the bill color of the somewhat larger drake may be slightly more intense than that of the female. Sometimes referred to as African mallards or geelbeks by local inhabitants, yellow-billed ducks are among the most common of African ducks, and the population may actually be increasing in some regions as a result of man-made surface water areas that have been created by urban mining and agricultural developments. These ducks are shy and wary in areas where hunted, but can be tame where not persecuted. They breed under a variety of circumstances and have been recorded at heights exceeding 8000 feet on the Nyika Plateau of Zambia. When swimming, they often ride very high in the water.

While the South African yellow-billed duck (*A. u. undulata*) is very familiar to most waterfowl propagators, the Abyssinian race (*A. u. ruppelli*) is practically unknown (although it was apparently common in collections prior to the Second World War). The two forms are similar, but individuals of the Abyssinian subspecies are significantly darker and browner, with deeper yellow bills. South African yellowbills breed rapidly in captivity, but must be managed carefully because they will quickly hybridize with mallards.

African black ducks (*Anas sparsa*) are not typical representatives of the tribe, and there is some speculation that they may be distantly related to the shelducks. The sexes are similar, but females tend to be smaller and darker. The bend of the wing is armed with a bony knob, the function of which is obscure (it may play a role in either courtship or defense). Bright iridescent blue-green speculums and yellow feet

8.18

8.19

8.18 *Pair of South African yellowbills. The bird in the background is feeding. Yellowbills are more slender and graceful than the common mallard and are common in South Africa, where they can frequently be encountered in fairly large flocks. They typically frequent waters in open country, reedy ponds, and even salt lakes.*

8.19 *Aged male Abyssinian yellowbill. About the same size as the South African yellowbill, members of this race are generally darker and browner, and the pale margins of the feathers are less broad. The bill color also tends to be a shade deeper.*

are particularly distinctive, and relatively long tails suggest that these ducks may perch, but this has not been well documented. Males are noted for a whistling peep-like call, while the female vocalization is merely a loud quack that is heard constantly during flight.

Rather wary and unsociable birds, African black ducks do not appear to be particularly common in any part of their range, but may be relatively plentiful in some localized areas. Considered to be almost exclusively a year-round river species, they prefer waters which run fairly swiftly and locations where vegetation overhangs the bank. (They are not always confined to such wooded country, however, and on rare occasions will utilize waters that are slow moving, even stagnant.) Diving readily in rapids for food, they are relatively specialized feeders, apparently foraging mainly on items of animal origin, such as aquatic insects, larvae, crustaceans, small larval amphibians, and perhaps even fish. However, they also consume aquatic vegetation, and appear to be particularly fond of acorns. Activity is greatest at dawn or dusk, and they generally pass the day at regular sites under overhanging branches, where they lie hidden and well camouflaged.

These highly territorial and aggressive birds exhibit no gregarious tendencies and are usually observed in pairs or small parties. They fly fast and low over the water, often with their wing tips almost touching the surface. When they swim, their bodies float low. Pair bonds of African black ducks are strong and may exceed two years in duration; and breeding pairs fiercely defend their section of river territory. Sometimes, nests are built on top of driftwood that is caught in trees along riverbanks, although several nest sites have been recorded in tree cavities. Once the young have hatched, the nest may be used as a brood site for a week or so. Monitor lizards reportedly prey upon the eggs and young. Non-breeding birds are not territorial and presumably constitute a sizeable segment of the overall population.

Three subspecies of African black ducks have been described, although the Gabon race (*A. s. maclatchyi*) will probably ultimately prove to be without basis. The blue-black bill of the South African form (*A. s. sparsa*) distinguishes it from the other two races, which have pinkish black bills. The Abyssinian (Ethiopian) black duck (*A. s. leucostigma*) is a high-altitude species which occurs in appropriate habitat up to 14,000 feet, whereas the other two subspecies frequent the lowlands. The South African race is said to be the most attractive, and is the best-known form in captivity, but even though a few have been sporadically bred over the years, only a handful of aviculturists are familiar with them. The two pink-billed races are virtually nonexistent in collections, although *leucostigma* was formerly kept at the Wildfowl Trust, and at least one bird is currently maintained in Delacour's superb collection at Cleres, France. All African black ducks that I have observed tended to be apprehensive and very secretive, nervously pumping their heads if they sensed they were being watched. They also seem to probe and root in the grass much more than typical dabblers. As a rule, they can be dangerous to other waterfowl in collections, but there are exceptions.

From a behavioral standpoint, the **bronze-winged duck** (*Anas specularis*) is among the most interesting of all ducks. They can possess very distinct personalities and may become very tame in captivity. In the wild, they appear to be fearless, and are often indifferent to the presence of a human intruder (I have been able to approach to within 15 feet of feeding pairs). Preferred habitat includes heavily forested rivers, relatively fast flowing streams, and mountain lakes in the southern third of South America. In flight, they usually follow the

8.20

8.21

8.20 - 8.21 *South African black ducks. Shy and unsociable birds, they can be rather aggressive. They may feed in swift-moving water by standing on protruding rocks and probing under stones with their bills. The pair bond is strong, but whether or not the drake is involved in brood care or defense has yet to be documented.*

course of a river, and seldom fly over land. Few nests have been observed by qualified naturalists, but *specularis* apparently nests most often on river islets, and the few documented nests were well concealed in tall grass and well lined with down. Pair bonds are reasonably strong, much more so than with more typical dabblers, and males may be involved in rearing the young (although this has yet to be fully documented). Apparently, this rather sedentary species may establish not only breeding territories but foraging territories as well.

Their beautiful iridescent bronzy-purple speculums, from which the vernacular name is derived, are particularly brilliant when the sun strikes them at the right angle. Immaculate white throats and cheek patches are also quite flashy, and oval-shaped white areas in front of the eyes produce a spectacled effect, which has prompted some observers to call them spectacled ducks. The female's vocalization is so dog-like that the natives refer to them as "pato perros," or the dog-ducks, while the male's call is totally different, consisting of a loud trilled whistle. (There may be a close relationship between these and the crested ducks [*Lophonetta*], but following more traditional taxonomic placement, I have retained these latter ducks with the shelducks. Johnsgard, however, recommends that the crested ducks be moved into the dabbler tribe.)

In captivity, bronze-winged ducks may be pugnacious to other waterfowl, but they can be so personable and charming that this unpleasant trait is not held against them by most aviculturists. Breeding pairs must be maintained separately, and I know of one bronze-

8.22

8.22 *Pair of bronze-winged ducks.*

8.23 *Group of bronze-winged ducks loafing on a sandbar at the middle of a river, in the extreme southern part of Argentina.*

highly nomadic species, they can be considered opportunistic omnivorous feeders, and they readily consume insects.

Essentially a nondescript little duck, *gracilis*, like the other grey teal, is characterized by bright red eyes. Their speculums are black, with green streaks in the center and a border of white on the leading edge; and in flight, a prominent wedge-shaped white patch on the upper wing is clearly evident. Both sexes look essentially alike, but males tend to be slightly larger and darker. As with some of the northern swans and geese, their heads, necks, and breasts may sometimes be stained a bright reddish orange—a condition brought about by the presence of iron deposits in shallow stagnant water.

These grey teal have colonized New Zealand and New Caledonia on their own, and the last major drought-induced invasion from Australia occurred in 1967. The New Zealand population probably does not exceed 18,000 to 20,000 individuals, and the scarcity of suitable shallow water areas is quite possibly the major factor in determining the extent of this population. While these birds are totally protected in New Zealand, some are nevertheless shot each year.

Not at all particular about nest sites, Australian grey teal may choose locales on the ground (near or far from water), under rocks, in rabbit burrows, and in tree hollows as well. In one instance, a pair selected a tree hollow some 30 feet above the ground, but descended all the way down inside the tree to build the nest at almost ground level. Getting out would seem difficult enough for the female, but incredibly, the newly-hatched young were somehow able to scamper up and exit

8.23

winged duck that killed an adult crane. During the nonbreeding season, on the other hand, I have observed small flocks (possibly immatures) in southern Argentina, so it is possible that their temperaments are more tolerable at this time of year, at least in the wild. Unfortunately, few collections possess these fascinating ducks—although they have become more available in recent years as greater breeding success has been achieved.

The four races of **grey or austral teal** (*Anas gibberifrons*) occupy the Australasian region, and may represent an intermediate link between the mallard group and the green-winged teal complex. Grey teal perch readily on trees and rocks, and demonstrate an inclination to nest in holes. For dabbling ducks, they are surprisingly capable divers.

Australian grey teal (*A. gibberifrons gracilis*) are among the most numerous, widespread, and mobile of Australian wildfowl. Some flocks contain thousands of birds, and when disturbed they may circle overhead in large black masses. They breed throughout the year and respond rapidly to rain, often beginning to lay within two weeks of rising water. During severe drought years, little or no breeding will occur. Some evidence suggests that males may assist in brood care. A

through the elevated entrance hole. The Australian grey teal is the only one of the four races that is commonly maintained and readily bred in wildfowl collections.

The East Indian teal (*A. g. gibberifrons*) and Rennell Island teal (*A. g. remissa*) are essentially very similar to the Australian grey teal. They differ mainly in size and distribution, although the East Indian race is also readily distinguished by a rather high forehead. Those birds which occupy Rennell Island (southern Solomon Islands) are the smallest of the group, are darker than those which reside in Australia, and have smaller bills and lower foreheads. Due to limited distribution, the insular forms are extremely vulnerable to changing conditions. When, for example, exotic fish (*Tilapia*) were introduced to the single lake on Rennell Island (a small island measuring 50 by 10 miles), they apparently had an adverse effect on the teal, and in fact, the last confirmed sighting of *remissa* occurred in 1959. It is quite possible that they are already gone.

The Andaman or oceanic teal (*A. g. albogularis*) is the most distinct of the four austral teal, both physically and behaviorally. Inhabiting the Andaman, Landfall, and Coco islands in the Indian Ocean, these ducks are in general subject to a great deal of individual variation, and

8.25

8.25 *Australian grey teal. The breeding season of this species is erratic and varies throughout its range — it can occur at any time of year. They are generally the first ducks to appear on any newly-formed water area. During times of drought, the inland birds may move in large numbers to deep lakes in the highlands, or to salt water bays and estuaries along the coast — but under more typical conditions, these areas support few grey teal. While they undoubtedly have wide habitat tolerances, grey teal are most typically birds of low rainfall areas and are best adapted to a lifestyle in the inland regions, and as a rule, the greatest concentrations can be encountered there. During major flood years, hundreds, and even thousands, of square miles of formerly arid land may be covered by water. During such times, immense nomadic flocks of grey teal may appear, and extensive breeding activity can take place. Every tree and stump may contain a nest, and countless numbers of eggs may also be laid on the ground. As hatching commences, almost every depression will contain large numbers of ducklings. Breeding may continue as the water dries up, and as it recedes, hundreds of ducklings of various ages tend to concentrate into the rapidly dwindling pools. If the water dries up too rapidly, duckling mortality can be very high and many nests will be abandoned.*

8.24

8.24 *Male East Indian grey teal. Individuals of this race are readily separable from the other rather similar grey teal by their conspicuous swollen foreheads. They are also smaller and darker than the representatives of the more familiar Australian subspecies that is pictured in plate 8.25. The sexes are basically alike, but females tend to be slightly smaller and paler in color, and their eye color may not be quite as intense. Females are noted for a loud, penetrating, often-repeated quack; males produce only a muted "peep." While they are relatively common and widespread throughout the East Indies (particularly in the Celebes), these teal are practically unknown to contemporary aviculturists. Where they are subjected to hunting pressure, they tend to become wary. They may feed by sifting through the mud at the water's edge, or by upending in the shallows, but also filter the surface of the water, where they collect insects and seeds. The seven to eight cream-colored eggs are incubated by the female alone for 24 to 26 days.*

8.26

8.27

8.26 *Bernier's or Madagascan teal at Lake Bermamba. Possibly rare and endangered, these teal are little known and have only rarely been photographed. They are unfortunately not offered protection and are apparently suffering as a result of direct persecution.* PHOTO BY JOANNA LUBBOCK

8.27 *Andaman teal drake. These handsome birds are certainly the most distinctive of the grey teal complex. They are vulnerable because of human alteration of their specialized habitat, and in order to insure their continued survival, it appears that sanctuaries will be required. One has already been established on Rees Island.*

as a result two races have been described (although only one of these has been substantiated). Drakes usually have more white on the face, but this is also subject to a significant amount of variation. The white is usually restricted to large eye rings and the throats of the females. Dorsal feathers are edged with gray, producing a distinct scalloped effect. These birds are prone to partial albinism, a condition which may indicate inbreeding.

The somewhat nomadic Andaman teal nest on the ground or in generally inaccessible hollow trees, and the drakes assist in brood care. Frequently perching in mangrove trees or on rocks exposed at low tide during the day, they may feed in wet rice fields after dark. A vulnerable race, *albogularis* is particularly threatened by developments such as drainage programs and settlements. They are practically unknown to contemporary aviculturists, and as of early 1979, the several pair at the Wildfowl Trust constituted the entire captive population. No breeding has occurred in recent years, but some were successfully reared at the London Zoo during the early years of this century.

The little-known **Bernier's or Madagascan teal** (*Anas bernieri*) inhabits the west coast of Madagascar between sea level and 4500

feet. Their distribution is apparently very limited and, indeed, may be restricted to but two lakes (Bemamba and Masama)—although it is possible that they are more widespread than has been reported. The population estimates for Lake Bemamba are not encouraging (probably no more than 120 teal in 1973) and the Lake Masama population is even less (estimated at 60 ducks in 1970). The species is not protected and may, in fact, already be endangered. Natives hunt them with dogs and reportedly also take eggs to eat. Delacour believes they have always been relatively rare.

Bernier's teal resemble the other austral teal somewhat, and some biologists feel that they may merely represent an erythristic or reddish form; hence their status as a valid full species is regarded with suspicion by some taxonomists. But curiously, their speculums appear rather velvety black, lacking any hint of the metallic luster that is typical of the grey teal complex, and for this and other reasons they do appear to be rather distinct. Habitat preferences include regions where grassland savannahs, mangroves, and mature forests converge. Most often encountered as pairs or in small groups, up to 30 or 40 of these teal may congregate in small flocks. These rare birds have not only virtually

8.28 *Drake chestnut teal. Nest sites of this species are varied. They may be located on the ground in long grass or other vegetation, in rock crevices, or even in tree cavities. Nest predation by snakes is apparently high.*

8.29 *New Zealand brown teal drake. Until the 1880s, these birds were relatively abundant throughout the country, but they went into a rapid decline thereafter. They swim and dive well but are not strong fliers.*

never been maintained in captivity, they have seldom even been observed (although Delacour did have a female in France in the 1930s that survived for six years). Nests and eggs have never been described by a qualified biologist.

Chestnut or chestnut-breasted teal (*Anas castanea*) of southern Australia are so named for the gorgeous chestnut-colored breast of the drakes in breeding plumage. Males also have iridescent green heads that are accentuated by brilliant ruby-red eyes, and appear to have a rather indistinct eclipse plumage. Although these beautiful teal have definitely declined in some areas, they are still more numerous than is commonly believed, particularly in coastal areas. Tasmania appears to be their stronghold at present, and they are highly regarded as game-birds by Australian hunters. While essentially sedentary, they will move about locally in response to changing water conditions and food supplies. On occasion, they have been known to perch in trees. They may breed more than once a year, and males rejoin the females after the ducklings have hatched, remaining with the family until the young fledge (a trait which is generally atypical of the tribe). In some instances, the nest may be used as a brooding site.

Chestnut teal and grey teal are very similar in many respects and may hybridize in captivity, although they nest side by side in the wild and there are few authenticated records of natural hybrids. (Some authorities believe, however, that hybridization could be more common than the record indicates, since the results may not be obvious.) Female chestnut teal closely resemble grey teal, but can be distinguished by their slightly larger size and their darker color, particularly about the head and shoulders; they also lack the light throat. These birds have long been popular with aviculturists, and while they are not particularly widespread in collections, they breed readily.

Two of the three races of the **brown teal** (*Anas aucklandica*) are not unlike the chestnut teal in appearance, but behaviorally brown teal tend to be much more aggressive. The New Zealand race (*A. a. chlorotis*) is noted for two distinct color phases, and albinism is not particularly uncommon. Males usually have a greenish head color, as well as a distinct white eye ring. Females somewhat resemble female chestnut teal, but are easily distinguished by their whitish eye rings and dark brown (instead of red) eyes; they are also more brownish overall. Brown teal favor shady swampy streams and tidal creeks, and are considered to be essentially a crepuscular or even nocturnal species. Mated pairs form strong pair bonds (which are perhaps even permanent), and compared to most other dabbling ducks they produce remarkably large eggs. Females alone incubate, and it is not known whether or not males participate in brood care.

The New Zealand brown teal is the most widespread and may be the most abundant of the three races overall, but even it is thought to be rare. At one time considered relatively common, these birds had disappeared from most of their former haunts by the 1920s, with the loss of small ponds and swampy habitat contributing greatly to their extensive decline. It is also possible that some of the early decline can be attributed to introduced poultry diseases, against which the native teal had no immunity. Currently, the total population is estimated at approximately 1000 teal (although this figure may be conservative), with most of the population concentrated on the Barrier Islands.

In recent years, however, the New Zealand Wildlife Service has been very successful in breeding *chlorotis* within a controlled environment, and several restocking programs are in progress. During the 1970-71 season, ten captive-bred pairs which had been previously released on Kapiti Island (just off the southwest coast of the North Island) produced 45 young that reached the fledging stage. In 1973, additional releases were attempted at four other locations. In conjunction with Ducks Unlimited (N.Z.), the New Zealand Wildlife Service hopes to ultimately produce and liberate up to 1000 brown teal over the next ten years to supplement the wild population.

After brown teal were first bred at the Wildfowl Trust in 1960, quite a number were reared. Unfortunately, all the subsequent young were derived from only six adult birds, and this population soon suffered problems associated with inbreeding (such as infertility); ultimately, they all but died out, and only two or three can currently be accounted for outside of New Zealand. Brown teal are extremely aggressive and belligerent—as dangerous to other waterfowl as they are to each other in a mixed collection. Pairs must be housed separately, although single non-breeding birds are not nearly as aggressive.

The other two obscure races of brown teal are flightless (or nearly so) and inhabit small islands south of New Zealand. Flightlessness may better adapt the teal for terrestrial life and for diving as well; it undoubtedly conserves energy, and may prevent loss of breeding stock through aerial dispersal. The Auckland Island teal (*A. a. aucklandica*) appears to be holding its own at this point, although they are extremely rare and are perhaps even gone on Auckland Island itself. At least 24 pairs inhabit Ewing Island, and the teal occur on at least six other rather inaccessible islands as well, so the population can be considered fairly secure. (In 1974, optimistic population estimates suggested that 1200 to 1500 might survive.) On Auckland Island, introduced feral cats and pigs (as well as the ubiquitous rats) abound, and are primarily responsible for the decline of the brown teal there. The remains of teal found at skua middens indicate that these gull-like birds may be major predators on all islands. Petrel and rabbit burrows are sometimes utilized by the teal when seeking protection. Reportedly, the gapes of their mouths have become hardened as an adaptation for catching and consuming spiny isopods.

The Campbell Island race (*A. a. nesiotis*) is rather similar to *aucklandica*, but is slightly smaller and browner. In the opinion of some ornithologists, the differences are so slight that the validity of the subspecies must be viewed with suspicion. Until recently, only a dozen or so individuals had ever been observed, and it was speculated that

8.30

8.30 *New Zealand brown teal drake. These birds have relatively strong pair bonds, and it is possible that males may be involved in brood defense.*

8.31 - 8.32 *Auckland Islands flightless teal on Rose Island. This rare and endangered race occupies small, inaccessible islands that are not infested with introduced cats, pigs, and rats. For the moment, they appear secure.*
PHOTOS BY NEW ZEALAND WILDLIFE SERVICE

8.31

they may have been stragglers from the Auckland Islands. The total museum collection of this duck numbers only three specimens (one collected in 1886 and two in 1944).

This flightless teal was believed extinct for a number of years, but on November 12, 1975, the New Zealand Wildlife Service reported the sighting of five individuals on Dent Island, a tiny island of only a few acres located about a mile and a half off the west coast of Campbell Island. Dent Island is characterized by steep slopes, which are extensively covered with tussock grass-type vegetation, and it is fortunately not infested with the introduced black rats and cats that inhabit the larger island. (The ducks on Campbell Island were exterminated shortly after the introduction of rats in 1810.)

Rodney Russ, a New Zealand Wildlife Service biologist, captured one of the "rediscovered" teal and studied it for a week before releasing it back on the island. He suggests that the race certainly deserves its subspecific status, and that *nesiotis* probably was not derived from wind-blown stragglers from the Auckland Islands, but constitutes instead a separate resident population. Russ also reported that the population probably does not exceed 20 pairs, but that the ducks are relatively secure for the time being, due to isolation and the ruggedness of the island and the rough seas which surround it. It has been strongly recommended that Dent Island be designated a sanctuary, and that all future visits be strictly regulated. The tiny size of the island is of some concern, since the limited amount of appropriate habitat may have a limiting influence on the size of the population, and some consideration is being given to establishing an additional breeding population on another predator-free island.

It is of interest to note that the Campbell Island brown teal are fond of probing in the peat. In fact, the tell-tale "probes" in the peat constituted the most abundant sign of the teal's presence. While they occupy appropriate habitat from a few feet above sea level almost to the summit of the island, present available evidence suggests that these teal seldom, if ever, venture into the sea. Often, they frequent small gullies which maintain a trickle of water, small soaks, and/or pools. Like their counterpart on the Auckland Islands, these ducks tend to retreat into petrel burrows when threatened.

The **South American green-winged or speckled teal** complex (*Anas flavirostris*) is not as well known as the green-winged teal of the north. All four subspecies—the Chilean, sharp-winged, Andean, and Merida teal—lack the vivid colorful hues of their northern relatives, are all very similar in appearance to one another, and are only partially migratory. The sexes are essentially alike, although females tend to be smaller and duller, with slightly darker heads and less colorful bills.

Andean teal (*A. f. andium*) and Merida teal (*A. f. altipentens*) are very obscure high-altitude ducks, with the former race occurring up to the limit of the snow and seldom encountered below 11,000 feet. Little is known about both of these more northerly forms of speckled teal, but they are noted for their lead-blue (rather than yellow) bills, and both are larger and significantly darker than the more familiar Chilean and sharp-winged teal. Merida teal are somewhat lighter in color than *andium*, with less speckling on the head and neck, and it is also said that the green of the speculum lacks the purplish bronze reflections. Neither of these races is apparently abundant anywhere, nor have they ever been maintained in captivity.

The Chilean teal (*A. f. flavirostris*) is undoubtedly the most common of the speckled teal, both in the wild and in captivity. These agile birds often perch in trees in wooded regions, and are most adept at eluding

8.33

8.34

8.35

8.33 *The Campbell Island teal was, until recently, considered extinct. Still very insecure, the total world population may not exceed 30 to 50 teal. They are restricted to a tiny jagged island just off the west coast of Campbell Island.* PHOTO BY RODNEY RUSS (NEW ZEALAND WILDLIFE SERVICE)

8.34 *Mounted specimen of the Andean teal. The blue-billed forms of speckled teal are little-known. They breed where suitable cover is present in the highlands of Colombia and Ecuador, in marshes and along the margins of lakes.* PHOTO BY GLEN SMART

8.35 *Chilean teal are common throughout much of their range. Often nesting close to human dwellings, they tend to be relatively tame if not taken advantage of. In some regions, they may take over the bulky stick nests of the monk parakeet, forcing the psittacines out and disposing of their eggs.*

both human hunters and hawks by flying between tree trunks at great speed. Widespread throughout southern South America, they also occur on the Falkland Islands, and in 1971 a small resident population of 40 to 50 individuals were discovered inhabiting Cumberland Bay on South Georgia Island. Relatively adaptable, Chilean teal may nest on the ground, in clay banks, and in a variety of other sites that include the abandoned stick nests of the colonial monk parakeet; and in some regions, nests may be located up to a mile from water. During courtship, the elongated feathers at the back of the neck of the male may be partially erected. Their call consists of a high clear whistle that is reminiscent of a song bird. Drakes may remain with the hen once she emerges with the brood, but not always.

To the untrained eye, Chilean and sharp-winged teal (*A. f. oxyptera*) are practically identical, but sharp-winged teal are slightly larger, longer, and paler in color. In addition, the speckling on their chests is smaller and does not extend as far back along the sides, and the scapulars are comparatively long and sharply pointed (obviously, the origin of the vernacular name). Sharp-winged teal are rather limited in distribution compared to the widespread Chilean race, and mainly occupy the high plateau of the Andes above 12,000 feet, where they are one of the most abundant anatids of Lake Titicaca. Both of these races of speckled teal (particularly *flavirostris*) tend to be tame and sociable, and are relatively common in wildfowl collections.

The **northern green-winged teal** (*Anas crecca*) is a relatively abundant species that is well known to waterfowl hunters, who hold it in high regard. Among the smallest of northern puddle ducks, these birds tend to migrate in larger flocks than most waterfowl. Swift and erratic fliers, they dart about in flight in the manner of a flock of shorebirds, and their rapid wingbeats create a pleasant whistling sound. During the fall migration, there is a tendency for the sexes to segregate, with drakes generally departing earlier than their mates and usually not moving as far south. Courting birds may engage in much whistling and bowing, and the high-pitched whistling chirp of the drake is similar to the call of a tree frog or a cricket. During courtship, amorous males are prone to rape unattached females. Nests are often extremely well concealed in thick vegetation, and can be very difficult to locate.

Although they are mainly birds of freshwater habitats, green-winged teal sometimes frequent coastal areas, and from time to time perch on low limbs of dead trees. Essentially, they are regarded as vegetarian, but it is interesting to note that those inhabiting Alaska may sometimes gorge themselves on putrid salmon. Of the three races, two are common in captive waterfowl collections; but in general, birds of this species tend to be very elusive and nervous, and are therefore seldom visible. The American birds appear to be *slightly* less nervous than their Old World counterpart and, as a result, are apt to breed more readily.

Full-color drakes of the American (*A. c. carolinensis*) and European (*A. c. crecca*) races can be readily differentiated, because the European green-winged teal have a highly visible horizontal white line between the grey flanks and the back. This is lacking on the American birds, but is replaced by a broad vertical white band extending down the side of the breast. In addition, the metallic green band which extends from the eye to the nape of *carolinensis* is not totally, nor distinctly, bordered by a narrow creamy line, as it is with *crecca*. Females of all three races are practically identical, although European hens can be distinguished from *carolinensis* because they have a white and buff front border instead of pale brown on the speculum. Mem-

8.38

8.36

8.37

8.36 *Pair of sharp-winged teal. The bird in the foreground is feeding. A high-altitude species, these attractive little teal are seldom observed below the 12,000-foot level of the Andes in Peru, Bolivia, Chile, and northern Argentina.*

8.37 *American green-winged teal drake in full color. These are not shy birds, and where not molested they will loaf a great deal during the day, either ashore or in the water. They are not at all uncommon, and the continental population probably numbers between seven and ten million birds.*

8.38 *Male European green-winged teal. Because of their small size and swift and erratic flight style, their aerial speed has often been over-estimated; it rarely exceeds 50 miles per hour.*

bers of the European subspecies are slightly smaller and are simply referred to as common teal in the Old World, where they are among the most abundant of Eurasian ducks. They are rarely, but regularly, seen along the east coast of North America.

The Aleutian race (*A. c. nimia*) is practically identical to the European green-winged teal, but it is somewhat larger, and the cream outline around the eye may be slightly less distinct. Whether or not these Alaskan birds truly constitute a valid subspecies remains to be seen. They may be the most common dabbling duck of the Aleutian Island chain, and apparently are not migratory—which is a rather puzzling trait for a northern dabbler. Curiously, these ducks have never been maintained in captivity.

Like the red-breasted goose, the drake **Baikal or spectacled teal** (*Anas formosa*) almost appears to be artificial; perhaps even hand-painted. These fast-flying ducks are indescribably beautiful, with an elaborate and unique head pattern that must be viewed up close to be fully appreciated. Appropriately, the literal translation of their Latin name means "beautiful duck." The low clucking vocalizations of the males have prompted the Russians to give these birds such vernacular names as "gurglers" or "bubbling teal." They breed in eastern Siberia, north of Lake Baikal, from whence they take their common name. A variety of habitats are utilized by these striking birds, but typical breeding habitat lies within the forest zone, around ponds and along streams in low vegetation.

Huge flocks of Baikal teal formerly wintered in the flooded rice fields and freshwater marshes of Korea and Japan; and while they are currently not as common as they once were, these ducks are still said to be one of the most common dabblers of eastern Asia, despite hunting pressure in both Russia and China. One huge Korean flock seen in 1964 was reported to be at least two miles in length, containing tens of thousands of ducks—and at least one wintering flock in Japan was said to consist of as many as 100,000 teal. Apparently, Baikal teal are a nocturnal species, and the Russians report that the ducks sometimes converge on highways at night to feed on soybeans spilled from transport vehicles. It seems that they are more prone to feed ashore than in the water and may in fact forage some distance from the water. They demonstrate a fondness for acorns.

Curiously, Baikal teal molt into eclipse plumage much later in the year than most species. Males in eclipse plumage resemble females, but can be differentiated by their less extensive white throats and the obscurity of the white spot at the base of the bill. Drakes usually assume their breeding plumage in October, but it remains dull for approximately three months because the feathers of the head and neck are bordered with dull grey. This gradually wears out, and the full brilliance of the ornate plumage becomes evident in January or February. Baikal teal do very well in wildfowl collections and are delightful additions—but unfortunately, they are relatively shy and breed infrequently. Also, they are not readily available, and females are particularly scarce. In view of their current rarity in captivity, it is interesting to note that between 1911 and 1914, Baikal teal were the ducks most commonly imported into Europe.

An equally beautiful bird in its own way is the **falcated or bronze-capped duck** (*Anas falcata*)—which fortunately breeds much more freely than the Baikal teal and is well established in captivity. Full-color drakes of this species are noted for long curved scapulars that droop over the flanks, and also for a long shaggy crest that shimmers with an iridescent bronzy-green to chestnut-purple color. In addition, a very

8.39

8.40

8.39 *Aleutian green-winged teal drake. During the warmer months, these nonmigratory teal seek fresh-water ponds and lakes and tend to nest in grassy areas. However, during the winter they shift to marine beaches, where they commonly feed at low tide in pools and shallow-water areas among the exposed reefs.*
PHOTO BY KARL KENYON

8.40 - 8.41 *(Above and Opposite Page) Baikal teal drakes in full nuptial plumage. Displaying males often tilt their heads back, thus exposing their black throats. Males may take leave of their incubating mates to molt in groups, usually at sites not very far from the nesting females. Nesting habitat is variable, and nests have even been discovered under large branches and in piles of driftwood. Baikal teal are strong fliers, but their flight is not as swift nor erratic as the green-winged teal. They spend a good deal of time ashore, and when feeding in the water are not prone to dive.*

8.42

8.43

8.42 *Adult drake gadwall. These birds are noted for a distinct whistling sound produced by their wings when in flight. When necessary, they will dive for food.*

8.43 *Coues's gadwall. Known from only two specimens, this obscure insular duck became extinct in 1874.*

8.44 *Falcated duck drake. A large segment of the population winters in Japan, where they are seldom observed far from salt water. However, they do move inland to feed in rice fields and freshwater lakes.*

8.44

prominent small white spot is usually visible just above the base of the upper mandible, and they have beautiful green speculums that are quite evident in flight.

Falcated ducks are undoubtedly related to the gadwall, and are probably also more closely related to wigeons than their ornate appearance would indicate. They are roughly the same size as a gadwall, and females closely resemble gadwall hens, except that their legs and feet are dark rather than yellowish, they are slightly more brownish overall, and the proportionally larger head is generally darker. The call of the drake is a piercing shrill whistle that is suggestive of a curlew, whereas the call of the female is similar to that of the gadwall hen.

Like the Baikal teal, these ducks are migratory, breed in eastern and central Siberia, and when engaged in long-distance flights, tend to fly in formation. While they are considered to be essentially a freshwater species, they may utilize marine habitats in winter, and are said to be surprisingly capable divers. Primarily vegetarian, they also consume aquatic insects and small molluscs.

According to some observers, the overall population of falcated ducks may be declining, due to drainage and cultivation of suitable marshland habitats in China. However, while their numerical status is not really clear, there appears to be no definite evidence that the overall population of these ducks is suffering a significant decline— even though they are regarded as a valuable food source in China and Russia, and may be harvested for their beautiful ornamental feathers as well.

Both falcated ducks and Baikal teal are observed fairly regularly in the Aleutian Islands in Alaska. In essence, the Aleutians bridge the North Pacific to Asia, with some 70 named islands extending westward from the Alaskan mainland for approximately 1000 miles, to within 500 miles of the Kamchatka Peninsula of the Soviet Union. It is therefore not surprising that so many "out-of-range" species are encountered there, and since these islands are important for the survival of a number of species, it is fortunate that most of them are incorporated into the United States National Wildlife Refuge System, totalling more than 2,720,000 acres.

The **common gadwall** (*Anas s. strepera*) is not nearly as flashy as the Baikal teal or falcated duck, but is a rather elegant duck nevertheless. Essentially a continental species of Eurasia and North America, gadwall are not normally associated with the coast. Significantly less gregarious than mallards or pintails, they tend to be somewhat shy and retiring, preferring waters with a great deal of cover; and they also appear to be more prone to dive than most of the surface-feeding

8.45

ducks. Drakes have a peculiar high, reedy, frog-like quack.

In flight, gadwall are fairly easily identified by a distinctive flight profile, whistling wings, and prominent white patches on the dorsal wing surfaces. (They are, in fact, the only North American puddle duck with white in the speculum.) Gadwall hens may superficially resemble other female dabblers, but they can be fairly readily differentiated by their proportionally narrower bill with dull orange sides. They are also much more delicate in appearance than mallard females, and generally float higher on the water with their posteriors somewhat elevated.

While gadwall are mainly vegetarian, they may supplement their diet with snails and other aquatic invertebrates, especially during the breeding season. They sometimes obtain food by expropriating the food of other waterfowl species or coots. The overall population has been steadily increasing during the past decade, and they enjoy one of the most extensive ranges of all ducks. As a rule, these ducks nest on the ground in thick cover, but they may also seek open areas, often in association with gulls and terns; and they appear to prefer island sites, usually close to the water. In captivity, they can be prolific breeders, and are common (but not prominent) in most collections.

Coues's gadwall (*A. s. couesi*) was a dwarfed insular duck. Now extinct, it is known from but a single pair obtained in 1874 on Washing-

ton Island, some 1000 miles south of Hawaii. As might be expected of an isolated inhabitant of a tiny island, it was extremely vulnerable to change and was probably exterminated shortly after the arrival of man and his animals. Almost nothing is known about it, and *couesi* was gone practically before it was known to exist. Migrating common gadwalls that have gone astray have been recorded in the Marshall Islands, and it appears likely that the Coues's gadwall evolved from stock which may have become stranded in a similar fashion centuries ago.

The three species of wigeons are very ornamental and often rather wary. The northern forms are noted for extensive grazing habits, and not surprisingly, their short necks and bills are ideally suited for grazing, with distinct goose-like serrations along the edges to facilitate cutting grass. The sexes of both the American wigeon (or baldpate) and European wigeon differ significantly in appearance, whereas male and female South American Chiloe wigeons are very similar, with the males being only slightly larger and brighter (especially on the head). Wigeon drakes have delightful whistles, but the female merely quacks. In flight, their wings produce a rustling sound.

Baldpates (*Anas americana*) are so named because of a creamy-white stripe on the drake's forehead that creates the illusion of a bald spot when viewed from a distance. Aside from the white foreheads, other conspicuous field marks are their dark green eye patches, purplish grey bodies, and white flank patches. These ducks fly swiftly but erratically, in irregularly shaped but compact flocks, and their ability to wheel and turn in unison matches that of the teal. Considered to be the most terrestrial of the North American ducks in the genus *Anas*, baldpates ride high in the water, sometimes pivoting lightly as they daintily peck at the surface for food. Interestingly, they commonly associate with diving species, such as redheads and even coots, and as these more efficient divers pop to the surface with food, the baldpates will claim a portion of it (they have also been known to poach from canvasbacks and brant geese). While essentially vegetarian, they also appear to be fond of molluscs and insects. Regarded as relatively nervous and alert birds, they are at the same time curious. They are quick to take flight when alarmed, but may nevertheless frequent city parks during the winter. This species is one of the most abundant of American sporting ducks, with a total population that may exceed 6,000,000 birds.

Drakes of the slightly smaller **European wigeon** (*Anas penelope*) can easily be distinguished from their American relatives by their russet-red heads, which are topped by a distinctive golden-buff crown stripe. Females of the two species are very similar, except that the head of the European female is tinged with red, while that of *americana* is always grey. (A grey European color phase is also known, however, and this can make accurate identification a bit more difficult.) As a rule, *penelope* also generally exhibits more color contrast between its head and neck and the breast, and the scapulars are white instead of dusky.

8.46 *Pair of European wigeons. During the winter, these attractive ducks are more inclined to occupy coastal habitat than inland areas.*

8.47 *Chiloe wigeon. This species generally nests on dry ground, often in thistles or tall grass. Upon occasion, nests are located some distance from the water.*

In flight, the white coloration of the upper forewing is very conspicuous. Like the American wigeon, drakes in eclipse plumage rather closely resemble females but have white upper wing coverts.

European wigeons tend to be more vocal and less aquatic than baldpates, and swim slightly lower in the water. They are among the most abundant of Eurasian waterfowl, and along the southeast coast of China and Japan they are said to be the most common wintering ducks. Rather shy birds, they often fly in tightly formed flocks, but may also string out in long straggling lines. The distinctive musical whistle of the male may be uttered frequently. Like baldpates, they sometimes associate with other aquatic species (such as foraging swans and diving ducks), and will pirate food that the others bring up from the bottom.

Wintering birds sometimes gather in compact flocks numbering in the thousands to graze on short grass. North American sightings of European wigeons are not uncommon, but up to four pairs were observed on a single pond on Amchitka Island in the Aleutians in 1972. While it has yet to be documented that they nest there, it appears likely that some breeding may be taking place.

South American **Chiloe wigeons** (*Anas sibilatrix*) are similar in habits to their northern relatives. Generally, they are more or less sedentary, but may undertake limited migrations. In flight, they are easily identified by the large crescentic white patches on each forewing, a bright white rump, and rust-colored flanks. Throughout much of their range they are relatively common, and in regions where they have not been molested or persecuted they tend to be tame. When excited, they call almost continually.

During the nonbreeding season, Chiloe wigeons become very social and gregarious and may flock up in the hundreds, both during migration and on their wintering grounds to the north. In addition,

thousands may gather during the molt. They appear to have significantly stronger pair bonds than other wigeons, and unlike the others, males *may* take part in the rearing of the young. Drakes are also unlike their northern counterparts in that they are not noted for an eclipse plumage.

In October of 1966, a dead emaciated male was recovered on Signey Island (in the South Orkney Island Group), just north of the Antarctic Peninsula. Thus, Chiloe wigeons join the very small number of waterfowl species that have managed to cross the hostile South Atlantic (Drake Passage) separating the tip of South America from Antarctica. In 1972, another specimen was collected on South Georgia Island, approximately 1000 miles east of their normal range. All three species of wigeons are firmly established in captivity and can generally be considered rather dependable breeders. They are a hardy group that can usually be readily mixed with other species, but during the breeding season they may turn aggressive.

The pintail complex is comprised of three distinct species, with many races. **Bahama or white-cheeked pintails** (*Anas bahamensis*) are perhaps the most attractive species, being particularly noted for the brilliant red coloration at the base of their bill, which is almost wax-like in appearance. This basal bill color is slightly more intense on the drakes, and males also possess more immaculate white cheeks and

8.48 *Lesser Bahama or white-cheeked pintail. These attractive little ducks are partial to coastal areas, and demonstrate a decided preference for salt or brackish water habitats. They particularly like tidewater mangrove swamps, and may also be encountered at the mouths of rivers near salt lakes. Their tropical and subtropical distribution is somewhat spotty, and in some areas, their numbers have declined. Bahama pintail tend to become rather shy and wary where subjected to hunting pressure in the Caribbean, and they are quite capable of effectively hiding in dense vegetation. They are considered to be excellent eating. The sexes are similar (although males are slightly larger), and they do not undergo an eclipse plumage. In many respects, these birds are intermediate between the African red-billed pintail and the Chilean pintail, and hybrids with the latter species in the wild have been reported. While they may wander to some extent, these pintails are essentially sedentary, and they are usually observed in small flocks. The few nests that have been seen in the wild were located in mangrove thickets. Six to ten eggs are incubated by the female alone for 25 days. It has yet to be definitely established whether or not the males are involved in brood care, but probably they are not.*

8.49 *Niceforo's pintail — probably extinct.*
8.50 *Chilean pintail.*
8.51 *Greater Bahama pintail drake.*
8.52 *Lesser Bahama pintail.*
8.53 *Galapagos pintail.* PHOTO BY GARY R. JONES
8.54 *South Georgia pintail.*
8.55 *Silver Bahama pintail.*

throats, as well as longer tails. Another conspicuous feature is the green speculum, which is accentuated by buff-colored borders.

Three geographical races of this pintail have been described, with the northern or lesser form (*A. b. bahamensis*) inhabiting brackish or salt water habitats throughout the Caribbean and northern South America. The Caribbean population has been seriously reduced on some islands by over-hunting and nest predation by introduced mammalian carnivores. This race is sometimes referred to as the summer duck, and at one time they may have been abundant in Florida. The southern or greater Bahama pintail (*A. b. rubrirostris*), which is larger and slightly darker, occupies much of central South America.

The Galapagos pintail (*A. b. galapagensis*) is an island race and is absurdly tame. Smallest and slenderest of the group, they are not as brightly colored as other pintails, and the white on their cheeks and throats is less well-defined. This race is the sole indigenous anatid of the Galapagos Archipelago (although small numbers of blue-winged teal may winter in the islands, and there also is a single record of a southern black-bellied whistling duck). The restricted insular distribution of *galapagensis*, combined with a limited amount of appropriate waterfowl habitat, increased tourism, and the problems associated with introduced predators, place this race in a more vulnerable position than its mainland counterparts. The unstable nature of the volcanic islands which they inhabit also presents some problems. For example, some 2000 teal may have perished in June of 1968 when the floor of the Fernandina Crater Lake (Narborough Island) collapsed and fell almost 1000 feet.

In captivity, a white form of the Bahama pintail has been developed that aviculturists refer to as the silver pintail. These birds are a delicate silvery grey overall, but retain the normal blue and red bill. The lesser Bahama pintail is the only one of the three races which is well established in captivity, although *rubrirostris* was apparently rather common at one time. Pure greater Bahama pintails are currently rare (at least in America), while the Galapagos subspecies is nonexistent in any collection and has never been bred, although it was formerly kept at the Wildfowl Trust.

The **yellow-billed pintail** group (*Anas georgica*) includes three rather similar forms. Most familiar is the Chilean or brown pintail (*A. g. spinicauda*), which is by far the most abundant of South American waterfowl and probably greatly exceeds in number all other anatid species on that continent combined. They range from swampy prairies at sea level up to the 14,000-foot level of the Andes and appear to be essentially freshwater birds. Reportedly, they will sometimes nest in deserted parrot nests, and it is possible that the male offers some assistance in rearing the young (at least in the case of the South Georgia race).

One of the three yellow-billed pintail subspecies, the Niceforo's pintail (*A. g. niceforoi*), is very rare, and some naturalists believe that it is probably already extinct. It is (or was) thought to be sedentary and occupied selected habitats in the eastern Andes of central Colombia, between 3200 and 10,000 feet. These ducks differ slightly from the Chilean race in that they are generally darker and redder, the top of their heads are somewhat blackish, the tail is less pointed, and the bill is both longer and less upturned. This obscure bird has been observed by only a handful of field ornithologists, and its natural history is almost totally unknown. Apparently, *niceforoi* has never been handled by an aviculturist.

Another race, the South Georgia pintail (*A. g. georgica*), is presently not considered endangered—although they are heavily preyed upon by skuas, and the presence of introduced rats has also proved to be locally detrimental. At one time, the population was significantly reduced by food-seeking whalers, but unlike the great whales, the pintail outlasted the whalers and is now frequently encountered in the debris of derelict whaling stations. Sometimes considered a full species and referred to as the yellow-bill pintail, these birds represent the sole endemic anatid of this remote South Atlantic island.

South Georgia pintail are smaller, darker, and shorter-billed than their continental relatives, with 16 tail feathers instead of 14. As a rule, they are very inconspicuous, except for their bright yellow bills; but the short, shrill whistle of the males (which is oft-repeated in flight) frequently reveals their presence. Their relatively long necks are clearly a mechanism for obtaining food in deep water, where they have little competition from other duck species. I have observed them feeding in a variety of places: in freshwater tarns, in tide pools, on offshore rocks, and on kelp-strewn beaches in association with elephant seals, fur seals, and subantarctic penguins. Totally protected now, the population probably numbers several thousand ducks.

In January of 1975, a small anatid that was possibly a member of this race was observed on Breaker Island, adjacent to the Antarctic Peninsula. While other southern sightings of waterfowl have been reported (including several *georgica* in the South Shetland Islands between 1916 and 1922), the 1975 observation constitutes the record for the southernmost sighting of any waterfowl species.

While a few South Georgia pintail have found their way into waterfowl collections over the years, only the Chilean race (*spinicauda*) is well-known. At the same time, even this subspecies is not overly common, because they are rather nondescript compared to many other waterfowl species. They adapt well and are not difficult to propagate.

Best known of the pintails are the members of the **blue-billed pintail** complex (*Anas acuta*). Of these, the common or northern pintail (*Anas a. acuta*) is by far the most familiar. Better known to waterfowlers as the sprig, these ducks are perhaps second only to mallards as gamebirds, and are among the most numerous of the world's waterfowl. Slender and trim, with long tails and necks, they have a very elegant and graceful profile. The long, thin, pin-like tail feathers of the drake account for a quarter of the bird's total length and are responsible for its descriptive vernacular name.

The particularly long necks of these birds may be an adaptation for upended feeding in deeper water, but may also be of value in seeing over the tall grass that covers much of their preferred habitat. In the water, they float higher than most dabblers. While these pintails do feed at night, they are most active during the early morning and late evening hours. Primarily vegetarian for much of the year, they have taken advantage of agricultural activity in some regions, and readily forage in croplands. Nesting females tend to feed heavily upon aquatic insects.

They are highly mobile, and in flight the long pointed wings and elongated tails of these birds make them easy to recognize. Often, they will zig-zag rapidly down from great heights before leveling off for a landing, and the peculiar hissing or swishing sound produced by the rapid wing beats of a flock overhead is audible for a considerable distance. Many of their courtship antics are aerial and can be spellbinding to observe. At times, many amorous males may pursue a single

8.56

8.57

8.56 *South Georgia pintail flying over southern elephant seals.*

8.57 *Northern pintail landing.*

8.58 *Wintering northern pintail.*

8.58

8.59 *Kerguelen pintail.*

8.60 - 8.61 *Puna teal. Largest and most distinctive of the three versicolor teal, this race inhabits the Andean highlands (above 12,000 feet) of Peru, Bolivia, and Chile. The sexes are similar in appearance, but the slightly smaller females have much duller speculums that lack the bluish (and sometimes greenish) reflections.*

female to the point where she may die of exhaustion. Drakes are noted for a soft whistle, and during courtship they may call out with a high-pitched chirp. Hens usually croak in a rather undabbler-like way, but at times they sound like female mallards. In the New World, pintails tend to be prairie nesters, frequently in areas that are relatively dry. Nests are often not well concealed, and as a result, nest predation can be high.

The range of northern pintails extends far into the prairies and tundra of the Arctic, where they are one of the most abundant dabblers in both the Eastern and Western hemispheres. In some years, the American segment of the population alone may exceed 10,000,000 individuals. Some migrate from Alaska to Hawaii for the winter, although almost half of the migrating American pintails congregate in California. Pintails, as a group, are among the most popular of the captive waterfowl and are known as prolific breeders.

The Kerguelen Island pintail (*A. a. eatoni*) and Crozet pintail (*A. a. drygalskii*) are rather obscure races, and like many insular forms, these little-known birds tend to be tamer than their mainland counterparts. There is also a tendency for males to lose their distinctive plumage on remote islands, possibly because the reduced number of resident species means that species recognition signals are less critical.

Kerguelen (or Eaton's) pintail inhabit Kerguelen Island, a desolate island of 1318 square miles extent located in the south Indian Ocean. They are very agile on the ground and surprisingly strong fliers as well. During low tide, they feed on the tidal flats and are known to be efficient divers, although their wings are not used underwater. Interestingly, their bills are relatively short when compared to their northern cousins, and this can probably be correlated with their habit of feeding partly on crustaceans. They are afforded total protection and are reportedly "abundant." Pairs of this race have been introduced, and are now apparently breeding, on New Amsterdam and St. Paul Islands, approximately 1000 miles to the northeast.

The Crozet race inhabits Crozet Island (approximately 425 square miles in extent), some 800 miles west of Kerguelen Island. These birds are very similar in appearance to *eatoni*, but do not have barred markings on their sides. Their status as a valid subspecies is very shaky,

as is their population status. The Crozet Island birds are rare, and even though a few Kerguelen pintails exist in collections, *drygalskii* has probably never been seen by an aviculturist.

The **silver teal** complex (*Anas versicolor*) has been subdivided into three races: the northern and southern silver (or versicolor) teal, and the more distinctive puna teal, which is the largest of the three. Puna teal (*A. v. puna*) are flashy because of their striking hyacinth-blue bills. Like the other silver teal, they exhibit little external dimorphism. They inhabit the upland plateau country of the Andes up to 10,000 feet (which is known as puna country) and are among the most common ducks on Lake Titicaca. Some ornithologists believe this teal should be elevated to full species status, because it nests side by side with the smaller versicolor teal in the Argentine Andes with no evidence of hybridization. These handsome birds have increased in captive anatid collections during the past few years, and they breed fairly readily.

The two races of versicolor teal are shy, quiet little ducks of the lowlands. They apparently form strong pair bonds, and when conditions are suitable, reportedly produce up to four broods a year. Males may assist in rearing the young, and this may explain in part the high degree of productivity. The wide, dark brown caps of these birds contrast sharply with their distinctive pale cream cheeks, and their rather long, deep blue bills are enhanced by a yellowish orange patch.

Although both races are similar, the southern versicolor teal (*A. v. fretensis*) is larger and darker, and characteristically has more yellow on the bill. With both subspecies, the sexes are almost alike but can be distinguished because the females are slightly smaller and browner, with less distinct dorsal barring. These are popular avicultural birds, but unfortunately they are not particularly numerous in collections, primarily because they are not commonly bred. In America at least, the northern race (*A. v. versicolor*) appears to be slightly more common.

The somewhat gregarious **Hottentot teal** (*Anas hottentota*) is the smallest of African wildfowl; indeed, it is among the tiniest of all ducks. In many ways, these birds appear to be smaller versions of the aforementioned versicolor teal. However, the sexes are easier to tell apart, because the secondary feathers of the drake are a dark metallic

8.62

8.62 *Hottentot teal. These tiny ducks are most often encountered in shallow freshwater marshes or ponds that are surrounded by reeds and papyrus, and which have an abundance of floating leaf plants (such as water lilies).*

8.63 *Southern versicolor teal stretching. These little ducks seek grassy ponds, open freshwater marshes, and flooded areas bordering rivers and lakes.*

8.64 *Northern versicolor teal roosting on a log over the water. In flight, the green speculums of these birds (which are lined with white both front and behind) are quite conspicuous.*

8.65 *Red-billed pintail. These attractive ducks forage extensively ashore, and in some areas they are considered agricultural pests.*

iridescent green, whereas those of the female are dark olivaceous brown, with a less glossy iridescence. In addition, female crowns tend to be browner and their facial markings are less contrasting.

Hottentot teal feed mainly during the pre-dawn and twilight hours or at night. When disturbed, these retiring and unobtrusive little ducks tend to seek shelter in vegetation bordering the water rather than fly. Although they have a wide but rather localized distribution in the wild, Hottentot teal are not at all common in captivity because they are rather reluctant breeders. Some propagators are of the opinion that they must be contained within a covered aviary in a full-winged state, rather than pinioned, if they are to be successfully bred. This supposition is not correct, however, and despite their small size, Hottentot teal are surprisingly hardy and competitive.

The **red-billed pintail or teal** (*Anas erythrorhyncha*) is a silent and undemonstrative (but nevertheless active) bird that occurs in southeast Africa. Superficially, they resemble the Bahama pintail, and even though the two species will readily hybridize in captivity, some authorities believe they are not as closely related as one might initially suspect (although a number of other taxonomists suggest otherwise). The sexes are similar, but females are generally somewhat smaller and duller, particularly in regard to their bills.

A highly nomadic and mobile species, red-billed pintail are not particularly shy and are often found in the company of other ducks. In some regions, they are extremely common, and vast concentrations may occur when conditions are suitable. Reportedly, one flock of over 500,000 was observed, although this is quite exceptional. Depending on their mood, these birds either ride high or low in the water. They are considered to be one of the best of Africa's sport ducks (at least in South Africa).

Red-billed pintail are noted for their terrestrial feeding habits, and are considered agricultural pests in some areas when they congregate in rice fields. However, they also feed on such animal fare as worms, insects, crustaceans, occasional tadpoles, and perhaps even fish. Like many other tropical ducks, they have a breeding season which is long and irregular. Currently well established in wildfowl collections, they are not particularly difficult to breed.

8.63

8.65

African **cape teal** (*Anas capensis*), or cape wigeons as they are sometimes known, may be distantly related to green-winged teal. These attractive little ducks have a distinctive pink bill with a black base, which is slightly upturned at the tip. The bill is bordered with long lamallae or tooth-like projections, indicating that filter feeding may be more important to these birds than has been reported. Eye color is highly variable, ranging from yellow to brown or deep orange to red. Females are similar to their mates, but tend to be slightly smaller, paler (except for the head), and perhaps less speckled. Drakes have rudimentary crests that can be elevated during periods of excitement.

Cape teal are surprisingly capable divers for dabbling ducks, swimming underwater with closed wings. They seek shallow water (either fresh or brackish), usually in arid areas. Essentially a nocturnal species, they tend to keep to themselves and spend much time ashore. Both sexes are silent as a rule, but drakes may utter a high-pitched clear

8.67

whistle, whereas the females produce a nasal-sounding quack. In flight, their bright metallic green speculums with black edges are very noticeable, and during courtship they are very agile on the wing.

Cape teal are one of the few dabbler species in which the male actively participates in rearing the ducklings, and the fact that both parents rear the young is no doubt at least partially responsible for the apparent low incidence of duckling mortality. It appears that these ducks may breed throughout the year, but most intensely between March and May. In areas where the species is common, some broods may merge. The population may be increasing as a result of the development of dams, reservoirs, and irrigation projects.

Generally a tame and confiding species, cape teal adapt well to a controlled environment, but they must nevertheless be closely observed when kept in a small aviary with other small waterfowl, since some individuals can become rather aggressive. All the same, they are very popular, and are not uncommonly bred. In San Diego, they have a very extended breeding season, and young have been produced in every month except December.

Cape teal are good parents, and will vigorously defend their young against birds many times their size. A pair at Sea World was exceptional in this regard, and would unhesitatingly attack potential predators (such as western gulls or black-crowned night herons) that ventured near their ducklings. I was amused one day to see a very surprised gull take off with the little defending cape teal firmly attached

to its tail. It was not until the duck was lifted completely clear of the water that it released its grip on the gull. After being accosted several times in such a manner, the intruder gave up and departed for good.

The handsome **Salvadori's duck or teal** (*Anas waigiuensis*) is the only anatid indigenous to New Guinea. It is among the least known of all the waterfowl, and in fact, the first reported nest in the wild was not even recorded until 1959. The relationship of these birds to other wildfowl species has yet to be adequately defined, and formerly they were placed in a separate genus (*Salvadorina*). However, their current placement in the genus *Anas* appears justified on the basis of recent feather protein analysis.

These little ducks inhabit relatively high altitudes, occurring between 1600 and 12,000 feet. Though unquestionably specialized, they occupy a variety of habitats, ranging from highland lakes and mountain streams to rather sluggish muddy streams. Their slender bodies are shaped somewhat like those of torrent ducks, suggesting a lifestyle associated with rushing rapids. Shy and nervous, they can be rather aggressive, and are probably quite territorial. They appear to be essentially nocturnal, are considered to be accomplished divers, and feed almost entirely on invertebrates.

No population estimates are available, but even though Salvadori's ducks are not common, they are also not presently considered to be rare either. There are some fears, however, that the introduction of competitive insectivorous fish into New Guinea rivers may prove to be disadvantageous, since these fish may compete with the ducks for food. Full government protection has been extended to *waigiuensis* since 1968, but this probably means little, since law enforcement in the jungles of primitive New Guinea can be not only difficult but downright dangerous as well.

In many respects, Salvadori's duck is similar to the more typical dabbling ducks, but some aspects of their lifestyle deviate from the norm significantly. For one thing, they are obviously not gregarious, and the pair bond is very strong, with pairs possibly remaining together throughout the year. Also, the clutch size is surprisingly small, usually only three to four relatively large eggs—perhaps indicating that egg predation is not prevalent. (In contrast, a typical mallard clutch would contain some 10 or 11 eggs.) The few nests that have been seen indicate that ground nesting is typical, and young have been seen riding on the backs of females (although both sexes are actively involved in brood care). These ducks also have a rather prolonged breeding season, but this is not particularly unusual for a tropical species.

The sexes are essentially alike, although males are slightly larger and their voices differ. A whistling note is typical of the drake (with vocalizations being infrequent), whereas the female emits only a harsh quack. Males have wing spurs and the legs and feet are yellowish. Bills of both sexes are a conspicuous bright yellow, which can vary in intensity and may be tinged or spotted with black at times. Secondaries are mostly iridescent green or purplish black, with broad white tips that form a conspicuous white stripe along the trailing edge of the speculum. There is no eclipse plumage. The relatively long tail is sometimes held almost vertical, particularly when the birds are alarmed.

Very few specimens of this most interesting species have been maintained in captivity, which explains in part why so little is known about them. The numerous problems associated with acquiring them are practically insurmountable, and it is unlikely that Salvadori's duck

8.68

8.66 (Opposite Page) *Salvadori's duck. A little-known New Guinea species, these small ducks were still practically unknown as recently as the 1920s. When alarmed or excited, they cock their tails in such a way that the white underside becomes conspicuous, and this probably functions as a social signal to their mates.* PHOTO BY PAUL JOHNSGARD

8.67 *Cape teal. Nesting females demonstrate a fondness for islands, and nests may be some distance from the water, often placed among small trees or thorny bushes. When the young fledge at about seven weeks of age, they resemble the adults.*

8.68 *Salvadori's ducks are aggressive and the limited amount of data available suggests that only one pair per pond is advisable in captivity. They dive readily for food, and apparently feed primarily on aquatic insects.* PHOTO BY LADY PHILIPPA SCOTT

8.69 *Drake blue-winged teal. These teal sometimes seek the company of other waterfowl, and appear to be particularly fond of associating with the wary black duck. (It is possible that the black ducks serve as lookouts for the teal.)*

8.70 *Male garganey teal in color. This species demonstrates a tendency to wander considerable distances and stragglers have been recorded from such remote locales as the Hawaiian Islands and even Midway Island.*

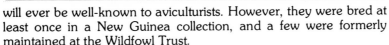

will ever be well-known to aviculturists. However, they were bred at least once in a New Guinea collection, and a few were formerly maintained at the Wildfowl Trust.

The seven species of blue-winged ducks include the blue-winged teal, the garganey, the cinnamon teal, and the four shovelers. Although these ducks may differ in many respects, all share a blue-grey coloration on the wing and certain behavioral traits. Rather specialized, they are most common in temperate climates, and are not noted for high arctic breeding ranges. The northern forms are highly migratory, the subtropical representatives are essentially sedentary, and the southern species are at least partially migratory.

The **blue-winged teal** (*Anas discors*) is a familiar and common duck of interior North America. Their range has been greatly reduced through cultivation and destruction of suitable habitat, but even though the overall population has declined during the past few decades, they still remain one of the more numerous of ducks and are regarded as one of America's most popular sporting birds.

Drakes in nuptial plumage are very attractive and are particularly noted for a distinctive white crescent in front of the eye. The male's sibilant whistle of "tseet, tseet, tseet" is easily differentiated from the weak quack of the female, and these twittering calls are clearly audible in flight. When not courting, however, the males are relatively quiet.

These rather social but shy teal may perch on stumps, large tree limbs or boulders in shallow-water areas. They generally nest around prairie potholes, sloughs, or ponds, and in shallow marshes—but they will seek appropriate sites in lakeside and boreal forest regions as well.

Blue-winged teal are among the swiftest of ducks in flight, often flying in compact flocks, and much of their courtship activity is aerial. As a rule, they winter farther south (and in greater numbers) than any other North American anatid, and banded individuals have been recovered in Brazil and Peru—the farthest south that any *banded* northern duck in the Western Hemisphere has ever been recovered. (A male in "good" condition was observed on South Georgia Island on June 20, 1972, in association with South Georgia pintail and Chilean teal.)

Two races of blue-winged teal have been described, but the validity of the Atlantic subspecies (*A. d. orphna*) is very suspect. Supposedly, these maritime birds are differentiated from the nominate race (*A. d. discors*) by their larger size and appreciably darker color, and they allegedly breed in the salt or brackish tidal marshes of the Atlantic seacoast. It is more likely, however, that these relatively minor differences are due mainly to individual variations. Aviculturists have long worked with blue-winged teal, and they are both highly regarded and easily maintained.

The unobtrusive and generally quiet **garganey teal** (*Anas quer-quedula*) is in many respects the Palearctic counterpart of the blue-winged teal. In habits, however, the garganey are more like northern shovelers, and I have often observed groups of them feeding in a manner suggestive of shovelers. They are probably not typical representatives of the blue-winged duck complex, and are certainly the least specialized of the group. Drakes are noteworthy for the extraordinarily long period of time they remain in eclipse plumage (up to nine or even ten months), and full-color males are not generally seen until late winter. In eclipse, they resemble females, but like the blue-winged teal drakes, their more colorful upper wing pattern sets them apart.

The cricket-like sounds produced by the drakes have caused them to be known as "cricket teal" in the Old World, and their calls have also been described as crackling or rattling; but females merely quack. In flight, the garganey's wings produce a characteristic hiss that experienced waterfowlers can even identify in the dark. In England, they are also known as summer teal, because they occur in that country during the summer months.

Most garganey normally winter in Asia and Africa, where they gather together in flocks numbering in the tens of thousands. (In January of 1971, for example, some 200,000 were wintering in the Senegal River Delta of Gambia and Senegal alone.) They are not particularly common in Europe but are apparently very abundant in the Soviet Union, with a range that extends all the way across that huge nation. Breeding habitat is generally located in the steppes and consists of deciduous forests, lowland lakes, ponds, and ditches surrounded by luxurious marginal vegetation. Garganey teal have been sighted in North America on occasion (especially in the Aleutian Islands), and there is some recent evidence which suggests that a small American population may exist. Stragglers have also been recorded as far south as Australia and New Guinea.

Essentially a species of inland fresh water, garganey teal are seldom seen on the sea except during migration, but on occasion they do winter in coastal marshes. Their flight is fast and agile, and they usually feed during the day in pairs, small groups, or even large flocks (although in India they are considered nocturnal feeders). As a rule, these birds are indifferent to the presence of man, unless they have been previously subjected to persecution or repeated disturbance. For some unexplainable reason, this very handsome species is scarce in American wildfowl collections, but they are well known to European aviculturists, and more have been sent to the New World in recent years.

As the vernacular name suggests, drakes of the five subspecies of **cinnamon teal** (*Anas cyanoptera*) are basically cinnamon in color. To the untrained eye, the various forms appear to have few discernible differences, and the validity of some of these races may in fact be subject to challenge. Cinnamon teal are in many respects very much like little shovelers. Their bills, for example, are slightly enlarged, and the eye colors of the sexes differ; and while this dimorphism is common among shovelers, it is not typical of blue-winged teal—suggesting that cinnamon teal may be intermediate between the two. In eclipse plumage, males are still distinguishable from their mates by their pale yellow to reddish eyes (females usually have hazel eyes); and during the breeding season, drake eye color intensifies to bright orange-red. Aside from the fulvous whistling duck and ruddy duck, cinnamon teal are the only ducks to nest in both North and South America.

8.71

8.72

8.73

8.71 *Drake garganey teal.*

8.72 *Two pair of garganey teal feeding in shoveler-like fashion.*

8.73 *Male Andean cinnamon teal. Largest of the five recognized races of cinnamon teal, these birds occupy the Andean plateau of Peru and Bolivia.*

The Andean race (*A. c. orinomus*) is the largest of the cinnamon teal, and has the longest bill of the five forms. Limited in distribution to the arid country above 12,500 feet in Peru and Bolivia, they are particularly common in the Lake Titicaca region. The Argentine subspecies (*A. c. cyanoptera*) ranges throughout the southern third of South America (including the Falkland Islands). Drakes of this race are slightly brighter red than the more familiar northern cinnamon teal, and these birds are considered to be less graceful in shape. The tropical race (*A. c. tropica*) is the smallest of the group, with males that are characterized by their spotted breasts, sides, flanks, and vents. They occupy the lowlands of Colombia up to 3000 feet.

Borrero's cinnamon teal (*A. c. borreroi*) is also found only in Colombia, but is limited to the moist highlands and the western Andes, between 7500 and 11,500 feet. Fifty percent of the males are said to be spotted on the breast, sides, and flanks, and they also tend to be somewhat darker than the teal of Argentina. A combination of habitat destruction and over-hunting has reduced this population to perhaps the point of no return. None have been observed in recent years, and it is conceivable that they are already gone.

The well-known northern cinnamon teal (*A. c. septentrionalium*) is a common North American sporting duck west of the Rocky Mountains, where it replaces the blue-winged teal. Much of the population migrates to Mexico and Central America to spend the winter. As a rule, these are rather quiet, trusting ducks and are relatively slow to take alarm. During the breeding season, they become very active, and pursuit flights are frequent, with drakes often rushing at one another. More than 50 percent of the population breeds in Utah, where nest predation by California gulls can be heavy.

The hens of this species are strikingly similar to female blue-winged teal, and it takes a competent expert to reliably differentiate them in the field. But cinnamon teal hens have slightly longer bills and wings,

8.74 *Argentine or southern cinnamon teal prefer shallow water to feed in, and they often forage in a manner that recalls the feeding behavior of shovelers.*

8.75 *The northern or common cinnamon teal is a well-known western species. In appropriate habitat, nesting densities can be as high as 100 pairs per square mile. Reproductive success can fluctuate, since these birds tend to breed in areas where botulism has traditionally been a significant cause of mortality.*

the slope of their foreheads is theoretically more gradual, and they are also a shade more reddish and less distinctly marked. In addition, the blue shoulder patch has a chalky tone that contrasts with the more waxy appearance of the patch on *A. discors*. Northern cinnamon teal are well-known to aviculturists and breed readily within a controlled environment. Argentine cinnamons are becoming more established, but this is not true of the Andean race, for even though a few *orinomus* have been in collections, little breeding success has been achieved with them. To my knowledge, *tropica* and *borreroi* have never been kept.

Shovelers are named for their shovel-like spatulate bills, which are obviously a specialized feeding adaptation. This peculiar bill has apparently evolved to allow the bird to suck in water as it moves along and then to squirt it out again at the sides, filtering out food particles in the process with long comb-like lamellae that line the edge of the bill. Interestingly, ducklings hatch with typical duck bills, but as they mature the bills enlarge. Often, shovelers feed in a line, with the trailing birds capitalizing on food particles churned to the surface by the leading birds. Comically, they often end up going around in a circle, since the lead duck will sometimes swing about and begin to follow the trailing bird. Single birds may swim in a tight circle to create a whirlpool in order to bring food to the surface. They seldom upend to feed, nor do they dive very often.

The **northern or common shoveler** (*Anas clypeata*) has the most developed bill of the group, and is popularly known as the spoonbill (or sometimes as the "smiling mallard"). Preferred feeding habitat for these ducks consists of permanent freshwater areas that are rich in plankton. On the wing, they have a peculiar humpbacked posture, and although their flight can usually be considered direct and relatively slow, they may also twist and turn in the manner of green-winged teal. During takeoff, their wings produce a characteristic loud buzzing sound, a noise which is perhaps associated with territory defense. Generally, they are rather quiet birds that can sometimes be fairly tame, and they will tolerate human presence if unmolested. The population appears to be increasing, at least in North America.

Drakes in breeding plumage are among the brightest of northern ducks, but unlike mallards and other northern dabblers they sometimes do not molt into the bright nuptial dress in the fall, staying in eclipse plumage until February. Common shovelers are reported to be polyandrous, with females associating with more than one male—but this has never been fully substantiated, and such behavior is unlikely, since shovelers as a rule form rather strong pair bonds. Drakes tend to be more territorial than most ducks, and may remain on their territories almost until the young hatch.

Interestingly, because of their superficial resemblance to mallards and their relatively poor taste, these ducks are sometimes colorfully referred to as "neighbor's mallards," because some hunters tend to give them to their neighbors while retaining the more tasty mallards for themselves. Shovelers are very popular with aviculturists, are rather easy to propagate, and can be found in almost any waterfowl collection.

The elegant **Argentine red shoveler** (*Anas platalea*), which ranges throughout the southern third of South America, may represent an intermediate link between the other shovelers and the cinnamon teal complex, since they have been known to interbreed with the teal (at least in captivity). Their conspicuous black bills are relatively small when compared to the rest of the shovelers. Like the cape shoveler, but unlike the other species, they have no eclipse plumage. They may be either resident or migratory, with the migratory urge being greatest at the northern and southern extremes of the range. They have been recorded as stragglers to the Falkland Islands.

These attractive birds seek brackish lagoons and shallow inland waters, where they tend to be naturally tame and relatively nonvocal. When they do vocalize, their calls have been described as "wooden-sounding." They appear to be fairly common in some localities, and

8.76 Male Argentine red shoveler. These lovely ducks have been little studied in the field, but they apparently prefer nesting areas that are surrounded by coastal lagoons or estuaries.

8.77 Drake northern shoveler. Because of the disproportionate size of its bill, the wings of a flying shoveler appear to be abnormally far back on the body. In flight, the bill may be carried at a downward tilt, and even at rest, the bill is often held angled downward — almost as if it were too heavy to be supported horizontally by the short, thick neck.

8.78 Drake Argentine red shoveler.

during the nonbreeding season, I have encountered them in the company of other waterfowl. In eastern Argentina, they are considered a gamebird species. Red shovelers are not nearly as common in captivity as *A. clypeata*, but breeding success in recent years has been far greater than it formerly was and they are becoming more available.

The **South African or cape shoveler** (*Anas smithi*) is possibly the least known of the group. Generally, they are the dullest of the shovelers in coloration, but the bright yellow eyes, legs, and feet of the males contrast sharply with their black bills, and their blue shoulders and white-edged green speculums are conspicuous in flight. Females are similar to their mates, but are generally duller in overall color, with no iridescence on the upper parts. Their calls are rather like a snort or a belch.

Cape shovelers may be year-round breeders and appear to be significantly less territorial than the other members of the tribe; on some islands, they have been known to nest in loose "colonies." Sometimes, courting males engage in aerial displays, while nonbreeding birds are relatively silent and tend to gather in large flocks. Essentially freshwater birds, they may frequent tidal estuaries, lagoons, and saline pans as well. Mainly, they are diurnal feeders, and although they

usually feed in typical shoveler fashion, I have occasionally observed them ineffectively snapping at passing flying insects. They particularly favor fertile waters that are rich in planktonic organisms, such as sewage disposal ponds. South African hunters consider them to be an indifferent gamebird species, and despite their rather limited distribution, the population may be increasing in some areas. Cape shovelers are poorly represented in American wildfowl collections, not because interest is lacking, but rather as the result of a general unavailability of the species. They are more common in Europe, and are well established at the Wildfowl Trust.

The closely related Australian and New Zealand shovelers are collectively referred to as the **Australasian shoveler** (*Anas rhynchotis*). Both are quite colorful, with distinctive white crescent-shaped cheek patches (although these are less pronounced on the Australian birds). The New Zealand race (*A. r. variegata*) which is more brightly colored overall, is distributed throughout the country, but is most common in the rich coastal wetlands. Their range is currently somewhat reduced, but the population appears to be stable and may even be on the increase. Formerly, they occurred on the Chatham Islands as well, but they have been gone from there for a number of years.

8.79 *Group of foraging New Zealand shovelers, with grey teal and New Zealand grey ducks in the background.*

8.80 *Pair of Australian or blue-winged shovelers.*

8.81 *Cape or South African shovelers.*

8.82 *New Zealand shoveler drake. These ducks frequent inland waters and coastal lagoons, and tend to avoid streams in forested areas. They are widespread and the population is probably increasing.*

8.83 *Male cape shoveler. These birds mix freely with other waterfowl species. During the breeding season, they are generally encountered in pairs or small groups; but on occasion, flocks may contain as many as 600 ducks.*

The Australian or blue-winged shoveler (*A. r. rhynchotis*) is locally known as the "stinker," because of the offensive smell produced when one is cooked. They have never been particularly common, and unfortunately, their numbers have declined significantly during the past half century. At the present time, they are most abundant in inland regions, because swamp drainage has drastically altered their former coastal habitats. Australian shovelers are nomadic birds, which are usually observed in small, widely dispersed groups. They can be very wary and, as a rule, are quiet and unobtrusive. Very few birds of either race exist in wildfowl collections outside of Australia. The New Zealand shoveler is somewhat more abundant than *rhynchotis*, but is far from common in captivity and not firmly established, at least not in North America. They are no more difficult to maintain than the other shovelers, but propagation has been surprisingly challenging as the ducklings are somewhat delicate.

The **marbled teal** (*Marmaronetta* [*Anas*] *angustirostris*), is included with the dabblers, but exhibits some behavioral and anatomical similarities to pochards which suggest that it may be more closely related to them. It may, in fact, represent an intermediate ancestral link between the two tribes (although some aviculturists suggest a possible relation-

8.84

ship to the crested ducks). Most contemporary taxonomists place the marbled teal in the monotypic genus *Marmaronetta*, but Delacour still believes it to be a true *Anas*.

Both sexes usually have shaggy crests, although some females lack crests and the male's is somewhat larger. In addition, the relatively long and narrow bill of the male is uniformly grey, whereas the female's is often pale, or cream colored, or olive-green near the base—but this is not a reliable indicator of sex. (Females may also have less distinct eye stripes.) Unlike all other members of the genus *Anas*, these birds do not have a metallic wing speculum, nor do they have an eclipse plumage.

Marbled teal are enchanting little birds, rather quiet, retiring, and unobtrusive. Drakes may utter a weak nasal squeak during courtship, and females are noted for a kind of low croaking note which is not typical of dabbling females. Preferred habitat consists of lowland sheltered ponds, and brackish or salt water marshes that contain much vegetation. Almost exclusively vegetarian, these birds readily dive while foraging. In some regions of Spain, they may nest in the reed roofs of old huts, but their nests are more typically placed in dense thickets or in burrows with tunnel-like entrances.

8.85

8.84 *Pair of marbled teal. Throughout much of their range, the population of these enchanting little ducks is greatly reduced. Their habitat requirements are rather strict, and uncontrolled development of remaining habitat will undoubtedly continue to affect the teal adversely. At times, these birds will roost on low overhanging branches. They generally feed in shallow water, but occasionally will forage ashore and even in corn fields. Essentially vegetarian, they may also ingest aquatic insects and their larvae, worms, and small molluscs.*

8.85 *Marbled teal. These birds tend to be gregarious, sometimes even when nesting (particularly in Spain, where nests may be as close as three feet to one another). Shy and unobtrusive by nature, marbled teal generally spend much time on reed-covered lakes and slow-moving rivers.*

While marbled teal are not presently considered an endangered species, the population has declined significantly throughout much of their range, and they are believed to be among the rarest of Europe's breeding anatids. There are perhaps less than 100 pairs in Spain, and these remaining birds represent a mere fraction of the numbers that formerly occurred in the region. (At the turn of the century, marbled teal were considered to be one of the most common of Spanish ducks.) They have rapidly declined in Pakistan as well, and restocking with captive-reared birds has not yet met with much success.

Their total range in North Africa, southern Europe, and the Near East is very restricted because of limited suitable habitat—with the result that they are extremely vulnerable to development and other forms of persecution brought about by an expanding human population. During the winter, they become more gregarious, and in 1972 some 10,000 wintering marbled teal were accounted for in Iran. The total current population is estimated at about 21,000 ducks. Fortunately, a healthy captive breeding population exists and they are popular with most breeders.

The remainder of the species that are tentatively placed with the dabbling ducks are most puzzling taxonomically, since they are clearly no more closely related to one another than they are to the more conventional members of the Anatini. With the exception of the ringed teal, all are extremely rare or virtually nonexistent in wildfowl collections.

The South American **ringed teal** (*Calonetta leucophrys*) is one of the most attractive and dainty of waterfowl, and while the male is undeniably more colorful, the hens can be just as striking in their own subtle way. Drakes of this species are unusual in that they do not undergo an eclipse molt but retain their bright breeding plumage year-round (a trait which endears them to aviculturists). The call of the male is a wheezy soft whistle, while that of the female is a harsh cat-like scream.

Ringed teal perch readily and are cavity nesters. At times, they have been observed using the bulky stick nests of the monk parakeet. Pair bonds are strong and may even be permanent, but males do not appear to be involved in incubation. (There is some data which suggest otherwise, but this remains to be documented.) However, drakes do actively assist in rearing the young, and in some cases may be more attentive than their mates; on rare occasions, they may actually chase the hen away. Ringed teal inhabit tropical forested country and appear to be rather scarce, although there is no information which suggests that they are rare. They demonstrate some migratory tendencies, and in flight their wings produce a pleasant whistling sound.

On the basis of behavior and skeletal anatomy, some specialists believe that ringed teal should be included with the perching ducks in the tribe Cairinini. Johnsgard has already shifted them over to this group, but such a move must be considered tentative, since analysis of feather proteins suggests a closer relationship with the dabblers. In recent years, ringed teal have become very popular avicultural birds, and in certain collections they are extremely prolific breeders. While they do very well pinioned, many breeders maintain them in a full-winged state in heavily planted and covered aviaries to capitalize on their perching abilities. Their popularity is enhanced by the fact that they can be readily mixed with other smaller, more delicate species without fear of harm.

8.87

The recently extinct **pink-headed duck** (*Rhondonessa caryophyllacea*) was certainly not the most attractive of waterfowl, but its highly unusual coloration made it one of the most distinctive of the anatids all the same. Traditionally lumped with the dabblers, this strange species has recently been subjected to anatomical re-evaluation, and based on this work, it appears they might be more appropriately included in the pochard tribe. Johnsgard has, in fact, already moved them, and this shift appears justified on the basis of their pochard-like shape alone.

Essentially blackish brown from the neck down, males were characterized by their bright pink heads and hind necks, and the slight tuft behind the head. Even the narrow bill was bright pink, while the eyes were brownish orange, and the legs and feet were rather brownish. In flight, the light pinkish buff speculum and pale shell-pink underwings were said to contrast greatly with the otherwise dark bodies. Females were slightly smaller but similar, although the pink on their heads and necks was not quite as bright nor as sharply demarcated.

The tragic loss of the pink-headed duck is perhaps symptomatic of our troubled times. While it was last reliably sighted in the wild in 1935 (in the Darbhanga district of Bihar Province, India), the species was not afforded full protection *until 1956*—a classic example of too little, far too late. (A small group of *Rhodonessa* was reported in the mid-1960s near the Burmese-Tibetan border, but the severe political problems in that region make it impossible for foreigners to enter and confirm their possible existence. There have also been recent reports of pink-headed ducks being seen or shot in India, but these may be explained by the rather close resemblance between the pink-headed duck and the red-crested pochard, which may be its closest relative. In the field, the two species could conceivably be confused.)

8.86 (Opposite Page) *Male ringed teal. A fairly migratory species, these birds may move northward several hundred miles into southern Brazil during the nonbreeding season. Most of the population apparently breeds in northwestern Argentina and Paraguay.*

8.87 *The perching abilities of ringed teal are clearly illustrated here.*

8.88

8.89

8.90

8.88 *Museum skin of the extinct pink-headed duck (male).*

8.89 *Old mount of a female pink-headed duck. The pochard-like shape is clearly evident.*

8.90 *This old photograph, taken by the eminent Indian ornithologist Dr. Salim Ali in November of 1929, is of great historical interest because it shows no less than three living pink-headed ducks in the famous English collection of Alfred Ezra. Aviculturists will also be interested to note the number of cotton teal that were maintained on an open pond.*

Pink-headed ducks were never common in recent times but were said to be more abundant over 100 years ago, when the Duars of eastern Bengal in India occasionally observed them while hunting tigers from the backs of elephants. Not regarded as prime table birds, they were nevertheless offered from time to time in the markets of Calcutta. Ironically, the ducks were highly sought by affluent colonial "sportsmen," not only because of their highly unusual coloration but also because of their *scarcity*. It is possible that they were once more common than believed, since their preferred habitat of thickly vegetated swampy grasslands and jungle areas would perhaps have prevented close observation. Furthermore, they were said to be shy and rather secretive birds which tended not to flush easily.

No doubt their demise was hastened by direct persecution, such as hunting, but as is the case with many imperiled animals, it was habitat alteration and destruction that ultimately sealed their doom. Essentially an Indian species (also found in central Burma), their center of distribution was in an area today referred to as Bangledesh—a region perhaps best known for its unbelievably dense human population. As the wetlands were drained and converted to cropland, the relatively specialized pink-headed duck was apparently unable to cope with the rapid changes and pressures, and as a result, simply died out.

Very little is known about their natural history, but pink-headed ducks appear to have been omnivorous feeders. Foraging mainly on the surface of the water, they were accomplished divers as well. The vocalization of the male has been described as a wheezy whistle and that of the female as a low quack. A number of accounts indicate that pink-headed ducks sometimes perched in trees. During the winter, they gathered in small flocks (up to 40 birds upon occasion), but generally, they were encountered in small parties. The ground nests, which were sometimes (but not always) situated close to water, were circular in shape and well constructed of dry grass and a few feathers. Clutch sizes varied between five and ten eggs, and the white eggs were rather peculiar in that they were almost perfectly spherical in shape.

A few pink-headed ducks were maintained in captivity over the years, and the species was first seen in Europe at the London Zoo in 1894. Unfortunately, no captive birds ever demonstrated any inclination to breed, although they were hardy, not quarrelsome, and required no special care. Delacour himself possessed a few in the late 1920s and he once suggested to me that they were "rather stupid." Some captive birds lived up to 12 years. The last specimen died either in 1936 or 1939—but rumors persist about a male in the famous Ezra collection (England or India) that allegedly survived until 1945. All that presently remains of the mysterious pink-headed ducks are rapidly fading memories and some 80 skins.

Pink-eared ducks (*Malacorhynchus membranaceus*), on the other hand, are still relatively abundant, and range widely throughout inland Australia and Tasmania. These little birds resemble shovelers because they have huge lead-grey spatulate bills, but their bills have developed to a much greater extreme, and the sides of the upper mandible droop down to form large flaps at the sides—and unlike shovelers, even the ducklings have the modified bill upon hatching, suggesting a specialized lifestyle from the very beginning.

The overhanging bill flaps are quite soft and pliable, and may serve to channel the water during feeding so that the ducks can more readily filter out algae and plankton. At the same time, even though pink-eared ducks are highly specialized feeders, I have also observed them upending in the manner of typical dabbling ducks, and they feed to some extent on small aquatic invertebrates as well. Like the shovelers, these ducks sometimes engage in communal foraging behavior; but usually only pairs (sometimes trios) feed together. Having said all this, it is nevertheless clear that any resemblance to shovelers in form and feeding behavior is strictly superficial; the two are not related in any way, and their resemblance is simply a result of convergent evolution. A taxonomically peculiar species, pink-eared ducks exhibit affinities with no less than three waterfowl tribes: dabblers, perching ducks, and shelducks.

The small pink patch behind the eye is the source of their vernacular name, but they are sometimes more appropriately referred to as zebra ducks because of their bold black and white stripes. The pink patch, while very bright, is often very difficult to observe (and is absent altogether on immatures), and these birds lack the metallic speculum that is so typical of dabblers. Both sexes are virtually identical in appearance (although females are slightly smaller), and both call with a musical chirrup or clear twittering whistle that is frequently uttered on the wing (although the vocalization of the female is somewhat lower in pitch). Pink-eared ducks are reputed to have a relatively unstable flight, which has been described as "weak and fluttering," but they fly very well and, in fact, are both agile and maneuverable. They often swim with their tails up and their rumps held high, and seldom leave the security of the water except to roost. Surprisingly, when they do so, they perch readily. They are not prone to dive, except when wounded or perhaps when engaged in courtship displays.

The greatest breeding concentration is generally in the southeast portion of the continent. Depending on climatic conditions, these ducks appear to be capable of breeding at any time of the year, and they may do so at a different time and place from year to year. However, when water conditions do not meet their specifications, no breeding may take place. Nest sites may be built in a variety of locales, from ground level up to 30 feet above water—on logs, on fence posts or flat limbs, in the crotches of trees, and even in the nests of other waterbirds. The nest is lined solely with their own thick down, which is somewhat oily and readily clings to itself. During years of intense breeding activity, several nests may be built on top of one another, and up to 60 eggs have been recorded from a single hollow (probably the result of competition for nest sites). Seven eggs, however, is the normal clutch size. Males remain within the vicinity of the brood, but may not be involved in defense of the young.

Pink-eared ducks are highly mobile, and are considered to be the most nomadic of all Australian waterfowl. They primarily prefer dry

8.91

8.92

8.93

8.91 *Pink-eared ducks perch readily when ashore.*

8.92 *The specialized and highly-modified bill of the pink-eared duck is clearly illustrated here.*

8.93 *Dozing pink-eared duck.*

8.94 *(Overleaf) Trio of pink-eared ducks.*

8.95 *Duckling of the New Zealand blue duck. Note that even at this early age, the peculiar lateral lobes of the upper mandible are clearly evident.*

8.96 *Adult male blue duck. Pair bonds of this species are apparently strong. The female alone incubates, but the male remains nearby, often concealed. Young assume the appearance of adults at about six months of age.*

8.97 *(Opposite Page) Portrait of a drake Chilean torrent duck.*

8.96

inland areas where the rainfall does not exceed fifteen inches a year, but their distribution is erratic, and is determined by the availability of stagnant saline water. These birds are not particularly uncommon, and hunting is even permitted in some states. However, as the rivers become more controlled, and more water is diverted for irrigation and other purposes, suitable habitat will undoubtedly disappear—and with the habitat will go this charming, highly-specialized species.

Usually tame and confiding, pink-eared ducks may occasionally be seen on the water in city park lakes. Often encountered in huge flocks, they commonly associate with grey teal. Like many endemic Australian avian species, they are practically unknown to aviculturists outside of Australia (as of early 1979, only three could be accounted for at the Wildfowl Trust)—and this is most unfortunate, because these little ducks are among the most beautiful and unique of the wildfowl. They have apparently been bred in Australia under semi-natural conditions.

The **blue or mountain duck** (*Hymenolaimus malacorhynchos*) is one of the few indigenous waterfowl species of New Zealand. Although it formerly occurred down to sea level, it now occupies a narrow ecological niche along the banks of remote and fast-moving high mountain streams. Habitat requirements of these birds are very specific, and only the torrent duck, harlequin duck, and possibly the Salvadori's duck display similar preferences. The call of the male is a strong, shrill whistle (a type of vocalization which appears to be characteristic of species that frequent loud, fast-water habitats). Females, however, utter only a rasping quack. Mainly crepuscular feeders, blue ducks are extremely specialized in their almost total dependence on the aquatic insects that abound in the highly oxygenated waters.

Their specialized feeding habits are reflected by modifications of the bill. Peculiar soft black lateral lobes of the upper mandible overhang the lower bill, and these may function as a "tool" for scraping or sucking algae and invertebrate animal life off of submerged rocks.

Generally, these ducks feed in water that is too shallow for diving; and indeed, they are not particularly adept under the water and use their wings when engaged in such activity. Both sexes are similar in that they have yellow eyes and wing spurs, but the smaller females tend to have less brownish spotting on the breast. Interestingly, the pinkish white bill color can vary in intensity, depending on the bird's emotional state, and this color variation has been described as "blushing."

Although they rarely take to the air, blue ducks are strong and accomplished fliers. They are not gregarious, and their lifestyle is such that one would expect the pair bonds to be strong and pairs to remain together year-round; however, this has yet to be fully documented. Rather territorial, they will vigorously defend their particular section of a stream. Nest sites appear to be variable and include natural burrows, log hollows, trees, cliff ledges, and clumps of tussock grass, usually close to the water. Successful nest sites of previous seasons may be re-used. As with Salvadori's duck and torrent ducks, the clutch size is abnormally small, consisting merely of four to five fairly large eggs. Males assist in the rearing of the young.

Blue ducks are no longer common, perhaps in part because they tend to be quite tame and confiding when encountered—and man formerly took advantage of their trusting ways. Now fully protected, they have nevertheless suffered as a result of habitat destruction, and introduced predators have taken their toll as well. The introduction of trout could be particularly detrimental, because it may increase competition for limited food sources (especially the caddis fly larvae) on which the birds greatly depend. The current population is believed to be on the order of 5000, and it is possible that these ducks would not still exist if they did not inhabit such inaccessible and remote areas.

No blue ducks are currently found in collections outside New Zealand, although they were kept at the Wildfowl Trust at one time. In recent years, New Zealand Wildlife Service biologists have been somewhat successful in captively rearing them, and are hoping that ultimately they can be re-introduced into their former haunts. Their reproductive potential is low, however, and in the long run the preservation of remaining habitat will probably be the key to their continued survival. Little can be said about their relationship to other waterfowl species, except that *Hymenolaimus* does exhibit some similarities to perching ducks, and preliminary study of feather proteins indicates that they are probably not particularly closely related to the Anatini (although this analysis was not helpful in determining what they *are* related to).

Of all the diverse forms of wildfowl, perhaps none is more spectacular and unusual than the obscure South American **torrent ducks** (*Merganetta armata*); not only because of their vivid external appearance and design, but also because of their extraordinary behavior and extremely specific habitat requirements. Torrent ducks comprise a very distinct monotypic genus, with a total of six races currently described. However, it is probable that the Argentine (*M. a. berlepschi*), Bolivian (*M. a. garleppi*), and Turner's (*M. a. turneri*) torrent ducks represent variants of the Peruvian race (*M. a. leucogenis*), and will be ultimately discarded. Johnsgard considers the torrent ducks distinct enough to warrant a separate tribe of their own—the Merganettini—which, using his new taxonomic arrangement, he places between the perching ducks and the dabbling ducks. There is also some evidence (based on feather protein analysis) which indicates that they may be more closely related to the perching ducks—or even the shelducks—than their physical appearance would suggest. It could be

8.98 *Female Chilean torrent duck. These highly-specialized, little-known ducks often display a pronounced sexual dimorphism. The larger males are perhaps more colorful, but the females are also undeniably beautiful.*

8.99 *Drake Bolivian torrent duck. While six subspecies have been described, it is unlikely that more than three are valid.*
PHOTO BY PAUL JOHNSGARD

8.100 *Male Chilean torrent duck. For the most part, adults are rather silent birds, but when excited, drakes are prone to call out with a shrill whistle or unduck-like squeaking chatter. These calls are clearly audible above the roar of the rushing torrents that are a major part of their habitat.*

8.101 *Male Peruvian torrent duck. The fast-water habitat of the species is clearly illustrated here. These birds demonstrate a strong attachment to a particular stretch of river, and the extent of their territories is variable depending on the terrain. Territories are probably relatively permanent, and for the greater part of the year torrent ducks are encountered as pairs. Due to their strict habitat preferences, the species is vulnerable; but in general, they do not appear to be endangered at the moment.*
PHOTO BY GARY R. JONES

that their closest living relative is the equally puzzling Salvadori's duck of New Guinea.

The head plumage of the male is strongly patterned in contrasting black and white stripes, with long white feathers extending back from the head and down the side of the neck. Drakes occupying northern portions of the range, such as the Colombian race (*M. a. colombiana*), are much paler in color than males that inhabit more southern regions, such as the Chilean subspecies (*M. a. armata*). Males are in general larger and heavier than their mates, and much more striking and conspicuous—but the hens are every bit as attractive in a more subdued way. Females are characterized by rich somber rusty brown underparts and throats (contrasting with their greyish dorsal regions). Both sexes have rosy-red bills and reddish legs, as well as iridescent green speculums.

All races of torrent ducks are confined to turbulent fast-flowing rivers and streams of the Andes, and their preference for cold, clean, fast-rushing streams (or torrents) is responsible for their descriptive vernacular name. They measure approximately 17 inches in length, with elongated torpedo-shaped bodies that are clearly designed specifically for swimming against the swiftest of currents. Noted for relatively long stiff tail feathers, they also possess peculiar spurs at the joint of the wing, with those of the male being superior in size. (The function of these carpal spurs is unknown. They may serve some purpose in courtship or defense, but fights between rival males have not been reported. It has also been suggested that the spurs might be useful in securing the bird in turbulent waters, but this supposition has yet to be documented by field observation, and since the spurs of collected birds show little signs of wear, it is highly unlikely that this is their function.) Obviously, these ducks have adapted themselves to the same type of demanding lifestyle and habitat as the blue duck of New Zealand, but the two forms do not appear to be particularly closely related.

Even though the general range of torrent ducks is geographically immense, stretching down the entire 5000-mile length of the Andes, they are actually very localized in distribution because of their highly specialized ecological requirements, and nowhere can they be considered common. While usually considered a high-altitude species (occupying habitats at least as high as 14,000 feet), they also occur at sea level—particularly in the southern portion of their range, where the mountains diminish in height, precipitation increases, and the slopes are covered with a progressively thicker forest. Torrent ducks are obviously a very vulnerable species, and any violation of their habitat will undoubtedly have an adverse effect on them. However, while the northern population may be suffering some decline, those to the south appear more secure.

Almost everything about torrent ducks is specialized: their body design, their feeding method, their nest, their reproductive biology, and even their ultra-specific food requirements. Analysis of stomach contents has demonstrated that their diet consists almost exclusively of insect larvae—particularly those of the caddis fly and (to a lesser degree) stone and May flies. These favored insect larvae inhabit only the rocks and stones in the oxygen-rich waters of fast-flowing mountain rivers and streams. No trace of vegetable matter, fish, or molluscs has been discovered in the diet of torrent ducks.

The stiff tail feathers and large webbed feet of these ducks may enable them to stand securely on slippery rocks, even when the rock surfaces occur at a steep angle. Their narrow flexible bills are well suited to exploring the innumerable cracks and niches among the partially or wholly submerged rocks. For the most part, adults are relatively silent birds—but when excited, drakes tend to whistle or to emit a high-pitched unduck-like squeaking chatter that is clearly audible above the roar of the rushing water. (As noted elsewhere in this book, sharp, clean calls also typify the blue, Salvadori's, and harlequin ducks—all species which occur in noisy fast-water habitats.)

Torrent ducks are not at all gregarious, and pairs occupy exclusive breeding (and even foraging) territories. The population density of even prime stream habitat probably does not exceed one pair per half mile. The breeding season appears to be rather prolonged, particularly in the north, where weather extremes are less severe. While very few nests have been seen, it appears that torrent ducks are typically cavity nesters. In at least one case, a female occupied a burrow excavated by a kingfisher, and a ledge and a ground nest have been described as well. Pair bonds are long and probably permanent.

Very little information regarding incubation period is available, but it would appear to be extraordinarily long—perhaps as long as 40 to 44 days (although pipping has been reported to commence as early as the 38th day). If the sparse data available on the incubation period of torrent ducks do prove to be accurate, then *Merganetta* has the distinction of having the longest recorded incubation of any living species of waterfowl.

Only the female incubates, and she may spend extended periods of time off the nest (when she is joined by the male)—which perhaps explains, at least in part, the long incubation period. Not surprisingly, the clutch size is small, consisting of three to four relatively large eggs.

Following hatching, ducklings leap from the nest site when called by the female, and immediately appear to be at ease in the hostile environment, taking to the turbulent water without hesitation. In addition, they are well developed upon hatching and even have stiff quills in the tail, perhaps to assist them in maintaining their balance on the slippery rocks. (However, it is probable that quite a few of the young are swept away and ultimately lost.) Both sexes apparently participate in rearing the young. When searching for torrent ducks in southern Argentina, I was told of instances in which adults were seen to carry young on their backs, but I was unable to verify this behavior.

Torrent ducks are virtually unknown to aviculturists, and to most field biologists as well. Two adult males of the Chilean race reside in the New York Zoological Garden, where they were hatched from eggs collected in Chile in 1969. In late 1978, a joint venture involving the Wildfowl Trust, Sea World, and a private aviculturist resulted in the acquisition of four fertile eggs from Chile. These were taken to England in a portable self-contained field incubator, and fortunately, all hatched (producing one male and three females). *Merganetta* has

8.102 *Male Bolivian torrent duck. All the torrent ducks inhabit cold, clear, well-oxygenated waters. This habitat generally consists of rivers and torrents with rapids and waterfalls, usually interspersed with stretches of more placid water.* PHOTO BY PAUL JOHNSGARD

8.103 *Turner's torrent duck male.* PHOTO BY PAUL JOHNSGARD

8.104 *Male Colombian torrent duck.* PHOTO BY PAUL JOHNSGARD proved to be among the most challenging of all waterfowl to get established in captivity, but limited work with them has already suggested that they are hardy and long-lived once acclimatized.

The final species to be considered with the dabbling ducks is the peculiar **freckled duck** (*Stictonetta naevosa*) of southern Australia, which is also known as the monkey or oatmeal duck. Johnsgard has placed the freckled duck in a new monotypic tribe, the Stictonettini—arguing that while it is fairly duck-like in form and foraging behavior, it exhibits a number of anatomical traits which suggest affinities with swans and geese.

For one thing, the downy young are not patterned, a trait that is common with swans and geese but which is completely unknown with the dabblers. In addition, the trachea of the male loops outside the sternum (as it does with the magpie goose and to some extent with northern swans), and the voicebox is similarly shaped to that of a swan. Likewise, the leg scale pattern, the simple plumage lacking a speculum, the vocalizations, and even threat and courtship displays are somewhat swan-like. Furthermore, unlike most ducks, freckled ducks apparently have but a single annual molt.

It is possible that this species is the sole survivor of a very ancient waterfowl lineage, which really has no other close living relatives. In fact, the Australian ornithologist Harry Frith suggests that it is a rather unique primitive species, which may be closer to the original stock of the family Anatidae than *any* other present day species.

Freckled ducks are relatively large birds, with males averaging in excess of two pounds, and they derive their vernacular name from the small buff-colored freckles on the head and upper parts. Females are similar to males but are slightly smaller, and they may be lighter in

8.105

8.106

8.105 *Freckled ducks.*
PHOTO BY A. EAMES

8.106 *Pair of freckled ducks with grey teal on the bank.*
PHOTO BY CHRIS SPIKER

8.107 *Pair of freckled ducks. The red basal portion of the drake's bill indicates that the bird is in breeding condition. Essentially a sedentary species, these ducks normally have little need to wander because of the relatively permanent nature of their habitat. However, if need be, they do have the ability to move and exploit newly-formed habitats, particularly if forced to do so by a prolonged drought.*
PHOTO BY A. EAMES

8.108 (Opposite Page) *Mallards at dusk.*

8.107

color about the head, with a less contrasting pattern of freckles. Both sexes have high pointed crowns, although the drake's is somewhat higher. The basal half of the drake's proportionally long bill is greenish

gray for most of the year, but during the breeding season it becomes a brilliant red-orange.

These ducks appear to be quite fearless in the wild, but their general lack of alertness and tameness gives one the impression that they may simply be stupid. Usually, they occur in small groups of four or five birds, and a flock of more than 20 is unusual, although during severe dry spells several hundred may congregate. During the nonbreeding season, they become very nomadic and are characterized by extensive, often erratic movements, particularly in times of severe drought. Their vocalizations have been characterized as either pig-like grunts or the mewing of a cat, and one of their calls has even been colorfully described as "like a belch backwards." At times, they may also utter trumpet-like or flute-like whistles. Despite all this colorful imagery, however, they can be considered a relatively nonvocal species.

Freckled ducks are thought to be the rarest of Australian ducks—although they *may* not be as many people believe. They occur at widely separated locales, but the actual extent of their range is rather small, and they are essentially limited to inland southeastern Australia and the southwest portion of western Australia. They are subjected to some hunting pressure, but the main threat is loss of appropriate habitat. While apparently not endangered for the moment, the species is insecure and very vulnerable, and uncontrolled drainage programs could have fatal consequences.

Unlike most dabblers, freckled ducks do not appear to be capable of springing directly from the water during takeoff. They have a slightly hunched appearance in flight and fly a good deal more swiftly than some of the literature indicates. Not infrequently, they associate with other duck species, even in flight. Essentially nocturnal, they tend to retire during the day to dense cover, where they remain very inconspicuous. Sometimes, they perch on floating logs or flooded posts and timbers.

Freckled ducks are primarily surface feeders, and generally forage by filter feeding with only the bill submerged, but they do occasionally upend as well. In some respects, they feed like a stiff-tail, and the bill shape shows some stiff-tail features. They forage extensively on algae, but also consume tiny fish, minute molluscs, insects, or crustaceans (although the larger animal fare probably constitutes a relatively minor portion of their diet). If need be, they are surprisingly skilled divers, and readily resort to underwater escape if threatened during the flightless molt.

The nest is well constructed for that of a duck and is usually located either at water level or in tangled flood debris at the base of a tree. Falling water levels may cause the nests to be elevated later in the season. The clutch size is five to ten (average seven) cream or ivory colored eggs, and apparently the female alone incubates for 26 to 28 days. Based on the little data available, it seems as though the pair bond is not strong during incubation, since males have not been seen near incubating females. The fledging period is rather long, and it is not known whether drakes participate in brood rearing.

Stictonetta has yet to be studied in great depth, and much remains to be learned about their natural history. They have been kept in captivity on rare occasions in Australia, but have never been seen outside the country. As with some of the other little-known waterfowl species, the lack of knowledge about them is perhaps a reflection of the unavailability of captive birds necessary for detailed long-term studies. The future in this regard does not appear to be very bright, and this I consider to be most unfortunate.

9
Eiders
Somateriini

All four species of eiders are highly specialized diving ducks. Circumpolar in distribution, they inhabit the cold arctic and subarctic zone, with ranges that sometimes overlap considerably. A number of specialists include the eiders in the sea duck tribe Mergini, but others feel strongly that eiders probably evolved from an offshoot of the dabbling ducks—possibly when some dabbler species invaded the marine coastal habitat. (Eiders were originally included with the sea ducks by Delacour and Mayr in 1945, but Delacour shifted them to the present tribe in 1956. Recently, however, Johnsgard has proposed that they be moved back to the Mergini.)

These ducks have long been famous for their thick, heavy down, which has been used by man as an insulating material since before the beginning of recorded history. Eider down is extremely soft, light, and cohesive, with the best thermal quality of any known natural substance. Fortunately for the eiders, synthetics have been developed in recent years that are almost as effective—but no synthetic yet produced is able to match the combined insulating quality and lightness of the genuine article, so many people still prefer down. It is said that eider down will retain its cohesiveness and elasticity for almost 30

9.2

9.1 (Opposite Page) *Drake king eider on a tundra pond along the north coast of Alaska in July. This particular bird is entering the initial stages of the eclipse molt.*

9.2 *Full-color male eiders are considered to be among the most beautiful of all birds, as illustrated by this spectacled eider. A high arctic species, spectacled eiders are almost totally unknown to most people.*

years. In North America at least, natural eider down is an expensive luxury, and most of the down used comes from domestic geese and is imported from China.

Unbelievable amounts of eider down have been marketed over the years, and some historians suggest that ten tons of cleaned down (or more) were bartered annually during the early part of this century in Russia alone. There is reason to view such figures with suspicion, however, since ten tons of down would represent the harvest of more than 500,000 eider nests.

There is some evidence that early Vikings may have harvested eider down, and activity of this kind still continues today in Norway and Iceland. Colonies of these birds are managed and pampered in those countries to such a degree that they are considered eider farms. In Iceland alone, there may be as many as 200 such farms, producing an average annual yield of perhaps 8000 pounds of processed down. The normal yield of each nest is a little more than half an ounce, and the going price for the down is currently around 30 dollars per pound, with ten pounds of raw down reducing to about one pound of cleaned down. As many as 3000 pairs of eiders may occupy some farms, and in the past a few farms had as many as 12,000 pairs. During the early

9.3

1960s, the aggregate total consisted of approximately 250,000 pairs, but it is undoubtedly somewhat less today. (Times are changing in Iceland, and more and more people are turning to more lucrative vocations, such as commercial fishing. This in turn affects the eiders, for significant numbers become trapped annually in nets set for lump-fish. Pollution in coastal waters has also contributed to eider mortality, although it is somewhat less serious today than it was during World War II.)

Eiders nesting on farms are strictly protected, and in some instances, man-induced colonies have been established in suitable areas that are surrounded by predator-proof fences. Nesting holes in walls or in the ground have been provided for the birds, and some eider hens have become so trusting that they even nest inside buildings. Avian predators such as gulls and ravens are shot on sight and are poisoned, while mink are hunted with dogs. If not controlled, egg predators can cause considerable damage. In 1973, for example, ravens alone caused the loss of more than 12,000 eggs at Aethey, Iceland. During normal years, down is collected as the clutch is set, and then gathered again midway through incubation. The hen is then left alone to rear the young, and thus the reproductive potential is theoretically not compromised. When the nest is abandoned, down is collected for a third time.

The three larger eider species are extremely heavy-bodied birds, but are strong fliers nonetheless. They fly unexpectedly fast, and several species tend to move low over the water, often in single file; sometimes, these wavering lines have an undulating motion that is beautiful to watch. The migratory urge of most eider species, unlike that of many northern ducks, is not strong, although they migrate locally within given areas. At the same time, some king eiders may move east and west as far (and as regularly) as many other anatid species may migrate north and south. Such migratory movements are chiefly diurnal and are governed by climatic conditions. In general, members of the tribe prefer to winter as far north as possible, wherever there is open water and a food source, regardless of ambient air temperature.

Eiders are among the most pelagic of ducks, spending the majority of their time at sea, frequently in the roughest waters. Like many oceanic species, these birds have acquired anatomical and physiological modifications which enable them to ingest salt water, including enlarged glands above the eyes that facilitate the excretion of excess salt through their nostrils. Proficient divers, eiders depend greatly upon their wings to assist them in underwater propulsion, unlike the divers of the pochard and stiff-tail tribes. The legs and feet of eiders are huge, and although they may appear to be cumbersome on land, they are actually quite at ease ashore and can move with surprising rapidity.

All species are omnivorous, consuming both aquatic vegetation and large quantities of small molluscs, crabs, and other crustaceans. Their diet varies seasonally, depending on the availability of specific food items, but they appear to prefer food of animal origin, particularly when at sea. Some eiders, especially the Pacific eider, may have purple-tinted bones—an odd pigmentation that is thought to result from the consumption of large quantities of green sea urchins. (Alaskan sea otters, which also feed extensively on green sea urchins, have purple-tinted bones as well.) Fish are rarely eaten in the wild, although captive eiders will ravenously consume an astounding number of them daily. Bill shapes vary from species to species, but they are, in general, relatively narrow with strongly hooked nails at the tip.

9.3 King eiders in flight. Once the female commences incubation, males depart and head for traditional molting sites at sea. For such bulky birds, they fly deceptively fast.

9.4 European eider nest and eggs in Scotland. Eiders demonstrate a phenomenal homing ability and frequently return to the same nest area that they used in previous seasons, sometimes even to the same nest. When old nests are re-used, the hen will usually churn up the bowl with her bill, presumably to allow air to circulate and dry the contents.

9.5 Pacific eider nest and eggs. The normal clutch size is three to four eggs, and while incubation may commence with the laying of the first egg, it usually does not start until after the third egg.

9.6 (Opposite Page) Pacific eider female flying over mudflats on the northwest coast of the Alaskan Peninsula.

9.4

9.5

9.7 *European eider brooding young in Scotland. Eiders may use old nests of other species such as scoters, mergansers, and gulls — and in Spitsbergen, they may even occupy barnacle goose nests. At times, they have been known to take possession of gull nests, complete with eggs.*

All eiders are ground nesters, generally locating their nests on the tundra near the coast or bordering freshwater pools. Some seek the security of small coastal islands that are free of mammalian predators. Interestingly, when nesting habitat is limited, females may engage in serious battles over nest sites. In some areas of northern Europe, common eiders may nest beneath the floors of boathouses, under inverted wooden boxes, or in abandoned fishing boats near the shore. Incubating females can be remarkably trusting, and some of them will almost allow themselves to be picked up. The nest itself is well camouflaged and heavily lined with the famous eider down, which effectively protects the relatively large olive-green eggs.

Reportedly, female common eiders do not feed during incubation and are reluctant to leave the nest for any reason. On the other hand, spectacled eider females may desert the nest for short periods during incubation, and although very little food is usually taken during these excursions, they may bathe, preen, and drink. Common eider females may lose considerable weight during incubation (perhaps even half their body weight), and it may be that they are more resistant to starvation than males—either because they have a lower metabolic rate or because they have a greater ability to lay on subcutaneous fat. Interestingly, drakes in captivity do appear to be more delicate and difficult to maintain, particularly during the summer molt.

If frightened from the nest, hens often defecate on the eggs, and since this results in an extremely foul-smelling nest, it has been suggested that such behavior might serve as a predator deterrent. According to Gross (1938), ''the spray of filth accompanied by thrashing wings will confuse and discourage some of the eiders' enemies.'' Speaking from firsthand experience, it has also been known to discourage some biologists. (Because eiders do not eat during incubation, it is likely that the fecal material is quite different from that of feeding birds, and the especially odiferous, greenish, and rather oily excrement is possibly the result of the action of anaerobic bacteria.)

The female incubates and rears the brood without assistance from the male. Near the beginning or midway through incubation, males (and subadults) usually desert the breeding grounds to undertake a pre-molt migration. They generally depart abruptly and collectively, disappearing almost overnight to gather in huge flocks at sea. (In the case of the king eider, high density molting locations may be as much as 1000 miles from their breeding locales.) Their departure is important, because the modest food resources of the arctic breeding grounds are then exclusively available for the females and their young.

While drakes are not involved in care or protection of the nest, eggs, or ducklings, the pair bond is extremely strong *prior* to egg laying, and it has been suggested that this close association protects the female from other males while she is feeding. Generally, drakes outnumber the females, and since the females have limited access to food during incubation, they must build up sufficient fat reserves prior to egg laying and incubation.

In nuptial plumage, eider drakes are unquestionably among the fanciest and most beautiful of ducks. All species have a subtle green pigmentation on the head, and colorful velvety facial patches arranged in elaborate patterns, as well as long and curved ornamental wing feathers. Unlike dabbling ducks, eider males may take up to three years to acquire full breeding plumage, even though they may be capable of breeding within two years. Females are dressed in a well-camouflaged brown, and since they habitually nest on the ground in the open, this protective coloration is an invaluable asset. The eclipse plumage of the larger eider drakes is not similar to the brown coloration of the hens, since it is decidedly more black, and some white on the wing is retained.

Eiders are very important to the Eskimos and other northern natives, and large numbers are harvested annually for food, even though people in more ''civilized'' areas do not consider them culinary delights. (Presumably, their extensive diet of marine invertebrates makes

the flesh unpalatable.) But the traditional Eskimo way of life is extremely harsh, and they are greatly dependent on eiders and their eggs as dietary supplements. Furthermore, I have found eiders to be quite palatable, if properly prepared.

Incredibly beautiful robes of male eider skins were formerly fashioned by some Eskimo tribes, but unfortunately, these ancient art forms are rapidly disappearing along with the traditional Eskimo way of life. Twenty to twenty-five skins were required for one parka, and in some instances two parkas were worn—the under one with the skin facing out, and the outer one with the skin facing in. (Interestingly, even the ancient Chinese used eider skins to create luxurious garments.)

The native harvest of eiders has been considerable in the past, with Siberian natives in some areas capturing between 12,000 and 14,000 molting flightless eiders (mostly kings) annually. In recent years, however, the eiders have been subjected less and less to such exploitation. Common eiders were formerly hunted by some Eskimos with bolas weighted with ivory balls, walrus teeth, or fragments of walrus tusks. The bola was skillfully flung at flying eiders approaching in the fog, and on occasion as many as three ducks could be brought down on a successful throw. Egging is still commonly practiced in some regions, and can be considered locally detrimental.

Eiders are relatively uncommon in captive wildfowl collections and are almost never kept in the more southern areas, since they are extremely susceptible to thermal stress and to such fatal mycotic diseases as aspergillosis. Maintaining the drakes through the molt in good condition has also proved to be most challenging. Oddly, eiders in northern collections appear to suffer from cold in freezing weather if ice-free water is not available to them.

Once acclimated, however, these ducks appear to do remarkably well, and are not at all troublesome to other birds. The common eider is the only species to be found in captivity in any numbers, and it is

bred fairly regularly by some propagators. It is unfortunate that the eiders as a group are so difficult to acquire and acclimate, because they are among the most beautiful and interesting of the waterfowl—and also because their high arctic ranges preclude all but a relatively few privileged people from ever seeing and enjoying them.

Some taxonomists have divided eiders into two well-defined branches: the lesser eider group, which consists of only the little Steller's eider; and the more typical greater eider group, which includes all the others. The **common eider** complex (*Somateria mollissima*), of eider down fame, has been sub-divided into five and possibly six or even seven races. But even though these various races may be geographically distinct, most are not easy to separate visually because of their similar appearance. The principal differences concern body size, intensity of head color, extent of feathering along the bill, and bill color.

9.8 *American eider drake in full color. This bird is very alert, but eiders often swim very low in the water, generally with their heads drawn back.*

9.9 *American eider drake in eclipse plumage. Unlike most ducks, the large eider males in this plumage do not resemble their mates. They are much darker as a rule, their upper wings remain white, and there are often varying amounts of white on the breast. They are generally out of color between July and November.*

9.9

Both sexes of all common eider races have a peculiar membraneous extension of the bill that forms a Y-shaped frontal shield or process extending up almost to each eye. The shapes of these processes vary with each race. Basically, drakes in color are a contrast in black and white, with much of the head, chest, neck, and back being white; whereas the belly, sides, rump, and tail are black. The white chest is often pinkish in color. In contrast to most water birds, these eiders are light above and dark below.

The head profile of the common eider is very sloping, recalling that of a canvasback duck. In the American race (*S. m. dresseri*), the slope is somewhat broken by a slight dome at the forehead, whereas the slope in birds of the European race (*S. m. mollissima*) is perfectly straight. Drakes of these two races can also be readily separated by the form of the Y-shaped frontal shield, since it is decidedly more pointed at the tips on the slightly larger European eiders. These two subspecies are the most commonly maintained eiders in captivity, although in recent years a few Pacific eiders have been incorporated into several collections.

The Pacific eider (*S. m. v-nigra*) is not only the largest of North American ducks, it is the largest duck of the Northern Hemisphere, and males sometimes weigh more than six pounds (which is larger than a small goose). Whereas drakes of most other subspecies have rather greenish bills, males of this race are characterized by bright orange bills. They also have a distinctive black inverted "V" on the

9.10 *American eider female. While not nearly as flashy as their mates, females do possess a subtle beauty.*

9.11 *The rounded membraneous extension of the bill of this American eider drake quickly differentiates it from the European eider illustrated in plate 9.12.*

9.12 *European eider drake.*

9.13 *Pair of Pacific eiders, largest of Northern Hemisphere ducks. Drakes of this species in color are easily separated from the other common eiders because of their conspicuous orange bills and the black "V" on the throat.*

throat, with the apex pointing directly toward the chin. The northern eider (*S. m. borealis*) is apparently an intermediate form between the American and Pacific eiders, and drakes in full color typically have yellow to orange bills. The females of this race are also supposedly more rufous in color. Some males of this population may also have a black "V" on the throat, and in fact, individuals from most races of *mollissima* have been encountered with at least traces of the throat chevron—a fact that may demonstrate a close ancestry. King eider drakes also display the black "V" on the throat, and interestingly, at least two specimens of spectacled eiders have shown this same feature as well (although faintly).

The Faeroe's eider (*S. m. faeroeensis*) is a poorly defined subspecies, which has been challenged by some authorities. Smallest of the common eider complex, these ducks typically have smaller bills, with short and narrow frontal processes that are dark olive-grey; and the females are said to be darker than those of the nominate race. They are locally common in their stronghold on the Faeroe Islands to the north of Great Britain. Like some of the eiders of Iceland, they are apparently non-migratory. Another unsubstantiated race, the Hudson Bay eider (*S. m. sedentaria*) has also been described, and members of this group are supposedly the palest of the eiders. Some authorities consider the eiders from Iceland, southern Greenland, northern Norway, and Spitsbergen to be intermediate between *borealis* and *mollissima*, and so *S. m. islandica* sometimes appears in the literature. The validity of these latter two races is suspect.

Common eiders are well named, since they are relatively common, and the European race alone may exceed 2,000,000 birds. However, like most sea birds, they are extremely vulnerable to oil pollution, particularly in wintering areas where they gather in huge numbers. A major spill at the right time and place could have a significant negative impact on the population, regardless of its size. Between 1969 and 1971, for example, some 28,000 eiders became oiled and were subsequently lost in the offshore waters of Denmark alone.

Frequently feeding in shallow waters, common eiders are especially fond of bivalve molluscs. They can easily crush the shells with their powerful bills, but nevertheless swallow most of the molluscs whole, since their gizzards are highly developed and can easily grind up the tough shells. Common eiders are very dependent on the presence of the blue mussel. This is particularly true of the Pacific eider, to such an extent that it is possible that no other North American duck is so dependent on a single food species. At times, Pacific eiders forage at the water's edge as the tide rises and falls over large mudflats. Feeding areas can be readily identified by the tell-tale craters in the mud that the birds create as they probe for molluscs.

When diving, these ducks use their feet and their half-folded wings as they descend; but once the bottom is reached, they depend solely on the powerful thrusts of their feet to keep them down and maintain their stability. Powerful fliers, they may alternately flap their wings and glide (a behavior which is not characteristic of waterfowl in general) and they may hold their heads below the body level as well.

Although eiders may prefer to migrate over water, they do not hesitate to fly over points of land that project out into the sea. Eskimos have traditionally taken advantage of this habit, shooting many as they cross over such "eider passes." Perhaps the greatest and most famous of these passes is located at Point Barrow, Alaska, where a million or more eiders pass annually. When the eiders are migrating, Eskimo subsistence hunters from the town of Barrow establish a duck camp at the base of the point. Almost everyone in camp carries a shotgun, including young children, and I have even observed a number of pre-adolescent girls shooting. Undeniably, many eiders are shot, but the actual percentage taken compared to the number that fly over is relatively low, probably no more than one percent. According to my calculations, during the summer migration of drake king eiders, at least five shots were fired for every eider dropped. Tragically, many drop as cripples and are not recovered, and along one of the more inaccessible beaches I counted some 30 king eider carcasses that had washed ashore within a 200-yard stretch. When a flight of king eiders appears on the horizon, Eskimo hunters commence whistling, hooting, and hollering, and quite often the eiders swing toward them, presumably to investigate the source of the commotion. To my great surprise and delight, my own attempts to attract flying eiders in this fashion were just as successful.

9.14 *Eskimo hunter at Point Barrow. Eiders have been taken at eider passes by northern natives since time immemorial, but the use of firearms in recent years has greatly increased the Eskimos' success.*

9.15 *Subadult Pacific eiders. These bulky ducks are most at home on the sea. They do come ashore at times to roost on sandbars or rocks. They walk with a distinctive rolling gait and their posture is often erect. The cooing call of the drake in foggy weather has a ghostly quality, and once heard it is not easily forgotten.*

9.16 *Northern eider drake in color. Intermediate between the Pacific and American eiders, birds of this race usually have yellowish to orange bills.*

9.17

9.18

The American race of common eider (*dresseri*) has been steadily increasing in southern regions in recent years. In 1905, for example, only a single pair of eiders were known to have nested along the entire coast of Maine. By the 1940s, however, they had increased to 2000 pairs; and by 1967, some 20,000 pairs were nesting in the area. Large numbers of eiders winter along the entire northeastern coast of the United States, and as many as 500,000 eiders have been observed off the coast of Massachusetts alone.

Common eiders are noted for their colonial nesting, and this tendency can be regarded as an anti-predator adaptation. In one island colony in Penobscot Bay, Maine, up to 389 nests per acre have been recorded. Pacific eiders also tend to be colonial in the Aleutians, and on some islands adjacent to the north slope of Alaska as well. But generally, they nest in relatively dispersed fashion on the Yukon-Kuskokwim Delta and in similar regions, usually within two miles of the beach. Atypically, there is a small, dense colony of *v-nigra* that nests in the crumbling ruins of a long-abandoned cannery at Nelson Lagoon, on the north coast of the Alaskan Peninsula, where I observed nests situated within feet of one another.

At the onset of the breeding season, common eider drakes repeatedly call out with a dove-like cooing sound. These vocalizations are totally unlike any other waterfowl calls, and Johnsgard theorizes that the particular notes may be produced by inhalation rather than expiration. Females, on the other hand, utter repetitive, hoarse, grating quacks that are distinctly grunt-like.

Gull and raven predation during nesting can be significant, and both eggs and young are preyed upon. Depending on the area, this predation can be incredibly destructive, and the extent of it can vary significantly from year to year. Egg predation in some colonies of European eiders can be as high as 70 per cent, mostly attributable to glaucous gulls. In one study, it was estimated that only 6000 young survived to fledging age out of 73,500 eggs. Persistent gull attacks may ultimately drive an incubating female from the nest, but some of the more determined eiders will fend the intruders off. Since nests may be located some distance from the water, the overland trek to the water can be very hazardous for the ducklings. Once they reach the water, they are still not totally secure, since gulls will sometimes swoop down and snatch them.

Shortly after the ducklings hatch, the hen leads the brood to tidal pools or, in some areas (particularly in Europe), directly to the sea. Initially, the ducklings feed from the surface of the water, and are evidently quite fond of mosquito larvae, but they develop rapidly into efficient divers. Ducklings of a number of broods may merge together into a single large concentration of young, called a créche or nursery, and presumably this behavior increases survival potential. Créches sometimes mingle and subdivide throughout the rearing period, so groups with young of various ages are not uncommon. On the average, 10 to 100 young may be found in a créche, with as many as 10 guard females, but sometimes the assemblages may contain as many as 500 young. In some areas, mixed créches of eiders and snow geese have even been reported.

Once the family departs the nest, the bond between parents and offspring may be rather weak and the young are often attended to by unattached females—so-called "aunties." It is believed that this strange arrangement is of benefit to the successful females, for it allows them to feed heavily and quickly regain the weight lost during incubation. Conversely, in other locales the young remain with their own

9.17 *Glaucous-winged gulls. In many areas, gulls are the major predators with which nesting eiders must contend, and they can inflict heavy losses upon newly-hatched young. Gulls may also parasitize feeding adults, by diving on them and forcing the eiders to drop their food.*

9.18 *Incubating Pacific eider. Eiders have powerful bills and jaws, and can crush large mussels with ease. When occupying coastal habitat, they frequently feed most extensively on a falling tide (especially at ebb tide), but tend to rest on a rising tide.*

9.19 *Recently-hatched European eider duckling. Even at this early age, eiders look like eiders.*

9.19

mothers until they are independent, and during long travels across open sea, small ducklings have been observed to rest on the backs of their mothers.

The majestic **king eider** (*Somateria spectabilis*) is one of the most distinctive of all birds, and drakes in nuptial dress certainly cannot be confused with any other species. Their short bills are at such times bright orange to violet-red, and the prominent fleshy shield at the base of the bill expands to form a huge yellow or orange decorative knob. Outlined in black, this fatty knob is clearly evident, even in flight, and some Eskimos consider it to be a great delicacy (to the point that they may bite it off to eat as soon as they capture one of the ducks). Rather soon after courtship, the knob decreases in size, and like the bill, fades considerably. During courtship, their legs and feet are vivid yellow, with dusky webs, but they become somewhat duller later in the season.

Large males may weigh in excess of three and a half pounds. Their pale, puffy, pearly blue crests are very beautiful, and the decorative head skins are (or were) used by many northern native peoples in a variety of artistic ways; along with the head skins of other eiders, for example, they were sewn into handsome mats. At rest, king eiders appear to be white in front and black at the rear, with a white patch near the base of the tail and a conspicuous black "V" outlining the throat. In flight, their large white wing patches, which contrast with the black back, make it easy to distinguish them from the other eiders. One modified scapular feather on each side protrudes to form a small distinctive triangular "sail." Contrary to some reports in the literature, their eyes are black or dark brown, not yellow.

Female king eiders are similar to the hens of the common eider, although they are slightly smaller and decidedly redder, with a shorter bill that gives the head a more rounded appearance. The feathers along the top of the bill extend forward to above the nostrils, and there are also crescent-shaped dark markings on the feathers of the back and sides. The bill is greenish grey to yellowish green, and during the summer the frontal process may be somewhat swollen. Hybrids between king and common eiders have been reported in the wild, most often in Iceland (even though Iceland is outside the normal breeding range of the species). It would appear that they are more closely related to common eiders than to spectacled eiders.

King eiders may live and breed farther north than any other waterfowl species, with the possible exception of the oldsquaw duck. Cir-

9.20 *European eider escorting ducklings in Scotland. As the ducklings grow older, they may merge into large groups to be reared collectively. However, in some instances young may be reared to fledging age by their own mother. On the average, it is estimated that eight weeks or so are required for fledging.*

9.21 *King eider drake. During the summer or molt migration in late June or early July, hundreds of thousands of male king eiders can be observed in flight along the north coast of Alaska. Later in the year, the females commence their migration, to be followed shortly thereafter by the young of the year. When landing, these ponderous birds sometimes make a long glide when approaching, and may touch down very hard on the water with a big splash.*

9.22

9.23

9.22 *Red fox. These and arctic foxes are leading predators of eiders. Like all eiders, king eiders are preyed upon by both avian and mammalian predators, and for this reason they may nest rather closely together on predator-free islands, often in association with nesting geese and gulls.*

9.23 *King eider nest and eggs. The down is much darker than that of the common eider. Additionally, the four to six eggs are generally smaller, more slender, and paler in color.*

9.24 *King eider drake.*

9.24

cumboreal in distribution, they inhabit areas not commonly frequented by man, and so the full extent of their population is not known. They occur not only in Alaska, Canada, and Siberia, but in Scandinavia, Spitsbergen, and Greenland as well. Even during the winter, they remain as far north as ice-free seas permit, and up to 100,000 may gather to molt along the western coast of Greenland alone.

Due to their relatively inaccessible high arctic ranges and their rather infrequent contacts with man (other than Eskimos), there is a tendency for the average person to think that they are rare. This supposition is not only incorrect but grossly in error, since the breeding population of Victoria Island, Canada, alone may exceed 800,000 king eiders. These birds may even be more numerous than oldsquaw ducks, and some biologists suggest that they *may* be the most abundant of *all* wild ducks.

King eiders can be relatively long-lived, and there are records of wild individuals attaining 15 years of age. Natural catastrophes can be responsible for tremendous losses, however. During the spring of 1964, for example, it was calculated that some 100,000 eiders (most of which were *spectabilis*) perished in Alaska (presumably from starva-

tion)— simply because the sea ice was unusually late in breaking up. During such times, the early migrants are very weakened, and can be forced down by adverse winds, ice-fog, and freezing sleet.

King eiders appear to be especially fond of echinoderms and feed extensively on such organisms as sand dollars, sea urchins, sea stars, brittle stars, and even sea cucumbers (they will also take some crustaceans). When at sea, they may rest on drifting ice. Like oldsquaw, they are well known as superior divers, and dives of 180 feet have been reported (although this depth has been disputed by some). They often fly abreast in long wavering lines, sometimes only a few feet above the water, and their flight is more buoyant and maneuverable than that of the common eider. I have occasionally seen them flying in "V" formations as well. They frequently call during migratory flights and the low, grating, croaking vocalizations of the drake have been likened to those produced by a large frog. Females call out with a variety of croaks and grunts, although they may also "hiss" or cluck.

Unlike some members of the Somateriini, king eiders are not social nesters. Their nests are widely scattered, and these aggressive ducks are reportedly intolerant of other eiders if they attempt to venture too close. However, if fox population densities are high, they may form

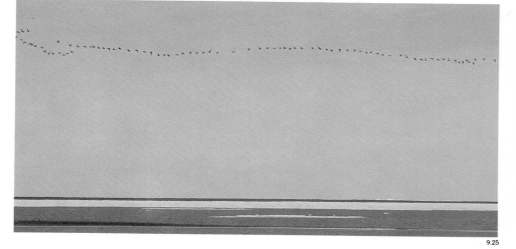

9.25

9.27

9.28

9.29

9.26

9.30

"semi-colonies" and concentrate on secure river islands. Nests may be located up to a quarter mile from water, and are often situated on dry (sometimes rocky) slopes.

Typical nesting habitat consists of regions with tundra ponds and lakes, and hummocky marshes which are sometimes surrounded by fresh water. During years of particularly adverse weather, the reproductive potential can be severely compromised. The four to six eggs are smaller and paler than those of the common eider, incubation usually takes between 22 and 24 days, and the young are generally reared on fresh water instead of salt. King eiders are even more prone to establish créches of young than the common eider, and there are records of créches of more than 100 young (often of various ages) attended by only a few adults—and in some cases, by no adults at all. This regal species has been maintained by only a handful of propagators over the years, and has been irregularly bred since the first captive breeding in 1961. Unfortunately, it seems unlikely that they will be well established in captive collections in the near future.

The bizarre **spectacled or Fischer's eider** (*Somateria fischeri*) is so distinct from the common or king eider that, until quite recently, it was placed in the genus *Lampronetta*. Its descriptive vernacular name was

9.25 Migrating king eiders often fly in long undulating strings or in wedge formation. In the latter formation, one side is generally significantly longer than the other. Migrational movements are influenced by weather, and in extremely cold climates they are subject to fluctuation, because the timing of the spring thaw and fall freeze-up is highly variable. In the spring, the king eider is one of the first to migrate, and often has the farthest to go. Pair bonds are apparently formed at sea prior to arrival on the breeding grounds.

9.26 King eider female on nest. Upon arrival on the breeding grounds, females may lead their mates about, uttering a moaning or growling sound as they inspect the terrain for suitable nesting sites. Nest sites vary, but the eiders frequently use the polygonal surface cracks that are created by frost.

9.27 Group of king eiders.

9.28 Migrating king eiders at times travel in small amorphous groups, maintaining no particular shape for very long.

9.29 Subadult male king eider.

9.30 Even on flat terrain king eider females can be difficult to locate. However, if an observer faces the sun, their location can sometimes be revealed by the sunlight reflecting off their feathers. They sometimes exhibit a tendency to take their young to sea at an early age. Those that nest along the coast may lead their broods downstream to the sea or may go overland from pond to pond until the coast is reached.

obviously derived from the large round satin-white patches with narrow black borders that surround the eyes of the drakes. The feathers which comprise these conspicuous "spectacles" are extremely soft and velvety. Females have less well-defined greyish spectacles, and even newly-hatched ducklings have obvious dark spectacle markings. These ducks have from time to time been described in the literature as grotesque, but while I am admittedly prejudiced, I regard them as incredibly beautiful.

Spectacled eiders are medium-sized, chunky ducks, with drakes weighing up to three and a quarter pounds. Their flight is much swifter and more agile than the larger eiders. Curiously, the upper bill of these birds is feathered all the way to the anterior end of the nostrils or beyond, a very unique feature. The iris is whitish, ringed by pale blue, and although the eyes are sometimes difficult to see, they contrast sharply with the dark brown eyes of all the other eiders. The drake's bill is a much more vivid yellow-orange (or red) than some of the literature indicates, whereas that of the female is greyish blue. The dark plumage areas of the male are not the typical eider black, but have instead a lustrous silver greyish cast. The contour of the hind part of the male's head is not smooth like the king eider's; instead, it rather resembles an uneven haircut. The shaggy greenish chest is apparently not normally raised during display. Drakes in non-breeding plumage are rather grey to greyish black overall, whereas their heads become grey and the spectacles are darker grey.

Spectacled eiders are little known and are undoubtedly the rarest of the eiders, and they may have the most limited distribution. Like the emperor goose, they almost exclusively inhabit the shores, waters, and deltas of the Bering Sea, along the Siberian north slope and western coastal Alaska. Due to their remote ranges, these eiders are not subjected to much sport hunting, although some are taken by Eskimos, who claim that they are better eating than king eiders, particularly the females. Eggs are harvested by Siberian natives, and Eskimo artisans formerly made good use of their distinctive head skins, sometimes fashioning incredibly beautiful vests from them.

The status of this eider is not well-known, and a number of biologists believe they may be declining. Approximately 50,000 to 70,000 pairs nest in the Yukon-Kuskokwim Delta of Alaska, and in some regions of prime habitat they may be the most abundant of nesting ducks. There are also some Eskimo reports of spectacled eiders nesting on St. Lawrence Island. Up to 3000 pairs occupy other portions of Alaska, and some 30,000 to 40,000 pairs breed in Siberia, where they are widespread but not particularly common in any one locale. Thus, some 200,000 adult spectacled eiders can usually be accounted for on the breeding grounds. Subadults are seldom observed in these areas, and since these non-breeding birds may constitute a major portion of the population, it is possible that the total population numbers some 300,000 to 500,000 individuals.

To this day, the question of where spectacled eiders spend the winter remains one of the most perplexing and intriguing of ornithological mysteries. No large concentrations of molting or wintering spectacled eiders have ever been observed, and virtually nothing is known of their whereabouts or activities once they depart the breeding grounds. In fact, only a dozen or so winter sightings have been documented, and these were relatively widely scattered. Presumably, they winter somewhere in the Bering Sea, possibly along the southern edge of the ice pack. Chris Dau, who is one of the world's foremost eider experts, suggests it may be necessary to attach transmitters to eiders leaving the

9.31 *Spectacled eider drake, perhaps one of the most beautiful and unusual of all birds. These eiders sometimes fly in compact flocks, which generally contain less than 50 ducks. During the spring, spectacled eiders are most often encountered alone or in pairs, in small bunches, or in strings — and they may be loosely associated with other waterfowl, especially with the king eider.*

9.32 *Spectacled eider female. Females of breeding age can be differentiated from subadult females by their darker color, non-mottled breasts, and more uniform overall wing color.*

9.33 *Even at two days of age, the spectacled eider duckling is readily identifiable. Females are very attentive to their young, and while some brood merging does take place, it is not nearly as prevalent as with king or common eiders. The ducklings are generally reared on fresh or slightly brackish water, and they are capable of flight at about 53 days of age.*

breeding grounds, and track their movements via orbiting satellite. Locating them may be of extreme importance, because it is probable that they concentrate in a relatively limited area, and this makes them extremely vulnerable to either natural or man-associated catastrophes. Since subadults are seldom encountered on the breeding grounds, it is conceivable that if their whereabouts could be pinpointed, the wintering location would be revealed . . . but this remains to be seen.

The Bering Strait and adjacent areas of the Bering and possibly Chukchi Seas are thought to serve as major staging areas in the spring, and pair bonding may occur at this time of the year, since the pair bond is already formed when the ducks arrive on the breeding grounds. There appears to be a definite correlation between ice conditions and the timing of arrival on the breeding grounds, and if the ducks do not arrive at the right time nesting may be delayed for several weeks to allow the tundra to become free enough of snow for nest construction. The eiders generally arrive in mid- to late May (at least in the Yukon Delta), and by the end of June most of the drakes have already departed, usually midway through incubation. Many of the males I have observed in late June appeared to be already entering the initial stages of the eclipse molt.

Nesting habits of spectacled eiders suggest a limited tendency to form colonies, and I have observed incubating females separated by only 40 to 50 feet. In some regions, they may nest in conjunction with small gulls and terns; and in western Alaska, *fischeri* nest in relatively close association with emperor, cackling, and Pacific white-fronted geese, as well as black brant, whistling swans, and Pacific eiders. Most nests I have seen were located within several feet of the edge of small tundra ponds, although nests are at times constructed some distance from water. Frequently, they can be found on small peninsulas or islands, but in Alaska the ideal islands are generally usurped by breeding cackling geese. On rare occasions, mixed clutches with cackling geese have been reported, and in at least one case, eider and greater scaup eggs shared the same nest. As a rule, Alaskan spectacled eiders nest in proximity to salt water, but I have observed them at least 20 miles up river, and in some parts of Siberia they are said to penetrate further inland than any other eider. When on the breeding grounds, they behave more like dabbling ducks, but at sea they feed extensively on molluscs, one of their most favored food items.

Drakes are almost entirely nonvocal, even during the breeding season, but do have a faint "hoo-hoo" call. Females sometimes growl, or produce short guttural croaks. When calling ducklings, they may cluck and the ducklings themselves have a slurred whistling note. The incubation period is 24 to 25 days, and incubating hens can be very closely approached before they will flush. Nest failures in many regions can be attributed to the predatory activities of gulls, jaegers, and arctic and red foxes; and while these predators normally concentrate on eggs or young, remains of adult eiders can sometimes be encountered around fox dens. The ducklings are reared to fledging size on fresh or brackish-water tundra pools, rather than at sea. This species appears to be less prone to merge broods than some of the other eiders, and the females are very attentive to the young. Most of the Alaskan females and young have departed the breeding areas by mid-September.

Due to their general inaccessibility, very few of these beautiful eiders have been maintained in waterfowl collections; in fact, they weren't captively bred until 1976 at the Wildfowl Trust. Removal of eggs from

9.34

9.35

9.36   9.37   9.38

9.34 *Adult spectacled eider at the edge of an Alaskan tundra pond. When at sea (at least in the spring), these handsome ducks may rest on floating ice.*

9.35 *Adult spectacled eider female flying over a portion of the Yukon-Kuskokwim Delta. In late May or early June, females move ashore to prospect for nest sites.*

9.36 *Incubating spectacled eiders are "tight sitters" and flush reluctantly. The low incubating profile of the hen is well illustrated here.*

9.37 *Spectacled eider nest and eggs. Nests of previous seasons may be re-used. Nest sites are often exposed early in the season but become more concealed as new vegetation grows in.*

9.38 *Subadult male spectacled eider.*

the laying female in subsequent years at Slimbridge stimulated the production of a second clutch, but due to the short length of the Arctic summer it is unlikely that replacement clutches are laid in the wild. Aviculturists are working diligently to get this fine species established in captivity, but until this is accomplished, they will remain little known and almost totally unavailable.

Smallest of the Somateriini are the **Steller's eiders** (*Polysticta stelleri*), which seldom exceed two pounds in weight. These petite ducks are also infrequently referred to as either Russian (Siberian) or lesser eiders, and are known as "Scotchies" by the inhabitants of the western Alaskan Peninsula. Some authorities question whether or not they are actually "true" eiders, and while they possess many of the physical attributes of the eiders and construct nests in a similar manner, there can be no denying that they are the least eider-like of the tribe. Steller's eiders appear to be much more specialized in their feeding than their larger counterparts, and have a long thin bill, that is somewhat reminiscent of the bill of the extinct Labrador duck. Possibly, they represent an ancestral link between the Labrador duck and the larger eiders.

Drakes in nuptial plumage are quite elegant and most colorful, and they have sometimes been described as birds in a clown costume. The shiny white head of the drake is broken by a black eye spot and a very

9.39

9.39 *Steller's eiders. A group of five adult drakes and a single female (at left). These attractive birds are the least eider-like of the eiders and are apparently the most specialized as well. Their bills are soft-edged and this suggests that they have different feeding techniques. Compared to the larger eiders, they are very comfortable ashore, walking (and even running) with ease. Groups of these little eiders commonly rest on sandbars, beaches, and flats exposed by the falling tide. Wintering birds along the Scandinavian coast are said to be quite tame and can be encountered rather close to shore.*

peculiar "tuft" of plush pale green feathers on the back of the head is flanked by small black marks. A faint green spot is located in front of the eye, and the black chin and throat merge to form a distinctive black collar, which extends down the middle of the back to the tail. The chest, breast, and sides are colored a rich chestnut and a conspicuous black spot is located just in front of and below the folded wing (but this is often obscured). Flanks, rump, lower belly, and tail coverts are black. Long decurved and pointed scapulars, which are striped with iridescent blue-black and white, spread out over the rear of the folded wing. The dark brown tail is wedge-shaped and is comparatively long.

Interestingly, Steller's eiders are also noted for prominent blue mallard-like speculums, which other eiders and most of the diving ducks lack. (The harlequin duck is the only other sea duck with a speculum, and the wings of the two species are remarkably similar in appearance.) The bill and feet of *stelleri* are blue-grey and the bill lacks feathering along the side and top, another unusual trait for an eider. The nondescript hens are essentially dark brown sprinkled with light buff, and are considered to be the darkest of the eiders. While the larger eider drakes in eclipse plumage are distinctly darker than their mates, Steller's eider males in summer dress rather resemble females, except for the white they retain on their upper wing.

These trim little ducks do not have the bulky appearance that is characteristic of the larger eiders and, as a rule, they ride higher in the water and may swim with their tails angled upward. In fact, they more closely resemble active dabbling ducks. Generally flying higher than other eiders and with a more maneuverable flight style, they are the swiftest of the Somateriini. When taking flight, they rise more easily and steeply than their larger and heavier relatives, although a run over the surface of the water is still necessary before they can become airborne. When large flocks rise simultaneously, the roar of thousands of wings can sometimes be heard up to a mile away. In flight, their wings whistle like those of the goldeneye, only louder, and in foggy weather they are generally heard long before they are seen. They are occasionally observed flying in the company of oldsquaw. Rather quiet on the whole, drakes murmur a low crooning or growling note during courtship that is not audible over long distances, and at times they may also call out with a sound that approximates the bark of a

9.40

9.41

small dog. Females have a hoarse wigeon-like call, and as a rule are considerably more vocal.

The bills of Steller's eiders are noteworthy because the lateral portions of the distal half of the upper mandible are rather soft and fleshy, indicating that the ducks probably feed more extensively on soft animal material, which they apparently swallow underwater. Unquestionably, their selection of food is governed by availability and season, but they are opportunistic feeders and appear to prey heavily on soft-bodied crustaceans, such as isopods and amphipods— although they also relish barnacles and small bivalve molluscs, particularly little blue mussels. When Steller's eiders forage in fresh water, such as a tundra pond, insect larvae may constitute a major portion of their diet. In the case of some captive birds I have maintained, I have seen them working over algae-covered rocks and logs, presumably feeding on the algae.

9.40 *Long-tailed jaegers prey heavily on Steller's eiders. They are capable of snatching up ducklings with ease.*

9.41 *Large numbers of subadult Steller's eiders can be encountered in the lagoons along the northwest coast of the Alaskan Peninsula. When taking off, these smallest and trimmest of the eiders rise more steeply and easily than their larger, more cumbersome relatives. They also fly higher and faster, and their flight is much more buoyant. Once airborne, their wings produce a loud whistling sound, and this noise may serve to keep the birds together during foggy weather.*

9.42 *Bald eagle. It is believed that these large raptors may prey upon adult Steller's eiders.*

9.43 *Steller's eider drake in full color. These little eiders are about the size of a lesser scaup but have a more elongate shape. Unless extended, their necks are very inconspicuous. Courting males sometimes swim rapidly and then rear up suddenly in the water to expose their conspicuous tawny undersides. Even during courtship, they are relatively nonvocal. As a rule, their courtship displays are more rapid than those of the greater eiders, and involve more aerial activity.*

9.43

While there is no doubt that Steller's eiders are capable divers, they often feed in the shallows, and I have frequently observed large numbers of them foraging at the water's edge during a falling tide. As the tide receded, large mud tidal flats and runoff channels were exposed and the little eiders commonly swam and waded in these areas. They often left the water to probe in the mud, somewhat like a dabbler. They "chattered" loudly, and their feeding activity suggested a form of filter feeding. When ashore, they are the most agile of the eiders, walking or running with surprising ease.

In shallow waters along the Bering Sea coast of the Alaskan Peninsula, such as in Izembek and Nelson Lagoons, their feeding activity can result in extensive shore wear, due to their habit of probing and agitating the mud and sand with their feet. In such habitat, maximum feeding usually occurs at low tide, when food items are most available, and when the tide is high they return to diving. It is not unusual for a thousand or more Steller's eiders to dive simultaneously, and as a result of their synchronized, almost military-like behavior, they are sometimes referred to as "soldier ducks." A large raft of feeding eiders throws up a spray that is visible for great distances. When diving, their wings are partially opened, and although some accounts suggest that propulsion is accomplished by short jerky wing movements, I have personally never seen them use their wings underwater. Like puddle ducks, they also commonly upend to feed in shallow waters, and at times they tend to feed in long irregular lines.

Steller's eiders can be considered extremely gregarious, except when breeding, and during the winter they are among the most social of all waterfowl. Sometimes they pack together so densely that the sea appears to be covered with a solid living multicolored carpet. Wintering eiders along the north coast of the Alaskan Peninsula may exceed 200,000 individuals, and this must be considered a major wintering area for much of the population, although another segment winters along the Kamchatka Peninsula and around the Kurile Islands to the south. Once the eiders depart from the breeding grounds, they don't move far—and unlike most northern anatids, their movements are relatively restricted. Essentially, they move as the ice pack advances and follow its retreat.

Non-breeders remain gregarious throughout the year. In mid-June of 1977, for example, I observed some 26,000 Steller's eiders in Nelson Lagoon, and by the end of July, more than 50,000 were in the area. Most of these were obviously subadult birds, but perhaps one in a hundred was a fully-colored drake. Some of these flocks contained in excess of a thousand individuals, and the birds rafted together so tightly that they practically touched one another. They even roosted collectively, and it was not uncommon to see several thousand eiders ashore at the water's edge. Because of their small size and their tendency to feed in shallow water, it is possible that the highly gregarious nature of these birds is an anti-predator adaptation. Adults are apprehensive when bald eagles and gyrfalcons are nearby, indicating that they may be a prey species for these two large raptors. Generally, when one of the predators is sighted the eiders will take to the wing immediately instead of diving.

Steller's eiders are noted for their discontinuous breeding range that may be even more restricted than the range of the spectacled eider. In North America, it extends from the Alaskan Peninsula up the coastal

9.44

9.45

9.46

9.44 *Incubating Steller's eider in typical nesting habitat. These birds generally seek sites on the tundra where there are numerous ponds that have elevated margins or dry areas interspersed between them. They may also nest on ridges near the sea or in slight depressions between small hummocks. Because they are solitary nesters, incubating birds can be extremely difficult to locate. Much of the natural history of this species remains to be learned, but presumably, late spring thaws have an adverse effect on their reproductive potential.*

9.45 *Large group of Steller's eiders (mostly immatures) roosting at the water's edge, Nelson Lagoon, Alaskan Peninsula.*

9.46 *Flock of Steller's eiders. Note that most are females or subadults, although a few adult drakes are visible.*

9.48

9.47

9.47 *Steller's eider nest and eggs. The down is a very dark sooty brown, and may be one inch thick. Usually, there is much vegetation intermingled with the down. Egg laying commences in early to mid-June (sometimes later), and these birds produce larger clutches than the other eiders. The seven to eight pale buff eggs darken as they become nest-stained. The incubation period is not known.*

9.48 *Small flock of adult Steller's eiders. The time of their arrival on the wintering ground is highly variable. In some years, most (if not all) of the population arrives in August, but in other years their arrival may be delayed until November.*

9.49 *(Opposite Page) Steller's eiders with young. Note that two females are leading the brood, which suggests the possibility of brood merging. The young are reared on tundra ponds, brackish inlets, or occasionally on salt water. Young may be abandoned while they are still flightless when the females undertake a molt migration. By the end of August, most of the young are flying, suggesting a fledging period of approximately 50 days.*

arctic slope to the Canadian border, and nesting birds have also been recorded from St. Lawrence and Nunivak Islands. The majority of the population, however, probably breeds in northeastern Siberia, west to the Lena River. They are not known to *regularly* nest further east than the Yukon border, but there are a few isolated records for northern Europe and central and western Siberia. Most Steller's eiders banded in the fall by federal biologists at Izembek Bay have been recovered in Siberia.

Often, these little eiders even court collectively, and as a rule, their displays are rapid and may be performed without vocalizing. Some of their courtship antics take place in the air, and a number of males may pursue a single female. Just prior to copulation, mated pairs separate from the flock (apparently to avoid interference), and following breeding they rapidly rejoin the group. In light of their extremely gregarious nature, it is surprising that Steller's eiders demonstrate *no* colonial nesting tendencies whatsoever. Nests are widely scattered, and due to the dark down lining of the nest and the low profile of the incubating hen, a nesting eider can be easily overlooked. The nest can be difficult to locate even when being sought, and one almost has to step on an incubating bird to force it to flush. Nest sites are not unlike those selected by oldsquaw ducks, and may not be as close to water as is typical with most eiders. Preferred breeding habitat consists of lowland tundra, usually well away from the sea; but in some areas, they may be closer to the coast.

Egg laying usually occurs in early to mid-June. Larger clutches are produced than with other eiders, averaging seven to eight pale olive-buff eggs—and incredibly, the incubation period is not known to this day. My field observations along the north coast of Alaska suggest that some brood merging is typical, for I saw several broods exceeding ten ducklings, with more than one female in attendance. While there are some accounts in the literature indicating that drakes assist in the rearing of the young, I have not seen any indication of such behavior, although unlike other eiders, males may remain with the hens almost until the eggs are due to hatch. Ducklings are a uniform dark brown and are noted for a buff eye ring that extends back over the ear as a pale cinnamon stripe. They are most distinctive in that the toenails and edges of the foot webs may be yellowish, greatly contrasting with the olive-grey legs and feet. Egg predation and duckling mortality are apparently high, and by the time the young are half grown the brood size may be reduced by 50 percent.

Steller's eiders are practically unknown to aviculturists. Although a few eggs and adults have been collected in recent years, none have been bred in captivity to date. The overall captive record, while admittedly very limited, would seem to suggest that they are rather delicate, but I have not found this to be the case at all. Once wild-caught adults are acclimated, they appear to be relatively hardy, even in southern climates, and I am convinced that they will be captively bred within the next few years. Until they are established, however, they will remain mysterious to most people, for unfortunately, very few individuals have had an opportunity to see them, either in the wild or in collections.

10
Pochards
Aythyini

Also known as diving ducks, the 15 species of pochards are considered to be near relatives of the dabbling ducks, but are more completely oriented toward aquatic lifestyles. In general, they are noted for short heavy bodies, relatively large heads, long necks, and proportionally large feet—and as a group, they are remarkably homogenous, both behaviorally and anatomically. Most inhabit the Northern Hemisphere, although four species occur south of the equator; and with the exception of the tropical and subtropical species, all are migratory.

Pochards are excellent divers and feed extensively underwater. Like other groups of ducks that dive, their legs are set far back on their bodies to facilitate more efficient underwater propulsion. Dives are usually preceded by a vigorous forward leap. Unlike dabbling ducks, which typically have an unlobed hind toe, this toe on pochards is distinctly lobed, a modification that presumably aids them substan-

10.2

tially in underwater swimming. Most members of the tribe seldom wander far from water, and because of the placement of their legs, they move with a shuffling gait when ashore. They are essentially freshwater ducks, but do not necessarily shun salt water, particularly during the winter.

Pochard wings are fairly short and sharply pointed, and they usually cannot take to the wing without effort. Most species must patter along the surface of the water for some distance before they gain sufficient speed to take to the air—but once airborne, they fly swiftly. In most instances, the sexes are not at all alike in appearance, and curiously, it appears that with some species the sexes may forage at different underwater depths (a situation that may be more widespread than the limited amount of data suggests). Indeed, these diving differences may help to explain why there may be partial winter segregation of the sexes of certain species.

Although normally monogamous, some pochards have been reported to exhibit polygamous tendencies. During courtship display, drakes may greatly expand their brightly colored irises by contracting their pupils, thereby flashing their eyes. Nests are generally situated in thick cover, over shallow water or on the ground not far from water. Drakes often depart the nest site prior to the hatching of the young, and may join with other males while the hens incubate and rear the young without assistance. A number of species exhibit parasitic nesting behavior. Diving ducks in general are less demonstrative than dabbling ducks, and as a group, the pochards are not particularly vocal; the drakes even less so than their mates. The dietary preferences of these ducks cover a broad spectrum, from the chiefly vegetarian to the almost exclusively carnivorous. Some species winter on the sea in large flocks, and during such times they are very vulnerable to oil spills and other forms of coastal pollution.

The red-crested and rosy-billed pochards, along with the two races of southern pochards (South American and African), are collectively known as the narrow-billed pochards, and are grouped together in

10.1 (Opposite Page) *Drake red-crested pochard in full color. Among the most distinctive of the pochards, these birds typically float higher in the water than most diving ducks.*

10.2 *Drake redhead duck beginning a dive. To gain momentum, diving pochards often rear up out of the water and plunge forward vigorously. Pochard legs are placed rather far back on the body to facilitate underwater propulsion, and their feet are relatively large.*

10.3

10.4

the genus *Netta*. All are less specialized than the rest of the tribe, and as a result, they are less inclined to dive and are more comfortable ashore. Males are characterized by their bright red eyes and low, squeaky voices.

Essentially a lowland species, the Eurasian **red-crested pochard** (*Netta rufina*) is by far the flashiest of the narrow-billed group. Its rich golden chestnut crest is extremely distinctive and has the appearance of a neatly fashioned head of hair; and much of the upper wing is white—a feature that is particularly conspicuous in flight. As with all pochards, the female is well camouflaged in dull brown plumage, which lacks the distinctive disruptive patterns that typify female dabbling ducks. Drakes in eclipse plumage resemble their mates, except for their red bills and eyes. Both sexes swim high in the water and are considered to be moderately wary. Primarily vegetarian, they feed extensively on aquatic vegetation of various types, but may also consume some food of animal origin, such as tadpoles, small fish, crustaceans, and molluscs. (However, some of this latter fare may be ingested accidentally.)

Unique among the waterfowl, these birds engage in ritualized courtship feeding—a behavior that is apparently restricted to mated pairs, and which may serve to reinforce the pair bond. While the female waits on the surface, the male dives and brings her food offerings, sometimes even inedible items. During courtship, male red-crested pochards may utter a hoarse rasping sound that has been described as a suppressed wheeze. As with a number of other pochards, they are sometimes parasitic nesters, and dump nests are not uncommon. Thirty-nine eggs were found in one such nest, but normal clutches consist of 6 to 12 eggs.

Red-crested pochards are not considered good gamebirds, but they are very popular with aviculturists because of their handsome appearance and even temperament, and they may be encountered in many waterfowl collections. They are easy to maintain, and breed readily; but they will sometimes hybridize with the rosybill, so these two species should be kept separate, at least during the breeding season.

The South American **rosy-billed pochard** (*Netta peposaca*) is well named, since the bright rosy colored bill of the drake rises up at the base to form an impressive bulbous facial shield. Both the intensity of the color and the size of the facial knob increases when the males are in breeding condition. These highly social birds are among the most common of South American diving ducks. Argentine hunters consider them to be indifferent gamebirds, while farmers in some districts regard them as an agricultural menace because they tend to feed on rice crops. The farmers, as a result, are prone to destroy nests they encounter, but despite this persecution, the population has remained fairly stable. During the austral winter, rosybills congregate in large numbers, and while their movements are mainly local, limited migrations may be undertaken.

Dabbler-like in many respects, rosybills seldom dive and spend considerable time ashore. During the breeding season, males may growl whereas the females quack hoarsely. Nests are usually placed in the water amid aquatic vegetation, and dump nests are not particularly uncommon. In Argentina, hatching success can be low for some unexplained reason. Broods may merge, and in one unusual instance, 52 ducklings were reportedly tended by a single female. Common in wildfowl collections, the rosybill is held in high esteem—because they are easily bred and very popular, and perhaps also because they are colorful year-round.

The two races of **southern (or red-eyed) pochards** (*Netta erythrophthalma*) are virtually indistinguishable, although those of the South American subspecies (*N. e. erythrophthalma*) are theoretically slightly larger. The head of the drake is a very dark chestnut color, glossed with violet, and in flight its white speculum is very conspicuous. Like the aforementioned rosybill, these birds assume no obvious eclipse plumage. Little field work has been done on the South American race, but presumably their behavior parallels that of their Old World relatives. African southern pochards (*N. e. brunnea*) are said to be among the fastest flying ducks on that continent. They are most often observed in small groups, but flocks containing up to 300 ducks have been re-

10.5

corded during the nonbreeding season. Often, they are encountered on large stretches of deep open water.

Both of the southern pochards are essentially nonmigratory, but they may move about a great deal locally in search of food (as is typical of many tropical ducks). These wary ducks swim low in the water with the head held high, frequently with the tail pointed downward to the degree that it is submerged. They commonly upend to feed, instead of diving. Apparently, breeding takes place year-round, although most reproductive activity appears to coincide with the arrival of the austral spring rains, at least in Africa. While there is at least one account of a male apparently assisting with brood care, such behavior is probably exceptional.

Southern pochards are rather timid and quiet, and are not bothersome to other birds in wildfowl collections. Considering the bright red eyes and the subtle beauty of the males, it is surprising that they have never been particularly common in captive collections, at least in North America. But this may reflect general unavailability rather than disinterest on the part of aviculturists. It appears that at this time there are no pure South American red-eyed pochards in captivity, and even in the wild, this subspecies is apparently insecure. It may be that the population has undergone a rather severe decline throughout much of its range, for reasons yet undetermined.

The other twelve species of pochards are all incorporated into the genus *Aythya*, and are collectively referred to as the broad-billed pochards. (American representatives are sometimes known as bay ducks.) As a rule, they are generally more aquatic, have much broader bills, and are much more accomplished divers; and as a result, they are

10.6

10.5 *African southern pochard male. A species of open water, these pochards are frequently encountered near the edges of emergent shoreline vegetation. While they are effective divers, they often upend, and on occasion they will forage ashore. They are essentially vegetarian, but may also ingest small snails, aquatic insects, and crustaceans.*

10.6 *African southern pochard female. Although they are not nearly as colorful as their more flashy mates, females do possess a subtle beauty.*

10.7 *South American southern pochard male. (This individual may have some African blood in it.) The two races are practically identical but the slightly larger New World drakes are said to be somewhat darker and less brownish in overall coloration. The distribution of these pochards is notably spotty, and in recent years the population may have undergone a significant decline.*

not as comfortable ashore. Less striking in appearance than the previously described narrow-billed pochards, they nevertheless have a crisp clean look that makes them very attractive.

The **canvasback** (*Aythya valisineria*) is by far the most distinctive of all the pochards; not necessarily because of its color, but rather because of its graceful build and aristocratic profile. A long sloping forehead and elongated bill give these birds a shape quite unlike any other waterfowl species (with the possible exception of the common eider), and this singular profile is even evident on newly-hatched young. Drakes in eclipse plumage resemble females, but retain their reddish eyes and darker heads.

Largest of the pochards, canvasbacks are considered to be one of the best tasting of all ducks, and many waterfowlers (who refer to them as "cans") regard them as the most magnificent of all gamebirds as well. Their superior succulent taste is attributed to their habit of feeding extensively on wild celery buds; and indeed, their species name is derived from the latin word for wild celery. But these birds can be greedy, gluttonous feeders, and are not above gorging themselves on the rotting flesh of dead salmon—and birds consuming such fare are not deemed to be as tasty.

Canvasbacks are wary and difficult to approach; but at the same time, they can be inquisitive. Drakes are generally silent, except during some nuptial displays, when they may croak, peep, coo, or even growl. During pair bond formation, they may engage in aerial chases. As with many pochard species, males usually outnumber females. Typically, these birds fly in rather small flocks, and are among the fastest flying of all wildfowl, having been reliably clocked at more than 70 miles per hour. (This is still relatively slow, of course, when compared to the unbelievable speed of the peregrine falcon, which may attain a velocity of 160 to 180 miles per hour when diving on its prey.) Flocks of canvasbacks often fly at considerable heights, and while their formations are usually irregular, they sometimes employ the "V" formation. In the air, they appear to be unusually long-necked and have a very characteristic flight profile.

The population has declined in recent years for a number of reasons. For one thing, habitat destruction has been widespread, and these superb ducks have been unable to adapt to take full advantage of agriculture and field feeding. Also they are very dependent on the presence of prairie potholes and these are disappearing at an alarming rate. Redhead ducks, which often associate with canvasbacks, tend to parasitize their nests, and the adaptable racoon, which has extended its range in recent years, has also proved to be an effective deterrent to nesting success.

Canvasbacks are probably more adversely affected by drought than any other species of North American waterfowl, and exceptionally dry years can be disastrous for them. During the 1930s, and again in the late 1960s and early 1970s, the population dropped significantly for this reason. On the other hand, excessive flooding or unseasonably cold weather can also result in a significant amount of nest desertion. Clearly, this is a specialized species which does poorly if it is too dry, too wet, or too cold. Then too, a large portion of the population winters in areas that experience high ship traffic (including oil tankers)—such as San Francisco Bay, Chesapeake Bay, and the Gulf Coast—and as a result, the wintering ducks are exposed to much oil pollution, which has become a significant cause of mortality.

The combination of all these factors—sensitivity to climatic changes, habitat destruction and alteration, predation, and coastal

10.8

10.8 - 10.9 *Canvasback duck. In the fall, and to a lesser extent in the spring, these regal ducks may associate with other species, most notably with redhead ducks and lesser scaup. However, they are seldom seen with other waterfowl when in flight. In areas where they are not molested, canvasbacks can be considered reasonably tame. They will sometimes poach food from feeding swans.*

10.9

pollution—makes the canvasback a very vulnerable species, and the population must be closely monitored if the species is to survive. They are not yet considered rare, but as is the case with any highly specialized species, a population crash can occur with surprising rapidity. Canvasbacks are not among the more common waterfowl in collections, but aviculturists regard them very highly, and despite the fact that they are generally considered reluctant captive breeders, propagators that concentrate on them enjoy a fair degree of success in raising them.

The Old World counterpart of the canvasback is the **European or common pochard** (*Aythya ferina*), which is intermediate in shape and color between the canvasback and the North American redhead duck. European pochard drakes somewhat resemble the yellow-eyed male redhead, but their brilliant red eyes and more rounded heads provide a means of easy identification. Their flanks and dorsal areas are also significantly lighter in color, and their shorter bills are dark slate with a broad pale silver-grey band. (With redheads, the band is narrow and poorly defined.) Like the redhead, canvasback, ring-necked duck, and Baer's pochard, common pochard males in eclipse plumage retain their brilliant eye color, which contrasts with the dark female eye.

European pochards are very gregarious, and tend to be unwary if not persecuted. Drakes are noted for a peculiar soft wheezing or whistling call, while females simply grunt hoarsely. Sometimes, these birds will nest in association with black-backed gulls. Unlike their American counterparts, they have adapted well to human pressure, and the overall population appears to be prospering, even increasing. Stragglers have been sighted in the Aleutian and Pribilof Islands, Alaska. European pochards are fairly common in captivity, but they are not widespread in American wildfowl collections, perhaps due to their close resemblance to the redhead.

The familiar **redhead duck** (*Aythya americana*) is a fairly specialized species, and its population level is subject to much fluctuation from year to year. As with the canvasback, the breeding range of these birds has diminished significantly, and they have also been subjected to some overhunting. During the 1960s and early 1970s, in fact, many concerned waterfowl biologists considered the status of this species precarious, and the overall population has probably declined as much or more than almost any other duck in North America. The introduction of Eurasian carp to many of the redhead's traditional feeding grounds has resulted in a reduction of favored aquatic plants (such as wild celery), and will undoubtedly be responsible for habitat degradation.

During the winter, redheads may raft up in the tens of thousands, and as many as 80,000 to 90,000 have been observed in the vicinity of Cedar Key, Florida. During the summer of 1977, I observed a number of redheads (and even canvasbacks) in the region of Old Chevak on the Yukon-Kuskokwim Delta, Alaska, somewhat out of their normal range. (Presumably, the severe drought in the western states that year was responsible for much of the wayward North American waterfowl movement that took place at that time.) During such dry periods, clutch sizes are generally smaller and overall production of young is down.

Redheads depend more on food of vegetable origin than most of the other pochards, with this type of sustenance often exceeding 90 percent of their total intake. Drakes tend to be more vociferous than most members of the *Aythyini*, and their call has been compared to a

10.10

10.12

10.11

10.10 *European pochard male. Like their American relatives, this species demonstrates a tendency to engage in parasitic nesting. Usually, these very gregarious birds nest near water, and in some areas (such as Tibet) they may nest at altitudes exceeding 2000 feet. When involved in short local flights, flocks of these pochards may travel in compact groups, but when they fly long distances they tend to form long wavy lines or wedges.*

10.11 *Drake redhead. When nesting, this species prefers extensive marshy areas with shallow water openings, cattail marshes, or potholes bordered by emergent vegetation (such as bulrushes, sedges, cattails, cane, etc.). Nests are generally constructed over water, but on occasion they are located on land as well. Vegetation may be pulled over the top of the nest for added concealment. Nests are generally well-dispersed, but concentrations occur where there is good cover and sufficient water. Some females are apparently completely parasitic nesters, and redhead eggs have even been discovered in the nests of American bitterns.*

10.12 *Recently-hatched redhead duckling.*

10.13

10.13 *Male Australian white-eye or hardhead. These birds frequent extensive deep water areas and are usually encountered in the still reaches of large swamps or lakes. But they are equally at home in the swift, turbulent tributaries of inland rivers at flood stage. While the visits of these birds to rice crops are at times much publicized, the overall damage done appears to be negligible. A population decline has been associated with drainage and flood-control projects, and continued loss of habitat will undoubtedly adversely affect these specialized ducks.*

cat meowing. Strong and swift on the wing, these ducks may skillfully wheel and turn in flight. To some extent at least, redheads are parasitic nesters, and this inclination undoubtedly results in a great wastage of eggs. Many times, eggs may be deposited in the host nest after incubation commences, which indicates that redhead egg laying is not synchronized with that of the host species. As a result, the redhead eggs will probably fail to hatch with those of the host, and will be abandoned and subsequently lost. Brood merging tendencies have been recorded among redheads, and older broods are often observed unattended by adults. These ducks are very common in waterfowl collections and can be regarded as fairly reliable breeders.

The four forms of white-eyed ducks are all very similar in appearance and obviously take their names from their distinctive eye color. The **Australian white-eye** (*Aythya a. australis*) is colloquially referred to as the hardhead, and together with the Banks Island race, is known as the Australasian white-eye. As one might expect, the eye of the hardhead drake is a very conspicuous white, but the iris of the female is brown. Both sexes have a broad white bar near the outer end of the bill, but this is much narrower and paler on the female, and she is also lighter in color overall. Wintering flocks of 800 to 1000 hardheads are typical, but during periods of extreme drought, flocks up to 80,000 have been recorded. These swift-flying nomadic ducks tend to be rather shy and wild, and Australian waterfowl hunters regard them as superior gamebirds for this reason. They feed mainly on aquatic plants, but roughly ten percent of their diet is material of animal origin, including water beetles, black swimmers, molluscs, crustaceans, and small fish.

Like most Australian waterfowl, hardheads depend greatly on proper water conditions during the breeding season, and if there is not enough water, breeding may not occur at all. Water availability is very cyclic, and where thousands of ducks may breed one year, there may be none the following year if circumstances are unfavorable. It is quite clear that physiological changes associated with reproduction are synchronized to the fluctuations in water levels.

Hardheads have periodically invaded New Zealand, but although the species was at one time fairly common in that country, there have been no recent reliable sightings. Intense drought tends to promote extensive wandering, and Australian white-eyes have also been recorded in Indonesia, New Guinea, and New Caledonia, as well as other Pacific islands. Formerly, they were among the most common ducks of the Australian southeast coast, but they are rare there now, primarily as a result of agricultural development, and only the inland populations have remained secure. As a specialized species, these pochards are quite sensitive to habitat alteration, and the continuation of swamp-draining programs will certainly accelerate the population decline.

A closely related but smaller subspecies inhabits Banks and Gaua Islands in the southern Pacific (and possibly New Caledonia and the New Hebrides as well). Theoretically, the Banks Island white-eye (*A. a. extima*) is more blackish brown about the head and throat, but its validity as a separate race has been challenged. Two other additional races have also been proposed for the birds of New Guinea and east

238

Java, but both have been rejected. The Banks Island birds have not found their way into anatid collections, but Australian white-eyes are fairly well-known to aviculturists, and although the latter are far from common (at least in the New World), they are sporadically bred.

The **Madagascan white-eye** (*Aythya innotata*) is noted for its relatively limited distribution, since it is restricted to the northeastern portion of the island on its intermediate plateau, at altitudes between 3000 and 4000 feet. While these birds are much like the redhead in shape and proportion, and the displays of the two are similar, the Madagascan species is clearly a white-eye. It is, in fact, not unlike the ferruginous white-eye, but is somewhat larger and darker overall.

Delacour collected several Madagascan white-eyes in 1929, and by 1930 had propagated them to the point that they were fairly well established in France and England. Unfortunately, however, none survived the ravages of the Second World War, and they are totally unknown to contemporary aviculturists. They are not well-known to field ornithologists either, and to date no nests or eggs have been described. Delacour considered them localized but comparatively common in the late twenties. The current status of the species is unknown, but considering its limited range and rather specialized habitat, it must be considered vulnerable.

Smallest and daintiest of pochards is the **common or ferruginous white-eye** (*Aythya nyroca*), which ranges widely throughout the lowlands of Eurasia and North Africa. Females of this species are smaller, duller, and browner overall than their mates, and have brown eyes. In flight, a white bar on the wing becomes very noticeable. Unlike some

other pochard species, this bird tends to be unwary, and is not easily alarmed—but it is secretive, and instead of fleeing when threatened, it tends to seek concealment in reeds. In some parts of southeastern Europe and Kashmir, ferruginous white-eyes number among the most common of the local breeding birds, but they tend to be somewhat less gregarious than other pochards. During the breeding season, males very effectively flash their white irises and call out with high-pitched whistles. At the same time, drakes can be quarrelsome, and hens often have to hide to escape their aggressive attentions. Nests may be associated with those of gulls. Seldom observed in salt water, these pochards concentrate during the winter in the Mediterranean region, the Persian Gulf, the Nile Valley, India, and Burma. Ferruginous white-eyes are common in captivity and not troublesome to other species, but they may fight among themselves. They breed with a fair degree of regularity, and are attractive additions to any collection.

Baer's pochards or Siberian white-eyes (*Aythya baeri*) are superficially similar to the aforementioned species, although their proportions differ. With these birds, the blackish heads and necks of drakes are distinctly glossed with iridescent green in the breeding season. During periods of excitement, the black pupils of their eyes may almost disappear in the straw-colored irises. Females resemble males, but are dark-eyed and duller in coloration, may have a brownish spot between the eye and bill, and do not have the head iridescence.

These pochards have been little studied in the field. Reportedly, however, they are often encountered on swift-running waters or during the winter on lowland jungle pools. Apparently, they are fairly rare

10.15

10.14 - 10.15 *Drake ferruginous or common white-eye. This species is able to rise more easily from the water than some of the other pochards. At times, they can practically spring into the air. While partially gregarious during the winter, they seldom mix with other species during the breeding season. In Europe, the population has declined from that of former years.*

throughout much of their range, although they seem to be relatively common in coastal regions of eastern Russia and Manchuria. They breed in China, but migrate as far south as Burma during the winter. Shyer and wilder than ferruginous white-eyes, they are also stronger and faster on the wing, rise more easily into the air, and are more at ease ashore. Some reports claim that *baeri* feed extensively on frogs during the spring, and while little data are available on their diet, the fishy, almost inedible, taste of their flesh suggests that they probably depend mostly on items of animal origin. Until recently, Baer's pochards were unknown to most aviculturists, but a number of propagators have been successful with them in recent years and they are currently fairly well established.

The **tufted duck** (*Aythya fuligula*) of Iceland, Europe, and Asia is the only pochard with a long crest at the back of its head—a feature that is very pronounced on the drakes, but only rudimentary on the females. The dark heads and necks of males in breeding plumage are glossed with green and purple, which accentuates their bright golden-yellow eyes. Females have light-colored eyes as well, although the color is not nearly as brilliant. Tufted ducks tame readily, and when left undisturbed, they will even occupy city lakes and ponds. They are quick to utilize inland water areas that are artificially created by the construction of reservoirs or gravel pits, and marshland ditches as well. The population is apparently on the increase, particularly in the west, although these fine ducks are threatened to some degree in the Baltic Sea by oil

10.16

10.18

10.17

10.16 - 10.17 *Drake Baer's pochard or Siberian white-eye. These two pictures illustrate how different the same duck may appear under varying lighting conditions. A great deal remains to be learned about the natural history of this species. During the breeding season, these pochards appear to prefer treeless habitat instead of forested regions, and during migration they reportedly occupy rapidly-flowing rivers — habitat that is not normally associated with pochards.*

10.18 *Two tufted duck drakes and a female. This species may nest singly or colonially, and typical nesting habitat consists of lake islets, ponds, rivers, and coastal areas. Nests are generally well concealed, and located close to water or on matted floating vegetation. Young are sometimes abandoned before they can fly, but even if they are tiny, the ducklings often survive if the weather remains favorable.*

pollution. They are regularly observed in the Aleutian Islands, and at least eight were recorded on a small pond on Amchitka Island in 1972. While it has not yet been documented, such numbers suggest that some limited breeding might be taking place on Amchitka.

It is not unusual for tufted ducks to nest in gull and tern colonies, perhaps as a protective measure, since the gulls may drive off crows and other egg thieves. Rather frequently, eggs will be laid in the nests of other species, and eggs have been found not only in coot nests but, interestingly, in the nests of grouse as well. These popular ducks are widespread in waterfowl collections, and are fairly commonly bred.

Curiously, the ring about the bill of the North American **ring-necked duck** (*Aythya collaris*) is much more conspicuous than the faint chestnut ring around the neck, to the extent that it might be more appropriate to refer to these birds as ring-billed ducks. The long, partially-raised feathers on the drake's crown give the head a very angular shape, and these birds are also noted for a distinct vertical white wedge on the side of the body, located just in front of the folded wing—a feature that is particularly obvious when they are on the water. Females somewhat resemble redhead hens, but can be quickly and accurately identified by their smaller size and distinctive head shape. In addition, they have a rather conspicuous white eye ring, a ringed bill, and a broad grey wing stripe that is visible in flight. Contrary to the opinion of some writers, ring-necked ducks are probably more closely related to the "true" pochards (canvasback, redhead, and Eurasian pochard) than to the scaups and tufted ducks, even though they more closely resemble the latter.

Ring-necked ducks are essentially freshwater birds of the interior, and can be found more often in shallow water and dense vegetation than the other North American pochards. They rise from the water with greater ease than do most diving ducks, producing an unmistakable whistle with their wings as they do so. Males produce a purring or whistling note when vocalizing, but with the exception of some courtship displays, these little ducks are relatively quiet.

More adaptable than canvasbacks and redheads, ring-necked ducks have markedly expanded their range east of the Great Lakes during the past 30 years or so. They will even breed in regions that have been subjected to agricultural and human disturbance, and there is no cause for concern about their status at the moment. At times, they tend not to be wary and are said to decoy easily. Surprisingly, even

10.19

though they are one of the most attractive of the pochards, they are not particularly common in wildfowl collections. For some reason, they are not as easy to breed as some of the other *Aythya* species, although some propagators breed them fairly regularly.

The rather somber **New Zealand scaup** (*Aythya novae-seelandiae*) is the only scaup of the Southern Hemisphere. In its country of origin, this species is sometimes incorrectly referred to as the "black teal." These birds are not nearly as numerous as they once were, and they are particularly vulnerable because they tend to be rather tame and are reluctant to fly. However, they have been afforded full protection since the 1930s, and there are positive signs that they are responding favorably. The establishment of man-made reservoirs is considered beneficial in this regard, since it somewhat compensates for lost habitat. A large segment of the existing population (approximately 2000) winters at Hamurana Springs, Rotorua (North Island). Liberated

10.20

10.19 *Pair of ring-necked ducks. When at rest, these ducks ride high in the water. They prefer shallow waters with much dense vegetation, and are primarily associated with freshwater marshes. Females are persistent re-nesters, and they will often set again if the first clutch of eggs is destroyed early. Unlike most diving ducks, ring-necked ducks escort their young to cover if danger threatens, rather than to open water.*

10.20 *Drake New Zealand scaup or "black teal." Although their numbers are greatly reduced from former times, these birds now appear to be holding their own, and the population may even be increasing somewhat. Habitat loss has been detrimental, but in some cases the creation of artificial lakes for hydroelectric projects has provided new habitat.*

captive-reared stock have apparently done well.

Both sexes have broad blue bills, but the dark-eyed females differ markedly from their yellow-eyed mates in that they are generally brownish overall, except for a distinct white patch at the base of the bill. Preferred habitat consists of inland lakes and lagoons, usually near the coast, and New Zealand scaup are apparently nocturnal feeders. Drakes are noted for a soft whistle, whereas the hens utter muted quacks. Nests may be lined extensively with down, and these scaup often nest in a rather colonial fashion. Not overly common in American collections, they are more numerous in Europe, where they are commonly bred. Indeed, some 364 were produced from three original pair at the Wildfowl Trust between 1958 (when the species was first bred) and 1975. Interestingly, thus far there has been no sign of problems associated with inbreeding.

The greater Pacific, European, and lesser scaup are all essentially alike, except for size and minor color variations. Some authorities contest the legitimacy of the two races of **greater scaup** (*Aythya marila*), since they appear to be practically identical, although drakes of the American race (*A. m. mariloides*) tend to be slightly smaller and

darker on the back than those from the Old World race (*A. m. marila*).

Lesser scaup (*Aythya affinis*) are also very similar to greater scaup, but greater males can be distinguished by their superior size, paler backs, and the greenish iridescent sheen of their heads; whereas the head sheen is more purple on the lesser scaup, and they characteristically have a higher and more angular head. In addition, greater scaup drakes generally exceed two and one half pounds, and there is also more white on their wings (a feature that is more easily observed during flight). The white wing patch is one of the most reliable ways to differentiate these birds, since both sexes of both species have it. The white normally extends onto the primaries of the larger species, whereas it is generally restricted to the secondaries on the lesser scaup. The ranges of these two scaup species somewhat overlap, and this can greatly complicate accurate field identification, often making it next to impossible to distinguish the two from a distance.

Their call—a discordant "scaup, scaup"—may be the origin of their vernacular name, although some authorities suggest that their common name may have actually been derived from their diet of scallops or scalps, which are both words for shellfish. During the breeding season, greater scaup may vocalize in flight. At other times, they also have a low soft musical cooing or crooning call. On the whole, however, they can be considered to be rather silent ducks. They are omnivorous, but appear to prefer molluscs, and in some areas, herring gulls often rob wintering scaup of their food. In Scotland, they may feed on grain around sewage outfalls that are fed by breweries or distilleries.

Greater scaup have the most northerly range of the genus, and occupy a wide area throughout the Northern Hemisphere. As a rule, breeding territories may overlap and are not well defended. Nesting takes place rather late in the season, and as with some of the other pochards, they may nest in association with gulls and terns. Large clutches of sizeable eider-like eggs are produced, and some instances of nest parasitism have been reported. The young are often reared on open water and ducklings may be subjected to a great deal of predation. For much of the year, greater scaup are associated with salt water and are little affected by storms.

Lesser scaup are sometimes colloquially known as "bluebills." Much more abundant than their larger relatives, they are among the most numerous of all North American diving ducks—certainly, the most populous diving ducks of the interior. They more commonly frequent fresh water than *marila*, but during the winter they may raft up in tremendous numbers on salt water. Fifty thousand or more may form a single flock, covering several hundred acres of water; and this gregarious tendency is responsible for colorful local names like "raft duck" and "troop duck." Sometimes, these birds are encountered on

city park lakes. Lesser scaup fly in compact but irregular formations, and are prone to dart about a great deal in flight. They tend to be somewhat more nervous than their larger relatives.

During the breeding season, females are apt to return to the area in which they were hatched, but this is not necessarily the case with the drakes. Broods are sometimes combined, and adults occasionally abandon the young while they are still in down. These ducks are late migrants, often moving south just ahead of freezing water. The overall population appears to be stable, but wintering birds are vulnerable to oil pollution. Scaup of both species make delightful additions to captive waterfowl collections, and are not infrequently bred. The European birds are seldom seen in America because they are, for all practical purposes, the same as *mariloides*.

10.21 (Opposite Page) *European scaup drake. On occasion, males of this species have been observed with females and young, but most abandon their mates midway through incubation. Some brood merging has been noted (i.e., one female with 30 young). European scaup may nest singly or colonially, and often nest in association with gulls or terns.*

10.22 *Pacific greater scaup female winging over the Alaskan tundra.*

10.23 *Pair of lesser scaup. Like their larger relatives, these scaup may merge broods — in one instance, 64 young were observed being tended by seven females — but broods may be reared singly as well. Normally shy, these birds can become tame during the winter and may even take food from the hand. Opportunistic gulls may pirate food from foraging scaup.*

10.24 *Pacific greater scaup drake. On occasion, the nests of this species are built in rather dense concentrations, with nests situated within two feet of one another (or closer). Wintering birds may drift feed, and when they float beyond favored feeding areas they will fly back upstream and drift by again.*

11
Perching Ducks
Cairinini

A mong the most bizarre and heterogeneous of the waterfowl are the 12 species of perching ducks which comprise the tribe Cairinini. They range in size from among the largest of the waterfowl to the very smallest; and some are considered to be the most beautiful of all birds, while others have the ignoble distinction of being perhaps the least attractive of all wildfowl. Superficially, there are few similarities which would indicate that most perching ducks are even remotely related to one another, and the sheer diversity of this collection of anatid misfits appears to have no end—but the required anatomical and behavioral similarities do exist nevertheless.

Johnsgard has advocated moving the perching duck tribe up into a position between the shelducks and dabbling ducks, based on tracheal similarities, the appearance of downy young, and evidence of hybridization; and he has also urged that the ringed teal be moved from the dabblers to this tribe. However, other authorities have suggested that dabbling and perching ducks should be merged into a single tribe.

As their collective name implies, perching ducks are clearly more arboreal than any of the other waterfowl tribes. They generally nest in tree cavities or holes, often very high up—although several species, such as the spur-winged goose, will also nest on the ground. In

11.2

11.1 (Opposite Page) *Drake wood duck in full color. Considered by many to be the most beautiful of waterfowl, the wood duck has staged a remarkable comeback. During the early part of this century, the species almost became extinct.*

11.2 *Bathing male spur-winged goose. The appearance of these birds is misleading. Despite the fact that they are among the largest of waterfowl and are referred to as "geese," they are actually perching ducks.*

keeping with their arboreal lifestyles and their use of cavities as nest sites, these birds have sharp toenails which facilitate entry to and egress from the nest hole. The nails are even prominent on ducklings, and enable them to easily scamper up and out of the elevated entrance.

Some of the smaller members of the tribe have relatively large eyes, which perhaps indicates a preference for shady areas or a nocturnal lifestyle. Most have fairly wide and rounded wings, and some have relatively long legs. A number of species exhibit a significant amount of iridescent color throughout the plumage, including even the females. Pair bonds are usually seasonal (with possible exceptions), and in a number of cases are very weak or even absent. As with most ducks, drakes do not become involved in the complexities of rearing a family, although pygmy geese and Brazilian teal will sometimes remain together as a family unit. With only two exceptions—the wood and mandarin ducks—all species inhabit tropical or subtropical regions and are essentially nonmigratory.

The two races of **Brazilian teal** (*Amazonetta brasiliensis*) are included with the Cairinini primarily because their habits suggest that

they may represent an evolutionary link between the dabbling ducks and the perching ducks. The metallic coloring of their wings, along with their bright orange-red legs, greatly enhances the appearance of these otherwise rather nondescript ducks; and, in fact, the brilliant metallic green coloration of the outer secondaries cannot be adequately described in words. (Unfortunately, this green is seldom visible unless the wings are extended.) They also have rudimentary black manes, and the species is not noted for an eclipse plumage. The sexes differ in that the male has a dark red bill, whereas the female's is olive-grey; females are smaller; and hens have a distinct white spot in front of and above the eye, as well as a larger one at the base of the bill. Additionally, their leg color is not nearly as intense as that of the male.

Brazilian teal tend to be very vocal. The squeaky whistle of the drake is strong and piercing, whereas the call of the hen is a loud, deep quack. In some areas, the Indians refer to these birds as "Roppong"—a name derived from their call. These little teal are considered to be among the most common of Brazilian waterfowl in their preferred habitat of thickly vegetated jungle lagoons, but they avoid coastal and mangrove swamps. They are generally not encountered in large flocks, and are usually seen in small groups of 10 to 20 individuals or family parties. Apparently, they are less dependent on the availability of tree hollows than some of the other perching ducks, and will also nest on or near the ground. They may use abandoned nests of other species, and there is some speculation that they may nest on cliffs as well. Pair bonds are strong and may, in fact, be permanent; and both sexes are involved in brood care.

The lesser Brazilian teal (*A. b. brasiliensis*) has two distinct color phases, a light and a dark. The greater Brazilian teal (*A. b. ipecutiri*), which is sometimes known by the vernacular name of Schuyl's teal, is obviously larger. There is some evidence that there may be more races than just these two, and this possibility is being investigated. Brazilian teal have become relatively common in waterfowl collections in recent years, even though some aviculturists consider them rather aggressive for their small size. I have not necessarily found this to be the case, but they are definitely not inclined to let other birds (even larger ones) bully them. Once established, they tend to be incredibly prolific breeders, and may produce two or three broods a year. At times, drakes may take over sole responsibility for the young, thereby freeing the female to produce an additional clutch. Whether or not this behavior occurs in the wild, I can't say.

The **maned goose or Australian wood duck** (*Chenonetta jubata*) is not a goose at all, although it is somewhat reminiscent of a small goose in its proportions and goose-like bill. Like true geese, these birds graze extensively (particularly at night), and this similarity of feeding behavior accounts for the similar shapes of the bills. (At one time, they were included with the shelducks.) The somewhat longish and uneven nape feathers (or "mane") are responsible for the vernacular name. Prime habitat consists of lightly timbered country with water nearby, and they range extensively throughout much of Australia.

Maned geese do not perch as readily as the more typical members of the Cairinini, and they are decidedly more terrestrial. In the water, they are rather slow and awkward swimmers. During the breeding season, these birds become more arboreal and seek tree hollows (even green ones), usually close to water. But if appropriate nest cavities are scarce, they may select a site up to a mile from water. The pair bond is strong, perhaps even permanent. Females alone incubate, but the drakes may establish a brood territory, particularly if

11.3 *Drake greater Brazilian teal. The female alone incubates, but the male is involved in the rearing of the young.*

11.4 *Female maned goose or Australian wood duck.*

11.5 *Male lesser Brazilian teal. Except for their size, these birds are virtually identical to the greater Brazilian teal shown in plate 11.3. They fly swiftly and easily through trees.*

11.6 *Male maned goose. Although these wary birds have been subjected to some sport hunting pressure, they appear to be thriving.*

11.7 *Drake wood duck. In areas where they are not molested, these beautiful ducks can be considered almost tame. They generally feed from the surface of the water, and although they are not prone to upend, they will dive for food and have been known to catch fish. Wood ducks are also rather adept at catching insects that fly close by. At times, they will forage in cultivated fields and even in farmers' hog lots. In flight, their wings produce a subdued whistling sound.*

there is little water in the vicinity, and will drive off other males. Adults are essentially herbivorous, but the ducklings feed extensively on small insects until they are three to four weeks of age. As with many waterfowl species, immatures resemble females.

At the conclusion of the breeding season, the somewhat nomadic maned geese will typically congregate in large flocks of several hundred. Upon occasion, these flocks may contain several thousand birds, and at such times extensive crop damage may occur in some regions, since they tend to gather in cultivated and irrigated areas. Extremely shy and very wary as a rule, these birds are popular Australian game-birds, although hunting has not been detrimental thus far. Maned geese are not troublesome in waterfowl collections, and despite the fact that they are not consistently bred, they are delightful additions.

The North American **wood duck** (*Aix sponsa*) and its close relative, the mandarin duck of Asia, are among the most beautiful and striking of all birds and, consequently, they are very common in waterfowl collections the world over. The Latin name for the wood duck is unusually apt and poetic, since it can be loosely translated to mean "a water bird in bridal dress," and drakes in nuptial plumage are adorned

with gorgeous colors and patterns of astonishing complexity. Their popular name is based on their fondness for wooded areas.

Also known as summer or Carolina ducks, wood ducks are among the most popular of American ducks, and have long been prized by duck hunters, not only for their superb flesh, but also for the resplendent breeding plumage of the drake, which is highly sought by trout fly tiers for the creation of special trout flies. Omnivorous feeders, these ducks will consume seeds and other parts of aquatic vegetation, aquatic and land insects, and crustaceans; and some individuals have been observed to dive and catch fish. They also appear to be more fond of acorns than any other North American anatid, crushing the nuts in their gizzards.

In the water, wood ducks ride very high, and in flight they characteristically bob their heads to such a degree that Johnsgard describes them as "rubber-necked." Their tails are relatively long, which facilitates more maneuverable flight in heavily wooded areas, and they readily fly through thick timber with great speed and skill. The female has a peculiar squealing call; and while the drake is usually silent, he does utter a low goldfinch-like call. It has been suggested that the loud call of the hen may have evolved because of the visual restrictions of their thickly-wooded habitat. Where not molested, wood ducks tend to be unwary and almost tame. They may gather in large communal roosts in wintering areas, and up to 5000 have been reported at a single roost site.

As a result of over-exploitation and severe habitat loss—particularly the removal of old dead trees and snags as the great American forest was cut—the wood duck population drastically declined during the early part of this century. By 1918, the species was thought to be virtually extinct, and there were probably more birds in captive collections than in the wild. The species was then afforded rigorous protection, and was fortunately able to stage a remarkable, almost

11.8

11.9

11.8 *Raccoon. Nesting wood ducks and their eggs may be preyed upon by these arboreal marauders.*

11.9 *Female wood duck on nest in a pine tree. While these birds are normally considered cavity nesters, they do on rare occasions construct nests.*

11.10 *Wood duck male. Currently, the greatest threat to this species is an alarming rate of habitat destruction. But wood ducks are also subjected to some hunting pressure and some are unintentionally caught in muskrat traps. In addition, a certain percentage of nest-hunting females are lost when they become trapped in chimneys. Predators, such as bull and rat snakes, snapping turtles, bull frogs, and alligators also take a large toll.*

11.10

unbelievable, comeback. Artificial nest boxes were installed in many areas to compensate for lost tree cavities, and hundreds of captive-reared wood ducks were liberated; and incredibly, these once endangered ducks may now be the most common nesting ducks in the eastern United States. As inspiring as this story is, however, the threat of indiscriminate habitat destruction still hangs over these birds.

The relatively specialized wood duck is totally dependent on wooded areas with sufficient water, as well as the availability of a number of appropriate tree cavities of suitable size for nesting. Holes that are too small for prowling racoons to enter are particularly favored, and hens generally select a nest site in trees standing in water, 30 to 65 feet (or more) above the ground—although a few have been recorded as nesting on the ground, and I know of at least one case in which a nest was *built* in a pine tree. Drakes remain with their mates longer than most ducks, usually until the eggs pip. If a clutch is lost early, wood ducks demonstrate a propensity to re-nest, and are therefore able to maintain a fairly high level of productivity. Two successful clutches in one season is not particularly unusual. After hatching, the tiny duck-

lings, responding to a call from the hen, unhesitatingly leap from the nesting hole and float to the ground like so many balls of fluff. Due to their light weight and thick down, they usually drift to the ground unharmed, but occasionally a duckling will experience a rough landing and may be momentarily stunned.

While the hens are not nearly so colorful or striking as their handsome mates, they possess a subtle beauty of their own. They rather closely resemble mandarin duck females, but can easily be distinguished from the latter by their slightly larger size and darker color. The conspicuous white eye stripe of the wood duck is also much broader and does not extend nearly as far back on the head. Even though wood ducks are apparently closely related to mandarin ducks, it is interesting that very little interbreeding between them has been recorded, despite the fact that they are often maintained together in captivity.

For centuries, the beautiful **mandarin duck** (*Aix galericulata*) has been famous in Chinese and Japanese art and literature. References to the mandarin duck can be found in the songs or odes collected by the followers of Confucius in the Fifth or Sixth Century B.C., and pairs of caged mandarin ducks were formerly given as gifts at Chinese weddings, as symbols of marital fidelity. The gorgeous drake of this species is perhaps best characterized by the curious dorsal orange-gold "sails" that extend up along its flanks, and its strange orange-chestnut "side whiskers." The inner vane of the twelfth secondary feather has been modified and greatly enlarged to produce the sail-like structure, and these peculiar feathers are flattened against the body during flight. Males in eclipse plumage resemble their mates, although they are readily distinguishable by the retention of the dark red bills.

Like wood ducks, mandarins are comfortable ashore, perch readily, and are partially migratory. As a rule, they are relatively silent, but the male infrequently utters a sharp rising whistle. Their breeding habits parallel those of their American relatives, but I have noted that mated pairs (at least in captivity) are more prone to engage in mutual preening. Their pair bonds are strong, and while essentially cavity nesters, they will also nest on the ground sometimes. Rather gregarious birds, they tend to be active in the pre-dawn and twilight hours.

The current status of mandarin ducks in the wild is not particularly encouraging. Habitat loss and alteration may be proving to be detrimental, and since mandarins are no longer regarded with the reverence they once were, they are undoubtedly subjected to some hunting pressure. In a protein-starved country such as China, any source of meat is important, and these relatively tame birds are easy prey for hunters. They were formerly quite common in Japan, but the population has been significantly reduced, even though over 11,000 wintering birds could be accounted for in 1976. Encouragingly, mandarins are still apparently rather common throughout much of their range, and there is a small feral population of approximately 300 to 400 birds in Britain, descendants of ducks that were imported from China and liberated many years ago. Among the most popular of all aviary birds, these ducks are widely kept on ornamental ponds. Fortunately, both mandarins and woodies thrive in captivity, and thousands are raised annually. When kept together, however, wood ducks dominate and are more productive.

Pygmy geese, as the vernacular name implies, are among the smallest and daintiest of waterfowl, and do resemble diminutive geese, complete with goose-like bills. But, of course, they are not geese and are not even closely related to them. All four forms inhabit the tropics

11.11 *Pair of mandarin ducks. This Old World counterpart of the wood duck is equally beautiful. Female mandarins from Korea tend to be darker than those which occur elsewhere and they have pink bills, which has led some to believe that the Korean birds may be a separate subspecies.*

11.12 *Drake mandarin. In flight, the crest is depressed along the neck and the distinctive "sails" are flattened against the body.*

11.13 *Pair of mandarin ducks engaged in synchronized courtship behavior.*

11.12

11.13

11.11

11.14

of Australia and Asia, and all are related closely enough to one another to be incorporated into the single genus *Nettapus*. They favor ponds, sluggish rivers, or bays that have an abundance of aquatic vegetation. Essentially vegetarian, they feed on the seeds and other parts of water lillies; and while they do not ignore aquatic insects, such as water beetles and their larvae, such fare probably does not constitute a major portion of their diet. They fly well, and are said to be capable of springing directly from the surface of the water like a dabbler. They are poorly adapted for prolonged movements on land and are seldom encountered ashore. Their large eyes suggest a nocturnal existence.

These birds are very seldom maintained in wildfowl collections because they are extremely delicate and difficult to acclimate. They do not transport well, and appear to be especially susceptible to shock, dehydration, pneumonia, and rat predation. Many propagators believe that pygmy geese must be kept full-winged within an enclosed, heavily planted aviary if they are to survive and propagate, but since so few have been maintained and bred over the years, such generalizations may be premature. In captivity, they seldom leave the security of the water, except to perch on a branch over it. Most of the captive Asian pygmy geese I have observed tended to be very nervous and apprehensive, and resorted to very rapid jerky head pumps whenever approached too closely. This behavior has also been noted with the African species, but was not nearly as intense. Hopefully, once pygmy geese are established in captivity and propagation commences, the resulting progeny will be more amenable to long-term maintenance.

The **African pygmy goose** (*Nettapus auritus*) is the smallest and perhaps the most elegant of the group, and enjoys a large range throughout a major portion of the continent, including even Madagascar. Some duck enthusiasts consider them to be the most beautiful of the African waterfowl, and the large pale green patches on the sides of the male's neck, as well as its yellow bill, are indeed most distinctive. The black wings are adorned with a prominent white bar, which is evident in flight and is a reliable way to identify them. When the birds are on open water, their bright colors and distinct patterns are very conspicuous. But these same colors and patterns serve as perfect camouflage when the pygmy goose is in its natural setting of reed-lined cul-de-sacs along quiet, rather deep waterways, where there is an abundance of water lilies and other aquatic vegetation. Not particularly vocal as a rule, the male has a high-pitched whistle or twittering call, while the female merely quacks weakly.

It is not unusual to observe these ducks roosting in trees, and in fact, their favored nest sites are located in tall hollow trees, standing in water. Nests have also been recorded in the thatched roof of an occupied African hut, in ant hills, and in the nests of other birds, including the huge nest of a hammerkop stork. In swampy areas, they may nest on the ground, perhaps to escape the deadly arboreal black mamba, a snake that frequently explores tree cavities. African pygmy geese were bred for the first time in captivity in 1975, but unfortunately, they are maintained in only a handful of collections.

The other three types of pygmy geese are rather similar to *auritus* behaviorally, but are primarily green and white in coloration. The **green pygmy goose** (*Nettapus pulchellus*), of tropical northern Australia and southeast New Guinea (as well as the small islands of Ceram and Buru), does not range inland more than 50 or 60 miles, and is strictly limited to the flood plains and swamps of coastal rivers. Like all pygmy geese, their distribution is governed by the availability of

11.14 *African pygmy goose male. Almost totally aquatic, pygmy geese seldom come ashore; but when they do, they perch readily. In areas where they are not persecuted, these diminutive birds can be tame and confiding. Fortunately, they are too small to be considered a game species, and their relatively large range has thus far spared them from the negative effects of habitat destruction.*

11.15 *Pair of hammerkop storks. While pygmy geese are normally considered cavity nesters, they have been known to utilize the nests of these storks on occasion.*

11.16 (Opposite Page) *African pygmy goose drake. These rather quiet little ducks are considered by many to be the most beautiful of South African ducks. The sexes are similar, except that the slightly smaller females are somewhat duller overall than their mates and lack the distinctive green and white facial pattern. Their heads are rather greyish, with darker crowns and hind necks, and they have a dark eye stripe. Immatures resemble females, but they are noted for more distinct eye stripes, and their breasts and flanks are more buff in coloration.*

11.15

permanent, lily-covered deep-water lagoons. Females are slightly smaller and duller than their mates, with less distinct flank barring, and the green of the neck does not continue to the front. They are swift fliers, and tend to fly low over the water. On the wing and at rest they often utter a shrill chirruping whistle continuously. They are not particularly wary, but their small size has prevented them from being subjected to much man-related persecution, such as over-hunting.

Unlike the other forms of pygmy geese, which prefer to feed from the surface by upending, the green pygmy goose often secures food by diving. While their range overlaps that of the other Australian pygmy goose, their favored foods differ significantly enough to preclude competition. This species favors the flowers and seeds of water lilies, whereas the white-quilled pygmy goose seeks pond weeds and the seeds of aquatic and shoreline grasses. During the breeding season, the aggressive males may engage in territorial disputes that can be vicious, often involving underwater pursuits, but during the dry season they may flock together in relatively large numbers. The pair bond is surprisingly strong, perhaps even permanent. While they typically seek arboreal nesting cavities, these birds occasionally nest on the ground. During incubation, males remain in the vicinity of the nest site, and rejoin the hens when they emerge with the brood.

The **Australasian pygmy goose** (*Nettapus coromandelianus*) is commonly referred to as the cotton teal (or ''quacky-duck'' in India). Their flight is effortless, and has been compared to that of a gigantic bee—strong and swift, with rapid whirring wing beats, and a great deal of agile turning and twisting. They often fly fairly low over the water, or just skim over the treetops. In the water, they ride high, and although they dive well, they seldom do so except to escape an enemy. Generally, they are encountered in pairs or small flocks, but up to 500 have been recorded in a single flock during the nonbreeding season. As a rule, the cotton teal is considered a sedentary species; but those nesting in the north, particularly in China, do move south to pass the winter. Because of its large range, the species is probably secure for the moment.

The Indian (*N. c. coromandelianus*) and Australian (*N. c. albipennis*) races are practically identical, although the Indian cotton teal tends to be slightly smaller. Some of the more dated literature indicates that males of the Australian population do not have a noticeable eclipse plumage, but this is now known to be incorrect. Both sexes are similar, but the females tend to be duller and less iridescent dorsally, and lack the distinct breast band. In addition, their eyes are brown instead of red.

In some areas, individuals of the Asian race have become so trusting that they have been known to nest under the roofs of pagodas and temples and, considering their nervous temperament in captivity, this is somewhat surprising. Ducklings have reportedly been pushed from the nest cavity by the female, and in one case, the female was allegedly seen carrying the ducklings down on her back.

The Australian birds are frequently referred to as white-quilled or white pygmy geese. In flight, males of this race are noted for a call which consists of a rapid staccato trumpeting. Their breeding habitat is limited to coastal Queensland, and because of this localized, restricted range, they are considered to be among the rarest of Australian wildfowl. Unfortunately, in recent years the population has declined significantly, and although white-quilled pygmy geese are not in immediate danger, habitat alteration could seriously compromise their continued survival.

Over the years, captive maintenance of the cotton teal has been attempted more often than that of any other pygmy geese. Despite all efforts, however, a mere handful remain in collections today, and it was not until 1978 that they were finally *successfully* bred. Sadly, the current state of the avicultural art is such that it will probably be many years before any of the pygmy geese are well established—but as impossible as it may appear now, it will come to pass. There are, after all, a number of species now thriving within controlled environments that only a few years ago were believed to be impossible to maintain. Both the green and the white-quilled pygmy geese have been kept in Australian collections, but are virtually unknown to propagators outside of Australia.

The two bizarre **comb ducks** (*Sarkidiornis melanotos*), or "knob-billed geese," occur not only in Africa and Asia, but in South America as well. Although widely separated geographically, the two subspecies are very similar, except that the male neotropical birds (*S. m. caruncu-*

11.19

11.20

11.18

11.21

latus) are slightly smaller and much darker along the flanks than their Old World relatives (*S. m. melanotos*). Named for the black leaf-shaped caruncle or fleshy knob which adorns the basal two-thirds of the upper bill, drakes of both races are twice the size of the females, weighing up to four and a half pounds. The comb enlarges during the breeding season, but is very much reduced in size the remainder of the year. The dark dorsal parts are glossed with violet, purple, bronze, and green; and when males are in full breeding color, their heads and necks are tinged with yellow, as are the undertail feathers.

Although it may seem farfetched, these large and ungainly birds perch readily and reportedly even cling to the sides of trees with their strong claws—somewhat resembling monstrous woodpeckers. In the air, they fly in "V" formation, and they tend to wander a great deal. Their flight is not rapid but is powerful and is characterized by slow, distinct wing beats. At times, comb ducks can be gregarious, but they are more commonly observed alone or in small groups. In Africa, they are not considered superior gamebirds, and are regarded as agricultural pests in some districts. As a rule, these are quiet ducks, but males sometimes utter a croaking whistle or hiss, and females grunt weakly.

Tree cavities are favored as nest sites, but comb ducks are not at all adverse to nesting on the ground, and may also utilize the nests of other birds, including those of vultures, fish eagles, storks, etc. Most sites are near water, and sometimes more than one female will use the same nest. In fact as many as 54 eggs have been recorded in a single

11.17 (Opposite Page) *Green pygmy goose drake. When these birds are seeking a nest site, the male is usually the first to fly up to a prospective hollow — but it is the female that inspects it.*

11.18 *Old World comb duck male in breeding condition. While comb ducks may nest in long grass or amongst stones, they usually nest in tree cavities, sometimes as far as a mile from water. Successful sites may be used year after year.*

11.19 *Male white-quilled or white pygmy goose. Considered rare, these perching ducks are extremely susceptible to any significant habitat alteration.*

11.20 *Indian pygmy goose (or cotton teal) male. These little ducks are essentially nocturnal — indeed, this photograph was taken at night. Cotton teal have a rapid flight and can easily fly between trees.*

11.21 *Drake Old World comb duck. These rather shy birds are normally observed in small groups or alone (at least in South Africa), but at times they may gather to form flocks of a hundred or more birds.*

11.22 *South American comb duck drake. Essentially, these ducks are the same as their Old World counterparts, but males tend to be slightly smaller and are significantly darker along the flanks. Restricted to tropical and temperate areas, they are normally associated with ponds, wooded swamps, savanna lagoons, and sluggish tree-lined streams. They are considered by some to be a distinct species.*

11.23 *Female muscovy duck. Pure muscovies bear little resemblance to domestic muscovies and are a rather attractive species.*

11.24 (Opposite Page) *Drake muscovy duck. Adult males may weigh as much as nine pounds, but despite this, they are powerful fliers.*

nest. Little down is used to line the nest. Comb ducks exhibit some polygamous tendencies, and in captivity they are perhaps best maintained in trios, as amorous males can become aggressive toward a single female and she may be abused. The Old World race is much more common in waterfowl collections, and while they are not commonly bred, some propagators have done particularly well with them.

The **muscovy duck** (*Cairina moschata*) is familiar to most people, but is very rare in the *pure* form outside of its native Central and South America. Along with the white-winged wood duck and Hartlaub's duck, muscovies constitute a subgroup collectively known as the greater wood ducks. All three species are large heavy-bodied birds, and their relatively short legs are set well forward on the body, giving them a distinct horizontal stance. All have broad wings that are armed with a bony knob at the bend, and drakes exhibit a slight swelling of the forehead during the breeding season. The three species of greater wood ducks replace one another in comparable areas of the tropical forests of Asia, Africa, and Central and South America, and their closest relatives appear to be the comb ducks.

In the 1500s, when the Spaniards first invaded South America, they discovered that the Indians had already domesticated the huge muscovy duck; and, in fact, Columbus noted upon his arrival in the West Indies that the natives had domesticated ducks which were as large as geese. However, just when muscovies were initially domesticated has never been accurately established. Domestic muscovies have since become common barnyard fowl the world over, but these birds have evolved into massive, grotesque, multi-colored creatures through generations of captive breeding. Typically, they have huge, ugly facial warts. Wild birds, on the other hand, are essentially black with conspicuous white wing patches (the extent of which may vary with age), and the black facial protuberances are very reduced in size.

Pure muscovies are considered to be quite handsome, lacking the coarseness of their domestic counterpart. The erectile forecrown crest is very decorative, as is the blackish bill with pinkish white bars, and the bright green and purple reflections of their upper parts. Immediately following the molt, these ducks have a lovely velvety appearance. Often double the size of their mates, muscovy drakes can be extremely aggressive and may hiss loudly when threatened. When fighting, they use not only their wings, but their powerful clawed feet as well. In flight, their wing beats are slow and labored, but they are often effective and strong fliers nonetheless, and for such cumbersome birds, they fly deceptively fast.

Some polygamous tendencies have been demonstrated by this species, and pair bonds are virtually nonexistent. Primarily forest ducks, they are said to be very fond of termites, frequently tearing a termite nest apart to get at the insects within. They have also been observed eating other insects, small fish, and even little reptiles. Highly regarded as superior table birds, they have been hunted to such an extent in many regions that they have been exterminated; but due to their widespread range, they can still be considered abundant in areas that are removed from human habitation. Because most aviculturists are unfamiliar with the pure muscovy, they are thought of as barnyard birds and are unpopular for this reason. As a result, they are surprisingly rare in collections, but they breed prolifically for those who do maintain them.

All three of the greater wood ducks are quarrelsome, and some propagators even consider them to be violent. The muscovy is the worst of the group in this regard, whereas there is a significant amount

11.25 *Group of muscovies in Guatemala.*

11.26 *White-winged wood duck male bathing. It is possible that no more than 200 pairs of these gravely endangered birds exist in the wild. When annoyed or threatened, they hiss and raise their wings in such a manner that the prominent white wing patches are very conspicuous. In flight, pairs may call out with a prolonged and vibrant wailing honk.*

of variation in individual temperament with the other two forms. Male muscovies will also fight among themselves, and unless a relatively large area is available, breeding pairs in captivity should be maintained in separate facilities. All the same, they can usually be safely mixed with smaller ducks and teal, since these are apparently not viewed as competitors.

White-winged wood ducks (*Cairina scutulata*) are large, broad-winged, short-legged ducks which are rather cumbersome in overall appearance. The white on their heads is extremely variable and may range from extensive to almost none, but females generally have less white than their mates. Hens are also slightly duller in color, moderately smaller, with thinner necks and finer heads—but the species can be most accurately sexed by eye color, since females have eyes that are dark brown while drakes have lighter and redder (or yellowish) eyes. The bill color is a deep yellow or orange, blotched with greyish black, and that of the male swells up at the base during the breeding season.

Even though white-winged wood ducks are large and bulky, their flight is strong and surprisingly swift. They readily fly through tree branches and often pass the day perched in high trees. Probably nocturnal, they avoid direct sunlight, and are thus restricted to the deep shady forests of Assam and southeast Asia (ranging, on occasion, up to 5000 feet). The pair bond, if it does exist, is apparently weak. Males, however, may remain in the vicinity of a female with young, but

what role they play in brood rearing, if any, is unknown.

These birds invariably call in flight, and during the breeding season, they are noted for a trumpeting call or a prolonged wailing honk that has been described as "ghostly." Apparently, this strange call is the reason why the Assamese have named them "spirit ducks." White-winged wood ducks are omnivorous, and readily consume seeds, aquatic vegetation, insects, worms, molluscs, frogs, and possibly even small snakes and fish. However, their diet may vary seasonally.

These intriguing ducks are thought to be very rare and are considered endangered—a plight that resulted from over-hunting and the uncontrolled felling of the primary rain forests. Delacour believes that they rightly belong on the endangered species list, but he also suggests that they may not be quite as rare as many people suggest, since they live more or less in small isolated groups and may easily be overlooked. Their distribution is widespread in southern Sumatra, and in certain regions they are considered by some to be "common." The total wild population is estimated at under 200 pairs. On occasion, they may be encountered in cleared regions and disturbed forest, and they appear to be fairly well-known to Sumatran natives; perhaps even nesting in fairly close proximity to some villages. Few nests have been seen in the wild, but these ducks appear to favor decaying tree hollows.

In recent years, the Wildfowl Trust has been very successful with white-winged wood ducks, and over 100 were reared between 1971 and 1977; as a result, their future seems somewhat assured, at least in the captive state. Pairs have been established in other collections, and the species was bred for the first time in America in 1978. However, in captivity these birds appear to be very susceptible to avian tuberculosis, a source of major concern to aviculturists, and a problem that is probably more acute in areas such as England, where the climate is damp. (Sunshine can greatly reduce the incidence of TB, but as previously noted, the species prefers shady areas.) Inbreeding may also become a major problem if a few wild-caught, unrelated birds are not occasionally added to the captive gene pool.

Hartlaub's ducks (*Pteronetta hartlaubi*), while possibly not uncommon in the rain forests of tropical west and central Africa, are seldom seen elsewhere. Apparently, they are still relatively abundant, but no doubt the wanton clearing of the forests will sooner or later adversely affect the population. The subtle beauty of the Hartlaub's duck is highlighted by a large bluish grey patch on the wing, which is generally not visible when the wings are closed but is very obvious in

flight. Smaller and much trimmer than both the muscovy and white-winged wood ducks, they nevertheless have similar proportions. The amount of white on the head of the drake is subject to a great deal of individual variation, but it is possible that as males mature the extent of white on the head increases; whereas adult females are generally noted for little or no white at all. Usually, sex can be reliably ascertained by eye color, since females have a distinctly darker eye. They are usually slightly smaller and duller as well, and the pale bill markings near the tips of their bills and below the nostrils are generally more pinkish grey (rather than yellowish as in the male). This is also subject to some variation, however, and I have seen females that had considerably more colored area on the bill than males. In addition, most of the drakes I have seen lacked the colored area about the nostrils.

The call of the male has been described as somewhat high-pitched and wheezy. Females often utter a relatively loud quack. Preferred habitat consists of secluded shaded streams, ponds, and creeks. Their sedentary habits somewhat parallel those of the white-winged wood duck, and like those birds, they appear to avoid direct sunlight. Hartlaub's ducks are rather trusting and often perch in trees overhanging the water. The species has been studied little in the wild and nests have apparently never been documented. Unlike the other two greater wood ducks, these birds appear to have a definite pair bond and data obtained by observing captive pairs suggest that males may even be involved in brood defense.

11.27 *White-winged wood duck. The decline of this species has been caused by a number of factors, but the most detrimental at this stage is the alarming loss of undisturbed primary rain forests in Southeast Asia.*

11.28 *Male western Hartlaub's duck. The beautiful blue wing patches are generally not visible when these birds are at rest.*

11.29 *Drake western Hartlaub's duck bathing. While no wild nests have been seen by qualified biologists, there can be little question that these ducks are cavity nesters. The female alone incubates, but the limited amount of data available suggests that both sexes aggressively defend the brood.*

11.30 *Mount of the so-called eastern Hartlaub's duck. These ducks are noted for much more white on the head than their "western relatives," but they are not regarded as a valid subspecies by most authorities.*

11.31 *Portrait of a male spur-winged goose. These large ducks can be common on larger stretches of water in South Africa. They are also found along streams and rivers where there are open grassy flats, with adjacent tall grasses and water weeds in which the birds can find shelter.*

Some authorities consider the possibility of two races, but Delacour suggests that the white-headed eastern birds (*P. h. albifrons*) of the upper Congo (which may sometimes have white napes and chins as well) may merely represent variants, not worthy of racial distinction. The occurrence of Hartlaub's ducks in collections is very sporadic, particularly in America—although in recent years a few pairs have been imported from Europe. If the breeding success achieved with them thus far in Europe is a reliable indicator, they should be well established in collections in the New World within a few years. They were bred for the first time at the Wildfowl Trust in 1959, but the first captive breeding in North America did not occur until 1977. Some propagators don't trust them with other birds, and I am aware of one particularly nasty individual that attacked and killed a flamingo.

The two races of African **spur-winged geese** (*Plectropterus gambensis*) are the largest and oddest of the perching ducks; and indeed, they are among the most peculiar of all waterfowl. Large males are said to weigh almost 20 pounds, but despite this they are still considered to be ducks and not geese. Apparently, they are not related to magpie geese as some biologists have suggested, although they do superficially resemble them. Some museum workers have speculated that a number of prominent skeletal features seem to indicate that these birds may be aberrant shelducks.

Some purists feel that these birds are downright ugly and ungainly, but beauty is in the eye of the beholder, and in my opinion, they are not quite as ugly as many authorities would have us believe. The dark upper parts are glossed with bronze and green, and in flight, large white wing patches are very conspicuous. Females are generally smaller and not as colorful as their mates. The large spurs located at the bend of the wing provide them with both their name and dangerous weapons. When threatened, the huge males tend to huff and can be very formidable, but normally, they utter a high squeaky chatter-like whistle at the same time that seems somewhat incongruous, perhaps even ludicrous. Interestingly, the females are practically mute, and spur-winged geese are notoriously wary and shy.

Rather than select a cavity to nest in as do other perching ducks, spur-winged geese are more prone to construct a substantial nest in high grass on dry land. But they may also utilize old nests of other birds, or may even choose to nest in a hole in a large termite mound. The pair bond is apparently very weak, and may be nonexistent. Ranging throughout the African continent, they are fond of cultivated areas, avoid large forests and the desert, and are especially attracted to flood plains, where groups of 50 or more may graze on grasses in shallow water. Essentially a sedentary species, they may engage in seasonal movements. They are fairly adaptable, and can still be encountered in inhabited areas; and in some agricultural regions, they tend to trample crops and are regarded as pests. Primarily vegetarian, they will from time to time take small fish. In general, spur-winged geese are regarded as inedible, but are still subjected to some hunting

pressure. They fly heavily but swiftly, perch readily, and commonly associate with the ubiquitous Egyptian goose. During the molt, up to 2000 have been seen together. Both adults and goslings are said to be preyed upon by crocodiles.

Spur-winged geese appear sporadically in waterfowl collections—the northern race (*P. g. gambensis*) more so in America than the black or southern subspecies (*P. g. niger*). The knob on the head of the black spur-winged goose is not as pronounced as it is on the northern or Gambian race, and they also lack the distinctive naked red patch on the throat. In general, *niger* is a much trimmer bird. However, the two races apparently hybridize in the wild, for I once saw a specimen collected within the range of the southern subspecies which clearly exhibited characteristics of both races.

Because of their great size and large wing spurs, many aviculturists consider spur-winged geese dangerous to the unsuspecting public, but some individuals tame very rapidly. If confined to limited areas, they can be spiteful to other birds, and even though they have been maintained for many years, they are not commonly bred. They are however, fairly well represented in a number of collections, although their numbers may merely reflect the species' capacity for long life.

11.32 *Spur-winged geese are notoriously wary and are not easily hunted. In addition, their flesh is quite tough so they are not considered to be prime gamebirds.*

11.33 *During the middle of the day, spur-winged geese usually rest on grassy banks or in short aquatic vegetation. They are most active at dawn and dusk, and much of their feeding is done at night, particularly if the moon is bright.*

11.34 *Black spur-winged goose. Darker than the spur-winged geese to the north, these birds are relatively abundant.*

11.35 *Nile crocodiles are said to prey upon both adult spur-winged geese and their goslings.*

12
Sea Ducks
Mergini

To a certain extent, the common collective name of this tribe is misleading, since it implies an almost totally pelagic existence for all members of the group. It is true that scoters, goldeneyes, harlequins, oldsquaws, and mergansers are all strongly aquatic in their lifestyles, and are all considered to be among the most accomplished of waterfowl divers—but in general, they often *nest* rather far inland near fresh water, and a few species seldom (if ever) go near the sea. It is conceivable that they may merely represent specialized perching ducks which have adapted to an underwater feeding lifestyle (and this is certainly thought to be the case with goldeneyes and mergansers), but their taxonomic relationship to other wildfowl groups remains to be clearly defined. Eiders are also considered with the Mergini by some anatid specialists.

Sea ducks are mainly diurnal foragers, which feed primarily underwater on animal matter, such as mussels and other molluscs, crustaceans, insects, and fish. When diving, most of them normally open their wings and use them for underwater propulsion. As a rule, they are rather poorly equipped for terrestrial locomotion (even though some species, such as the mergansers, are quite mobile when ashore).

12.2

Since many of them are associated with the sea for a major portion of the year and commonly ingest salt water, they have special glands which remove excess salt from the blood stream and discharge it through the nostrils. These supraorbital glands are located directly above the eyes, and not surprisingly, there appears to be a definite correlation between gland size of a particular species and the degree to which it frequents salt water.

With some notable exceptions, sea ducks are medium-sized to fairly large birds, which range in color from solid velvety black to the most unbelievable combination of colors imaginable; and the degree of external sexual dimorphism is often extreme. Most have non-iridescent speculums. All but the oldsquaw are generally rather quiet. When nesting, most prefer sites in tree hollows or other cavities, but several (like the scoters) typically nest on the ground, and a number of species may nest in gull or tern colonies. With the exception of only two species of mergansers, all sea ducks inhabit the arctic and temperate regions of the Northern Hemisphere. Even the vast ocean is not a significant factor in limiting their distribution, since harlequin and oldsquaw ducks, one species of goldeneye, two of the mergansers, and two of the scoters have ranges that extend far into both the Eastern and Western hemispheres.

12.1 (Opposite Page) *Bufflehead drake bathing. These tiny birds, like many of the sea ducks, nest in regions well away from the sea and utilize salt water habitat only during the winter. Wintering birds sometimes engage in synchronous feeding — and when doing so, whole flocks may disappear underwater simultaneously.*

12.2 *Adult male Pacific white-winged scoter. Scoters are large, chunky birds that often have gaudy and multi-colored bills, but which are rather dull and nondescript otherwise.*

The three species of scoters are circumboreal in distribution, and very much at home on the sea. Adult males are essentially black in overall coloration, and they might be considered nondescript were it not for their distinctive, often brightly colored and peculiarly shaped bills. Unlike most northern ducks, they have no real eclipse plumage, although their heads and necks may become duller and the underparts somewhat browner during the nonbreeding season. When winds are strong or adverse, scoters usually fly so low that they skim the wave crests, and unlike eiders, they prefer to fly around projecting points of land instead of crossing over them. They feed primarily on material of marine animal origin (which may exceed 90 percent of their diet), and are particularly fond of blue mussels, easily swallowing medium-sized specimens whole. (Mussels measuring one inch by two inches have been removed from white-winged scoters.) This predilection makes them unpopular in areas where valuable shellfish beds are located, such as in Puget Sound, because wintering flocks can have a significant impact on commercial shellfish production.

Ironically, despite the fact that scoters can be among the most numerous of offshore wintering birds, very little is really known about them—and this is especially true of their behavior following their

winter. In my observations of surf and white-winged scoters along the Pacific coast, most winter flocks I have seen have consisted primarily of full color drakes, with a relatively small percentage of female-plumaged birds (some of which may have been immature males). These observations have included numerous sightings as far south as the Sea of Cortez in Mexico and as far north as the San Juan Islands in southern Canada. Such a separation on the wintering grounds *might* be related to availability of food, or possibly even to different foraging techniques. On the other hand, I have also seen large wintering flocks (particularly surf scoters) in which the sex ratios were equal. Their distribution on the wintering grounds is obviously a question which requires a great deal more study.

The peculiar **surf scoter** (*Melanitta perspicillata*) has the dubious distinction of being the least studied duck in North America. It is perhaps the most attractive of the scoters, since the bills of adult drakes are strangely swollen at the top and sides and adorned with an elaborate pattern of reddish orange, yellow, black, and white, with a distinct squarish black patch near the base. The top of the bill is feathered nearly to the nostrils. Adult males are very velvety black overall, but rather less glossy than the other species, with scarlet to

12.3

12.3 *Two drake surf scoters flying low over the water. At sea, these scoters feed primarily on molluscs, but will also consume crustaceans, echinoderms, and other marine invertebrates. They also eat herring eggs and have been known to take fish on occasion. Normally considered to be North American residents, they may also breed in northeastern Siberia. Unfortunately, sea ducks in general are specialized and are highly vulnerable to oil spills and other types of coastal pollution. (Most of the surf scoters pictured in this chapter were oil spill casualties.)*

arrival on the arctic breeding grounds. Scoter nests are notoriously difficult to locate, because they are not necessarily oriented to lake or pond shores and may be hundreds of feet back from the waterline, often well concealed under the low spreading branches of a pine or spruce tree. Indeed, surf scoter eggs were discovered for the first time by biologists scarcely a century ago and downy young were not seen until 1920.

It is relatively easy to sex adult scoters, but subadult birds are another matter altogether, because the different plumage sequences are not at all well known and can be extremely confusing, even for the most experienced waterfowl specialist. Not infrequently, there is considerable disagreement on what little is known. Most of the literature indicates that males become fully colored within two years, but my observations have led me to believe that as much as three years (or more) may be required. (As an example, several European white-winged scoter drakes of known age that I examined at the Wildfowl Trust were at least two years old and were far from being in what I would call adult color.) Likewise, while two-year old scoters may be capable of breeding, it is unlikely that they breed before their third year.

While it is not well documented, there is some evidence which suggests that the sexes *might* migrate to different areas during the

orange legs and feet, and black webs. The eye of the drake can be either pale blue or yellowish to greyish white.

Full color drakes also have a very conspicuous white forehead patch (which may vary greatly in size and shape), as well as a long white triangular patch on the nape with the apex pointing down the back of the neck—two features that have inspired the vernacular name "skunk-head coot." The size of the nape patch is also variable and may be an indication of age. Interestingly, the white nape patch is comprised of hairlike white feathers and forms a short mane. Some of the literature indicates the nape patch is lost during the nonbreeding season, and in the case of several captive scoters at Sea World the patch was certainly indistinct during this time. As late as December, I have seen males (presumably adults) which had conspicuous forehead patches but not nape patches, and while this may indicate that the nape patch is indeed lost during the summer molt, the aforementioned captive birds had clearly regrown their white napes by that time. (I have also examined some adult males which had a very thin but distinct white line at the base of the neck, just above the chest. This has been briefly mentioned in some of the more technical literature and is apparently uncommon.)

Compared to their rather exotic and ornate mates, females are relatively nondescript. Essentially dark brown above, they are some-

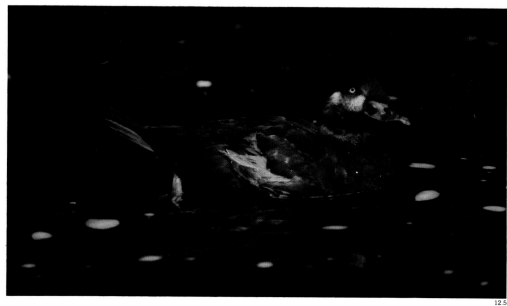

12.4 Adult drake surf scoter in full color. Note the trace of white at the base of the neck. Pairs are generally formed on the wintering grounds, and they may keep close company. It is said that if the female is shot, the drake will repeatedly return to its stricken mate.

12.5 Adult female surf scoter. Much of the literature indicates that mature females have dark eyes, but as illustrated here, such is not always the case. The white facial patches are subject to much individual variation and some females may have hardly any white on their faces.

12.6 Subadult male surf scoter. This bird, photographed in December, has a well-defined white nape patch, but the forehead patch is just beginning to appear. The plumage is still slightly brownish and the bill is less colorful than that of a fully mature bird.

12.7

12.8

12.7 *Female surf scoter — presumably immature. At this stage, the eyes are definitely dark, but they may lighten in color as the bird ages.*

12.8 *Immature male surf scoter, presumably a first-year bird. The eyes are dark at this age, and the bill shows only a trace of the color to come. The cheeks are darker in this case than those of a female, and there is no sign of the distinctive white nape or forehead patches which typify the adult drake. The ages of all scoters pictured are unknown — because the different plumage sequences are little known, and also because the coloration of these birds appears to be subject to much individual variation. However, their sexes were accurately ascertained by vent sexing.*

before the onset of the second winter. Some authorities state that males are sometimes totally black by the end of their first year, but those that I would call year-old birds are blotchy black with bills not fully colored. More and more, it is becoming evident that the only foolproof way to accurately document the seemingly complicated and inconsistent plumage sequences of these birds is to acquire a number of fertile eggs and hatch them under controlled conditions. The resulting young could then be hand reared and plumage changes could be followed as they occurred.

Unlike other scoters, the surf scoter is believed to be an exclusive North American resident which is restricted to the boreal forests of Alaska and Canada during the breeding season (although over 140 stragglers have been recorded in Europe). However, it may be that some individuals breed across the Bering Strait in adjacent Siberia as well. Pitifully little is known about their reproductive biology, but breeding habitat apparently consists of sites along the margins of fresh water lakes, ponds, rivers, or bogs, in dense but not necessarily tall vegetation. However, nests have been located some distance from water and are invariably well concealed. The few described nests suggest that while they resemble those of the white-winged scoter, they were even flimsier. The five to seven creamy or pinkish buff eggs are incubated by the female alone, and although the incubation period has not been established, it is probably no more than 27 to 28 days. There is some evidence that brood merging might be typical. This behavior appears to be relatively common with a number of high arctic pelagic species and it may possibly enhance duckling survival potential. It is also possible that the young are abandoned by the female prior to fledging as with the white-winged scoter.

Surf scoters are even less vocal than the other species, but courting drakes do have a low throaty croak and a bubbling whistle or gurgle, while females are noted for a crow-like caw or croak. Their flight is much more maneuverable than that of the larger white-winged scoter, and their wings produce a humming rather than whistling sound that may be audible for 400 yards. Worldwide, they are the least common of the scoters, with a population probably numbering about 750,000.

Once the breeding season has passed, surf scoters return to the sea, where they prove the aptness of their vernacular name by frequenting the surf and diving through large breaking waves with apparent ease. Often, they associate with other ducks, including eiders and other scoter species. I have frequently encountered them in association with wintering black brant and courting California gray whales in the fertile offshore waters of western Baja California. As an example, in early February 1979 I counted no less than 5000 surf scoters between Punta Abreojos and Laguna San Ignacio, a distance of less than 15 miles.

Not much is recorded about their feeding habits, but I have often watched wintering birds feed extensively on mussels. Many surf scoters wintering in the bays of southern California appear to be rather indifferent to human activity, even when it is intense, and on numerous occasions I have been able to approach within 10 to 20 feet of scoters feeding on mussel-covered rocks or pilings. While the full extent of the surf scoter's diving ability is not known (or that of the other sea ducks as well, for that matter) it appears that most foraging dives do not exceed 20 to 30 feet. Along the northeast American coast, they are said to congregate around the mouths of estuaries because the bottom in such areas tends to be sandy. The density of preferred food items is presumably greater.

what paler below, although some individuals are significantly darker than others. As a rule, their crowns are somewhat darker than the rest of the plumage. Adult female eyes may be pale grey or yellow to nearly white (rather than always brown as some authorities suggest), but this appears to be subject to some variation. A faint nape patch may be present, along with two indistinct whitish facial patches (one between the eye and bill and the other in the ear region). However, these patches are also quite variable and may be indistinct or even absent, especially the smaller one in front of the eye. The bill is greenish black, and as with the male, it has a distinct black squarish spot at the base and a prominent "Roman nose" look to it. Legs and feet are usually a dullish orange-yellow.

Juvenile surf scoters somewhat resemble adult females, except that they are generally paler and browner, the breast and belly tends to be whitish, and the eyes are said to be dark brown. The white facial patches can be more conspicuous than those of adult females and may merge together. Theoretically, the nape patch is never present on yearling birds and the crowns are darker, forming a head pattern somewhat like that of the female black scoter. Immature males supposedly acquire black feathers and white napes gradually during their first winter, but not the white forehead patch, which in theory appears

This species, like all scoters, is extremely difficult to acclimate to captive conditions, and this is most unfortunate because sea ducks are frequent victims of oil spills. The survival rate of oil-soaked birds in general is discouragingly low, and rehabilitation of recovered victims (particularly those that are specialized, such as the sea ducks) is no easy task. I have worked with hundreds of oiled surf scoters (mostly males) over the years, and am of the opinion that they are one of the most difficult sea duck species to successfully rehabilitate. Force feeding is often required for months, and it can take a year or more to get them totally waterproofed. In addition, most salvaged scoters I am familiar with have been rather heavily parasitized by a variety of internal worms, which is a further complication. However, even apparently healthy wild-caught adults have proven to be surprisingly difficult to get started, even compared to other scoter species, particularly the white-winged scoter. Acclimated scoters appear to do well on a diet of dry commercial food such as trout, dog, or cat chow.

Delacour believes that surf scoters are no more difficult to acclimate than the other scoters, but speaking as one of the few biologists who has been privileged to work with all three scoter species simultaneously, I do not agree. Once acclimated, however, even surf scoters appear to be reasonably hardy (although males can be delicate in the molt), and a male did survive for ten years at the San Diego Zoological Garden. Scoters in general can be rather aggressive once they are established, but most of their threat behavior is apparently bluff with little actual physical contact. All the same, gaping scoters with their disproportionately large bills can easily intimidate other birds. Unlike white-winged scoters, surf scoters tend to be rather secretive. Scoters as a group are poorly represented in captivity, and the surf scoter is almost nonexistent. It is unlikely that *any* of the scoters will be common in captivity in the foreseeable future.

Appropriately enough, **white-winged scoters** (*Melanitta fusca*) are named for the prominent white secondaries and white-tipped upper wing coverts of both sexes, but the white is really only conspicuous during flight and is scarcely visible when the birds are at rest. These are not only the largest and chunkiest of the scoters, but one of the largest of all ducks as well, with adult drakes weighing up to four pounds. Like most of the sea ducks, white-winged scoters must patter rapidly over the water for some distance into the wind before attaining the necessary speed to take off. Once airborne, their flight appears to be labored and very ponderous, and their heavy heads and thick necks are very

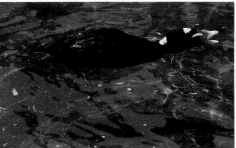

12.9 *Subadult male surf scoter. In this case, the belly is still white but the dorsal surfaces are black. The bill is not fully colored, and the white forehead patch is not evident. However, the white nape patch is beginning to appear and the hair-like white feathers are visible.*

12.10 *Adult drake surf scoter in molt. While the forehead patch remains, the nape patch may be lost during the summer molt. However, it does not necessarily reappear at the end of the summer as some authorities suggest. This photograph was taken in December, and the nape patch had not yet reappeared. Note also the light-colored eyes.*

12.11 *Adult male surf scoter in a threatening posture.*

12.12

12.13

noticeable. However, they fly deceptively fast. Habitually flying low over the water in loose flocks or long lines, they frequently shift formation, with their wings typically producing a whistling sound that is often audible half a mile away. Sometimes, feeding flocks synchronize their dives. They can be unwary almost to the point of being "tame," particularly as first year birds. Except for nesting females, they almost never venture ashore and are particularly clumsy when they do so.

During the breeding season, courting drakes utter calls that range from croaks or bell-like high-pitched whistling notes to growling or soft purring, while a low whistling note typifies the female. Often, these birds will move inland for considerable distances to breed, and their nests are generally well concealed (even from above) in extremely dense cover. Flushed females may experience some difficulty in flying through the trees. At times, when they nest in association with gulls or terns, the nests may be more open. Brood merging is typical, and aggregations exceeding 100 downy ducklings have been recorded. In at least one case, a wild hybrid between the white-winged scoter and a common goldeneye has been reported.

Duckling mortality can be incredibly high. In a three-year study in Finland, for example, 7418 eggs were laid and some 84 percent hatched, but only 3.2 percent were reared to fledging size. The low survival rate in *this* case was attributed to over-crowding in brood rearing areas, extremely loose parent/duckling bonds, and sensitivity to harsh climatic and environmental conditions (including low water temperature). Fortunately for the species, however, such mortality is apparently not typical elsewhere, and even though the overall European population may have declined in recent years, white-winged scoters are not at all uncommon. In fact, they are the most abundant of the North American scoters (perhaps a million birds).

Overall, white-winged scoter drakes are glossy black, although the sides and flanks may have a brownish tinge, the secondaries are white, and there is a distinct comma-shaped dash (or "eye-hook") under each eye. Non-breeding males tend to be duller and browner in color. Their feet are deep red and the eyes range from pale grey to white. Adult females are dark brown dorsally and somewhat lighter below, with brown eyes. The white on their wings corresponds to that of the male, and typically, they have two variable whitish facial patches—a small one in front of and below the eye, and a larger one behind and below the eye. However, these whitish areas can be very indistinct or absent altogether, and curiously, the white is more obvious on birds with worn plumage. The long and broad bills are generally dull black, but in some cases small amounts of white or pink may be present.

Juveniles are similar to adult females, but are generally paler, with white mottling on the breast and white facial markings that tend to be somewhat larger and more pronounced. In theory, males lose the juvenile facial patterns and begin to grow most of their black feathers during the first year, but the underparts remain light. The iris should be white by the second winter (i.e., approximately 15 to 18 months). By the end of the second year, they are supposed to resemble adult drakes, but this seems to be subject to a great deal of individual variability.

Altogether, there are three (possibly four) races of white-winged scoters. All are very similar, and the major differences involve the size, shape, and color of the adult male's bill, which is extraordinarily long and broad and can be very swollen at the base. European white-winged or velvet scoters (*M. f. fusca*) have bills that are less swollen and less colorful than the other races. In the case of adult drakes, the

12.16

12.14

12.15

12.12 (Opposite Page) *Drake Pacific white-winged scoter running over the surface of the water prior to becoming airborne.*

12.13 (Opposite Page) *Adult drake Pacific white-winged scoter. The light-colored eyes, the distinctive white "eye-hook," and the huge multi-colored bill are clearly illustrated.*

12.14 *Adult female American white-winged scoter.*

12.15 *Adult male Pacific white-winged scoter. While not evident when the birds are at rest on the water, the white wing patch from which the species takes its name is highly visible when they take flight.*

12.16 *Portrait of an adult female Pacific white-winged scoter.*

12.17 *Adult female Pacific white-winged scoter. Essentially diurnal feeders, these birds may also be active at dusk or twilight, or even at night. They tear mussels loose from the bottom with their powerful bills and bring the larger ones to the surface, where they may swallow them with some difficulty. Once swallowed, the shellfish are readily ground up in the gizzard. In prime nesting areas, these scoters may nest relatively close together (i.e., 20 nests on a half-acre island). The young often gather in loose assemblages, and in one case, a single female was observed with 84 young (all under two weeks of age).*

12.17

sides of the black upper mandible characteristically are rich yellow with some areas of whitish grey on top. On the other hand, the bills of the other races are multicolored and elaborately patterned with yellowish orange, reddish pink, black, white, and orangish yellow. However, color intensity and even pattern appears subject to some variation. American white-winged scoters (*M. f. deglandi*) have shorter bills than their European relatives, the culman knob is more pronounced, and the feathering extends farther down the bill. The Pacific population (*M. f. dixoni*) is considered by some to be racially distinct, but has not really gained wide acceptance. They supposedly have even shorter, blunter, and broader bills, with a more evident culman knob. On a few adult males, I have noted a slight amount of white feathering around the base of the upper mandible, particularly in the area of the hump. In the case of the Asian race (*M. f. stejnegeri*), the basal knob is so high that it extends over the nostrils, and it is so pronounced that the birds are known to the Soviets as "hump-billed turpans." The Asian bill coloring apparently approximates that of *deglandi*.

The size and extent of the diagnostic white comma under the eye is also quite variable, but it is typically smallest on drakes of the nominate race. Whether or not the females of the various races can accurately be separated is a subject for debate, although velvet scoter females are said to have longer bills than those of other races.

While there are relatively few white-winged scoters in captivity, the scanty evidence available suggests that they are much more hardy and adaptable than the surf scoter. Indeed, I have worked with a number

of wild-caught adults which acclimated surprisingly rapidly to captive conditions, and while some were rather aggressive, particularly when hungry, others became incredibly tame and would even eat from the hand. Undoubtedly, the longest surviving captive specimen is a female I acquired as an adult from the infamous Santa Barbara oilspill of 1969. She was still thriving in early 1979. (A banded adult female European white-winged scoter was recovered after 12 years, 6 months.) There are a number of velvet scoters in European collections, but most of these were acquired initially as fertile eggs.

The two races of **black scoters** (*Melanitta nigra*) are the smallest of the scoters, and in North America at least, they have the distinction of being the blackest of all ducks. They differ from other scoters in that they tend to be more vocal, are somewhat wary, seem less prone to associate with other waterfowl, are considerably more inclined to take flight, and are also capable of rising from the water with greater ease and more grace. In flight, the very narrow outer primaries produce a whistling sound. Despite a rather heavy build, they are relatively buoyant in the water, and when swimming they sometimes hold their proportionally longer tails at a forty-five degree angle.

Almost exclusively marine during the nonbreeding season, black scoters frequent the open sea just off the coast (often in the vicinity of broad estuaries) and tend to avoid rough water if possible. They seldom come ashore, and when they do, walk upright with an awkward and rather peculiar gait. Generally, they breed rather late and nesting may not commence until mid- to late June. Courting males produce a melodic vocalization that is suggestive of the call of a curlew, but they also have distinct twittering calls, which contrast greatly with the hoarse croaks of the females. During courtship activities, small parties of drakes may raft up on little ponds and direct their attention to a single female, but despite all the activity it is probable that most successful pair bonds are formed prior to arrival on the breeding grounds.

Breeding habitat is generally located inland. Nests are widely dispersed, usually well concealed amid tundra vegetation or dwarf heath, and often sheltered by tall herbaceous plants or shrubs. All nests I have observed were located in tall grass on tiny islands in Scottish lochs, and while the literature indicates that the nests are lined with grasses, mosses, lichens, and down, those I am familiar with were relatively flimsy and lined with only minor amounts of very dark down. Six to nine large cream to pinkish buff eggs are laid, and are incubated solely by the female for 27 to 28 days. Once the clutch is set, the males abandon their mates and depart to undergo the molt at traditional sites, presumably at sea. As a rule, black scoters are less prone to merge broods than their near relatives.

The two races are quite similar. Adult drakes of both are almost totally black, with the head, neck and upper parts often glossed with dull purple. Unlike the other scoters, *both* sexes have dark brown eyes and their legs are black. The different races can be distinguished from one another by the amount of yellow on the otherwise black bill of the adult drake. The European males (*M. n. nigra*) have a distinct bump at the base of the upper mandible, as well as a relatively restricted amount of yellow. Johnsgard suggests that maximum bill enlargement may not take place until at least the third year, and I agree. It is also said that the bill nail is more curved in both sexes of European black scoters, and males have a very narrow dark brown or orange-yellow eye ring, which can be quite distinctive when viewed at close range. American black scoter drakes (*M. n. americana*) are noted for a much smoother bill profile, with the bill being different in shape and somewhat shorter. In addition, the amount of yellow on the bill is much more extensive.

Also known as common scoters, black scoters are probably the most abundant of the scoters worldwide, despite the fact that they are the least common in the New World. Well over half a million birds of both races occupy North America and western Europe alone, and in parts of Russia they are said to be second only to the oldsquaw in abundance. American black scoters may be more common in eastern Asia, particularly around Kamchatka, than they are in the Western Hemisphere.

Adult females of both races superficially resemble female redcrested pochards because of their two-toned head pattern. The head is dark brown above and brownish white along the sides, on the neck, chin, throat and foreneck. Overall, they are dark brown dorsally but tend to be mottled brown and white ventrally. Juveniles resemble females but are paler above and whiter below, and it seems unlikely that drakes attain their full color until the third year.

Black scoters have been kept from time to time in captivity. A pair of wild-caught adults resided in the Delacour collection from 1928 to at least 1940, but they were apparently lost sometime during the German occupation of France. The European race was bred on Long Island in 1970, and to my knowledge, this was the first captive scoter breeding ever achieved. They were bred a second time in 1978 in a private collection in Great Britain. Almost without exception, the

12.18

12.19

12.20

12.21

12.18 *Velvet scoter drakes. These two birds are at least two years old and are not yet in adult color. The bird to the rear is even less colorful than the one in the foreground, even though both are presumably the same age. As with the other scoters, plumage sequences appear to be subject to much individual variation.*

12.19 *Pair of adult European black scoters (female in background). These birds are poorly represented in wildfowl collections, but they occur more frequently than the other scoter species. Most captive European black scoters were initially acquired as fertile eggs.*

12.20 *Adult drake European black scoter in full color. Males of the European race are easily separated from their American counterparts by the protruberances at the base of the upper mandible and the restricted amount of yellow on the bill.*

12.21 *Nest and eggs of the European black scoter. Note the flimsy construction and scanty lining.*

12.22

12.23

12.24

12.22 *Female American black scoter. This species often nests on top of grassy hummocks. On occasion, more than one female will lay in the same nest. While they will sometimes associate with surf scoters and greater scaup, these birds generally keep to themselves, particularly the males.*

12.23 *Group of adult American black scoters. These particular birds were all salvaged from an oil spill. Black scoters are sometimes prone to fly in lines just over the water's surface. They may rise and fall or form up in bunches, then space out again in irregular lines.* PHOTO BY GLEN SMART

12.24 *Pair of American black scoters (drake on left). These birds are somewhat different from the other scoters in certain respects. They are much more noisy and somewhat wary, are considerably more inclined to take to the wing, and are rather less inclined to associate with other waterfowl.* PHOTO BY PHIL STANTON

12.25 *(Opposite Page) Adult male Labrador duck. A painting of this extinct bird can be found on page 353.*

12.26 *(Opposite Page) Adult drake Pacific harlequin duck in full color at a waterfall. Few species can compare with the beauty of these magnificent ducks, but in the wild they can be surprisingly difficult to see.*

majority of American black scoters that have found their way into wildfowl collections originated as salvaged birds (i.e., victims of oil-spills, gunshot birds, etc.).

The extinct **Labrador duck** (*Camptorhynchus labradorius*), or pied duck, was a wigeon-sized bird that may have represented an intermediate link between the scoters (or eiders) and the harlequin duck. As far as is known, the range of these ducks extended from Labrador south to Chesapeake Bay, and formerly they were regularly observed in the sandy bays and estuaries of Long Island and New Jersey. The distinctive bills of adult males were black, with a large orange or flesh-colored band near the base below the nostrils. The bills were relatively soft around the edges, perhaps indicating a diet of soft shelled invertebrates as well as specialized foraging techniques. Curiously, these beautiful ducks were sometimes caught by fishermen using mussels as bait on trotlines, suggesting that they also fed on mussels to some extent. Old accounts suggest they were swift fliers with whistling wings. Seldom observed in flocks, *labradorius* was usually described as shy and difficult to approach.

Very little is known about the natural history of the Labrador duck, since the species was officially declared extinct in 1875. (A possible specimen was allegedly shot in 1878, but this has never been confirmed.) The cause of their rapid extinction has never been definitely established. They were probably never very numerous to begin with,

and possibly had a rather limited breeding range. Certainly they were hunted, but apparently no more than any other waterfowl—and perhaps less, since their flesh was said to be fishy. (They were not considered good table birds, but a number were taken for the market nevertheless.) Their down had some commercial value, and their ornate plumage may have been used in the feather trade; and activities of egg collectors may have also contributed to the decline.

It seems quite possible that Labrador ducks were already declining before the arrival of European man. They may have ultimately been victims of their own over-specialization, since very specialized foraging techniques and food preferences would have made them unable to cope with changes in the molluscan fauna that may have been brought about by an increased human coastal population. At the same time, the possibility that an unknown disease struck them down cannot be totally dismissed. All of the theories that have been proposed to explain their rapid disappearance are based on speculation, and it appears unlikely that the mystery will ever be fully resolved. All that

remains today of this beautiful sea duck are some 54 skins and a few separate skeletal items deposited in various museums throughout the world. The unfortunate Labrador duck was gone practically before man knew it was in peril; within 90 years of its description in 1789, it had disappeared. Dr. Paul Johnsgard perhaps best described its demise with the astute observation that: "It disappeared so swiftly and quietly that it is not only difficult to compose a suitable epitaph, but also impossible to write a complete obituary."

Few species can compete with the elegant beauty of the **harlequin duck** (*Histrionicus histrionicus*). Webster defines harlequin as a variegated pattern, but this description hardly does justice to these gorgeous birds, and it seems more likely that the vernacular name was taken from Harlequin the clown, a stock character in a classic 18th Century Italian comic opera and *commedia dell'arte*. Harlequin the clown always appeared in a mask of many bright and contrasting colors and this description more closely matches the species. Males in nuptial plumage are elaborately patterned with different hues of slate grey, black, white, and reddish chestnut. Their bills are relatively short and stout, and the wings are adorned with metallic blue speculums, a unique feature among sea ducks. Although drakes appear gaudy at close range, the harlequin plumage is a classic example of confusion camouflage; from a distance, they can be surprisingly inconspicuous. They blend in with the rocky beaches on which they often sit, and an

with grace. Harlequin ducks are not very noisy birds throughout most of the year, but males can be vocal at times and have a high-pitched squeal or a low descending whistle which ends in a trill. Their call has been likened to the squeaking of fighting mice, and as a result, the vernacular name "sea mice" is sometimes applied. The shrill calls are clearly audible above the rushing water. The female is characterized by a hoarse croak.

Harlequin ducks reside on salt water during the winter months, particularly near rocks and ledges where the surge is strong. It seems almost incongruous that a species which appears so delicate can thrive under such wild and inhospitable conditions. They are well adapted for prying chitons and other molluscs from underwater rocks. As a rule, harlequin ducks are characterized as being extremely unwary, particularly at sea, and I have often watched them feed but 10 or 15 feet away, totally unconcerned about my presence. But when they are persecuted, they quickly become educated and tend to be much more wary.

During the breeding season, harlequins move inland to nest, favoring fast-moving mountain streams. At such times, they remain well dispersed and are very territorial, usually being observed only as singles or family groups, never in flocks. (Contrary to some accounts, flocks are not uncommon at sea.) Once they move inland, their lifestyle recalls that of the New Zealand blue duck or the South

12.27 *Adult female Pacific harlequin duck. A wide variety of predators prey on these beautiful ducks. In Iceland, feral mink and ravens are a great threat, while arctic foxes reportedly stalk sleeping harlequins in the Soviet Union. Gyrfalcons may also take them at sea in a rather bizarre fashion. The raptors are hidden by large waves during storms, and are thus able to strike the low-flying ducks aerially before they can dive. As with female scoters, there is considerable variation in the intensity and extent of the white head patches.*

12 27

observer scanning a bay full of ducks will usually become aware of harlequins last.

Eclipse-plumaged males resemble their mates except that their underparts tend to be darker and they retain a brighter upper wing coloration. Females are perky little ducks which are rather duller than males when in full color. Their secondary feathers are essentially dark olive brown, but are glossed with a purplish sheen. In addition, there are two white spots on the head—a small rounded one above and in front of the eye (sometimes quite indistinct), and a larger one behind the eye. The cheeks can be whitish (the extent and intensity of which can be variable), and in the case of several females I have seen, the entire head was mottled with white, perhaps an indication of advanced age.

Very buoyant swimmers, harlequins commonly swim with their tails cocked partially up, frequently bobbing and jerking their heads in a coot-like fashion. When at sea, they tend to swim and fly in compact little groups and sometimes flocks. Ashore, they stand about and walk

American torrent duck (although they are not closely related). They are efficient but reluctant fliers, and when they fly are apt to follow the exact course of the stream, generally within six feet of the water. Their wings may be partially opened when swimming underwater but are probably not used in propulsion—although I have observed them on occasion weakly flap their wings underwater in the manner of an alcid. In fast-moving streams, they head into the current and are said to walk along the bottom with their wings closed, in a fashion similar to dippers.

Harlequins usually arrive at the breeding streams already paired. Their nesting requirements are rather exact, and a single pair may occupy up to a mile of appropriate stream habitat. Females may return to a nest site used successfully in previous years. In some areas, nests may be washed out if the spring runoff is heavy, resulting in high nest failure and duckling mortality. During incubation, hens are known to be "tight sitters." Sometimes, even if touched they will not flush, although they may hiss and attempt to bite the intruder. This reluc-

12.28

12.28 *Group of Pacific harlequins skittering over the surface of the water to gain flight speed. Harlequins inhabit regions where the light is often rather subdued, and in such light the gaudy colors and patterns of the adult drakes are simply not obvious. When at sea, these ducks are often encountered in compact little groups (both in the air and on the water), and they seldom mingle with other waterfowl — although they are sometimes seen with black scoters. During the breeding season, when they are occupying inland stream habitat, they do not form flocks.*

12.29 *Female Pacific harlequin duck with young on a fast-flowing stream in southeastern Alaska. Even in turbulent waters, recently-hatched harlequins are at ease and can dive skillfully. They also skitter over the surface of the rough water with surprising speed. Due to the shortage of food in glacial streams, breeding pairs tend to avoid them. In some cases, the young may be abandoned when only half grown. Apparently, some 60 to 70 days are required for fledging.*

12.29

12.30 *Drake Pacific harlequin duck in nuptial plumage. Among the most gorgeous of all ducks, these birds are fortunately not subjected to a significant amount of hunting pressure. (However, adult males were formerly taken by northern natives for their skins, which were utilized in artistic ways.) Pacific harlequins appear to be at ease on ice floes, although they normally avoid icy areas. If danger threatens, they tend to dive rather than fly, particularly when occupying inland stream habitat. At times, they may dive from the wing.*

tance to flush, combined with their preference for wild mountainous breeding habitat, makes nesting sites extremely inconspicuous, and relatively few have been found. (In treeless Iceland, however, the habitat is more open and the task is considerably easier.) Surface nests are more prevalent than hole nests, and nests are usually well concealed under dense vegetation, in rock crevasses, or on islands.

The five to ten creamy buff eggs are incubated by the female alone for 28 days. Upon hatching, the ducklings are very agile. They immediately take to the turbulent rivers and streams, and are able to skitter across the top of the water with surprising speed and skill—although they do tend to keep close to projecting rocks or quiet backwaters near the river bank for the first few weeks. Incredibly, they are able to dive in the foaming rapids when only a few days old. Males generally desert the hen once incubation commences, although I have on occasion seen *pairs* with recently-hatched young in eastern Alaska. The departure of the males is perhaps related to the availability of appropriate food, since the supply may be limited to begin with because of the specialized requirements of this species.

The two described races are practically identical, and the females of both are essentially indistinguishable from each other. But drakes of the Pacific population (*H. h. pacificus*) are said to have heavier bills, less rich color overall, and paler chestnut crown stripes that do not extend as far forward. These supposed differences notwithstanding, however, there is a significant amount of overlap between the two races, and the validity of the Pacific race is regarded with suspicion; indeed, it is usually ignored. The western population is a hundredfold more abundant than the eastern (*H. h. histrionicus*), and after the oldsquaw duck, harlequins are possibly the most numerous duck along the Aleutian Island chain in Alaska, with 600,000 to a million birds occupying the area in the fall. The extent of the Siberian population is unknown. Even during the breeding season, I have observed rafts containing hundreds of harlequins along the Bering Sea side of the Alaska Peninsula; presumably, these flocks consisted of nonbreeding subadult birds. Fortunately, because so much of their range is in remote regions, far from human habitation, these beautiful ducks have apparently suffered little from habitat destruction and hunting.

Sadly, relatively few harlequin ducks have been maintained in captivity over the years, and most that have been kept were obtained either as eggs or recently-hatched ducklings (although a number of adults have been collected in recent years). Due to their specialized feeding requirements, the ducklings are somewhat difficult to raise. But once maturity is attained, they are very hardy and competitive, even in southern areas, if cool clean water is provided. Wild-caught adults can be acclimated, but not without some initial difficulty, and while they tame readily (some individuals will eat from the hand), waterfowl obtained as adults are typically not as apt to breed as those that are hand raised from eggs. After many years of hard frustrating work, Chuck Pilling of Seattle succeeded in breeding harlequins for the first time in 1977. This achievement can be considered a major breakthrough, but it undoubtedly will be a number of years before these magnificent ducks are firmly established in captivity. Most of the harlequins in European collections originally came from Iceland as eggs.

Oldsquaw ducks or long-tailed ducks (*Clangula hyemalis*) are unique among waterfowl in that the drakes have two totally different seasonal ornamental plumages, and each is as distinct and beautiful as the other. In addition, they also have a very brief dull eclipse plumage.

12.32

12.31 *Pair of Atlantic harlequin ducks. Strong fliers, these ducks will generally follow the course of a stream rather than fly overland. In Iceland, they tend to fly under bridges instead of over them. They float high in the water when swimming and characteristically bob or jerk their heads with each leg stroke. At sea, they appear to relish chitons, which they are somehow able to pry off rocks.*

12.32 *Pair of flying oldsquaw in breeding plumage.*

12.31

During the late fall and winter, males are mainly white, whereas their nuptial plumage is blackish brown. The females also have different breeding and winter plumages. The black and pink bills of the old-squaw drakes are stout and rather high basally. Trimmest of the sea ducks, with a low but buoyant swimming profile, they often cock their long tails at a forty-five degree angle (although they are commonly held nearly horizontal as well). They fly swiftly in a characteristic way, and because the wings typically are not raised much above the level of the body, they have a somewhat "hunched" appearance in the air. As a rule, they tend to fly in irregular flocks or straggling lines, commonly twisting and turning in flight like shorebirds, and swinging from side to side so that the dark upperparts and white bellies show alternately. Oldsquaw are rarely found in association with other waterfowl.

These ducks are the most vocal of American ducks, and rather appropriately, the rich and melodious call of the drakes is the origin of both their common and scientific names. The vernacular name old-squaw originated with the Cree Indians, who believed that their constant chatter sounded like that of a complaining squaw, whereas their scientific name literally translates to "noisy winter duck." Alaskan Eskimos refer to them as hohohalic, after their call, and white men sometimes think the Eskimos are calling them "alcoholic." Early fur traders of the upper Yukon referred to them as organ ducks. (Females are noted for only a low quack.)

Oldsquaw are not considered a prime game species, and even Eskimos do not actively hunt them, possibly because they are small compared to other equally available sea ducks. Those that I have handled had a very distinct fishy smell, but if properly prepared they are quite edible. Eggs are sometimes collected by northern natives for human consumption, and down is also collected, because its quality rivals that of the eiders. Like king eiders, flocks of flying oldsquaw tend to be curious and can be attracted by whistling and hooting.

Oldsquaw are perhaps best known for their unexcelled diving ability. It is reported that a number of these ducks were recovered from fish nets set at the unbelievable depth of 240 feet, although their normal foraging dives probably do not exceed 20 feet. The problem of oldsquaw entangling themselves in fishing nets cannot be dismissed as minor, particularly during the winter months. During the winter of 1952/53 alone, for example, over 19,600 oldsquaw were entangled and drowned in gill nets in the Great Lakes, and in the winters of 1949/50 and 1950/51, more than 100,000 oldsquaw may have perished in nets, particularly in Lake Michigan. (An associate of mine astutely suggests that such losses say more about flaws in fishing techniques than about the diving ability of the species.) Fortunately, in recent years fishing activities have been less intensive in these areas, and as a consequence, losses have not been as severe. Huge winter flocks of oldsquaw sometimes occur in deep waters far from shore, although they frequently will utilize shallow coastal areas as well. They sometimes dive from the wing. While many do move south to winter, a large segment of the population remains in the arctic, with as many as 500,000 wintering in the vicinity of St. Lawrence Island, Alaska.

Because oldsquaw and other sea ducks are at the top of the food chain, they may be adversely affected by the presence of DDT and other chlorinated hydrocarbon pesticide residues in their food. Up to 32 parts per million of the DDT metabolite DDE have been found in

275

12.34

12.35

12.33 (Opposite Page) *Flock of oldsquaw in the spring, flying over the ice pack of the Beaufort Sea, Alaska. These are restless, active, noisy ducks. When landing in haste, they plunge headlong downward and splash breast first into the sea, sending up a sizable shower of spray.*

12.34 *Drake oldsquaw. These ducks often travel in irregular masses, straggling lines, or bunches. They will often fly low over the water and then suddenly swing upward 200 feet or more. Their flight is buoyant and rather unduck-like, and flocks produce a swishing sound when on the wing.*

12.35 *Male oldsquaw or long-tailed duck in full nuptial plumage on tundra pond in Alaska. This species is perhaps the most abundant of arctic-nesting ducks, but due to their often inaccessible high arctic breeding ranges, the total extent of the population is not known. However, the breeding population of North America alone may be on the order of three to four million birds.*

the fat reserves of these ducks, and residues of such magnitude may not only cause eggshell thinning, but also could affect the survival of adult birds. PCBs (polychlorinated biphenyls) in the environment are also considered to be particularly detrimental. In addition, these birds are also extremely vulnerable to oil spills. Nevertheless, oldsquaw are among the most numerous of all arctic ducks, perhaps exceeded only by the king eider. Due to the huge and inaccessible range of the species, accurate population counts are not possible, but estimates range as high as 10,000,000 individuals.

The breeding range is circumpolar and females construct well-concealed nests which may be difficult to locate (except in areas where nesting densities are high, such as the Yukon Delta). Quite often, the nests may be a considerable distance from the coast, and may even be hundreds of feet from water. At times, oldsquaw may nest in association with terns. When a hen departs the nest, she camouflages the eggs so skillfully with her dark sooty-brown down, grass, and rubbish, that the nest is rendered practically invisible. The six or seven eggs are incubated for some 24 to 25 days, and ducklings are generally reared on freshwater ponds or lakes. If danger threatens, the female leads the brood to the security of open water. The young may be abandoned by the female at a relatively early age and groups of parentless young may flock together. They fledge in the incredibly short period of 35 days, which probably represents the shortest fledging period of any arctic duck.

Like many of the sea ducks, oldsquaw are unfortunately very poorly represented in waterfowl collections. This situation is somewhat para-

12.36 *Female oldsquaw on nest. At times, oldsquaw may nest in a somewhat colonial fashion, particularly on islands that are safe from terrestrial carnivores. In one case, 29 nests were constructed on an islet measuring no more than 60 yards in circumference. More typically, nests are well dispersed and are notoriously difficult to locate.*

12.37 *Drake oldsquaw in late fall. When they are in full winter plumage, the black cheek patches of these birds are greyer. This is the only duck species that has two ornamental plumages. PHOTO BY PAUL JOHNSGARD*

12.38 *Male European goldeneye. These cavity-nesting ducks may mix clutches with other species, including goosanders, smew, mallards — and even tawny owls, jackdaws, and starlings.*

12.39 *(Opposite Page) Pair of oldsquaw. On occasion, oldsquaw will rest on floating ice. They rarely associate with other waterfowl.*

doxical, considering that they are both extremely numerous and extremely hardy in the wild, and are able to exist under the harshest of conditions in the Arctic. That they should seemingly be so delicate in captivity is very frustrating to the aviculturist; but the sad fact is that most high arctic waterfowl are very delicate because they have highly-specialized lifestyles and are also extremely susceptible to many fatal diseases when removed from their natural environment.

Even now, oldsquaw are maintained in but a handful of collections, but in 1978 they were bred in at least two English collections. Interestingly, on at least one occasion fertile eggs were obtained from a female which was bred by a male only one year old, even though sea ducks normally require at least two years to attain sexual maturity. Delacour once told me of a hybrid he produced in the 1930s which resulted

from a cross between a male oldsquaw and a female chestnut teal. It could be that if conditions are adequate, the species may not be as difficult as the scanty record suggests. It is imperative that they be provided with clear, cool water—probably the deeper the better. Based on those which have been maintained, these birds tend not to mix readily with other waterfowl. As of early 1979, at least one pair in England was approaching 13 years of age.

Unlike the preceding sea ducks, the two species of goldeneyes adapt well to captive conditions, but curiously, they are still rather uncommon in all but the more sophisticated collections. Their descriptive vernacular name is based on their bright golden-yellow eyes, but the distinct whirring of their wings in flight is the origin of the nickname "whistlers." Typically, they fly in tight formations, and sometimes rise from the water in rapid spirals. They are generally heard before they are seen. The call of the common goldeneye has been described as similar to that of the nighthawk.

The two races of **common goldeneyes** (*Bucephala clangula*) are virtually identical. However, the European birds (*B. c. clangula*) are typically slightly smaller and shorter than their American counterpart (*B. c. americana*), and they have less broad bills—but there is much overlap. Common goldeneye males are easily distinguished from the drakes of the closely-related **Barrow's goldeneye** (*Bucephala*

islandica) by the shape of their conspicuous white round cheek patches, since those on the Barrow's goldeneyes are crescent-shaped. Females of the two species are almost impossible to accurately identify in the field, but female *clangula*, during the breeding season, have dark bills with yellow tips, while those of female *islandica* are more yellow and stubbier. The extent of yellow bill color is subject to variation, but as a rule, females with the greatest amount of yellow are most common in the Rocky Mountain population and are seldom observed elsewhere. Possibly these two populations constitute separate races of Barrow's goldeneye, but the variation in bill coloration may simply be related to the fact that the western breeding population overlaps the range of the common goldeneye. Very few *documented* hybrids have been reported. Males of both species are quite similar in appearance to their mates during the summer molt, but tend to have darker heads; and they sometimes exhibit a trace of white cheek patterning as well.

There are also distinct differences in the head shapes of the drakes of the two species. With the common goldeneye, the head is strikingly

12.40 Two pair of Barrow's goldeneye. Note the yellow bills of the females. Competition for prime nest sites is keen, and in addition to other birds, goldeneye have to compete with bushy-tailed wood rats, flying squirrels, and red squirrels. The young depart the nest cavity in a manner that has been described as "literally pouring out." Brood territories are fiercely defended by the female, and intruding young from other broods may be drowned or severely beaten by a defending female.

12.41 Pileated woodpecker. Goldeneye favor the deserted cavities of this species and those of the flicker as nesting sites. The cavities may be enlarged by natural decay — and, in fact, flicker cavities are generally too small for the goldeneye until such decay has occurred.

peaked, almost triangular in shape, whereas the head of the Barrow's goldeneye is more rounded and somewhat bulbous. Interestingly, there are also some striking internal differences, since the skull of *islandica* rises much more abruptly from the bill. A greenish iridescent sheen on the head typifies *clangula* males, whereas a similar sheen on the Barrow's is characteristically more purplish. The downy young of the two species are virtually indistinguishable, except for very minor differences in foot color and slightly different head shapes.

Goldeneyes are almost exclusively cavity nesters. In Iceland, however, where trees are not present, Barrow's goldeneyes may nest on the ground under dense shrubs and they will readily take to artificial nesting boxes (in some cases, even boxes attached to the sides of houses). They probably do not breed until their second year, but first-year females may "prospect" for nest sites. During the breeding seasons, female common goldeneyes may often perch on large branches, but generally they fly directly in and out of the nest cavity. Their breeding habitat requirements are strict, with prime habitat consisting of tall forest growth with hollow trees, generally close to biologically productive cold-water lakes, pools, or rivers. They are partial to abandoned woodpecker holes as high as 60 feet above the ground, which are often used in successive years. On very rare occasions, they have been known to utilize rabbit burrows in the Old World. At one time, goldeneyes were subjected to much adverse human-associated pressure in Europe when deforestation brought about the large-scale elimination of hollow trees. However, the practice of installing artificial nest boxes has been very successful in reversing the downward population trend in some areas. The boxes are accepted very readily, in much the same way that wood ducks took to artificial boxes in North America.

The relatively large eggs vary in color from deep olive to dull pale green. Nest sites as close as possible to the water are preferable, but when appropriate sites are not available, hens may select a cavity some distance away, and in several instances common goldeneyes have been observed leading their broods as much as two miles overland to reach water. Young have been observed riding the backs of swimming females, even though the ducklings are proficient swimmers and divers by their second day of life. Curiously, female Barrow's goldeneyes establish definite brood territories which are vigorously defended against the intrusion of all ducks. Indeed, in areas of dense concentration, significant duckling mortality can take place if territorial boundaries are violated.

Goldeneyes are very attractive birds, particularly during the breeding season. At that time, common goldeneye drakes whistle a great deal (as opposed to uttering a variety of clicking and grunting sounds like the Barrow's goldeneye), and they engage in a variety of elaborate and highly-ritualized courtship displays. Indeed, their courtship may be the most spectacular and complex of any northern duck. Drakes may, for example, swim around a female and suddenly thrust their heads back almost to their tails, while kicking up a spray of water several feet into the air behind them. Immediately after copulation, drakes fully expand their crests and hold their necks straight up while rapidly swimming away.

Goldeneyes, particularly older birds, are typically rather shy and only infrequently associate with other ducks. On the other hand, young ones can be remarkably tame, to the point that some observers have referred to them as "stupid." They prefer fresh water (particularly during the breeding season) and are accomplished divers, but the

sers choking to death on oversized fish are not uncommon). Often referred to as saw-bills or fish ducks, mergansers of both sexes have elongated feathers on the head or nape which form crests of various shapes.

The fish-eating habits of these birds have attracted adverse attention from some sport fishing interests and hatchery operations, while their rank flesh has discouraged many hunters from urging their conservation as a game species because they consider them to be "trash birds." A number of commercial fishing interests have repeatedly advocated reduction or elimination of fish-eating birds on salmon waters. There is some evidence that a number of local merganser populations have been adversely affected by overuse of DDT or other non-selective chlorinated hydrocarbon pesticides—a situation that occurs because fish-eating birds are at the top of the food chain, and pesticide residues are more concentrated in the food they eat. Nevertheless, at least the common merganser has demonstrated a remarkable degree of tenacity, and has managed to maintain a sizable population despite sustained campaigns for its extermination.

Among the smallest of the fish ducks is the **smew** (*Mergus albellus*) a petite diurnal merganser of northern Eurasia. Drakes in nuptial plumage are among the whitest of all ducks and are easily recognizable due to their conspicuous black masks; in addition, males have a frontal crest which is elevated during display. During the eclipse plumage phase, the larger males resemble females, but are typically darker on the chest and belly, with a more extensive area of white on the upper wing. Eye color is variable, particularly with older birds, ranging from reddish brown to pearly grey. Unlike typical mergansers, the bills of smew are rather short and stout and appear to be the least specialized of the fish ducks. Sometimes known as "white nuns," these beautiful birds prefer flooded woodlands with an abundance of dead broad-leafed trees, and they also frequent the back waters of large rivers (where they may be locally common). They tend to avoid fast-flowing streams and torrents, and are seldom observed on the open sea.

Smew have a delicate appearance, and scarcely exceed a teal in size. They tend to be relatively shy and rarely vocalize, although during courtship drakes will croak, utter a hissing whistle, or produce a soft rattling call that is almost mechanical sounding. Females can do little more than croak hoarsely. Highly mobile and restless, smew tend to fly rapidly and noiselessly, and they have the ability to leap from the water as easily as a dabbler.

In the water, they are relatively buoyant swimmers, and when ashore they walk well with a characteristic upright stance. They are accomplished divers, and pairs often dive in unison, but they rarely venture below six feet. Small fish, frogs, crustaceans, and aquatic insect larvae are their preferred food items, and they often feed cooperatively. Considered quite a hardy species despite their fragile appearance, they very reluctantly retreat southward as winter advances, and often the water must be completely frozen before they will move on. Wintering flocks can be comparatively large, and feeding groups of up to 750 birds have been recorded in the Netherlands.

It appears that smew (along with the hooded merganser of America) may represent an evolutionary link between the larger mergansers and the goldeneyes; indeed, smew often associate with common goldeneye and the two species have been known to hybridize. Both readily take to artificial nest boxes put out for goldeneye, particularly if nesting sites are scarce. In some cases, broods of mixed species may merge, a tendency that has been noted with other members of the

12.49

12.50

12.51

12.49 *Pair of smew. Full-color drakes of this Eurasian species have recently been reported along the Atlantic coast of North America, but there is at least one record of a female observed in New York as far back as 1960. Like most sea ducks, smew probably don't normally breed before their second year, but I have seen year-old birds copulating — although admittedly, the female was an unwilling participant.*

12.50 *Smew duckling. Like most mergansers, smew are typically cavity nesters. In Asia, however, they may breed beyond the limit of the trees and therefore nest on the ground, usually under creeping cedars. Preferred habitat consists of drowned woodlands with many dead trees and oxbows, or other backwaters of large rivers. As a rule, they tend to avoid fast-flowing streams and mountain torrents.*

12.51 *Smew drake in nuptial plumage. A hardy species, these fish ducks may feed under the ice as long as unfrozen patches of water are available. Groups may fly in oblique lines or in "V" formations when moving long distances, but at other times they are more likely to form up in bunches.*

Mergini as well. Preferred nest sites consist of natural cavities or woodpecker holes, most notably those of black woodpeckers (*Dryocopus martius*). Interestingly, much of the smew range coincides with that of the black woodpecker, suggesting a dependence with regard to reproductive requirements.

Overall, the smew population may be on the increase, at least in Europe. During January of 1976, a lone drake smew was observed in Rhode Island, and although this is the first documented sighting of a colored male off the Atlantic coast of North America, smew are observed fairly regularly in the Aleutian Islands of Alaska. Another Rhode Island smew (possibly the same one) was observed in January of 1977. Unlike their New World counterpart, the hooded merganser, smew are relatively uncommon in captivity. Only recently have a few been incorporated into American collections, and they weren't captively bred in the United States until 1975. Currently, they are being

12.53

bred with a greater degree of regularity, and within a few years they will probably be fairly well established in American collections.

The **hooded merganser** (*Mergus cucullatus*) is the only fish duck indigenous to North America. They are very wary and retiring birds, and despite the fact that males are strikingly patterned in black and white with bright yellow eyes, they are difficult to observe because they are generally well concealed by the thick underbrush and trees of their preferred habitat. As a rule, they tend to congregate in the vicinity of freshwater sloughs, streams, ponds, and swamps, and they perch readily on fallen trees and branches overhanging water. Primarily fish eaters, they will also readily take frogs, tadpoles, crustaceans, and small molluscs.

The most distinctive characteristic of these birds is a large and elegant erectile crest resembling a hood, which is the obvious origin of their common name. Males in nonbreeding plumage resemble their more somber-colored (but nevertheless attractive) mates. However, they tend to be more mottled about the head and neck, with a greater amount of white on the upper wing. Their eyes also remain brighter, but are not as brilliant as when they are in nuptial garb. Like other forest species, these mergansers have relatively long tails and this gives them a great maneuverability in flight. They habitually fly low and very fast, twisting and dodging through the trees; and during flight, the crest is compressed along the neck, giving the head an oblong appearance.

12.52 (Opposite Page) *Hooded merganser male. Although these beautiful birds are essentially a North American species, stragglers have been reported from Hawaii and some Caribbean Islands. They may typically roost on snags, logs, and rocks, but are prone to perch in trees only during the breeding season.*

12.53 *Trio of smew (a male and two females). Smew are buoyant swimmers and are capable of taking off with relative ease. Their flight is quite maneuverable and they are able to fly with assurance in limited spaces.*

12.55

12.54

12.54 *Pair of hooded mergansers on a wintery pond.*

12.55 *Trio of hooded merganser drakes in nuptial plumage. These birds are active daytime feeders and forage rather frequently in rapidly-flowing water. Loss of habitat, as a result of forest cutting and drying of streams, continues to be troublesome — and the introduction of pike into various northern lakes has proved to be hazardous to ducklings. On the other hand, hooded mergansers take to artificial nest boxes readily (particularly those which are adjacent to water), and this somewhat compensates for the loss of prime nesting trees.*

When on open water, courting drakes behave in a way that quickly calls attention to them—expanding their throats to almost unbelievable proportions and uttering a long guttural call that can be heard as far as half a mile away in still air. These vocalizations have been compared to the voice of the pickeral frog; and consequently, the swamp people of Georgia refer to hooded mergansers as "frog ducks." Amorous ducks may even pursue their mates underwater.

Hens frequently select nesting cavities as much as 75 feet above the ground, and since trees that are close to water are preferred, there is considerable competition for such prime sites. On rare occasions, they may nest in the hollow of a fallen tree, particularly if it is close to water. Like many hole-nesting species, they demonstrate a strong homing tendency and may return to the same nesting tree of previous seasons. The white oval eggs are surprisingly large, and the incubation period is relatively long (approximately 32 days). Hooded mergansers will sometimes share a cavity with a nesting wood duck, and usually when this occurs, it appears that neither species is very successful. Even in captivity, the two species may compete for the same nest box, and mixed clutches are not infrequent. Interestingly, ducklings in the water may gather together in a tight compact group that somewhat resem-

bles a swimming muskrat—an instinctive behavior that may be useful in deceiving roving aerial predators such as sharp-shinned hawks. Broods of different females do not merge as do those of some other mergansers. During the winter, they tend to move toward the coast, but are said to generally avoid salt water environments. This generalization may not be totally accurate, however, for I have often observed wintering birds in marine environments, particularly in Puget Sound and around the San Juan Islands in British Columbia, Canada.

In captivity, hooded mergansers are among the most desirable of all waterfowl species, and some propagators have been exceedingly successful in breeding them. Curiously, while they are prolific egg layers, fertility has traditionally been a problem. For some unknown reason, drakes often come into breeding condition well in advance of the hens, and males can be observed courting as early as the fall, almost as soon as they come back into color. Indeed, I have observed them copulating as early as November. If maintained in flocks, the drakes may court collectively. During the 1978 season, this species hybridized with the American goldeneye, a cross that has also been recorded in the wild. The young are more difficult to rear than dabblers, but not nearly as difficult as some of the other Mergini.

12.56 *Female hooded merganser. In many ways, the drab color of the female is as attractive as the more showy plumage of the male. This species is prone to set a replacement clutch if the first is lost. At the onset of incubation, most of the drakes depart, presumably to traditional molting sites. The young may be abandoned prior to fledging.*

12.57 *Drake hooded merganser with crest depressed.*

Mergansers (smew and hoodies in particular) are extremely curious, and will pick up and play with just about anything, often swallowing it. If care is not exercised, foreign body impaction can occur and losses may result. I once lost a male goosander that had a four-inch-long nail, a paper straw, and a number of rocks in its stomach.

The **Brazilian merganser** (*Mergus octosetaceus*) is either one of the rarest of ducks or is merely unknown because of its secretive ways and inaccessible habitat. Apparently, these birds are extremely shy, and they were considered extinct by some biologists until they were "rediscovered" in 1947. The first recorded nest (in a tree cavity) was not seen until 1954. It is possible that Brazilian mergansers are more common than generally believed and that isolated, sedentary populations of this elusive merganser may occupy the valleys of remote rivers and streams in certain districts of Brazil, Paraguay, and Argentina. On the other hand, because of their remote habitat, they could disappear before anyone recognized that they were in trouble.

Like the only other southern merganser (the Auckland Islands merganser), Brazilian mergansers exhibit little external dimorphism except for size—females being somewhat smaller with shorter bills. They are similar to the red-breasted merganser in size and propor-

tions, and Delacour described them as having a black head and neck with a distinct greenish reflection. Most of the literature indicates that they are basically greenish brown dorsally, with a conspicuous white patch on the wing, but the greenish cast was practically indiscernible on museum specimens I have examined. (Conceivably, it could have faded after years in a museum drawer.) On the whole, they appear to me to be rather like very dark versions of red-breasted mergansers. The lower neck, breast, and sides are grey, but may be finely veined with hoary white. The remainder of the ventral surfaces are broadly and irregularly barred with brown and white. Both sexes have very long occipital crests, with that of the female being less developed. The iris is said to be brown, the bill greyish black, and the legs and feet rosy red.

Brazilian mergansers are usually observed in pairs, and appear to prefer lowland rivers and small streams, especially where these are interspersed with rapids. Almost all reports indicate that they invariably fly close to the surface of the water, always following the river's course. It is believed that these interesting birds spend their entire lives along a small portion of a selected river. Feeding mainly by day, they demonstrate a preference for rapids where fish are abundant and easy

12.58

12.59

12.60

12.61

12.58 *Auckland Island merganser, now extinct.*

12.59 *Live mounts of the little-known Brazilian merganser.*

12.60 *Wintering red-breasted mergansers loafing ashore. When not nesting, these birds are generally encountered in pairs or small groups. But where food is plentiful, they occasionally gather in scattered bunches, which may contain thousands of ducks.*

12.61 *Red-breasted merganser drake in breeding plumage. This species typically nests on the ground, but the presence of overhead cover is apparently a prerequisite and open nest sites are exceptional. On occasion, the female may have a path (even a tunnel) through the vegetation to the water.*

to obtain. By most accounts, they are exceedingly silent birds, although vocal activity probably increases during the breeding season. The black and white hawk-eagle (*Spizastur melanoleucus*) is apparently a major predator.

There are no indications that the population is in trouble, but their limited range and specific habitat requirements suggest a relatively small population. The inaccessibility of their haunts is such that for the time being they are afforded some degree of security—but as with most small, specialized populations, the Brazilian merganser is frighteningly vulnerable to habitat alteration and other changes. Unfortunately, these intriguing birds are almost totally unknown to both aviculturists and field ornithologists alike. They have never been maintained in a collection, but if they are like other mergansers, they could easily be established if birds were to become available.

The **Auckland Islands merganser** (*Mergus australis*) was less fortunate than its Brazilian counterpart, and it appears unlikely that it will be rediscovered. This insular austral merganser was first recorded in 1840 and was apparently gone by the first decade of the 20th century. For a change, *modern man* may not have been totally responsible for its disappearance, since the species was already rare and possibly close to extinction at the time of its discovery. It may be, however, that pre-European man contributed greatly to its decline and possible extirpation in New Zealand, since merganser bones have been discovered in the middens of the Moa-hunting Polynesians. In addition to natural predators such as skuas, falcons, large fish, eels, sea lions, and egg-eating rails, introduced species such as dogs and rats undoubtedly took their toll.

Once the population was gone from New Zealand and was confined to the Auckland Islands, these mergansers were probably never very abundant, and even under optimum conditions, it is unlikely that more than several hundred birds could have survived in the limited appropriate habitat available on the islands. Some writers have suggested that Auckland Islands mergansers were flightless but apparently they could fly, although the wings were definitely reduced in size. Both sexes resembled a female goosander, but were smaller and darker, with males being somewhat superior in size and having larger crests. The color of the head and neck was dark reddish brown, and as with other mergansers, the secondaries and coverts had white patches—although males had double white bars and females had a single bar of white. The crest was relatively short, the iris brown, the bill black and orange, and the legs orange. Some 25 or 26 skins (four ducklings, twelve males, and nine females), three skeletons, and a preserved specimen are known to exist in various museum collections. Like the Labrador duck, the Auckland Islands mergansers were essentially gone before modern man recognized that they were in serious trouble.

The two subspecies of **red-breasted mergansers** (*Mergus serrator*) are obviously named for the cinnamon breast that drakes exhibit in nuptial plumage. Both races tend to be much more gregarious than the superficially similar goosander, are more apt to be found on salt water, and spend a rather large amount of time ashore for sea ducks. Females are much smaller and trimmer than the female goosanders, and lack the sharp color contrast between the head and throat. Their crests are much more ragged and pronounced, while the bills are relatively thin, with almost an upturned look to them. Drakes in eclipse plumage can be distinguished from the very similar females by their darker chins and backs, the greater amount of white on their upper wings, and their redder eyes.

12.62 *It is not uncommon for red-breasted merganser drakes to court one another, particularly early in the breeding season. At times, nests may be rather close together, but this is usually more an indication of preferred nesting areas than of a tendency toward social nesting. Some dump nesting has been documented (with eggs even being dumped in the nests of other species), and up to 56 eggs have been recorded in a single nest. Broods may merge, and in one case 64 young (not necessarily the same age) were observed together. Often, wintering birds feed cooperatively by arranging themselves in an arc and thrashing and splashing until fish are driven into the shallows, where capture is easier. Fish are usually caught and then manipulated into a head-first position prior to swallowing.*

Red-breasted mergansers are reportedly shy, but this is not always the case. I can vividly recall one occasion when I was observing hundreds of wintering mergansers in Florida. The ducks were so trusting that a dozen or so were feeding at my feet, and one individual was so intent on foraging that it actually grabbed my foot. Although red-breasted mergansers readily dive, they more frequently swim about with their heads partially submerged searching for food. Sometimes, they engage in communal fishing activities.

Unlike other mergansers, they are more prone to nest on the ground than in tree cavities, and appear to prefer sites under boulders or amid thick vegetation. In some regions, such as Iceland, they demonstrate a preference for small island sites, and nest concentrations in such areas are approximately twice as dense as those on the mainland. Their complicated courtship repertoire is most intriguing and fascinating to observe. Drakes will sometimes display to females (or other males) by stretching their necks diagonally (the salute) and then rapidly lowering the neck and part of the twisted head into the water (the curtsy)—accompanying the entire performance with a cat-like mewing call.

Courtship may commence during the winter, or as early as late fall in captivity, and pairs are usually already formed when they arrive on the breeding grounds. Egg laying generally takes place from late May to mid-June, although it can be later. (On one occasion in Scotland, I saw a pair court and copulate while the male was already in eclipse plumage. This occurred during the third week of June and none of the mergansers in that area had commenced laying.) Ducklings on occasion will ride the backs of swimming females, and some brood merging tendencies have been demonstrated.

The two described races are essentially identical, but birds of the Greenland race (*M. s. schioleri*) tend to be larger, and to have broader and stronger bills and longer wings than those of North America and Eurasia (*M. s. serrator*). Also, the Greenland birds tend not to be migratory, and adult females are said to have paler heads and upper backs. There is, however, a great deal of overlap, and the Greenland subspecies is not accepted as valid by many contemporary ornithologists. Red-breasted mergansers are not particularly common in wildfowl collections, nor are they bred regularly. However, they thrive under captive conditions and are not troublesome to other birds, at least not on larger ponds. The Greenland birds are totally unknown to aviculturists.

The **Chinese merganser** (*Mergus squamatus*) is little known and apparently rare. It somewhat resembles the red-breasted merganser, and the two species are probably closely related. The red breast is lacking, however, and the feathers along the sides and flanks of both sexes of *squamatus* are marked in such a way that the birds appear to have large scales, bringing about the often-used name of scaly-sided merganser. (The scaly-sided appearance of the female is much more pronounced than most illustrations indicate.) Chinese mergansers probably represent an intermediate form between the goosander and the red-breasted merganser. The dark greenish black throat of the male is characterized by an indistinct white line which extends upward toward the chin, and the crest is extraordinarily long.

These birds have received little or no attention from western biologists. Scanty evidence suggests that at one time they were not particularly uncommon in certain areas, as in the valleys of the Iman and Sitze rivers in China. Currently, however, the overall population is apparently declining in all areas of its restricted range. Lacking more accurate data, we must consider the species rare, possibly even endangered. Ornithologists have expressed concern over the fate of the specialized Chinese merganser because of its extremely restricted breeding range, which makes it very susceptible to increased hunting pressure and changing forestry practices. There are some indications that it may be preyed upon by the introduced North American mink.

Apparently, *squamatus* avoids narrow tributaries in which it is difficult to dive, and tends to frequent only those rivers which are surrounded by forests. Reportedly, they are reluctant fliers. Their white down suggests that cavity nesting is typical, and while only two nests have been documented, both were in tree hollows. These distinctive mergansers have never been maintained in captivity outside of China, and unless drastic political changes occur they will remain virtually unknown to anyone outside of that country. Hopefully, the recent opening of diplomatic relations with the United States may facilitate study by western biologists. As of 1978, there were two specimens at the Shanghai Zoo.

The three remaining mergansers are all collectively referred to as **common mergansers** (*Mergus merganser*). Known as goosanders in

12.63 *Pair of Chinese or scaly-sided mergansers. Found in China for the most part, these little-known birds have been, on rare occasions, reported in Korea as well. During the breeding season, they inhabit the fast-flowing mountain streams of the Sikhote-Alin Mountains, in the middle and upper coniferous forest zone. Their status is not know, but they are believed to be rare.* PAINTING BY BONNIE PILSON

12.64 *Pair of red-breasted mergansers. When feeding in water that is too shallow for effective diving, foraging mergansers may swim along with their heads partially underwater, and they may even keep their heads entirely underwater for rather long periods of time.*

12.65 *(Opposite Page) American merganser underwater. Like all mergansers, these ducks are efficient divers and underwater swimmers.* PHOTO BY TONY MERCIECA

the Old World, these birds are the largest and most widespread of the fish ducks. The name goosander refers in a somewhat exaggerated fashion to their "goose-like" size. Males average three and a half pounds, and lack the full trailing crest that is characteristic of most other mergansers. Like the other northern merganser drakes in eclipse plumage, males can be differentiated from their mates by their larger size and a greater amount of white on their upper wings.

Typically, these birds fly very low over the water in long, evenly-spaced lines, and their flight silhouette is more like that of a loon or cormorant than of a duck. Vocalizations usually consist of hoarse croaks, but males also have a bell-like call and a peculiar courtship call which Johnsgard describes as a curious twanging note, similar to that produced by a guitar. Natural arboreal nesting cavities are preferred, such as those excavated by the black woodpecker; but they will nest on the ground if appropriate cavities are scarce, and they have also been observed nesting in rock crevices, artificial nest boxes, holes in walls, chimneys, and even abandoned buildings. Females can be very aggressive toward courting males, frequently jabbing at them with

12.66

12.67

12.66 *Female goosander. On occasion, nest-seeking females become trapped in chimneys. In Sweden, duck lovers may provide nest holes in their attics, and at times, up to four pairs of goosanders may occupy a single attic. If clutches are lost early, they may be replaced. Flying females are capable of maneuvering through closely-spaced tree branches.*

12.67 *Goosander drake in nuptial plumage. These ducks are less apt to winter on salt water than red-breasted mergansers. They feed in rapids as readily as they do in quiet waters. Breeding drakes will threaten adult males that violate their territories, but will tolerate females and even subadult males.*

their bills. Swimming females occasionally carry the young on their backs. It is believed that young, unfledged mergansers are heavily preyed upon by owls, most notably the barred owl.

Common mergansers are less apt to gather together in large wintering flocks than the red-breasted merganser (although flocks exceeding 10,000 birds have been recorded), and they are also less prone to engage in cooperative feeding. At the same time, they are rarely observed feeding singly, and it is possible that birds feeding in small groups have greater success than birds feeding alone. When foraging in shallow water, they may occasionally take frogs, snakes, inverte-brates, and even small mammals (such as shrews) as well. While the prey is generally brought to the surface before swallowing, smaller fish may be ingested underwater. North American mergansers are some-times robbed of their prey by bald eagles and various gull species.

Some drakes in the wild have a beautiful salmon-pink tinge to their white underparts, but curiously, this pinkish cast is usually lost when they are maintained in captivity. Because of this color, common mergansers are sometimes known as "salmon bellies" in certain por-tions of their range. The loss of the pink may be attributable to captive diets, but it is also said that the salmon tinge of the white underparts fades shortly after death. (Interestingly, this phenomenon is apparently not restricted to common mergansers, since Delacour told me of two male Chinese mergansers he collected in China in 1925 which also had a very deep salmon color on their light ventral surfaces.)

All three races are very similar in appearance, but the European goosander (*M. m. merganser*) is the largest, and is distinguished from the others by the strongly hooked tip of the bill. To me, at least, their bills appear to be more maroon in color than the reddish bills of the American race (*M. m. americanus*). New World males can be reliably distinguished from their two Eurasian counterparts by their prominent black wing stripe, which is visible when the wing is closed but most conspicuous in flight. This wing bar is not lacking on the other two races, but its presence is obscured by the white upper secondary coverts.

The American and Asiatic subspecies are approximately the same size, although the Asian goosander (*M. m. orientalis*) has a slightly shorter and less heavy bill, somewhat longer wings, and legs that are theoretically proportionally shorter. In addition, *orientalis* is said to have more black on the upper back, whereas the lower back is paler and more freckled with white. Some taxonomists have expressed doubts as to the validity of the eastern race. In India, little egrets take

12.68

advantage of the cooperative feeding action of wintering Asian mergansers by leap-frogging back and forth over the foraging ducks and taking up advance positions on the bank, where they seize fish that have become stranded in the shallows in their frenzy to escape from the mergansers.

Common mergansers adjust well to captivity, but they are not overly common or popular with aviculturists—perhaps because they will snatch and consume recently-hatched ducklings of other species without hesitation. Goosanders are not uncommon in European collections but are virtually unknown in North America, probably as a result of their similarity to *americanus*. Although the larger mergansers are not often bred, this is probably a reflection of their relative scarcity in collections rather than a reluctance to breed on the part of the birds. In 1978, an interesting hybrid was produced, resulting from a cross between an American merganser and a redhead duck.

12.69

12.68 *Goosander duckling. If orphaned, even at quite an early age, goosander young are capable of survival if the weather is not too harsh.*

12.69 *American merganser male. Full-color drakes are easily distinguished from their Eurasian counterparts by the presence of a rather distinct dark wing stripe. If startled when ashore, these wary birds tend to run to the water in an upright posture. Like harlequin ducks, they follow the bends of a river when in flight, and they are capable of flight speeds approaching 50 miles per hour. If alarmed, they may disgorge their food in order to become airborne — and in the case of one bird that was caught by hand, the fish it was trying to eject from its throat was a carp weighing more than one and a quarter pounds.*

13
Stiff-tailed Ducks
Oxyurini

Even the most casual waterfowl observer is bound to find the quaint, dumpy little ducks of this tribe among his or her favorites, for their antics can be most amusing and charming. So distinctive is their appearance and behavior, in fact, that all stiff-tails are easily distinguished from other waterfowl (with the possible exception of the white-backed duck). Only nine species have been described, but the overall range of the group is extremely large. Most stiff-tails inhabit the Southern Hemisphere, living primarily in tropical, subtropical, and warm temperate regions, and their center of distribution appears to be in the Americas.

Appropriately enough, these charming birds are named for their distinctive stiff tail feathers, which the drakes often hold parallel to the surface of the water or cock jauntily up into the air. The tail plays a major role in courtship displays, and is especially useful as a brake when landing. Also, the stiffening of the feathers (which increases resistance to bending) makes it possible for the birds to use their tails as very effective rudders when swimming underwater.

Stiff-tails demonstrate no apparent close relationship to any other group of ducks, but the white-backed duck may ultimately prove to be an exception in this regard, and Johnsgard has therefore already moved them to the whistling duck tribe. Excluding white-backed and

,13.2

13.1 (Opposite Page) Argentine ruddy duck drake in a typical stiff-tail habitat of thick emergent aquatic vegetation. Because of their small size and elusive nature, stiff-tails in the wild are not conspicuous and there is a persistent tendency to believe that they are rare. As a result of their dependence on specialized wetland habitat (which is rapidly disappearing in many areas), a number of stiff-tail populations must be considered vulnerable, although they are not yet endangered. PHOTO BY MAURICE RUMBOLL

13.2 Diving North American ruddy duck drake. As is typical of most stiff-tails, the legs of ruddies are located well back on the body and their feet are large. Such an arrangement increases their underwater swimming capabilities, but it severely compromises terrestrial locomotion and they are practically helpless ashore. When drakes are out of color, as this bird is, the bill turns blackish and the ruddy plumage is replaced by greyish brown feathers, but the white cheeks are retained. PHOTO BY TONY MERCIECA

musk ducks, all stiff-tails exhibit distinct sexual color dimorphism, and the sexes are similar in size. Males of most species are characterized by blue bills, which can be very colorful during the breeding season; but this color is lost when the season is over. Usually, bills are quite broad, with a recurved nail at the tip. The dense plumage is typically grebe-like and shiny, without any suggestion of metallic coloration, and most species do not have a "true" eclipse plumage, although they do go out of color. They have feet which are relatively large, and the short, thick necks of the males are inflatable.

Stiff-tailed ducks are almost exclusively aquatic and very efficient divers. They can remain submerged for up to 30 seconds while foraging, and they are also able to simply sink below the surface of the water without a ripple, a trait they share with the grebes. (Not surprisingly, these unobtrusive ducks can be very elusive.) Most are essentially vegetarian, and feed by straining aquatic plant seeds and insect larvae from the muddy bottom ooze of swamps, ponds, lakes, and sheltered lagoons. (An exception is the musk duck, which is primarily carnivorous.) Stiff-tails prefer fresh or brackish water, particularly if there is an abundance of floating and submerged vegetation, along

13.3

13.3 *North American ruddy duck drake in full breeding color — a plumage that is generally assumed from April to August. The low swimming profile of the species is evident here. In flight, the axis of the body is tilted downward slightly, but these grebe-like birds fly with surprising speed. They tend to travel by night and feed by day. As a rule, ruddy ducks do not associate with other waterfowl, but they may keep company with coots or even gallinules.*

13.4 *During courtship, ruddy ducks engage in numerous unorthodox activities, including the ring-rush illustrated here. To begin, drakes quickly snap their partially spread stiff tails downward. Then, with a shower of spray, they rush forward to within several feet of a female and come to an abrupt stop. Both wings and feet propel the birds, and it may be that their stiffened submerged tails support them during the skitter. During such movements, ruddy drakes move surprisingly fast and their aquatic scamper is accompanied by a short series of ascending and descending staccato sounds that are produced as the large feet strike the surface of the water in rapid succession. The wings may also produce a ringing sound.*

13.4

with reeds and rushes; but several species do frequent salt water at certain times of the year.

Their relatively short rounded wings, combined with their heavy bodies, make these birds rather labored fliers. They must kick and flap across the surface of the water for some distance prior to becoming airborne—and once up, their flight tends to be rapid and jerky. Masked and black-headed ducks appear to be unlike the others in this regard, since they reportedly can leap directly into flight from the water if need be. Generally, stiff-tails fly only as a last resort, even if frightened or threatened, preferring instead to dive in an effort to escape danger.

On land, they are practically helpless, because their legs are placed far back on their bodies. This anatomical arrangement increases their diving efficiency, but compromises their terrestrial locomotion to such a degree that when they are ashore they may move like injured birds, pushing both feet together while leaning forward on the breast. As a group, these ducks tend to be nocturnal, and spend most of the day dozing on the water. Like most waterfowl, when sleeping they tuck their bills into the scapular feathers between the bases of the wings, and often draw both feet up into the flank feathers. If there is a brisk wind, sleeping stiff-tails are sometimes blown across the top of the water like floating balls.

Usually, drakes are unvociferous and retiring, but they often become quite active during the breeding season, and their complicated stereotyped courtship displays can be very striking. At such times, their vocalizations are relatively simple, but the nuptial antics which accompany them can be extremely varied. For example, calls may be modified by inflatable throat sacs, or extended by instrumental sounds such as drumming and rattling with the bill, or even supplemented with other mechanical noises such as splashing. In most cases, the females are quiet, but they may produce rattling, wheezing, or purring sounds. Unlike most anatids, stiff-tails are inclined to "construct" elaborate nests, which are sometimes even domed over and well disguised. In many cases, they modify the nests of other birds and bend vegetation down over them. When nests extend over the water, they may be equipped with ramps leading down to the water, and in some cases, females utilize a floating platform that is anchored.

Members of the genus *Oxyura* produce the largest egg in relation to body size of any living duck. Interestingly, the clutch size is also relatively large, the incubation period is short, and little (if any) down is used to line the nest. A typical clutch consists of seven or eight eggs, the total weight of which may exceed the weight of the female that laid them. This is remarkable, considering that some species three times as large (such as mallards or canvasbacks) produce eggs substantially smaller, and a mallard egg represents only 5.3 percent of the adult's weight. It has been postulated that the large stiff-tail eggs are part of a functional adaptation that permits the development of unusually precocious young, which are able to forage independently by diving soon after hatching. Several other wildfowl species, such as torrent ducks, demonstrate similar tendencies, and ducklings of these species must also be able to dive and navigate swift currents immediately after departing the nest site.

Incubation periods for the tribe range from 20 to 33 days and, with the exception of the black-headed duck and the white-backed duck, the female incubates without assistance from the male. In some instances, the ducklings become independent of the adults within a week or two—and in the case of the black-headed duck, which is a

13.5 *On occasion, ruddy ducks will roost ashore or on submerged rocks, as this male is doing — but they are clearly uncomfortable when they do so. If threatened, they tend to dive rather than fly, and if need be, they are capable of submerging without producing a ripple. Population estimates of the North American ruddy duck range as high as half a million birds, but there are those who believe that they do not exceed several hundred thousand individuals.*

13.6

13.7

13.6 *Female North American ruddy ducks are not nearly as bright and colorful as their mates, but they are just as feisty and appealing. When agitated, females (and sometimes ducklings) tend to gape, raise their scapular feathers, and hiss at an intruder.*

13.7 *Courting ruddy duck performing the bubbling display, which is the major sexual display of these birds. During most of their displays, ruddies cock their tails vertically but usually do not spread them. When the tail is tilted upward, the conspicuous white area under the tail is brought into view and males may attempt to impress females by swimming directly in front of them and displaying it (the tail-flash display). If a courted female is too closely approached by a second courting drake, the first male may rush at the competitor with its bill gaping, its head near the water, and its back feathers ruffled. This threat position has been descriptively referred to as the hunched rush.*

parasitic nester, the ducklings are reputed to be completely independent upon hatching.

The ruddy duck complex is composed of the familiar **North American ruddy duck** (*Oxyura j. jamaicensis*), and three South American varieties. The northern ruddy duck is the best known of the stiff-tails and is one of the most appealing and popular of all waterfowl—by far the most common stiff-tail in captivity. The shape, behavior, and lifestyle of these charming little ducks recalls that of an animated wind-up toy, and during the breeding season, the brilliant powder-blue bill and snow-white cheek patches of the active male are not easily overlooked. Lengthened feathers over the drake's eyes protrude not unlike little horns, and during the breeding season, males assume a predominantly reddish plumage, which is obviously the origin of their vernacular name. Ruddy ducks have been dubbed with at least 95 colorful colloquial names, ranging from "bumblebee buzzer" and "dinky" to "chuck-duck" and "spatter." (They are sometimes called blue-bills as well, but this name is more appropriately applied to the lesser scaup.)

Although ruddy ducks do not have a true eclipse plumage, there is a distinct contrast between winter and summer coloration, and during the nonbreeding season the ruddy plumage is lost (although the white cheek patches remain). Unlike most other waterfowl, which are dull in coloration for only a brief time, ruddy duck drakes may remain drabbly colored all winter. Females are much more somber in color, but are just as feisty in disposition, and are often highly aggressive toward the drakes, frequently gaping at them with outstretched necks and ruffled scapulars.

The enchanting behavior of the drakes during courtship is perhaps even more distinctive than their physical appearance. Communal courtship activity is not particularly uncommon, and the numerous nuptial displays take many forms. A courting male may "strut" about on the water, with the tail tilted forward until it almost touches his head. Or the bright blue bill may be continuously slapped against the inflated chest—producing a distinct drumming sound as air is forced out from beneath the feathers, and causing a ring of bubbles to form around the breast. (Not surprisingly, such behavior is known as the "bubbling

13.8 *Pair of North American ruddy ducks with two ducklings. Because males in nuptial plumage are often observed in the company of females with young, it has been said that drakes are actively involved in brood care. But their association with the hens during such times is merely a reflection of continued interest in breeding. Nest sites are generally located in dense emergent vegetation and they also utilize old coot nests, muskrat houses, or at times feeding platforms. If the water level is unstable and nesting birds are flooded out, there is a tendency to lay eggs in dump nests, and as many as 80 eggs have been recovered from a single such nest. Ruddies may also deposit their eggs in the nests of other species, including those of other waterfowl, grebes. American bitterns, coots, and even gallinules.*

display.'') The ability of the male ruddy duck to puff up its chest is due to a large tracheal air sac that is inflated during courtship rites.

Other performances in the nuptial repertoire include rapid pumping of the head up and down, and the tendency to scoot over the surface of the water with surprising speed. As the feet strike the water in rapid succession during the latter maneuver, a distinct clicking or popping sound is produced. The nuptial behavior is extremely ritualized, and once a given display commences, the sequence of movements is generally easy to predict. To the delight of onlookers, the aquatic strutting and displaying may continue for hours—but more often than not, the females are not particularly impressed with all this attention and treats the energetic drakes with total indifference.

While the females incubate, males may continue to court other females. However, when the ducklings hatch and the hens gather up the broods and lead them to the water, the drakes (still cloaked in their bright breeding dress) tend to puff up their chests, cock their tails upward, and join the females and young. For this reason perhaps, it has long been suggested that ruddy duck males assist in rearing the young—but in reality, little (if any) attention is actually paid to the young by the drakes. More likely, their association with the family at this time is due to a continuing sexual attraction for the hens, although their presence with the family may serve to distract predators from the ducklings as well. All the same, defense of the brood rests primarily with the female, and when danger threatens, the male will generally move away. Ruddy ducks exhibit some tendencies toward nest parasitism, and brood merging behavior has also been noted. In some areas, two broods a year may be produced.

Some authorities separate the ruddy duck of North America from those of the Caribbean Islands, and as a result, *O. j. rubida* sometimes appears in the literature. But whether or not these two populations are in fact distinct enough to warrant the creation of yet another subspecies remains to be seen. The current population of ruddy ducks in North America is probably well over half a million, but there has been a downward trend in recent decades. Most significant among the causes of this decline has been deterioration and alteration of marsh breeding habitat, but heavy losses of wintering birds caught in oil spills

can be considered a significant cause of mortality as well.

A small introduced feral population of ruddy ducks exists in England, and they are well established in many waterfowl collections. They are bred fairly regularly, but present special propagation problems, since the ducklings are notoriously more difficult to raise than the young of a dabbler, and require specialized brooders and rearing techniques. However, once these techniques are mastered, they can be reared with relative ease. As adults, they are hardy and require no special care, although they do best if clean, deep water is available.

Colombian and Peruvian ruddy ducks are both very similar behaviorally to the more familiar ruddies of the north, and are merely regarded as southern races. **Peruvian ruddy ducks** (*O. j. ferruginea*) are the largest and darkest overall of the three races, and drakes are characterized by their solid black heads, with the white on the head being reduced to only a small white spot on the chin. Superficially, full-color drakes closely resemble Argentine ruddy ducks, and while they weigh twice as much, this size difference is not easily discernible in the field. Peruvian ruddies inhabit the Andean lakes of Peru, Bolivia, and Argentina, and have been observed at altitudes of 14,500 feet. Apparently, they breed throughout the year. They are extremely rare in captivity, and as of early 1979, I was only aware of three pure ones in collections anywhere (two males and a female at the Wildfowl Trust). Reportedly, they have been bred in the past, but the birds involved may have been hybrids.

Drakes of the **Colombian ruddy duck** race (*O. j. andina*) are supposedly unique in having black and white mottled cheek patches, but I have seen North American ruddies with traces of black flecks in the white cheek patches. The mottled cheeks of the Colombian birds are subject to a significant amount of variation, and may range from almost pure white to solid black; but most typically they are black, irregularly spotted with white. Some of the older literature indicates that *andina* is slightly smaller than the nominate race, but they are both essentially the same size, although the bill of the Colombian drake may be somewhat larger. Females are said to have less distinct facial markings. The center of distribution is on mountain lakes and lagoons in central and eastern Colombia. They may sometimes gather in flocks ranging from 30 to 500 birds, but more typically, they are encountered in much smaller groups of five to ten. The status of this sedentary duck is not known, but like some of the other elusive stiff-tails, they may be more common than suspected.

In the minds of many waterfowl specialists, the position of the Colombian ruddy duck as a valid race is somewhat suspect, and I personally believe they merely represent an intergrade population between the ruddy ducks of the north and those of the south. In 1977, Sea World aviculturists bred a pair of ducks that had resulted from a cross between *ferruginea* and *jamaicensis;* and even though the drake of this pair had only slight traces of black on the cheeks, the subsequent generation produced males with distinctly mottled cheek patches, conforming to the description of Colombian ruddy ducks. These males were fully colored and courting in less than a year.

The third of the South American ruddy ducks is the **Argentine ruddy duck or lake duck** (*Oxyura vittata*), which is afforded full specific rank primarily because it occurs side by side with the Peruvian ruddy duck in some parts of its range with no evidence of hybridization. In addition, unlike the typical ruddy duck, these birds utilize nests that are not elaborate and are more like small, flattened grebe nests. Males in nuptial plumage are strikingly similar to birds of the Peruvian

13.9

13.10

13.11

13.12

13.15

13.9 - 13.10 (Opposite Page) *Peruvian ruddy duck drakes. These birds may nest at very high altitudes (up to 14,500 feet). The breeding season can be prolonged and the time of its occurrence varies, depending on locality and altitude.*

13.11 (Opposite Page) *Melanistic drake North American ruddy duck.* PHOTO BY JOSE A. OTTENWALDER

13.12 *Peruvian ruddy duck male.*

13.13 *Argentine ruddy duck male. The flight of these ducks is rather labored and their wings produce a buzzing sound.*

13.14 *Artificially produced "Colombian ruddy duck" drake. This individual is one of a pair which resulted from a cross between a northern ruddy duck and a Peruvian ruddy duck. It is likely that the ruddy ducks of Colombia merely represent an intergrade population and are not really a separate race.*

13.15 *A male "Colombian ruddy duck," produced from the pair of hybrid ducks mentioned in 13.14. Note that there is more black in the cheeks of the birds of this second generation.*

13.16 *Portrait of the duck pictured in 13.15 as it began to acquire its nuptial plumage.*

13.13

13.16

race, but they are not as large. They also have comparatively small and narrow bills, which are higher near the base, and they appear to have proportionally larger tails. In addition, the black color of the head and neck extends farther down in front and behind, the overall chestnut color is darker, and sometimes the throat is white. It is possible that these Argentine ducks are rather closely related to the blue-billed duck of Australia, and Johnsgard, in fact, refers to them as Argentine blue-billed ducks. (Their courtship displays are clearly more like the Australian birds than those of the other ruddy ducks.) Females rather resemble North American ruddies, but their heads are more distinctly striped with buffy white below the eyes, and they have white cheeks and throats.

Argentine ruddy ducks are decidedly birds of the lowlands, and even though their range is relatively large (extending throughout Chile and Argentina), they do not appear to be overly abundant anywhere. However, because they are by nature very secretive, their presence may have simply been overlooked, and it is possible that they are more common than suspected. Although Argentine ruddies are not regarded as particularly strong fliers, a number of these little ducks were reported on Deception Island during the austral summer of 1916/17, following a severe drought in Argentina. Deception Island is located directly north of the Antarctic Peninsula, some 500 to 600 miles south of the normal range of these ducks, and for birds that are not considered to be good fliers, such a crossing is a remarkable feat. During the nonbreeding season, small flocks of *vittata* may gather, and up to 400 have been recorded on a single lake. They are still quite rare in captive waterfowl collections, but are being bred with greater frequency, at the Wildfowl Trust in particular.

The **maccoa duck** (*Oxyura maccoa*) of Africa superficially appears to be a large Peruvian ruddy duck, but its bill is significantly broader and higher. Characteristically, these birds swim low in the water, and when disturbed, they may submerge to the point where only their heads, thick necks, and backs are visible. Their habitat includes the cooler highland lakes and ponds. Sometimes, they lay all or some of their eggs in the nests of other ducks—more often than not, in those of other maccoas.

Unlike the North American ruddy ducks, breeding males of this species are highly territorial and most intolerant of other drakes that invade their territories. Maccoas are polygamous, and a successful male may have a number of females nesting within his territory (eight were observed in one instance). Under natural conditions, males outnumber females, and the hens tend to ignore drakes defending marginal territories. These birds are normally rather silent and shy, but courting males produce harsh and rather bullfrog-like noises, as well as snoring, growling, or gargling sounds; or in some cases, a vibrating trumpet-like call. (The frog-like calls may be more closely associated with territory defense than actual courtship.) The breeding season is prolonged, perhaps up to ten months in length, but the most intense activity appears to take place between September and December. In at least one case, a male was observed to drown his mate during copulation.

The overall distribution of maccoa ducks is wide, but they are generally uncommon throughout the range; however, due to their broad distribution and nongame status, the population as a whole appears to be stable, at least for the moment. Maccoas are not particularly well established in captivity and are represented in relatively few

13.17 (Opposite Page) *Drake maccoa duck. These birds are probably closely related to the Argentine ruddy duck, and the downy young of the two species are strikingly similar, although maccoa ducklings have striped backs and a narrower cheek stripe. At times, these ducks can be encountered on impoundments or sewage-farm basins, where decomposing organic matter provides much invertebrate food.*

13.18 *Pair of Argentine ruddies or blue-billed ducks. Even though the distribution of these birds overlaps that of the larger Peruvian ruddy duck, and the two species nest side by side on lowland lakes, there is no indication of hybridization. The males are superficially similar to Peruvian ruddies, but females can be readily separated because those of the Argentine species have a whitish line extending from the nape to the bill, below the eyes.*

13.19 *Argentine ruddy duckling.*

13.20 *Maccoa duck female. The four to eight (average five) eggs are incubated by the female alone for 25 to 27 days. By the time the young are several weeks old, they are capable of fending for themselves.*

13.21

13.22

13.21 *Male Australian blue-billed duck. While this is a relatively nonvocal species, displaying drakes may produce a rapid low-pitched rattling note. Females sometimes utter a weak quack when startled. When these birds congregate on large lakes or swamps, they tend to pass the day far from shore in large rafts, but will move closer to shore to feed in the late afternoon and early morning. During the breeding season, they frequent the densest part of the swamp and become very secretive.*

13.22 *Australian blue-billed ducks are excellent divers and can easily swim a distance of 60 feet or more underwater when escaping from danger. During the winter, when they are occupying more open habitat, they are more apt to fly, but their takeoff is laborious and they must patter over the surface of the water for several yards before becoming airborne. Once up, however, they fly swiftly and well, albeit in a decidedly tail-heavy manner.*
PHOTO BY CHRIS SPIKER

collections. But a significant amount of success has been achieved with them in recent years at the Wildfowl Trust (where they were first bred in 1974), and like the Argentine ruddy duck, they may soon become more available to aviculturists.

The Australian counterpart of the maccoa is the **blue-billed duck** (*Oxyura australis*), which has a close resemblance to the maccoa and occupies the same type of ecological niche as do the other stiff-tails. These shy and retiring ducks are relatively numerous, and are widely distributed throughout southern Australia and eastern Tasmania, but (as with some other stiff-tails) because they are elusive, many people are not aware of how common they may be in some areas. During the winter, flocks of a thousand or more may congregate on large lakes and swamps—and in one unusual instance, 8000 were reported in a single flock. The population size appears to be limited only by the availability of permanent, deep-water swamps, but because their hab-

itat requirements are so specific, the species is rather vulnerable.

Like some of the other stiff-tails, blue-billed ducks tend to take over abandoned nests of other aquatic birds, and they seem to have relatively weak pair bonds. They don't appear to be very vocal, although displaying males utter a rapid, low-pitched rattling note; and when startled, females may utter a weak quack. Drakes can be aggressive to one another, and definite territories are established and defended. Males probably do not participate in brood care, and rarely associate with females after they reappear on the water with young.

Essentially vegetarian, *australis* will feed on small spiders, mites, molluscs, crustaceans, and midges as well. They dive for most of their food, but may also strip seeds from vegetation overhanging the water. At times, blue-billed ducks have been known to become entangled in gill nets set for fish, and some Australian hunters also consider them to be good gamebirds (although hunting pressure is relatively light). Few

13.23 *Drake white-headed duck. Less dainty and graceful in overall appearance than the more typical stiff-tails, these birds are noted for a distinctive hunched swimming posture. They are omnivorous feeders but apparently favor vegetable matter. They generally forage underwater, but on occasion they will dabble on the surface. Recently-hatched young are capable of diving within minutes of first reaching the water. However, ducklings must leap into the air in a vigorous manner to gain enough momentum for a dive. Adults may also leap forward to dive, but they can dive in a seemingly effortless way as well.*

13.24 *White-headed ducks may spend considerable time in marine lagoons, and as a result, they are equipped with salt glands. The presence of the glands is partially responsible for the shape of the bill. Sometimes, these ducks are observed at sea, usually in rocky bays. They are seldom seen ashore, but can stand and even walk without apparent strain.*

have ever been maintained in captivity outside of Australia, but it is likely that the Wildfowl Trust will acquire some in the near future.

The **white-headed duck** (*Oxyura leucocephala*), also known as the spine-tailed duck, is one of the most enchanting and interesting of the stiff-tails. Sadly, it is also one of the rarer Eurasian ducks, and the total population may not exceed 10,000 to 15,000 individuals, with perhaps no more than 30 or so pairs breeding in all of Europe. A few breed in Spain, North Africa, and Turkey, but most return to the Soviet Union after wintering in Turkey, Tunisia, or Pakistan. Their habitat requirements are strict, which has resulted in a localized distribution; undoubtedly, drainage of appropriate habitat and increasing agriculture (with the use of nonselective pesticides) has had a significant detrimental effect on the species. In fact, their currently fragmented distribution and disappearance from former breeding areas suggests that the species may be approaching a precarious state.

These ducks frequent salt water to a greater extent than most other members of the tribe, although their preferred habitat is shallow lagoons or brackish-water marshes surrounded by an abundance of tall aquatic vegetation. They have large, relatively high bills that are much swollen near the base, and presumably, the extra height is to accommodate the larger nasal glands that species associated with a salt or brackish environment usually have to facilitate the discharge of excess salt. The bill is also well shaped for grasping and tearing underwater vegetation, and the color of the bill changes to a brilliant blue during the breeding season. The extent of the black crown patch is very variable, and some males are almost completely black-headed (particularly those which occupy the eastern portion of the range). The white heads and dark crowns are retained by the males even when not in breeding plumage.

White-headed ducks are very heavy-bodied birds, and are not as

13.25

13.26

13.25 *Courting white-headed duck. During the breeding season, displaying males frequently rush at one another. Actual contact is apparently rare, however, and opponents generally escape by diving. These birds have a wide variety of courtship movements that have been closely analyzed only recently by animal behaviorists. Unlike the other stiff-tails, drakes if this species do not greatly expand their necks, but an extension of the neck accompanied by tail cocking (as illustrated here) is a commonly performed display.*

13.26 *Female white-headed duck with duckling. The characteristic high bill of the species is equally evident on the females and is even detectable on newly-hatched young. While these birds often utilize the nests of other aquatic avian species, they may also build their own. The site is generally located in the water in thick vegetation, and the nest itself may consist of a platform of dead reed stems and leaves that are woven into upright stems. Nearby vegetation is often bent down over the nest to form a roof. For reasons not clearly understood, these ducks are unusually late nesters. Females closely tend the ducklings, while males play no role in parental care.*

dainty nor as buoyant as typical members of the tribe. They appear to be more closely related to the ruddy ducks than to the other stiff-tails (although some similarities suggest a distant relationship to the maccoas). As is typical with stiff-tails, they are not comfortable away from the water, but occasionally they may come ashore all the same and walk some distance standing upright in the manner of a penguin. They sometimes preen at the water's edge as well.

A distinctive and very characteristic hunched swimming position gives these ducks the appearance of a giant water beetle. The waterborne nuptial displays of the drake are quite intriguing, and must be viewed and heard firsthand to be fully appreciated. They sometimes grunt or, if engaged in group display, may produce a mechanical-sounding tickering purr, while rapidly foot paddling in place and vibrating the tail. At times, the relatively long tail is cocked straight up, or the drakes may assume a hunched posture and present themselves broadside to a female. Often, they will rush at one another and chase each other underwater, and physical contact is not infrequent.

Many times, white-headed ducks use abandoned nests of other aquatic species, including those of coots; and, in fact, these ducks were not bred in captivity until such a nest was provided. Little or no down is used to line the nest, and the incubation period is 23 days, somewhat less than has been reported in some of the literature. The pair bond is weak (if it exists at all) and males do not consort with females after the ducklings emerge, deviating in this regard from the more typical ruddy duck behavior. The tiny ducklings dive in exactly the same way as the adults, including even the pre-dive jump. Relatively few white-headed ducks have ever been maintained in captivity; but fortunately, the Wildfowl Trust has been remarkably successful in breeding them in recent years and they may soon be established in other collections. In late 1978, some were sent to several American collections.

The elusive **masked duck** (*Oxyura dominica*), also called the white-winged lake duck, is not well known. Its vernacular name is derived from a distinctive black mask that characterizes the males during the breeding season. Native to Central and South America and the West Indies, these birds are significantly smaller than *jamaicensis*. They have comparatively long tails and heads which appear disproportionally large when they are in the water. Additionally, the dorsal and flank spotting is unique. During the breeding season, the blue bill of the drake intensifies in color. Females are rather similar in appearance to ruddy duck hens, but are characterized by the presence of two distinctive cheek stripes (rather than one), with the upper stripe passing through the eye. Adult males in nonbreeding plumage closely resemble their inconspicuous mates, although the upper wing is whiter and the facial striping shows less contrast. Immature males also resemble females, but are somewhat blacker on the crown.

Possibly, these are among the most inconspicuous and secretive of all ducks, and even though they are said to be "relatively abundant" in certain localities, they are rarely observed and I have not found them to be at all common anywhere—with the possible exception of northern Argentina. (On occasion, they have been observed in Texas and Florida, and have even been recorded as breeding in southern Texas.) Generally, when encountered in small groups, adult males appear to be considerably outnumbered by female-plumaged birds (some of which may be immature males). In areas where they are not molested by man, masked ducks can almost be considered tame.

It has been suggested that this elusive duck is the most isolated form of the typical stiff-tailed ducks, which may represent a less specialized evolutionary line than the others—and for this reason, the masked duck is sometimes placed in the separate genus *Nomonyx*. The bills of these birds are shaped much more like those of dabbling ducks than stiff-tails, and this structural difference is probably due to both a totally vegetarian diet and specialized foraging techniques. They appear to favor ponds and marshes that contain an abundance of floating leaf plants, and Johnsgard points out that this probably results from either a dietary preference or the availability of possible escape cover, or both. Frequently, masked ducks will surface from a dive with only their heads exposed above the water, and they will then often remain hidden beneath a lily leaf.

The flight of the masked duck is relatively strong and swift, and their white wing patches are very conspicuous when they are airborne. Unlike most other stiff-tails, they are said to be able to leap into the air without a running start, perhaps because of propulsion gained while they are underwater. But no matter how capable they may be as fliers, when danger threatens they usually resort to diving instead of flying. Their eggs, although similar to those of the ruddy duck, are significantly smaller and smoother, and lack the typical chalky shell. They may nest in rice fields (in Argentina, at least), and although the incubation period has not been definitely established, it is probably around 28 days. Drakes apparently do not associate with females that are tending young.

Unfortunately, masked ducks have never been available to aviculturists. As far as I know, they not only have never been bred, but have never even been maintained for any length of time in captivity (although wing-clipped birds may have been held for study purposes for short periods of time). There is no reason to believe, however, that they would be more difficult to keep than the other stiff-tails.

The two races of African **white-backed ducks** (*Thalassornis leuconotus*) are behaviorally quite different from typical stiff-tails in many respects, and much of their behavior and morphology suggests a closer affinity to the whistling ducks. They have not been studied intensively in the field, and scientific opinion is somewhat divided, but biochemical analysis of feather proteins supports a whistling duck relationship and Johnsgard has, in fact, already moved them to the Dendrocygnini. (He suggests that their closest living relative may be the Cuban whistling duck.) Downy young differ from those of whistling ducks in that they are not patterned, but the duckling distress calls are similar and, in addition, the scales of the tarsus form a reticulated pattern, a condition shared only with dendrocygnids and the equally puzzling freckled duck. Clearly, the white-backed duck is as much an aberrant stiff-tail as it is an aberrant whistling duck—and it may ultimately prove to be neither.

The stubby shape and posture of the white-backed duck makes them somewhat resemble a typical stiff-tail, but the distinctive rigid tail is lacking. Males and females are practically identical in size, shape, and color, and in some ways they have the appearance of dumpy grebes. They are really not well named, because the white back and white upper tail feathers are only visible when the birds are on the wing, which is not often. (Actually, the roundish white patch between the bill and the eye is much more diagnostic.)

Instead of diving when disturbed, these ducks tend to flatten out on the water in an attempt to make themselves less conspicuous. As a rule, they are very lethargic, and not nearly as active as some of the other representatives of the tribe; even during courtship, they appear to be rather undemonstrative. Vocalizations of adults recall those of

13.27

13.28

13.29

13.27 *Pair of masked ducks (male on left). Smallest of the stiff-tails, these little-known ducks are typically quiet and aloof, and they are seldom encountered in groups of more than 20 birds. They apparently fly more readily than is believed by most people. The four to six pale buff to buffy white eggs are decidedly smaller and smoother than those of the ruddy duck. While almost exclusively aquatic, masked ducks may nest on supporting vegetation or floating objects, and sometimes even at the water's edge or ashore.* PHOTO BY DALE CRIDER

13.28 *Typical masked duck country in the Dominican Republic. Tropical and subtropical swamps, or marshes that are densely overgrown with both emergent vegetation and extensive areas of floating leaf plants (such as water lilies and water hyacinths) are ideal habitats for these ducks. On occasion, they have been observed in mangrove swamps.*

13.29 *African white-backed duck male. These strange aquatic birds are seldom observed ashore. From time to time, they may rest on submerged objects. In this photo, the duck has pulled its legs into the flank feathers, although the foot is still clearly visible.*

guinea pigs or whistling ducks, and they may call when on the wing. Somewhat social, they are nevertheless not particularly gregarious, and although small groups may forage and even nest together from time to time, they are most often encountered in pairs or family units. In all probability, white-backed ducks are sedentary for the most part, but they may undertake occasional local movements.

Habitat preferences are identical to those of pygmy geese—quiet waters covered with water lilies. The nest consists of a floating mass of aquatic vegetation, which may be built up from an abandoned coot nest and is usually concealed from above. Little down is used to line the nest. The six to eight smooth-shelled eggs are rather large, pale rusty brown to light ocherous brown in color, and quite different altogether in appearance from typical stiff-tail eggs. In fact, they are among the darkest of waterfowl eggs, and it has been suggested that this may enable the white-backed ducks to distinguish their eggs from the bluish white ones of the maccoa duck, which sometimes parasitizes their nests.

Based on limited field data, it appears that pair bonds may be semi-permanent, but this has yet to be fully documented. Males do most of the incubating, a behavior which is atypical for stiff-tails but conforms to that of the whistling ducks. Incubation periods are reported to vary considerably, from 26 to 33 days (which is somewhat longer than most members of the tribe), and males also participate in rearing of the young. The downy offspring feed extensively on gnat larvae, whereas adults appear to be mainly vegetarian.

The two races of white-backed ducks are practically identical in appearance, except that those from Madagascar are smaller and darker than their mainland relatives. As a result of their distribution over a large range, the population of the mainland race (*T. l. leuconotus*) appears to be relatively stable and secure as a whole. The status of the Madagascan birds (*T. l. insularis*) is unknown, but luckily, because these little birds are considered to be inedible, they are not subjected to much hunting pressure. Nevertheless, their specialized habitat requirements would tend to make them vulnerable.

White-backed ducks are almost totally unknown to contemporary aviculturists. To my knowledge, as of early 1979 the entire captive adult population in the world consisted of 14 individuals: a single pair of Madagascan birds; an aged male and six recently acquired specimens of the African race deposited at the Wildfowl Trust, and five others in a private collection. Two *leuconotus* were reared for the first time in an English collection in 1978, and young of the Madagascan race were raised on several occasions back in the early 1930s. (Some African birds were hatched previously at the Wildfowl Trust but were not reared to maturity.) The extreme scarcity of *Thalassornis* in collections does not reflect disinterest on the part of aviculturists, but rather a general unavailability of breeding stock. Delacour summed up his experiences of many years ago by indicating that white-backed ducks are quiet, rather stupid little birds, which could easily come to grief on a large lake. On the other hand, I get the impression from those I've seen that they would probably thrive on a small pond if given half a chance.

The **musk duck** (*Biziura lobata*) has a discontinuous distribution in south and west Australia, as well as Tasmania. In appearance, it is undoubtedly one of the oddest of all waterfowl, and it is considered by some observers to be the most grotesque of ducks. For reasons unknown, the uropygial or preen gland of the male produces a strong musky odor during the breeding season, and this is responsible for the

13.31

13.32

13.30 (Opposite Page) *African white-backed duck male. These birds more typically assume a dumpy posture on the water (as illustrated in 13.31), but they sometimes swim with their necks extended and appear to be more alert.*

13.31 *African white-backed duck on quiet water.*

13.32 *The Madagascan white-backed duck is practically identical to its continental counterpart but tends to be slightly smaller and darker.*

13.33

rather descriptive vernacular name of the species. Interestingly, those that I have handled also had a distinct oily feel to them. Compared to the other stiff-tails, musk ducks are huge, and drakes weighing as much as eight and a half pounds have been reported (although four and a half pounds may be more typical, with the much smaller females weighing between two and three pounds).

These strange birds are considered to be the most specialized of the stiff-tails. They inhabit large permanent swamps, but they may move to saltwater estuaries during the austral winter and are sometimes even seen offshore. Extremely aquatic, they rarely come ashore, and when they do, they experience difficulty standing because their legs are placed so far back on the body. When moving on land, they are forced to slither across the ground on their bellies.

Fully mature adult males possess a large pendant-like pouch under the bill, which varies in size with age and season. This pouch is not hollow and cannot be inflated with air as some of the older literature indicates since there is no apparent connection with the windpipe. But it can be thickened considerably and distended at the base, and during periods of display it becomes turgid and enlarged. The turgidity is probably due to an increase in blood pressure, since the structure is well supplied with blood vessels. During the nonbreeding season, the pouch is loose and flaccid. In the past, writers tended to be much more florid in their use of language than those of today, and one cannot help but be amused at Captain George Vancouver's vivid musk duck description, which he penned in 1791: "A very peculiar one was shot, of a darkish gray plumage, with a bag like that of a lizard hanging under its throat, which smelt so intolerably of musk that it scented nearly the whole ship."

The courting antics of a musk duck drake are a sight to behold because they have a wide variety of movements and postures. Perhaps the most spectacular and bizarre display is the plonk kick, which is performed while the bird is relatively stationary in the water. The sequence begins with the head and tail being tilted upward, then the throat pouch is thickened and the cheeks and throat are expanded. Both legs are then simultaneously kicked, sending splashes of water backwards some seven to eight feet—and as the feet strike the water, a strange loud hollow "plunk" or "ker-plonk" resounds and echoes through the swamp. These mechanical sounds, which can be heard perhaps a half-mile away, were formerly thought to be vocal in origin.

Males have at least two distinctive calls—a cough-like sound, and an oft-repeated, shrill whistle that is clearly audible for several hundred yards. These calls are used to great effect when the drakes perform another spectacular display known as the whistle kick. To begin, they spread their tail and extend it forward so that it almost lies flat on the

back. The throat lobe is expanded to its fullest extent and the inflatable sac below the tongue is distended, causing the cheeks and throat to swell up considerably. Holding their heads low in the water with the bill tilted upward, they suddenly flick both feet simultaneously, splashing water out to the sides for several feet. With each splash, they utter a sharp clear whistle. This and other courtship sequences are commonly performed at night, perhaps because so many of them are so loud. Apparently, the displays of the eastern segment of the population are somewhat different from those of the west.

The literature indicates that it takes these birds "more than a year" to reach adulthood, but I suggest it could take considerably longer, if recent observations of two males and a female at the Wildfowl Trust are any indicator. It appears possible that the close presence of an older, dominate male may inhibit sexual maturity of a younger, subordinate male; and further, if the subordinate male is maintained with an adult female, she may intimidate him as well. The aforementioned dominant male at the Wildfowl Trust (which was at least seven years old) had a large throat pouch, whereas throat development was scarcely evident on the younger male (even though he was at least four years old). The older drake was maintained in a separate aviary, divided from the younger pair by a partition in the water that had a hole in it just large enough for the female to pass through. This

separation was necessary because it was feared that, in his zeal, the large male would kill her.

In June of 1978, the female laid an egg, which was unfortunately infertile. However, as a result of this nesting interest, the partition was removed one evening to allow the dominant male greater contact with the female—and not surprisingly, the subordinate male was immediately attacked. He scurried ashore and slithered through the grass with surprising speed, and since the older aggressive male continued hostilities, the younger male was ultimately removed from the aviary altogether for his own protection. The female was more circumspect, but she was finally overtaken and copulation was immediately attempted. It was apparently unsuccessful, however, and since the female was clearly in danger, the pair was separated and the partition replaced. (She subsequently laid another egg, but it too proved to be infertile. The whitish eggs were somewhat unusual for a stiff-tail in that they were not roundish but elliptical in shape.)

Musk ducks may come into breeding condition twice a year. Males establish territories and it is possible that more than one female will nest within a well-defended territory—but they apparently do not form pair bonds. As demonstrated by the Wildfowl Trust birds, the polygamous males are particularly aggressive during the breeding season, even to females. Copulation itself can be a brutal affair,

13.34 *The courting displays of the musk duck are no less spectacular than the physical appearance of the bird itself. This drake is performing a "whistle kick." Note that the tail is spread and lying almost flush along the back, and that the neck and cheeks are greatly inflated. The pendant lobe under the bill is expanded to form a turgid wedge. Given the name of this display, it should come as no surprise that the kick is accompanied by a sharp, clear whistle.*

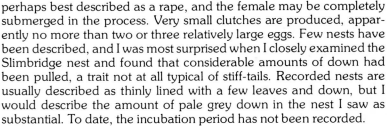

13.35

13.35 *Subadult male musk duck.*

13.36 *Drake musk duck with fish. These powerful ducks are almost exclusively carnivorous and will readily take a wide variety of life forms, including insects, crayfish, frogs, molluscs, and even young birds. Larger food items (such as a large fish) may be beaten on the water in an apparent attempt to break the prey apart so it can be more easily consumed.*

13.37 *Leopard seal with a half-eaten Adelie penguin. The behavior of the musk duck with large prey is surprisingly similar to that of the leopard seal. These large seals do not "pop" penguins out of their skins, as much of the literature suggests, but rather beat them apart on the surface of the water.*

13.36

13.37

perhaps best described as a rape, and the female may be completely submerged in the process. Very small clutches are produced, apparently no more than two or three relatively large eggs. Few nests have been described, and I was most surprised when I closely examined the Slimbridge nest and found that considerable amounts of down had been pulled, a trait not at all typical of stiff-tails. Recorded nests are usually described as thinly lined with a few leaves and down, but I would describe the amount of pale grey down in the nest I saw as substantial. To date, the incubation period has not been recorded.

The ducklings are essentially an unpatterned uniform dark brown-grey color except for their lighter brown bellies, and in this respect they are unlike the young of any other ducks, save those of the freckled duck. Unlike the other stiff-tails, *Biziura* ducklings are very reluctant divers. They often ride on the back of the female (yet another trait not shared by other stiff-tails), and reportedly, they will tightly grasp the nape feathers in such a way that the adults can dive carrying the young with them underwater. There are even some vague, unsubstantiated reports of flying females carrying young on their backs.

In addition, the ducklings are very dependent on the female for food, a characteristic they share only with magpie geese. When the female surfaces from a dive carrying food in her bill, the young approach her, uttering a food-begging call. Parental feeding continues throughout the juvenile rearing period, and young birds almost as large as adults have been observed being fed. This behavior is most curious, since young stiff-tails are usually incredibly independent, even when only a few days old. Johnsgard believes that this parent/chick feeding behavior may preclude a large clutch from the very start, since females could not possibly pay such close attention to more than a few ducklings.

Adults are always very pugnacious and quarrelsome. Essentially carnivorous, they consume all forms of small animal life, including molluscs, leeches, crustaceans, frogs, fish, and even other birds. I have observed captive birds eating six-inch-long fish without hesitation. (To break the fish down to eatable size, the ducks repeatedly slapped them on the surface of the water in much the same way that a leopard seal prepares a penguin for consumption.) On another occasion, I saw a male in an obviously excited state patrolling back and forth along a thickly vegetated bank. Upon closer examination, I discovered a brood of young dusky moorhens hidden in the vegetation. The musk duck could obviously hear them, and had the female moorhen not prevented them from entering the water, the chicks would surely have been eaten.

Because of their foul smell and poor taste, musk ducks have never been highly regarded by waterfowlers, but they were nevertheless smoked and eaten in former times when nothing better was available. Like the other Australian stiff-tail, the blue-billed duck, musk ducks occasionally become entangled in fish nets and drown, and mortality of this type can be surprisingly high in some areas. The species is not thought to be in any current danger, however, although loss of appropriate habitat could be deleterious.

As with many Australian birds, aviculturists have unfortunately had almost no contact with the musk duck. At the beginning of 1979, only three specimens existed outside of Australia—the aforementioned Slimbridge birds. Apparently, these intriguing birds have been captively bred in Australia, but even there, it has only occurred on very few occasions. Of course, considering their temperament and the need to maintain the sexes separately, it is unlikely that they would

13.39

ever enjoy wide appeal, even if they were readily available. They are definitely a connoisseur's duck.

The South American **black-headed duck** (*Heteronetta atricapilla*) is unique because it is essentially an obligate parasitic nester. That is, these birds apparently construct no nest whatsoever and lay their eggs in the nests of other species—something that no other waterfowl species is forced to do. Because this behavior is reminiscent of the parasitic cuckoos, black-headed ducks are sometimes referred to as "cuckoo ducks." (However, a female black-headed duck has been observed on at least *one* occasion with flightless young, and this casts some doubt upon their *total* dependence on other species.)

The black-headed duck is probably the most generalized of the stiff-tailed ducks both behaviorally and anatomically, and the current placement of these birds with the Oxyurini is due mainly to similarities in courtship and breeding biology, as well as some anatomical features. Their diving ability is rudimentary compared to the other stiff-tails, and as a result, they usually upend to feed like dabbling ducks; females even more so than the males. (In some of the earlier literature, these birds were included with the dabblers.) They are apparently incapable of submerging gradually like some of the typical stiff-tails. In addition, their relatively long and slender bills (which are slightly spatulate) are more adapted to surface feeding, and on numerous occasions I have seen them feed in a manner that resembles filter feeding. Mainly vegetarian, they may obtain at least a portion of their food by straining mud in shallow water. They rarely come ashore (except possibly to sleep), and although they walk rather poorly, they may stand in shallow water to preen.

Courtship behavior is peculiar, and one display of the black-headed duck has caused them to be referred to as "pato sapos" or toad ducks by some natives. In this "toad posture," the head is held low, the throat and cheeks are inflated to twice the normal size, and the head is pumped rapidly. A strange low grunt is produced, followed by a faint whistle. Females characteristically make a clucking sound, but as a rule are rather silent. They have no eclipse plumage but during the breeding season the base of the male's greyish blue-black bill becomes rosy-red, and that of the female may turn yellowish orange or yellowish pink.

Black-headed ducks do form definite pair bonds, but the bond is weak and no territory is defended (which is not surprising in light of their parasitic nesting habits). The eggs bear no resemblance to the characteristic thick-shelled, rough-surfaced eggs of the ruddy duck; and because black-headed ducks are not host specific, their eggs have been recorded in nests of not only other waterfowl, but those of coots, gulls, egrets, ibises, rails, and other birds as well. Altogether, *Heteronetta* eggs have been recorded from the nests of at least 18 species of birds—including even the nests of predatory snail kites.

Most of the eggs probably hatch, but current evidence suggests that the survival rate may not be high. (It is unlikely that a kite, for example, could rear a duckling.) Fortunately for the species, ducklings are reportedly capable of leaving the host within several days. To maintain a viable population, it is probable that a large number of eggs must be laid, and this may explain why the laying season extends up to three months. Ducklings are extremely downy and float very high on the water. They rather resemble the young of other stiff-tails, except for

313

13.40

13.41

13.40 *Female black-headed ducks may be larger than their mates. As illustrated here, they come ashore on occasion but are rather cumbersome when they do. These ducks are the only completely parasitic nesters among the waterfowl and they lay extraordinarily large eggs. They parasitize the nests of a great variety of aquatic birds but appear to prefer those of coots, at least in some regions. The eggs may fail to hatch in some cases, either because they get buried under the coot eggs or because they are laid too late to hatch simultaneously with those of the host species. Nevertheless, this bizarre reproductive arrangement is successful frequently enough to accomplish the continuation of the species. It is clear that their rather wide choice of hosts has worked to assure the success of the species far more effectively than dependency on a single species.*

13.41 *Black-headed duck duckling. Ducklings rather resemble other stiff-tail young but are more brightly colored and have thicker down — probably a necessity for a species that is not brooded. Recent observations support the theory that the young are essentially independent upon hatching. Black-headed ducks are not endangered, but their habitat requirements are rather critical.*

13.42 *(Opposite Page) Drake white-headed duck. The shape of this typical stiff-tail differs significantly from that of the black-headed duck.*

their yellow and brown spotted pattern, and a dark eye stripe (which is more like that on the downy young of some dabblers). The significantly thicker down is probably a requirement for a species that is not brooded. If startled, *Heteronetta* ducklings tend to freeze instead of diving as a typical stiff-tail would. Black-headed ducks fly easily and rapidly (but reluctantly during the day), and can become airborne without prolonged skittering over the water surface—presumably an adaptation to life in small pools, where a steep takeoff is often necessary. This is an ability they share with the masked duck, but is not typical of the other Oxyurini. Within their restricted range, these ducks can be considered reasonably common.

Due to their unavailability, little has been done with these ducks in captivity until recently. Breeding success was achieved for the first time in 1977 at the Wildfowl Trust, and the Assistant Director, Mike Lubbock, has made a number of observations that have added considerably to our knowledge of the breeding biology of this interesting species. In one case, a pair of black-headed ducks was observed to *force* an incubating Argentine red shoveler from the nest, and within five minutes the female *Heteronetta* was seen to lay an egg of her own.

Incubation periods were found to range from 20 to 25 days, and even though this is somewhat longer than that of the host species, in most cases the parasitic eggs hatched at *precisely* the same time as the other eggs in the nest. This hatching consistency was noted with a variety of species, and apparently, the pipping of the host eggs triggers a hatching response in the *Heteronetta* eggs so that all eggs in the nest hatch simultaneously. It is clear that the variability in the incubation period of the black-headed duck is a necessity if they are to successfully reproduce in such a bizarre manner. Data obtained during the captive rearing of the young support the theory that the ducklings are totally independent upon hatching.

Breeding success at the Wildfowl Trust has been so great that it seems likely that black-headed ducks will become established in other collections in the near future, and several were sent to America in 1978. Host species are obviously required if the birds are to be bred, and such ducks as Argentine red shovelers and rosy-billed pochards seem ideal for this purpose. The young are best reared in the manner of a typical stiff-tail.

14
Screamers
Anhimidae

Superficially, the three distinct species of neotropical screamers bear no resemblance whatsoever to typical wildfowl, but they are surprisingly closely related to ducks and geese, and this kinship is clearly demonstrated by a number of anatomical affinities. For this reason, they are included in the same order as the waterfowl, in the separate family Anhimidae. Nevertheless, their systematic position as second cousins to the waterfowl still appears farfetched. Considering their external appearance, it would be no real surprise to discover that they were modified gamebirds; and the real surprise is that they are not. When all is said and done, the evidence seems to leave no doubt that screamers and waterfowl do share a common ancestor.

Some ornithologists suggest that anhimids are linked with the rails and their allies, while others contend that they are relatives of the storks and other ciconiids. Most likely, however, screamers may repre-

14.2

14.1 (Opposite Page) *Black-necked screamer with young. Screamers, unlike true waterfowl, generally construct substantial nests of rushes and reeds on the ground. Like swans and whistling ducks, both sexes incubate.*

14.2 *Black-necked screamer in a swamp. The perching ability of these rather ungainly birds is well-illustrated here.*

sent an ancestral link between the curassows (arboreal gamebirds of South America) and the equally strange magpie goose. Like the magpie goose, screamers undergo a graduated wing molt and bypass the annual flightless period that is typical of all the other waterfowl.

The ungainly semi-terrestrial screamers have the appearance of birds that have been constructed from leftover avian parts. Standing three feet tall, they are about as large as a large goose, but their strong bills are relatively short, hooked at the tip, and *distinctly* fowl-like. The feathers of the head are short, soft, and downy; and the head is comparatively small and slender. The moderately long legs and feet are disproportionately large and thick, even for such massive birds, with a long hind toe that is located on the same plane as the front three (an advantage to a walking species), and these birds walk with a peculiar slow and deliberate gait that is somewhat dignified. Interestingly, although the long toes exhibit merely a trace of webbing,

screamers are excellent (if somewhat reluctant) swimmers. They are perhaps best known for two long, curved, extremely sharp spurs that protrude from the leading edge of their wings. These spurs may be up to two inches in length, and combined with the powerful wings, make screamers potentially dangerous, particularly during the breeding season. Broken-off spurs have been found buried in the breasts of some

14.4

screamers, indicating fierce battles. Males and females are essentially indistinguishable from one another.

Unlike most species of birds, screamers lack distinct feather tracts; instead, their feathers grow continuously over the body without bare spaces between tracts. This is considered to be a primitive trait that is shared only by ostriches, penguins, and African mousebirds or colies. Screamers are also the only living birds that have not developed an uncinate process—an overlapping rib projection that strengthens the rib cage by serving as a supporting cross strut. So far as is known, the only other avian species that lacked an uncinate process was *Archaeopteryx*, the earliest known fossil bird, which became extinct at least 140 million years ago.

Among their other unique features, screamers have developed the hollowness of their bones to a greater degree than any other living bird. Practically all of their bones are hollow, including even the end of the spine and the distal digits of the wings and toes. In addition, a network of air sacs lies under the loose skin, a condition which screamers share with pelicans and boobies. When the skin is squeezed, the air sacs crackle audibly. The function of these sacs is not known, but with such species as brown pelicans and boobies subcutaneous air sacs may serve as shock absorbers when they dive from considerable heights into the water. Screamers do not dive, although their surprising swimming ability is no doubt due in part to their skeletal pneumaticity and the presence of the subcutaneous air sacs.

Screamers inhabit marshes, wet grasslands, open savannahs, and forest lagoons of South America, where they are frequently observed walking on floating masses of vegetation. As large as they are, their long toes increase the surface area of the foot and more equally distribute their weight, making it possible for them to move about in much the same manner as the jacanas or lilly trotters. Mainly vegetarian, screamers feed principally on succulent grasses and seeds from aquatic plants. In captivity, they consume unbelievable amounts of lettuce.

Like most of the true waterfowl, screamers are strong fliers, but rise rather heavily. Once aloft, however, they frequently fly to considerable heights and may *soar* for hours with their long legs trailing behind them—another behavioral trait that sets them apart from typical waterfowl. Sometimes, they will spiral high up into the sky until they are almost out of sight, not unlike vultures, and in general, their flight characteristics parallel those of the magpie goose. They tend to be extremely gregarious, and may gather during the nonbreeding season in flocks numbering a thousand or more individuals.

Screamers are so named for their powerful, far-carrying vocalizations, which are sometimes clearly audible at a distance of two miles. The calls of the sexes are similar, although that of the male is slightly lower. Frequently, the screaming of one bird will stimulate others to join in, and the ensuing chorus can be deafening. During the breeding season, mates frequently call back and forth, and while the sonorous trumpeting vocalizations are rather pleasing at first, prolonged repetition can soon make them an annoyance. Their loud, unmelodic calls have made them unpopular with hunters, since they tend to give an alarm at the approach of danger, alerting game animals to impending peril. When alarmed, screamers are apt to retreat to the treetops, where they can easily view the cause of the disturbance from a safe distance. Apart from their loud calls, they are also capable of producing a throaty sound that somewhat resembles drumming, and this may possibly function as a close-range threat behavior. (Some of the literature indicates that these noises may be produced through distension of the subcutaneous air sacs.)

Anhimids possess a strong pair bond and may mate for life. Courtship displays are comparatively rudimentary and consist mainly of antiphonal calling or dueting, mutual preening, and a rapid opening and closing of the bill. Usually, they nest on the ground or in shallow water, constructing a rather large untidy nest of bushes and reeds. Both sexes participate in nest construction, and by the time it is completed, the nest may rise up several feet from a watery base. There is some evidence which suggests that some nesting material may be carried to the nest site, and if this is the case, it conforms with the behavior of some gamebirds but is totally unlike the nest building habits of typical waterfowl. The eggs are relatively large, have slightly granular shells which are white (sometimes tinged with buff or pale green), and two to six constitute a normal clutch. Incubation is shared by both sexes, and takes from 42 to 44 days; somewhat longer than most waterfowl, except for the torrent ducks. Upon hatching, chicks are covered with thick yellowish to greyish down which shades to white ventrally, and like the adults, their legs and feet are huge. Chicks somewhat resemble recently-hatched goslings except, of course, for the feet and bill. Newly-hatched screamers remain in the nest for only a short period and then wander about led by the parents, sometimes returning to the nest to roost at night. Because the preen glands of newly-hatched chicks are not functional, the adults will sometimes oil them from their uropygial glands.

All species are hunted to some extent by the natives—the **crested or southern screamer** (*Chauna torquata*) apparently more so than the others. Crested screamers are the most gregarious of the group and commonly graze in open grasslands or cultivated fields, often in association with domestic farm stock. They range throughout Brazil and Bolivia, and the northern half of Argentina. Noted for a conspicuous black collar of velvety feathers at the base of the neck, they also have a prominent crest of pointed feathers on the back of the head. Two color phases exist, one significantly darker than the other. The

14.5

14.6

14.3 (Opposite Page) *African jacana or lily-trotter. The extremely long toes of screamers and jacanas distribute their weight over a larger area and make it possible for them to walk on floating vegetation.*

14.4 (Opposite Page) *Unlike most true waterfowl, screamers do not have webbed feet. Interestingly, this does not appear to compromise their swimming ability.*

14.5 *African mousebird or coly. With the exception of mousebirds, ostriches, and penguins, screamers are the only birds that lack feather tracts. As a result, feathers grow at random all over their bodies.*

14.6 *Pair of crested screamers engaged in mutual preening (or allopreening). This "affectionate" behavior may serve to strengthen pair bonds.*

14.7

14.8

14.7 *The origin of the horned screamer's vernacular name is obvious. Curiously, the horn or spike is not rigidly attached to the skull, and this presumably precludes its use as a combat weapon.*

14.8 *Pair of black-necked screamers. Screamers are surprisingly powerful fliers, but tend to rise from the ground or water rather heavily. In flight, their wings produce loud swishing sounds.*

14.9 *Crested screamer with quarter-grown young. Upon hatching, screamers rather resemble newly-hatched goslings — except, of course, for their feet and bills.*

14.10 *Crested screamer. The distinctive spurs on the forward edge of the wing can be clearly seen on this bird. The powerful wings would be effective weapons even without the spurs, but the addition of these barbs makes screamers highly dangerous, particularly when they are nesting or defending young.*

14.9

14.10

14.11

14.12

14.11 *Portrait of a black-necked screamer. It is easy to see how screamers can be confused with gamebirds. Superficially, they appear to have little in common with waterfowl, but the required anatomical and behavioral similarities exist nonetheless and there can be no question that true waterfowl and screamers are rather closely related.*

14.12 *Crested or southern screamer. These birds inhabit tropical and subtropical areas in marshes, on wet savannas, and along lagoon borders. They are commonly observed with domestic cattle, particularly in Argentina.*

native name "chaja" is taken from their distinctive double-noted trumpeting call.

Northern or black-necked screamers (*Chauna chavaria*) are noted for clearly defined white cheeks and throats. They also have long crests, and as with the southern screamer, the bare skin about the eye is rosy in color. This species is currently restricted to the lowland marshes, river banks, and forest lagoons of northern Colombia and northwestern Venezuela.

The **horned screamer** (*Anhima cornuta*) is the largest of the group, weighing up to ten pounds. It derives its name from a weird frontal spike (which may be up to six inches in length) that curves forward from the forehead toward the bill. This spike (or "horn") grows continuously, but tends to break off if the length becomes excessive. It is not firmly attached to the skull and sways back and forth as the bird shakes its head, and since it lacks rigidity, it is unlikely that this strange projection serves any real function in combat. Its main value may be as a useful bluff device, making the birds appear to be more formidable than they actually are; or it may be associated with courtship, although it is carried by both sexes.

Horned screamers are not shy, but are the least vocal of the screamers. They have a call which sounds like "mo-hoo-ca," and this has led some Indians to refer to them as Mohookas. Both sexes have a bright orange iris, while the other two species are noted for dark eyes. Essentially a bird of the wet savannas and swampy forests of the tropical zone, they range widely but locally throughout northern South America, particularly east of the Andes. They frequent exposed river bars and banks, and are generally encountered in pairs. In former times, they occupied Trinidad, where they were incorrectly referred to as "wild turkeys."

Screamers are not rare in the wild. Not infrequently, they are maintained by the natives with their chickens, and it is said that the anhimids will defend their farmyard companions against birds of prey and other potential predators. In addition, they are efficient "watchdogs," raising a fuss whenever there is a disturbance. In this respect, they recall the behavior of African guinea fowl.

Up until a few years ago, screamers were not particularly uncommon in zoological collections, with the black-necked variety being the most common, at least in North America. However, due to severe avian import and quarantine restrictions, they are no longer as common in collections as they once were. Some zoos, particularly in South America, allow screamers to roam unrestricted about the grounds, a practice that I view as potentially dangerous. The long sharp spurs could easily injure an eye, and there is no question that an angry screamer could quickly maim—or even kill—a small child that might be tormenting it. Since screamers fiercely defend their young, they can be doubly dangerous during the breeding season.

As a rule, all screamers do very well in captivity, are relatively long-lived, and easy to maintain. However, they appear to be sensitive to cold and must be protected during the winter months, since their toes are susceptible to frostbite. The less tropical birds from more southern regions appear to be more hardy in this regard. Screamers have been bred from time to time, but these successes have been rather infrequent. Interestingly, those that I have bred tended to nest on top of something, such as a large box, rather than on the ground as they would in the wild.

15
Captive Display, Maintenance and Propagation

Mankind has been fascinated for centuries by birds of all varieties—in particular by waterfowl, pheasants, pigeons, parrots, and a number of exotic finches. As a result of this fascination, many generations have been moved to painstakingly provide for birds in captivity, and perhaps the greatest emphasis in captive maintenance has been placed on waterfowl. Of all the groups of birds in the world, the wildfowl seem to lend themselves best to display and propagation in a controlled environment; not only because so many of them are colorful and strikingly patterned, but also because of their dispositions, habits, and minimal maintenance requirements. Certainly, no other avian group has been so intensively maintained and propagated by man for strictly aesthetic or ornamental purposes. It was not until well into the 20th Century, however, that the role of propagation within a controlled environment began to emerge as a significant major conservation consideration.

The accomplished aviculturist is a highly motivated and skilled specialist, and for some endangered avian species this is most fortunate—because these birds are (or were) so close to extinction in the

15.2

wild that they would probably not survive without some human assistance. Certainly, this is true of the Hawaiian Nene goose, the Hawaiian duck or koloa, the Laysan teal, and possibly even the Aleutian Canada goose (to cite but a few of the endangered waterfowl). The decline and apparent subsequent recovery of the Nene is perhaps the most dramatic example of the importance of managed captive propagation, and serves to illustrate the expanding role of skilled aviculturists in a modern, rapidly changing, highly mechanized society.

In the late 1940s, biologists estimated that no more than 40 Nene geese survived in the highlands of Hawaii; hardly a viable population. These geese were probably never overly numerous, but there may have been as many as 25,000 of them on the islands during the 1800s. Why they declined so drastically is not known with certainty, but it is possible that they were unable to cope with predation by introduced non-native terrestrial predators—such as feral dogs and pigs, rats, and the infamous mongoose, which has been severely detrimental to many Hawaiian avian species. (Curiously, the mongoose was originally brought to Hawaii to control yet another introduced species, the rat.)

Generally, insular or island species are highly specialized life forms. Most have evolved in isolation, in an environment where terrestrial

15.1 (Opposite Page) *Often, proper management of a public wildfowl collection requires the construction of barriers to keep the birds where they belong and the people where they belong. There are many ways to accomplish this, but one of the most visually appealing is the use of barriers that are mainly psychological. In this instance, the birds are separated from the public by a thick hedge of natal plum (shown to the right of the photo), but other thick plant material can be effective as well. Natural barriers of this type are more difficult to establish initially than the more typical chain link fence, and they require more upkeep — but the end result is well worth the extra effort.*

15.2 *Ideally, public waterfowl exhibits should not only provide adequate facilities for ducks, geese, and swans, but should be botanical showcases as well. It is especially important in public situations to present the birds under optimum conditions — and this means giving much thought to the design of the water area, proper planting, water quality, appropriate viewing areas, etc. The needs of both visitors and birds must be kept in mind. Properly designed waterfowl exhibits must have the appropriate land/water ratio for the species that will be maintained within them. (Obviously, for example, a trumpeter swan will require more water than a puna teal.)*

predators are absent; and as a result, they have developed few, if any, defenses. In the absence of terrestrial predator pressure, some species have even degenerated to a flightless state and have become remarkably trusting. Unfortunately, their specialization makes insular species very vulnerable to changes in their environment, and in particular to man's interference with the ecological balance.

In the case of the Nene, man not only introduced exotic predators, but also subjected the geese to a great deal of hunting pressure. There are vivid accounts in the literature of commercial hunting parties returning from the mountains with muleloads of slaughtered Hawaiian geese. These were often sent by clipper ship to California to feed the Forty Niners, or were salted down for whaling ships. Hunting was prohibited in 1911, but by then the geese were virtually gone.

In a desperate effort to preserve the species, three Nene were sent to the Wildfowl Trust in England in 1950. This unique institution, founded by Sir Peter Scott in 1946, is dedicated to the study and preservation of the world's waterfowl, and is well-known internationally for its excellent achievements in the conservation of ducks, geese, and swans. The Nene stock sent to the Trust originated from a flock maintained by an Hawaiian rancher named Harold Shipman, who initiated captive work with the geese in 1918. At first, breeding success with the Nene at the Wildfowl Trust was limited, but gradually the results improved and hundreds have been reared. Ultimately, some 200 were sent back to the wilds of Hawaii. Fortunately for the Nene, the remoteness of their barren and inhospitable range has thus far prevented man from seriously altering their habitat, and upland habitat is still available to receive them.

Currently, the Wildfowl Trust, the Hawaiian Division of Fish and Game, and numerous zoological institutions and private aviculturists throughout Europe and America are producing hundreds of these geese annually, and some 1200 now exist in collections around the world. Thus far, some 1600 captively-reared Nene have been liberated on Hawaii and Maui. As of 1976, approximately 750 geese existed in the wild—650 on Hawaii and 100 on Maui. (Reproductive success has not been as great on Maui, and it may be that the larger amount of rainfall on that island is affecting the survival rate of the goslings.) Undoubtedly, without the assistance of captive propagation, the Hawaiian goose would have joined the extinct dodo years ago.

Other endangered species have faced (and are facing) similar tragic predicaments. During the years 1911-12, for example, the total population of Laysan teal was reportedly reduced to only seven individuals—and indeed, some authorities are of the belief that by 1930 the entire population may have consisted of but a single gravid female. If this is true, the entire world population arose from that lone female, incredible as it may seem. (Supposedly she laid a replacement clutch after the first was destroyed by a curlew.)

Laysan Island is merely a dot in the Pacific, only two miles long and one mile wide, consisting of little more than 700 acres with a single central lagoon of brackish water. Nearby Lisianski Island was also said to be inhabited by the teal during the early part of the 19th Century. Man's introduction of rabbits to Laysan Island was a main cause of the precipitous decline. The rabbits first arrived in 1903, and within 20 years they had consumed most of the native vegetation. The ducks began to disappear rapidly as a consequence. (Even prior to the rabbit era, however, Laysan teal were subjected to severe hunting pressure by commercial guano diggers, and there is also some evidence that Japanese feather hunters worked the island.)

Fortunately, rabbits no longer inhabit Laysan Island, but the teal population remains very cyclic, fluctuating from year to year. It was estimated at only 69 teal in 1977, but during 1978 the situation improved, and it may have increased to between 350 and 400 ducks. In all probability, the population has never exceeded 700, even during the best of years. These apparently drastic fluctuations may be natural, and could be related to weather (violent hurricanes) or to reproductive failure of the brine flies upon which the teal feed; or indeed, to other entirely unknown factors. The surviving teal on the island have evolved into essentially nocturnal insectivorous birds that are not dependent on the presence of fresh water.

Despite the remoteness of Laysan Island and official attempts to isolate the teal from human interference, the birds remain vulnerable in their natural habitat. The limited size of the island and the small size of the population make it impossible to assure a large enough gene pool to insure the survival of the species—and variable natural forces (such as storms, food supply, etc.) cannot be controlled at all. Due to the dedication of avicultural propagationists, however, there are currently hundreds of Laysan teal in waterfowl collections all over the world, and the chances of extinction have been greatly reduced.

This success, of course, should not be construed to imply that captive breeding is the answer to the plight of all endangered species—but it can be the answer for many (at least in the short run). Ultimately, the success of such activity in most cases must be judged by the degree to which species can be successfully re-introduced to their natural habitats. Tremendous numbers of captive-reared Nene, Aleutian Canada geese, masked bobwhite quail, and Swinhoe's pheasants have been re-introduced back into the wild. This has been a slow, long-term process and the evidence suggests that these releases have not always achieved the success initially hoped for. But there are positive signs that success can ultimately be achieved, as in the case of the Nene.

Perhaps the most difficult of all problems that re-introduction programs must overcome is the condition of the original habitat itself. If it has been completely destroyed or significantly altered, it must be restored to its former condition before re-introduction can be attempted. Obviously, if non-native predators were responsible for the decline of a species, it is unlikely that the birds can be re-established until the unwanted competitors are removed, or at least controlled. To this end, governments of the countries involved must be committed to the project, because a release program is doomed to failure without local support. Until such environmental and political problems can be solved, however, a captive reservoir of wildlife can at least be maintained and held in trust for future human generations until such time as their native homelands are suitable for their return.

Ironically, many of the people who are doing the most good in terms of propagation and public education are presently being subjected to well-meaning, but unjustified, attacks. Certain individuals and organizations naively (and bitterly) complain that there can be no justification whatsoever for maintaining an animal in captivity. Often, these attacks are based more on emotion than scientific fact—but many of the special-interest groups behind them are extremely vocal and well-financed, and lawmakers have tended to overreact by passing a great deal of overly restrictive, controversial, exotic animal oriented legislation. In some instances, it is difficult to fault the intentions behind *some* of these statutes, but the endless miles of bureaucratic red tape that they engender with regard to interpretation and enforcement is

15.3 (Opposite Page) *A small portion of the large flock of Nene that is maintained at the Wildfowl Trust in England. Hundreds of Nene are currently being reared in waterfowl collections around the world. The captive rearing of the endangered Hawaiian goose is one of the outstanding avicultural success stories, because it has been instrumental in assuring the survival of the species.*

15.4

making it increasingly difficult (if not impossible) for many propagators and even institutions to carry on with this essential work. The problem is so acute that many of the larger zoological institutions have been forced to retain the services of full-time bio-legislative analysts, and some private breeders no longer work with endangered species.

It is of especial interest to note that some legislation which was initially proposed to help preserve and protect wildlife may turn out to be *detrimental* to the survival of a number of species. Since life first appeared on this planet, millions of species have emerged and disappeared for a variety of reasons, but it would be a sad commentary on our times if some misguided individuals, organizations, or bureaucrats were permitted to legislate certain life forms out of existence. Extinction is final, and once it occurs, it is absolutely irreversible; the void is left for eternity. A destroyed painting or building can conceivably be re-created, but man with all his technical skill will never be able to resurrect the great auk, the Labrador duck, or the passenger pigeon. It is most tragic that many protectionist groups, while meaning well, may in some instances be doing more harm than good.

In many respects, the controversies regarding aviculture and endangered species have arisen from basic differences in philosophy. For example, there are some self-proclaimed experts who suggest that maintaining and propagating a species in captivity is totally pointless, because sooner or later the resulting progeny will no longer be exactly the same as the originals. There may conceivably be some slight validity to this argument, but the idea of abandoning captive work and letting nature take its course is still totally absurd. Personally, I would rather see one pair of the now extinct Labrador duck living in captivity (no matter how much they differed from the original birds) than a hundred perfect "pure" specimens lying on their backs in a dusty museum drawer.

Not unlike many of the species that propagators work with, American aviculturists may presently be an endangered species—but despite the bureaucratic harassment, the serious business of captive breeding continues. In this activity, numerous specialized techniques of professional management are utilized to achieve the highest possible level of success. Obviously, the serious aviculturist must consider such factors as water quality, enclosure size, habitat within an enclosure, mixing of compatible species, proper diet, adequate nesting facilities, etc.

To begin with, care must be exercised to make sure that closely related species are not maintained together, since hybridization must be prevented. Hybrids are significant and interesting taxonomically because they provide important clues for determining evolutionary relationships, but from a propagation standpoint the aviculturist has a greater obligation to maintain pure blood lines. Waterfowl are very prone to hybridize and more than 400 inter-species hybrids have been recorded. As a rule, a species is considered a distinct entity because it is reproductively isolated and rarely successfully mates with another species—but obviously, in the case of the waterfowl the rules regarding this matter have been somewhat bent. Subspecies are even more prone to hybridize. A subspecies is generally defined as a group of individuals of a species that shows variation in size and plumage as a result of geographic or ecological isolation. Occasionally, non-related birds of the same species must be brought into the collection to prevent the complications associated with inbreeding. If this is not done, the progeny will tend to become genetically weaker generation by generation, and the reproductive potential will fall off considerably.

Hybrids

15.4 *Redhead x American merganser.*

15.5 *A hybrid in the making — drake wood duck mating with an African yellowbill. While hybrids are interesting, and are often more colorful than either parent, hybridization should not be encouraged. One of the primary responsibilities of aviculturists is the maintenance of genetically pure bloodlines. But preventing hybridization involves constant vigilance on the part of the aviculturist.*

15.6 (Opposite Page) *European eider x European shelduck.*

15.5

15.7

There are numerous methods used to propagate and rear waterfowl—probably as many techniques as there are breeders, in fact. Some aviculturists prefer to leave the eggs with the adult, and allow them to hatch and rear their own young. Others remove the young shortly after hatching and hand rear them. The level of success obtained utilizing these methods depends entirely upon the circumstances and the species involved. Swans, for example, are usually quite reliable and generally can be depended upon to be good parents, while smaller species are not always as dependable, and the risk of predation is ever present. Frequently, eggs and young are lost merely as a result of carelessness on the part of the adults, or because of interference from other birds. For this reason, many experienced breeders remove the eggs and incubate them artificially, using specially bred bantam chickens or mechanical incubators for that purpose. While this method requires a great deal more work and skill, it significantly increases the reproductive potential. Then too, because a female that loses a clutch during early incubation will often lay an-

15.8

15.7 Collecting European black scoter eggs. Obtaining new blood from wild stock via eggs is usually advantageous since eggs travel better than newly-hatched young or adults (provided that adequate equipment, such as field incubators, etc., is available). Also, hand-reared young are more prone to breed in captivity than wild-caught adults. If incubated (or "hot") eggs are collected, they must be kept warm, and styrofoam containers are frequently used for this purpose until the eggs can be transferred to a portable field incubator. Natural down is often used to cushion the eggs during transport and to aid in keeping them warm.

15.8 - 15.10 As this aviculturist found out, collecting goose eggs can be hazardous. Geese fiercely defend their nests and can severely beat an intruder with their powerful wings — they are even capable of knocking a grown man to the ground. The gander is the main aggressor, but if pressed enough, the incubating female will also leave the nest and join in the battle.

15.11 A variety of waterfowl eggs in an electric forced-air incubator. With larger incubators such as this one, the eggs are turned automatically. Prior to being placed in either a mechanical incubator or under broody bantams, eggs are often stored, since it is far better to set a full clutch at once than to set single eggs as they are laid. Eggs can be safely stored for up to ten days, provided they are kept cool and turned daily.

15.12 (Opposite Page) The young of some species, such as this white-headed duck, require specialized care and modified rearing techniques. Stiff-tails are notoriously more difficult to rear than the young of dabblers and they should be started out immediately on water.

15.9

15.11

other, the removal of a clutch will often stimulate greater productivity. This is most significant with some of the rarer species, because theoretically twice as many birds can be reared—and in some cases, three fertile clutches may even result.

When eggs are collected for artificial incubation, they should be candled. Candling is simply the process of shining a strong light through the egg to visually determine fertility. By the tenth day, most experienced breeders can confirm fertility in this manner, and as incubation progresses they can also determine how far into incubation the egg is by merely examining the size and position of the air sac. Infertile and nonviable eggs should be removed from the incubators as soon as possible. If this is not done, they tend to spoil and can contaminate the good eggs—and if left too long, they can explode. When candling is not practical, as in the field, eggs can be "floated" in water to establish fertility and state of incubation. The axis along which the egg aligns itself, combined with the buoyancy it shows in the water, indicates the state of incubation. Non-incubated eggs can be safely stored at temperatures between 50 and 60 degrees Fahrenheit, but they must be turned daily and set within ten days. Recent work suggests that egg storage at even cooler temperatures (i.e., just above freezing) may be even *more* beneficial.

15.10

Many propagators use artificial or dummy eggs which approximate the size, color, and weight of the eggs of a specific species. As eggs are laid, they are removed and replaced with the dummy eggs. Replacement of the eggs with a substitute is important because it keeps the female faithful to the nest site and she will continue to lay. However, in the case of a few species, such as the garganey teal and pygmy goose, this technique can be considered counter-productive, since the nest site may be abandoned if disturbed. When down appears in the nest, it generally indicates that the entire clutch has been laid. The dummy eggs can then be removed and frequently the female will lay again. Once the total clutch is pulled, all signs of down should be removed and new nesting material added so that other birds might use the site.

If eggs are to be collected for artificial incubation, it must be done with a minimum of disturbance. Birds on the nest should not be flushed, as they may not return. In the case of larger geese and swans, removing eggs from an occupied nest can be hazardous. Defending swans and geese often attack without hesitation, and unless great care is exercised, serious injury can result to the aviculturist or the attacking birds (or both). Sometimes, clutches are not discovered until incubation has commenced, and if these "hot" eggs are collected, they must be kept warm and moved immediately to the incubator or broody bantam. A basket or other container filled with copious amounts of natural down is the best way to transport hot eggs. In the field, portable self-contained incubators will be required if incubated eggs are to be collected.

Waterfowl nest in a variety of ways. Some prefer the open while others seek thick vegetation, and still others are exclusively cavity nesters. Most hole-nesting ducks will readily take to nest boxes which, depending on the species involved, must vary in size. The diameter of the entrance hole and shape of the nest box can be very important, as some ducks have rather specific requirements. The inside of the vertical boxes must not be smooth because incubating females could easily be trapped within, and the boxes should be designed to facilitate easy egg removal. Placement of the boxes can also be extremely important, and in some cases they must be over water and ramped. In general, each pair of birds should have a variety of boxes to choose from.

In the case of collections where the general public has access, natural-looking nesting logs should be provided because the typical nesting box, although effective, is not visually appealing. Unfortunately, hollow logs of the appropriate size are often difficult to acquire, so many zoos are now creating their own "natural" logs. These artificial reproductions are often impossible to tell from real logs, and the birds do not hesitate to use them. Palm stumps make excellent nesting hollows as well. A chainsaw can be used to hollow them out and to cut entrance holes of appropriate size. The upright log should then be partially buried in the ground and sphagnum moss can be used as nesting material. The moss serves to keep the humidity up and is an excellent substrate for the eggs and incubating hen.

The lifestyles of most waterfowl are governed by the seasons. The availability of specific food material varies seasonally, for example, and these dietary shifts must be taken into account when captive diets are planned. This is particularly important for collections which are maintained in regions where winters are severe. During the winter, corn and grain should be increased to build the birds up—but, as the breeding season approaches the grain should be cut back and more protein added to the diet. Geese, in particular, tend to become too fat if

offered an abundance of grain throughout the year, and they may not lay as a result. Crushed oyster shell should also be available during the breeding season, to provide additional calcium and help prevent soft-shelled eggs. Some species, such as mergansers, eiders, buffle-heads, goldeneyes, scoters, etc., require high protein supplements throughout the year. These supplements can take the form of commercial dry dog food or trout chow, but some propagators prefer to offer whole fish to their eiders and mergansers.

Hand rearing young waterfowl can be a long, time-consuming process, and often very sophisticated techniques are required. The young of many species commence eating right away, while others can be most troublesome to get started. As a rule, young waterfowl do not require food for the first 24 hours after hatching, since the yolk sac is still in the process of being absorbed. Specialized species, such as scoters, harlequins, and oldsquaw ducks are particularly difficult to get eating, and often must be pampered and fed by hand for considerable lengths of time. Reluctant feeders can sometimes be stimulated to eat by the use of "starter birds," and mallard ducklings are often ideal for this purpose. They commence eating almost immediately, and as the reluctant feeders see the "starter" mallards eating, they too become interested. For this reason, many breeders maintain several pairs of breeding mallards. In this regard, it should be pointed out that it is usually much easier to successfully rear a brood of young than a single bird by itself.

A thorough knowledge of the natural history of the birds involved is very beneficial. For example, some propagators toss newly-hatched wood ducks or mandarin ducks into the air and let them drop to the ground, because this tends to calm them down in the brooders and encourages them to start eating. As bizarre as this may appear, it often works, because these species are cavity nesters in the wild, and the young frequently must fall some 60 feet or more to the ground to leave the nest. Apparently, the impact at the end of this fall, though slight because the ducklings are so thickly covered with down, is necessary. In the case of some species, such as the stiff-tails which are almost exclusively aquatic, the young can be notoriously difficult to hand raise. Due to their aquatic lifestyles, they should be started out on water in special brooders from the first day.

Hand rearing of young waterfowl always carries with it the risk of imprinting. While all waterfowl are essentially prone to imprint, geese are the most notorious in this regard. Newly-hatched young will readily attach themselves to the first moving objects they see and hear (even if human), and thus can become imprinted on a surrogate parent. Imprinted waterfowl undeniably make delightful pets, and may be ideal specimens for study due to their tractability, but unfortunately, such birds are generally reluctant to breed because they are more interested in their human companions than individuals of their own kind. To avoid imprinting, young waterfowl should be reared in groups (rather than singly), and they should be handled as little as possible.

Imprinting on surrogates is not restricted to a captive situation, of course; it occurs in the wild as well. There are numerous accounts of such behavior in the literature, and a classic example is one documented by Kenneth Abraham as recently as 1978 (Condor 80:338-40). In this case, five spectacled eider ducklings were being reared by a pair of arctic loons (*Gavia arctica*). When first observed, the two species were nesting within 35 feet of one another. However, the loon nesting attempt apparently failed, the female eider disappeared for reasons unknown, and the loons ended up with the eider ducklings.

Like most waterfowl young, eider ducklings forage independently upon hatching, so it was of interest to note that the eiders learned to take food from the loons, a species which normally feed their young on invertebrates. The ducklings were also observed to ride the backs of their foster parents in the manner of a loon chick. When aerial predators, such as glaucous gulls, were nearby, the loons would lead the ducklings to the security of emergent vegetation. For such extraordinary behavior to take place, it appears likely that either conspecific parental calls must be absent and the calls of both species similar, or the imprinting species must be susceptible to a wide range of auditory signals. Previous studies have shown that the young of ground-nesting ducks, in particular, tend to approach most rhythmic, repetitive auditory signals without discrimination.

A combination of these factors could account for the willingness of the ducklings to accept the loons as foster parents. However, in this case, it is the role of the loons that is of most interest. It is probable that the hatching of the ducklings near the end of the loon's incubation period (combined with their nest failure) was responsible for their receptiveness. The similarity in behavior of loon chicks and eider ducklings possibly reinforced their acceptance of the foster chicks. Thus, this rather bizarre interspecific adoption was successful only

15.14

15.13

because the ducklings appeared at the stage of the nesting cycle when the loons were hormonally receptive to the stimulus of young. Curiously, under more typical circumstances, the loons would probably have preyed upon the young eiders.

Developing young must have a balanced, nutritional diet. Swans and geese, in particular, should have unlimited quantities of chopped greens, and a diet that is too rich in protein can result in wing and leg problems. If the flight feathers of developing birds grow too rapidly, for example, the wing will droop or flop over, resulting in an oar-winged or angel-winged bird. If not corrected immediately, the bird will be disfigured for life. (Generally, however, if the wing is properly taped up for a few days the condition can be reversed.)

Most captive waterfowl are pinioned, since the removal of the distal portion of one wing creates an unstable aerodynamic condition which precludes flight. Pinioning is usually done at one or two days of age and is painless at that time. It is desirable that some husbandry techniques be standardized and therefore, males should be pinioned on the right and females on the left. The same applies to banded birds:

15.15

males should be banded on the right leg and females on the left. Waterfowl can be reliably vent sexed, and even day-old birds can be accurately sexed within a day or two of hatching by manipulating and inspecting the cloaca. Some birds may be left full winged and they usually tend to stay around the grounds. (To prevent the possible introduction of an exotic species into the surrounding local environment, however, it is advisable that only those species which occur naturally in the area be maintained in a full-winged condition.) Interestingly, a number of species, such as some whistling ducks and shelducks, can fly surprisingly well even when pinioned, because of their long secondaries.

The problems associated with properly maintaining and managing a waterfowl collection are almost beyond number. Disease, predation, adverse weather, vandals, thieves, etc., can all be troublesome in one way or another, and *all* breeders will sooner or later experience losses due to one or more of them. Unpredictable weather, disease, and even predation can be dealt with to some extent, but the wanton and barbaric actions of irresponsible vandals (human predators) are ex-

15.13 *For optimum breeding results in large mixed collections, it is advisable that a variety of nest boxes of different shapes and sizes be provided. Each pair of potential cavity nesters should have more than one box to select from, and in many cases, the boxes should be placed over water and ramped. The problem of nesting boxes is more difficult to solve in public institutions because aesthetic considerations are involved, whereas propagation is the top priority in private collections and overall visual appeal is of less importance.*

15.14 *Palm logs have been used successfully as nesting boxes in some collections. In this case, both wood ducks and mandarin ducks are inspecting the log (a mandarin female is perched on top).*

15.15 *A wide variety of different types of natural materials (such as vegetation, rocks, logs, etc.) can be used effectively and artistically to greatly enhance a wildfowl exhibit. Waterfowl can be hard on plants, but this does not mean that the two life forms cannot co-exist. Geese and swans are particularly detrimental to plants, but even with these species, attractive exhibits can be maintained if care is exercised in the selection of botanical specimens. In warmer climates, plants such as cycads, holly, yucca, etc., have all proven to be virtually bird-proof.*

stolen from the nest each spring. (Would-be falconers are prone to steal young birds of prey, for instance, and some of the illegal stolen nestlings are confiscated by federal and state wildlife authorities and brought in for rehabilitation.) Happily, a certain percentage of the salvaged birds can be restored to a condition where returning them to the wild is feasible. But more often than not, the injury or ailment is such that it permanently precludes a release attempt.

The challenges involved in creating aesthetic exhibits and efficient propagation programs at the same time are manifold, and although many of the problems involved are shared by both private aviculturists and public zoological institutions, the public facilities face additional challenges which are not of major concern to those with private collections. The private breeder's prime responsibility is successful breeding, and the overall visual impact of such an operation is relatively unimportant. At a public institution, on the other hand, both propagation and aesthetic surroundings should be of equal importance—and simultaneous public displays and breeding are frequently not compatible. This is less of a problem with wildfowl than most other avian groups, such as with pheasants, but even so, some compromises may be necessary (although I do not mean to imply that compromise means the abandonment of imaginative and innovative exhibit and propagation techniques).

Most public zoological institutions maintain and often propagate large numbers of ducks, geese, and swans, but exhibits may not visually present the birds under optimal aesthetic conditions. In the past, some zoos have been guilty of constructing either cage-like aviaries or huge concrete ponds or lakes for their wildfowl. As zoological institutions become more sophisticated, new philosophies and modern exhibit techniques continually emerge, and zoological gardens are changing much more rapidly than many workers in the field believed was possible. Today, most zoo specialists agree that wildlife must be presented under the best possible aesthetic conditions if the public is to appreciate and learn from the exhibit. Contrary to the opinion of many outspoken zoo critics, television animal documentaries are just not enough. Man needs to see, hear, smell, feel, and experience the presence of an organism to truly understand and respect it.

There are countless philosophies concerning the constitution of the ideal waterfowl exhibit, and while it is possible that all of my professional colleagues may not fully agree with my personal preferences, I am inclined to believe that the naturalistic exhibit approach is the most logical and effective. If the birds are displayed in tasteful surroundings that are devoid of wire, concrete, fences, unsightly feeding devices, nest boxes, and so forth, the exhibit potential is significantly increased. Naturally, various displays and husbandry techniques must vary according to climatic conditions and topography.

Water quality should be one of the primary considerations. A high water turnover rate is a major factor in maintaining clear water as well as reducing the incidence of contagious diseases, and in the case of some specialized species such as harlequin ducks, clean and clear water is an absolute necessity. As a rule, the colder the water, the better. If a ready source of fresh water is not available, high quality filters and heavy duty pumps may be utilized to maintain good water quality. To stimulate water movement, small waterfalls can be most effective and will also greatly enhance the visual impact of the exhibit.

Another factor to be considered is the depth of the water. Generally, if a high water turnover rate is possible, no more than two feet is

15.16

15.16 *One of the most effective ways to generate greater public interest is to encourage some controlled interaction between the birds and the visitors. The public may, for example, be given the means to feed the birds, since feeding from the hand establishes the needed rapport between visitor and birds very quickly. A feeding machine that dispenses specially prepared food can be seen on the dock.*

tremely difficult to reconcile—because they are so pointless. Fortunately, however, the ultimate successes that can be achieved usually outweigh the all too numerous problems.

One of the most frustrating situations a breeder must deal with is what to do with a pair of birds that refuses to breed. Sometimes, it is simply a matter of changing the mate, moving the pair to a different enclosure, or altering the diet. However, it is not always this simple, and in some cases a propagator may have to resort to trickery. Here again, a knowledge of the natural history of the birds involved is often helpful. A colleague of mine in Arizona makes use of such knowledge when he brings his Cape Barren geese into breeding condition by transferring them to a large grassy enclosure that is exposed to overhead sprinklers. The sprinkler system effectively simulates the spring rains of Australia, and since breeding commences with the arrival of the austral rains in the wild, the birds are stimulated to breed. As another example, white-headed ducks were not successfully reared in captivity until coot nests were made available to them—because this species frequently parasitizes the nests of other aquatic birds in the wild.

Aviculturists, as custodians of nature, have assumed a serious responsibility. In addition to the numerous maintenance and breeding commitments, many of these individuals are frequently called upon to treat sick or injured birds. Many of these casualties can be attributed to natural causes such as outbreaks of botulism or other diseases, but all too often, they are the results of unfortunate encounters with man. Thousands of stricken birds are treated annually for such maladies as gunshot wounds, poisoning, and injuries resulting from collisions with power lines and entanglements with fish lines or fish hooks. An increasing number of birds are also being trapped in oil spills or other pollutants. Even nestlings and eggs are not secure, and many are necessary, although for swans and some diving species three to four feet (or more) is desirable. If flamingos are maintained with the wildfowl, a water depth of at least four feet will be required to facilitate breeding. Exhibits with underwater viewing windows have some merit, particularly if such species as ruddy ducks, mergansers, pochards, etc., are contemplated.

The design or shape of the exhibit itself is also of great importance, and a free form unit is much more attractive than a symmetrical round, square, or oblong pool. Instead of one or two huge exhibits with many birds crowded into them, it is better to have a number of small, well done displays, since these will greatly enhance the visual impact of the overall exhibit and are much better for the birds. One of the most difficult aesthetic problems to solve is that of the physical barriers which surround an exhibit. Barriers of some sort are necessary not only to contain the birds, but also to restrict public entry into exhibit areas—with the latter problem often being the greater of the two. A most effective method from a visual standpoint is the use of "psychological barriers." In southern climates, for example, a closely planted compact hedge can be just as effective as a fence if it is thick enough, high enough, and wide enough to prevent the public from stepping over it, and unpalatable to the birds. Natal plum (*Carissa*) has proven to be one of the more effective plants for this purpose, because birds do not attempt to eat it and the branches bear countless thorns that discourage the public from attempting to get through it. Inevitably, there are places in the hedge through which birds can escape, but they tend to become rapidly conditioned to staying within the exhibit area, and when they do become so conditioned the barrier becomes essentially psychological. In cooler climates, several species of *Berberis* have also proved to be effective.

When creating a psychological barrier, it is wise to start with the largest and fullest plant specimens possible. Small plants generally require much time to mature and produce the desired effect. If larger plants are not available, low and unobtrusive fencing material can be woven between the shrubs. A great deal of patience is required if hedges are utilized, as the creation of barriers of this type is a long-term project that requires constant attention and maintenance. The greatest challenge, however, will be to get the public "conditioned" to stay where they belong. If visitors continue to violate exhibits, the judicious use of obnoxious plants (such as yuccas or holly) in certain areas can be helpful in discouraging passage. Despite all the difficulties that may initially be encountered in this type of approach, the end result is spectacular and well worth the effort. Low walls of natural stone have also proven to be very effective and have the added advantage of requiring no maintenance.

Propagators who maintain collections in regions where harsh winters occur are faced with a number of problems and challenges not familiar to their southern counterparts. Cold winters will preclude the use of many types of vegetation, especially tropical forms. Also, many wildfowl are very sensitive to cold weather, and such species as whistling ducks, ringed and hottentot teal, radjah shelducks, etc., should be moved indoors for the winter. The major problem associated with cold winters is that of freezing water. If ponds totally freeze over, the risk of losing birds due to dehydration, freezing into the ice, predation, etc., is great. (In the wild, when a duck freezes to the ice after leaving the water, gulls, raptors and other predators will quickly take advantage of the bird's misfortune.) Roosting islands that were secure during the summer are no longer predator-proof once a pond

freezes over. One of the most efficient means of maintaining open water is through the use of "bubblers" that inject compressed air into the water and create numerous bubbles. The bubbles keep the water constantly circulating and thereby prevent freezing. Recirculation pumps, which circulate the water from the bottom of the pond (where it is warmer) and gush it to the surface, will also help in maintaining open water.

Some wildfowl species tend to adhere to their traditional nesting schedules, regardless of climatic conditions. In other words, they nest during the same time of year as they would if they were still in their native homelands. Black-necked swans and Cape Barren geese, for example, come from the Southern Hemisphere and often commence nesting during the austral or southern summer. Unfortunately, this corresponds with the northern winter. If the eggs are left with the incubating female, great care must be taken to see to it that they do not freeze.

Whenever a zoological facility is open to the general public, there are certain unavoidable problems which must be contended with daily, such as visitors entering the exhibits or feeding unauthorized food items, theft of eggs, etc. For some reason, a number of visitors feel compelled to throw objects at the birds (frequently, these are coins, since clear water apparently stimulates the "wishing well syndrome"). If the overall aesthetic atmosphere of the institution is high, however, the aforementioned difficulties will not be as serious as they could be, so it is recommended that public exhibits be maintained in the best possible condition.

Some institutions encourage public contact with the animals, and visitors are allowed to feed the birds. Feeding machines with specially prepared waterfowl food can be provided for that purpose. It should be pointed out that even if there is a "no feeding" policy, some visitors will feed the animals anyway (usually with their unwanted garbage), so by providing food, management retains a degree of control over what (and how much) the birds are fed; also, the public tends to respond enthusiastically. A desirable side effect of public feeding is that the ducks, geese, and swans will become reasonably tame, and as a result, the agonizing problems associated with psychological stress will be minimized.

In most cases, quality wildfowl exhibits can also be botanical showcases. Over the years, horticultural personnel at various zoological institutions have experimented with an infinite variety of plant species, and have discovered (usually the hard way) which ones can withstand unrelenting avian pressure. As a general rule, the larger the waterfowl, the larger and hardier the plants must be. Geese appear to be the worst offenders, although swans can be troublesome as well, and these larger species are compatible with relatively few plants. Sweet-tasting, soft, succulent plants are usually doomed from the start, and flowers do not fare well either with most species. Junipers, pines, palms, bird-of-paradise plants, cycads, coral trees, etc., have proved to be at least partially bird-proof, but even under the best of conditions, constant upkeep and specimen replacement is a necessity. In public institutions, this requires a good rapport between the avicultural staff and horticultural personnel.

It is most desirable to maintain captive wildfowl in areas that best suit their temperaments and requirements. For example, there should be heavily planted exhibits for those species that tend to be secretive, grass lawns for grazers, and so forth. For the smaller and more delicate forms, Korean grass (*Zosia*) has proven to be relatively durable, at

15.17 (Overleaf) Small islands will do much to increase the aesthetic appeal of an exhibit, and they also provide secure roosting and nesting sites. In the situation illustrated, the birds are maintained on salt water, which greatly reduces the incidence of disease. To solve the problem of fresh drinking water, small waterfalls can be provided. Freshwater species adapt quickly to saltwater if a freshwater drinking source is readily available. The overall effect of a waterfowl exhibit can be intensified significantly if the unit is as natural-looking as possible. This means, among other things, the facing of unsightly cement pool edges with natural stone or rock. If large rocks are used, they should be angled down into the water so the birds can come ashore with ease. Clean, clear water is highly desirable, not only for health reasons, but also because it increases the educational potential of a zoological exhibit by making it possible for viewers to see the birds underwater.

least in warm climates. Once established, this grass is beautiful and lush, and is an excellent ground cover—and most important, the birds are not inclined to eat it. Zosia remains green year round, and has a tendency to cover everything, including the edges of pools, rocks, the bases of larger plants, etc. Unfortunately, it is fairly expensive and requires a great deal of time to mature.

For geese and other grazers, a sturdy lawn of golf fairway grass (such as hybrid bermuda) is excellent. The birds graze constantly, and if the proper number of birds are maintained, it is not even necessary to mow the lawn. If exhibits are designed correctly and contain enough lawn space, it is also possible to successfully maintain relatively large flocks of species that are somewhat colonial, such as black brant or red-breasted geese. Breeding potential is significantly increased by this, since gregarious species thrive in flocks. Even in the more open grassed exhibits, however, dense planted areas should be included to provide nesting areas and shady retreats.

Depending on the exhibit area and the species involved, a wide variety of materials can be used to enhance an exhibit and increase its aesthetic appeal, including rock, sand, river stone, logs, wood, bark, etc. The use of large rocks in the water is often effective, as they are not only attractive but provide secure roosting sites as well. Due to its light weight, feather rock has been effectively utilized in many zoological gardens, and huge boulders are particularly attractive. Naturalistic islands should be provided whenever practical, since they do much to improve the overall visual impact of the exhibit while providing needed nesting and roosting sites. Birds that use islands for such purposes will then be fairly secure from terrestrial predators, such as feral cats. The unsightly cement edges of ponds and islands should be faced with natural rock or other appropriate material. Dirt banks are not practical, because the waterfowl tend to eat them away.

The judicious use of driftwood can also be very effective, but the acquisition of wood and logs with character is a surprisingly difficult task, and if a great deal of care is not exercised in the selection of the appropriate piece, the desired effect can be lost. There are three basic methods of wood utilization: land use, water use, and a combination of land and water use. Any of the three methods (or perhaps a combination) can effectively pull an exhibit together. The "in the water" pieces are also beneficial to the diving duck species, because the divers tend to glean food underwater surfaces once mosses and other aquatic plants begin to appear.

The use of wood also allows exhibition of other avian species, such as macaws and cockatoos, within the wildfowl exhibits. This can be overdone, of course, but a touch of color and noise in certain areas can do a great deal to enhance the total visual impact of a public exhibit. Generally, wood in the water is best for this purpose because it prevents the parrots from departing the perch. (If they do manage to get to the shore, they can be disastrous to a planted area.) Psittacines which are used in this manner are usually tame and are taken in and out daily.

Other avian species can easily be maintained with waterfowl as well, including ibises, spoonbills, egrets, etc. Flamingos lend themselves perfectly to some exhibits, and in regions where conditions are suitable, free-roaming pheasants can enhance a facility as well. Within each exhibit, a variety of habitats or ecological niches should be provided, since this will render the exhibit much more flexible and make it possible to use it for a variety of species. Some institutions successfully exhibit fish in wildfowl displays, but speaking from per-

15.19

15.20

15.21

15.22

15.18 (Opposite Page) *Ground cover is always a problem, but the Korean grass (or Zosia) on which this fulvous whistling duck is loafing can be effective under certain conditions. This thick, lush grass requires no mowing and it can tolerate a certain amount of avian pressure. Unfortunately, it is a warm weather grass, is expensive, and requires much time to become established.*

15.19 *Driftwood can do much to increase the overall visual impact of a display and its effectiveness is further intensified if tame parrots are included in the exhibit. These scarlet macaws are taken in and out daily.*

15.20 *A mixed exhibit containing waterfowl and Chilean flamingos. Some waterfowl do best if maintained in small flocks. With northern geese, a lawn of sturdy grass should be provided.*

15.21 *A scenic waterfowl exhibit which includes a greater sulphur-crested cockatoo and a pair of scarlet macaws. Note that the psittacines are kept on perches which are in the water. This prevents them from leaving the logs and venturing into the planted areas (where they could cause real havoc). Plants and parrots do not mix.*

15.22 *Blue-eared pheasant. Traditionally, pheasants have been maintained in aviaries to increase breeding potential. As a rule, they are much more "flighty" than waterfowl and do not lend themselves nearly as well to open exhibits — but they can thrive if conditions are suitable, and a number of collections have pheasants roaming free on the grounds. In such cases, the gamebirds are not pinioned and they tend to roost in trees at night, a habit that reduces the incidence of terrestrial predation. (All collections are plagued by feral cats.)*

15.23

15.23 *The black-crowned night heron at the top of this photo is patiently waiting for an opportunity to snatch up the downy European shelduck duckling in the water. The constant threat of predation is one of the major reasons why most experienced breeders prefer to hand-rear young under more controlled conditions.*

15.24 *A U.S. Fish and Wildlife Service biologist holding a female Pacific eider that has been marked with a numbered nasal tag. Due to extreme variations in climatic and topographic conditions (as well as the mobility and elusiveness of the various species involved), it is unfortunately not always practical to obtain all the data required in the field. Wildfowl within a controlled environment can provide a viable alternative. These "living laboratories" can greatly supplement field studies. Collections are particularly valuable for long-term research. Interestingly, behavior in captivity does not appear to differ significantly from that in the wild and the information obtained is therefore most meaningful; indeed, much of our current knowledge of waterfowl comes from captive studies.*

15.25 *(Opposite Page) Family of Falkland Island kelp geese. Even though no kelp geese currently exist in any wildfowl collection, the science of aviculture is rapidly advancing and there can be no question that these birds will be established sometime in the future. The next generation of aviculturists will undoubtedly wonder why we of this era considered the kelp goose "difficult."*

15.24

sonal experiences, in the interests of good inter-departmental relations it is not advisable to place mergansers or other fish-eaters in units containing fish.

Most urban collections are plagued by large numbers of unwanted domestic pigeons, starlings, and sparrows, which tend to take over feeding areas. To prevent this, some consideration should be given to feeding the wildfowl underwater, especially since this also keeps the birds active and pleases the public greatly by giving them numerous opportunities to see the dabblers dabbling and the divers diving. Aside from the food that rock pigeons, European starlings, and English sparrows steal, they should also be discouraged from mingling with waterfowl because they present a definite disease threat. For this reason, a continual control program is strongly recommended.

Unfortunately, these opportunists are not the only unwanted intruders. *No* avian collection is totally free of predators. Aside from mice and rats, the most cunning and dangerous terrestrial predators are feral cats, and they must be removed immediately. In my own experience, a single cat is one too many. Feral dogs and coyotes are

also very troublesome. In addition, collections in coastal areas frequently attract large numbers of gulls, black-crowned night herons, and great blue herons, and all of these can be most detrimental. They are not only a serious threat to fish in open ponds, but can be responsible for the loss of young birds as well. On one occasion, I saw a black-crowned night heron kill a large, month-old black-necked swan. Western gulls are particularly competitive, and will take young waterfowl without hesitation the moment they emerge from the nesting site. These skilled predators are quick to take exposed eggs as well. Needless to say, the public is not impressed with these types of avian interaction.

Over the years, numerous methods have been devised to protect valuable collections from the great variety of predators. Many breeders bury the lower portion of their perimeter fences in an effort to discourage digging predators, while others use electrified strands of wire along the top and bottom of the fence to thwart climbing carnivores. Some aviculturists light their entire collection at night in an attempt to reduce losses, and in the Midwest, a few breeders have even gone so far as to keep a hand-raised great horned owl on the premises, in the belief that this will prevent other owls from coming in and establishing a territory. A few collections are totally covered with wire mesh. Regardless of all the work that goes into these efforts, however, it is obvious that predators can only be controlled, not totally eliminated. Alligators, corvids, otters, raccoons, foxes, owls, snakes, snapping turtles, skunks, weasels, and coyotes are just a few of the opportunists that will always be around to test the patience and diligence of a propagator.

During the breeding season, a great deal of knowledge about specific breeding behaviors is also necessary, as individual dispositions may alter drastically at that time. Aggressive species such as the larger swans, sheldgeese, Cape Barren geese, and bronze-winged ducks (to name but a few) must be closely observed when in breeding condition if they are exhibited with species of comparable size—for they can turn savage. If a mixed exhibit is desired, the unit must be relatively large. From an exhibit potential standpoint, it is desirable to maintain species of varying sizes, colors, shapes, and habits together, such as whistling swans with ruddy ducks.

As discussed previously, perhaps the most important consideration is breeding potential. An effective breeding program has always been part of the proper management of a collection, but it is becoming ever more important due to the plight of many species—especially since increasingly strict restrictions relative to avian acquisition, importation, and federal quarantine are making it extremely difficult (if not impossible) to acquire new birds.

Zoological institutions have great social, cultural, and biological potential; but some changes in contemporary zoo management thinking will be required if that potential is to be realized. If an institution elects to display a species, it is obligated to provide the best exhibit possible without compromising breeding potential. This suggests that many collections will have to specialize, leaving the huge broad-spectrum collections to institutions in large urban areas. One of the major goals, of course, is to have all species in zoological institutions exhibited under natural or seminatural conditions. Once this is accomplished, the outspoken zoo critics will probably fade away, institutional educational programs will improve significantly, and the reproductive potential will be even greater. The *ultimate* goal is to have all captive populations self-sustaining.

16
Epilog
Man and the Future of Waterfowl

When one considers the status of most waterfowl populations, it is heartening to note that most species are at least holding their own for the present; and despite the numerous detrimental activities of man, it is perhaps encouraging that only one species of North American waterfowl (the Labrador duck) has been driven to extinction during historical times. Having said this, it is nevertheless true that man's impact on waterfowl has been essentially negative, and the problems that humans create for waterfowl are such that they will undoubtedly get worse before significant improvement is achieved (even though waterfowl as a group have probably been protected and managed more by man than any other form of wildlife).

In the minds of many, it is hunters who should be held accountable for the present plight of wildfowl. As a result, the concept of hunting itself is being increasingly challenged in the United States by anti-hunters, who claim that man does not have the right to kill and that hunting is therefore immoral. Hunters, of course, counter by contend-

16.2

16.1 (Opposite Page) *Whooper swan in the sunset.*

16.2 *Family of emperor geese.*

ing that it is man's nature to hunt, and that it is no more immoral to do so than to raise cattle for slaughter. Like all such controversies, both sides have valid arguments, but the major issues are unfortunately clouded by uncompromising passions, and it is therefore obvious that the issue will not be easily resolved. In considering the positions of both sides, it is interesting to note the results of a recent survey. Various outdoor-oriented groups were queried about their knowledge of wildlife, and anti-hunters scored *lowest*, while sport hunters were rated somewhat higher. Significantly, bird watchers scored the highest.

From a biological standpoint, certainly, anti-hunting groups have some potent arguments. They point to the dramatic increase in hunters during the past century, and to the great decrease in appropriate wildfowl habitat that has taken place at the same time. They question whether or not the resource can absorb the increased pressure.

Hunting is undoubtedly a very big business, on which more than two billion dollars is spent annually in the United States alone—over $500 million just on ammunition. Each year approximately 16 million licensed hunters harvest over 120 million birds in the United States, and an additional 10 million are taken in Canada. At least three million of these hunters *actively* hunt waterfowl, along with 400,000 in Canada, and approximately 17 million ducks are shot in North America alone (without taking into account non-retrieved cripples, which may account for an additional 15 percent). In addition, native Eskimos and Indians may take 100,000 to 200,000 waterfowl annually, exclusive of eggs.

Despite this seemingly heavy kill, however, most wildfowl populations usually regain their normal levels each year through normal production, and it appears that the resource can absorb hunting pressure to a considerable degree if managed properly. Also, in order to retain some sort of realistic perspective, it is important to keep in mind that more than 57 million birds are slaughtered each year on the nation's highways—and as many as 1,250,000 birds may perish annually in the United States alone when they collide with glass windows, tall buildings, lighthouses, televison towers, power lines, and other man-made structures.

In my opinion, anti-hunting organizations tend to tar all hunters unfairly with the same brush, accusing all of them of indiscriminately gunning down any wildlife that ventures within range. To my mind, there is a considerable difference between the beer-guzzling weekend skyblaster, who shoots whatever moves, and the dedicated waterfowler. The true sportsman appreciates the intricate and delicate relationship between man and nature, and understands that it must be preserved—and the actual bagging of game is not necessarily the prime consideration for such an individual. To suggest that all hunters are bad is almost as ludicrous as insinuating that all non-hunters are good.

In one very vital area, in fact, hunters have directly and indirectly done far more good for waterfowl than the vocal anti-hunters. There can be no question that the greatest threat to the continued existence of wildfowl (and most other life forms as well) is the alteration, destruction, or total loss of appropriate habitat—and money raised from hunters has helped to set aside, preserve, and even improve large tracts of land for this purpose. Not too many years ago, there were millions of acres of wetlands and marshes in the continental United States. However, by 1968 wetlands had declined from some 127 million acres to only 75 million acres. Of this, only nine million acres are considered to be prime wildfowl habitat, although the remainder is used to some degree by waterfowl. It is estimated that some 200,000 acres of wetlands are being lost each year and no major change in this rate is anticipated. This continued loss is extremely alarming, because without appropriate habitat wildlife simply cannot survive, no matter how much protection is afforded to specific species.

The millions of dollars generated by the annual sale of duck stamps and hunting licenses (both federal and state) have made possible the establishment and maintenance of countless wildfowl refuges. It is estimated that since the duck stamp concept was initiated in the 1930s, more than 72 million stamps have been sold. In excess of 200 million dollars have resulted, and this has been used to acquire some 2.1 million acres of wetlands. Approximately $12 million are currently collected each year from the sale of federal duck stamps alone.

In addition, numerous private organizations *actively* raise funds to acquire, restore, and preserve the critical habitat of ducks, geese, and swans. The largest and best known of these groups, Ducks Unlimited, has alone committed over $60 million for breeding habitat restoration in Canada. There is no doubt that without such diligent long-range programs for habitat acquisition and restoration, some waterfowl populations would have declined significantly, while others conceivably could have disappeared altogether. It has been sarcastically said, of course, that these pro-hunting organizations only raise funds to per-

16.3 (Opposite Page) *Flight of Pacific black brant winging over San Ignacio Lagoon, Baja California, Mexico.*

petuate their sport, and this may be true. But in the long run, it matters not why an essential deed is done; the important thing is that it *is* done. At any rate, some 18.5 million acres have been set aside in over 1000 major federal, state, and private refuges in North America.

The preservation of wetlands is of benefit not only to waterfowl, but to man as well. From a biological standpoint, pristine marshes and estuaries are not just stinking, bug-inhabited swamps as many developers would have us believe. Far from it! They are, in fact, among the most biologically productive of all habitats on Earth, and literally thousands of diverse life forms depend on them for their survival. The loss of wetlands will ultimately mean the loss of many forms of wildlife that man values most. Furthermore, the aesthetic value of marshes and wetlands is such that it is just not possible to measure such losses in human terms. Certainly, a monetary value cannot be attached to these natural wonderlands—especially when one considers that they are *irreplaceable*.

While I am not a hunter, and have devoted my professional life to seeking a means of perpetuating the existence of waterfowl and other wildlife, I can appreciate the responsible hunter's point of view all the same. Perhaps I could be a great deal more sympathetic to anti-hunting groups if they were as active in raising funds for waterfowl studies and habitat acquisition as they are in clouding the issues with emotional rhetoric. Clearly, before any progress is made in bringing together these two widely opposing schools of thought, compromises will be required on both sides. Effective, long-term conservation can only be attained by working together.

Hunting, of course, is not the only controversial issue concerning the frightening plight of many of this planet's life forms. In recent years, oil spills and other forms of pollution have become increasingly detrimental to aquatic birds. Thousands of birds are trapped annually, and the mortality rate can be incredibly high. Unhappily, if the oil itself does not kill the bird, the treatment of salvaged birds often does. When the coating of oil is manually removed with a solvent, most of the bird's natural oils are lost, and the structure of the feathers is broken down as well. As a result, a bird frequently cannot become adequately waterproofed again until it undergoes a molt, and this may require up to a year. Meanwhile, the birds must be kept out of the water to prevent chilling (and possible drowning), and they may perish as a result, since they are not adapted to life ashore. They are, for one thing, very susceptible to deadly avian diseases such as aspergillosis, a fungal infection which attacks the lungs and air sacs. Of course, most birds oiled on the high seas die there and decompose, and their fate is therefore largely a matter of speculation.

Due to improved methods of cleansing, the mortality rate of birds recovered from oil spills has decreased significantly in recent years. But the kills are still far too large, and clearly, prevention of oil spills and other forms of pollution is the most effective means of protecting aquatic and pelagic life. In light of ever-expanding world energy demands, the need to continue and expand offshore drilling must be acknowledged, and the need for raw materials cannot be minimized—but at the same time, the potentially severe environmental hazards that are associated with such activities must be recognized and solved as well. Likewise, the need to drill in places like the Alaskan north slope brings with it the possibility of a major fracture in an oil pipe line (from an earthquake or other cause)—which could result in biological disaster with extremely long-term detrimental effects for the countless species that depend on the fragile Arctic as major breeding

grounds. If environmental concerns are totally cast aside in the quest for additional energy sources, the quality of life will significantly decrease. It has been suggested that man can have both wildlife and kilowatts, but not in the same place nor at the same time—and while this may not necessarily be totally true, it does provide provocative food for thought.

Some cynics suggest that man will always be the extremely destructive force that he has always been. But, with all due deference to the totally committed pessimists, I believe there is cause for at least some guarded optimism. In this era of ecological enlightenment, man at long last has come to recognize that he has serious responsibilities concerning his surroundings and fellow creatures—and to recognize also that our own survival may depend on what we do now. The need to

conquer or alter surroundings had survival value at one time in man's history and so it became part of his nature. Now that this compulsion has proved to have numerous negative and deadly aspects as well, hopefully man will be able to adopt another survival tactic in its place—or at least modify the old ways enough to prevent complete disaster. The need to conquer or alter surroundings may be man's nature, just as it is the nature of a successful predator to kill in order to survive, and some do suggest that expecting man to change his habits now is comparable to expecting a predator to become vegetarian. But I believe the change is not so drastic as that. After all, even with mankind's terrible excesses, there has always been a compassionate and benevolent side of the species as well. Consider, for example, that man is the only animal who possesses the capacity to mourn the loss of

another species. Perhaps it is not so much that we must totally alter our nature, but rather that we must consider more seriously the alternatives, while we still have a choice.

The choices that are open to us are, of course, limited by the current status of human society. We must accept the fact that some "growth and progress" is inevitable in a world seriously handicapped by a mushrooming human population. However, such growth must be carefully planned and *controlled* to avoid as much as possible doing irreparable harm to the environment and the living things in it. For some species, it is already too late—the die has already been cast and their fate is sealed. And, of course, nothing can be done about those species which have already vanished. But hopefully, something constructive can be done about most of the other imperiled life forms, and

those which are likely to become endangered in the future.

Extinction and death are two unpleasant words that conjure up the same meaning . . . finality. While extinction is undoubtedly an essential part of the evolutionary process, there can be no question that man has greatly accelerated the process, particularly during the last century. In most cases, the environment has been altered so rapidly that many species have not been afforded sufficient time to adapt to changing conditions and have died off in ever-increasing numbers. *Homo sapiens* must be forced to acknowledge that no matter how technically advanced the human race becomes, no-one can claim the moral or ethical right to decide which species should survive and which should perish. No earthly life form is capable of making that awesome decision.

16.4 *Flock of lesser Magellan geese flying over the snow-covered mountains of Tierra del Fuego.*

16.5 (Overleaf) *Lesser snow geese at dusk.*

An ecosystem can be as large and complex as the entire planet Earth, or as seemingly insignificant as a mere drop of swamp water, but no matter what its size, an ecological network is most fragile indeed—far too delicate to be tampered with too often. If such a network is visualized as a massive spider web, it is not too difficult to see what could happen if we continue to be intolerant of the surrounding environment. The demise of a species, the loss of a river or a marsh, or the pollution of an ocean represent the plucking away of the strands that hold the web together. Obviously, the deletion of a certain number of strands can be tolerated, but one is forced to wonder just how many strands can be detached before the entire system collapses. Once that point is reached, of course, the question really becomes academic.

There are those in our society who claim that we can easily survive without the Laysan teal, the Nene goose, or even the trumpeter swan. In a certain sense, this point cannot be argued, for man has survived despite the disappearance of the dodo, the great auk, the passenger pigeon, and the Labrador duck, as well as countless other life forms; although admittedly, life is a little less without them. In another sense, however, man cannot long survive his fellow creatures if current trends continue to accelerate. After all, the plights of the numerous endangered species provide us with a foretaste of the future that may await us. In general, these life forms are endangered today because they are more specialized than man, and tend to be adversely affected more rapidly and drastically by environmental alterations than we more adaptable humans are. But it is all a matter of degree and time. As the negative environmental factors continue to accumulate, the other species may go first . . . but we shall probably not be very far behind. Or if we do manage to survive the demise of the majority of the Earth's species, we may find ourselves sharing an almost dead planet with the even more adaptable rat, cockroach, domestic pigeon, and English sparrow. In my mind, this might be a fate worse than death.

Waterfowl constitute but a small fraction of the animals in this world, but because they are obvious and colorful, they easily capture the imagination of an observer—and grasping the spirit and essence of these wondrous birds will certainly enrich our lives and make it easier to appreciate other forms of life, at a time when this kind of appreciation is sorely needed. Certainly, anything that helps us to appreciate the frailties of the natural world more fully is especially important at this time in the history of the world, since the depth of our understanding is the hinge upon which the future of *all* life may turn. In the words of one of America's greatest conservationists, Aldo Leopold, "Conservation is a state of harmony between men and land"—and, one might add, "its wild creatures." Unhappily, that necessary harmonious state is something we are going to have to strive for very hard to achieve.

In the old days, miners used to carry canaries with them into the bowels of the earth because the birds were more sensitive to the presence of poisonous gas. If the bird died, the miners had time for a choice—continue and risk death, or back off. It is clear that our canaries are dying, and a decision must be made now—before it is too late.

16.6 (Opposite Page) *We can only hope that the sun is not literally setting for the waterfowl of the world, and that our descendants will know these fascinating birds as viable life forms rather than memories.*

16.6

Waterfowl are cosmopolitan in distribution and have exploited practically every habitat on Earth. Major topographic boundaries, such as mountains and oceans, have presented no great obstacles to their diffusion because so many of them are superior fliers. They inhabit every continent except Antarctica and some forms even live on remote oceanic islands. In general, however, anatids have been most successful in the north temperate regions and in the seasonally productive Arctic. In such regions, severe climatic conditions during part of the year make it necessary for most species to migrate to warmer areas to pass the winter. In more tropical areas, where there is a reliable source of food year-round, most species do not migrate.

Major Global Climatic Regions

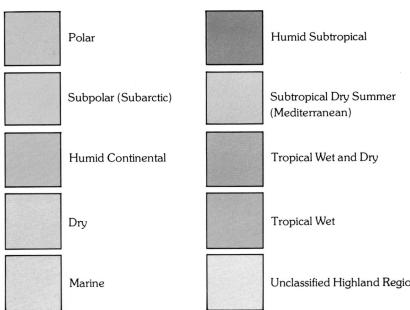

Polar

Subpolar (Subarctic)

Humid Continental

Dry

Marine

Humid Subtropical

Subtropical Dry Summer (Mediterranean)

Tropical Wet and Dry

Tropical Wet

Unclassified Highland Regions

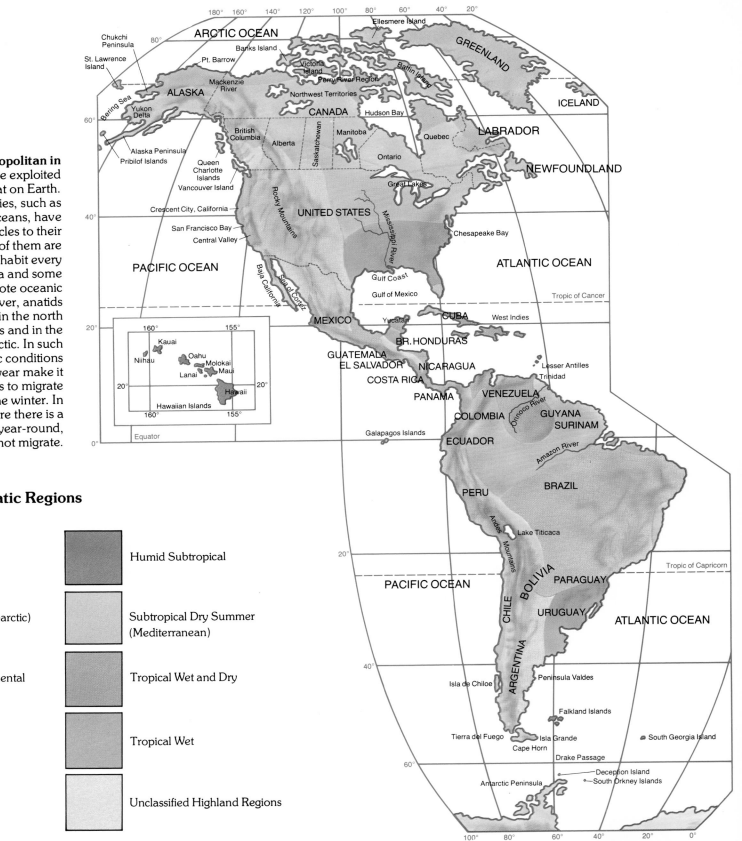

ARCTIC OCEAN

GREENLAND

Svalbard (Spitsbergen) (Nor)

Taymyr Peninsula

Wrangel Island (USSR)

Kanin Peninsula

Novaya Zemlya

Yamal Peninsula

Khatanga River

Verkhoyansk Mts

Yana River

Kolyma River

Anadyr River

NORTH ATLANTIC

Arctic Circle

ICELAND

Ob River

Lena River

Siberia

Komandorski Islands (Commander Islands)

Faeroe Islands

North Sea

Norway

Sweden

Finland

Attu Island (US)

Buldir Island (US)

UNITED KINGDOM

Kamchatka Peninsula

Amchitka Island (US) (Aleutian Islands)

River Thames

SOVIET UNION

FRANCE

Danube River

Lake Baikal

Sakhalin Island

Khor River

Kuril Islands

SPAIN

ITALY

Black Sea

Caucasus Mts

Caspian Sea

Aral Sea

Mongolia

Amur River

Ussuri River

Iman River

PORTUGAL

Manchuria

Vladivostok

CHINA

KOREA

JAPAN

Mediterranean Sea

IRAQ

AFGHANISTAN

Szechuan Province, China

Honshu

Morocco

ALGERIA

LIBYA

EGYPT

JORDAN

Persian Gulf

IRAN

PAKISTAN

Himalaya Mountains

Mt. Everest

TIBET

Shanghai

Yangtze River

Spanish Sahara

Sahara Desert

Nile River

Red Sea

SAUDI ARABIA

OMAN

Assam

Ganges River

Bihar State

Orissa State

Tropic of Cancer

Senegal River

NIGER

CHAD

SUDAN

YEMEN

ARABIAN SEA

INDIA

BURMA

LAOS

TAIWAN

Luzon

PHILIPPINES

Mariana Islands

SENEGAL

MALI

Kordofan Plateau

THAILAND

CAMBODIA

VIETNAM

Tinian

Saipan

GUINEA

GHANA

Blue Nile River

White Nile River

NIGERIA

ETHIOPIA (Abyssinia)

Andaman Islands (India)

GUAM

LIBERIA

IVORY COAST

CENTRAL AFRICAN REPUBLIC

CEYLON

Nicobar Islands (India)

PACIFIC OCEAN

CAMEROON

SOMALIA

Malay Peninsula

Palau Island (Pelew)

GABON

UGANDA

KENYA

Equator

CONGO

ZAIRE

SUMATRA

BORNEO

Moluccan Islands

Ceram

TANZANIA

Celebes

Buru Island

NEW GUINEA

New Britain

Solomon Islands

INDONESIA

ANGOLA

JAVA

Papua

ZAMBIA

East Indies

CORAL SEA

Rennell Island

SOUTHWEST AFRICA

MALAWI

MOZAMBIQUE

Cape York Peninsula

New Hebrides

RHODESIA

INDIAN OCEAN

Northern Territory

BOTSWANA

MADAGASCAR

Mauritius

Tropic of Capricorn

TRANSVAAL

Reunion

AUSTRALIA

SOUTH AFRICA

Western Australia

Queensland

South Australia

INDIAN OCEAN

Cape of Good Hope

Darling River

New South Wales

Murray River

North Island

Victoria

NEW ZEALAND

Crozet Island

Bass Strait

Flinders Island

Kerguelen Island

Tasmania

South Island

Auckland Island

Macquarie Island

Campbell Island

ANTARCTICA

351

Waterfowl Bill Types

Waterfowl exploit an enormous variety of food sources, and in general, the shapes and sizes of their bills reflect not only their dietary preferences but their foraging techniques as well. Bill shapes are not necessarily reliable indicators of close taxonomic relationships, since similarities in shape may merely be the result of similar lifestyles. For example, the bills of eiders and steamer ducks may appear superficially similar—but this is because both groups frequent the sea and feed extensively on hard-shelled molluscs, and they are not closely related.

A. Grazing (white-fronted goose)
B. Fish-eating (red-breasted merganser)
C. Dabbling, Surface-feeding (Baikal teal)
D. Filter-feeding (pink-eared duck)
E. Bill Shape Modified by Salt Glands (surf scoter)
F. Tearing Underwater Vegetation (Bewick's swan)

PAINTINGS BY MARK HALLETT

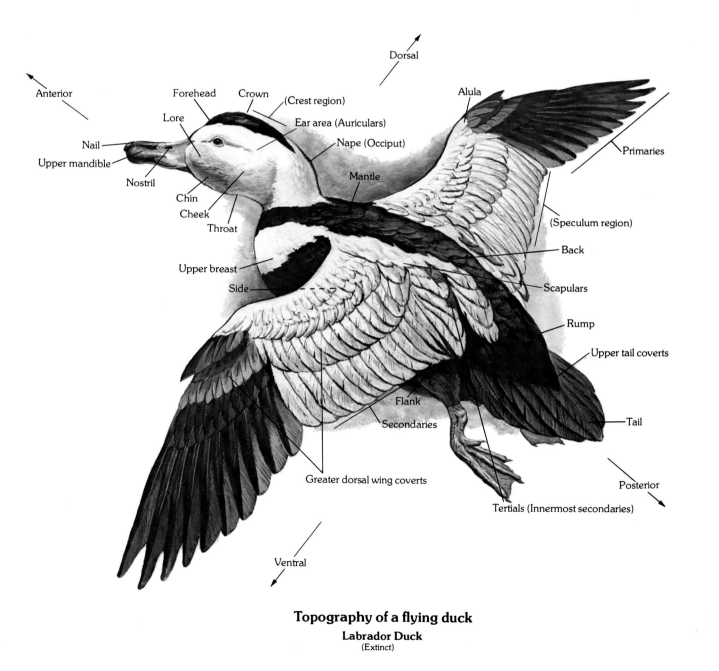

Dorsal

Anterior

Forehead   Crown   (Crest region)

Lore   Ear area (Auriculars)

Nail   Nape (Occiput)

Upper mandible

Nostril   Mantle

Chin

Cheek

Throat

Upper breast

Side

Alula

Primaries

(Speculum region)

Back

Scapulars

Rump

Upper tail coverts

Flank

Secondaries   Tail

Greater dorsal wing coverts

Tertials (Innermost secondaries)

Posterior

Ventral

Topography of a flying duck
Labrador Duck
(Extinct)

Appendix 1
A Concise Reference Guide to the Waterfowl

The following listing of the waterfowl of the world is, with few exceptions, arranged according to the systematic work of Delacour and Mayr. Most of the information concerning distribution, nesting, status, etc., is of necessity quite brief and general, and is mainly intended for comparative purposes.

To give the reader some idea of the relative sizes of the birds listed, I have chosen to include the average weights of males and females of each species (and subspecies where possible) rather than measurements. This is because measurements are readily available in the technical literature and can also be somewhat difficult for the nonspecialist to interpret. Weights, on the other hand, are not so readily available and are also perhaps more meaningful to the general reader. In using weights for purposes of comparison, however, a certain amount of caution is advisable, since the weights of birds may fluctuate drastically from season to season.

For the purposes of this section, *average* yearly weights have been used where possible, although the reader should bear in mind that variances of up to 40 percent (and even 50 percent) may occur, particularly with those species that are highly migratory. (Seasonal weight changes are not nearly as extreme with tropical or subtropical species.) In a number of cases, I was forced to resort to museum study skins for the weights of the more obscure species and subspecies, and I note with some dismay that the weights of surprisingly few are recorded. Usually, either no weights were available at all or they were recorded on only one or two specimens. In some instances, the weights of the different sexes have been combined and averaged in this listing, and the same is also true of some races. When this has occurred, it has been indicated.

The data on Status In Captivity in this listing is as accurate as it is feasible to make it, and is current up to early 1979. However, situations can alter rapidly in the field of aviculture and the current status of a specific form can change with surprising speed. The data presented include both private and public collections.

KEY:

♂ = Male   ♂♂'s = Males
♀ = Female   ♀♀'s = Females

1000 grams (g) = 1 kilogram
1 kilogram (kg) = 2.21 pounds
1 pound = 454 grams
1 ounce = 28 grams

VERNACULAR NAME	LATIN NAME	DISTRIBUTION	AVERAGE WEIGHTS	NESTS, EGGS AND INCUBATION	STATUS/ WILD	STATUS/ CAPTIVITY
Sub-Family: ANSERANATINAE Tribe: ANSERANATINI (Magpie Goose)						
Magpie Goose	*Anseranas semipalmata*	N. Australia, S. New Guinea	♂ 2,766g ♀ 2,071g	Average 8-9 roundish, glossy wt. eggs. Usually form trios (1 ♂ ; 2 ♀). All 3 incubate: 28 days. Goslings fed by adults.	Relatively abundant. Population stable with some indications of local decline.	Relatively rare outside of Australia. Has been bred on few occasions (San Diego, Wildfowl Trust and Cleres, France). Can be aggressive.
Sub-Family: ANSERINAE Tribe: DENDROCYGNINI (Whistling Ducks)						
Spotted Whistling Duck	*Dendrocygna guttata*	Philippines, New Guinea and numerous East Indies Islands.	♂ 800g ♀ 800g	Up to 11 wt. eggs. Cavity nesters. Both sexes incubate: 30-31 days.	Abundant and widespread.	Quite rare but bred more regularly in recent years. Not well established. Can be aggressive.
Eyton's (Plumed) Whistling Duck	*D. eytoni*	Eastern Australia. Widespread, mainly in tropical or grassland habitats. Occasional vagrants to Tasmania and New Guinea.	♂ 788g ♀ 792g	8-14 wt. eggs. Ground nests, concealed in vegetation. Both sexes incubate: 28-30 days.	Abundant and widespread; may be increasing in some regions, possibly as a result of cattleman activities.	Relatively common but not known to be prolific breeders, (at least not in America).
East Indian Wandering Whistling Duck	*D. a. arcuata*	Widespread throughout the East Indies including the Philippines and Indonesia.	Slightly smaller than *D. a. australis*	6-8 (up to 15) wt. eggs. Nests on ground concealed by vegetation or in cavity. Both sexes incubate: 28-30 days.	Apparently abundant.	Reasonably well established. Breeds readily but prone to hybridize with other dendrocygnids, particularly *D. bicolor*.
Australian Wandering Whistling Duck	*D. a. australis*	Tropical N. Australia, S. New Guinea.	♂ 741g ♀ 732g	6-15 wt. eggs. Nest is usually a scrape on the ground in vegetation. Both sexes incubate: 28-30 days.	Very common in tropical regions.	Not maintained outside of Australia. Probably has been bred.
Lesser Wandering Whistling Duck	*D. a. pygmaea*	New Britain Islands; (possibly also Fiji Islands).	Smaller than *D. a. australis*	Presumably same as nominate race.	Status unknown but due to limited distribution is probably vulnerable.	Essentially unknown to aviculturists, but several pair maintained at the Wildfowl Trust.
Fulvous Whistling Duck	*D. bicolor*	Widespread: Africa, Asia, North and South America.	♂ 675g ♀ 690g	8-16 wt. eggs. Ground nesters but also utilizes tree crotches and hollows. Both sexes incubate: 24-26 days.	Very common and secure due to extensive range.	Extremely common and breeds readily. Well established everywhere.
Cuban (Black-Billed) Whistling Duck	*D. arborea*	West Indies (Bahamas, Cuba, Haiti, Jamaica, Puerto Rico, Virgin Islands, Leeward Islands, Martinique).	♂ 1,150g ♀ 1,150g	8-12 wt. eggs. Nest sites variable; on ground, in palm trees, cavities, etc. Both sexes incubate: 30 days.	Considered an endangered species but can be locally common, but generally declining throughout range.	Not uncommon and bred fairly regularly. Well established. Can be aggressive.
Javan (Lesser) Whistling Duck	*D. javanica*	Widespread throughout Indonesia, India, Malay Peninsula, Indochina, Ceylon, coastal S. China, etc.	♂ 450-600g ♀ 450-600g	8-10 wt. eggs. Nest sites variable including abandoned nests of other birds. Both sexes incubate: 27-28 days.	Very common and widespread.	A delicate species which has become surprisingly rare in recent years. Seldom bred.
White-faced Whistling Duck	*D. viduata*	Discontinuous distribution: tropical South America and Africa, including Madagascar and Comoro Islands.	♂ 686g ♀ 662g	6-12 wt. eggs. Nests generally on ground or in reeds over water but sometimes uses cavities. Both sexes incubate: 26-28 days.	Very common, particularly in Africa.	One of the most popular of whistling ducks; relatively common and breeds fairly frequently, but sporadically.
Northern Black-Bellied (Red-billed) Whistling Duck	*D. a. autumnalis*	Extreme S. Texas to to Panama.	♂ 816g ♀ 839g	12-16 wt. eggs. Cavity sites preferred but may nest on ground. Both sexes incubate: 28-31 days.	Fairly common and most populations are apparently stable.	Very common in American collections and breeds readily.

VERNACULAR NAME	LATIN NAME	DISTRIBUTION	AVERAGE WEIGHTS	NESTS, EGGS AND INCUBATION	STATUS/ WILD	STATUS/ CAPTIVITY
Southern Black-Bellied Whistling Duck	*D. a. discolor*	E. Panama south to N. Argentina (absent on west side of Andes south of Ecuador).	Similar to nominate race.	Same as nominate race.	Presumably same as nominate race but no accurate population estimates available.	Rare in American collections but more common in Europe where it is easily reared.

Tribe: ANSERINI (Swans and True Geese)

VERNACULAR NAME	LATIN NAME	DISTRIBUTION	AVERAGE WEIGHTS	NESTS, EGGS AND INCUBATION	STATUS/ WILD	STATUS/ CAPTIVITY
Coscoroba Swan	*Coscoroba coscoroba*	Southern third of South America, Falkland Islands.	♂ 4.6kg ♀ 3.8kg	4-7 creamish wt. eggs. Bulky ground nest near water; lined with much down for a swan. Incubation by ♀ alone: 35 days.	Not overly abundant but there are no indications of a population decline.	Not uncommon and reasonably well established. Difficult to breed initially but established pairs often produce for years. Can be aggressive.
Black Swan	*Cygnus atratus*	Australia (except extreme N. central region), Tasmania. Introduced to New Zealand.	♂ 6.27kg ♀ 5.10kg	4-10 (aver. 5 or 6) pale green eggs. Large bulky nests. In some regions may be colonial nesters. ♂ may sometimes incubate: 35-40 days.	Very common and may be increasing in some areas.	Well established and hundreds are reared annually.
Mute Swan	*C. olor*	Eurasia (British Isles to Mongolia). Introduced to North America, Australia, New Zealand and South Africa.	♂ 12.2kg ♀ 8.9kg	4-8 pale greenish-blue eggs. Some semi-feral populations are rather colonial. Incubation generally by ♀ alone: 35-36 days.	Extremely common in many regions. Have benefitted from man's influence to some degree.	One of the most popular of all captive birds; commonly bred. Can be aggressive and dangerous to other birds.
Black-necked Swan	*C. melano-coryphus*	Southern third of South America, Falkland islands.	♂ 5.4kg ♀ 4.0kg	4-8 cream-colored eggs. Large bulky nests; sometimes partially floating. Incubation by ♀ alone: 36 days.	Population relatively stable. Can be locally common.	Not uncommon but not abundant either. Bred regularly in some collections and the species has become more established in recent years. Can be aggressive.
Whistling Swan	*C. c. columbianus*	Breeds on North American tundra (mainly N. of Arctic Circle from Alaska to Hudson Bay); winters along both Atlantic and Pacific coasts.	♂ 7.1kg ♀ 6.2kg	3-5 wt. eggs. Nests on tundra along shores of lakes or ponds, occasionally on islands. Incubation by ♀ alone: 30-32 days.	Relatively common; population estimated at approximately 100,000 swans.	Common but rarely bred. Breeding more frequent in recent years due to acquisition of hand-raised stock.
Bewick's Swan	*C. c. bewickii*	Breeds in N. Russia from Kanin Peninsula to the Lena Delta. Winters in the British Isles and N. Europe.	♂ 6.4kg ♀ 5.0kg	3-5 wt. eggs. Tundra nest sites. Incubation by ♀ alone: 29-30 days.	Probably fairly secure but vulnerable. 6-7,000 wintering birds accounted for in Europe. Western segment may not exceed 10,000 swans (although this may be as high as it has ever been).	Quite rare (particularly in America) but regularly bred at the Wildfowl Trust.
Eastern Bewick's (Jankowski's) Swan	*C. c. jankowskii*	Breeds on tundra of E. Asia from Lena River Delta to the Kolyma River Delta. Winters China, Japan and Korea.	Slightly larger than nominate race.	Presumably same as *C. c. bewickii.*	Extent of population not known, but possibly exceeds that of the nominate race. May not be a valid subspecies.	Very rare. Apparently has never been bred.
Whooper Swan	*C. cygnus cygnus*	Breeds throughout Eurasia and Iceland, (possibly Japan). Winters in Great Britain, N.W. Europe, Asia Minor, N. India, China, Japan and Korea.	♂ 10.8kg ♀ 8.1kg	4-6 wt. eggs. Huge nests. Incubation by ♀ alone: 31-40 days. (31-32 days probably typical.)	Relatively common, possibly as many as 100,000 swans.	Well established and fairly regularly bred. Can be aggressive.
Trumpeter Swan	*C. c. buccinator*	North America; S. interior Alaska, Alberta, British Columbia, Wyoming.	♂ 11.9kg ♀ 9.4kg	4-8 (aver. 5) wt. eggs. Nests may be in the water or on top of muskrat lodges. Incubation by ♀ alone: 33-37 days.	Formerly endangered, now only considered threatened. Population currently probably exceeds 5-6,000 swans.	Fairly well established but not common. Bred regularly in some collections. Can be *very* aggressive and dangerous to other birds.

VERNACULAR NAME	LATIN NAME	DISTRIBUTION	AVERAGE WEIGHTS	NESTS, EGGS AND INCUBATION	STATUS/ WILD	STATUS/ CAPTIVITY
Swan Goose	*Anser cygnoides*	Breeds S. central Siberia east to Kamchatka, south to central Asia and N. Mongolia. Winters N. China and Japan.	♂ 3,500g ♀ 2,850- 3,450g	5-8 wt. eggs. Nest typically located in grass, lined with dry grass and down. Incubation by ♀ alone: 28 days.	Little known, but appears to be greatly declining in some regions. Over hunting, disturbance and habitat destruction have contributed to the decline.	Well established but many captive birds are not pure. Easily bred.
Western (Yellow-billed) Bean Goose	*A. f. fabalis*	Breeds N. Scandinavia and N. Russia. Winters in Europe from Great Britain south to the Mediterranean and Black Sea.	♂ 3,198g ♀ 2,843g	4-6 wt. eggs. Previous year's nest may be reused. Building mostly by ♀ but ♂ *may* assist. ♀ alone incubates: 27-29 days.	Difficult to ascertain due to numerous similar races. Some decline in wintering birds in parts of Europe. Considering all races, certainly in excess of 100,000 geese.	Well established in European collections; less so in America. Breeds easily.
Johansen's Bean Goose	*A. f. johanseni*	Breeds in forests of W. Siberia, east to the Khatanga River. Winters in Iran, Turkestan and W. China.		Presumably same as nominate race.	Not known. Validity of race contested by some biologists but Delacour believes it to be a good subspecies.	Not known in captivity.
Middendorf's Bean Goose	*A. f. middendorfi*	Breeds in forests of E. Siberia (Khatanga to Kolima region). Winters in Japan and E. China.		Presumably same as nominate race.	Extent of population unknown, but may be rare.	Very rare. Has possibly been bred.
Russian Bean Goose	*A. f. rossicus*	Breeds on tundra of arctic Russia and Siberia. Winters in Europe, Russia, W. Siberia, Turkestan and China.	♂ 2,668g ♀ 2,374g	Presumably same as nominate race.	Extent of population unknown.	Fairly well established in a number of Eurasian collections. Extremely rare in America.
Thick-billed (Eastern) Bean Goose	*A. f. serrirostris*	Breeds along the tundra shores of Siberia. Winters in Korea, China and Japan.		Presumably same as nominate race.	Extent of population unknown, but wintering birds in Japan have increased from 1500 to 5000 between 1970 and 1976, but this figure may include some *middendorfi*.	Very rare. Some hybrids, but few pure specimens. Pure ones have been bred at least once.
Pink-footed Goose	*A. brachyrhynchus*	Breeds in E. Greenland, Iceland and Spitzbergen. Winters in N.W. Europe.	♂ 2,620g ♀ 2,352g	3-5 wt. eggs. Nests typically on open tundra (sometimes in small colonies), also on inaccessible ledges and cliffs. Incubation by ♀ alone: 26-27 days.	Tends to fluctuate. During 1974/75 some 89,000 wintering in Britain and Ireland, followed by substantial reduction. Population probably fairly secure.	Well established, more so in Europe than America. Does not breed freely in most American collections.
European White-Fronted Goose	*A. a. albifrons*	Breeds in N. Russia and Siberia east to Kolima River where it probably intergrades with Pacific race. Winters in England, North Sea, shores of Mediterranean, Caspian Sea and N. India.	♂ 2,290g ♀ 2,042g	5-6 wt. eggs. Both sexes *may* participate in nest building. Nests of previous years may be reused. Incubation by ♀ alone: 27-28 days.	May be the most numerous of Old World Geese. Numbers in the hundreds of thousands.	Very common in European collections where it breeds readily. Rare in America.
Pacific White-Fronted Goose	*A. a. frontalis*	Breeds Alaska, St. Lawrence Island and E. Siberia. Winters W. United States (east to Louisiana), and N. Mexico, China and Japan.	♂ 2,404g ♀ 2,222g	3-7 wt. eggs. Nests widely scattered; site may be on incline or top of low hill, or small island. Incubation by ♀ alone: 21-28 days.	Very common; at least 200,000 in North America alone. Extent of Siberian population not known.	Common and bred fairly regularly. Not well known in Europe.
Greenland White-Fronted Goose	*A. a. flavirostris*	Breeds W. coast of Greenland. Most winter in Ireland, occasionally in E. North America.	♂ 2,543g ♀ 2,526g	3-7 wt. eggs. Tends to nest on hillsides. Incubation by ♀ alone: 26-27 days.	Indication of slight overall population decline. At least 12,000 currently exist. The small size of this race makes it vulnerable.	Common in European collections and bred regularly. Pure specimens rare in America.

VERNACULAR NAME	LATIN NAME	DISTRIBUTION	AVERAGE WEIGHTS	NESTS, EGGS AND INCUBATION	STATUS/ WILD	STATUS/ CAPTIVITY
Gambel (Interior) White-Fronted Goose	*A. a. gambelli*	Breeds probably in the Mackenzie Basin of Canada (Old Crow Flats) and adjacent western Alaska. Winters along Gulf Coast (Texas, Louisiana, and N. Mexico).	♂ 3,180g ♀ 3,060g	Not known, but presumably similar to nominate race.	Not really known, but rare; possibly 2,000 geese.	Extremely rare; has been bred at the Wildfowl Trust and in private collection in Montana.
Tule White-Fronted Goose	*A. a. elgasi*	Breeding range unknown but possibly in the taiga zone south of the Alaskan tundra. Winters in Sacramento Valley of Calif.	♂ 2,993g ♀ 2,861g	Not known, but presumably similar to nominate race.	Extremely rare and very vulnerable. Possibly 1,500 geese. Some 100-150 shot annually in California.	Very rare. Has been bred at least once in private Montana collection.
Lesser White-Fronted Goose	*A. erythropus*	Breeds in subarctic regions from Scandinavia eastward to the Pacific coast. Winters in S. Europe, Egypt, S.W. India, China and Japan (rarely).	♂ 1,440- 2,300g ♀ 1,300- 2,100g	3-8 wt. eggs. Typically nests on tundra under dwarf birch vegetation or in rocky areas on mountains. ♀ alone incubates: 25 days.	Population may exceed 100,000 individuals. Apparently secure for the moment.	Well established, particularly in Europe; less so in America.
Western Greylag Goose	*A. a. anser*	Breeds in Europe east to the Caucasus in Russia. Winters in Europe, North Africa, Turkey, Iraq and Iran.	♂ 3,531g ♀ 3,105g	5-6 wt. eggs. In favored areas, nests may be relatively concentrated. Incubation by ♀ alone: 28-29 days.	Population tends to fluctuate, but appears to be secure. Increasing in some areas.	Abundant in Europe, but rather uncommon in America. Breeds rather readily.
Eastern Greylag Goose	*A. a. rubrirostris*	Breeds throughout central Russia east to N. Mongolia, Manchuria, and S.E. Siberia. Winters south to Asia Minor, India and N. Indochina.	♂ 3,860g ♀ 2,720g	Presumably essentially same as nominate race.	Not known but may be suffering due to a greatly disrupted and generally declining range.	Less common than *anser*, but well established in European collections. Virtually unknown in America.
Bar-Headed Goose	*A. indicus*	Breeds on high mountain lakes in S.E. Russia, N. India and W. China. Winters in N. India, N. Burma.	♂ 2,000- 3,000g ♀ 2,000- 3,000g	4-6 wt. eggs. Some colonial nesting tendencies. Nest sites varied but islands preferred. Incubation by ♀ alone: 27 days.	Indications are that there has been a significant population decline in recent years, particularly in the northern parts of the range, i.e., no more than 2,000 in Russia.	Relatively common and breeds readily. Currently well established.
Lesser Snow (Blue) Goose	*A. c. caerulescens*	Breeds N. coast of Alaska east to Baffin Island, Canada. Also on Wrangle Island, Siberia. Winters in the Central Valley of California, Gulf Coast and rarely in China and Japan.	♂ 2,744g ♀ 2,517g	4-5 wt. eggs. Among the most colonial of nesting geese. ♀ alone incubates: 22-23 days.	Perhaps the most numerous of wild geese. Population greatly exceeds 1 million birds. Secure but can be considered vulnerable.	Very common in collections everywhere and bred often.
Greater (Atlantic) Snow Goose	*A. c. atlanticus*	Breeds in Greenland and Baffin, Devon and possibly Grinnell Islands, Canada. Winters along Atlantic coastline south to North Carolina.	♂ 3,310g ♀ 2,812g	Essentially the same as nominate race but not so colonial. Incubation by ♀ alone: 23-24 days.	Recovered from a low of 2-3,000 in 1900 to in excess of 100,000. (Liberal population estimates number as high as 200,000 geese.)	Very few pure specimens in captivity. (Most have hybridized with *caerulescens*). Not well established.
Ross's Goose	*A. rossi*	Breeds mainly in Perry River region of Canadian Northwest Territories. Winters mostly in Central Valley of California but some wintering farther east in recent years; i.e., to the Gulf Coast.	♂ 1,315g ♀ 1,224g	3-5 wt. to pinkish eggs. Very vulnerable to predation. May nest in association with lesser snow geese. ♀ alone incubates; 20-22 days.	More common than believed. Population *possibly* exceeds 70,000 geese.	Becoming more established but still can be considered relatively uncommon. Significant breeding success in recent years.
Emperor Goose	*A. canagicus*	Breeds coastal W. Alaska, St. Lawrence Island and N.E. coast of Siberia. Winters Aleutian Islands and Alaska Peninsula.	♂ 2,812g ♀ 2,766g	4-6 wt. eggs. Less down in nest than most geese. ♀ alone incubates: 24-25 days.	Stable and secure for the time being. Population certainly exceeds 100,000 individuals.	Not well established, but becoming more so. If managed properly, breeds fairly regularly. Has a tendency to become too fat which will preclude breeding.

VERNACULAR NAME	LATIN NAME	DISTRIBUTION	AVERAGE WEIGHTS	NESTS, EGGS AND INCUBATION	STATUS/ WILD	STATUS/ CAPTIVITY
Nene (Hawaiian) Goose	*Branta sandvicensis*	Non-migratory. Island of Hawaii and introduced to Mauai (Haleakala National Park).	♂ 2,212g ♀ 1,923g	3-5 wt. eggs. Nests usually located in vegetated areas surrounded by recent lava flows, typically above 6,000 foot elevation. ♀ alone incubates: 29 days.	Endangered. Recovered from a low of less than 50 in the late 1940s to well in excess of a thousand. As of 1976, some 750 in the wild and 1,250 in captivity. Captive reared stock has been liberated to supplement wild population.	Common, but not yet widespread in collections, but becoming well established. Breeds readily.
Atlantic Canada Goose	*B. c. canadensis*	Breeds in E. Labrador, Newfoundland, and Anticosti and Magdalen islands. Winters along Atlantic coast from Nova Scotia south to Florida.	♂ 3,809g ♀ 3,310g	4-6 creamy wt. eggs. Most nests located near water. ♀ alone incubates: 28 days.	Common. *Most* races of Canada geese are secure and are probably more numerous now than they ever have been.	Well established. Commonly bred. Captive Canada geese tend to readily hybridize, therefore, many individuals in collections are of mixed blood.
Interior (Todd's) Canada Goose	*B. c. interior*	Breeds N. Quebec, Ontario and E. Manitoba and S. Hudson Bay. Winters S. Ontario, south to Atlantic coast to Florida and Louisiana.	♂ 4,212g ♀ 3,856g	4-6 wt. eggs. Like most Canada goose races, nest sites require good visibility, fairly dry nest foundation, close proximity to water and isolation. Incubation by ♀ alone: 25-28 days.	Secure.	Apparently reasonably well established and has been bred.
Giant Canada Goose	*B. c. maxima*	Formerly widespread on Great Plains from Manitoba and Minnesota south to Arkansas and Tennessee. Most of the population today is probably restricted to Wildlife Refuges and *may* have been derived from captive-reared stock.	♂ 6,523g ♀ 5,514g	4-6 wt. eggs. May nest on top of muskrat lodges. Incubation by ♀ alone: 26-28 days.	Apparently secure; at least 54,600.	Fairly well established but "pure" specimens not common.
Western (Great Basin) Canada Goose	*B. c. moffitti*	Breeds throughout the Great Basin region including southern Canada. (Discontinuous breeding range.) Does not migrate far but moves to S. British Columbia, N. W. Wyoming to Arkansas, south to California and Baja California.	♂ 4,334g ♀ 3,930g	4-6 wt. eggs. Prefers island sites. ♀ alone incubates: 26-28 days.	Secure.	Well established and is not uncommonly bred.
Lesser Canada Goose	*B. c. parvipes*	Breeds central Alaska eastward to Hudson Bay, Canada and south to Prairie Provinces. Winters in S. United States: California to Louisiana and Mexico.	♂ 2,766g ♀ 2,471g	4-6 wt. eggs. ♀ alone incubates: 25-28 days.	Secure.	Presumably well established. Not a well defined race.
Alaska (Taverner's) Canada Goose	*B. c. taverneri*	Breeds from central Alaska to the Mackenzie River Delta. Winters western states to Texas and Mexico.	♂ 2,241g ♀ 2,059g	4-6 wt. eggs. Incubation by ♀ alone: 25-28 days.	Secure.	Fairly well established.
Vancouver Canada Goose	*B. c. fulva*	Breeds along coast of and on islands of British Columbia, and S. Alaska north to Glacier Bay. Mainly non-migratory but some winter in N. California.	♂ 4,625g ♀ 3,537g	4-6 wt. eggs. Incubation by ♀ alone: 26-28 days.	Not as abundant as some races, but not thought to be declining.	Rare; seldom bred.

VERNACULAR NAME	LATIN NAME	DISTRIBUTION	AVERAGE WEIGHTS	NESTS, EGGS AND INCUBATION	STATUS/ WILD	STATUS/ CAPTIVITY
Dusky Canada Goose	*B. c. occidentalis*	Breeds along Prince William Sound, Cook Inlet to Copper River Delta, Alaska. Somewhat sedentary but may winter in Oregon.	♂ 3,754g ♀ 3,131g	Essentially the same as *fulva*.	Some indications of population decline. Rather vulnerable; subjected to hunting pressure and breeding habitat may be exposed to development.	Not well established and not commonly bred. Not many pure birds.
Aleutian Canada Goose	*B. c. leucopareia*	Breeding presently restricted to Buldir (possibly Amchitka and Agattu Islands). Formerly occurred throughout the Aleutian Islands as well as Commander and Kurile Islands, and possibly western Alaska.	♂ 1,954g ♀ 1,927g	4-6 wt. eggs. May nest on steep slopes. Incubation by ♀ alone: 24-28 days.	Rare and endangered. Restricted breeding distribution. Population supplemented with captive-reared stock. Wintering areas closed to the hunting of "dark" geese. Population is increasing—estimated at 1,600 + in 1978.	Well established at federal Wildlife Research Centers (Patuxent, Amchitka and N. Dakota) but not widespread in private collections. Bred fairly regularly by federal biologists and at Wildfowl Trust but has proven to be a rather difficult race to propagate.
Bering Canada Goose	*B. c. asiatica*	Thought to have bred on Commander and Kurile Islands (USSR).		Not known.	Extinct. Undoubtedly not a valid race; more likely a variant of *leucopareia*.	Never kept.
Cackling Canada Goose	*B. c. minima*	Breeds along western Alaskan coast. Winters from S. British Columbia to S. California.	♂ 1,930g ♀ 1,360g	4-6 wt. eggs. In some regions can be considered somewhat colonial (i.e., 100 nests per sq. mile). Incubation by ♀ alone: 24-30 days (26 days average).	Common and secure.	Well established and bred regularly. One of the most desirable of the Canada geese.
Richardson's (Baffin Island) Canada Goose	*B. c. hutchinsii*	Breeds on Melville Peninsula, Southhampton, Baffin and Ellesmere Islands, Canada and W. Greenland. Winters in Texas and Mexico.	♂ 2,041g ♀ 1,865g	4-6 wt. eggs. Incubation by ♀ alone: 24-26 days.	Common.	Well established.
Barnacle Goose	*B. leucopis*	Breeds in N.E. Greenland, Spitsbergen, Novaya Zemlya and other W. Siberian Islands. Winters in Scotland, Ireland, Norway and Holland.	♂ 1,672g ♀ 1,499g	4-6 wt. eggs. May nest colonially. Sometimes nests on slopes or even on rocky ledges. Incubation by ♀ alone: 24-25 days.	Appears to be increasing but is vulnerable. Population probably on the order of 50,000 geese, possibly more.	Well established and bred regularly, particularly in Europe.
Russian (Dark-Bellied) Brant	*B. b. bernicla*	Breeds N. Europe and Asia, mainly on Taimyr Peninsula. Winters along coast of England and N.W. Europe.	1,410g average of both sexes combined. Sample size: 313 geese.	3-5 wt. eggs. Semi-colonial nesters in areas of dense concentrations. Nest heavily lined with thick down. Incubation by ♀ alone: 22-26 days.	Apparently increasing; from 16,500 in 1955/57 to 80,000 in 1973/74. However, the population is subject to extreme fluctuations.	Fairly well established in European collections. Extremely rare in America. Bred sporadically.
Atlantic (Light-Bellied) Brant	*B. b. hrota*	Breeds along coasts and islands of E. arctic Canada, N. Greenland and Spitsbergen. Winters along Atlantic coast of N. America and Iceland.	♂ 1,542g ♀ 1,270g	Essentially same as nominate race.	Population fluctuates greatly due to unfavorable climatic conditions (and perhaps over-harvesting). Estimated at 90,000 geese in 1975.	Not abundant and not bred often.
Black (Pacific) Brant	*B. b. orientalis*	Breeds along coast regions and islands of W. Arctic Canada, N. Alaska and Siberia. Winters mainly along Pacific coast of N. America from Vancouver island to Baja California. Also Japan, N. China and Korea.	♂ 1,494g ♀ 1,354g	Essentially same as nominate race.	Population more stable than other races. Probably exceeds 140,000 geese.	Relatively common in *some* collections but not widespread. Not commonly bred.

VERNACULAR NAME	LATIN NAME	DISTRIBUTION	AVERAGE WEIGHTS	NESTS, EGGS AND INCUBATION	STATUS/ WILD	STATUS/ CAPTIVITY
Lawrence's Brant	*B. b. nigricans*	Breeding area unknown. Wintered off coast of New Jersey.		Not known.	Extinct. Probably not a valid race.	Never kept.
Red-breasted Goose	*B. ruficollis*	Breeds on Siberian tundra from the Ob to the Khatanga Rivers. Winters along the Black Sea, Caspian Sea and north end of the Persian Gulf.	♂ 1,315-1,625g ♀ 1,150g	3-7 cream-colored eggs. Semi-colonial. May nest in association with peregrine falcon or other raptor. Incubation by ♀ alone: 23-25 days.	Rare (possibly endangered) and declining. Suffering both on wintering and breeding range. Loss of wintering habitat, over hunting, decline of the peregrine falcon and disturbance are main contributions to population decline. Total population probably does not exceed 15,000-25,000 geese.	Relatively rare but more common in Europe. Most desirable of captive geese. Bred sporadically.

Sub-Family: ANATINAE
  Tribe: TADORNINI (Shelducks and
    Sheldgeese)

VERNACULAR NAME	LATIN NAME	DISTRIBUTION	AVERAGE WEIGHTS	NESTS, EGGS AND INCUBATION	STATUS/ WILD	STATUS/ CAPTIVITY
Crested Shelduck	*Tadorna cristata*	W. Russia and Korea.		Unknown.	Extinct. Known from only 4 specimens: 3♂ ; 1♀ ; (only 3 remain). One unconfirmed sighting in 1964.	Never seen by 20th century aviculturists. Possibly kept by the Japanese in the early 1700s.
Ruddy Shelduck	*T. ferruginea*	Breeds from S.E. Europe east to S.E. China. Winters in southern part of breeding range and N. Africa, India, Burma, Thailand and S. China.	♂ 1,200-1,640g ♀ 950-1,500g	8-12 cream-colored eggs. Nests in cavities and even in abandoned buildings. Incubation by ♀ alone: 27-29 days.	Population probably secure because of huge range, but is declining in Europe—possibly less than 50 breeding pairs.	Common and well established. Breeds readily. Can be aggressive.
Cape Shelduck	*T. cana*	South Africa. (Cape Province, Orange Free State and Transvaal)	♂ 1,758g ♀ 1,417g	6-13 cream-colored eggs. Nests often in burrow of aardvark, porcupine, etc. May be located some distance from water. Incubation by ♀ alone: 30 days.	Even though the range is restricted, the species can be considered common and possibly increasing.	Well established. Will readily hybridize with ruddy shelduck, hence some captive specimens are not pure.
Australian Shelduck	*T. tadornoides*	S. and S.W. Australia, Tasmania.	♂ 1,559g ♀ 1,291g	10-14 creamy-wt. eggs. Nests in burrows, tree cavities or on ground in vegetation. ♂ establishes a brood territory. Incubation by ♀ alone: 30-32 days.	Relatively common and secure.	Fairly common and reasonably well established. However, in America they are not bred frequently. Can be aggressive.
New Zealand (Paradise) Shelduck	*T. variegata*	New Zealand; more common on South Island.	♂ — ♀ 1,260-1,340g	5-11 (8 aver.) creamish eggs. Nest sites in cavities or above ground in tussock grass. Incubation by ♀ alone: 30 days.	Apparently secure and re-occupying former areas of its range.	Relatively abundant and widespread. Bred regularly by some propagators (in *most* collections breeding is sporadic). Can be aggressive.
European (Common) Shelduck	*T. tadorna*	Breeds in Europe eastward to Central Asia and E. Siberia. Range discontinuous. Winters southern portion of breeding range, N. Africa, Iran, India, S. China and Japan.	♂ 980-1,450g ♀ 801-1,250g	7-12 (aver. 9) creamish eggs. Nest sites variable but include cavities, burrows, hay stacks and occasionally, open nests. Incubation by ♀ alone: 30 days.	Common and perhaps increasing. Western segment of population alone exceeds 130,000 birds.	Very common and frequently bred. Not so aggressive as the larger shelducks.
Moluccan (Black-Backed) Radjah Shelduck	*T. r. radjah*	Resident in Moluccas, New Guinea and associated islands.	♂ 750g (Aver. of both races combined). ♀ 839g	6-12 wt. eggs. Nest sites generally in a tree near water. Incubation by ♀ alone: 30 days.	Apparently secure.	Relatively common and frequently bred in recent years in *some* collections.
Australian (Red-Backed) Radjah Shelduck	*T. r. rufitergum*	Northern and eastern tropical Australia.	♂ 934g ♀ 839g	Same as nominate race.	Not uncommon but extremely vulnerable to overhunting and habitat destruction.	Almost non-existent in collections outside of Australia (probably no more than 6 aged individuals).

VERNACULAR NAME	LATIN NAME	DISTRIBUTION	AVERAGE WEIGHTS	NESTS, EGGS AND INCUBATION	STATUS/ WILD	STATUS/ CAPTIVITY
Egyptian Goose	*Alopochen aegyptiacus*	Resident in Africa south of the Sahara, also Nile Valley, and occasionally extreme N. Africa and S. Europe. (Small feral population in Great Britain.)	♂ 1,900-2,550g ♀ 1,500-1,800g	6-12 (aver. 7) creamy-wt. eggs. Nest site variable; burrows, other bird nests, in trees, cliffs, on ground, etc. Incubation generally by ♀ alone but possibly sometimes by ♂ as well: 30 days.	Extremely common. Has adapted well to human intrusion.	Very common and widespread. Breeds very readily. Can be dangerous to other waterfowl; very aggressive.
Orinoco Goose	*Neochen jubata*	Resident in Orinoco and Amazon River basins, south to Paraguay and N. Argentina.	♂ — ♀ 1,250g	6-8 cream, brownish or pale greenish eggs. Usually nests in hollow trees. Nest well lined with wt. down. ♀ alone incubates: 30 days.	Fairly common and apparently secure.	Relatively common and reasonably well established. Regularly bred in some collections; but breeding is usually sporadic.
Abyssinian Blue-Winged Goose	*Cyanochen cyanopterus*	Highlands of Ethiopia (usually above 8,000 feet). Has the most restricted range of all the sheldgeese.	♂ — ♀ 1,520g	4-9 creamish eggs. Little known of wild reproductive biology. Possibly nocturnal, Reportedly ♀ alone incubates: 30-34 days.	The species is vulnerable due to presumed small population size and restricted range. The effects of the recent war are not known.	Fairly well established and regularly bred by some breeders. Not widespread in collections. Can be aggressive.
Andean Goose	*Chloephaga melanoptera*	Highlands of S. Peru, Bolivia, Argentina and Chile (usually above 10,000 feet).	2,730-3,640g (weights of both sexes combined)	5-10 creamish eggs. Nest generally a relatively simple scrape amongst sparse vegetation. Incubation by ♀ alone: 30 days.	Population size not known but probably secure for the moment due to relatively inaccessible habitat.	Reasonably well established but not widespread. Bred fairly frequently. Can be aggressive.
Lesser (Upland) Magellan Goose	*C. p. picta*	Southern third of South America. Winters in Northern portion of range.	♂ 2,834g ♀ 2,721-3,200g	5-8 creamish-wt. eggs. Nest sites vary but generally near water. Incubation by ♀ alone: 30 days.	Despite persecution, very common, and it remains the most abundant of the sheldgeese.	Well established and fairly common, especially in America. Not particularly difficult to breed.
Greater Magellan Goose	*C. p. leucoptera*	Falkland Islands, Tierra del Fuego and southern Patagonia.	Somewhat larger than nominate race.	Presumably essentially same as nominate race.	Relatively small size of population makes it vulnerable but apparently secure for the moment.	Well established in Europe, (less so in America, but becoming more so in recent years). Will hybridize with *picta*. Both races can be aggressive.
Patagonian (Lesser) Kelp Goose	*C. h. hybrida*	Coastal regions of Tierra del Fuego, S. Patagonia, S. Chile and Chilöe Islands.	♂ 2,607g ♀ 2,041g (aver. of both) races combined)	3-7 deep cream eggs. Nests usually within 30′ of high tide line on low cliff ledges, in tall tussock grass, etc. Incubation by ♀ alone: 30 days.	Relatively common and population appears to be stable.	None currently in captivity. Extremely difficult to acclimate. Has been bred at least once.
Falkland (Greater) Kelp Goose	*C. h. malvinarum*	Resident: Falkland Island coasts.	See nominate race.	Essentially same as nominate race.	Same as nominate race.	Has been attempted but few have survived over a year. None currently in captivity.
Ashy-Headed Goose	*C. poliocephala*	Southern third of South America; Falkland Islands.	♂ 2,267g ♀ 2,200g	4-6 pale buff eggs. Usually nests in tall grass but also may utilize hollows of burnt trees. ♀ alone incubates: 30 days.	Fairly common but may be suffering some decline locally.	Very popular and reasonably well established. Bred regularly in some collections.
Ruddy-Headed Goose	*C. rubidiceps*	Southern third of South America; Falkland Islands.	♂ 2,000g ♀ 2,000g	5-8 deep cream eggs. Nests generally in tall grass but on the Falkland Islands may use abandoned penguin burrows. Incubation by ♀ alone: 30 days.	Drastic decline in continental population; possibly an endangered species. Possibly less than 1,000 geese left on mainland. 40,000 said to inhabit the Falklands, but this figure may be optimistic. Introduced foxes extremely detrimental.	Becoming more established in recent years but not common. Bred fairly regularly in some collections.

VERNACULAR NAME	LATIN NAME	DISTRIBUTION	AVERAGE WEIGHTS	NESTS, EGGS AND INCUBATION	STATUS/ WILD	STATUS/ CAPTIVITY
Cape Barren (Cereopsis) Goose	*Cereopsis novae-hollandiae*	Islands off S. Australian coast, in the Bass Strait. Winters on the mainland along the coast.	♂ 5,290g ♀ 3,770g	3-6 wt. eggs. Nests usually on the ground but have been reported in trees as high as 18′ above ground. ♀ alone incubates: 35 days.	Considered endangered by some but population appears to be increasing. Population estimates range between 5,000-20,000 individuals.	Fairly well established and can be considered rather dependable breeders. Can be extremely aggressive.
Flying Steamer Duck	*Tachyeres patachonicus*	Extreme southern portion of South America; Valdez Peninsula (Argentina) south to Tierra del Fuego on the Atlantic coast and north to approximately 37° So. latitude (Chile) on the Pacific coast. Falkland Islands.	♂ 3,073g ♀ 2,616g	5-9 ivory-colored eggs. Typically, nests are placed on small islets, usually well concealed in grass or other vegetation. Moves inland during the breeding season. ♀ alone incubates: not definitely established but probably between 30-40 days. ♂♂'s assist in brood care.	Fairly abundant and the population appears to be secure for the time being.	Never been successfully maintained.
Magellanic Flightless Steamer Duck	*T. pteneres*	Coastal regions of extreme southern South America: Range approximates coastal range of flying steamer duck. Additional taxonomic work may disclose that the range is more restrictive; i.e., Beagle Channel and W. coast of Chile.	♂ 6,039g ♀ 4,111g	5-8 ivory-colored eggs. Nest usually well concealed and close to water. Sometimes nests in forests. Incubation probably by ♀ alone. Incubation period not definitely established but probably between 30-40 days. ♂♂'s assist in brood care.	Relatively common and not currently in danger.	Very few specimens in collections. Not at all established. Apparently has been bred in Europe. Very aggressive.
Falkland Flightless Steamer Duck	*T. brachypterus*	Resident on Falkland Islands. (Possibly Atlantic coast of South America as well)	♂ 4,303-4,420g ♀ 3,400g	5-8 buff-colored eggs. Usually nests in grass along the coast but may utilize abandoned penguin burrows. Nests well lined with down. Incubation by ♀ alone: 28-40 days (aver. 34 days). ♂♂ assists with brood care.	Widespread and common in appropriate habitat.	Established in several collections and occasionally bred. However, generally not widespread and rare. Very aggressive.
Patagonian Crested Duck	*Lophonetta (Anas) s. specularioides*	Central Chile and W. central Argentina south to Tierra del Fuego. Falkland Islands.	♂ 1,070-1,180g (aver. of both races combined) ♀ 900g	5-8 creamy eggs. Nests in boggy areas on clumps of marsh grass. ♀ alone incubates but ♂ participates in rearing of the young: 30 days.	Common and widespread.	Common and bred regularly. Can be aggressive.
Andean Crested Duck	*L. s. alticola*	Andes of Chile and N.W. Argentina, north to Bolivia and Peru.	♂ 1,078g ♀ 866g (sample size: 1 pair)	Essentially same as nominate race except that they favor mountain lakes between 10-15,000′ in elevation.	Relatively common and probably secure.	Not so common as nominate race (although formerly more common) but reasonably well established. Does not breed as readily as *speculariodes*. Can be aggressive.

Tribe: ANATINI (Dabbling Ducks)

VERNACULAR NAME	LATIN NAME	DISTRIBUTION	AVERAGE WEIGHTS	NESTS, EGGS AND INCUBATION	STATUS/ WILD	STATUS/ CAPTIVITY
Blue (Mountain) Duck	*Hymenolaimus malacorhynchos*	Restricted to highland streams of New Zealand.	♂ 887g ♀ 750g	4-8 (aver. 5) pale buff eggs. Nest sites variable — usually on ground under vegetation, hollow logs, etc.; normally near water. ♀ alone incubates and ♂ assists in tending the brood: 31-32 days.	Population much reduced from former times (estimated at approx. 5000 in the mid-1970s). Considered to be rare and is *very* vulnerable.	Has been kept sporadically in the past. None currently in any collection outside of New Zealand. Has been bred by N.Z. Wildlife Service biologists.

VERNACULAR NAME	LATIN NAME	DISTRIBUTION	AVERAGE WEIGHTS	NESTS, EGGS AND INCUBATION	STATUS/ WILD	STATUS/ CAPTIVITY
Salvadori's Duck	*Anas waigiuensis*	New Guinea, above 1,300 feet.	♂ 462g ♀ 469g	3-4 creamy wt. eggs. Few wild nests described, usually in depressions under vegetation near water. Incubation presumably by ♀ alone. Incubation period not definitely established but is probably at least 28 days. ♂ possibly participates in brood care.	Not thought to be rare as yet but rather vulnerable. No population estimates available.	None currently in captivity. Difficult to acclimate. Has been bred in a New Guinea collection and has been maintained at the Wildfowl Trust in the past.
South African Black Duck	*A. s. sparsa*	Resident: South Africa north to Rhodesia and Mozambique.	♂ ♀ 952-1,077g	4-8 deep cream eggs. Nest sites typically located along grassy river banks or among driftwood. Tree sites have also been reported as well as ground burrows. ♀ alone incubates: 28 days. Highly territorial and ♂ *may* assist in brood care.	No accurate population estimates available but not thought to be rare.	Maintained in but a handful of collections. Not well established. Bred only sporadically. Can be very aggressive and at times secretive.
Abyssinian Black Duck	*A. s. leucostigma*	Resident in Central Africa from Ethiopia and Central Sudan south to Zaire and Tanzania.	♂ 1,081g (2 specimens) ♀ —	Presumably same as nominate race.	Significantly less abundant than nominate race, particularly in the west. No population estimates available.	As of early 1979, only one bird in captivity. Apparently has never been bred.
Gabon (West African) Black Duck	*A. s. maclatchyi*	Resident in Gabon and possibly Cameroon.		Presumably same as nominate race.	May not constitute a valid race.	Probably never been kept.
European (Eurasian) Wigeon	*A. penelope*	Breeds in Iceland, across Europe and Asia. Winters from British Isles south to N. Africa as well as India, Ceylon, S.E. Asia and Japan.	♂ 720g ♀ 640g	7-11 (aver. 9) creamy eggs. Nests well hidden and rather widely dispersed. Incubation by ♀ alone: 23-25 days.	Very common. At least 1 million birds in western segment of population.	Well established; more so in Europe. Commonly bred.
American (Baldpate) Wigeon	*A. americana*	Breeds throughout north-western North America. Winters along Pacific coast south to Costa Rica and Atlantic coast south to Mexico; West Indies and extreme N. South America.	♂ 770g ♀ 680g	7-9 creamy eggs. Sometimes nests rather far from water. Nests well concealed. Incubation by ♀ alone: 24-25 days.	Very common. Possibly more than 6 million ducks.	Well established and abundant in collections everywhere. Commonly bred.
Chiloe Wigeon	*A. sibilatrix*	Breeds southern third of South America. Some winter movement north to Uruguay, Paraguay, and S. Brazil. Resident in the Falkland Islands.	♂ 939g ♀ 828g	5-8 pale buff eggs. Typically nests on ground in tall grass, often considerable distance from water. Incubation by ♀ alone: 26 days; ♂ *may* assist in brood rearing.	Relatively common and the population appears to be secure.	Common and fairly well established. Breeds readily. Can be aggressive during the breeding season.
Falcated Duck	*A. falcata*	E. Asia south of the Arctic Circle, east to Kamchatka and south to Lake Baikal and Mongolia. Winters in Japan, Korea, E. and S. China and Burma.	♂ 713g ♀ 585g	6-9 (aver. 8) creamy eggs. Nests usually concealed in tall grass or small bush cover. Incubation by ♀ alone: 24-25 days.	No population estimates but there is no evidence which suggests a *significant* population decline.	Reasonably well established and bred fairly regularly in some collections.
Gadwall (Gray Duck)	*A. s. strepera*	Breeds throughout W. North America, Europe eastward to Kamchatka. Winters in S. Europe, Asia Minor, the Himalayas, China, Japan, N. Africa, India, British Columbia to Baja California and along the Atlantic coast to the Gulf Coast, Yucatan, and West Indies.	♂ 990g ♀ 850g	8-12 pale pinkish eggs. May nest colonially on favored islands. Nests usually well concealed. Incubation by ♀ alone: 26 days.	Extremely common and may be increasing in some areas. Probably in excess of several million in North America alone.	Very common and well established. Breeds readily.

VERNACULAR NAME	LATIN NAME	DISTRIBUTION	AVERAGE WEIGHTS	NESTS, EGGS AND INCUBATION	STATUS/ WILD	STATUS/ CAPTIVITY
Coues's Gadwall	A. s. couesi	Limited to Washington and New York Islands of the Fanning Island Group. (Southwest Pacific).		Not known.	Extinct. Known only from a single pair collected in 1874.	Never kept.
Baikal Teal	A. formosa	Breeds N.E. Asia south to Lake Baikal. Winters in Korea, Japan and China.	♂ 437g ♀ 431g	6-9 greenish eggs. Nest sites variable including in small holes, in vegetation, in piles of driftwood, etc. Incubation by ♀ alone: 25 days.	No population estimates but despite hunting pressure is considered one of the most common dabblers of E. Asia.	Not abundant. Apparently large surplus of males. Infrequently bred for reasons that are not clear.
European Green-Winged Teal	A. c. crecca	Breeds throughout Eurasia and Iceland. Winters southern portion breeding range, N. and central Africa, Asia Minor, India, S.E. Asia, Malaya, E. China and S. Japan.	♂ 329g ♀ 319g	8-10 yellowish wt. eggs. Nests extremely well concealed. Incubation by ♀ alone: 21-23 days.	Very abundant; over a million ducks in western segment of population alone.	Well established and regularly bred in European collections. Rare in America. Because they are nervous and elusive, they are not prominent.
American Green-Winged Teal	A. c. carolinensis	Breeds throughout North America from Alaska to as far south as California and N. New Mexico. Winters in S. United States, Mexico and occasionally to Central America and the West Indies.	♂ 360g ♀ 340g	Essentially the same as nominate race.	Extremely common; population probably exceeds 3 million ducks.	Well established (particularly in America) and breeds fairly readily, but is secretive.
Aleutian Green-Winged Teal	A. c. nimia	Resident in the Aleutian Islands. Nonmigratory.	♂ 352g ♀ 385g (Sample size: 3/3)	Presumably similar to nominate race.	Restricted range, but can be common locally. Said to be the most common dabbler in the Aleutians.	Never been kept.
Chilean Speckled Teal	A. f. flavirostris	Breeds throughout southern third of South America. Winters in Uruguay and Brazil. Resident in the Falkland Islands and South Georgia Island.	♂ 429g ♀ 394g	5-8 creamy-wt. eggs. Nest sites vary depending on locality, but may be on ground, tree nest of monk parakeet, etc. Incubation by ♀ alone, but ♂ may assist in brood rearing: 24 days.	One of the most common of South American ducks.	Well established and breeds readily.
Sharp-Winged Speckled Teal	A. f. oxyptera	Resident in the Andes of central and southern Peru, W. Bolivia, N. Chile and N. Argentina.	Slightly larger than the nominate race.	Essentially same as nominate race, but tends to favor holes of banks or escarpments as nest sites.	Rather limited distribution but can be locally common.	Fairly well established but less so than flavirostris. These two forms will readily hybridize.
Andean Speckled Teal	A. f. andium	Resident in the central and eastern Andes of Colombia and N. Ecuador.	Larger than nominate race.	Not really known, but presumably similar to nominate race.	Limited distribution and is apparently not common.	Probably has never been kept.
Merida Speckled Teal	A. f. altipetans	Resident in the Andes of Venezuela and E. Colombia.		Not really known, but presumably similar to nominate race.	Very limited distribution and apparently not common.	Probably has never been kept.
Cape Teal	A. capensis	South Africa north to the eastern Sudan and Ethiopia.	♂ 419g ♀ 380g	7-8 pale to deep cream eggs. Inland nest sites preferred, usually located among small trees and thorny bushes. Nests not necessarily located near water. ♀ alone incubates but both sexes assist in brood care: 25-26 days.	Widespread and fairly common. May be increasing in some localities.	Well established (particularly in recent years) and is easily bred. Can be aggressive.

VERNACULAR NAME	LATIN NAME	DISTRIBUTION	AVERAGE WEIGHTS	NESTS, EGGS AND INCUBATION	STATUS/ WILD	STATUS/ CAPTIVITY
Madagascar (Bernier's) Teal	*A. bernieri*	Western Madagascar.		No nests have been described, but reported clutch sizes range from 2-4 to 8-10. Incubation period unknown.	Apparently very rare and possibly declining. It is probably an endangered species. 120 estimated on Lake Bemamba in 1973 and 60 at Lake Masama in 1970.	Only record is of a female acquired by Delacour in the 1930's which lived six years.
East Indian Grey Teal	*A. g. gibberifrons*	Resident in Indonesia and East Indies.	Slightly smaller than *gracilis*	4-14 (aver. 7) creamy wt. eggs. Nest sites variable, including hollow limbs, burrows, etc., but usually on the ground. Incubation by ♀ alone but it is possible that ♂ *may* participate in brood care: 24-25 days.	No population estimates available but due to large range, the race is probably secure. Apparently not common in Java.	None in captivity, but has been kept in the past. Has probably been bred but there are no records.
Rennell Island Grey Teal	*A. g. remissa*	Rennell Island (Solomon Islands).	Smallest of the grey teal.	Not known but presumably somewhat similar to nominate race.	Unknown but undoubtedly vulnerable due to limited insular distribution. Introduced exotic fish considered detrimental. Possibly already extinct; not seen since 1959.	Little known and has probably never been kept.
Australian Grey Teal	*A. g. gracilis*	Resident in Australia, Tasmania, New Zealand, New Guinea and associated islands.	♂ 507g ♀ 474g	Same as nominate race.	One of the most common and widespread ducks of Australia.	Well established and breeds readily.
Andaman (Oceanic) Grey Teal	*A. g. albogularis*	Resident on Andaman Islands, also on Landfall and Great Coco Island.	—425g (Weights of both sexes combined)	May nest in tree hollows. Incubation period not recorded but presumably similar to nominate race.	Vulnerable due to small insular distribution, relatively small population size, and tendency to inbreed. Continual habitat disruption will undoubtedly be detrimental.	Several pairs currently at the Wildfowl Trust. Was bred during the early part of the century.
Chestnut Teal	*A. castanea*	S. Australia and Tasmania.	♂ 595g ♀ 539g	9-10 deep cream eggs. May breed more than once a year. Nests usually on ground but may also be in rock crevices or tree cavities. Incubation by ♀ alone, but ♂ *may* participate in brood rearing: 28 days.	Fairly common although much reduced from former years. More common in Tasmania.	Reasonably well established but not particularly widespread. Bred regularly in some collections.
New Zealand Brown Teal	*A. aucklandica chlorotis*	New Zealand.	♂ 665g ♀ 600g	5-7 dark cream, relatively large eggs. Nests generally located in dry and secluded places, often close to water. Incubation by ♀ alone: 27-30 days.	Quite rare and much reduced from former times. Some restocking in progress from captive-reared birds. Total population est. at approx. 1000 teal but this est. may be conservative. Most common in the Barrier Islands.	Rare. As of early 1979, very few outside of New Zealand (possibly no more than 2 males). N.Z. Wildlife Service biologists have reared a number for restocking purposes.
Auckland Island Brown Teal	*A. a. aucklandica*	Auckland Islands (Adams, Disappointment, Rose, Ocean, Ewing and Enderby Islands).	♂ — ♀ 450g	3-4 light tan eggs. Nests well concealed under vegetation and may be near soggy water courses. Incubation period unreported, presumably by ♀ alone.	Extremely rare but apparently secure due to inaccessibility. Total population unknown but at least 24 breeding pairs on Ewing Is. alone (also occurs on 6 other small islands as well). Total population may exceed 1200 to 1500 teal; (possibly optimistic).	None in captivity. A specimen at the London Zoo lived for 17 months (1895).

VERNACULAR NAME	LATIN NAME	DISTRIBUTION	AVERAGE WEIGHTS	NESTS, EGGS AND INCUBATION	STATUS/ WILD	STATUS/ CAPTIVITY
Campbell Island Brown Teal	*A. a. nesiotis*	Campbell Islands.		Not known but presumably similar to *aucklandica*.	Extremely rare. "Rediscovered" in 1975 on Dent Island after thought to be extinct. Total population probably does not exceed 20 pairs but somewhat secure due to isolated distribution. Very vulnerable.	Never been kept.
Northern Mallard	*A. p. platyrhynchos*	Breeds throughout Northern Hemisphere. Winters in southern portion of breeding range south to N. Africa, Persian Gulf, India, S. China, Japan and N. Mexico. Well established introduced populations in New Zealand and Australia.	♂ 1,261g ♀ 1,084g	8-10 greyish or buffish green eggs. Nest sites vary considerably but generally on ground, often some distance from water. Incubation by ♀ alone: 28 days.	One of the most abundant of all wild ducks. The North American segment of the population alone numbers in the millions.	Extremely common everywhere and is easily bred. Hybridizes readily.
Greenland Mallard	*A. p. conboschas*	Resident in coastal S.W. Greenland. Does not migrate, but does move to the coast during the winter.	Slightly larger than nominate race.	Presumably similar to nominate race although more than 1 year may be required for sexual maturity.	Relatively common within its restricted range.	Rare. Regularly bred at the Wildfowl Trust. Not well established in other collections.
Florida Duck	*A. p. fulvigula*	Resident in Florida to Louisiana and Texas. (Includes the so-called mottled duck, *A. f. maculosa*.)	♂ 1,030g ♀ 968g	6-12 greenish-wt. eggs. Similar to nominate race. Incubation by ♀ alone: 27-28 days.	Relatively common; perhaps several hundred thousand ducks.	Well established but not widespread. Breeds regularly.
Mexican Duck	*A. p. diazi*	Southern New Mexico, Texas and Arizona south to central Mexico.	♂ 1,036g ♀ 980g (Sample size; 1 pr.)	4-9 greenish eggs. Nests usually placed in thick grass, and arched runways may lead through vegetation. Incubation by ♀ alone: 26-28 days.	Considered by some biologists to be an endangered race. The population is estimated at 30 to 40,000 ducks. No more than 1000 pure birds north of Mexican border.	Pure specimens rare. Not well established or widespread.
Hawaiian Duck (Koloa)	*A. wyvilliana*	Resident on Hawaiian Islands (apparently now restricted to the island of Kauai). Captive-reared stock released on the islands of Oahu and Hawaii.	♂ 670g ♀ 573g	6-13 greenish-wt. eggs. Nests usually on ground, sometimes in cane fields or in grass bordering irrigation ditches. Incubation by ♀ alone: 26-28 days.	Rare and vulnerable. Considered endangered. The population may be on the order of 3000 individuals (1967).	Widespread and common but apparently relatively few "pure" specimens outside of Hawaii. Readily hybridizes with Laysan teal.
Laysan Teal	*A. laysanensis*	Resident on Laysan Island (900 miles west of Hawaii).	♂ — ♀ 450g	4-8 greenish-wt. eggs. Nests on ground generally under vegetation. Incubation by ♀ alone: 26 days.	Endangered and very vulnerable. Population noted for extreme fluctuation. Reduced to 7 individuals in 1911/12 but has been as high as 500. In 1977 it was thought that 69 teal occupied the island but by 1978, was estimated at 350-400 ducks.	Common and well established. Breeds fairly regularly.
North American Black Duck	*A. rubripes*	Breeds N.E. North America. Winters in southern portion of breeding range south to Gulf Coast, Florida and Bermuda.	♂ 1,330g ♀ 1,160g	9-10 greenish eggs. Nest sites variable. Tendency to renest if eggs taken by predators. Incubation by ♀ alone: 27-28 days.	Relatively common but recent surveys suggest a decline. Possibly numbers some half million ducks. Interbreeding with common mallards may be a significant problem.	Well established but not widespread. Easily bred.

VERNACULAR NAME	LATIN NAME	DISTRIBUTION	AVERAGE WEIGHTS	NESTS, EGGS AND INCUBATION	STATUS/ WILD	STATUS/ CAPTIVITY
Meller's Duck	*A. melleri*	Eastern Madagascar. Also on Mauritius (possibly introduced). Formerly on La Reunion Island.		8-10 yellowish-wt. eggs. No wild nests have been described. Incubation by ♀ alone: 27-29 days.	No population estimates available. Can be considered vulnerable and some biologists consider it rare, perhaps even endangered. 20 pairs throught to occupy Mauritius (1977) but the population numbered in hundreds in the 1930s.	Rare and not at all established. After an absence of a number of years, they have recently been incorporated into several collections where they have been bred.
South African Yellow-Billed Duck	*A. u. undulata*	Resident in South Africa north to Angola, Zaire, Uganda and Kenya.	♂ 954-844g ♀ 817-677g (average of both races combined)	4-10 (8 aver.) buff eggs. Nest sites generally in areas of thick grassy vegetation (usually near water). Incubation by ♀ alone: 27 days.	One of the most abundant of ducks in South Africa.	Common and well established. Readily hybridizes with closely related species.
Abyssinian Yellow-Billed Duck	*A. u. ruppelli*	Resident in Upper Blue Nile and Abyssinian Lake region of N.E. Africa.	See nominate race.	Presumably similar to nominate race.	No population estimates available, but apparently not as common as *undulata*.	Very rare and not at all established. As of early 1979, only one aged male could be accounted for in North America.
Indian Spotbill	*A. p. poecilorhyncha*	Resident throughout Indian subcontinent. Ceylon.	♂ 1,230- 1,500g ♀ 790- 1,360g	7-9 wt. or grayish eggs. Nests are generally on the ground, usually near water. Incubation by ♀ alone: 28 days. Some evidence which suggests ♂ assists in brood rearing.	No population estimates available but appears to be relatively common.	Well established and frequently bred. Prone to hybridize with closely related forms.
Burma Spotbill	*A. p. haringtoni*	Resident in Burma, E. Assam and Yunan.		Presumably similar to nominate race. Two clutches of 6 and 14 eggs have been recorded.	Extent of population is unknown. May not be a valid race.	None currently in collections. Some were kept by Delacour between 1925 and 1930. They bred fairly readily.
Chinese Spotbill	*A. p. zonorhyncha*	Breeds E. Siberia, Manchuria, N. China, S. Sakhalin, Japan and the Kurile Islands. Winters south to S. China and Taiwan.	♂ 1,156- 1,340g ♀ 750-980g	Presumably similar to nominate race.	Apparently widespread and common.	Recently re-established. Commonly bred but not widespread.
New Zealand Grey Duck	*A. s. superciliosa*	Resident throughout New Zealand as well as Macquarie, Auckland and Campbell Islands.	♂ 765-1,275g ♀ 623-1,275g	5-13 pale greenish-wt. eggs. Nest sites variable but generally located on the ground. Incubation by ♀ alone: 28 days.	Relatively common but has hybridized with the introduced mallards, particularly in urban areas.	Fairly well established but not widespread. Breeds readily.
Pelew Island (Lesser) Grey Duck	*A. s. pelewensis*	Pelew Islands (east of Philippines), N. New Guinea, Solomon Islands, Fiji, Samoa, Tonga, Tahiti, New Caledonia, New Hebrides, etc.	(Smallest of the three races)	Presumably similar to nominate race.	No population estimates but probably secure due to wide range.	Not abundant nor widespread, but breeds fairly readily.
Australian Grey (Black) Duck	*A. s. rogersi*	Widespread throughout Australia. Also resident in S. New Guinea, Tasmania, East Indies, Indonesia, Celebes, Moluccas, etc.	♂ 870-1,400g ♀ 805-1,280g	Similar to nominate race but also may nest in elevated tree cavities or in the deserted nests of other birds.	Probably the most numerous of Australian ducks.	Fairly well established but not particularly widespread. Breeds freely. Prone to hybridize.
Philippine Duck	*A. luzonica*	Resident on Philippine Islands.	♂ 906g ♀ 779g	8-14 (aver. 10) pale green eggs. Curiously, no wild nests have been described. Incubation by ♀ alone: 25-26 days.	Conflicting reports ranging from "rare" to "very abundant." It may be declining.	Well established and widespread, but totally pure specimens are less common. Breeds fairly readily. Prone to hybridize.

VERNACULAR NAME	LATIN NAME	DISTRIBUTION	AVERAGE WEIGHTS	NESTS, EGGS AND INCUBATION	STATUS/ WILD	STATUS/ CAPTIVITY
Bronze-Winged (Spectacled) Duck	*A. specularis*	Southern third of South America (forested regions).	♂ 1,130g (1 specimen) ♀ 990g	4-6 deep cream eggs. Few nests in the wild recorded, but appear to prefer small islets in the middle of a river. Apparently the ♀ alone incubates but ♂ *may* participate in brood care: 30 days.	No estimate of population size but apparently fairly common and stable.	Relatively rare and not widespread. Bred more frequently in recent years. Can be aggressive.
Northern Pintail	*A. a. acuta*	Breeds throughout Northern Hemisphere. Winters south to N. Africa, Persian Gulf, India, S.E. Asia, S. China, Taiwan, Hawaiian Islands, S. North America and Central America to Panama and West Indies.	♂ 850g ♀ 759g	8-10 creamish eggs. Tends to nest in fairly dry areas, often a mile from water. Nests often not well concealed. ♀ alone incubates: 21-26 days.	One of the most abundant of wild ducks. The North American segment of the population alone undoubtedly exceeds 6 million ducks.	Very common and well established. Breeds readily.
Kerguelen Pintail	*A. a. eatoni*	Resident on Kerguelen Island (S. Indian Ocean). Introduced to New Amsterdam and St. Paul Islands.		3-6 pale olive green eggs. Nests are well built of grass and are usually situated in tussock grass near water (or on rocky cliffs). Incubation by ♀ alone: 26 days.	Limited distribution but apparently relatively "abundant."	Quite rare. Not established but is bred in a few collections.
Crozet Pintail	*A. a. drygalskii*	Resident on Crozet Island.		Not recorded—but presumably similar to *eatoni*.	Limited distribution and are said to be "uncommon." This may not be a valid race.	Has probably never been kept.
Chilean (Brown) Pintail	*A. georgica spinicauda*	Breeds from the highlands of Peru and Bolivia south to Chile, Argentina and Tierra del Fuego. Winters as far north as S. Brazil. Resident on the Falkland Islands.	♂ 776g ♀ 705g	4-10 (aver. 7) creamy eggs. Nest sites variable, ranging from mere scrapes on bare ground to sites in thick vegetation. Incubation by ♀ alone: but ♂ *may* assist in brood care: 26 days.	One of the most abundant and widely distributed of South American waterfowl.	Fairly common and well established.
South Georgia Pintail	*A. g. georgica*	Resident on South Georgia Island.	♂ 660g ♀ 610g (sample size: one pair)	5 cream-colored eggs. Nests generally well concealed in tussock grass. Presumably the ♀ alone incubates: 26 days. ♂ *may* assist in brood care.	Exploited by whalers but currently appears to be secure. At least several thousand pairs inhabit the island.	None currently in captivity although a few have been maintained in the past at the Wildfowl Trust. Apparently has never been bred.
Niceforo's Pintail	*A. niceforoi*	Eastern Andes of Central Colombia.		Little known but presumably similar to *spinicauda*.	Probably extinct.	Apparently has never been kept.
Lesser (Northern White-Cheeked) Bahama Pintail	*A. b. bahamensis*	Resident in N. Venezuela, Guianas, N. Brazil and the Caribbean Islands.	♂ 474-533g ♀ 505-633g	6-10 creamy eggs. Reportedly nests in mangrove thickets among the roots. Incubation by ♀ alone: 25 days.	No population estimates available but the overall population appears secure. However, it is not so common on some Caribbean Islands.	Relatively abundant and widespread and is not infrequently bred.
Greater (Southern) Bahama Pintail	*A. b. rubrirostris*	Breeds in Argentina (formerly in Chile) but also occurs in S. Brazil, Paraguay, Uruguay and Bolivia.	♂ 710g ♀ 670g	Little field data but probably similar to nominate race although mangrove thickets are probably not used.	No population estimates available but apparently the population is stable.	Difficult to ascertain because of hybridization with the lesser race. Formerly was the most common of the two races but pure individuals are currently rare. Breeds readily.
Galapagos Pintail	*A. b. galapagensis*	Resident in the Galapagos Islands.		Up to 10 pale brown eggs. Nests generally in dense vegetation near water. Incubation presumably by ♀ alone: 24-25 days.	Limited distribution and, although in no current danger, is certainly vulnerable. Population estimated at approx. 2000 + teal.	Has been kept in the past at the Wildfowl Trust but none currently in captivity. Has never been bred.

VERNACULAR NAME	LATIN NAME	DISTRIBUTION	AVERAGE WEIGHTS	NESTS, EGGS AND INCUBATION	STATUS/ WILD	STATUS/ CAPTIVITY
Red-Billed Pintail	*A. erythrorhyncha*	Throughout South Africa north to S. Congo, S. Sudan, Kenya, Uganda, Tanzania and Madagascar.	♂ 617g ♀ 566g	5-12 (aver. 10) greenish-wt. eggs. Nests typically located near water in grass or other vegetation. Incubation by ♀ alone: 25-27 days.	Widespread and can be locally common.	Relatively widespread and well established. Has been bred frequently in recent years.
Northern Silver (Versicolor) Teal	*A. v. versicolor*	Breeds S. Brazil, Uruguay, Paraguay and Bolivia south to S. Central Argentina and central Chile. Winters in Bolivia, Paraguay and Brazil.	♂ 422g ♀ 373g	7-10 creamy pink eggs. Nests generally on the ground in grassy or rushy vegetation. Incubation by ♀ alone: 25-26 days.	Fairly widespread distribution but is apparently not overly abundant.	Not common although is bred regularly in some collections. More numerous than *fretensis* in America.
Southern Silver Teal	*A. v. fretensis*	Breeds S. Chile and S. Argentina to Tierra del Fuego; resident on the Falkland Islands.	Slightly larger than nominate race.	Presumably similar to nominate race.	Apparently more numerous than nominate race.	Not common nor well established. Bred fairly regularly in some collections (particularly in Europe).
Puna Teal	*A. v. puna*	Resident in puna zone of the Peruvian, Bolivian, and Chilean Andes.	Largest of the 3 *versicolor* races.	5-6 pale pinkish eggs. Nests in tall, coarse grass (usually in dry situations); often not close to water. Incubation by ♀ alone: 25-26 days.	Relatively common and said to be one of the most abundant ducks of the Peruvian Andes.	Relatively widespread and well established. Bred fairly regularly.
Hottentot Teal	*A. hottentota*	Angola, Zambia, E. Congo, Malawi, N. Mozambique, Tanzania, Kenya, Uganda, S. Ethiopia, Sudan south to the Cape.	♂ 224-253g ♀ 224-253g	6-8 creamy eggs. Nests typically placed in cattails, grass or other vegetation. Incubation by ♀ alone: 24-27 days.	Widespread but rather localized distribution. Not overly abundant but appears to be secure.	Relatively rare and not well established. More common in Europe; bred sporadically. Apparent surplus of males in America.
Garganey	*A. querquedula*	Wide breeding range throughout N. Eurasia. Winters in Africa (Egypt, Kenya, N. Africa) Mediterranean region, S. Arabia, India, Indochina, Philippines and occasionally East Indies.	♂ 240-542g ♀ 220-445g	8-11 (aver. 9) pale straw-colored eggs. Nests in tall grass or dense herbage. Apparently prefers meadows. Incubation by ♀ alone: 22-23 days.	Widespread and secure. Wintering African population sometimes reaches 2 million teal.	Common in Europe but rare in America (less so in recent years). Breeds fairly readily but is more difficult than most teal.
Prairie Blue-Winged Teal	*A. d. discors*	Breeds throughout interior of North America. Winters from Gulf Coast south through Central America to South America, occasionally as far as Chile and central Argentina.	♂ 360g ♀ 332g	10-12 creamy to olive wt. eggs. Nests in grass approx. 1' tall. May renest if nest is lost to predators. Incubation by ♀ alone: 21-24 days.	Despite some overall population decline, they are still considered one of the most abundant of North American dabblers. Average breeding population probably exceeds 5 million.	Very common and well established. Breeds freely.
Atlantic Blue-Winged Teal	*A. d. orphna*	Breeds Atlantic seaboard from New Brunswick, Nova Scotia south to North Carolina. Partially sedentary, but some may migrate to the West Indies or South America.	Said to be slightly larger than nominate race.	Presumably similar to nominate race but tends to breed in salt or brackish tidal marshes.	Not known but probably not a valid race.	Probably has been kept but not differentiated from *discors*.
Northern Cinnamon Teal	*A. cyanoptera septentrionalium*	Breeds W. North America from British Colombia south to N.W. Mexico. Winters in S.W. states south to Central America and N.W. South America.	♂ 408g ♀ 362g	6-14 wt. to pinkish-buff eggs. In ideal habitat nesting densities high (up 100 nests per sq. mile). Nests generally well concealed. Incubation by ♀ alone: 24-25 days.	Relatively abundant and total population undoubtedly exceeds one million teal.	Very common and well established. Breeds readily.
Argentine (Southern) Cinnamon Teal	*A. c. cyanoptera*	Breeds throughout southern third of South America. Winters in Brazil. Resident in the Falkland Islands.		Little studied in the wild but probably similar to *septentrionalium*. Generally nests among rushes.	No population estimates available but is apparently not particularly rare.	Well established in some collections but not widespread. Not difficult to breed.

VERNACULAR NAME	LATIN NAME	DISTRIBUTION	AVERAGE WEIGHTS	NESTS, EGGS AND INCUBATION	STATUS/ WILD	STATUS/ CAPTIVITY
Andean Cinnamon Teal	A. c. orinomus	Andean plateau of Peru and Bolivia.	Largest of the cinnamon teal.	Little known but presumably similar to the other races.	No population estimates available but there is no evidence which suggests it is rare.	Very rare and *may* have been bred on a few occasions. As of early 1979 only one "pure" ♂ could be accounted for.
Borrero's Cinnamon Teal	A. c. borreroi	Colombian Andes between 7,500 and 11,500 feet.		Not known.	Very rare and possibly already extinct.	Has probably never been kept.
Tropical Cinnamon Teal	A. c. tropica	Colombia (Upper Cauca Valley, lower parts of Cauca and Magdalene drainages) below 3000 feet.	Smallest of the cinnamon teal.	Not known.	Extent of population not known but probably not abundant.	Has probably never been kept.
Argentine Red Shoveler	A. platalea	Southern third of South America. Falkland Islands.	♂ 608g ♀ 523g	5-8 creamy eggs. Nesting habitat consists of dry areas surrounding coastal lagoons. Incubation by ♀ alone and there is some evidence which suggests ♂ participates in brood care: 25 days.	Appears to be relatively common but there are no population estimates.	Not particularly common nor widespread, but becoming more so in recent years. Breeds fairly readily.
Cape (South African) Shoveler	A. smithii	South Africa but sometimes north to S.W. Africa, Botswana and Rhodesia.	♂ 688g ♀ 597g	5-12 (9-10 aver.) creamy eggs. In some areas partially colonial nesters. Nests generally within 30' of water. Incubation by ♀ alone: 26-28 days.	Rather limited distribution but is considered fairly common.	Rare and not at all established; at least not in North America. Bred sporadically.
Australian Shoveler	A. r. rhynchotis	Resident in E. Australia with discontinuous distribution on west coast. Tasmania.	♂ 667g ♀ 665g	9-12 greenish eggs. Nests on ground with sparse cover often some distance from water but nest sites are variable. Incubation by ♀ alone: 24-28 days.	Not overly common with evidence of population decline. Fairly secure for the time being but is very vulnerable.	Very rare outside of Australia. Not established nor widespread. Bred sporadically and ducklings not particularly easy to rear.
New Zealand Shoveler	A. r. variegata	New Zealand.		Similar to nominate race.	Widespread and apparently increasing. Not as numerous as in former years.	Slightly less rare than nominate race and not firmly established. Bred occasionally (more so in Europe).
Northern (Common) Shoveler	A. clypeata	Breeds throughout Eurasia, W. North America. Winters in southern parts of breeding range south to N. & E. Africa, India, Persian Gulf, Burma, India, S. China, S. North America to Honduras.	♂ 410-1,100g ♀ 420-763g	7-14 greenish-buff eggs. Nests generally well concealed in low vegetation usually near water. Said to be polyandrous but probably is not. Some brood merging. Incubation by ♀ alone: 23-28 days.	Very common and may be increasing, at least in North America. Approx. 2 million in North America alone.	Very common, widespread and well established. Breeds readily.
Pink-Eared (Zebra) Duck	Malacorhynchus membranaceous	Nomadic throughout Australia and N. Tasmania (particularly in Darling and Murray River Basins).	♂ 404g ♀ 344g	3-11 (aver. 7) wt. to creamy wt. eggs. Nests usually elevated (from a few inches to 30') above the water. ♀ alone incubates but ♂ *may* assist in brood rearing: 27 days.	Can be common but population prone to fluctuate. Very vulnerable to habitat alteration.	As of early 1979, only three outside of Australia (Wildfowl Trust). Have been bred under semi-natural conditions in Australia. Rather delicate.
Marbled Teal	Marmaronetta (Anas) angustirostris	Breeds in S. Spain, N. Africa, Cyprus, Syria and Iraq to Caspian and Aral Seas, south to W. Pakistan. Winters in N. Africa, eastward to N. India.	♂ 240-600g ♀ 250-550g	10-11 creamy eggs. Nest sites variable but usually on ground concealed by low bushes or coarse dry grass. ♀ alone incubates: 25 days.	One of the rarest of European ducks and is very vulnerable. Population may exceed 21,000 individuals but is apparently declining.	Widespread and well established. Breeds readily.

VERNACULAR NAME	LATIN NAME	DISTRIBUTION	AVERAGE WEIGHTS	NESTS, EGGS AND INCUBATION	STATUS/ WILD	STATUS/ CAPTIVITY
Freckled (Monkey) Duck	Stictonetta naevosa	Australia; limited to S.W. Western Australia and the Murray-Darling Basin of W. Australia.	♂ 969g ♀ 842g	5-10 (aver. 7) cream or ivory eggs. Breeds only during flooded conditions. Nests built over water. Moderate amount of down in nest. Apparently ♀ alone incubates: 26-28 days.	Considered to be among the rarest of Australian ducks. Loss of appropriate habitat could doom the species. No population estimates available.	None in captivity. Never bred.
Ringed Teal	Callonetta (Anas) leucophrys	Breeds in N.W. Argentina and Uruguay and also inhabits E. Bolivia, Paraguay and S.W. and S. Brazil.	♂ 190-360g ♀ 197-310g	6-12 wt. eggs. Little studied in the field. Cavity nesters and may utilize stick nests of the monk parakeet. Incubation by ♀ alone but ♂ assists in brood care: 26-28 days.	No population estimates available but not thought to be rare.	Fairly widespread and well established. Not difficult to propagate.
Pink-Headed Duck	Rhodonessa caryophyllacea	Formerly in N. India and probably also Assam, Manipur, Bengal, Bihar and Orissa.	♂ 935g ♀ 840g	5-10 ivory-wt. (nearly round) eggs. Nests in tall grass generally well concealed. Incubation period unknown; presumably by ♀ alone.	Extinct. Last recorded definitely in the wild in 1935.	Some 20-25 specimens (between 1874 and 1935) maintained outside of India. Some lived up to 12 years but never bred. By 1935 the last bird died —as did the species.
Chilean Torrent Duck	Merganetta a. armata	Chilean Andes and adjacent regions of Argentina S. to the tip of Tierra del Fuego.	♂ 440g ♀ 315-340g	3-4 buff eggs. Few nests reported but included ledges, cliffs, bank cavities and under vegetation. ♀ alone incubates but ♂ participates in brood rearing: 43-44 days.	Population relatively secure due to inaccessibility of habitat. However, it is a highly specialized species and as such is extremely vulnerable to habitat destruction.	As of early 1979 only two adult males in America. Four young (1/3) hatched in England from eggs collected in Chile (1978). Very difficult to acclimate. Has never been bred.
Peruvian Torrent Duck	M. a. leucogenis	Andes of central and S. Ecuador and Peru.		Presumably same as nominate race.	Evidence of some population decline; relatively rare.	Never been kept.
Turner's Torrent Duck	M. a. turneri	Peruvian Andes; known only from Tinta, Cuzcan Andes and Rio Victor (Department of Arequipa) Peru.		Presumably same as nominate race.	Probably not a valid race and perhaps should be included with leucogenis.	Never been kept.
Bolivian (Garlepp's) Torrent Duck	M. a. garleppi	Bolivian Andes.		Presumably same as nominate race.	Probably not a valid race and possibly should be included with leucogenis.	Never been kept.
Berlepsch's (Argentine) Torrent Duck	M. a. berlepschi	Andes of N.W. Argentina.		Presumably same as nominate race.	Probably not a valid race and possibly should be cluded with leucogenis.	Never been kept.
Colombian Torrent Duck	M. a. colombiana	N. Ecuadorian, Venezuelian and Colombian Andes.		Presumably same as nominate race.	Relatively rare and is apparently declining, particularly in the north.	Never been kept.

Tribe: SOMATERINII (Eiders)

VERNACULAR NAME	LATIN NAME	DISTRIBUTION	AVERAGE WEIGHTS	NESTS, EGGS AND INCUBATION	STATUS/ WILD	STATUS/ CAPTIVITY
European Eider	Somateria m. mollissima	Breeds along coastal region of Eurasia (including Scotland and Iceland) from Scandinavia east to Novaya Zemlya. Rather sedentary but may winter as far south as France and even Spain and Italy.	♂ 2,253g ♀ 2,127g	3-6 dark olive-green eggs. Nest sites variable. May nest in tern colonies. Nests heavily lined with down. In some areas, can be very colonial. Brood merging typical. Incubation by ♀ alone: 25-30 (aver. 26-27) days.	Very common and widespread; population certainly numbers in the millions. (Over 1 million in Iceland alone.) However, like all seabirds, very vulnerable to oil spills.	Well established, particularly in Europe (relatively rare in America). Bred fairly regularly.

VERNACULAR NAME	LATIN NAME	DISTRIBUTION	AVERAGE WEIGHTS	NESTS, EGGS AND INCUBATION	STATUS/ WILD	STATUS/ CAPTIVITY
Pacific Eider	*S. m. v-nigra*	Breeds on arctic coasts and islands of N.E. Siberia, Commander and Aleutian Islands and coasts of N. Alaska east to Victoria Island, Canada. Winters in the Bering Sea, primarily around the Aleutian Islands and Alaska Peninsula.	♂ 2,600g ♀ 2,500g	5-8 (aver. 4) dark olive green eggs. Nests generally scattered but tends to be colonial in some regions. Nests usually between boulders above the beach or in grassy vegetation. Incubation by ♀ alone: presumably 25-30 days.	Relatively common and secure due to inaccessible range; may exceed 300,000 eiders.	Very rare and not established. As of early 1979, probably no more than 30 in captivity. Infertile eggs have been laid but has yet to be bred.
American Eider	*S. m. dresseri*	Breeds along coastal Labrador, Newfoundland, Quebec, Nova Scotia and Maine. Winters from the Gulf of St. Lawrence south to Massachusetts and E. Long Island.	♂ 2,000g ♀ 1,500g	3-5 dark olive green eggs. Habits similar to nominate race.	Common and increasing in some areas. Population probably exceeds a million birds.	Fairly well established (particularly in America) but not at all widespread. Bred sporadically.
Northern Eider	*S. m. borealis*	Breeds N.E. coast of Canada south to South-hampton Island, N. Labrador and W. Greenland. Winters from S. Greenland and Labrador south to Nova Scotia and Maine.	♂ 2,000g ♀ 1,810g	3-5 dark olive green eggs. Nest sites vary but apparently prefers areas sheltered by rocks, and boulder-covered iselts. Incubation by ♀ alone: 25-30 days.	Extent of population unknown but apparently not rare.	Rare and not established. Perhaps no more than a dozen in captivity. Apparently has been bred in Canada.
Faeroe Eider	*S. m. faeroeensis*	Resident on Faeroe Islands.	♂ — ♀ 1,703-2,223g	Presumably similar to nominate race.	Limited distribution but considered locally common. This race is suspect.	Presumably has never been kept.
Hudson Bay Eider	*S. m. sedentaria*	Breeds along coasts and islands of Hudson Bay south to James Bay. Winters around the Belcher Islands.	♂ 2,500g ♀ 1,575-1,825g	Presumably the same as *borealis*.	Extent of population unknown. Not recognized as a valid race by some authorities.	Probably has been kept but not separated from *dresseri*.
King Eider	*S. spectabilis*	Circumpolar breeding distribution: Greenland, N. Russia, Siberia, N. Alaska, Arctic coast of Canada and probably N. Labrador. Winters from the Aleutians south (occasionally to California) and along the Atlantic coast from Greenland to New-foundland with strays farther south.	♂ 1,830g ♀ 1,750g	3-6 bright olive eggs. Prefers islands but are also common on the tundra. Nests widely scattered. Tendency to merge broods. ♀ alone incubates: 22-24 days.	Very common and widespread. The North American segment of the population alone may exceed 1½ million eiders.	Rare and barely established (more so in Europe). Bred sporadically.
Spectacled (Fischer's) Eider	*S. fischeri*	Limited distribution. Breeds from E. Siberia from the Chukot Peninsula to the Yana River Delta, east to coastal N.W. Alaska, particularly in the lower Kuskokwim Delta. Winter grounds unknown but presumably in the Bering Sea.	♂ 1,630g ♀ 1,630g	4-6 olive eggs. Nests usually along edge of tundra ponds near the coast, often not well concealed. Incubation by ♀ alone: 24 days.	Despite rather limited distribution, the population may number 300,000-500,000 eiders. Some biologists suggest that they are declining.	Extremely rare. First bred at the Wildfowl Trust in 1976. Certainly less than 50 in captivity as of early 1979.

VERNACULAR NAME	LATIN NAME	DISTRIBUTION	AVERAGE WEIGHTS	NESTS, EGGS AND INCUBATION	STATUS/ WILD	STATUS/ CAPTIVITY
Steller's Eider	*Polysticta stelleri*	Breeds along coastal regions of extreme N. Alaska from Wainwright to Pitt Point, also portions of Alaska along Bering Sea, St. Lawrence Island, westward to Novaya Zemlya in Arctic Siberia. Winters mainly in the Aleutian Islands but also at the Commander and Kurile Islands, Kamchatka and Kenai Peninsulas and N. Finland and Norway.	♂ 860g ♀ 860g	7-8 pale olive buff eggs. Nests well scattered and well camouflaged. May be on flat tundra or on a slight hummock or in a depression between hummocks. Some apparent brood merging. ♀ alone incubates: Incubation period not definitely established but is probably in the 22-24 day range.	Population appears to be relatively stable and secure for the time being and may number 500,000 eiders.	Extremely rare and represented in but a handful of collections. Some wild-caught adults recently incorporated into several collections. Certainly less than 60 in captivity as of early 1979. Has never been bred.

Tribe: AYTHYINI (Pochards)

VERNACULAR NAME	LATIN NAME	DISTRIBUTION	AVERAGE WEIGHTS	NESTS, EGGS AND INCUBATION	STATUS/ WILD	STATUS/ CAPTIVITY
Red-Crested Pochard	*Netta rufina*	Breeds from the Lower Danube through S. Russia to W. Siberia, south to N. Syria, Iran and W. China. Winters in India, Burma, N. Africa and E. Mediterranean.	♂ 1,135g ♀ 967g	6-12 greenish or light stone-colored eggs. Nest sites variable, often at edge of water, in dense vegetation, or on floating mats of aquatic vegetation. Incubation by ♀ alone: 26-28 days.	Common and secure. Probably in excess of 200,000 in western portion of the range alone.	Well established and common. Breeds very readily.
South American (Southern) Pochard	*N. e. erythropthalma*	N. half of South America.	♂ 600-977g (Aver. of both races combined) ♀ 533-1,000g	Little studied but presumably similar to *brunnea*.	Status not well known but the population apparently has undergone a substantial decrease in recent years throughout much of its range, for reasons which are not clear.	Rare. As of early 1979, it is possible that no pure ones exist in captivity. Has apparently been bred in the past.
African (Southern) Pochard	*N. e. brunnea*	Eastern Africa from S. Sudan, E. Zaire, Angola, Uganda, Kenya, Tanzania, Malawi, Zambia south to Rhodesia and South Africa.	See nominate race.	6-15 (aver. 9) creamy wt. eggs. Nests usually near water in grass or over water in aquatic vegetation. ♀ alone incubates: 26 days.	Widespread and common.	Reasonably well established but not widespread (more common in Europe). Bred regularly but not commonly.
Rosy-Billed (Rosybill) Pochard	*N. peposaca*	Breeds in central Chile, central Argentina north to S.E. Brazil, Uruguay and Paraguay. Winters north to Bolivia and south central Brazil.	♂ 1,181g ♀ 1,004g	8-12 (aver. 10) greenish or cream eggs. Most nests are in the water amid dense vegetation. Will dump eggs in nests of other species. Incubation by ♀ alone: 25-28 days.	One of the most abundant of South American diving ducks.	Widespread and common. Well established. Commonly bred. Will hybridize with *N. rufina*.
Canvasback	*Aythya valisineria*	Breeds from central Alaska south to N. California, east to Nebraska and Minnesota. Winters in S. Canada south along the Pacific and Atlantic coasts to central and south Mexico.	♂ 1,252g ♀ 1,154g	8-10 bright olive eggs. Nest typically constructed in aquatic vegetation fairly close to open water. Some dump nesting tendencies. Incubation by ♀ alone: 24-25 days.	Population tends to fluctuate in response to climatic conditions. Very vulnerable to habitat destruction and oil pollution. Currently in excess of a million ducks, but may be declining.	Fairly well established but neither widespread nor common. They are reluctant breeders but some propagators have been particularly successful with them.
European (Eurasian) Pochard	*A. ferina*	Breeds in Europe through central Eurasia to W. China. Winters from southern breeding range south to N. Africa, Nile Valley, Persian Gulf, India, Burma, S. China and Japan.	♂ 998g ♀ 947g	6-9 olive eggs. Typically nests in reef beds, often on floating mats of aquatic vegetation. May dump eggs. Incubation by ♀ alone: 24-28 days (aver. 25 days).	Very abundant and possibly increasing. At least 1 million pochards make up western segment of the population.	Common and well established in European collections (almost nonexistent in America). Regularly bred.

VERNACULAR NAME	LATIN NAME	DISTRIBUTION	AVERAGE WEIGHTS	NESTS, EGGS AND INCUBATION	STATUS/ WILD	STATUS/ CAPTIVITY
Redhead	*A. americana*	Breeds from central Canada south to S. California, New Mexico, Minnesota, Nebraska and Old Mexico. Winters from Washington east to the middle Atlantic states south to the Gulf coast, Mexico and Guatemala.	♂ 1,080g ♀ 1,030g	7-8 pale buff to greenish eggs. Usually nests in dense aquatic vegetation but sometimes nests on dry land. Somewhat parasitic and may merge broods. ♀ alone incubates: 24 days.	Total population has declined significantly and while they are still fairly numerous, their status is shaky. Very vulnerable. Population probably numbers between 1 and 1½ million ducks.	Common and well established. Bred fairly regularly.
Ring-Necked Duck	*A. collaris*	Breeds N. North America from New England north to Nova Scotia and west through the forested parts of S. Canada to the Mackenzie District. Winters along Pacific coast from British Columbia to Baja California, Mexico, Central America (to Panama) and along Atlantic coast from Massachusetts southward, including the West Indies.	♂ 790g ♀ 690g	8-12 greyish to buffy wt. eggs. May nest on floating mats of vegetation but also ashore, usually close to water. Incubation by ♀ alone: 26-27 days.	Relatively common and apparently increasing and extending their range. Current population estimates suggest approximately ½ million ducks.	Curiously, relatively scarce and not widespread but are apparently fairly well established. Rather reluctant breeders.
Australian White-Eye (Hardhead)	*A. a. australis*	Widespread throughout Australia. Also Tasmania and possibly E. Java, Celebes, New Guinea, New Caledonia and formerly in New Zealand.	♂ 902g ♀ 838g	9-12 pale cream eggs. Breeding dependent on spring rainfall. Nests generally in the water on aquatic vegetation. Incubation by ♀ alone: 25 days.	Has declined, particularly along the coast in Australia. Can be common locally but is very vulnerable and continued marsh and swamp drainage could endanger it.	Fairly well established but not widespread and not particularly common. Bred regularly but not commonly (more so in Europe).
Banks Island White-Eye	*A. a. extima*	Banks and Gaua Islands (north of the New Hebrides Island group).	Slightly smaller than nominate race.	Little studied but presumably similar to *australis*.	No population estimates available but it is undoubtedly very vulnerable.	Apparently has never been kept.
Baer's Pochard (Siberian White-Eye)	*A. baeri*	Breeds E. central Asia from Transbaikalia to the lower Ussuri River and the Amur and possibly also on Kamchatka. Winters in S.E. China, also to Assam, Burma and rarely in Japan.	♂ 880g ♀ 680g	6-9 cream to pale brown eggs. Little studied in the field but apparently nests along lake shorelines and and river banks in dense vegetation. Incubation by ♀ alone: 27 days.	Relatively rare throughout much of its range but is considered common along the coast of the U.S.S.R. and E. Manchuria. No population estimates are available but is overall probably not as rare as some of the literature suggests.	In recent years, has become reasonably well established but is not particularly widespread. Bred regularly but not commonly.
Ferruginous White-Eye	*A. nyroca*	Breeds in Europe eastward to W. Siberia and south to S. Tibet, Kashmir, Turkeston, Iran and northern Africa. Winters in in Burma, Persian Gulf, Nile Valley and Mediterranean region.	♂ 583g ♀ 520g	7-11 pale buff or yellowish grey eggs. Typically nests close to water, often on floating mats of aquatic vegetation. ♀ alone incubates: 25-27 days.	Total extent of population unknown but at least ¼ million occupy the western part of the range.	Common and well established. Breeds fairly readily.
Madagascar White-Eye	*A. innotata*	North and east Madagascar.		5-6 buffy grey eggs. Wild nests have not been described. Incubation by ♀ alone: 26-28 days.	Status is not known but due to limited distribution and rapid deforestation of Madagascar, it could be threatened and is certainly vulnerable.	None currently. Formerly in European collections but all were lost during World War II.
Tufted Duck	*A. fuligula*	Breeds in Iceland, Europe and throughout most of Eurasia to Pacific coast. Winters in southern portions of breeding range south to northern Africa, Nile Valley, Persian Gulf, India, S. China and the Philippines.	♂ 1,116g ♀ 1,050g	6-14 (aver. 10) greenish-grey eggs. May nest in gull or tern colonies. Nest sites variable. Incubation by ♀ alone: 23-25 days.	Common and increasing in some portions of its range. Total extent of the population is unknown but in excess of 800,000 winter in Europe alone.	Common and well established. Bred fairly regularly.

VERNACULAR NAME	LATIN NAME	DISTRIBUTION	AVERAGE WEIGHTS	NESTS, EGGS AND INCUBATION	STATUS/ WILD	STATUS/ CAPTIVITY
New Zealand Scaup (Black Teal)	*A. novae-seelandiae*	New Zealand. Also on Auckland and Chatham Islands.	♂ 695g ♀ 610g	5-8 cream eggs. Nests usually placed in dense cover at edge of lake or other water source. Extensive amount of down. Incubation by ♀ alone: 27-30 days.	Formerly relatively rare but is responding to total protection and has started to reoccupy areas of former abundance. Population undoubtedly exceeds 2000.	Relatively well established and bred fairly regularly (particularly in Europe).
European Greater Scaup	*A. m. marila*	Breeds in Iceland, Scandinavia, N. Eurasia east across Siberia perhaps to the coast where it may intergrade with *mariloides*. Winters along coastal regions of W. Europe, E. Mediterranean, Black Sea, Persian Gulf and N.W. India.	♂ 1,250g ♀ 900-1,200g	8-10 brownish to olive eggs. Nest sites variable ranging from thick vegetation to cracks in rocks. Often well concealed. May nest in gull or tern colonies. Some parasitic nesting tendencies. ♀ alone incubates: 24-28 days.	Apparently relatively abundant although no overall population estimates available; at least 200,000 winter in Europe alone.	Common and bred relatively frequently in Europe. Essentially absent in American collections.
Pacific Greater Scaup	*A. m. mariloides*	Breeds along coast of Ungava Bay, Newfoundland, and N. Hudson Bay west to the Bering Sea coast of Alaska. Also mainland E. Asia west to Lena River. Winters along coast from Alaska to California, Gulf of St. Lawrence to South Carolina, coasts of Japan, Korea and China.	♂ 1,000g ♀ 976g	Essentially same as *marila*.	Common and apparently stable. At least 200,000 in North America alone.	Fairly well established but due to hybridization with *affinis*, totally pure specimens are not particularly common. Bred regularly but not commonly. Relatively rare in Europe.
Lesser Scaup	*A. affinis*	Breeds inland regions of N.W. North America from central Alaska to Nebraska. Winters from mid-Atlantic states to West Indies and Colombia and along the west coast from British Columbia to Mexico.	♂ 850g ♀ 800g	8-10 olive to stone-colored eggs. Nests generally within 150' of pot holes or marshes. Sometimes builds floating nests. May nest in association with terns. Incubation by ♀ alone: 23-25 days.	Population appears to be relatively stable and they are among the most numerous of North American pochards. The population certainly numbers in the millions.	Well established and bred fairly regularly.

Tribe: CAIRININI (Perching Ducks)

VERNACULAR NAME	LATIN NAME	DISTRIBUTION	AVERAGE WEIGHTS	NESTS, EGGS AND INCUBATION	STATUS/ WILD	STATUS/ CAPTIVITY
Lesser Brazilian Teal	*Amazonetta b. brasiliensis*	Resident in Colombia and Venezuela south to S. Brazil.	♂ 380-480g ♀ 350-390g	6-8 pale cream eggs. Not as prone to utilize cavities as most members of the tribe. May nest in vegetation surrounded by water, possibly on cliff faces or in tree nests of other avian species. Incubation by ♀ alone but ♂ is involved in brood care: 25 days.	Said to be one of the commonest ducks of Brazil.	May be common but not differentiated from *ipecutiri*. Certainly hybrids exist. Can be slightly aggressive.
Greater Brazilian Teal	*A. b. ipecutiri*	Resident in Buenos Aires Province, Argentina north to Uruguay, E. Bolivia and S. Brazil.	♂ 600g ♀ 580g (Sample size 2/1)	Essentially same as nominate race.	No evidence which suggests it is rare.	In recent years has become well established and widespread. Breeds very readily.
Maned Goose (Australian Wood Duck)	*Chenonetta jubata*	Throughout Australia, including Tasmania.	♂ 815g ♀ 800g	8-11 creamy eggs. Breeding is dependent on arrival of rains. Typically nests in tree hollows, up to a mile from water. Incubation by ♀ alone, but ♂ assists in brood care: 28 days.	Although subjected to much hunting pressure, there is no indication of population decline.	Relatively well established and widespread. However, they are reluctant breeders and are only bred sporadically (but regularly).

VERNACULAR NAME	LATIN NAME	DISTRIBUTION	AVERAGE WEIGHTS	NESTS, EGGS AND INCUBATION	STATUS/ WILD	STATUS/ CAPTIVITY
Mandarin Duck	*Aix galericulata*	Breeds in extreme E. Asia from the Amur and Ussuri Rivers south to Korea, E. China and Japan. Winters in southern portion of the breeding range, S.E. China and occasionally to Formosa. There is a well established feral population in Great Britain.	♂ 440-550g (weights of both sexes combined) ♀ 440-550g	9-12 creamy wt. eggs. Typically selects tree cavity near or overhanging water but rarely do nest on the ground. Incubation by ♀ alone: 28-30 days.	Apparently fairly secure (although vulnerable), but may have suffered local declines.	Well established and widespread. Breeds readily.
North American Wood Duck (Carolina Duck)	*A. sponsa*	Breeds throughout E. North America from Lake Winnipeg and S. Nova Scotia south to Texas, Florida and Cuba and along the Pacific coast from British Columbia to California. Winters in the southern half of the breeding range.	♂ 680g ♀ 539g	13-15 wt. eggs. Nests in tree cavities (often high up), often over water. Readily takes to artificial nest boxes. Incubation by ♀ alone: 30 days.	Very common, particularly considering the species was virtually extinct in the wild during the early part of the 1900's. The population certainly exceeds 1 million ducks.	One of the most common and popular of all captive waterfowl. Breeds very freely and often.
African Pygmy Goose	*Nettapus auritus*	Wide range in Africa from the Cape north to Senegal and Ethiopia. Also inhabits Madagascar.	♂ 285g ♀ 260g	6-12 creamy-wt. eggs. Nests usually in tree cavities but also on ground, cliff holes, termite mounds, thatched roofs, etc. alone incubates: 23-26 days. It is not known if the ♂ actively participates in brood care.	Considered to be relatively common.	Rare; probably no more than 20 in captivity as of early 1979. Was first bred in 1975. All forms of pygmy geese are notoriously delicate.
Indian Pygmy Goose (Cotton Teal)	*N. c. coromandelianus*	Resident throughout India, S.E. Asia, Malay Peninsula, N. Luzon (Philippines), Indonesia, N. Celebes and N. New Guinea	♂ 255-312g ♀ 185-255g	6-8 (up to 14) creamy wt. eggs. Typically selects tree hollows but has also been known to nest in buildings. Incubation presumably by ♀ alone and the role of the ♂ during brood rearing is not really known. Incubation period not established but probably in the 22-24 day range.	Fairly common throughout much of their range but apparently relatively rare along the Malay Peninsula and in the East Indies.	Very rare. Has been attempted often but has never been established. Certainly less than 20 in captivity. Was bred for the first time in 1978 by the New York Zoological Society (♂ was on breeding loan from the Wildfowl Trust).
Australian (White-Quilled) Pygmy Goose	*N. c. albipennis*	Resident in N.E. Australia; coastal regions of E. Cape York Peninsula south to Townsville.	♂ 403g ♀ 380g	Similar to nominate race.	One of the rarer Australian ducks but is reasonably common in some areas. The total population has declined significantly. Can be adversely affected by loss of appropriate habitat.	Never been kept outside of Australia; apparently has never been bred.
Green Pygmy Goose	*N. pulchellus*	Resident in N. Australia from the Fitzroy River to Rockhampton, Queensland. Also in S. New Guinea, Ceram and Buru.	♂ 310g ♀ 304g	8-12 creamy wt. eggs. Typically nests in tree hollows. Incubation presumably by ♀ alone and ♂ may be involved in brood care. Incubation period not established but probably in the 22-24 day range.	Not particularly abundant but can be locally common within appropriate habitat. Appears to be secure if habitat remains intact.	Never been kept outside of Australia. A few currently in Australian collections but has never been bred.
Hartlaub's Duck	*Pteronetta hartlaubi*	Guinea west to Zaire and S.W. Sudan. Resident.	♂ 800-940g ♀ 800-940g	9 (or more) cream eggs. Little studied in the wild and no nests described but presumably in tree hollows. ♀ alone incubates but ♂ apparently is involved in brood defense: 32 days.	No population estimates available, but if the rain forests are cut, no doubt the species will suffer. The race *albifrons* appears to be invalid.	Rare although in recent years it has become more established. Bred sporadically and some birds currently being brought to America from European collections. Bred for the first time in North America in 1977 by Seattle Zoological Garden. Can be aggressive.

VERNACULAR NAME	LATIN NAME	DISTRIBUTION	AVERAGE WEIGHTS	NESTS, EGGS AND INCUBATION	STATUS/ WILD	STATUS/ CAPTIVITY
White-Winged Wood Duck	*Cairina scutulata*	Assam, Manipur, Bangladesh, Burma and locally south through the Malay Peninsula to Java and Sumatra.	♂ 2,945-3,855g ♀ 1,925-3,050g	6-13 greenish yellow eggs. Few wild nests have been documented but probably seeks decaying hollows. Presumably ♀ alone incubates: 33-35 days. ♂ may remain with the family but their involvement in brood care is not known.	Considered to be endangered species but may be more common than suspected. However, in many portions of the range, it is very rare and decreasing, and the population may number less than 200 pairs.	Rare but well established at Wildfowl Trust where it is breeding regularly (100 reared between 1971-77). Some pairs sent to other collections on breeding loan in recent years. Bred for first time in America in 1978 by National Zoological Park. Can be aggressive.
Muscovy Duck	*C. moschata*	Resident from S. Mexico south to South America from the coast of Peru on the west to Santa Fe, Argentina in the east.	♂ 2.0-4.0kg ♀ 1.1-1.5kg	8-15 wt. (w/greenish sheen) eggs. Little studied in the wild. Typically nests in tree hollows but also nests on ground. ♀ alone incubates: 35 days.	While extirpated in some areas it remains widespread and fairly abundant.	As a "pure wild" species very rare but breeds readily. Birds with domestic blood are quite common. Very aggressive.
Old World Comb Duck	*Sarkidiornis m. melanotos*	India, Burma, Thailand, Laos, S.E. China, Madagascar and Africa from Gambia and the Sudan south to the Cape.	♂ 1,300-2,610g ♀ 870-2,325g (aver. of both races combined)	8-12 pale cream eggs. Nest sites variable and while they do use hollows, ground sites in tall grass cover near water are apparently more common. Incubation by ♀ alone: 30 days.	Appears to be relatively common and secure over much of its range but has apparently disappeared in Ceylon.	Fairly well established but not particularly widespread. Rather reluctant breeders but some propagators have been successful with them. Trios do better than pairs.
South American Comb Duck	*S. m. sylvicola*	E. Panama and Trinidad south on the east side of the Andes to N. Argentina.	See nominate race.	Presumably similar to *melanotos*.	No population estimates available but no indication of a decline. Probably not as secure as *melanotos*.	Not as abundant as nominate race nor as well established. Bred sporadically.
(Gambian) Spur-Winged Goose	*Plectropterus g. gambensis*	Resident from Gambia, Kordofan and White Nile south to the Zambesi.	♂ 5.4-6.8kg (rarely to 10kg) ♀ 4.0-5.4kg (aver. of both races combined)	6-15 wt. eggs. Nest sites variable but are usually on the ground in grass or reed beds, but also among rocks in termite mound cavities or in the nests of other large birds. Incubation by ♀ alone: 30-32 days.	Among the commonest of the larger African waterfowl and has adapted to human encroachment.	Neither rare nor common. A captive self-sustaining population does not exist as yet because they are bred only infrequently. However, they are long-lived. Can be aggressive.
Black Spur-Winged Goose	*P. g. niger*	Resident from at least Botswana south to the Cape of Good Hope.	See nominate race.	Presumably similar to *gambensis*.	Same as nominate race.	Relatively rare and has been bred at least once. Not well established.

Tribe: MERGINI (Sea Ducks)

VERNACULAR NAME	LATIN NAME	DISTRIBUTION	AVERAGE WEIGHTS	NESTS, EGGS AND INCUBATION	STATUS/ WILD	STATUS/ CAPTIVITY
Labrador Duck	*Camptorhynchus labradorius*	Bred probably in Labrador (or farther north) Wintered south to Chesapeake Bay but mainly along Long Island.	♂ 864g ♀ 482g	Clutch size not recorded but eggs probably pale olive to yellowish brown. Virtually nothing is known about its reproductive biology.	Extinct; the last one was recorded in 1875.	Apparently was never attempted in captivity.
Atlantic Harlequin Duck	*Histrionicus h. histrionicus*	Breeds in Iceland, Greenland, Baffin Island and N. Labrador (and perhaps Newfoundland). Winters in its breeding range and south to Long Island.	♂ 680g (aver. of both races combined). ♀ 540g	4-8 creamy eggs. Nest sites generally well concealed and surface nesting is more typical than hole-nesting. Incubation by ♀ alone: probably 28-29 days.	Population size is relatively small compared to the Pacific race; i.e., probably no more than 500 in Iceland. However, it appears to be stable.	Very rare and occurs in but a handful of collections (mostly in Europe). Virtually all captive birds acquired as eggs in Iceland. As of 1978, had not been bred.
Pacific Harlequin Duck	*H. h. pacificus*	Wide range. Breeds from N. and E. Asia and Bering Sea Islands, Alaska and the Yukon south to central California and Wyoming. Winters in or near the breeding range, south to California.	See nominate race.	Essentially the same as *historianicus*.	Often not considered as a separate race. Total extent of population not known but very common. Up to a million wintering harlequins in the Aleutian Islands alone.	Very rare and exists in no more than a dozen collections. Was bred for first time in 1977. In recent years some wild-caught adults have been incorporated into collections.

VERNACULAR NAME	LATIN NAME	DISTRIBUTION	AVERAGE WEIGHTS	NESTS, EGGS AND INCUBATION	STATUS/ WILD	STATUS/ CAPTIVITY
Oldsquaw (Long-Tailed) Duck	*Clangula hyemalis*	Circumpolar breeding range which includes arctic North America, Greenland, Iceland, N. Eurasia and Bering Sea islands. Winters south to Europe, Black Sea, Caspian Sea, Japan, California, Great Lakes, S. Greenland south to South Carolina.	♂ 800g ♀ 650g	6-7 olive buff eggs. Prefers islands on tundra ponds. May nest in tern colonies. Nests well concealed and notoriously difficult to locate. Incubation by ♀ alone: 24-26 days.	One of the most abundant of arctic ducks. At least 3-4 million in North America alone. Approximately a quarter of a million pairs occupy W. Russia.	Very rare and not established. Has proven to be very delicate. Has only been bred once or twice prior to 1978 when young were reared in at least two private collections in England. Small flock established in 1978 at the Game Bird Center in Salt Lake City, Utah.
European Black Scoter	*Melanitta n. nigra*	Breeds in Iceland, Scotland, Spitsbergen and N. Eurasia to Khatanga River. Winters chiefly off coastal areas of W. Europe and on the Mediterranean, Black and Caspian Seas.	♂ 1,108g ♀ 1,006g	6-9 creamy to pinkish buff eggs. Nests can be well concealed. May nest on tiny islands. Incubation by ♀ alone: 27-28 days.	Extent of population not known but are not rare and can be considered abundant. At least 150,000 winter in W. Europe alone. However, like all seabirds, scoters are extremely vulnerable to oil spills.	Rare. Virtually nonexistent in America. Was bred once in 1970; again in 1978. A pair survived over 12 yrs. in Delacour's collection in France. Most obtained as eggs.
American (Pacific) Black Scoter	*M. n. americana*	Breeds in Alaska from Bristol Bay north to the Kotzebue Sound and Mt. McKinley and N. Siberia from the Lena-Yana watershed to the Anadyr Basin. Also on the Kamchatka Peninsula and Kurile Islands. Winters along the Asian and North American Pacific coast, Great Lakes and North American Atlantic coast.	♂ 1,087g ♀ 815g	Essentially the same as *nigra*. Generally nests well inland and nests well dispersed.	Least common of the American scoters but not at all rare. Over a quarter of a million breed in Alaska alone. 400,000 may winter in Alaska.	Very rare, almost nonexistent. Virtually all in captivity were salvaged from oil spills. Never been bred. Can be difficult to initially acclimate.
Surf Scoter	*M. perspicillata*	Breeds from W. Alaska east through the Canadian Yukon and Northwest Territories to S. Hudson Bay and the interior of Quebec and Labrador. Winters along Atlantic coast south to Florida (also Great Lakes) and along the Pacific coast south to Baja California including the Sea of Cortez.	♂ 1,000g ♀ 900g	5-7 creamy to pinkish-buff eggs. Few nests have been described. Usually well concealed, often far from water. Brood merging may take place. Incubation period has not been definitely established but probably in the 27-28 day range. Incubation by ♀ alone.	While considered the least abundant of the 3 species of scoters it is by no means rare. The population may be on the order of ¾ of a million scoters.	Virtually nonexistent (6 at Sea World, San Diego, as of early 1979). Almost all that have been kept were acquired as salvage or oil spill birds although in recent years a few wild-caught adults have been acquired. Very delicate although a male survived 10 years at San Diego Zoo. Has never been bred.
European White-Winged (Velvet) Scoter	*M. f. fusca*	Breeds in N. Eurasia from Scandinavia to possibly the mouth of the Khatanga River. Winters offshore Norway to Spain and on the Caspian Sea.	♂ 1,727g ♀ 1,492-1,658g	9-10 creamy to buff eggs. Nests generally in heavy vegetation (often woodlands). Nests well concealed, even from above. May nest with gulls and terns. Incubation by ♀ alone: 26-27 days.	The extent of the population is not known but some 30,000 winter in the Baltic area of Europe alone.	Rare. Represented in a few European collections (none in America). Most obtained as eggs (i.e., Finland). Has never been bred.
Asiatic White-Winged Scoter	*M. f. stejnegeri*	Breeds in E. Asia from the Alta to the Kamchatka Peninsula (possibly also the Commander Islands). Winters off the coast of E. Asia south to Japan and China.		Presumably similar to nominate. race.	No population estimates.	Has probably never been kept.
American White-Winged Scoter	*M. f. deglandi*	Breeds in N.W. Canada from Hudson Bay to S. Manitoba (possibly to North Dakota). Winters on the Great Lakes and south along the Atlantic coast to South Carolina.	♂ 1,542g ♀ 1,223g	Similar to nominate race.	No reliable population estimates but certainly numbers in the hundreds of thousands.	Virtually none. Salvage or oil spill birds become available from time to time. Has never been bred.

VERNACULAR NAME	LATIN NAME	DISTRIBUTION	AVERAGE WEIGHTS	NESTS, EGGS AND INCUBATION	STATUS/ WILD	STATUS/ CAPTIVITY
Pacific White-Winged Scoter	M. f. dixoni	Breeds in N.W. Alaska, winters along Pacific coast south to Baja California.		Similar to nominate race.	It is doubtful if this race can be separated from deglandi. Nevertheless, at least ¼ million winter in the Aleutian Islands alone with perhaps another 150,000 wintering south down the Pacific coast.	Very rare. In recent years, a few wild-caught adults have been collected. A female salvaged from the January 1969 Santa Barbara oil spill was still alive in early 1979. Has never been bred.
Bufflehead	Bucephala albeola	Widespread breeding range throughout N. North America from S. Alaska to S. Hudson Bay south to N. California and N.W. Wyoming. Winters along Pacific coast from the Aleutians to central Mexico and along the Gulf and Atlantic coasts from S. Canada to Texas. Also in the interior where open water occurs.	♂ 450g ♀ 330g	8-9 creamy to pale olive buff eggs. May return to site used in previous years. Typically nests in tree cavities, usually close to water. May dump nest. Incubation by ♀ alone: 30 days.	Fairly common and appears to be increasing in the midwest and eastern states but has declined in the far western states. At least ¾ of a million birds make up the population.	Not particularly common nor widespread but reasonably well established. Bred regularly by some propagators. Ducklings can be difficult to raise.
Barrow's Goldeneye	B. islandica	Two distinct populations. Breeds in Iceland, S.W. Greenland and N. Labrador and from S. Alaska and the Mackenzie District south to California and Wyoming. Winters along Pacific coast south to central California and down the Atlantic coast to the mid-Atlantic states as well as Greenland and Iceland.	♂ 1,110g ♀ 800g	9-11 bluish-green eggs. Typically nests in tree cavities but in treeless Iceland, will nest on the ground in other cavities or under dense vegetation. In Iceland, nesting densities high —up to 600 pair/per sq. kilometer. Incubation by ♀ alone: 32 days.	Accurate population estimates not known but several thousand in Iceland and at least 150,000 make up western segment of population. Probably some 200,000 total birds.	Reasonably well established and fairly widespread. Bred regularly but not commonly. Most original breeding stock obtained from Iceland eggs (at least in Europe).
European Goldeneye	B. c. clangula	Breeds in Iceland and throughout N. Eurasia to Pacific coast. Winters in southern limits of the breeding range; Europe south to the Mediterranean, Persian Gulf, N. India, Burma, S. China and Japan.	♂ 990-1,158g ♀ 710-799g	9-11 greenish eggs. Generally use tree cavities and may re-use the same cavity of previous year. Will also use artificial nest boxes. Incubation by ♀ alone: 27-32 (aver. 30) days.	Relatively common and apparently somewhat stable although is increasing in some areas after a downward trend. At least 400,000 in western segment of the population alone.	Relatively common and well established in Europe but virtually absent in America (at least 2 pair as of early 1979). Bred regularly in some collections.
American (Common) Goldeneye	B. c. americana	Breeds throughout N. North America from central Alaska to S. Labrador and Newfoundland, south through the forested regions of Canada and N. and N.E. parts of the United States. Winters along the Pacific coast from Alaska south to California and in the interior wherever open water is present. Also down the Atlantic coast from Newfoundland to Florida.	♂ 997g ♀ 815g	Essentially the same as clangula.	Relatively common. Certainly in excess of 1 million ducks.	Relatively well established (particularly in America) but not particularly abundant. Bred regularly but not commonly.
Smew	M. albellus	Breeds throughout N. Eurasia from N. Scandinavia to E. Siberia. Winters along coasts and lakes of Europe to the Mediterranean, the Caspian Sea, Iran, N. India, S. China and Japan.	♂ 540g-935g ♀ 515g-650g	6-9 creamy-buff eggs. Preferred nest sites are in the hollows of broad-leafed trees (often relatively low to the ground). Will mix clutches with other species. Incubation by ♀ alone: 28 days.	Overall population estimates not available but the species is not thought to be uncommon. Some 40,000 winter in Europe.	Fairly well established and bred regularly in some collections (but not commonly). Rare in America but more have become available in recent years. Were not bred in the New World until 1975.

VERNACULAR NAME	LATIN NAME	DISTRIBUTION	AVERAGE WEIGHTS	NESTS, EGGS AND INCUBATION	STATUS/ WILD	STATUS/ CAPTIVITY
Hooded Merganser	*Mergus cucullatus*	Discontinuous North American distribution. Breeds from S.E. Alaska south to N.W. states and wooded portions of New Brunswick and Nova Scotia south to the Great Lake states east to the Atlantic coast. Less frequent breeding southward through the Mississippi Valley to the Gulf Coast. Winters along Pacific coast south, south to Mexico and along the Atlantic coast from New England south to the Gulf Coast.	♂ 680g ♀ 540g	9-11 wt. eggs. Typically nests in tree cavities, usually close to water. Competition for prime sites is keen and may mix clutches with other species (i.e., goldeneye). Incubation by ♀ alone: 32-33 days.	Accurate population estimates are difficult due to their wooded habitat but they probably number between 75-100,000 birds. Because they are specialized, the species is vulnerable and loss of appropriate breeding habitat will have an adverse effect.	Well established and relatively widespread. Bred fairly regularly but there is a high incidence of infertility (perhaps because ♂♂'s come into breeding condition before the ♀♀'s).
Brazilian Merganser	*M. octosetaceus*	Resident in S.E. Brazil, E. Paraguay and N.E. Argentina.		Clutch size unreported—eggs; light cream. Little known. Only 1 nest has been described; in a hollow cavity adjacent to a river. Incubation period unknown. Young have been observed with both parents present but the role of the ♂ in brood care is unknown.	Probably not as rare as the lack of data on the species would suggest and *may* possibly be common locally. As long as appropriate habitat is not violated, the species should be secure, but they are vulnerable.	Apparently has never been kept.
Common Red-Breasted Merganser	*M. s. serrator*	Wide breeding range throughout Northern Hemisphere including Iceland. Winters mostly on salt water from the southern limits of the breeding range south along the coastlines of Europe, Asia and North America.	♂ 1,133-1,209g ♀ 907-959g	9-10 deep buff eggs. Will use cavities but also commonly nests on the ground under boulders or in thick vegetation. Incubation by ♀ alone: 32 days.	No world-wide population estimates available but not uncommon although local populations have suffered due to pesticide pollution and control measures by fishing interests. Over ¼ million in North America and some 100,000 winter in Europe.	Not common nor widespread but bred sporadically in some European collections. Rare in America although some wild-caught adults have been acquired in recent years.
Greenland Red-Breasted Merganser	*M. s. schioleri*	Resident in S. Greenland.	Slightly larger than nominate race.	Presumably similar to nominate race. 7-15 eggs. May nest in association with eiders or terns, and at times on ledges with kittiwakes and gulls.	A poorly defined race which may not be distinct from *serrator*. No population estimates available.	Apparently has never been kept.
Auckland Islands Merganser	*M. australis*	New Zealand: Limited to Auckland Islands in historical times.		Little information available. One brood of 4 ducklings recorded which was attended by both parents.	Extinct. Last record of the species was in 1902.	Never kept.
Chinese (Scaly-Sided) Merganser	*M. squamatus*	Breeds possibly in north and east Manchuria. Also in Ussuriland from central and S. Sikhote-Alim range (from the Khor River basin to the Iman River Basin). Several records for Korea.		No description of eggs (probable clutch size: 8-12). Only two nests have been described, both in hollow trees. Presumably incubation by ♀ alone. Incubation period is unknown.	Apparently rare with restricted breeding range. Is undoubtedly vulnerable and recent reports suggest the population is declining throughout its range.	Apparently has never been kept outside of China. As of 1978, at least two in the Shanghai Zoo.

VERNACULAR NAME	LATIN NAME	DISTRIBUTION	AVERAGE WEIGHTS	NESTS, EGGS AND INCUBATION	STATUS/ WILD	STATUS/ CAPTIVITY
Eurasian Goosander	*M. m. merganser*	Wide breeding range throughout N. Eurasia from Iceland, Scotland, Switzerland, Poland, Romania, Scandinavia east to Kamchatka and Kurile and Commander Islands. Winters in southern limits of breeding range south to the Mediterranean, Black and Caspian Seas, N. India, Assam and China.	♂ 1,670g ♀ 1,535g	9-10 creamy eggs. Usually nests in natural tree cavities but will use artificial boxes, and where trees are not available, will nest on ground amid boulders or under vegetation. Incubation by ♀ alone: 32-35 days.	No overall population estimates available but apparently is not rare. Some 80,000 winter in European locations.	Not abundant or widespread but loosely established in some European collections. Virtually absent in American collections Bred rather sporadically. Can be aggressive.
American Merganser	*M. m. americanus*	Widespread breeding range throughout N. North America from S. Alaska east to Newfoundland and south to California and New Mexico and the Great Lake states and New England. Winters on both salt and fresh water from the southern limits of its breeding range south to California and Florida.	♂ 1,600g ♀ 1,200g	Similar to nominate race.	Widespread and reasonably common. Probably in excess of ½ million birds.	Somewhat rare and not widespread (very rare in Europe). Bred very sporadically. Can be aggressive toward other waterfowl and may consume ducklings.
Asiatic Goosander	*M. m. orientalis*	Breeds in N.E. Afghanistan east to Tibet and Szechuan, China. Winters in southern limits of breeding range, south to N. India, N. Burma and S.W. China.	♂ 1,250- 1,500g ♀ 910- 1,195g	Presumably similar to nominate race.	No information available with regards to population size nor relative abundance.	Apparently has never been kept.

Tribe: Oxyurini (Stiff-Tailed Ducks)

VERNACULAR NAME	LATIN NAME	DISTRIBUTION	AVERAGE WEIGHTS	NESTS, EGGS AND INCUBATION	STATUS/ WILD	STATUS/ CAPTIVITY
Black-Headed Duck	*Heteronetta atricapilla*	Breeds in central Chile, Argentina and central Paraguay. Also occurs in Uruguay, S. Brazil and Bolivia.	♂ 513g ♀ 565g	White eggs. Unique; appears to be almost totally parasitic with regards to nesting. At least 14 host species, not restricted to waterfowl. Ducklings almost entirely independent upon hatching. Incubation by host species: 20-25 days depending on incubation period of host species; i.e., hatching synchronized with eggs of host. Aver. 2 eggs per host nest.	Apparently fairly common but very dependent on marshy habitats. Vulnerable; loss of appropriate habitat would certainly be detrimental.	Established only at Wildfowl Trust where a number have been bred there since the first breeding in 1977. A few pairs sent to other collections (several to America in early 1979). Like most stiff-tails, ducklings are specialized and require special care. Adults easily maintained. Host species required for propagation.
Masked Duck	*Oxyura dominica*	Widespread but rather localized distribution from S. Texas and Gulf coast regions of E. Mexico, West Indies and Central America to the lowlands of Columbia to N. Argentina.	♂ 406g ♀ 339g	4-6 wt. eggs (up to 18 have been recorded for Cuba). Few nests studied but in Argentina and Cuba, nests located in rice fields; also in rushes next to water. Nests well concealed and may be roofed. Tendency to dump nest. Incubation by ♀ alone: presumably 28± days.	Does not appear to be particularly common anywhere with the greatest recorded densities in Argentina. However, due to elusive habits, may be more common than believed. Due to wide ranges, the species is probably secure for the moment.	Has apparently never been permanently kept. Clipped wing specimens may have been maintained for short periods of time, for study purposes.

VERNACULAR NAME	LATIN NAME	DISTRIBUTION	AVERAGE WEIGHTS	NESTS, EGGS AND INCUBATION	STATUS/ WILD	STATUS/ CAPTIVITY
North American Ruddy Duck	*O. j. jamaicensis*	Breeds mostly interior N.W. North America from central British Columbia and S.W. Mackenzie District southwest through the Great Plains to Colorado. Limited local breeding in Ariz., Texas, Calif., central Mexico and West Indies. Winters both Pacific and Atlantic coasts (including Gulf Coast) from British Columbia and Delaware south to Guatemala.	♂ 550g ♀ 500g	6-9 chalky wt. eggs. Some dump nesting and parasitic tendencies. Nests usually well concealed in dense aquatic vegetation. Incubation by ♀ alone: 23-24 days (with ranges of 20-26 days). After young hatch, ♂ rejoins the ♀ but is not involved in brood care. Two broods may be reared annually in some areas.	Remains fairly abundant despite declines in recent years due to habitat destruction and wintering oil spill losses. The population may be in excess of ½ million birds, but possibly less. The species is vulnerable.	Fairly well established and reasonably common, but not overly widespread. Bred regularly by some propagators. Nests fairly readily but ducklings can be difficult to rear. Adults are easily maintained if good water is available.
Colombian Ruddy Duck	*O. j. andina*	Lakes and marshes of the central and eastern Colombian Andes.	Essentially the same size as *O. j. jamaicensis.*	Presumably similar to *O. j. jamaicensis.*	No definite population data available but there is no evidence which suggests they are either rare or declining. The race may represent an intergrade population between *jamaicensis* and *ferruginea.*	Probably no "pure" specimens from Colombia have ever been kept. However, similar birds artificially produced at Sea World (San Diego) by crossing *jamaicensis* and *ferruginea.*
Peruvian Ruddy Duck	*O. j. ferruginea*	Andean lakes from S. Colombia to Chile and lowland lakes and marshes of central Chile and Argentina south to Tierra del Fuego.	♂ 817-848g ♀	Similar to nominate race.	Not known but said to be relatively abundant in some localities.	Very rare. As of early 1979 only 2 pure males and a female could be accounted for (none in America). May have been bred previously but it is possible hybrids were involved.
White-Headed Duck	*O. leucocephala*	Fragmented breeding range along the W. Mediterranean, Black and Caspian Seas to Turkestan. Winters N. coast of Africa through the Nile Valley, Turkey, Persian Gulf and N. India.	♂ 737g ♀ 593g	6-8 wt. eggs. Nests in thick vegetation immediately adjacent to open water. Nests of other aquatic species (i.e., coots) not infrequently used. Little down in nest. Incubation by ♀ alone: 23 days.	Rare and apparently declining in many areas. Considered by some to be endangered. Total world population probably does not exceed 10,000-15,000 birds. Habitat requirements rather strict.	Established only at Wildfowl Trust where it is currently bred regularly. A few pairs have been distributed to other collections (several to America in early 1979).
Maccoa Duck	*O. maccoa*	East Africa from the highlands of Ethiopia and Kenya to E. Zaire and Uganda south to the Cape.	♂ 450-700g ♀ 450-700g	4-8 bluish-wt. eggs. Nests usually in or next to water in thick aquatic vegetation. Very territorial and polygamous. Incubation by ♀ alone: 24-27 days.	Fairly widespread and not threatened. Apparently most common in Kenya and Rift Valley.	Rare and as of early 1979 few in America. Fairly well established at the Wildfowl Trust where it was first bred in 1974 and is currently regularly reared there.
Argentine Ruddy (Blue-Billed) Duck	*O. vittata*	Southern third of South America. Breeds in Tierra del Fuego, Chile, Argentina to Uruguay. Winters in Paraguay and S. Central Brazil.	♂ 610g ♀ 560g (Sample size 1/1).	3-5 chalky wt. eggs. Nests are generally well concealed in aquatic vegetation and tend to be nearly flat. Incubation by ♀ alone: presumably 23-28 days.	No reliable population estimates but not thought to be rare. However, it is vulnerable and depends greatly on large and permanent marshes.	Rare and barely established in most collections. As of early 1979, very few in America. Bred regularly at the Wildfowl Trust.
Australian Blue-Billed Duck	*O. australis*	Discontinuous distribution along coast of West Australia and in the Murray and Darling River systems and adjacent coast regions of Victoria and South Australia. Also in Tasmania.	♂ 812g ♀ 852g	5-6 light green eggs. Nests generally in dense swamp or marsh vegetation. Will rarely use nest of other species (i.e., coot). Incubation by ♀ alone: 26-28 days.	Does not appear to be particularly rare but distribution is limited to appropriate habitat. Destruction of such habitat would undoubtedly have a negative impact.	Have never been maintained outside of Australia, but has been bred there. Rare, even in Australian collections.

VERNACULAR NAME	LATIN NAME	DISTRIBUTION	AVERAGE WEIGHTS	NESTS, EGGS AND INCUBATION	STATUS/ WILD	STATUS/ CAPTIVITY
Musk Duck	*Biziura lobata*	Southern and western Australia as well as Tasmania.	♂ 2,398g ♀ 1,551g	1-3 pale greenish wt. eggs. Nests generally in aquatic vegetation but also on low tree branches where they touch the water, low stumps, etc. More down in nest than typical stiff-tails. Incubation by ♀ alone: incubation period has yet to be established. ♀♀'s feed ducklings.	Secure for the present but greatly dependent on the preservation of marsh and swampland habitat. Some losses attributed to human fishing activities.	Rare. As of early 1979 two males and a female at the Wildfowl Trust were the only ones outside of Australia. Infertile eggs laid at Slimbridge in 1978. Has apparently been bred in Australia under semi-wild conditions. Very aggressive.
African White-Backed Duck	*Thalassornis l. leuconotus*	Resident from E. Nigeria and S. Ethiopia south to the Cape (although absent in the Congo Basin).	♂ 650-790g ♀ 625-765g	5-7 rich brown eggs. Nests usually in aquatic vegetation (often in deep water). Nests are often ramped and concealed from above. Incubation by *both sexes* (perhaps more so by ♂): 26 (?) to 29-33 days.	Widespread and can be abundant locally. Does not appear to be threatened. Habitat loss would undoubtedly be detrimental.	Quite rare. As of 1978, only 12 in 2 collections; of these 6 were obtained in mid-1978. Successfully reared for the first time in a private British collection in 1978. None in the New World.
Madagascar White-Backed Duck	*T. l. insularis*	Madagascar, up to 2,500 feet.	Slightly smaller than nominate race.	Presumably same as nominate race.	Status unknown but is perhaps locally common. However, at the rate land is being reclaimed in Madagascar, there may be some cause for alarm in the future.	As of early 1979, only one pair at Wildfowl Trust. Was bred in the early 1930s.

Appendix 2
Photographing Waterfowl

Photographing wildlife can be one of the most exhilarating of endeavors—and from time to time, one of the most frustrating. Few experiences can match the excitement and the feeling of accomplishment that comes when one discovers that the image captured on film is exactly what was seen through the viewfinder; or better yet, that it is as beautiful and perfect as the image that was seen in the mind's eye. Conversely, no despair seems deeper than the feeling one gets upon discovering that the "picture of a lifetime" has been muffed. Both of those feelings are well-known to me, but happily, the positive aspects far outweigh the negative ones, and wildlife photography remains one of the most gratifying and therapeutic activities I can imagine.

It must be initially pointed out that I am a biologist first and a photographer second. I have not spent an undue amount of time pondering the sophisticated subtleties of the photographer's art, nor have I studied the subject in any systematic way. What I know about photographing wildlife and nature has been learned the hard way, by trial and error over the last fifteen years—by going out and doing it. I have definite ideas and feelings about what makes a good wildlife photograph, and have also discovered a few "tricks of the trade" over the years. But I do not pretend that my methods are the only ones, and certainly, other photographers using totally different techniques have been equally successful.

Among the essential ingredients of successful wildlife photography are dependable equipment, an infinite amount of patience, some basic knowledge of the lifestyle of the animal involved, and a feel for what constitutes a good picture. While it is undeniable that some superior pictures happen by accident, in most instances they are planned and require some degree of work and skill.

Good, reliable equipment is an absolute necessity, since a craftsman is generally only as good as his tools. Needless to say, whatever equipment is used, the photographer must be thoroughly familiar with the peculiarities of the equipment, because lack of experience with new or unfamiliar camera gear can result in missed opportunities. As a general rule, heavy, bulky, or extremely complex equipment should be avoided. For one thing, field conditions vary significantly and can often be arduous; for another, most wild animals are quite mobile, and will not stand still while one heaves some ponderous piece of hardware into position.

Many contemporary wildlife photographers depend on 35mm single-lens reflex (SLR) cameras with interchangeable lenses. The advantages of such equipment are many, including light weight, compactness, and an almost limitless selection of different types of lenses and films. There are many quality makes available, but I personally prefer Nikon equipment, because it is extremely well made and durable, and is able to withstand the rigors of the field. (Its disadvantage is the expense.) My equipment must be able to endure what I endure, whether it be the blistering heat of sand dunes in the desert or the bone-chilling cold of glaciers in the Antarctic. Then too, I occasionally fall from a tree or cliff, and the gear must be durable if it is to survive. I am very hard on my equipment.

The growth of wildlife photography in recent years has been made possible in large measure by the emergence of reliable, lightweight, readily available telephoto lenses. Perhaps the main factor governing the successful photography of wild animals is their natural wariness. Telephoto lenses are an absolute necessity, since there is often no other way to get close to some animals. In general, the longer the lens, the heavier and less sharp or crisp it will tend to be, and lenses exceeding 300mm will usually require the use of a tripod. Zoom lenses are convenient and have improved significantly in recent years, but some quality is sacrificed for the increased versatility, and as a rule, zoom lenses are optically inferior to a fixed focal length lens. In other words, a single lens cannot be expected to do everything. Bayonet-mounted lenses are much more practical in the field than those that screw in.

My basic lens is a 200mm, which is somewhat smaller than the lenses many accomplished field photographers use. In my opinion, the light weight and extremely sharp detail that is possible with this lens more than offsets the apparent size disadvantage. Longer lenses and bulky tripods are fine for use in a blind, when mobility is not required, but I seldom photograph from a blind and enjoy the stalk, depending on my skills in that regard to compensate for the use of a smaller lens. If a longer lens is required, as when the subject is some distance out on the water, I may depend on lenses up to 1000mm in length.

I strongly recommend that at least two cameras of the same make always be taken on field trips of any duration. I generally use one camera with a 200mm telephoto lens, loaded with a high-speed Ektachrome film, and the other with a 55mm macro-lens and Kodachrome film. The macro-lens (which focuses to infinity) is well suited for scenics (such as habitat material) and for close-up work as well (nests, eggs, recently-hatched young, etc.). Just as important, extended field work may involve weeks and sometimes months away from civilization, and camera repair shops are not part of the scene. With two cameras, one always has a backup unit, should one fail. If both cameras malfunction (and this has happened to me), it is sometimes possible to cannibalize one to repair the other. As a rule, it is far better to have two good cameras with a few basic lenses than to have a single camera with many superfluous accessories or gadgets.

A camera with a built-in through-the-lens (TTL) exposure meter is also recommended. Undeniably, meters of this type may not be quite as accurate as a hand-held meter for general shooting, but they are definitely superior for telephoto work. It is very difficult for a broad-spectrum light meter to accurately measure light intensity around the head of a duck that may be 100 feet away, although some skilled photographers are able to do it. I do strongly recommend that shots be bracketed; that is, several pictures should be taken that are slightly over and underexposed. In this way, if the meter is misreading to a certain extent, insurance pictures have been secured.

With almost *every* aspect of photography, each photographer has his or her preference with regard to every piece of equipment and type of technique. So it is with viewfinders and focusing. My preference is a split-image focus system rather than the more commonly used grid system. I usually attempt to focus on the *eye* of my subject, and find that split-image focusing gives me sharper results. When photographing flying birds, however, there are some disadvantages with split-image viewfinders because focusing is more finite.

Almost *every* photographer has definite ideas about what are the best films, and they will voice an opinion at the drop of a hat. When choosing film, the basic thing to keep in mind is that *no* film is perfect in all respects. Different types of film are created for different purposes, and no single film can do it all. Therefore, it is always necessary to compromise to a certain extent in determining which film best suits your purpose. Because most of my work is done with a telephoto lens (which requires a certain light level), and I work in the field under variable light conditions, I most often use a high-speed color film (ASA 160 to 200). Frankly, some of my colleagues have been critical at times of my apparent dependence on film of this nature, since they believe that high-speed film is not totally accurate with respect to color and that it tends to be grainy when enlarged. I leave this to the reader to decide for himself, for most of the plates in this volume were shot with a high-speed Ektachrome film. While I do concede that some Kodachrome colors (ASA 64) may be more brilliant, it must also be pointed out that brilliant colors don't mean much if it is not possible to take the pictures. Films with low ASA ratings are not practical in low light conditions or when photographing fast-moving subjects (i.e., flying birds). Simply stated, without high-speed color film, many of the pictures in this book would not have been possible.

I personally never use black and white film, since I learned long ago (the hard way) that it is always possible to convert color pictures to black and white if required, but not vice versa. Unless one is engaged in taking art shots, it is simply impossible to depict brightly-colored birds adequately with black and white film. (There are, of course, many superb photographers who will totally disagree with me on this point, but as I pointed out previously, everyone has an opinion on film.) Regardless of the type of film used, the photographer should be thoroughly familiar with its strong points and its limitations. A great deal of test shooting may be required before familiarity with a new type of film is ultimately achieved.

One extremely important point to keep in mind is that in the field, film is the cheapest thing there is. Therefore, one should carry an adequate supply of film and be prepared to over-shoot. In nature, there are usually no retakes. Opportunities to capture animals and events on film may never present themselves again in exactly the same way, so it is far better to over-shoot than to lament later that more pictures should have been taken. Obviously, this philosophy will require the discarding of a large number of pictures that don't quite make it—but it does greatly increase the chances of securing the superb pictures sought. The final selection(s) of a series will require a very critical review (unless sequential behavioral activities, etc., are involved). For example, while exposure, focus, and composition may be perfect, the position of the subject may not be optimal. I have been forced to discard a number of seemingly "perfect" pictures merely because the subject happened to be blinking at the instant when the shutter release button was pressed. At times like that, it becomes painfully evident that there is a considerable difference between pho-

tographing inanimate objects, such as trees or mountains, and unpredictable wild animals. In some instances, I am happy to salvage a single picture from an entire roll, but as I say, the acquisition of that sometimes superior picture would not have been possible had not a series been taken.

When photographing wildlife, attempt to shoot at a shutter speed of at least 1/250 of a second. Birds, as a rule, are in constant motion, and many of their movements are surprisingly fast. Where flight shots are concerned, the faster the shutter speed, the better. I prefer 1/1000 of a second or even faster if possible, especially with swift-flying ducks. Admittedly, on some occasions one may be forced to shoot at 1/60 of a second or lower, and in such cases, a tripod is recommended. The results, however, are not often exceptional.

I seldom use accessories. With the exception of a polarizing filter, I am not inclined to use filters, except that I do recommend an ultraviolet (or skylight) filter, but this is more for lens protection than for effect. The polarizing filter is used only when shooting down into the water on very bright days. Unless I am doing sequential behavior work, I seldom use a motor drive unit. In the field, they are bulky, heavy, and noisy, and they are not always dependable under unpredictable field conditions, particularly in very cold areas. I use available light almost exclusively, and tend not to use a strobe unit unless absolutely necessary.

Patience is perhaps the key to successful wildlife photography. Birds in particular come and go as they please, and they are not necessarily attuned to human timetables. Many species, for example, are most active at dawn or dusk and may sleep for a good part of the day, and good pictures of birds with these habits are simply not likely at high noon. Some pictures will require physical discomfort. Photographing on the tundra during the summer, for example, can be hot and miserable. One prays for a slight breeze, and if the wind does not materialize, the photographer must be prepared to be consumed by the most tenacious and savage mosquitos imaginable. To obtain certain pictures, it has sometimes been necessary to crawl through the mud on all fours for hours. Often, just as everything is about perfect, the bird(s) will flush seconds before the finger reaches the shutter release button.

Photography in sub-zero temperatures is equally challenging, and in places such as the Antarctic, it can even be painful. It is difficult to photograph with heavy gloves, for instance, so they must come off regardless of how cold it is. Extreme conditions can be hard on equipment as well, and cameras must be winterized. This involves the removal of all the oil in the camera and its replacement with specialized synthetic lubricants which are resistant to freezing. If this is not done, the oils will freeze and the camera is useless. Extremely cold weather can also rapidly drain the power from batteries, so it is recommended that extra meter batteries, etc., be available. The film also freezes and tends to become brittle. It can break if wound too fast, and winding the film too rapidly may also cause sparks that will leave static lines across the exposure. Once film is frozen, film speed may be reduced by as much as one *f* stop, so bracketing exposures is essential. Sometimes, a shift in the color balance may occur (particularly toward the blue) as a result of ultraviolet light reflected from the sky by snow crystals. A skylight filter should help to reduce this effect.

In many respects, waterfowl are better pictorial subjects than most forms of wildlife. Their size, form, color, and behavior lend themselves more readily to this type of art. Often, the reflective quality of the water can also be used to great advantage. Conversely, depending on light conditions, water reflections can be very harsh. In particular, bright water or snow often "confuses" the exposure meter and false readings can result. Under these types of conditions, I usually stop down at least one half of an ƒ stop.

It is not wise to photograph at mid-day, since the intense sunlight generally creates too much contrast. I consider the softer light of late afternoon to be ideal for most wildlife photography. Species which are brightly colored and well patterned, such as wood or mandarin ducks, are often better photographed on overcast days. Do not be hesitant about shooting in the rain, for interesting effects can sometimes be obtained and the behavior of the birds is often different. As a rule, front-lit pictures are more effective than those lit from overhead or behind.

I am particularly fond of sunset pictures of wildlife. Many of these that I have taken over the years required hours (and sometimes days) of preparation. One has to first compose the picture mentally, and then seek the ideal vantage point from which to take best advantage of the background, sun, and birds. This means knowing in advance what time the sun will set, exactly where on the horizon it will drop, and in the case of flying birds, when and from what direction they will appear on the scene. Of course, this is not always successful, and often I have been thwarted at the last moment when the birds inexplicably altered their route or did not materialize at the appointed time. Shooting directly into the sun, even if it is setting, can have a confusing effect on the light meter. Needless to say, photography of this nature requires a rather large amount of bracketing.

Most photographers will be afforded relatively few opportunities to film exotic species in the wild, and captive collections offer a good alternative. If a few minor points are kept in mind, pictures of birds within a controlled environment can often equal or better those taken in the field. The main advantages are that most birds in such a situation can generally be rather closely approached and tend not to be flighty. It is best to photograph only one species at a time, and if the picture must contain mixed species, shoot only those which would occur together naturally in the wild. Make sure that no signs of captivity, such as cement, food dishes, wire, etc., are visible. Try to photograph the non-pinioned side of the bird, and avoid shooting the birds in positions where the bands on their legs are visible. This, of course, is not always possible, but a little effort will go a long way.

Often, the desired bird may be dozing, sleeping, or otherwise inactive. A sharp clap of the hands or a loud whistle will usually serve to attract its attention. Waterfowl, as a rule, do not sleep deeply and are capable of becoming instantly alert if startled. Naturally, the more familiar the photographer is with the behavior of the birds, the greater the chances for good pictures. Certain actions of some species are such that their next moves are fairly predictable. This knowledge often allows the alert photographer to be prepared in advance for difficult-to-obtain action material.

Attempt to photograph the subject under a variety of conditions and poses. There is a great deal more to this than merely shooting a duck on the water. Usually, birds swimming directly toward or directly away from the camera do not produce good pictures. I always attempt to compose my pictures in such a way that cropping will not be required later, and relatively few of the plates in this book have required much cropping as a result. It is advantageous to photograph on the same plane as the subject, and this may involve lying down on the ground. Avoid shooting down on birds, if possible, as this does not portray them to best advantage.

Obtaining good flight shots or shooting from a moving boat at birds in the water (or in flight) can be very difficult and extremely frustrating. In such cases, it may initially appear that much film is wasted, but this is not necessarily the case. I know from bitter experience that merely snapping several exposures of flying birds will rarely produce a good picture. Flight photography requires almost simultaneous focusing and adjusting of ƒ stops as the bird passes areas of different light intensity (although some of the newer cameras automatically compensate for changing light conditions). Photography of this kind can be very traumatic, and while the subject may often be in focus, the exposure will be off. This is particularly true with birds that jump into the air from the ground or small ponds. Once they hit the skyline, which they can do deceptively fast, the light intensity will change.

In the field, opportunities for flight shots can occur at any time, so the camera should be carried at all times in such a manner to facilitate instantaneous use. Pictures of birds flying at or directly away from the photographer are usually a waste of time, and in any case, subjects flying parallel allow the photographer a bit more time to focus. Even when shooting into a flock, it is advantageous to concentrate on a single bird rather than the group.

In summary, it is obvious that each photographer will have his or her own ideas as to what will work best for them. Regardless of the techniques employed, patience and constant practice will be required. Even the "perfect" picture can be improved upon if the photographer continually strives for it, and some particularly sought after pictures may even require years to ultimately obtain. The plate of the pair of Patagonian kelp geese in flight on page 146 is a case in point. It literally took me years to get a picture that satisfied me—and my current satisfaction with the picture does not imply that I don't think I could do better if I kept at it. It is well to keep in mind that the really good pictures can be very elusive indeed.

There is one final point that I cannot stress too strongly. In the field, the photographer is always an intruder, and as such, he or she has a number of serious responsibilities and obligations. The opportunity to photograph wildlife under any conditions should be viewed as a rare privilege, and the life forms involved must be treated with care, respect, and understanding. This is particularly true during the breeding season, when great care must be exercised in order to avoid compromising the potential success of a nesting attempt. In some cases, the mere presence of a well-meaning photographer can disrupt a nesting bird. If the nest is lost, it matters not whether the disturbance was intentional or unintentional. Even if the nest is not abandoned, human activity around a formerly concealed nest can attract the attention of alert predators. If nests and eggs are to be photographed, this must be done quickly so that the eggs do not cool, and they must be covered with the down when finished. In the case of concealed nests, the vegetation and cover should be restored to its former state. I usually move back some distance and remain in the vicinity long enough to confirm that the nesting female has returned. It goes without saying that all litter, such as film wrappers, must be carried out. Without a field ethic, photography in the wild cannot really be justified, regardless of the results obtained on film. In other words, the ends do not necessarily justify the means.

Glossary

ABERRANT — Exceptional; divergent; having a marked difference (or differences) from other members of the group with which it is classified.

ACCLIMATE — Adapting to a new environment.

ADDLE — To become rotten.

AFFINITY — A relationship between groups of birds indicating a common ancestor.

ALBINISM — The abnormal absence of color.

ALCIDS — A group of birds which includes the puffins, murres, auks, etc.

ALLOPREENING — Mutual preening.

ANAEROBIC — Occurring in the absence of free oxygen.

ANALOGUE — A structure adaptively similar to another but of a basically different nature.

ANATIDAE — The family of birds that includes ducks, geese, and swans.

ANHIMIDAE — Family of birds closely related to waterfowl; the screamers.

ANTHROPOMORPHIC — The ascription of human feelings and motives to something not human.

ANTIPHONAL — Pertaining to the act of calling back and forth between two individuals; Duetting.

ARBOREAL — Adapted to a lifestyle in the trees.

ARCHAEOPTERYX — Extinct, reptile-like bird; the earliest known avian fossil.

ASPERGILLOSIS — Disease usually caused by the fungus *Aspergillus fumigatus*, which is often present in decaying vegetation.

AUDIO IMPRINTING — Imprinting by voice.

AUSTRAL — Southern or southerly; occurring in the Southern Hemisphere.

AVES — The taxonomic class which contains all birds.

AVICULTURE — Science of captive husbandry and propagation of exotic birds.

AVIFAUNA — The birdlife of an area.

BALEEN — Specialized horn-like plates which extend down from the roof of the mouth in the toothless whales (Mysticeti), used to filter food organisms; whalebone.

BILLABONG — In Australia, a stagnant backwater or minor branch of a stream.

BIOME — Major habitat type.

BIOTA — The living plants and animals of a region.

BIVALVE MOLLUSCS — Molluscs with two shells (i.e., a clam).

BLOOD FEATHER — Flight feather supplied with blood, as during the molt.

BOOBY — A small gannet.

BOREAL — Northern or northerly.

BOTULISM — Form of food poisoning affecting aquatic birds, caused by the anaerobic bacterium *Clostridium botulinum* (Western duck sickness, limber neck).

BRACKISH — Somewhat salty; a mixture of both salt and fresh water.

BRANT — North American name for the brent goose.

BROOD — Noun: A collective term for the young produced by a pair of birds; Verb: To cover young with wings and body.

BUCCAL — Pertaining to the mouth (buccal cavity).

BULLA — A hollow, thin-walled, bubble-like bony prominence associated with the syrinx in many male ducks.

CANDLING — Process of passing a strong light through an egg to determine fertility.

CARACARA — Specialized, carrion-feeding hawk.

CARNIVOROUS — Flesh-eating.

CARRION — Dead and putrefying flesh.

CARUNCLE — A fleshy enlargement of skin, usually on the head or neck.

CAUDAL — Pertaining to the tail, or the region of the tail.

CERE — Basal fleshy covering of the upper mandible above the nostrils (as in birds of prey, parrots, etc.).

CERVICAL VERTEBRAE — Neck vertebra.

CHATTERING — Sound produced by feeding waterfowl.

CHEVRON — Flight organized in "V" or wedge formation.

CICONIID — Pertains to birds in the order Ciconiiformes (i.e., herons, storks, etc.).

CIRCADIAN — Applied to a biological rhythm of about a day (*circa* 24 hours).

CIRCUMBOREAL — Referring to a distribution that encompasses the northern regions of both western and eastern hemispheres.

CIRCUMPOLAR — Referring to a distribution that encompasses the polar land masses of both western and eastern hemispheres.

CLASS — A major category in taxonomy, ranking above the order and below the phylum.

CLINE — Gradual change, usually in the color or size of a species, occurring in part or all of its geographical range.

CLOACA — The common chamber which receives the rectum, ureters and gonaducts.

CLUTCH — The total number of eggs laid by one female during a single nesting attempt and incubated simultaneously.

COB — Male swan.

COMMISSURE — The line of juncture between the closed mandibles when viewed laterally.

CONVERGENT EVOLUTION — Process whereby unrelated animals (usually from different regions) evolve similar adaptations (and appearances) because they occupy similar ecological niches.

COVERTS — Small feathers which overlie the bases of the flight feathers, and the several rows of smaller feathers between the bases of the flight feathers and the leading edge of the wing.

CRACIDS — Family of Central and South American gamebirds (i.e., curassows, guans, and chachalacas).

CRECHE — A nursery; an assemblage of flightless young representing several families, often attended by few adults.

CREPUSCULAR — Active at twilight.

CREST — A tuft of lengthened feathers on the head, erect or capable of being erected.

CROWN — Top of the head.

CRYPTIC — Adapted to conceal; concealing coloration.

CRUSTACEAN — A class of animals, consisting mostly of aquatic arthropods, which have a chitinous exoskeleton (i.e., shrimp, lobster, crab, etc.).

CULMAN — The dorsal ridge of the upper mandible, extending from the forehead to the tip.

CULMAN KNOB — Knob on the ridge or upper border of the maxilla.

CURASSOW — Gamebird of Central and South America.

CURSORIAL — Adapted to running or walking.

CYGNET — Young swan.

DABBLING — A method of feeding utilized by surface-feeding ducks.

DEWLAP — A hanging fold of skin under the neck.

DIMORPHISM — Occurring in two forms (i.e., color).

DIPPER — A small passerine bird, famous for walking along the bottom of rushing streams.

DISTAL — Farthest from the trunk or midline of an organism; referring especially to the segments of the appendages.

DIURNAL — Active during the day.

DORSAL — Pertaining to the back, or (in a more general sense) to the upper surface of the body.

DOWN — Specialized feathers which usually cover the young of precocial species; soft underfeathers of adult wildfowl.

DRAKE — Male duck.

DUCKLING — Downy young of a duck.

DUETTING — Male and female of a pair calling together, or almost together, and responsively.

DUMP NEST — Nest in which more than one female deposits eggs, seldom incubated.

ECHINODERM — A taxonomic group of radially symmetrical coelomate marine animals, consisting of starfish, sea urchins, sand dollars, etc.

ECLIPSE PLUMAGE — The dull female-like plumage worn by the males of most Northern Hemisphere ducks while growing new flight feathers.

ECOLOGICAL NICHE — The particular part or parts of its habitat in which an animal lives or seeks its food.

ECOSYSTEM — The living animals and plants of an area; their relationships with one another and their environment.

EIDER PASS — A projection of land into the sea, over which migrating eiders pass.

ENDEMIC — Confined to, or indigenous to, a certain area or region.

ERYTHRISTIC — A rufous or reddish plumage variation.

ESTUARY — A water area where a river current joins the ocean tide.

EXTIRPATE — Wipe out locally, as to remove totally by hunting.

FALCATED — Sickle-shaped.

FAMILY — A taxonomic group, more comprehensive than the genus and more restrictive than the order. Always ends with "-idae," as in Anatidae.

FEATHER TRACT — Specific regions on the skin of a bird where feathers grow.

FERAL — Wild; undomesticated. Used especially of stocks which have escaped from domestication and returned to the wild state.

FERROUS — Relating to, or containing, iron.

FERRUGINOUS — The color of rusty iron.

FLEDGE — To acquire the feathers necessary for flight.

FULVOUS — Dull yellowish brown; tawny.

FURCULA — The "wishbone" of birds, formed by the fusion of the right and left clavicles (collar bones).

GAGGLE — A flock. Normally pertains to a group of geese when not in flight.

GALLINACEOUS — Pertaining to galliform birds (i.e., pheasants, quail, grouse, etc.).

GAMEBIRDS — Gallinaceous birds.

GANDER — Male goose.

GENUS — A taxonomic group, more comprehensive than the species but less comprehensive than the family or tribe.

GIZZARD — The part of a bird's stomach with strong muscular walls, used for grinding food.

GONAD — One of the primary sex glands that includes the ovaries and testes.

GONADUCTS — The ducts which lead from the gonads to the cloaca (♂ = vas deferens; ♀ = oviduct).

GOSLING — Young goose.

GREGARIOUS — Social; tending to associate with others of one's kind.

GRIT — Particles of stone of varying coarseness, taken in by birds that eat vegetable matter, and used to grind their food to pulp through the action of powerful stomach muscles.

GUT — The alimentary tract from mouth to cloaca.

HABITAT — The place or type of site where a plant or animal naturally or normally lives.

HAMMERKOP — An African stork.

HERBIVORE — Plant-eating animal.

HOLARCTIC — The northern regions of the Northern Hemisphere, including both the Palearctic and Nearctic regions.

HOMOLOGUE — A structure basically equivalent to another, but possibly adapted in a different way.

HONKER — Local name for the Canada goose.

HUMERUS — The upper bone of the forelimb; in man, the upper arm.

HYBRID — Offspring of parents of two different species, generally of unlike genetic constitution.

ICONOGRAPHY — Pictorial material relating to or illustrating a subject.

IMPRINTING — A behavior pattern speedily established early in the life of a member of a social species, involving recognition of (and attraction to) identification characters for its own kind or for a surrogate.

INBREEDING — Production of young by closely related individuals (i.e., brother x sister, father x daughter, etc.).

INCITING — Functional or ritualized threatening movements and/or calls of female ducks, associated with the formation and maintenance of pair bonds.

INCUBATION — The application of heat to an egg, either by an adult bird or artificial means (such as an incubator).

INSULAR — Having an island distribution.

IRIS — Opaque, contractile diaphragm, located in the aqueous humor in front of the lens of the eye.

JACANA — A long-legged, long-toed tropical wading bird.

JAEGER — A gull-like bird normally associated with the Arctic.

LAMELLAE — Thin plates which line the bill of many species of waterfowl.

LAPPET — A small fold or flap, especially one hanging pendant; a wattle.

LITTORAL — Pertaining to the shore. Usually, the tidal zone of the ocean, but can also apply to the shallow edges of a lake.

LORES — The space between the eye and the bill.

MANTLE — Feathers of the back.

MANUS — The distal portion of the forelimb. In man, the hand.

MAORI — Polynesian natives of New Zealand.

MARITIME — Relating to, or bordering on, the sea.

MELANISM — An unusual dark plumage resulting from increased amounts of black pigment.

MOLLUSCS — Any of a large phylum of invertebrate animals having a soft unsegmented body that is usually enclosed in a calcareous shell (i.e., clam, oyster, etc.); shellfish.

MOLT — The renewal of plumage, wherein old feathers are shed and new ones grow to replace them.

MOLT MIGRATION — Regular movement to specific regions for purposes of molting.

MONOGAMOUS — Pairing with only one member of the opposite sex.

MONOTYPIC — A taxonomic category that has only one unit in it.

MONTANE — Pertaining to mountains. Applied particularly to the avifauna of elevated areas in which the bird life is strikingly different from that of adjacent areas at lower altitudes.

NAPE — The part of the neck behind the occiput.

NARES — Paired openings of the nasal cavities.

NEARCTIC REGION — One of the six zoological regions of the world, comprising North America and northern Mexico.

NEOLITHIC — Of or relating to the latest period of the Stone Age.

NEOTROPICAL — One of six zoographical regions of the world, comprising the lowlands of Mexico south to South America and the West Indies.

NOCTURNAL — Active at night.

NUPTIAL — Pertaining to the breeding season.

OCCIPUT — The back part of the head, between the crown and nape.

OFFAL — The viscera and trimmings of a butchered animal that are removed in dressing.

OMNIVOROUS — Eating both plant and animal food.

OOLOGY — The study of bird eggs.

ORDER — A category of taxonomic classification ranking above the family and below the class. Names of orders end in "-iformes," as in Anseriformes.

ORNITHOLOGY — The study of birds.

PALEARCTIC REGION — One of the six zoographical regions of the world, comprising Europe, North Africa, Asia, the Himalayas, and the Atlantic Islands.

PALEONTOLOGY — The study of animals and plants of former ages from their fossil remains.

PASSERINE — Pertaining to the avian order Passeriformes (i.e., songbirds), the largest order of the class Aves.

PELAGIC — Frequenting the high seas.

PEN — Female swan.

PHOTOPERIOD — The length and intensity of light during a day, particularly as its fluctuations affect the growth, maturity, and behavior of an organism.

PHYLUM — One of the primary divisions of the animal kingdom, below the kingdom and above the class (i.e., all vertebrates form a phylum).

PHYSIOLOGY — The study of the functions and activities of living matter (i.e., cells, tissues, organs, etc.); in particular, the physical and chemical phenomena involved in the processes of life.

PIED — Two or more colors in blotches.

PINION — To restrain a bird from flight, especially by removal of the distal portion of one wing.

PIPPING — The act of breaking through the eggshell during the hatching process (referred to as chipping in the Old World).

PLANKTON — Minute animal and plant life passively floating or weakly swimming in a body of water.

PNEUMATICITY — A condition marked by the presence of air cavities.

POLISH MUTE SWAN — Albinistic mute swan.

POLYANDRY — Mating of one female with several males.

POLYGAMY — Mating of one male with several females.

POLYMORPHIC — Having, assuming, or occurring in a variety of forms (i.e., color).

POTHOLE — A sizable and rounded depression, often water-filled.

PRECOCIAL — Descriptive of birds whose young, upon hatching, are well developed, covered with down, able to move about, and to feed themselves (i.e., waterfowl).

PREEN — To clean and dress the feathers with the bill.

PRIMARY FEATHER — One of the major flight feathers attached to the manus.

PROGENITOR — An ancestral form.

PROPAGATE — To cause, continue, or increase through sexual or asexual reproduction.

PROTECTIONIST — Radical, often militant, conservationist.

PSITTACINES — Parrots or parrot-like birds.

PUNA — The dry, grassy alpine zone of the central Andes.

PYGOSTYLE — The fused caudal portion of the vertebral column.

QUILL — Main flight feathers (primaries and secondaries).

RACE — A subdivision of a species (often geographic); a subspecies.

RAFT — A large group (i.e., "a raft of scaup").

RAPTOR — A bird of prey.

RESONANCE — The production of secondary vibrations that increase the volume of a sound.

SAGITTAL — Pertaining to a vertical plane drawn from the head to the tail of a bilaterally symmetrical animal, dividing the body into right and left portions.

SALINE — Consisting of or containing salt.

SALT GLANDS — Specialized glands (usually located above the eye) which facilitate the excretion of excess salt through the nostrils.

SCAPULARS — Feathers of the humeral feather tract.

SECONDARY FEATHER — One of the flight feathers, attached to the ulna.

SEDENTARY — Not migratory; resident all year.

SEXUAL DIMORPHISM — Condition where the sexes of the same species differ externally.

SKEINS — A flock of wildfowl in flight, particularly when in long and uneven lines.

SKITTER — To glide or skip lightly or quickly along a surface, as with some waterfowl prior to taking flight.

SNAIL KITE — Specialized hawk which feeds chiefly on snails.

SPATULATE — Narrowed and then abruptly expanded toward the end; spoon-shaped.

SPECIATION — The process by which new species are formed.

SPECIES — A category of biological classification, ranking immediately below the genus but above the subspecies.

SPECULUM — A metallic or brightly colored area on the wing that differs in color from adjacent feathers; sometimes iridescent, usually involving the secondaries.

SPUR — A horny modification of the skin surrounding a bony core.

STERNUM — The breastbone, which in waterfowl is deeply keeled.

SUBCUTANEOUS — Under the skin.

SUBSPECIES — A geographically defined aggregate of local populations which differs taxonomically from other such subdivisions of the species.

SUNGREBE — A tropical American, Asian, or African bird related to cranes and rails.

SUPRAORBITAL — Above the eye.

SWAN UPPING — Traditional English ceremony involving the capture and marking of young mute swans on the River Thames.

SYMPATRIC — Living in the same area.

SYRINX — Sound-producing structure in the trachea of birds.

TAIGA — Boreal or northern coniferous forest.

TARN — Small mountain lake or pool.

TAXONOMY — Classification of plants and animals according to their anatomy, behavior, and evolutionary relationships.

TEMPERATE ZONE — The area or region between the Tropic of Cancer and the Arctic Circle in the Northern Hemisphere, or between the Tropic of Capricorn and the Antarctic Circle in the Southern Hemisphere.

TERRITORY — An area defended by an organism, which includes a nesting site and a variable foraging range.

TERTIALS — Innermost secondary feathers, especially in cases where these differ in shape and color from the other flight feathers that are attached to the ulna (generally an obsolete term).

TRACHEA — Windpipe.

TREADING — Copulation.

TRIBE — A category of taxonomic classification below the family and above the genus, unique to waterfowl.

TUNDRA — Frozen or half-frozen swamp with vegetation largely of mosses and lichens, located between the regions of ice and the taiga.

TYMPANIC MEMBRANE — Eardrum.

ULNA — A bone of the forelimb.

UNCINATE PROCESS — A thick bony plate, either fused to or articulating with an avian rib. It projects upward and backward to overlie the next succeeding rib, thus strengthening the rib cage.

UROPYGIAL GLAND — A gland located dorsally at the base of the tail. Its secretions contain fatty acids and related substances which are used in the preening of epidermal structures, especially the feathers. Largest in aquatic birds.

VANE — The flat, expanded part of a feather bordering the shaft.

VENT — The cloaca.

VENT SEXING — Determining the sex of a bird by manipulating the cloaca.

VERNACULAR NAME — Name of an animal in a popular language (as opposed to its scientific Latin name).

WATTLE — An appendage which hangs from the throat of some birds.

XEROPHYTIC — Adapted to life in dry conditions.

Bibliography

(Major References)

Abraham, K. F., "Adoption of Spectacled Eider Ducklings by Arctic Loons," *Condor*, 80:339-340, 1978.

Ali, S. and S. D. Ripley, *Handbook of the Birds of India and Pakistan*, Volume I, Oxford University Press, London, 1968.

Alison, R. M., *Breeding Biology and Behavior of the Oldsquaw*, Ornithological Monographs (No. 18), American Ornithologists' Union, Adlers Press, Inc., Lawrence, Kansas, 1975.

Allen, G. A., Jr. (ed.), *Keeping and Raising Wild Geese in Captivity*, Allen Publishing Company, Salt Lake City, Utah, 1965.

_____, *Wild Waterfowl and Its Captive Management*, 2 Volumes, A.G.B.B.A., Allen Publishing Company, Salt Lake City, Utah, 1970-74.

American Ornithologists' Union, *Checklist of North American Birds*, 5th ed., Lord Baltimore Press, Inc., Baltimore, Maryland, 1957.

Anderson, D. R. and Charles Henny, *Population Ecology of the Mallard (I. A Review of Previous Studies and the Distribution and Migration from Breeding Areas)*, United States Fish and Wildlife Service, Resource Publication 109, Washington, D.C., 1972.

Austin, O. L. and Arthur Singer, *Birds of the World*, Golden Press, New York, 1961.

Bailey, A. M., *Birds of Arctic Alaska*, Colorado Museum of Natural History, Popular Series (No. 8), 1948.

_____, *Birds of Midway and Laysan Islands*, Denver Museum of Natural History Bulletin No. 12, 1956.

Bailey, A. M. and J. H. Sorensen, *Subantarctic Campbell Island*, Denver Museum of Natural History Proceedings (No. 10), 1962.

Banko, W. E., *The Trumpeter Swan: Its History, Habits and Population in the United States*, North American Fauna (No. 63), United States Fish and Wildlife Service, Washington, D.C., 1960.

Bellrose, F. C., *Ducks, Geese and Swans of North America*, Wildlife Management Institute, Stackpole Books, Harrisburg, Pennsylvania, 1976.

Bennett, L. J., *The Blue-winged Teal, Its Ecology and Management*, Collegiate Press, Ames, Iowa, 1938.

Benson, C. S., R. K. Brooke, R. J. Dowsett, and M. P. S. Irwin, *The Birds of Zambia*, William Collins Sons and Company, Ltd., Glasgow, Scotland, 1971.

Bent, A. C., *Life Histories of North American Wildfowl*, 2 Volumes, United States Natural History Museum Bulletin No. 126, 1925.

Blake, E. R., *Birds of Mexico*, University of Chicago Press, Chicago, Illinois, 1953.

_____, *Manual of Neotropical Birds*, Volume I, University of Chicago Press, Chicago, Illinois, 1977.

Boyd, H. and M. A. Ogilvie, *Wildfowl Trust Annual Report*, Volume 18, Wildfowl Trust, Slimbridge, England, 1966.

Boyd, H. and P. Scott, *Wildfowl Trust Annual Reports*, Volumes 12-17, Wildfowl Trust, Slimbridge, England, 1961-66.

Brunn, B., *Birds of Europe*, Golden Press, New York, 1971.

Bull, J. and John Farrand, Jr., *The Audubon Society Field Guide to North American Birds: Eastern Region*, Alfred A. Knopf, Inc., New York, 1977.

Clancey, P. A., *Gamebirds of South Africa*, Purnell and Sons, Capetown, South Africa, 1962.

Cogswell, H. L., *Water Birds of California*, University of California Press, Berkeley, California, 1977.

Cottam, C., "Food Habits of North American Diving Ducks," *United States Department of Agriculture Technical Bulletin*, No. 643:1-139, Washington, D.C., 1939.

Cramp, S. and K. E. L. Simmons (eds.), *The Birds of the Western Palearctic*, Volume I, Oxford University Press, London, 1977.

Delacour, J., *The Waterfowl of the World*, 4 Volumes, Country Life, Ltd., London, 1954-64.

Delacour, J. and E. Mayr, "The Family Anatidae," *Wilson Bulletin*, 57:3-55, 1945.

Dementiev, A. P. and N. A. Gladkov (eds.), *Birds of the Soviet Union*, Volume IV, Russia, 1952. Translated by Israel Program for Scientific Translations, United States Department of Interior and National Science Foundation, Washington, D.C., 1967.

Dill, H. H. and F. B. Lee (eds.), *Home Grown Honkers*, I.W.W.A., United States Fish and Wildlife Service, Washington, D.C., 1970.

Duplaix-Hall, Nichole (ed.), *International Zoo Yearbook*, Volume 13, Section I, Zoological Society of London, 1973.

Einarsen, A. S., *Black Brant: Sea Goose of the Pacific Coast*, University of Washington Press, Seattle, Washington, 1965.

Elman, R. and W. Osburne, *The Atlantic Flyway*, Winchester Press, New York, 1972.

Erskine, A. J., *Buffleheads*, Canadian Wildlife Service, Ottawa, Canada, 1972.

_____, *Populations, Movements and Seasonal Distribution of Mergansers*, Report Series No. 2, Canadian Wildlife Service, Ottawa, Canada, 1972.

Farmer, D. S. (ed.), *Breeding Biology of Birds: Proceedings of a Symposium on Breeding Behavior and Reproductive Physiology in Birds; National Academy of Sciences*, Washington, D.C., 1973.

Fjeldsa, Jon, *Guide to the Young of European Precocial Birds*, Villadsen and Christensen, Denmark, 1977.

Fleming, R. L., Sr., R. L. Fleming, Jr., and Lain Singh Bangdel, *Birds of Nepal With Reference to Kashmir and Sikkim*, Arun K. Mehta at Vakil and Sons, Ltd., Bombay, India, 1976.

Frith, H. J. *Waterfowl in Australia*, East-West Center Press, Honolulu, Hawaii, 1967.

Frith, H. J. (consulting ed.), *Reader's Digest Complete Book of Australian Birds*, Reader's Digest Services, PTY, Ltd., Sydney, Australia, 1977.

Gabrielson, I. N. and F. C. Lincoln, *The Birds of Alaska*, Wildlife Management Institute, Stackpole Books, Harrisburg, Pennsylvania, 1957.

Gill, L., *A First Guide to South African Birds*, Maskew Miller, Ltd., Capetown, South Africa, 1964.

Godfrey, W. E., *The Birds of Canada*, National Museum of Canada Bulletin No. 203, Biological Series No. 73, Ottawa, Canada, 1966.

Gore, M. E. J. and Pyong-oh Won, *The Birds of Korea*, Taewon Publishing Company, Seoul, Korea, 1971.

Grizimek, B. (ed.), *Animal Life Encyclopedia*, Volume 7, Van Nostrand Reinhold, Ltd., New York, 1972.

Gross, A. O., "Eider Ducks of Kent Island," *Auk*, 55:387-400, 1938.

Hanson, H. C. and R. L. Jones, *The Biochemistry of Blue, Snow and Ross' Geese*, Southern Illinois University Press, Carbondale, Illinois, 1976.

Harris, M., *A Field Guide to the Birds of the Galapagos*, Taplinger Publishing Company, Inc., New York, 1974.

Heinzel, H., R. Fitter, and J. Parslow, *The Birds of Britain and Europe*, William Collins Sons and Company, Ltd., London, 1974.

Hochbaum, H. A., *The Canvasback on a Prairie Marsh*, 2nd ed., Wildlife Management Institute, Washington, D.C., 1959.

Hoffman, R., *Birds of the Pacific States*, Houghton Mifflin Company, Boston, Massachusetts, 1927.

Hester, E. F. and J. Dermid, *The World of the Wood Duck*, Houghton Mifflin Company, Boston, Massachusetts, 1972.

Humphrey, P. S., D. Bridge, P. W. Reynolds, and R. T. Peterson, *Birds of Isla Grande*, Smithsonian Institution, University of Kansas Museum of Natural History, 1970.

Hyde, D. O. (ed.), *Raising Wild Ducks in Captivity*, International Wild Waterfowl Association, E. P. Dutton and Company, New York, 1974.

Johnsgard, P. A., *Handbook of Waterfowl Behavior*, Cornell University Press, Ithaca, New York, 1965.

———, *Waterfowl, Their History and Biology*, University of Nebraska Press, Lincoln, Nebraska, 1968.

———, *Waterfowl of North America*, Indiana University Press, Bloomington, Indiana, 1975.

———, *Ducks, Geese and Swans of the World*, Indiana University Press, Bloomington, Indiana, 1978.

Johnson, A. A. and W. H. Payn, *Ornamental Waterfowl*, Spur Publications Company, Hampshire, Great Britain, 1974.

Johnson, A. W., *The Birds of Chile and Adjacent Regions of Argentina, Bolivia and Peru*, Volume I, Platt Establecinientos Graficos, Buenos Aires, Argentina, 1965.

Kerklots, G. A. C., *The Birds of Trinidad and Tobago*, Collins Clear-Type Press, London, 1961.

King, B. F. and E. C. Dickinson, *A Field Guide to the Birds of Southeast Asia*, Houghton Mifflin Company, Boston, Massachusetts, 1975.

Kortright, F. H., *The Ducks, Geese and Swans of North America*, American Wildlife Institute, Washington, D.C., 1943.

Lack, D., *Evolution Illustrated by Waterfowl*, Hazell Watson and Viney, Ltd., Aylesburn, Great Britain, 1974.

Land, H. C., *Birds of Guatemala*, Livingston Publishing Company, Wynnewood, Pennsylvania, 1970.

Lekagul, B., *Bird Guide of Thailand*, Association for the Conservation of Wildlife, Bangkok, Thailand, 1968.

Leopold, A. S., *Wildlife of Mexico: The Game Birds and Mammals*, University of California Press, Berkeley, California, 1959.

Linduska, J. P. (ed.), *Waterfowl Tomorrow*, USDI/BSF&W, United States Government Printing Office, Washington, D.C., 1964.

Mackworth-Praed, C. W. and C.H.B. Grant, *Birds of Eastern and North Eastern Africa*, Longmanns, Green and Company, London, 1952.

Matthews, G.V.T. and M. A. Ogilvie, *Wildfowl Trust Annual Reports*, Volumes 19, 21-29, Wildfowl Trust, Slimbridge, England, 1968, 1970-78.

Meyer de Schauenesee, R., *The Species of Birds of South America With Their Distribution*, Livingston Publishing Company, Narbeth, Pennsylvania, 1966.

Meyer de Schauenesee, R. and W. H. Phelps, Jr., *A Guide to the Birds of Venezuela*, Princeton University Press, Princeton, New Jersey, 1978.

Moreau, R. E., *The Bird Faunas of Africa and Its Islands*, Academic Press, New York, 1966.

Murphy, R. C., *Oceanic Birds of South America*, Volume II, American Museum of Natural History, New York, 1936.

Newman, K. (ed.), *Birdlife in Southern Africa*, Purnell and Sons, PTY, Ltd., Capetown, South Africa, 1971.

Ogilvie, M. A., *Ducks of Britain and Europe*, T. and A. D. Poyser, Ltd., Hertfordshire, England, 1975.

———, *Wild Geese*, T. and A. D. Poyser, Ltd., Hertfordshire, England, 1978.

Olrog, C. C., *Las Aves Sudamericanas*, Universidad Nacional de Tucman, Argentina, 1968.

Owen, M., *Wildfowl of Europe*, MacMillan Ltd., London, 1977.

Palmer, R. S. (ed.), *Handbook of North American Birds*, Volumes 2 and 3, (Waterfowl, Parts 1 and 2), Yale University Press, New Haven, Connecticut, 1976.

Paterson, A., *Birds of the Bahamas*, Durrell Publications, Brattleboro, Vermont, 1972.

Peterson, R. T., *A Field Guide to the Birds*, Houghton Mifflin Company, Boston, Massachusetts, 1947.

———, *A Field Guide to Western Birds*, Houghton Mifflin Company, Boston, Massachusetts, 1961.

Pospahela, R. S., D. R. Anderson, and C. Henny, *Population Ecology of the Mallard (II. Breeding Habitat Conditions, Size of the Breeding Population and Production Indices)*, United States Fish and Wildlife Service, Resource Publication 115, 1974.

Pough, R. H., *Audubon Water Bird Guide*, Doubleday and Company, Inc., New York, 1951.

Prozesky, O. P. M., *A Field Guide to the Birds of Southern Africa*, Collins Clear-Type Press, London, 1970.

Raikow, R. J., *Evolution of Diving and Adaptations in the Stifftail Ducks*, University of California Publications in Zoology, Volume 94, University of California Press, Berkeley, California, 1970.

Ridgely, R. S., *A Guide to the Birds of Panama*, Princeton University Press, Princeton, New Jersey, 1976.

Riggert, T. L., *The Biology of the Mountain Duck on Rottnest Island, Western Australia*, Wildlife Monographs (No. 52), Wildlife Society, Washington, D.C., 1977.

Robbins, C. S., G. Bruan, and H. S. Zim, *Birds of North America: A Field Guide to Their Identification*, Golden Press, New York, 1966.

Robertson, C. J. R., *Birds in New Zealand*, A. H. and A. W. Reed, Wellington, New Zealand, 1974.

Ryder, J. P., *The Breeding Biology of Ross' Goose in the Perry River Region, Northwest Territories*, Report Series No. 3, Canadian Wildlife Service, Ottawa, Canada, 1967.

Savage, C., *The Mandarin Duck*, A. and C. Black, London, 1952.

Schwartz, C. W. and E. R. Schwartz, *The Gamebirds of Hawaii*, Board of Agriculture and Forestry, Hilo, Territory of Hawaii, 1949.

Scott, P., *A Colored Key to the Wildfowl of the World*, Wildfowl Trust, Slimbridge, England, 1957.

———, *The Swans*, Houghton Mifflin Company, Boston, Massachusetts, 1972.

Scott, P. and H. Boyd, *Wildfowl Trust Annual Report*, Volumes 7-10, Wildfowl Trust, Slimbridge, England, 1955, 1957-59.

Serle, W. and G. Morel, *A Field Guide to the Birds of West Africa*, William Collins Sons and Company, Ltd., Glasgow, Scotland, 1977.

Slater, P., *A Field Guide to Australian Birds (Non-Passerines)*, Livingston Publishing Company, Wynnewood, Pennsylvania, 1972.

Smythies, B. D., *The Birds of Borneo*, Oliver and Boyd, London, 1960.

———, *The Birds of Burma*, Oliver and Boyd, London, 1953.

Snyder, D., *The Birds of Guiana*, Peabody Museum, Salem, Massachusetts, 1966.

Sowls, L. K., *Prairie Ducks*, Wildlife Management Institute, Washington, D.C., 1955.

Sturgis, G., *Field Book of Birds of the Panama Canal Zone*, G. P. Putnam and Sons, New York, 1928.

Swan, L., "Goose of the Himalayas," *Natural History*, pp. 68-75, December 1970.

Udvardy, M. D. F., *The Audubon Society Field Guide to North American Birds: Western Region*, Alfred A. Knopf, New York, 1977.

Van Tyne, J. and A. H. Berger, *Fundamentals of Ornithology*, John Wiley and Sons, Inc., New York, 1961.

Welty, J., *The Life of Birds*, W. B. Saunders Company, Philadelphia, Pennsylvania, 1962.

Wetmore, A., *The Birds of the Republic of Panama*, Volume 150, Part I, Smithsonian Miscellaneous Collections, Washington, 1965.

Whistler, H., *Popular Handbook of Indian Birds*, Gurney and Jackson, London, 1949.

Wildash, P., *Birds of South Vietnam*, Charles E. Tuttle Company, Tokyo, Japan, 1968.

Williams, J. G., *A Field Guide to the Birds of East and Central Africa*, Houghton Mifflin Company, Boston, Massachusetts, 1963.

Wilmore, S. B., *Swans of the World*, Taplinger Publishing Company, New York, 1974.

Woods, R. W., *The Birds of the Falkland Islands*, Compton Press, Ltd., Wiltshire, Great Britain, 1975.

Yamashina, Y., *Birds in Japan*, Tokyo News Service, Ltd., Tokyo, Japan, 1961.

Index

In this listing, references to material to be found in the text are printed in regular type, references to material to be found in captions are enclosed in parentheses, and plate numbers are printed in italic. Plate reference numbers do not refer to pages but to the position of the plate within a chapter. (For example, plate *1.26* is the twenty-sixth plate in Chapter One.)